INTO ALL THE WORLD

INTO ALL THE WORLD

Emergent Christianity in Its
Jewish and Greco-Roman Context

Edited by

Mark Harding and Alanna Nobbs

WILLIAM B. Eerdmans Publishing Company
Grand Rapids, Michigan

Wm. B. Eerdmans Publishing Co.
2140 Oak Industrial Drive N.E., Grand Rapids, Michigan 49505
www.eerdmans.com

Published 2017
Printed in the United States of America

26 25 24 23 22 21 20 19 18 17   1 2 3 4 5 6 7 8 9 10

isbn 978-0-8028-7515-0

Library of Congress Cataloging-in-Publication Data

A catalog record for this book is available from the Library of Congress

"You will be my witnesses in Jerusalem,
in all Judea and Samaria,
and to the ends of the earth."

Acts 1:8

*To Edwin Judge
Pioneer, Mentor, Friend*

CONTENTS

Like the previous two volumes in this series edited by Mark Harding and Alanna Nobbs, namely, *The Content and Setting of the Gospel Tradition* (Eerdmans 2010) and *All Things to All Cultures: Paul among Jews, Greeks, and Romans* (Eerdmans 2013), this third (and final) volume brings together contributors with close but varying links to the Department of Ancient History at Macquarie University and/or the Australian College of Theology (ACT).

As the title indicates, the volume takes the story of the spread of Early Christianity into the Jewish and Greco-Roman world of the first century. All contributions have been anonymously refereed and refined in the light of any comments received. Nevertheless, the views remain those of the individual authors, as is fitting in areas where scholarly differences may be ongoing.

The Ancient History Department at Macquarie University has long had a focus on papyri and inscriptions relating to the Greco-Roman and Jewish setting of the New Testament, as shown for instance in the series New Documents Illustrating Early Christianity (Eerdmans, 10 volumes to date). The Department and its Ancient Cultures Research Centre are also home to the Society for the Study of Early Christianity, which hosts seminars, conferences, and visiting speakers.

The Australian College of Theology is a major provider of theological education, and operates in Australia and New Zealand as a network of affiliated colleges.

While this volume, like its two predecessors, emanates from the Australian context, many of the contributors have profitable links with the Society of Biblical Literature, and regularly attend its North American and International meetings. Indeed the ACT and Macquarie University have for the past two years held a joint reception at the North American SBL to further cement these links.

Thanks are due to the Board of Directors of the Australian College of Theology for a subvention towards formatting and editing, to Philip Walker-Harding for formatting, and to Gina Denholm for subediting and proofreading.

While the editors take joint responsibility for the work, I wish to acknowledge the major contribution of Mark Harding, whose name comes first not simply alphabetically.

We wish to thank the William B. Eerdmans Publishing Company for their constant support and helpfulness over the life of this series. We also wish to thank our colleagues whether their work is represented here or not, for ready assistance, and especially, and, finally, our spouses and families.

Alanna Nobbs
Professor of Ancient History
Macquarie University
27 January 2016

CONTRIBUTORS

Mark Harding

Mark Harding is the former Dean of the Australian College of Theology and an Honorary Associate of Macquarie University. He has postgraduate degrees from London University, Macquarie University, and Princeton Theological Seminary where he completed a PhD in New Testament in 1993. He is the author of *Tradition and Rhetoric in the Pastoral Epistles* (Peter Lang, 1998) and *Early Christian Life and Thought in Social Context* (T&T Clark, 2003).

Alanna Nobbs

Alanna Nobbs is Professor of Ancient History and former deputy Director of the Ancient Cultures Research Centre at Macquarie University. Her teaching, research interests, and publications are in Greek and Roman historiography (including New Testament background), and in the history of Christianity especially as seen through the papyri.

Bradley J. Bitner

Brad Bitner is Tutor in New Testament and Greek at Oak Hill College (London). He received an MAR from Gordon-Conwell Theological Seminary (2000) and completed a PhD in Ancient History at Macquarie University (2013). His thesis was published in the SNTS Monograph Series by Cambridge University Press in 2015 as *Paul's Political Strategy in 1 Corinthians 1–4: Constitution and Covenant.*

Edward Bridge

Edward Bridge is a Tutor in Ancient History at Macquarie University as well as the Moderator for New Testament units in the ACT Master of Arts degree programs. He has taught previously at Tahlee Bible College, and served for a time as Ministry Assistant at St Andrews Presbyterian Church, Newcastle. He has a PhD from Macquarie University in Ancient History (in Hebrew Bible; 2011), and an MPhil in New Testament from Griffith University (2001). He is well published in biblical studies journals, focusing on language use in the Hebrew Bible/Old Testament; and has entries in the *Lexham Bible Dictionary*, and in *New Documents Illustrating Early Christianity, Volume 10*, as well as being the assistant editor for that volume.

Johan Ferreira

Johan Ferreira is currently Professor in Oriental Studies at Minzu University in Beijing and an Honorary Research Associate at the Centre for Early Christian Studies, Australian Catholic University. He served as a Lecturer in Biblical Studies at Brisbane School of Theology from 1996 to 2014. He has postgraduate degrees from Princeton Theological Seminary where he completed a ThM in 1992 and the University of Queensland where he completed a PhD in 1996. He is the author of *Johannine Ecclesiology* (Sheffield Academic Press, 1998), *The Hymn of the Pearl: The Syriac and Greek Texts with Introduction, Translations, and Notes* (Strathfield, NSW: St Pauls Publications, 2002); *A Concise Classical Hebrew Grammar* [in Chinese] (Beijing, 2006), *A Concise Koine Greek Grammar* [in Chinese] (Shanghai, 2009), *Early Chinese Christianity: The Tang Christian Monument and Other Documents* (St Pauls Publications, 2014), and *A Reader's Greek New Testament* [in Chinese] (A Kernel of Wheat Ministries, 2014). He has also published numerous articles in biblical and oriental studies in a range of scholarly journals and is a member of the *Studiorum Novi Testamenti Societas* (SNTS). He teaches in the areas of ancient languages, biblical studies, and oriental history and cultures.

Chris Forbes

Christopher Forbes is a Senior Lecturer in Ancient History at Macquarie University, where he teaches New Testament history, Hellenistic history and Greco-Roman history of ideas. He completed his PhD in Ancient History at Macquarie University under the supervision of Professor E. A. Judge in 1987. His thesis was published by Mohr Siebeck in 1995 as *Prophecy and Inspired Speech in Early Christianity and its Hellenistic Environment*. He has published various articles on the intellectual and cultural context of the early Christians and is a regular contributor to the conferences of the Society for the Study of Early Christianity held annually at Macquarie University.

Lydia Gore-Jones

Lydia Gore-Jones is a PhD candidate at Macquarie University. Her area of research is the history of Second Temple Judaism and early Christianity, with a special interest in the study of pseudepigrapha and apocalyptic literature. She also works as a Tutor in Ancient History at Macquarie University.

James R. Harrison

James Harrison, Professor and Director of Research (Sydney College of Divinity), completed his PhD in Ancient History at Macquarie University under the supervision of Professor E. A. Judge and Dr Chris Forbes in 1997. His book *Paul's Language of Grace in Its Graeco-Roman Context*, published by Mohr Siebeck, was the 2005 Winner of the Biblical Archaeology Society Publication Award for the Best Book Relating to the New Testament published in 2003 and 2004. His latest monograph, published by Mohr Siebeck in 2011, is *Paul and the Imperial Authorities at Thessalonica and Rome: A Study in the Conflict of Ideology*. He is also the coeditor, with L. L. Welborn, of *The First Urban Churches: Methodological Considerations* (SBL Press, 2015). James is an Honorary Associate at Macquarie University and a regular contributor to the conferences of the Society for the Study of Early Christianity, held annually at Macquarie University.

Stephen Llewelyn

Stephen Llewelyn is a former lecturer at Macquarie University in the discipline of Ancient History where he taught Hebrew and the history of First and Second Temple periods of Israel and Judah. His research interests cover these periods and the texts that they produced, as well as the field of New Testament studies. He has also been the editor of the series *New Documents Illustrating Early Christianity*, volumes 6–10.

Tim MacBride

Tim MacBride lectures in New Testament and Homiletics at Morling College, an affiliated college of the Australian College of Theology. His research interest is the intersection between rhetorical approaches to the New Testament and homiletic theory. He completed a ThD through the Australian College of Theology in 2012, which was published by Wipf and Stock in 2014 as *Preaching the New Testament as Rhetoric.*

Paul McKechnie

Paul McKechnie is an Associate Professor (CoRE) in Ancient Cultures at Macquarie University. He teaches Greek and Roman history, and early Christianity, and has research interests in Ptolemaic Egypt and the early Christian churches. His published works include *The First Christian Centuries* (Leicester, 2001).

Ian K. Smith

Ian Smith was appointed Principal of Christ College, an affiliated college of the Australian College of Theology, in 2010. He has been a lecturer in New Testament at Christ College since 1995. He served as the Head of the Department of Bible and Languages of the Australian College of Theology from 2006 until 2010. He holds postgraduate degrees from the University of New England, the Australian College of Theology, and the University of Sydney, where he completed a PhD in New Testament in 2002. He is the author of *Heavenly Perspective: A Study of the Apostle Paul's Response to a Jewish Mystical Movement at Colossae* (T&T Clark, 2006).

Murray J. Smith

Murray Smith lectures in Biblical Studies (Greek and New Testament) at Christ College, Sydney (formerly the Presbyterian Theological Centre). He holds Masters degrees from the University of Sydney (Reformation History), Macquarie University (Early Christian and Jewish Studies), and the Australian College of Theology (Divinity). His Macquarie University PhD thesis concerns "Jesus and the Logic of His Coming in Earliest Christianity." His publications include articles on the Gospels, Paul and his letters, and the Didache.

David Starling

David Starling teaches New Testament at Morling College, where he serves as the head of the Bible and Theology Department. His PhD studies were at the University of Sydney. His doctoral thesis, on Paul's use of exile imagery, was published as *Not My People: Gentiles as Exiles in Pauline Hermeneutics* (de Gruyter, 2011). Subsequent books which he has written or coedited include *Theology and the Future: Evangelical Assertions and Explorations* (T&T Clark, 2014), *UnCorinthian Leadership* (Cascade, 2014), *The Gender Conversation* (Wipf & Stock, 2016), and *Hermeneutics as Apprenticeship* (Baker, 2016). His current research projects include commentaries on Colossians, Ephesians, and 1 Corinthians.

L. L. Welborn

Larry Welborn is Professor of New Testament and Early Christianity at Fordham University and Honorary Professor of Ancient History at Macquarie University. He is the author of several books, including *Politics and Rhetoric in the Corinthian Epistles* (Mercer, 1997), *Paul, the Fool of Christ: A Study of 1 Corinthians 1–4 in the Comic-Philosophic Tradition* (T&T Clark, 2005) and *An End to Enmity: Paul and the "Wrongdoer" of Second Corinthians* (de Gruyter, 2011). He is currently preparing the *Hermeneia* commentary on *First Clement*. With Dale B. Martin, he serves as book series editor of *Synkrisis: Comparative Approaches to Early Christianity in Greco-Roman Culture*, published by Yale University Press.

Bruce W. Winter

Bruce Winter completed his doctoral thesis at Macquarie University that was subsequently published on *Philo and Paul among the Sophists*. He taught at Moore Theological College and subsequently at Trinity Theological College, Singapore before being appointed the Warden, Tyndale House, University of Cambridge for almost two decades. He subsequently became the Principal of the Queensland Theology College, Brisbane. His additional monographs include *Seek the Welfare of the City*, *After Paul Left Corinth: The Influence of Secular Ethics and Social Change*, *Roman Wives and Roman Widows*: *The Appearance of "New" Roman Women and the Pauline Communities* and most recently *Divine Honours for the Caesars: The First Christians' Responses*. He has been a Senior Research Fellow in Ancient History, Macquarie University since 2003.

ABBREVIATIONS

1 Apol.	Justin, *First Apology*
1 Clem.	1 Clement
1 En.	1 Enoch
1QpHab	Habakkuk Pesher, from Qumran Cave 1
1QS	Rule of the Community, from Qumran Cave 1
2 Bar.	2 Baruch
2 Clem.	2 Clement
2 En.	2 Enoch
AB	Anchor Bible
ABD	David Noel Freedman, ed. *The Anchor Bible Dictionary*. 6 vols. New York: Doubleday, 1992
ABSA	*Annual of the British School at Athens*
Adv. Jud.	*Adversus Judaeos*
Aen.	Virgil, *Aeneid*
AGJU	Arbeiten zur Geschichte des Antiken Judentums und des Urchristentums
A.J.	Josephus, *Antiquitates judaicae*
AJA	*American Journal of Archaeology*
AJS	*American Journal of Sociology*
ASR	*American Sociological Review*
Alex.	*Alexander*
Alex. fort.	Plutarch, *De Alexandri magni fortuna aut virtute*
Amic.	Cicero, *De amicitia*
Anab.	*Anabasis*
ANF	*Ante-Nicene Fathers*
Ann.	Tacitus, *Annals*
An. post.	Aristotle, *Analytica posteriora*
ANRW	H. Temporini and W. Haase, eds. *Aufstieg und Niedergang der römischen Welt: Geschichte und Kultur Roms im Spiegel der neueren Forschung.* Berlin: de Gruyter, 1972–
Antichr.	Hippolytus, *De antichristo*
Ant. rom.	Dionysius of Halicarnassus, *Antiquitates romanae*
Apg	Apostelgeschichte
Apoc. Mos.	Apocalypse of Moses
Apol.	Tertullian, *Apologeticus*
Ars rhet.	Aristides, *Ars rhetorica*
ASE	*Annali di Storia dell' Esegesi*
AsJT	*Asia Journal of Theology*
As. Mos.	Assumption of Moses
Astron.	Manilius, *Astronomica*
Aug.	Suetonius, *Divus Augustus*
b. Avodah Zarah	Babylonian Talmud, Avodah Zarah
b. Ber.	Babylonian Talmud, Berakhot
b. Ketub.	Babylonian Talmud, Ketubbot

b. Meg.	Babylonian Talmud, Megillah
b. Sanh.	Babylonian Talmud, Sanhedrin
b. Shevu'ot	Babylonian Talmud, Shevu'ot
BA	*Biblical Archaeologist*
BAR	*Biblical Archaeology Review*
BBB	Bonner biblische Beiträge
BBR	*Bulletin for Biblical Research*
BCH	Bulletin du Correspondance hellénique
BDAG	Frederick W. Danker, ed. *A Greek-English Lexicon of the New Testament and Other Early Christian Literature.* 3rd ed. Chicago: University of Chicago Press, 2000
BECNT	Baker Exegetical Commentary on the New Testament
Ben.	Seneca, *De beneficiis*
BETL	Bibliotheca Ephemeridium Theologicarum Lovaniensium
BFER	*British and Foreign Evangelical Review*
Bib	*Biblica*
B.J.	Josephus, *Bellum judaicum*
BJRL	*Bulletin of the John Rylands University Library of Manchester*
BM Coins, Rom. Emp.	*British Museum Catalogue of Coins of the Roman Empire* (1923–)
BR	*Biblical Research*
BTB	*Biblical Theology Bulletin*
BZ	*Biblische Zeitschrift*
BZNW	Beihefte zur Zeitschrift für die neutestamentliche Wissenschaft
C. Ap.	Josephus, *Contra Apionem*
Cal.	Suetonius, *Gaius Caligula*
Caus. plant.	Theophrastus, *De causis plantarum*
CBQ	*Catholic Biblical Quarterly*
CBQMS	Catholic Biblical Quarterly Monograph Series
CD	Cairo Genizah copy of the Damascus Document
Cels.	Origen, *Contra Celsum*
CGTC	Cambridge Greek Testament Commentary
CH	*Church History*
Chron.	Malalas, *Chronographia*
CIL	*Corpus inscriptionum latinarum*
Claud.	Suetonius, *Divus Claudius*
CNT	Commentaire du Nouveau Testament
Comm. Isa.	Jerome, *Commentarius in Isaiam*
Comm. Jo.	Origen, *Commentarii in evangelium Johannis*
Cor.	Tertullian, *de corona militis*
CP	*Classical Philology*
CPJ	*Corpus Papyrorum Judaicarum.* Edited by Victor A. Tcherikover. 3 vols. Cambridge, MA: Harvard University Press, 1957–1964
CurBR	*Currents in Biblical Research*
De or.	Cicero, *De oratore*

Demon.	Isocrates, *Ad Demonicum*
Descr.	Pausanias, *Graeciae descriptio*
Dial.	Justin, *Dialogue with Trypho*
Diatr.	Epictetus, *Diatribai*
Did.	Didache
Dig.	Justinian, *Digesta*
Diogn.	Diognetus
Dom.	Suetonius, *Domitianus*
El.	Tibullus, *Elegiae*
Eng.	English
Ep.	Pliny the Younger, *Epistulae*
Ep.	Seneca, *Epistulae morales*
Ep. Arist.	Sextus Julius Africanus, *Epistule ad Aristidem*
Epist.	Jerome, *Epistulae*
ESV	English Standard version
ET	English translation
Eth. eud.	Aristotle, *Ethica eudemia*
Eth. nic.	Aristotle, *Ethica nichomachea*
EVV	English versions (of the Bible)
ExAud	*Ex Auditu*
Exp	*Expositor*
ExpTim	*Expository Times*
FGH	*Die Fragmente der griechischen Historiker*. Edited by Felix Jacoby. Leiden, Brill, 1954–1964
fl.	flourished
Flac.	Cicero, *Pro Flacco*
Flacc.	Philo, *In Flaccum*
frag(s).	fragment(s)
Frat. amor.	Plutarch, *de fraterno amore*
Galb.	Suetonius, *Galba*
Garr.	Plutarch, *De garrulitate*
Geogr.	Strabo, *Geographica*
Ger.	German
Gig.	Philo, *De gigantibus*
Gk.	Greek
Gos. Thom.	Gospel of Thomas
GR	*Greece and Rome*
GRBS	*Greek, Roman, and Byzantine Studies*
Haer.	*Adversus haereses*
HCSB	Holman Christian Standard Bible
Hist.	*Historiae*
Hist. eccl.	Eusebius, *Historia ecclesiastica*
HNTC	Harper's New Testament Commentaries
Hom. Luc.	Origen, *Homiliae in Lucam*
Hom. Rom.	Chrysostom, *Homiliae in epistulam ad Romanos*
HSCP	Harvard Studies in Classical Philology
HTR	*Harvard Theological Review*
HTS	Harvard Theological Studies

HUCA	*Hebrew Union College Annual*
IBS	*Irish Biblical Studies*
I.Eph.	*Die Inschriften von Ephesos* (1979–1984)
IG	*Inscriptiones Graecae* (1873–)
Ign. *Eph.*	Ignatius, *To the Ephesians*
Ign. *Magn.*	Ignatius, *To the Magnesians*
Ign. *Pol.*	Ignatius, *To Polycarp*
Ign. *Rom.*	Ignatius, *To the Romans*
Ign. *Smyrn.*	Ignatius, *To the Smyrnaeans*
IGRom.	*Inscriptiones Graecae ad res Romanas pertinentes* (1906–)
Il.	Homer, *Iliad*
In Apoc.	Victorinus, *In Apocalypsin*
Insc. lat. sel.	*Inscriptiones latinae selectae*
Inst.	Quintillian, *Institutio oratorica*
Int	*Interpretation*
ISBE	*International Standard Bible Encyclopedia.* Edited by Geoffrey W. Bromiley. 4 vols. Grand Rapids: Eerdmans, 1979–1988
Isthm.	Pindar, *Isthmionikai*
IVPNTC	InterVarsity Press New Testament Commentary
JBL	*Journal of Biblical Literature*
JECS	*Journal of Early Christian Studies*
JETS	*Journal of the Evangelical Theological Society*
JGRChJ	*Journal of Greco-Roman Christianity and Judaism*
JHS	*Journal of Hellenic Studies*
JNG	*Jahrbuch für Numismatik und Geldgeschichte*
Jos. Asen.	Joseph and Aseneth
JQR	*Jewish Quaterly Review*
JRS	*Journal of Roman Studies*
JSJ	*Journal for the Study of Judaism in the Persian, Hellenistic, and Roman Periods*
JSNT	*Journal for the Study of the New Testament*
JSNTSup	Journal for the Study of the New Testament: Supplement Series
JTI	*Journal of Theological Interpretation*
JTS	*Journal of Theological Studies*
Jul.	Suetonius, *Divus Julius*
KEK	Kritisch-exegetischer Kommentar über das Neue Testament
KJV	King James version
LCL	Loeb Classical Library
Leg.	Philo, *Legum allegoriae*
Legat.	Philo, *Legatio ad Gaium*
LNTS	Library of New Testament Studies
LXX	Septuagint
m. Ber.	Mishnah, Berakhot
m. Hull.	Mishnah, Hullin
m. Meg.	Mishnah, Megillah
m. Sanh.	Mishnah, Sanhedrin

Magn.	Ignatius, *To the Magnesians*
Mart. Pol.	Martyrdom of Polycarp
Metaph.	Aristotle, *Metaphysica*
Midr. Cant	Midrash Canticles (Song of Songs)
Midr. Exod	Midrash Exodus
Midr. Gen	Midrash Genesis
Midr. Lev	Midrash Leviticus
Midr. Ps	Midrash Psalms
Mil.	Cicero, *Pro Milone*
Mor.	Plutarch, *Moralia*
Mort.	Lactanctius, *De mortibus persecutorum*
MTSR	*Method and Theory in the Study of Religion*
NA²⁸	*Novum Testamentum Graece*, Nestle-Aland, 28th ed.
NASB	New American Standard Bible
Nat.	Tertullian, *Ad nationes*
Nat.	Pliny the Elder, *Naturalis historia*
Nat. d.	Cicero, *De natura deorum*
NCBC	New Cambridge Bible Commentary
NICNT	New International Commentary on the Old Testament
NIDNTTE	*New International Dictionary of New Testament Theology and Exegesis.* Edited by Moisés Silva. 5 vols. Grand Rapids: Zondervan, 2014
NIGTC	New International Greek Testament Commentary
NIV	New International Version
NIV11	New International Version (2011)
NIV84	New International Version (1984)
NovT	*Novum Testamentum*
NovTSup	Supplements to Novum Testamentum
NRSV	New Revised Standard Version
NSBT	New Studies in Biblical Theology
NTOA	Novum Testamentum et Orbis Antiquus
NTS	*New Testament Studies*
OCD	S. Hornblower and A. Spawforth, eds. *Oxford Classical Dictionary.* 3ʳᵈ edition. Oxford: Oxford University Press, 1996
Oct.	Minucius Felix, *Octavius*
Off.	Cicero, *De officiis*
OGIS	W. Dittenberger, ed. *Orientis graeci inscriptiones selectae.* 2 vols. Leipzig: S. Hirzel, 1903–1905
Or.	*Orationes*
Orest.	Euripides, *Orestes*
Pan.	Epiphanius, *Panarion*
Pan.	Pliny, *Panegyricus*
PaP	*Past and Present*
Pers.	Aeschylus, *Persae*
PGM	*Papyri Graecae Magicae: Die griechischen Zauberpapyri.* Edited by Karl Preisendanz. 2nd ed. Stuttgart: Teubner, 1973–1974

Phil.	Cicero, *Orationes philippicae*
Phil.	Polycarp, *To the Philippians*
Phld.	Polycarp, *To the Philadelphians*
Pisc.	Lucian, *Piscator*
PNTC	Pelican New Testament Commentaries
Poet.	Aristotle, *Poetica*
Pol.	Aristotle, *Politica*
Pomp.	Plutarch, *Pompeius*
Praec. ger. rei publ.	Plutarch, *Praecepta gerendae rei publicae*
PRSt	*Perspectives in Religious Studies*
Pss. Sol.	Psalms of Solomon
PSTJ	*Perkins (School of Theology) Journal*
Pulchr.	Dio Chrysostom, *De pulchritudine*
Quaest. conv.	Plutarch, *Quaestionum convivialum*
Quis div.	Clement of Alexandria, *Quis dives salvetur*
RAC	*Reallexicon für Antike und Christentum.* Edited by Theodor Klauser at al. Stuttgart: Hiersemann, 1950–
RB	*Revue biblique*
REL	*Revue des Études Latines*
Resp.	Plato, *Respublica*
RHE	*Revue de l'Histoire Ecclésiastique*
Rhet.	Aristotle, *Rhetorica*
Rhet. ad Her.	*Rhetorica ad Herennium*
Rhet. Alex.	Anaximenes, *Rhetorica ad Alexandrum*
Rhet. Gr.	L. von Spengel, *Rhetores graeci.* 3 vols. Leipzig: Teubner, 1853
Rom.	Ignatius, *To the Romans*
RSQ	*Rhetoric Society Quarterly*
Sat.	Juvenal, *Satirae*
SB	F. Preisigke, et al., eds., *Sammelbuch griechischer Urkunden aus Aegypten.* 1915–
SBET	Scottish Bulletin of Evangelical Theology
SBL	Society of Biblical Literature
SBLDS	Society of Biblical Literature Dissertation Series
SC	Sources chrétiennes
Scorp.	Tertullian, *Scorpiace*
SEÅ	Svensk exegetisk årsbok
SEG	*Supplementum epigraphicum graecum*
Senten.	Paulus, *Sententiae*
Sib. Or.	Sibylline Oracles
SIG	W. Dittenberger, ed., *Sylloge inscriptionum graecarum.* 4 vols. 3rd ed. Leipzig: S. Hirzel, 1915–1924
SJT	*Scottish Journal of Theology*
SNTSMS	Society for New Testament Studies Monograph Series
Spec.	Philo, *De specialibus legibus*
SPhiloA	Studia Philonica Annual
SR	*Studies in Religion*
ST	*Studia Theologica*

Strom.	Clement of Alexandria, *Stromata*
SwJT	*Southwestern Journal of Theology*
Symp.	Plato, *Symposium*
t. Ber.	Tosefta, Berakhot
t. Demai	Tosefta, Demai
t. Erub.	Tosefta, Eruvin
t. Hull.	Tosefta, Hullin
t. Sanh.	Tosefta, Sanhedrin
T. Ash	Testament of Asher
T. Gad	Testament of Gad
T. Job	Testament of Job
T. Jos.	Testament of Joseph
Tanh. Gen	Tanhuma, Genesis
TDNT	Gerhard Kittel, and Gerhard Friedrich, eds. *Theological Dictionary of the New Testament*. 10 vols. Translated by Geoffrey W. Bromiley. Grand Rapids: Eerdmans, 1964–1976
Tg. Zech	Targum Zechariah
Tib.	Suetonius, *Tiberius*
TL	*Theologische Literaturzeitung*
TNTC	Tyndale New Testament Commentary
Trist.	Ovid, *Tristia*
TS	*Theological Studies*
TSAJ	Texte und Studien zum antiken Judentum
Tusc.	Cicero, *Tusculanae disputationes*
TynBul	*Tyndale Bulletin*
TZ	*Theologische Zeitschrift*
UBS⁴	*The Greek New Testament*, United Bible Societies, 4th ed.
UBS⁵	*The Greek New Testament*, United Bible Societies, 5th ed.
Urb. cond.	Livy, *Ab urbe condita*
VC	*Vigiliae Christianae*
Vit. Apoll.	Philostratus, *Vita Apollonii*
v(v).	verse(s)
WBC	Word Biblical Commentary
WMANT	Wissenschaftliche Monographien zum Alten und Neuen Testament
WTJ	*Westminster Theological Journal*
WUNT	Wissenschaftliche Untersuchungen zum Neuen Testament
y. Ber.	Jerusalem Talmud, Berakhot
y. Demai	Jerusalem Talmud, Demai
y. Erub.	Jerusalem Talmud, Eruvin
y. Hor.	Jerusalem Talmud, Horayot
y. Sanh.	Jerusalem Talmud, Sanhedrin
y. Seqal.	Jerusalem Talmud, Sheqalim
y. Ta'an.	Jerusalem Talmud, Ta'anit
ZAC	*Zeitschrift für antikes Christentum*
ZIBBC	Zondervan Illustrated Bible Backgrounds Commentary
ZNW	*Zeitschrift für die neutestamentliche Wissenschaft*

ZPE	*Zeitschrift für Papyrologie und Epigrapfik*
ZPEB	*Zondervan Pictorial Encyclopedia of the Bible.* Edited by Merrill C. Tenney. 5 vols. Grand Rapids: Zondervan, 1968
ZTK	*Zeitschrift für Theologie und Kirche*

The Interaction between Ancient Historians and New Testament Scholars: A Critical Appraisal

Alanna Nobbs

Now that the third and last volume in this series has been completed, it seems appropriate to give an overview of what the series has attempted to do. It has brought together numerous scholars (mostly Australian, but all with close links to Australia) in Ancient History at Macquarie University working on the Jewish and Greco-Roman background of Early Christianity with those working on similar topics within the Australian College of Theology. In many cases, authors have links with both institutions, via postgraduate studies or other affiliation. Authors have variously contributed to one, two or three of the volumes. In each case the chapters have been anonymously refereed, revised accordingly, and allowed to stand as the author's considered opinion. In other words the editors have not attempted to synthesize.

Reactions to the first two volumes in the series have been generally favorable, as judged from the reviews.[1] Though Australian-based in essence, most if not all the contributors have benefited from international input and collaborations, in particular from North America via participation in the Annual Meetings of the Society of Biblical Literature, and in many cases the International Meetings of the Society also. The editors' decision to keep the volumes English-language based, in view of the expected readership's including undergraduates in Universities or seminaries, should not lead to the assumption that the contributors have ignored scholarship in other languages, German in particular.

Volume one, *The Content and Setting of the Gospel Tradition*,[2] went beyond the purely historical background to examine the textual tradition, both that from Biblical manuscripts and from inscriptions and papyri: an approach which in many circles is synonymous with the name of Macquarie. The physical environment (with up to date archaeological evidence) also constitutes "setting," and this is the topic of the opening chapter.

---

[1] See, for example, the review by Henry Wansbrough in *JTS* 66.1 (2015): 364–66 of the first volume, *The Content and Setting of the Gospel Tradition* (for publication details see n. 2 below). Wansbrough writes: "This all-Australian production is an impressive monument to the standard of learning, especially classical learning, at Macquarie University and the other universities at which the authors teach" (364).

[2] Edited by Mark Harding and Alanna Nobbs (Grand Rapids: Eerdmans, 2010).

The collection takes a broad view of the historical background of the New Testament and Christianity, which gives a distinctive flavor to this collaborative effort. Thus we find handled the noncanonical Gospels, the relationship of the Gospels as we have them to the Old Testament, their setting within Early Christian Literature, followed by specifics such as the parables, miracles, distinctives of Jesus' message and so on. This volume has the largest number of individual contributions and serves as a background to the series as well as to its own volume, so some of these areas are not covered in the later ones.

Volume two, *All Things to All Cultures: Paul among Jews, Greeks, and Romans*,[3] deals with the second major focus of the New Testament after the Gospels, namely, the career and influence of St Paul. It is acknowledged that there are significant differences in interpretations of Paul's chronology and his message (and indeed what is to be attributed to him). The virtue of such a collection is to expose readers to these and to enable them to see how the different views come about and how to navigate them. It is for this reason in particular that the two appendices contain versions of Pauline chronology which present a different interpretation from those of chapters two and three. These differences attest to the vitality of Pauline studies and the need for ongoing work of an historical, textual and archaeological nature. Further, the questions around Pauline authorship are looked at from different perspectives and with varying conclusions. Once again, the value of juxtaposing such differing conclusions lies in promoting further scholarship and enabling readers to appreciate the methods which have led to this result.

The present third volume, *Into All the World*, takes up some of these challenges to explore the impact of emergent Christianity in both its Jewish and Greco-Roman contexts. The first element is the impact on both Jews and Gentiles of the growth of the church and its mission to the Gentiles. As with our other volumes, there can be room for different views surrounding such matters as "The Parting of the Ways" and the dating and situation of the Book of Acts. Secondly, the volume considers the impact of Christianity on the Roman State and vice versa. It is here that current and very active controversies over the Imperial Cult, the book of Revelation, and the nature of imperial persecution are bought to the fore, again presented but not prejudged by the editors. The four sections of the book reflect the spread of Christianity, its relation to Jews, to the Roman state, and then finally to the verdict of Clement of Rome. He, fittingly, is given the last word on the perception of the church in Rome by the end of the first century. At this time, the Christian story is ready to be taken into the second century, and into an even wider geographical area. From that point, *Into All the World* extends beyond the scope of our series.

In considering where to go from here, I want to raise some themes which will repay further work in the belief that very little in the content of any of these three volumes is beyond having additions made to it. We might here paraphrase slightly the conclusion to the history of the Late Roman Empire by Ammianus

---

[3] Edited by Mark Harding and Alanna Nobbs (Grand Rapids: Eerdmans, 2013).

Marcellinus at the end of the fourth century AD: "We have set forth these things this far to the best of our ability. The rest we leave to loftier tongues."[4]

Nevertheless, it is fitting that volumes featuring interactions between Ancient Historians and New Testament scholars should emanate from what is sometimes seen as the Macquarie "schola."[5] Edwin Judge, the founder of the Department of Ancient History at Macquarie University, is recognized particularly in North America and Germany for his pioneering contribution in bringing these areas together. Mark Harding is a Macquarie Honorary and MA graduate, his thesis having been supervised by Judge; while Alanna Nobbs has taught Ancient History at Macquarie for forty-six years, twenty-four of those under Edwin Judge's headship.

Few would hold more authority in making such judgements than N. T. Wright. In his most recent book he discusses the effect of what he sees as a generation of study of the New Testament within its "social world."[6] He unequivocally attributes the "launching point" of the contemporary interest to Judge's short book *The Social Pattern of the Christian Groups in the First Century* published in 1960.[7] Ancient Historians, Wright contends, must be thoroughly grounded in the primary sources, and it is these, especially the documentary material, which can be so illuminating of life in the Ancient World. Judge, radically for his day, used these sources to analyze the groups to whom the Early Christian writings were addressed.[8] The majority of the contributors to the three volumes in the present series have been exposed to this method, the documentary foundations and method of which can be seen in the series *New Documents Illustrating Early Christianity*—ten volumes to date, and now published by Eerdmans. Four volumes of the collected writings of Judge have now been published. Each of these treats, from a slightly different perspective, the themes here identified by Wright.[9]

What conclusions might be drawn from the approach taken in the series? The strength of having the two disciplines interact lies in the integration of contemporary documentary sources from papyri, inscriptions and numismatics (and where possible archaeology also) with the literary material. In the case of the New Testament writings this is especially illuminating as there is a limited body of the New Testament (canonical and extracanonical) and many who work on them are extremely familiar with them, so that a new historical perspective

---

[4] Ammianus Marcellinus, *Res gestae* 31.16.9.

[5] Note, for example, the dedication of Bruce W. Winter's recent book *Divine Honours for the Caesars: The First Christians' Responses* (Grand Rapids: Eerdmans, 2015).

[6] N. T. Wright, *Paul and his Recent Interpreters* (Minneapolis: Fortress, 2015), 229–36.

[7] London: Tyndale, 1960. The book has now been reprinted in David M. Scholer, ed., *Social Distinctives of the Christians in the First Century: Pivotal Essays by E. A. Judge* (Peabody, MA: Hendrickson, 2008), 1–56.

[8] Wright, *Paul and his Recent Interpreters*, 230.

[9] Judge's collected essays have been thematically published in Scholer, *Social Distinctives* (with Larry Hurtado's comments hurtadoblog.https://larryhurtado.wordpress.com); James R. Harrison, ed., *The First Christians in the Roman World* (Tübingen: Mohr Siebeck, 2008); Alanna Nobbs, ed., *Jerusalem and Athens* (Tübingen: Mohr Siebeck, 2010); Stuart Piggin, ed., *Engaging Rome and Jerusalem: Historical Essays for our Time* (North Melbourne: Australian Scholarly Publishing, 2014).

can lead to surprising associations. The well-known phrase "render unto Caesar" becomes newly graphic when one is aware of the monuments and coins celebrating the Caesars in an intentionally overpowering way in the normal conduct of business in the first-century Roman world. For the classically trained historian, to enter at first hand the world of first century Rome can also give a new perspective. Despite for instance debates over dating of Acts, we have a credible geography of some of the Roman roads of Asia Minor as traversed by Paul in the Acts account.[10]

One important but hardly surprising conclusion is that neither group can afford to ignore rigorous training in the relevant ancient languages. While the New Testament may exist in a score or more of translations (which can be a problem in itself), the inscriptions and papyri may not, and in many cases require a paleographical or philological judgment between differing reconstructions. It was pleasing to see a reviewer comment favorably on the level of Classical language expertise in the series (see n. 1 above). Keeping this vital aspect of scholarship alive for both disciplines needs to be a priority for the subject in the twenty-first century. We cannot let the pool of such linguistically trained scholars and teachers dry up in our universities, colleges and seminaries.

Newer theoretical approaches to archaeology (while not as well-represented in these volumes), also need to be weighed up by both our bands of scholars. Source criticism, for long the lifeblood of New Testament criticism and formerly seen as one of, if not the prime, purpose of a classical training, is also vitally used by both groups in relation to their literary sources. For many if not most New Testament scholars a lot (even life issues) may hang on the reading of a particular text, in a way that is not so personal say for the historical accounts of Livy or Tacitus. This may account for the difficulties some feel in integrating the Paul of the Letters with the Paul of Acts. I have looked elsewhere at a roughly comparable situation between Cicero's own accounts of his role in the Catilinarian conspiracy with that attributed to him by Sallust.[11]

The purpose of this critical appraisal is not to obliterate the differences in training and purpose of the two disciplines—though several of the contributors, may I dare to suggest Paul Barnett, for example, might place themselves in both camps as occasion demanded it. Rather the series has hoped by the juxtaposition of the two to open new lines of enquiry and suggest new links. If both groups, working increasingly on common material (a situation that was not the case two generations ago), can continue to produce new insights by fruitful collaboration, the present editors will be well satisfied.

---

[10] Stephen Mitchell, *Anatolia: Land, Men, and Gods in Asia Minor*, 2 vols. (Oxford: Clarendon, 1993).

[11] Tom W. Hillard, Alanna Nobbs, and Bruce W. Winter, "Acts and the Pauline Corpus I: Ancient Literary Parallels," in *The Book of Acts in Its Ancient Literary Setting*, ed. Bruce W. Winter and Andrew D. Clarke, vol. 1 of *The Book of Acts in Its First Century Setting* (Grand Rapids: Eerdmans; Carlisle: Paternoster, 1993), 183–213.

1. The Acts of the Apostles as a Source for Studying Early Christianity

Chris Forbes

1. The Focus, Perspective, and Limitations of Acts

Imagine yourself as an airline passenger, traveling to a new city to spend a year there. You get your first view of your new place of residence as your plane comes in over the city to land. It is night and parts of the city are brilliantly lit up. The central business district is unmistakable and so are the main highways: rivers of moving lights. Whole areas stand out from the darkness as centers of twinkling activity. Others are just vague smudges of light and there are regions where nothing can be seen at all. Most frustratingly, even if you have a window seat, whole sections of your view are blocked by the wing of your plane and on the other side of the aircraft you can catch only fleeting glimpses past the heads of your fellow passengers. The plane turns and you briefly catch a new view from a completely new angle, but in moments it is gone as the plane slows down to approach the airport runway.

Studying the first thirty, fifty, or even one hundred years of the development of early Christianity has much in common with this imagined experience.[1] Some aspects of the period are vividly, though briefly, described in the evidence of the New Testament. The Acts of the Apostles is our only narrative account. It is rich with vivid vignettes, but it is also highly selective and often we cannot tell what the wider context of its narrative might be. The author's program is clearly signposted in the words of Jesus in Acts 1:8: "You will be my witnesses in Jerusalem, in all Judea and Samaria, and to the ends of the earth."[2] He

---

[1] The book of Acts can be studied from multiple perspectives, whether literary, sociological, theological, socio-rhetorical, feminist, post-colonial, "old school" historical or other, and (of course) using combinations of such methods. This chapter will focus almost exclusively on literary and historical approaches, and not even on all of those. My question will be: in what ways can historians make use of Acts as a source for the writing of the history of the early Christian movement? For a wide-ranging survey of a variety of different approaches to Acts, see Todd Penner, "Madness in the Method? The Acts of the Apostles in Current Study," *CurBR* 2.2 (2004): 223–93. The term "current" is, of course, necessarily relative.

[2] I will refer to the author of Luke's Gospel and Acts simply as "Luke" throughout this chapter. The actual identity of the author is controversial, but there seems no reason to repeat this point *ad nauseam*. On Acts 1:8, Brian Rosner and Richard Burridge, among others, note the connection between Luke's Gospel's movement towards Jerusalem and the movement in Acts from Jerusalem outwards. See Rosner's "Acts and Biblical History," in *The Book of Acts in Its Ancient Literary*

provides us with a sharply observed picture of the earliest Christian community in Jerusalem, a mere glimpse of Joppa and then of Samaria, a brief outline sketch of Antioch, and barely a mention of the countryside in between. We hear nothing *at all* of the village communities of followers of Jesus in Galilee (who in the early years must have made up the great majority of the "Jesus movement"). Then rapidly the view changes, as Syrian Antioch becomes the center of the activities of Barnabas and Saul/Paul. Next we are treated to brief sketches of Christian missionary activity on Cyprus, including dramatic encounters with "false prophets" and Roman governors. Suddenly, with little explanation, we find ourselves following Paul and Barnabas to Pisidian Antioch, a major city within the Roman province of Galatia in south-central Turkey, and then through a cycle of debates, conflicts and escapes in Iconium, Lystra, and Derbe, before their eventual return to (Syrian) Antioch.[3] From this point on, Paul's role in the narrative grows steadily until it is clear that it is his career that is the focus of the remainder of the book. For the purposes of Acts, it is Paul who will take the gospel "to the ends of the earth."

As noted above, Acts is our only narrative account of the earliest years of the social and religious movement that was to become Christianity. To its framework we can add a range of details drawn from other New Testament books, primarily the letters of Saint Paul himself. Even if we take this approach as far as we can, however, there is a great deal about which we simply know nothing at all. There are quite a number of New Testament books for which we do not know the place of composition, the intended audience, or the precise date. Instead Acts focuses relentlessly on the spread of the gospel to the north and then to the northwest, through Syria, modern Turkey, into Greece, and, eventually, on to Rome. We know from second- and third-century sources that Christianity also spread to the East (through modern Jordan and Syria into modern Iraq) and to the South (into Egypt), and there are some semi-historical traditions about how this spread happened, though on these subjects Acts tells us nothing whatsoever.

2. The Modern Historian's Problem: Varying Approaches

If the situation is as we have just described it, what is the historian of early Christianity to do about it? How do we fill the gaps in our historical information? Or if we cannot fill them, must we simply leave them blank, as a

---

Setting, ed. Bruce W. Winter and Andrew D. Clarke, vol. 1 of *The Book of Acts in Its First Century Setting*, ed. Bruce W. Winter (Grand Rapids: Eerdmans; Carlisle: Paternoster, 1993), 65–82 (70), and Burridge's "The Genre of Acts—Revisited," in *Reading Acts Today: Essays in Honour of Loveday C. A. Alexander*, ed. Steve Walton et al. (London: T&T Clark, 2011), 3–28 (18).

[3] The author takes it for granted that we know which Antioch he means. There were multiple Antiochs, Seleucias, Philippis, and Caesareas. This was the result of the penchant that ancient Kings (Antiochus I, II, and III, Seleucus I–IV, Philip II of Macedon), and later various Caesars had for naming cities after themselves (or accepting the compliment when others did).

story that cannot be told?[4] Different historians take a range of different approaches.

To some extent it is possible to fill out the picture with evidence drawn from later writings, or works of uncertain date. For Antioch in Syria, for example, we can draw on the evidence of the genuine letters of Ignatius, bishop of Antioch (ca. AD 115). Perhaps we can add the evidence of the (very different) early Christian work known as the Didache (or Teaching of the Twelve Apostles), usually thought to have originated in the neighboring Syrian hinterland, and perhaps also the evidence of Matthew's Gospel.[5] For the history of Christianity in Ephesus we may be able to draw on quite a range of writings: the Pauline Letter to the Ephesians, the first of the Revelation's "Letters to the Seven Churches," Ignatius's letter to the church in Ephesus, and perhaps more.[6] However, even when this approach has been taken as far as it can go, much remains uncertain and the results are relatively meager. Where can the historian turn for further information?

Historians agree that several of the documents making up the New Testament still show signs of the process of their composition. They contain "fossil remnants" of views less fully developed than their own. In some cases they may allow us to reconstruct, with various degrees of plausibility, the sources on which they were based. Thus, for example, at one time scholars regularly attempted to reconstruct what we could know of the "pre-Pauline Hellenistic Christian communities." They did this by starting with the evidence of Acts 6 and 7 and extrapolating by using what may reasonably be supposed to be traditional materials embedded in the Pauline letters. By removing any characteristically Pauline motifs, an approximation of the opinions of pre-Pauline followers of Stephen could be deduced. Perhaps the evidence of the Letter to the Hebrews could be factored in here as well.

The best-known example of this approach in contemporary scholarship is the full-scale attempt to reconstruct the hypothetical lost document known as Q. At its simplest, the "Q hypothesis" attempts to explain the many passages which the Gospels of Matthew and Luke share, but did not derive from Mark. Either one of these two gospel writers copied from the other, or both copied

---

[4] The problem I am dramatizing here is, of course, not unique to early Christian history. It is of the nature of *all* historical writing that it is based on incomplete, non-representative samples of information from the past. The case of the first thirty, fifty, or one hundred years of the early Christian movement is simply a vivid example of a universal problem.

[5] For an introduction to issues related to the letters of Ignatius see Paul Foster, "The Epistles of Ignatius of Antioch," parts 1 and 2, *ExpTim* 117.12 (2006): 487–95 and 118.1 (2007): 2–11, and for a later dating see Timothy D. Barnes, "The Date of Ignatius," *ExpTim* 120.3 (2008): 119–30. The dating of the Didache is highly controversial, with perhaps a majority of recent scholarship opting for a mid- to late first-century date. See the survey of Jonathan A. Draper, "The Apostolic Fathers: The Didache," *ExpTim* 117.5 (2006): 177–81. If Matthew's Gospel was written in Antioch as many suggest, then it becomes relevant here as well, and its literary relationship to the Didache becomes even more important. For a recent example of this synthetic approach, see Michelle Slee, *The Church in Antioch in the First Century C.E.: Communion and Conflict* (Sheffield: Sheffield Academic, 2003).

[6] For a recent example of this approach, see Paul Trebilco, *The Early Christians in Ephesus from Paul to Ignatius* (Grand Rapids: Eerdmans, 2007).

from a no-longer-extant common source or sources. The great majority of scholars argue for one substantial common source, conventionally known as Q. Having identified the passages in Matthew and Luke which seem to be derived from Q, scholars next attempt to reconstruct what Q must have resembled in its own right. Can we go further? In its original form, did Q have its own distinct point of view (as Matthew and Luke do)? Is it possible to reconstruct the overall theology of Q?[7] If so, can we reconstruct the "theological profile" of the people who originally formulated and used Q? If we can, is it possible to suggest at least the social, if not the actual, geographical location of their community?[8] If even approximate answers can be given to these questions, then we can fill at least some of the gaps that Acts has left in our overall picture of the development of early Christianity.

In reality, however, Q scholarship has gone much further than this. In particular, John Kloppenborg has been highly influential in arguing that it is possible to discern a number of stages in the literary development of Q and that these correspond to stages of development in the ideas of the "Q community/communities."[9] If Kloppenborg is correct, we can tell quite a complex story of the development of one important strand within early Christianity which would otherwise have been largely lost to history. We can do this by focusing our historical attention on the implicit, embedded evidence of the Q material in Matthew and Luke.

John Dominic Crossan takes this broad approach to its logical conclusion. In *The Birth of Christianity*[10] Crossan sets out to write a comprehensive history "discovering what happened in the years after the execution of Jesus."[11] He does this based substantially on the evidence embedded in the Q material and the Gospel of Thomas, and particularly on what he calls the "Common Sayings Tradition," that is, material common to both of them.[12] To this he adds material from the Didache, the Gospel of Peter and a range of other early Christian material (including the extant letters of Paul and other New Testament texts) set within a rich context of evidence drawn from Greco-Roman history, cultural anthropology and other sources. This approach allows him to propose that

---

[7] A positive answer would of course require us to be confident that the shared passages of Matthew and Luke we identify as Q constitute a valid sample of the original content of the work.

[8] Once again, a positive answer would require us to be confident that Q (and our understanding of it) really represented the overall views of a definable early Christian community. Such an interpretative move is often made for "the Matthean community" or "the Johannine community." However, (a) how sure can we be that the document on which we base this analysis (Matthew's Gospel, John's Gospel, or in this case Q) was the only, or even the primary, faith-document of an actual community? Also, (b) how sure can we be that the sample of Q available to us is representative of its original content?

[9] John S. Kloppenborg, *The Formation of Q: Trajectories in Ancient Wisdom Collections* (Philadelphia: Fortress, 1987), and a variety of other publications. A similar approach was taken to the traditions in Mark's Gospel by Burton L. Mack, in his *A Myth of Innocence: Mark and Christian Origins* (Philadelphia: Fortress, 1988).

[10] John Dominic Crossan, *The Birth of Christianity* (San Francisco: Harper, 1998).

[11] These words form the subtitle of the volume printed on the cover.

[12] See Crossan, *The Birth of Christianity*, 253–56, where the core of the idea of the Common Sayings Tradition is attributed to Stephen J. Patterson. See also Appendix 1, 587–91.

several (competing? complementary?) styles of early Christianity existed, which more conventional historical approaches have largely ignored.[13] What is remarkable is the extent to which the framework of the Acts of the Apostles—the *only* extant narrative dealing directly with the period—has been sidelined.[14]

3. Methodological Questions

I wish to emphasize that my intention in making the point about the sidelining of Acts is not to disparage Crossan's or Kloppenborg's projects, both of which are argued out in meticulous detail, and are often illuminating, and always erudite. Nor am I suggesting that their work is isolated. On the contrary, their rather different approaches have been part of a broader movement which is highly influential.[15] My point is to dramatize the question of historical methodology that such approaches raise. To what extent is it justifiable for a historian to focus on "reading between the lines" of our evidence, particularly if this is done at the expense of reading what is explicitly *on* the lines of one major piece of that evidence? How certain can we be of Kloppenborg's or Crossan's reconstructions of documents that no longer exist, or of the stages of development by which they were formed? Certainly not everyone has been persuaded of the value of the recent emphasis on Q. John P. Meier famously said:

> I cannot help thinking that biblical scholarship would be greatly advanced if every morning all exegetes would repeat as a mantra: 'Q is a hypothetical document whose exact extension, wording, originating community, strata, and stages of redaction cannot be known.' This daily devotion might save us flights of fancy that are destined, in my view, to end in skepticism.[16]

To this John Kloppenborg pointedly replied:

> Q is indeed a hypothetical document. Equally hypothetical, however, are Matthew and Luke's dependence upon Mark, something that Meier (along with

---

[13] For example, Crossan strikingly contrasts what he calls the "life tradition," originating in Galilee, with the more conventional "death tradition," originating in Jerusalem, with its focus on the importance of the sufferings and death of Jesus. He also distinguishes between a range of differing "eschatological" attitudes. See *The Birth of Christianity*, 258–71, 407–14, and 501–502. Crossan gives credit to Kloppenborg for the idea of the "two spheres" of early Christian theology.

[14] Crossan's index contains sixty-six references to Q, forty-five to the Gospel of Thomas, sixty-four to the Didache, thirty-one to the Gospel of Peter and a bare fifteen references to the Acts of the Apostles.

[15] Crossan himself emphasises that his "layers" (in Q and Thomas) are defined by tradition, while Kloppenborg's are literary-compositional. See his response to Question 60 in the "Seminar on Materials & Methods in Historical Jesus Research" originally posted on the XTalk Discussion List (https://groups.yahoo.com/neo/groups/crosstalk2/info), now available at https://web.archive.org/web/20080807060239/http://www.ntgateway.com/Jesus/crossan.htm. My thanks to Dr Mark Goodacre for locating this archived copy.

[16] John P. Meier, *A Marginal Jew: Rethinking the Historical Jesus*, vol. 2 (New York: Doubleday, 1994), 178.

Farrer and Goulder) apparently did not think it worthwhile calling "hypothetical." These too might be added to Meier's mantra. For that matter, the text that we call "Mark" is a hypothetical document. It is reconstructed on the basis of dozens of manuscripts, none earlier than the beginning of the third century CE. The substance lent to the text of Mark by the printing presses of the Deutsche Bibelgesellschaft should not be allowed to disguise the fact that "Mark" is not an extant *document*, but a *text* that is reconstructed from much later manuscripts with the help of hypotheses developed to account for the numerous disagreements between those manuscripts and the text-critical criteria that flow from those hypotheses. What we reconstruct as "the" text of Mark is, furthermore, only one in an imaginable series of texts extending from the initial draft(s) of Mark, to some putative "final form" of the gospel, to the texts of Mark used by Matthew and Luke. With the help of an anachronistic analogy of modern publishing, we designate one of that series as the "final" text of Mark and focus our reconstructive efforts on that hypothetical text.[17]

I take Kloppenborg's point, but his argument does not prove what he wants it to prove. Mark (and likewise Matthew and Luke) may indeed be hypothetical in the sense he defines. Q, however, is a hypothesis built on (a) the hypothetical Mark, (b) the (equally) hypothetical Matthew and Luke, (c) hypotheses about their literary relationship (Markan priority, Matthean and Lukan independence) and (d) Matthew and Luke's shared data which they do not share with the hypothetical Mark. However hypothetical Matthew, Mark, and Luke may be (and, I repeat, I take Kloppenborg's point), Q is necessarily several whole stages more hypothetical. Necessarily more hypothetical still is any theory about the stages of its composition, or the communities which may lie behind that development.[18]

The consequences of this fact must be taken seriously. Historical priority must be given to documents we actually have reasonably direct access to, as opposed to hypothetical, embedded, and no longer extant documents to which our access is necessarily limited. However, what this priority must mean has yet to be determined. Certainly it need not mean that we have no choice but to adopt the perspective of (in this case) Acts as the only possible perspective. Simply paraphrasing Acts is not the writing of history. Nor does it mean that the proposed evidence of Q or the "Common Sayings Tradition" is to be ignored. Surely, however, they, and all other non-extant sources, must be treated more tentatively and with greater caution than sources (even poor sources) of which we actually *have* texts.

---

[17] John Kloppenborg, "On Dispensing with Q?: Goodacre on the Relation of Luke to Matthew," *NTS* 49 (2003): 215.
[18] At least four major works dealing with Q published since Kloppenborg's ideas became well-known take fundamentally different approaches: Christopher M. Tuckett, *Q and the History of Early Christianity* (Edinburgh: T&T Clark, 1996), Dale C. Allison Jr., *The Jesus Tradition in Q* (Harrisburg: Trinity Press International, 1997), Alan Kirk, *The Composition of the Sayings Source: Genre, Synchrony, and Wisdom Redaction in Q* (Leiden: Brill, 1998), and (as part of a wider project) James D. G. Dunn, *Jesus Remembered. Christianity in the Making*, vol. 1 (Grand Rapids: Eerdmans, 2003), 147–58.

What follows is a limited survey of some, but not all, of the issues that need to be resolved in order to make the best use of Acts as a historical source. For reasons of space, issues to do with the authorship, dating, and sources of Acts have been largely set aside, to focus on the related questions of genre expectations and historical testability. In the Recommended Reading at the end of the chapter the reader is referred to some of the many recent thorough commentaries on Acts for more complete, integrated treatments of these issues.

4. The Question of the Genre of Acts: A Way Forward?

Before we can begin writing our proposed history of early Christianity, we need to decide what kind of evidence Acts provides us with. What kind of a piece of writing is Acts? What can we reasonably expect of it?

Over the last twenty years a clear scholarly consensus has emerged that the Gospels can be understood within the genre and conventions of Greco-Roman biography.[19] There is no equivalent consensus for Acts.[20] The first reason is that, alone among the books of the New Testament, Luke's Gospel and Acts present themselves to the reader as a two-part work.[21] Whatever Acts is, it is the sequel to Luke's Gospel. This complicates the question of genre. Clearly Acts is not in any normal sense a biography, even if Luke's Gospel is. The second half of Acts certainly focuses on the career of Paul, as a biography might, but what of the first half? Secondly, what of the definition implied by Acts 1:1, "In my former book, Theophilus, I wrote about all that *Jesus began* to do and to teach until the day he was taken up" (NIV)?[22] That certainly seems to suggest a high degree of continuity between Luke's Gospel and Acts. How

---

[19] This is primarily due to the work of Richard A. Burridge, *What are the Gospels?* (Cambridge: Cambridge University Press, 1992, 2004). The consensus does *not* suggest that the Gospels are not rich with Jewish elements, but that such material has been organized within the framework of an identifiable Greco-Roman genre, which would be thoroughly familiar to Greek-speakers, whether they were Greco-Roman or Jewish.

[20] For recent surveys of the question of the genre of Acts, see Thomas E. Phillips, "The Genre of Acts: Moving Toward a Consensus?" *CurBR* 4.3 (2006): 365–96, and Sean A. Adams, "The Genre of Luke and Acts: The State of the Question," in *Issues in Luke–Acts: Selected Essays*, ed. Sean A. Adams and Michael W. Pahl (Piscataway, NJ: Gorgias, 2012), 97–120.

[21] Acts 1:1 clearly expects its audience to identify the Gospel of Luke as "my former book, Theophilus, (in which) I wrote about all that Jesus began to do and to teach" (NIV). The question of the structural and thematic unity of the two works is more complex. For recent discussion, see I. Howard Marshall, "Acts and the 'Former Treatise,'" in Winter and Clarke, *The Book of Acts in Its Ancient Literary Setting*, 163–82; Michael F. Bird, "The Unity of Luke–Acts in Recent Discussion," *JSNT* 29.4 (2007): 425–48; Patrick E. Spencer, "The Unity of Luke–Acts: A Four-Bolted Hermeneutical Hinge," *CurBR* 5.3 (2007): 341–66, and the discussion of Craig S. Keener, *Acts: An Exegetical Commentary*, vol. 1 (Grand Rapids: Baker, 2012), 553–74. Common authorship is the overwhelming consensus of scholarship, despite the questions raised by Mikeal C. Parsons and Richard I. Pervo, *Rethinking the Unity of Luke and Acts* (Minneapolis: Fortress, 1993); Patricia Walters, *The Assumed Authorial Unity of Luke and Acts: A Reassessment of the Evidence* (Cambridge: Cambridge University Press, 2009), and Andrew F. Gregory and C. Kavin Rowe, *Rethinking the Unity and Reception of Luke and Acts* (Columbia: University of South Carolina Press, 2010).

[22] Or: what "Jesus did and taught from the beginning," NRSV; the ESV agrees with the NIV.

Chris Forbes

is Acts related to the conventions of ancient biography (if that is what Luke's Gospel is)? Its conventional title, *praxeis*, "acts" or "deeds," could be half of the conventional "words and deeds" that made up the content of biographies. Does the word "acts" on its own suggest history rather than biography?[23] Is Acts, then, a history?[24] From a modern commonsense perspective this looks like the obvious solution, and many scholars argue such a case. Since the publication of F. J. Foakes-Jackson, K. Lake and H. J. Cadbury's five-volume *The Beginnings of Christianity* (London: Macmillan, 1920–1933), the mainstream view in English language scholarship at least has been that Acts was intended as a piece of historical writing. It could be expected, then, to work within the conventions of ancient historical writing more broadly. The fact that Acts was a chronological narrative focused on events to do with the growth of a movement, with speeches illustrating important features of its theme, fits the history genre well.[25] Acts might be good historical writing (in ancient terms) or quite poor historical writing, but it seems that its *aim* was historical.

Two major points speak against such a view, however. First, in the Greco-Roman world, "histories" were normally works on a far grander scale than Acts. Herodotus's *History* had been written in nine books and a total of about 200,000 words. The scale of Thucydides's *History* is similar. Though incomplete, it weighs in at about 155,000 words. The surviving portion of Polybius takes up over 300,000 words and, closer to the date of Acts, the extant parts of Dionysius of Halicarnassus's *Roman Antiquities* come to 188,000 words, although the complete version would have been closer to 500,000. Josephus's *Jewish War* has just under 130,000 words and his *Jewish Antiquities* far more, about 207,000 words. Even Velleius Paterculus's brief *Roman History* (in Latin) has around 26,000 words. Acts, on the other hand, has only about 18,500 words. In

---

[23] See, for example, the comments of Aristotle, *Rhetoric* 1.1360a 35 and cf. Quintilian, *Inst.* 2.4.2. See also David E. Aune, *The New Testament in Its Literary Environment* (Philadelphia: Westminster, 1987), 78, for a brief review of other works described as or entitled the "Acts" of various people. Aune doubts that the category is useful for understanding the New Testament "Acts." To mention only one point, the New Testament "Acts" seems to be the only example which deals with the actions of more than one main character. On this point see Gregory E. Sterling, *Historiography and Self-Definition: Josephus, Luke–Acts, and Apologetic History* (Leiden: Brill, 1992), 314–15.

[24] Phillips argues that some version of the category "history" remains the dominant view in scholarship, with different scholars opting for different varieties of history ("The Genre of Acts," 375–82). James Dunn concurs, barely considering other options (*Beginning from Jerusalem* [Grand Rapids: Eerdmans, 2007], 68–73).

[25] Here the comment of Pervo, that "The speeches, often held to align Acts with historiography, are not consonant with the orations found in histories. Those tend to comment on or explain decisions, but the speeches in Acts are very often part of the narrative, provoking action or advancing the plot" (*Acts: A Commentary* [Minneapolis: Fortress, 2008], 17) seems to me to miss the point. Speeches in Greco-Roman histories do both things. See the discussion of David L. Balch, "ἀκριβῶς ... γράψαι (Luke 1:3): To Write the Full History of God's Receiving All Nations," in *Jesus and the Heritage of Israel: Luke's Narrative Claim upon Israel's Legacy*, ed. David P. Moessner (Harrisburg: Trinity Press International, 1999), 229–50. Pervo's further comment that "The book is devoid of a chronological framework" seems to me to be quite misleading, even given the qualifications of n. 101.

simple terms, ancient readers would have been unlikely to think of Acts as a history. It was not long enough or (in literary terms) grand enough.

Second, it has been forcefully argued that the way Acts begins, with a "recapitulatory reference" to Luke's Gospel, would probably not have reminded an ancient reader of the conventional style of the histories they knew.[26] There were accepted ways of explaining one's purposes and signaling one's intentions as a historical writer, built up over centuries, and Luke does not use them. It should also be noted that Luke's anonymity within his own narrative is atypical for ancient historical works.[27]

Partly as a result of the recognition of these points, a number of scholars have formulated refinements on or alternatives to this view. Some suggest Acts is related to shorter and more focused "historical monographs" (rather than major histories), perhaps those written closer to the biblical tradition such as 1 and 2 Maccabees.[28] Others propose that Acts is more closely related to "apologetic historiography," perhaps like that of Josephus.[29] Keener helpfully paraphrases "apologetic historiography" as works written by "authors with minority perspectives."[30] Adams distinguishes between apologetic works (written primarily for readers from the dominant culture) and self-definitional works (written primarily for readers within the minority), while admitting both audiences can be in view.[31] In the case of "apologetic historiography," however, the far greater scale of Josephus's work once again proves a difficulty for the parallel with Acts. It is true that there were shorter, more focused works of a

---

[26] On this subject see Loveday Alexander, "Luke's Preface in the Context of Greek Preface-Writing," *NovT* 28.1 (1986): 48–74; *The Preface to Luke's Gospel: Literary Convention and Social Context in Luke 1.1–4 and Acts 1.1* (Cambridge: Cambridge University Press, 1993); "The Preface to Acts and the Historians," in *History, Literature and Society in the Book of Acts*, ed. Ben Witherington III (Cambridge: Cambridge University Press, 1996), 73–103, and Pervo, *Acts: A Commentary*, 32–33. For critiques of Alexander's view see David E. Aune, "Luke 1.1–4: Historical or Scientific *Prooimion*?" in *Paul, Luke and the Graeco-Roman World*, ed. Alf Christophersen et al. (New York/London: T&T Clark, 2002), 138–48, and Sean A. Adams, "Luke's Preface and its Relationship to Greek Historiography: A Response to Loveday Alexander," *JGRChJ* 3 (2006): 177–91.

[27] On this point see Jacob Jervell, "The future of the past: Luke's vision of salvation history and its bearing on his writing of history," in Witherington, *History, Literature and Society*, 104–26 (111). There are, however, exceptions ("Xenophon, Diodorus Siculus, Dionysius of Halicarnassus, and others"), as Adams, "Luke's Preface," 181, points out. It should be noted that Luke's anonymity would be equally odd for a writer of biography.

[28] See the discussion of Darryl W. Palmer, "Acts and the Ancient Historical Monograph," in Winter and Clarke, *The Book of Acts in Its Ancient Literary Setting*, 1–29. One problem for this view is that historical monographs could also be long, indeed in some cases longer than general histories. There does not seem to be a commonly understood ancient term for "short historical monographs."

[29] This view is argued by Sterling, *Historiography and Self-Definition*.

[30] Keener, *Acts*, vol. 1, 91.

[31] Sean A. Adams, "Luke, Josephus, and Self-Definition: The Genre of Luke–Acts and its Relationship to Apologetic Historiography and Collected Biography," in *Christian Origins and Hellenistic Judaism*, ed. Stanley E. Porter and Andrew W. Pitts (Leiden: Brill, 2013), 451–56. See also Daniel Marguerat, *The First Christian Historian: Writing the "Acts of the Apostles"* (Cambridge: Cambridge University Press, 2002), 109, and Adams, "The Genre of Luke and Acts," in Adams and Pahl, *Issues in Luke–Acts*, 97–120.

historical kind being written, particularly in the period of the first centuries BC and AD. This was particularly so in Latin, with works such as Sallust's *Jugurthine War* (21,000 words) and *The Conspiracy of Catiline* (36,000 words), and later Velleius Paterculus's *Roman History* (ca. 26,000 words, as noted above). It is not clear, however, that these works constitute a genre ("short historical monograph"?), within the conventions of which Acts could be seen as working. Most recently, Doohee Lee has suggested that Acts can be understood in terms of some of the stylistic features of the sub-genre of "tragic history."[32] Overall, however, the mainstream view is well-expressed by Loveday Alexander:

> If we are to find a plausible location for Acts within the Greek historiographical tradition it should be … the more scholarly, less rhetorical side of history (archaeology, ethnography), and perhaps especially where the author and/or subject is non-Greek.[33]

Alternatively some argue that Acts, as part of a two-volume work, is most closely related to certain varieties of Greek semi-biographical writing. Charles H. Talbert proposed that Luke–Acts should be understood against the background of Greco-Roman philosophical biographies and "succession narratives."[34] These narrated the life of the founder of a philosophical movement and then followed it up with a narrative of the development of the "school" he had founded and its successive leaders. Acts, however, does not give us a succession of early Christian leaders. It does not have the expected "generational" structure.[35] Others have suggested that there is evidence of a genre of "lives" of *groups*, whether philosophical groups such as the Pythagoreans, or nationalities such as "the Greeks" or "the Romans."[36] Could Acts be best seen as a "life" of the early church, understood as a new "school

---

[32] Doohee Lee, *Luke–Acts and "Tragic History,"* WUNT 2.346 (Tübingen: Mohr Siebeck, 2013).

[33] Alexander, "The Preface to Acts and the Historians," 102. The most prominent scholar still comparing Acts to mainstream Greek historical writing is David L. Balch. See, for example, his "The Genre of Luke–Acts: Individual Biography, Adventure Novel, or Political History?" *SwJT* 33 (1990): 5–19, or his "ἀκριβῶς … γράψαι (Luke 1:3)," cited above.

[34] See Charles H. Talbert, *Literary Patterns, Theological Themes and the Genre of Luke–Acts* (Missoula: Scholars, 1974), *What is a Gospel?* (Philadelphia: Fortress, 1977), "Biographies of Philosophers and Rulers as instruments of religious propaganda in Mediterranean antiquity," *ANRW.* II.16.2 (1978): 1619–51, and most recently chapters 1–3 of his *Reading Luke–Acts in Its Mediterranean Milieu* (Leiden: Brill, 2003). One of the earliest of such works was the Life of Pythagoras by Aristoxenus, perhaps ca. 335 BC.

[35] Talbert suggests that the narrative of Acts would have been heard by its first audience as containing succession *motifs* ("Succession in Luke–Acts and in the Lukan Milieu," in his *Reading Luke–Acts in Its Mediterranean Milieu*, 19–55, 46–50), but whether this is sufficient to establish the genre of the work is a different matter, as Talbert is well aware.

[36] I believe the suggestion was first made by Richard Burridge in his *What are the Gospels?* 237–39, with reference to the fourth century BC work of Dikaearchus known as "the 'life' of the Greeks" (known only from fragmentary quotations in later writers). It is also developed by Talbert in his "Succession in Luke–Acts and in the Lukan Milieu," 29–30, with reference to Varro's first-century-BC work *On the Life of the Roman People*, and Iamblichus's (much later) *On the Pythagorean Way of Life*.

of thought" or a new "people"?[37] Here the question of the relationship between ancient categories of biography and history is clearly an issue.

Most recently, Sean Adams has suggested that there existed in antiquity a genre of "collected biography," first exemplified by the late fifth-century-BC work of Stesimbrotus of Thasos, conventionally entitled *On Themistocles, Thucydides, and Pericles*.[38] Other pre-Christian examples include Antiphon's *On the Life of the Champions of Virtue*, probably from the third or second century BC, Callimachus's *Pinakes* and works by Hermippus of Smyrna, Neanthes of Cyzicus, and Cornelius Nepos.[39] Adams also includes the succession lists of philosophical schools as a form of collected biography.[40] Far and away the best-known examples, however, are the *Parallel Lives* of Plutarch of Chaeroneia (ca. AD 120) and the *Lives of Eminent Philosophers* of Diogenes Laertius (ca. AD 250). In my view, the different categories of "collected biographies" are too diverse, and the parallels with Acts too limited, to make a decisive identification of genre possible. The brief portraits of the different early Christian leaders in Acts are not sufficiently biographical,[41] and the shift of focus in the narrative from one to another is not "succession" in any meaningful sense. Acts certainly displays some features of collected biography, but Adams is correct that "Acts' affiliation with collected biographies is not perfect."[42] Nonetheless, we are in Adams's debt for his sophisticated and detailed analysis.

Alongside the varieties of Greco-Roman historical and biographical literature, two other genres have been suggested for the Acts of the Apostles. Parallels have been drawn between Acts and works of epic poetry such as

---

[37] Jervell comments ("The future of the past," 112) that "It was unheard of in antiquity to write the history of a religious movement, since history was political history, dealing with significant events. A historian must have at least one qualification: political understanding. A newly formed sect was no suitable subject for a historian." This is broadly true, but does not really allow for the flexibility of the historical genre in the first century.

[38] Sean A. Adams, *The Genre of Acts and Collected Biography* (Cambridge: Cambridge University Press, 2013), 72. See also his briefer treatment, "Luke, Josephus, and Self-Definition: The Genre of Luke–Acts and its relationship to Apologetic Historiography and Collected Biography," in Porter and Pitts, *Christian Origins and Hellenistic Judaism*, 439–59. The known fragments of Stesimbrotus are collected by Jacoby in his *FGH I–III*, 107. See also *Brill's New Jacoby* (Leiden: Brill, 2007), 107. It should be noted that Adams's suggestion that Stesimbrotus's work was, in fact, written as a collected biography can be disputed. Sviatoslav Dmitriev raises the question: "Could it be that Stesimbrotos wrote separate biographies (if this term can be applied at all) of several Athenian politicians, which were then put together under his name (and under a new title?) at a later date?" (*Brill's New Jacoby* online, http://referenceworks.brillonline.com/entries/brill-s-new-jacoby/stesimbrotos-of-thasos-107-a107?s.num=13_#BNJTEXT107_T_1, accessed April 2015).

[39] Adams, *The Genre of Acts*, 92–96. On Antiphon see Jacoby, *FGH IV*, 1096; until Cornelius Nepos (who wrote in the mid-first century BC) none of these works survives whole. Adams's full listing of known "collected biographies" can be found in *The Genre of Acts*, 112–13.

[40] Adams, *The Genre of Acts*, 102–108.

[41] Adams correctly notes the lack of discussion of the births, childhood events, personal appearance, and deaths of the leading characters in Acts, *The Genre of Acts*, 169.

[42] Adams, *The Genre of Acts*, 171. He notes the geographic setting of Acts and the continuous narrative.

Homer's *Iliad* and *Odyssey*[43] and Vergil's *Aeneid*.[44] However, the fundamental facts of the scale of these different works, and the contrast between epic verse and prose narrative, have meant that very few have found these parallels persuasive. Far more influential has been the view of Richard Pervo, who has compared both the canonical Acts and the later apocryphal Acts with the narrative techniques of the Greco-Roman novel.[45] Pointing correctly to the social and literary level of these works, Pervo has argued that Acts has far more in common with popular novels than with the elite literature of history. He argues that novels are typified by a combination of what he calls themes, motifs, and modes.[46] (In what follows, comments in brackets are mine, not Pervo's, unless noted otherwise.)

Under "themes" he notes politics, patriotism, religion, wisdom, fidelity (particularly but not exclusively sexual), and social status. It is unclear whether "church politics" (the "apostolic council" of Acts 15) would count, and I doubt whether "patriotism" in any conventional sense applies as a theme in Acts. "Religion" is less clear. Obviously Acts is a religious work in modern terms. What would an ancient person think? In terms of "wisdom," there is little in Acts of "sententious utterances and conventional proverbs" (Pervo, 106). "Fidelity" (to ideals) is certainly exemplified by martyrdom in Acts 7, but in novels fidelity is almost always interpersonal and predominantly sexual. Acts provides no clear parallel. Though the "status" of particular leaders is certainly a topic in Acts, "questions of wealth, rank, education, birth, and social standing" (106) are only occasionally of significance.

As "motifs" Pervo notes travel, adventure and excitement (certainly prominent in Acts),[47] warfare (insignificant in Acts), aretalogy (accounts of the notable actions of a god: clearly relevant), miscellany ("the interest in what is exotic and bizarre," Pervo, 107: doubtful), court life and intrigue (occasional), and rhetoric (reasonably common). It is odd that Pervo does not include the topic of "separated lovers," a mainstay of the ancient novels, as either a theme or a motif.

"Modes" (closely related to genre, Pervo, 108) include the marvelous, the historical, the sentimental, the comic and satiric, the realistic, the didactic, the missionary, the pastoral (meaning the idealizing of the rural lifestyle: rare in

[43] See particularly Dennis R. MacDonald, *Does the New Testament Imitate Homer? Four Cases from the Acts of the Apostles* (New Haven: Yale University Press, 2003). For a full list of MacDonald's work in this area see the bibliography of Phillips, "The Genre of Acts: Moving Toward a Consensus?" 391.

[44] Marianne Palmer Bonz, *The Past as Legacy: Luke–Acts and Ancient Epic* (Philadelphia: Fortress, 2000).

[45] See particularly Richard I. Pervo, *Profit with Delight: The Literary Genre of the Acts of the Apostles* (Philadelphia: Fortress, 1987), and Pervo's *Acts: A Commentary*. For a convenient collection of the extant Greek novels in translation, see B. P. Reardon, *Collected Ancient Greek Novels*, 2nd ed. (Berkeley: University of California Press, 2008).

[46] For the "themes, motifs and modes" discussed here, see Pervo, *Profit with Delight*, 105–10. His comment (105) that the lists he gives "stress variation no less than repetition" should be noted.

[47] Pervo aptly notes (107) that "Trials, shipwreck, piracy, banditry, threatened rape, kidnapping, seduction, imprisonment, riots, execution, intended suicide, and apparent death appear to have been perpetual favorites of which readers simply could not get too much."

novels) and the tragic (lacking in novels). As generic modes, only "the historical" really applies to Acts, and that may not be as a novel.

There is much that is of value here. The essential problem for Pervo's case, however, is that many of the literary features he (correctly) identifies in Acts are simply not diagnostic of the genre of the novel. They may be characteristic of novels, but they are also commonplace in other genres. In many cases they are simply examples or features of skilled narrative writing, whether novelistic, historiographical, or other. Thus David Aune comments:

> The term "historical novel" should be reserved for novels that follow a historical sequence of events ... rather than applied to fictional narratives set in the real world.... The factual accuracy of Acts (variously assessed) is irrelevant to generic classification if Luke *intended* to narrate actual events. Luke's use of historical prefaces and his mention of sources are not found in novels.... Many of the episodes he discusses, with their constituent themes and motifs, far from being unique to novels and Acts, are found in both factual and fictional narratives in the Hellenistic world.[48]

As an example of Aune's point we might take one of the most commonly argued novelistic plot devices in Acts, the "storm at sea and shipwreck" motif which dominates Acts 27. Storms at sea, of course, are a reality as well as a literary motif, and there were famous cases narrated in historical works and in other genres. The storm that followed closely after the battle of Arginusae (406 BC) is narrated briefly in Xenophon, *Hellenika* 1.6.24–35, and with greater drama in Diodorus Siculus, *Hist.* 13.97–100. Various storms and consequent shipwrecks during the Punic Wars are described briefly by Polybius (*Hist.* 1.37, 39.6, and 54.6). Shipwreck is used as a vivid political metaphor in Polybius (*Hist.* 6.44.3–8). In the second century AD Diogenes of Oenoanda quotes a letter of the philosopher Epicurus describing his own experience of surviving a shipwreck while traveling from Athens to Lampsacus.[49] Finally, Josephus's *Vita* 13–16 briefly describes his own experience of shipwreck on a voyage to Rome. Here we have shipwrecks described in histories (both in narrative and as an editorial metaphor), in letters later transcribed into an inscription on stone and in an autobiographical work.[50]

---

[48] Aune, *The New Testament in Its Literary Environment*, 80. The genre of "historical novel" is neither as common nor as clearly defined as Pervo suggests (see Keener, *Acts* vol. 1, 64–65).

[49] See Plutarch, *Mor.* 1090e, and Martin Ferguson Smith, *Diogenes of Oenoanda: The Epicurean Inscription* (Naples: Bibliopolis, 1993), Fragment 72. On this account see Diskin Clay, "Sailing to Lampsacus: Diogenes of Oenoanda, New Fragment 7," *GRBS* 14 (1973): 49–59, and "The Philosophical Inscription of Diogenes of Oenoanda: New Discoveries 1969–1983," *ANRW* II.36.4: 2446–559, 3231–32, esp. 2513, 2542–48.

[50] On Paul's shipwreck see, for different points of view, Colin J. Hemer, *The Book of Acts*, 141–52, Brian M. Rapske, "Acts, Travel and Shipwreck," in *The Book of Acts in Its Graeco-Roman Setting*, ed. David W. J. Gill and Conrad Gempf, vol. 2 of *The Book of Acts in Its First Century Setting*, ed. Bruce W. Winter (Grand Rapids: Eerdmans; Carlisle: Paternoster, 1994), 1–47 (29–46), J. M. Gilchrist, "The Historicity of Paul's Shipwreck," *JSNT* 61 (1996): 29–51, and Pervo, *Acts: A Commentary*, 644–67.

Other themes, motifs, and modes, though they may be common in, or even characteristic of novels, are not exclusive to novels. Examples (and clusters of examples) can easily be found in other genres, including history and biography. For example, Pervo argues that "like ancient novelists, Luke frequently resorted to having speeches interrupted, a dramatic device."[51] His own footnote gives references to nine examples, and then adds that "the technique was (also) used by historians," but gives no examples. A range of examples is available.[52] This literary device was not restricted to novels.

More dramatically, miracle stories and visionary experiences are reported by Herodotus and a range of other Greek historians, not merely by novelists.[53] As with the example of interruptions to speeches above, this may or may not prove anything about the historicity of the phenomena, but it shows decisively that they cannot be taken as proof of genre. Likewise, trial scenes occur in Acts, the Greek novels, and a range of other genres, and can be studied from both an historical and a literary viewpoint.[54] Once again, remarkable escapes from captivity may occur in the novels and also in Acts, but the extraordinary escape of Moeragenes from the clutches of Agathocles in Alexandria in 202 BC (narrated by Polybius in *Hist.* 15.27.8–28.9) is a match for any of them. Features such as these therefore, even in combination, should not be used as diagnostic evidence of the genre "novel" for Acts. Further, as Keener argues, the evidence of Paul's letters makes it perfectly clear that we should expect such features as escapes from danger in any account of his life.[55]

Sean Adams usefully comments:

> Although Acts shows some similarities to ancient novels in its size, meter, and methods of characterization [and I would add, in the drama of its narrative], there are some notable differences … the structure of Acts as a whole differs notably from novels, since it is structured on multiple, near-discrete lives (e.g., the successive shift to focus on different disciples—Peter, Barnabas, Philip,

---

[51] Pervo, *Profit with Delight*, 76 and n. 108.

[52] For examples see Herodotus, *Hist.* 8.26.3, 8.59.1, 8.61.1, 9.11.2, Xenophon, *Anab.* 3.1.27, 3.1.31 and 3.2.9, Dionysius of Halicarnassus, *Ant. rom.* 11.4, and (in other genres), Homer, *Il.* 1.292. These examples come from Daniel Lynwood Smith, "Interrupted Speech in Luke–Acts," *JBL* 134.1 (2015): 177–91, and draw on his *The Rhetoric of Interruption: Speech-Making, Turn-Taking, and Rule-Breaking in Luke–Acts and Ancient Greek Narrative* (Berlin: de Gruyter, 2012). See also G. H. R. Horsley, "Speeches and Dialogue in Acts," *NTS* 32.4 (1986): 609–14, esp. 610–12, and Aune, *The New Testament in Its Literary Environment*, 127, who mentions interruptions in speeches in Josephus, in *B.J.* 1.629; 2.605; 3.485; 7.389 and in Herodian, *Hist.* 2.5.8.

[53] See William V. Harris, "Greek and Roman Hallucinations," in *Mental Disorders in the Classical World*, ed. William V. Harris (Leiden: Brill, 2013), 285–306 (esp. 289 and 295).

[54] The motif probably makes its literary debut in Plato's *Apology*. In Acts it has been studied from the historical viewpoint by, for example, A. N. Sherwin-White, *Roman Society and Roman Law in the New Testament* (Oxford: Oxford University Press, 1963), esp. chs. 1, 3 and 5, and Brian M. Rapske, *The Book of Acts and Paul in Roman Custody*, (Grand Rapids: Eerdmans, 1993). For the literary viewpoint see, for example, Sandra Schwartz, "The Trial Scene in the Greek Novels and in Acts," in *Contextualizing Acts: Lukan Narrative and Greco-Roman Discourse*, ed. Todd Penner and Carolyn Vander Stichele (Atlanta: Society of Biblical Literature, 2003), 105–37.

[55] Keener, *Acts*, vol. 1, 69. His wider appreciative critique of Pervo, *Profit with Delight*, 62–83, is well worth reading.

Stephen—and not just the main protagonists). Further, the storyline of these Acts characters lacks narrative closure, which is unacceptable in novels. For example, we do not know what happens to John, Philip, or Barnabas once their scenes are complete or whether or not they will return to the narrative ... Acts' use of sources is not a generic feature of novels.[56]

Finally, taking up Adams's comments about narrative closure, it should also be noted that the anti-climactic ending of Acts does not support the idea that it should be seen as a novel. The Greek novels are characterized by a high degree of narrative closure. Acts, on the other hand, ends with the central issues of Paul's appeal to Caesar and the success of the gospel in Rome and beyond completely unresolved.[57]

Pervo's overall case, that there is no need to critique Acts as poor historical writing because it is good novelistic writing, ultimately fails to persuade. Acts differs significantly from the genre of the Greek novels, and makes its claim to be historically based. The question of whether it succeeds as historical writing (of whatever particular kind) needs to be determined on better grounds than those suggested by Pervo. Luke does have weaknesses as a historian (see below), but as Pervo sensibly comments, "Historians duped by a legend or misled by a lie do not thereby become novelists."[58] Neither do historians who write dramatically, nor those who write selectively or with a particular interpretive bias, for who does not? As many commentators have noted, what Pervo has very effectively shown is that Luke is a skilled writer of popular narrative. Those skills, however, could equally be employed for the writing of popular-level historical, biographical, or novelistic narrative. Too many features of Acts suggest the gray area on the borders between popular history and biography for "novel" to be a convincing genre identification.

5. How Far Does *Genre* Take Us?

For three reasons, then, it seems that the question of the genre of Acts will not help us resolve the issue of the historical usefulness of Acts. First, there is insufficient consensus in scholarship as to which ancient genre best fits Acts. Second, there is agreement that in practice, ancient genres blur into one another in complex ways, and that this is particularly true in the first century period. Thus David Aune says:

> The "doctrine of literary forms" held by modern philologists emphasizes the supposed formal features of a literary genre at the expense of idiosyncratic

---

[56] Adams, *The Genre of Acts*, 151; cf. also 169–70. Cf. the comment of Keener, *Acts*, vol. 1, 67: "[N]ovels do not reveal the research, dependence on sources, and lengthy parallels to externally attested data ... that we find in Acts; few novelists would have been interested in such detailed correspondences."

[57] See Troy M. Troftgruben, *A Conclusion Unhindered: A Study of the Ending of Acts within Its Literary Environment* (Tübingen: Mohr Siebeck, 2010), 28–36 and 62–71.

[58] Pervo, *Profit with Delight*, 104.

features…. Ancient literature from the Hellenistic and Roman period is, in fact, often very difficult to identify in terms of strict literary forms….

A fascinating, yet problematic, development in the history of literature during the Hellenistic and Roman periods is the emergence of various 'new' genres through the transformation of earlier forms and their recombination in novel ways. The genre of the gospels is a problematic issue not dissimilar from the generic character of the *Vita Apollonii* of Philostratos, the *Satyricon* of Petronius, and the *De Iside et Osiride* of Plutarch. Yet the notion of "mixed genres," which some have applied to this type of literature is infelicitous, since it reflects a historical approach to genres which regards earlier forms as somehow normative. In many types of Greco-Roman literature, including the New Testament, there is often a tension evident between constituent literary forms (the part), and the total composition. To regard a "new" composition as merely a mixture of earlier genres destroys the possibility of viewing the composition in its totality as an entity greater than the mere sum of its parts. On the other hand, to ignore the particular literary history and conventions of the constituent literary forms impedes our understanding of the part.[59]

Similarly, Richard Burridge comments that "the borders between the genres of historiography, monograph and biography are blurred and flexible."[60]

Third, while the question of genre can help us understand the aims of an author and the expectations of an audience, it cannot resolve the question of whether those aims and expectations have been fulfilled. In other words, it is far too easy to make *genre* a more clearly-defined and diagnostic tool than is justified. Knowing what Acts is *not* (in terms of genre) can help us not to have faulty expectations of it. Knowing what it *is* (or might be, or might have been thought to be)[61] is both harder, and less helpful, than many have hoped. On this, despite their differences, Talbert, Alexander, and Pervo are agreed: "The biographical genre … offers no guarantees about historicity. The matter of the historical value of Acts must be determined on other grounds";[62] "We shall

---

[59] David E. Aune, "The Problem of the Genre of the Gospels: A Critique of C. H. Talbert's What is a Gospel?" in *Gospel Perspectives*, ed. R. T. France and David Wenham (Sheffield: Sheffield University Press, 1981), 2:9–60 (esp. 10 and 46).

[60] Burridge, *What are the Gospels?* 237; repeated in his "The Genre of Acts—Revisited," 28. Cf. the comments of Penner, "Madness in the Method," 256: "If the *progymnastic* exercises are any indication, ancient readers were actually encouraged from the earliest ages to mix genres and discourses, imitating patterns and conventions from a wide range of ancient narrative, from Thucydides to Homer … one is thus dealing with fairly flexible notions of genre and classification with respect to Acts." Similarly Adams, *The Genre of Acts*, 85, comments: "what we see here [in the Hellenistic period] is the strong generic relationship between history and biography and the blurring of genre boundaries." The comments of Pervo, asserting that "Unrestrained by the conventions governing elite literature, popular writers were able to blend genres and create new ones" (*Acts: A Commentary*, 18) miss the point: elite writers did the same things.

[61] Penner, "Madness in the Method?" in his survey of the genre issue (233–41), very reasonably raises the question, "Whose genre are we referring to—the author's or the reader's?" (234).

[62] Charles H. Talbert, "The Acts of the Apostles: Monograph or 'Bios?'" in Witherington, *History, Literature and Society in the Book of Acts*, 58–72 (esp. 72).

never solve the question of Acts' historicity by solving the genre question";[63] "The question of accuracy cannot be resolved by appeal to genre."[64]

6. The Historical Value of Acts

Opinions on the historical value of Acts vary widely. One of the central problems is that for much of the narrative, particularly in the first half of the book, there is no other direct evidence we can use to test the historical details of Luke's narrative. We simply have no other information on most of the events he narrates. There are exceptions, however. On a number of minor points of detail, there is a clear and undeniable tension between the evidence of Acts and other ancient sources of information. Here we will deal with two of the best-known examples.

6.1. Acts 5:35–37, the Report of Gamaliel's Speech in the Sanhedrin

Luke reports as follows:

> Then he [Gamaliel] said to them, "Fellow Israelites, consider carefully what you propose to do to these men. For some time ago Theudas rose up, claiming to be somebody, and a number of men, about four hundred, joined him; but he was killed, and all who followed him were dispersed and disappeared. After him Judas the Galilean rose up at the time of the census and got people to follow him; he also perished, and all who followed him were scattered." (Acts 5:35–37, NRSV)

The problem here is simple. The evidence of Josephus is very clear that Judas the Galilean's rising was "at the time of the census" of AD 6 (*B.J.* 2.118; *A.J.* 18.4). The revolt of Theudas, on the other hand, is placed by Josephus around AD 44–46 (*A.J.* 20.97–98), considerably later than that of Judas and indeed later than the dramatic date of Gamaliel's speech. Even if Luke had a direct source of information about the content of the speech (despite the fact that in 5:34 he explicitly says that the Christians were put outside the room),[65] Gamaliel cannot have known about a revolt by a Theudas, which was still roughly ten years in the future. Various suggestions have been made to alleviate the problem, but none is really satisfactory. The most likely solution is that

---

[63] Loveday Alexander, "Fact, Fiction and the Genre of Acts," *NTS* 44.3 (1998): 380–99 (esp. 394). See, similarly, Keener, *Acts*, vol. 1, 100.
[64] Pervo, *Acts: A Commentary*, 15. See also the comments of Penner, "Madness in the Method?" 240–41.
[65] Luke feels no need to explain his sources of information. "Luke at least twice reports conversations behind closed doors (Acts 5:34–39; 25:14–22) without clarifying whether the information was leaked or whether these conversations are his summary of what must have been said to produce the known outcome" (Keener, *Acts* vol. 1, 81). Keener later describes Acts 25:14–22 as "the strongest case for assuming Luke's reconstruction of a scene based on inference and plausibility" (i.e., rather than on direct information), *Acts* vol. 1, 102 n. 90. To Keener's two cases we should probably add Demetrius's speech to his fellow silversmiths in Acts 19:25–27.

Luke is simply mistaken. He knows of the revolt of Theudas, but has mis-remembered its date.[66]

6.2. Acts 9:27 on Paul's First Visit to Jerusalem, cf. Galatians 1:18

In Acts 9:26–27, a report of Paul's first visit to Jerusalem after his conversion, we are told as follows:

> When he had come to Jerusalem, he attempted to join the disciples; and they were all afraid of him, for they did not believe that he was a disciple. But Barnabas took him, brought him to the apostles, and described for them how on the road he had seen the Lord, who had spoken to him, and how in Damascus he had spoken boldly in the name of Jesus.

In Galatians, on the other hand, Paul himself reports:

> After three years I did go up to Jerusalem to visit Cephas and stayed with him fifteen days; but I did not see any other apostle except James the Lord's brother.

The difference between the accounts to do with the role of Barnabas is probably simply one of omission on Paul's part, but the issue of whom he saw among the Jerusalem leaders is more difficult. In Acts Barnabas brought Paul to "the apostles," but in Galatians Paul himself is very clear and emphatic that he met *only* with Peter and James and *not* the others. Both cannot be correct. The point may be minor, but on simple historical principles we must argue that Paul's letter, as both the earlier and the primary account, is to be preferred to the later, secondhand and more generalized account of Acts.[67]

At a more general level, there are well-known cases where there are tensions between the narrative of Acts and the incidental details mentioned in Paul's letters. The description of Paul's Thessalonian ministry in Acts suggests a period of less than a month (17:1–10), but the combination of 1 Thess 2:9 and

---

[66] The possibility that there were other revolutionaries named Theudas is sometimes raised, often with the suggestion that the name was quite common (e.g., Ben Witherington III, *The Acts of the Apostles: A Socio-Rhetorical Commentary* [Grand Rapids: Eerdmans, 1998], 239, and Darrell L. Bock, *Acts* [Grand Rapids: Baker, 2007], 250). Keener, on the other hand, says simply "Theudas, however, was a rare name, although it does appear" (*Acts*, vol. 2, 1232, but cf. Paul W. Barnett, *The Birth of Christianity: The First Twenty Years* [Grand Rapids: Eerdmans, 2005], 199–200 for other possibilities). Others argue that it is more likely that it is Josephus who is mistaken in his chronology (see again Witherington, *Acts*, 238–39). While thoroughly canvassing a range of possibilities, Keener clearly comes to the conclusion that it is most likely that Acts is mistaken (*Acts* vol. 2, 1230–33). Even as meticulous and conservative a commentator as Hemer simply refers to "the intractable Theudas problem" (*The Book of Acts*, 255). Jeffrey A. Trumbower, "The Historical Jesus and the Speech of Gamaliel (Acts 5.35–9)," *NTS* 39.4 (1993): 500–17 (esp. 502–03), is almost certainly correct to say that "It is obvious that Luke has heard of these figures and knows something about them; indeed, his depiction of them accords well with what Josephus says about them. He is simply confused about the chronology, and only on that of Theudas."

[67] Compare Martin Hengel, *Acts and the History of Earliest Christianity* (London: SCM, 1979), 86.

Phil 4:15–16 seems to suggest a longer period. Acts suggests the focus of Paul's activities was within the synagogue, while 1 Thess 1:9 suggests the majority of his converts were not Jewish, and 1 Thess 2:9 might well be taken to mean his evangelism took place while he supported himself financially by working. Acts 17:5 suggests that the opposition that forced Paul out of Thessalonica was instigated by the local Jewish community, but 1 Thess 2:14 seems to imply that the ongoing opposition to the church was from "your own compatriots" (though both of these could be true). Acts 17:4 suggests the newly-formed Thessalonian church contained a broad social range, from the elite women highlighted in the verse to others less notable. In contrast, 1 Thess 4:10; 5:14 and 2 Thess 3:6–12 suggest that the poor formed the majority of the congregation. This can be simply a matter of emphasis, however. Here, it seems to me, the case against Acts is far less decisive.

The best-known problem for the synchronization of Acts with the letters of Paul, however, is the complex and controversial chronology of Paul's visits to Jerusalem. Acts clearly describes four visits (9:26; 11:27–30; 12:25; 15:1–21). In Galatians Paul only refers to two (1:18; 2:1). This discrepancy in itself need not be a problem. Some of the visits may have been, from Paul's point of view, irrelevant to his case in Galatians. The difficulty is in matching Paul's visit referred to in Gal 2:1. Does it coincide with Acts 11 or Acts 15? Here, scholarship is deeply divided. This problem is of an essentially different kind from those above. The question is not *whether* the data of Acts and Paul's letters can be reconciled, but *which* of two suggested reconciliations does more justice to the evidence.[68]

The chronological data of Acts also need to be considered more broadly. Luke is not always precise in his indications of the passage of time. He locates events "not many days from now" (οὐ μετὰ πολλὰς ταύτας ἡμέρας, 1:5), "in those days" (ἐν ταῖς ἡμέραις, 1:15), "during these days" (ἐν δὲ ταῖς ἡμέραις ταύταις, 6:1, 21:15), with "some/several days" (ἡμέρας τινάς, 9:19, 10:48, 15:36, 16:12 and 24:24), or "many days" (πολλὰς ἡμέρας, 16:18). There are some cases where Acts is more precise, such as "after three days" (9:9), "on three Sabbath days" (17:2), "in five days … for seven days" (20:6; 21:4), "for three days" (28:7), "for three days … for seven days … three days later" (28:12, 14, 17), and the precise time notations in Acts 24–25. Overall, however, Luke's relative chronology is much stronger than his absolute chronology. Events make coherent sequences, but there are relatively few indications of overall periods of time, and still fewer precise dating references.

There are, however, a number of closely dateable points in Luke's narrative. When the newly converted Saul escaped from Damascus, let down in a basket through an opening in the city wall (Acts 9:25), his own firsthand account adds the detail that "the *ethnarch* under King Aretas guarded the city of Damascus in order to seize me" (2 Cor 11:32). We know from other sources that Aretas

---

[68] On this issue of Paul's visits to Jerusalem and the chronology of his career, see also David L. Eastman, "Paul: An Outline of His Life," in *All Things to All Cultures: Paul among Jews, Greeks, and Romans*, ed. Mark Harding and Alanna Nobbs (Grand Rapids: Eerdmans, 2013), 34–56.

IV *Philopatris* of Nabataea, who had considerable influence in and around Damascus, reigned from AD 9–39/40. This confirms the already strong impression that Paul's conversion must be dated at the latest to the mid-thirties AD.[69] The account of the death, in dramatic circumstances, of King Herod Agrippa (Acts 12:20–23, in whatever way it may be related to the parallel account in Josephus's *A.J.* 19.343), dates the events of chapter 12 to AD 44. The mention of the edict of Claudius expelling Jews from Rome in Acts 18:2 is less helpful because (a) the date of this edict within Claudius's reign is uncertain (though AD 49 is a strong contender) and (b) Acts does not indicate how long a period had passed since the edict.[70]

The most useful fixed point in Pauline chronology, however, is provided by the mention, in Acts 18:12, of the proconsulship of Gallio (Lucius Junius Annaeus Gallio). Gallio is a figure well known to historians as the elder brother of the famous philosopher and playwright, Lucius Annaeus Seneca. A fragmentary inscription discovered at Delphi, north of Corinth in central Greece, published in 1905, added crucial data. The inscription was authorized by Gallio during his term as proconsul and advertised what we might describe as a Roman "urban renewal project." It was aimed at revitalizing the ancient town of Delphi, home of the famous Oracle, which had fallen on hard times. The inscription notes that the emperor Claudius had been "acclaimed as Imperator for the twenty-sixth time … Consul for the fifth time, Censor." These details form part of a standard dating formula. They make it clear that the inscription was set up using an original document written before August 1 of AD 52 (by which time Claudius had been acclaimed Imperator for the twenty-seventh time). Gallio must have taken up office, assessed the problem, and referred the issue to Claudius, and the emperor written his reply, all before August 1 of 52 (though it is unclear how much before). On this basis it seems clear that Gallio took up office as Proconsul in Corinth in July of 51. The evidence of his brother Seneca's *Letter* 104.1 suggests he may have left Corinth

---

[69] There are complexities here both in terms of (a) Acts not mentioning the *ethnarch* and Paul not mentioning the threat from the local Jewish community within Damascus, and (b) the precise authority of the *ethnarch* in the region. Neither affects the chronological question. On (a) see Mark Harding, "On the Historicity of Acts: Comparing Acts 9.23–5 with 2 Corinthians 11.32–3," *NTS* 39.4 (1993): 518–38, and Martin Hengel and Anna Maria Schwemer, *Paul between Damascus and Antioch: The Unknown Years* (Louisville, KY: Westminster John Knox, 1997), 128–32. On Aretas more generally see 106–26. On (b) see Hemer, *The Book of Acts*, 164; Jane Taylor, "The Ethnarch of King Aretas at Damascus," *RB* 99 (1992): 719–28; Hengel and Schwemer, *Paul between Damascus and Antioch;* L. L. Welborn, "Paul's Flight from Damascus: Sources and Evidence for an Historical Evaluation," in *Historische Wahrheit und theologische Wissenschaft; Gerd Lüdemann zum 50. Geburtstag*, ed. A. Özen (Frankfurt: Peter Lang, 1996), 41–60; Rainer Riesner, *Paul's Early Period* (Grand Rapids: Eerdmans, 1998), 75–89; R. Wallace and W. Williams, *The Three Worlds of Paul of Tarsus* (London: Routledge, 1998), 80, 164–66; L. L. Welborn, "Primum Tirocinium Pauli (2 Cor 11:32–33)," *BZ* 43.1 (1999): 49–71; the discussion of Douglas Campbell, "An Anchor for Pauline Chronology: Paul's Flight from 'the Ethnarch of King Aretas' (2 Corinthians 11:32–33)," *JBL* 121.2 (2002): 279–302; Martin Hengel, "Paul in Arabia," *BBR* 12:1 (2002): 47–66 and of course the commentaries.

[70] For a discussion of the issues related to the edict of Claudius, see Riesner, *Paul's Early Period*, 157–201.

as early as October of the same year.[71] Paul's eighteen-month stay in Corinth (Acts 18:11) must have overlapped with Gallio's tenure, although it is unclear when in this eighteen-month period the hearing before Gallio took place. Paul may have been in Corinth for nearly eighteen months before Gallio's accession in mid-51. In that case Paul probably left for Asia before the end of September, after which travelling by sea became much more difficult. We cannot really hope to be more precise than this without further information, but Gallio's Delphic inscription at least specifies a clearly defined timeframe against which the events of Acts can be located.

7. The Portrait of Paul in Acts

The book of Acts does not only describe the specific events of Paul's missionary career. It also paints a portrait of his attitudes and methods. Many historians have detected degrees of tension between the portrait of Paul in Acts and the firsthand information of his letters.[72] It is often claimed that the Paul of Acts is a far more conventionally Law-observant Jew than the Paul of the letters.[73] Similarly, it is widely believed that the tensions between Paul and the leaders of the Jerusalem church, so apparent in (for example) Galatians, are smoothed over in Acts in a way that misrepresents the actual situation. Furthermore, it is clear that the author of Acts has a theological viewpoint that differs from that of Paul in his letters on significant issues.[74] The question is often asked whether Luke really understood the theology of Paul and whether he could have spent as much time with Paul as Acts seems to suggest he did. Certainly there is a contrast between the attitude to Greco-Roman culture in Paul's speech to the Areopagus in Athens in Acts 17:22–31 and the highly

---

[71] Seneca, *Ep.* 104.1. For a full discussion of the date of Gallio's proconsulship in Achaea see Riesner, *Paul's Early Period*, 202–11 and more recently, his brief discussion in "Pauline Chronology," in *The Blackwell Companion to St. Paul*, ed. Stephen Westerholm (Malden, MA: Wiley-Blackwell, 2011), 9–29 (esp. 14). For more background on Gallio and his legal decision in Corinth, see Jerome Murphy O'Connor, "Paul and Gallio," *JBL* 112.2 (1993): 315–31 and Bruce W. Winter, "Rehabilitating Gallio and his Judgement in Acts 18:14–15," *TynBul* 57.2 (2006): 291–308.

[72] Compare for examples, the very different estimates of Philipp Vielhauer, "On the 'Paulinism' of Acts," in *Studies in Luke–Acts*, ed. Leander E. Keck and J. Louis Martyn (Nashville: Abingdon, 1966), 33–50 (most recently re-published in *Paul and the Heritage of Israel: Paul's Claim upon Israel's Legacy in Luke and Acts in the Light of the Pauline Letters*, ed. David P. Moessner et al. (Edinburgh: T&T Clark, 2012), 3–17) and F. F. Bruce, "Is the Acts of Paul the Real Paul?" *BJRL* 58 (1976): 282–305.

[73] Compare, for example, Acts 16:1–3; 18:18; 21:17–26; 23:5–6; 24:14–21 and 26:5–8, with Rom 14:5–6; 1 Cor 9:19–22; 2 Cor 3:7–11; Gal 5:2–4; 6:15 and Phil 3:4–9.

[74] Probably the most striking case is the difference between Luke–Acts and Paul on the relationship between Jesus' death and the forgiveness of sins. Luke–Acts never articulates a theology of Jesus' death as a sacrifice for sin and Luke's Gospel omits Mark 10:45, "For the Son of Man came not to be served but to serve, and to give his life a ransom for many," saying only "I am among you as one who serves" (Luke 22:27b). Despite quoting Isaiah 53 at 8:32–33, the speeches in Acts do not present Jesus' death as an atoning sacrifice. Jesus' death is involved in the process of salvation, but the implied logic is different. The nearest Luke–Acts comes to a sacrificial understanding of Jesus' death is in Luke 22:17–20 and Acts 20:28.

critical attitude in Romans 1:18–2:16. Is the contrast merely situational, or does it represent a profound tension between two very different theologies?

It is often argued that Luke wrote Acts somewhere in the aftermath of the Jewish Revolt of AD 66–70. Commentators believe that by this time the tensions between "conservative Jewish Christianity" and the churches of Paul's Gentile mission had receded and could be portrayed as relatively minor issues overcome by a united decision, as Acts 15 suggests. If such unity had been the case at the time of the "Apostolic Council," it clearly did not remain so by the mid-50s AD, when Acts itself comments on the church of Jerusalem having "many thousands of believers … among the Jews, and they are all zealous for the law" (Acts 21:20–22). The essential question here is whether these differences between our sources represent relatively minor changes in perspective, perhaps due to differing historical contexts, or a fundamental tension between the firsthand evidence of Paul's letters and the later secondhand evidence of Acts.[75]

Likewise, it is often argued that Acts presents Paul as a miracle-worker,[76] whereas Paul's letters evidence a much more reserved attitude towards "signs and wonders."[77] Here, in my opinion, the contrast is overdrawn. Paul does object to "seeking signs," and is aware that they can be deceptive, but nonetheless he clearly believes himself to have worked miracles. Though this may cause unease among many modern readers, it clearly remains a significant feature of Paul's self-understanding as an apostle.[78] There is an important historical question here, but it is not one of a contrast between the evidence of Acts and that of Paul's own letters.

---

[75] For a variety of views on these issues, see, for example, John Clayton Lentz, *Luke's Portrait of Paul* (Cambridge: Cambridge University Press), 1993; Stanley E. Porter, *The Paul of Acts: Essays in Literary Criticism, Rhetoric, and Theology* (Tübingen: Mohr Siebeck, 1999) and "Was Paulinism a Thing when Luke–Acts was Written?" in *Reception of Paulinism in Acts*, ed. Daniel Marguerat (Leuven: Peeters, 2009), 1–14. See also Richard I. Pervo, "The Paul of Acts *and* the Paul of the Letters: Aspects of Luke as an Interpreter of the *Corpus Paulinum*," in Marguerat, *The Reception of Paulinism*, 141–56; Steve Walton, *Leadership and Lifestyle: The Portrait of Paul in the Miletus Speech and 1 Thessalonians* (Cambridge: Cambridge University Press, 2000); Reidar Hvalvik, "Paul as a Jewish Believer—According to the Book of Acts," in *Jewish Believers in Jesus: The Early Centuries*, ed. Oskar Skarsaune and Reidar Hvalvik (Peabody, MA: Hendrickson, 2007), 121–53; Thomas E. Phillips, *Paul, his Letters, and Acts* (Peabody, MA: Hendrickson, 2009); Stanley E. Porter, "The Portrait of Paul in Acts," in Westerholm, *The Blackwell Companion to Paul*, 124–38 and Michael B. Thompson, "Paul in the Book of Acts: Differences and Distance," *ExpTim* 122.9 (2011): 425–36.

[76] See for example Acts 13:8–11; 14:8–12; 16:18; 19:11–20; 20:10.

[77] See for example 1 Cor 1:22; 14:22; 2 Thess 2:9.

[78] See Rom 15:18–19; 1 Cor 2:4; 4:18–21; 2 Cor 12:12. On this subject see Jacob Jervell, "The Signs of an Apostle: Paul's Miracles," in his *The Unknown Paul: Essays on Luke–Acts and Early Christian History* (Minneapolis: Augsburg Fortress, 1984), 77–95; Bert Jan Lietaert Peerbolte, "Paul the Miracle Worker: Development and Background of Pauline Miracle Stories," in *Wonders Never Cease: The Purpose of Narrating Miracle Stories in the New Testament and its Religious Environment*, ed. Michael Labahn and Bert Jan Lietaert Peerbolte (London: T&T Clark, 2006), 180–99, esp. 195–99 and now Graham H. Twelftree, *Paul and the Miraculous: A Historical Reconstruction* (Grand Rapids: Baker Academic, 2013).

The chronological data of Acts, and the contrasting examples of historical inaccuracy, historical vagueness, and historical precision, offer both problems and possibilities for the historian. Along with the question of his portrait of Paul, they certainly raise the further question of the proximity of the author of Acts to the events he narrates. Was Luke a firsthand participant in any of the events he reports? In particular, was he a traveling companion of Paul?

8. The Puzzle of the "We Passages"

As is well-known, in several connected passages (Acts 16:10–17; 20:5–15; 21:1–18 and 27:1–28:16), the narrative shifts from the third person description of what "they" did, to a first-person plural description of what "we" did. This phenomenon has generated considerable discussion, which has settled into three main interpretative options. Some argue that the "we passages" are as they appear to be, the personal memoirs of the author, who distinguishes in this way between the times he was traveling with Paul and those when he was not.[79] Others argue that it is more likely that the "we passages" are indications of a written source used by the author, but not his own memoirs.[80] Still others argue for some variation on the theme that the "we passages" are a purely literary phenomenon, a stylistic device used by the author to "draw the reader in" to the story and that such a literary device was well known in ancient literature and would have been readily accepted by readers.[81]

No explanation is fully persuasive.[82] The first, arguing that the author of Acts was a traveling companion of Paul, struggles to explain why he "comes and goes" from the narrative in the way he does. The second, arguing that the author has made use of a source document written by someone else who was a traveling companion of Paul, suffers from the same problem. It also fails to explain why the author, who otherwise imposes his own style on his material in a way which makes it extremely difficult to detect his sources, leaves such an obvious clue as the "we" references in this case. The weakness of the third literary convention explanation is that its supporters have been unable to show that such a convention was in fact widely known in ancient literature. The choice between these three approaches must be made in conjunction with other arguments to do with the authorship and date of Acts, its portrait of Paul, and

---

[79] See, for example, Hemer, *The Book of Acts*, 312–34.

[80] See, for example, Porter, "The 'We' Passages," in Gill and Gempf, *The Book of Acts in Its Graeco-Roman Setting*, 545–74.

[81] See, for example, Vernon K. Robbins, "By Land and by Sea: The We-Passages and Ancient Sea Voyages," originally published in *Perspectives on Luke–Acts*, ed. Charles H. Talbert (Edinburgh: T&T Clark, 1978), 215–42, republished in *Sea Voyages and Beyond: Emerging Strategies in Socio-Rhetorical Interpretation* (Blandford Forum, Dorset: Deo, 2010) and more recently, "Sailing with Paul on Ideological Waters: The We-Passages in Acts," chapter 2 of the same volume, 82–113.

[82] See the careful survey of A. J. M. Wedderburn, "The 'We'-Passages in Acts: On the Horns of a Dilemma," *ZNW* 93.1–2 (2002): 78–98. For further discussion see William Sanger Campbell, *The "We" Passages in the Acts of the Apostles: The Narrator as Narrative Character* (Atlanta: Society of Biblical Literature, 2007), and Keener, *Acts*, vol. 3, 2350–74.

the evidence of the author's detailed knowledge of the regions through which Paul traveled. The relationship between these issues is dealt with in detail in the commentaries.

9. Cases of Historical Precision in Acts

As a contrast, there are a number of striking test cases where the details of the narrative in Acts can be confirmed from a wide range of other evidence. Some are simply background detail which any well-informed author could be expected to include. In other cases the details are so precise, yet so casually reported, and so marginal to the themes of the narrative, that it is hard to believe they are anything other than eyewitness reminiscences (whether those of the author himself, or those of his sources). Three rather different examples follow:

9.1. Cauda, Acts 27:16

Acts 27 describes the start of Paul's sea voyage from Caesarea to Rome. The ship shelters for a time at "Fair Havens, near the city of Lasaea" (27:8). Despite Paul's warning of danger due to the seasonal weather (27:10),

> the majority was in favor of putting to sea from there, on the chance that somehow they could reach Phoenix, where they could spend the winter. It was a harbor of Crete, facing southwest and northwest. (27:12)

Luke continues his narrative:

> When a moderate south wind began to blow, they thought they could achieve their purpose; so they weighed anchor and began to sail past Crete, close to the shore. But soon a violent wind, called the northeaster, rushed down from Crete. Since the ship was caught and could not be turned head-on into the wind, we gave way to it and were driven. By running under the lee of a small island called Cauda we were scarcely able to get the ship's boat under control. After hoisting it up they took measures to undergird the ship; then, fearing that they would run on the Syrtis, they lowered the sea anchor and so were driven. (27:13–17)

Much could be said about the circumstantial details here,[83] but for brevity's sake we will focus on one place name. Where is the island of Cauda located? The ancient evidence is confused. Ancient writers on geography disagree as to the island's precise location, but to quote Colin Hemer:

> The naming and placing of such rather obscure places as Lasaea and Cauda ought to be verified against contemporary epigraphical documents of those

---

[83] For example, for a sophisticated revisionist view of the ancient Mediterranean sailing seasons, see James Beresford, *The Ancient Sailing Season* (Leiden: Brill, 2013). Local conditions and vessel-type will now need to be factored into the often generalized discussions in standard introductions.

places rather than only against literary sources which may be inaccurate, or corrupted in transmission. We have offered documentary attestations of both, which, if not *in situ* (apart perhaps from the one fragment to Caudian Zeus), concern the external relations of both places, and evidently preserve the local, perhaps dialectal, forms…. Cauda, for instance, is precisely where a ship driven helpless before an east-northeast wind from beyond the shelter of Cape Matala might gain brief respite for necessary maneuvers and to set a more northward line of drift on the starboard tack. As the implications of such details are further explored, it becomes increasingly difficult to believe that they could have been derived from any contemporary reference work. In the places where we can compare, Luke fares much better than the encyclopaedist Pliny, who might be regarded as the foremost first-century example of such a source. Pliny places Cauda (Gaudos) opposite Hierapytna, some ninety miles too far east (*Nat.* 4.12.61). Even Ptolemy, who offers a reckoning of latitude and longitude, makes a serious dislocation to the northwest, putting Cauda too near the western end of Crete, in a position which would not suit the unstudied narrative of our text (*Geog.* 3.17.11).[84]

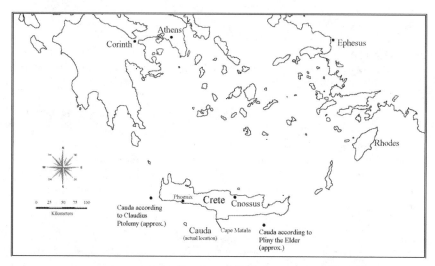

Location of Cauda

In other words, the description of the location of Cauda in Acts is confirmed by an inscription on the island itself, whereas two well-known geographical writers from the first and second centuries AD actually locate the island incorrectly. Clearly, it would not have been easy for the author of Acts to locate and name the island for the sake of its brief mention in the narrative without either his own notes of the voyage, or those of some other participant.

---

[84] Colin J. Hemer, "First Person Narrative in Acts 27–28," *TynBul* 36 (1985): 79–109 (99), and *The Book of Acts*, 142, 330–31. For Ptolemy's placement of the island see Alfred Stückelberger and Gerd Graßhoff, eds., *Ptolemaios Handbuch der Geographie* (Basel: Schwabe Verlag, 2006), Teil 1, 379 and Teil 2, map at 818–19.

9.2. Acts 24–25, Participants in Paul's Hearings at Caesarea

Consider the following extracts from Acts 24–25, the narrative of Paul's time in Caesarea:

> Five days later the High Priest Ananias went down to Caesarea with some of the elders and a lawyer named Tertullus, and they brought their charges against Paul before the governor. When Paul was called in, Tertullus presented his case before Felix (Acts 24:1–2). Several days later Felix arrived with his wife Drusilla (24:24). When two years had passed, Felix was succeeded by Porcius Festus (24:27). A few days later King Agrippa and Berenike arrived at Caesarea (25:13).

R. P. C. Hanson comments:

> This is a very remarkable piece of synchronisation on the part of the author.... It would have taken a very considerable amount of research for a later historian to discover that Ananias must have been the high priest contemporary with Paul at that point, that this took place in the period when Felix was married to Drusilla (who had been born in 38 and had had one husband already before Felix), and that not long afterwards Bernice (who had already had two husbands) was living for a period (a limited period) with her brother, during the procuratorship of Festus.[85]

Clearly it is possible that Luke could have done the necessary research to reconstruct this level of detail, could have received the details from some of those present, or could have been present himself (although the text does not suggest this). At one level it hardly matters which: the details he gives are thoroughly historically credible. However, at another level we are justified in asking which explanation seems most likely. James Dunn's comment reflects my own view:

> In an age when there were no almanacs [let alone the internet!] providing ready information regarding titles and dates of officials and no easy access to official records by someone of Luke's likely rank and status ... the accuracy of such details and representations as have just been listed can hardly be better

---

[85] R. P. C. Hanson, *The Acts*, The New Clarendon Bible (Oxford: Clarendon, 1967), 8. Compare the similar comments of Dunn, *Beginning from Jerusalem*, 81. The attempt of E. Jerry Vardaman to redate (among other things) the governorship of Festus on the basis of "micrographic" evidence on coins has not persuaded many (see the references of Jack Finegan, *The Archaeology of the New Testament: The Life of Jesus and the Beginning of the Early Church* [Princeton: Princeton University Press, 1992, reprinted 2014], vi, xxiv and *The Archeology of the New Testament: The Mediterranean World of the Early Christian Apostles* [London: Croom Helm, 1981, reprinted 2014], 5, 14, and footnotes on 236–38). As far as I can tell, Vardaman's research was never formally published beyond the summary results in "A Provisional Chronology of the New Testament: Jesus through Paul's Early Years," in *Chronos, Kairos, Christos, II: Chronological, Nativity, and Religious Studies in Memory of Ray Summers*, ed. E. Jerry Vardaman (Macon, GA: Mercer University Press, 1998), 313–20.

explained than by Luke's own involvement with those caught up in the events (or with the events themselves), or by his having access to eyewitness accounts of the events.[86]

9.3. Acts 19:23–41, especially v. 38: The Speech of the "Town Clerk" of Ephesus

In Acts 19 we are treated to a brief but vivid description of popular unrest in a Greek city under Roman rule. Demetrius the silversmith, concerned that the success of the Pauline mission would undermine his own business interests as well as the cult of Artemis itself, fomented popular opposition which developed into a riotous assembly in the city's famous theater.[87] Fanned in part by more generalized anti-Jewish sentiment (vv. 33–34), the anger of the demonstrators was finally only defused by a speech from the chief civil official, the *grammateus* or "town clerk."[88]

Once again, much could be said about circumstantial detail here.[89] One turn of phrase in the reported speech particularly catches the attention of the Roman historian. In verse 38 the *grammateus* says: "If therefore Demetrius and the artisans with him have a complaint against anyone, the courts are open, and there are proconsuls; let them bring charges there against one another." The courts are open and "there are *proconsuls*" (Gk.: *anthupatoi*, plural). This is very strange. Unless the phrase is simply a generalizing plural ("there are officials such as proconsuls")[90] the reference seems to make no sense. A *proconsul* was one of the highest officials of the Roman administration. Having held one of the two annual consulships in Rome, some years later such a person normally took up a major administrative position for a year or more as a proconsul. He was a governor of the highest rank, administering a major

---

[86] Dunn, *Beginning from Jerusalem*, 81.

[87] The theatre of Ephesus could probably accommodate roughly 20,000 people in this period. See the details in Keener, *Acts*, vol. 3, 2903.

[88] On the position of this official see Sherwin-White, *Roman Society and Roman Law*, 86–87 and the detailed notes in Keener, *Acts*, vol. 3, 2927–28.

[89] See, for example, the characteristic descriptions of Artemis as τῆς μεγάλης θεᾶς (the great goddess) in 19:27 and as τὴν θεόν (the goddess) in 19:37 (both in examples of reported speech), on which see Hemer, *The Book of Acts*, 121–22, and Steven M. Baugh, "Phraseology and the Reliability of Acts," *NTS* 36.2 (1990): 290–94. Other terms and phrases worth noting include the τινὲς τῶν Ἀσιαρχῶν (*Asiarchs*, "officials of the province") of 19:31, the title νεωκόρος (*Neōkoros*, "guardian of the temple") of 19:35, the ἀγοραῖοι (*agoraioi*, days the courts are open in the *agora*) of 19:38 and the ἐννόμῳ ἐκκλησίᾳ (*ennomō ekklesia*, regular assembly) of 19:39. See generally Hemer, *The Book of Acts*, 121–23; G. H. R. Horsley, "The Inscriptions of Ephesos and the New Testament," *NovT* 34.2 (1992): 105–68, esp. 136–38 and more broadly Trebilco, "Asia," in Gill and Gempf, *The Book of Acts in Its Graeco-Roman Setting*, 316–62. For a rather different approach to such "circumstantial detail," see Stephen Witetschek, "Artemis and Asiarchs: Some Remarks on Ephesian Local Color in Acts 19," *Bib* 90.3 (2009): 334–55. He argues (inconclusively, in my view) that in some cases such detail reflects the time of Luke's composition of Acts rather than Paul's time in Ephesus.

[90] Luke also uses the term, but (as expected) in the singular, in Acts 13:7, 8, 12 and 18:12. As Trebilco notes ("Asia," 356, n. 283), a similar (though not identical) generalising plural usage of the term occurs in Plutarch, *Mor.* 813e.

province on behalf of either the Senate and People of Rome, or the emperor himself (depending on the province).[91] There was only ever the *one* proconsul in a province at a time and it would be extraordinary for Luke's audience not to know this. Why then the plural, "proconsuls"?

We know from other sources of information altogether, that in either late 54 or very early 55, the newly enthroned Emperor Nero's mother, Agrippina, had the proconsul of the province of Asia, Marcus Junius Silanus, assassinated by poison.[92] For the period before his official replacement (probably by either Tiberius Plautius Silvanus Aelianus[93] or Marius Cordus[94]), his duties would normally have been undertaken by his senior *legatus*, or his three *legati* together.[95] Some have suggested that the two assassins, Publius Celerius and Helius, would have taken over the administration, but this is most unlikely.[96] Though neither Tacitus nor Dio Cassius fills in the details, it seems far more likely the *legati* carried on in the proconsul's place. Whatever the precise arrangements, for a brief period which is consistent with the chronology of Luke's account, Ephesus was probably administered by (officials acting as) "proconsuls," in the plural.

Now, what is remarkable here is not merely the coincidence of detail. That in itself is noteworthy. However, what sets this example apart is the casual nature of the reference and the fact that it is reported in a throwaway phrase in an abbreviated report of the speech of the *grammateus*. For those not familiar

---

[91] In the Republican period the proconsular year normally followed directly on the consulship. In the period under Tiberius (and later) there was usually a gap of as much as ten years or even more. See Ronald Syme, "Problems about Proconsuls of Asia," *ZPE* 53 (1983): 191–208 (191–92).

[92] The evidence is to be found in Tacitus, *Ann.* 13:1 and Dio Cassius, *Hist.* 61.6.4. Agrippina had previously had his brother Lucius Silanus killed and apparently feared he might engineer a coup in revenge.

[93] *Insc. lat. sel.* 986, a commemorative inscription of his career, makes it clear he held the post sometime after his consulship in 45, but not precisely when. See the translation in *Augustus to Nero: A Sourcebook on Roman History 31 BC–AD 68*, ed. David C. Braund (London: Croom Helm, 1985), 136–37. Richard Evans, *A History of Pergamum: Beyond Hellenistic Kingship* (London: Continuum, 2012), 158) suggests he held the position before Silanus, in 53–54.

[94] Evans, *A History of Pergamum*, 158 and n. 18 (on 203), suggests Cordus was Silanus's senior legate, and acted as proconsul after his murder, perhaps before being appointed proconsul in his own right in 55–56. This must remain speculative. See the cautious comments of Syme, "Problems about Proconsuls of Asia," 203.

[95] See the parallel case of the removal of Cn. Piso from the proconsulship of Syria after the death of Germanicus in AD 19, described in Tacitus, *Ann.* 2.74. In this case the rivalries between the legates and other Senatorials present led to the senior legate, Cn. Sentius, taking over Piso's position.

[96] This suggestion, for which see e.g., C. K. Barrett, *The Acts of the Apostles* (Edinburgh: T&T Clark, 1998), 2:937, proposing that "Helius and Celer … were temporarily in charge in Asia" was made as early as 1897 by H. M. Luckock, but is most unlikely. Thus briefly William M. Ramsay, "Some Recent Editions of the Acts of the Apostles," *Exp* 6.2 (1900): 321–35 (333–35). Not only would such an action have been unprecedented, in administrative terms, but the two were not of the requisite social rank to act on behalf of a proconsul. They were the managers of Nero's personal estate in the province and so his mother's agents "on the ground," but Celer was only an *eques* and Helius was a freedman. See Riesner, *Paul's Early Period*, 216–17, for a brief history of the discussion and note A. J. Woodman's case (Tacitus, *Annals*, trans. A. J. Woodman [Indianapolis: Hackett, 2004], 245 n. 4) that the customary abbreviation of Celerius's name to "Celer" is mistaken.

with the circumstances, it adds nothing to the narrative except a vague sense of puzzlement.[97] Whether the plural is generalizing and means "officials *such as* proconsuls,"[98] or specific and means "*officials* standing in for the proconsul," the reference fits the known context of 55–56 precisely.

Cases such as the three cited above can be multiplied.[99] What do such cases prove? C. K. Barrett comments:

> I once observed in a review that I had read many detective stories in which legal and police procedures were described with careful accuracy but in the service of a completely fictitious plot. The accurate accounts of the working of Greek cities cannot prove that Luke's main plot is not wholly or in part fictitious.[100]
> Accuracy in secular history does not prove that an author must be accurate also in Christian history, but it suggests that the author was not a reckless writer ready to follow any foolish tale. It is true that Luke believed in the possibility of supernatural, miraculous events, concerning which modern readers, including the modern Christian, may exercise some skepticism. He was not the only first-century writer to do so. Such features of his story do not discredit the rest; it is even possible that some of them may be true.[101]

Barrett's cautious balance should be maintained. The precision of Acts in contextual detail may justify a presumption of its accuracy in other matters, but it can *only* be a presumption. Alongside his care at the level of detail, Luke also has agendas and biases of his own. Any historian making use of his evidence

---

[97] In my view, this substantially weakens the argument of Richard Pervo, *Profit with Delight*, 71, that "those who point to the presence of good local color in Acts would be hard pressed to explain why this or that detail aids the reader in clarifying the legal entanglement or historical circumstance under discussion. What is beyond debate is that such details make the book vastly more interesting and readable." This may well be true for the case of Paul's trial before the assembled worthies in Caesarea Maritima, but I cannot see that it applies to the case of Cauda or to the apparently trivial details in Ephesus. In these two cases little indeed is added to Luke's narrative, either in terms of clarification or of interest, but "the debate over historical worth" may gain far more.

[98] Thus Barrett, *Acts of the Apostles*, 2:937, describing the usage as a "*pluralis categoriae*," with a reference to James Hope Moulton, ed., *A Grammar of New Testament Greek* (Edinburgh: T&T Clark, 1963), vol. 3 (by Nigel Turner), 26. But from Luke–Acts Turner notes only this passage, Luke 5:21 and Acts 21:28 (where "he [Paul] has brought Greeks into the Temple" actually means only one Greek, Trophimus the Ephesian). Is this a true parallel or just a rhetorical exaggeration? Generalizing plurals are actually rare in Luke–Acts. In two passages Luke tells us that, when there were two or more speakers present, "they" spoke, though common sense suggests that only one of them did (Acts 1:11 and 6:2; cf. Luke 5:21 above). Similarly (and notably also in Acts 19) when the seven sons of Sceva confront evil spirits (plural, vv. 12–13) it is *an* evil spirit (singular) which answers back to them and drives them off (vv. 15–16). None of these references are really "plurals of category" however, so I do not think a case can be made that such a thing is a feature of Lukan idiom. Other possible parallels (Acts 1:7, "times and seasons set by the Father," Acts 27:4) are even less impressive. Only Acts 27:4, "the winds were against us," cf. 27:13–14, "the wind (singular)" is really at all similar (or is it simply idiomatic variation?).

[99] For older scholarship, see the many works of William M. Ramsay, and Sherwin-White, *Roman Society and Roman Law*, chs. 1, 3, 4, 5, 7 and 8. More recently see the careful work of Hemer, *The Book of Acts*, and the massive detail of Keener's multi-volume commentary.

[100] C. K. Barrett, "The Historicity of Acts," *JTS* 50.2 (1999): 525.

[101] Barrett, "Historicity," 530–31.

needs to be aware of the attention to detail in Acts, but also of its perspective and its selectivity.

10. Historical Omissions in Acts

Probably the most striking gap in the information in Acts is its complete failure to mention the "collection for the poor among the saints in Jerusalem." The evidence of Paul's own letters makes it quite clear that this project was of great importance to him and that it was his ambition to deliver "the collection" to the Jerusalem church during his final visit there (Acts 21:17).[102] Yet in all its careful description of Paul's preparations for the Jerusalem visit and the visit itself, Acts studiously ignores the whole question of the collection. The most common interpretation of this remarkable omission is the hypothesis that, as matters turned out, the collection was not accepted by the leadership of the church in Jerusalem. It could not be delivered. Perhaps because of long-term sensitivity over the issue of Paul's approach to Gentile converts (perhaps exacerbated by the riot in Jerusalem and its consequences), the diplomatic effort embodied in the collection failed.[103] Paul's arrest and imprisonment soon after led indirectly to his appeal to Caesar, and hence to his journey to Rome, which the author of Acts uses as the climax to the whole narrative. Instead of telling the story of Paul's final visit to Jerusalem as a failure, Acts makes it the catalyst for his journey to Rome, in at least partial fulfillment of Jesus' mention of "the ends of the earth" (1:8).[104]

---

[102] For references to the collection in Paul's letters see Rom 15:26, 1 Cor 16:1–12, 2 Corinthians 8–9, Gal 2:10. For discussion of the significance of the collection to Paul, see Dieter Georgi, *Remembering the Poor: The History of Paul's Collection for Jerusalem* (Nashville: Abingdon, 1992); Sze-Kar Wan, "Collection for the Saints as Anticolonial Act: Implications of Paul's Ethnic Reconstruction," in *Paul and Politics*, ed. Richard A. Horsley (Harrisburg: Trinity Press International, 2000), 191–215; Stephan Joubert, *Paul as Benefactor: Reciprocity, Strategy, and Theological Reflection in Paul's Collection* (Tübingen: Mohr Siebeck, 2000); A. J. M. Wedderburn, "Paul's Collection: Chronology and History," *NTS* 48.1 (2002): 95–110; James R. Harrison, *Paul's Language of Grace in Its Graeco-Roman Context* (Tübingen: Mohr Siebeck, 2003), 291–321, David J. Downs, *The Offering of the Gentiles* (Tübingen: Mohr Siebeck, 2008); James D. G. Dunn, *Beginning from Jerusalem*, 932–47 and 970–72; Steven J. Friesen, "Paul and Economics: The Jerusalem Collection as an Alternative to Patronage," in *Paul Unbound: Other Perspectives on the Apostle*, ed. Mark D. Given (Peabody, MA: Hendrickson, 2010), 27–54, and L. L. Welborn, "'That There May Be Equality': The Contexts and Consequences of a Pauline Ideal," *NTS* 59.1 (2013): 73–90.

[103] For the hypothesis that Paul's assistance with the expenses of the Nazirite vows of four Jewish Christians, suggested by James (Acts 21:23), was a strategy to facilitate the acceptance of the Collection, see Jerome Murphy-O'Connor, *Paul: A Critical Life* (Oxford: Oxford University Press, 1996), 348–351.

[104] See Keener's useful note on the phrase, *Acts* vol. 1, 704–08. Hemer suggests that Acts 24:17 implicitly recognizes the collection (*The Book of Acts*, 188), noting (189) the critique of Haenchen.

11. Conclusions

This chapter deals with a subset of the issues that must be resolved if a modern historian is to use Acts responsibly in reconstructing the earliest history of the movement we call Christianity, and which Luke calls simply "the way." Unresolved questions of authorship, date of writing and the sources of information available to Acts have not been discussed in any detail. Other issues, such as the particular theological perspective of Acts, and the ways in which this influences the narrative, have barely been touched upon. Despite these omissions, I am aware that the chapter nonetheless raises far more questions than it can answer. This is appropriate. Studying history is a continuing process of evaluation and refinement. Supplying pre-packaged answers to broad scale historical questions may be part of the task. This chapter, however, has set out to illustrate the processes of interpretation and judgment that lie behind the deceptively simple surface of standard narrative accounts.

Acts is not a perfect source of information for the historian of earliest Christianity. This must not deter us from making use of it for everything it can provide. There *are* no perfect sources of information. If Acts focuses on the spread of the early Christian movement to the north and west, it cannot also, within the limits of its overall scale, tell the story of the growth of the movement in Egypt or eastward into Mesopotamia, or further. To tell the story of Paul, it must neglect the story of Thomas.[105] To focus on the strategic development of urban churches in Asia Minor and Greece, it must pass over the growth of the movement in the rural villages of Galilee and Syria. The very features that make an ancient source valuable for answering one kind of question disqualify it from answering others. To do more of these things Acts would have needed to be a far larger (and thus more expensive) work to produce and might not have survived as well as a result. There is little point lamenting Luke's selective and interpretative choices. He did not write with our needs in mind: how could he? The historian's task is to note the choices Luke made (whether conscious or subliminal); analyze the ways they shaped his narrative; evaluate the information he provides and integrate it into an overall reconstruction. Such a reconstruction must make the best sense of the available literary, epigraphic, archaeological, geographic, and other evidence. Hopefully the many difficulties of doing this will make us as historians, not uncritical, but charitable in our evaluation of Luke's contributions to our limited and fragmented information. Without his labors, we would know far less than we do and the history of the rise of the Christian movement would be far harder to write.

---

[105] Later church writers tell stories of Jesus' disciple Thomas traveling to the east as far as India, and Christian churches there still trace their origins to him, though the details of his travels are probably legendary.

Chris Forbes

Recommended Reading

Adams, Sean A. *The Genre of Acts and Collected Biography*. Cambridge: Cambridge University Press, 2013.

Adams, Sean A., and Michael W. Pahl, eds. *Issues in Luke–Acts: Selected Essays*. Piscataway, NJ: Gorgias, 2012.

Barrett, C. K. *The Acts of the Apostles*. 2 vols. Edinburgh: T&T Clark, 1998.

Dunn, James D. G. *Beginning from Jerusalem*. Grand Rapids: Eerdmans, 2007.

Keener, Craig S. *Acts: An Exegetical Commentary*. Four volumes. Grand Rapids: Baker, 2012–2015.

Marguerat, Daniel. *The First Christian Historian: Writing the "Acts of the Apostles."* Cambridge: Cambridge University Press, 2002.

Penner, Todd. "Madness in the Method? The Acts of the Apostles in Current Study." *CurBR* 2.2 (2004): 223–93.

Pervo, Richard I. *Acts: A Commentary*. Minneapolis, Fortress, 2008.

Talbert, Charles H. *Reading Luke-Acts in Its Mediterranean Milieu*. Leiden: Brill, 2003.

Walton, Steve, Thomas E. Phillips, Lloyd Keith Pietersen, and F. Scott Spencer, eds. *Reading Acts Today: Essays in Honour of Loveday C. A. Alexander*. London: T&T Clark, 2011.

Witherington, Ben, III. *The Acts of the Apostles: A Socio-Rhetorical Commentary*. Grand Rapids: Eerdmans, 1998.

2. The Johannine Purpose and Outline

Johan Ferreira

Among the canonical Gospels, the Gospel of John raises the most questions, demonstrates the deepest theological reflection, and attracts the greatest interest from readers and interpreters. Like a diamond refracting light in a myriad of colors, the Gospel of John illuminates our understanding of the significance of Jesus of Nazareth for human existence in inexhaustible ways. However, due to limitations in space, the following discussion is necessarily selective and seeks to provide only an introduction to some of the key ideas of Johannine thought. According to the scope of this volume, it will especially highlight the Gospel's engagement with the Greco-Roman world. Firstly, the discussion considers two key Johannine metaphors that encapsulate the vibrant heartbeat of the Gospel—mission. Secondly, it presents a brief overview of the content of the Gospel, highlighting its mission thrust and calculated interaction with the Greco-Roman environment.

1. Why Did John Write his Gospel?

Literary works, especially ancient ones, present readers with a number of questions that must be considered for both a correct overall assessment of the work and for understanding the finer details. Questions such as, "Who was the author? Who were the readers? What circumstances or challenges did the author address? Where do we locate the provenance of the work? And what traditions or sources were at the author's disposal?" are important for determining the meaning of the text.[1] However, the fundamental question to

---

[1] The so-called "Johannine Question" refers particularly to the identification of the author of the Gospel, but contains a raft of related questions concerning the historical reliability of the material, sources, compositional history, and theological tendencies. See Martin Hengel, *The Johannine Question* (London: SCM, 1989). A common view that has emerged over the last fifty years in critical scholarship is that the Gospel is the product of a community or school, with a prominent figure such as the apostle John standing behind the distinct style and theological perspective of the narrative. See R. Alan Culpepper, *The Johannine School*, SBLDS 26 (Missoula: Scholars, 1975); Oscar Cullman, *The Johannine Circle* (London: SCM, 1976); Raymond E. Brown, *The Community of the Beloved Disciple* (New York: Paulist, 1979). According to this view materials from different sources were edited over a lengthy period of time until the end of the first century AD when the Gospel was published in its current shape. Three sources or layers of tradition can be observed in the Gospel: (i) the Signs Source, which stems from Jerusalem; (ii) a Revelatory Discourse Source (*Offenbarungsreden*), which reflects

be addressed in the analyses of literary works concerns the matter of purpose, "Why did the author write the work?" When it comes to the four Gospels in the New Testament, the question regarding the individual evangelists' overall purpose determines how one understands and applies the Gospel narratives.

The Gospel of John, as most scholars argue, was probably the last of the canonical Gospels to be written, appearing in its final edition at the end of the first century AD when at least three other Gospels were already in circulation.[2] Why, then, would a person or a community who also stood in the apostolic tradition consider it necessary to write a fourth Gospel? Providentially, on closer investigation, we do not need to speculate in order to answer this question, since the Gospel of John provides the reader with a clear purpose statement. Towards the end of the Gospel we read: "Now Jesus also did many other signs in front of the disciples, which are not written in this book; but these are written in order that that you may come to believe that Jesus is the Christ, the Son of God, and in order that by believing you may have life in his name" (20:30–31).[3] Consideration of the purpose of the Gospel of John must start with a careful analysis of this statement; it provides an important hermeneutical key for unlocking the meaning of the whole narrative.[4]

In the Greek text, the purpose statement contains two final clauses, expressed with the conjunction *hina* (ἵνα: "in order that") followed by the verb in the subjunctive mood. The reader must first believe (ἵνα πιστεύ[σ]ητε) that Jesus is the Christ, the Son of God, and then the reader must receive or have life (ἵνα ... ζωὴν ἔχητε) in his name. Most discussions concerning the purpose of the Gospel have focused on the textual variant and the meaning of the first final clause. In some manuscripts the verb "to believe" occurs in the present subjunctive mood (πιστεύητε), whereas in others the aorist subjunctive (πιστεύσητε) is used.[5]

Samaritan or insipient Gnosticism; and (iii) a Passion Narrative, which shares much in common with the Synoptic traditions. It is argued by some that the final edition reveals the insertion of more traditional views by a so-called "ecclesiastical redactor" (Bultmann). It is interesting to note that this hypothesis corresponds in broad outline with early records regarding the life of the apostle John. After the resurrection of Jesus the ministry of John is located in Jerusalem (Acts 3:1; 4:13); it then shifts to Samaria (Acts 8:14; cf. Acts 8:5–6, 12–13, 40; 21:8–9), until John relocates to Asia Minor and Ephesus (Rev 1:4, 9). According to early church tradition, John lived out his last years in Ephesus where he published the Gospel of John in the reign of Trajan (AD 98–117). This tradition is preserved in Irenaeus (*Haer.* 3.1.1–2; 3.3.4) and Eusebius (*Hist. eccl.* 3.24.5; 6.14.5–7). See Rudolf Schnackenburg, *The Gospel according to St John*, Vol. 1, trans. Kevin Smyth et al. (New York: Crossroad, [1968] 1990), 77–103.

[2] See John Ashton, *Understanding the Fourth Gospel* (Oxford: Clarendon, 1993); Gary M. Burge, *Interpreting the Gospel of John: A Practical Guide* (Grand Rapids: Baker, 2013); and R. Kysar, *John, the Maverick Gospel*, 3rd ed. (Louisville: Westminster John Knox, 2007).

[3] Scriptural translations are by the author.

[4] On the various proposals for the Gospel's audience see A. Wind, "Destination and Purpose of the Gospel of John," *NovT* 14 (1972): 26–69.

[5] According to the Nestle-Aland edition of the *Novum Testamentum Graece*, the aorist reading is attested by ℵ², A, C, D, L, N, W, Ψ, f¹·¹³, 33, 𝔐; and the present by 𝔓⁶⁶ᵛⁱᵈ, ℵ*, B, Θ, 0250, 892ˢ, *l* 2211.

The discussion has pointed out that if the distinctive connotations of the present and aorist tenses are to be pressed, then the present could be translated as "in order that you may *continue to* believe," and the aorist as "in order that you may *come to* believe." Weighing up the external (the age, reliability, and geographical distribution of manuscript tradition) and internal criteria (the usual stylist preference of author/text) of textual criticism one may well argue that the aorist subjunctive is to be preferred and that it expresses an evangelical objective. The combination of the conjunction *hina* (ἵνα) with the finite verb *pisteuō* (πιστεύω) occurs nine times in the Gospel: on five occasions the aorist is used (1:7; 9:36; 11:15, 42; 13:19), on two occasions (6:29; 17:21) the present is used, and on the other two occasions (19:35; 20:31) some manuscripts have the aorist and others the present. Since the aorist is used in the majority of cases and a scribe amended the text of the Sinaiticus to the aorist subjunctive, presumably on the evidence of other manuscripts at his disposal, one may prefer the aorist reading above the present. The first final clause will then indicate that the Gospel, or at least the signs, intended to address non-Christians, and that its purpose was to convince them to believe that Jesus is the Christ.[6]

When one examines the seven signs presented in the Gospel, not including the miraculous catch of fish in the Epilogue, it appears that most of them resulted in people coming to believe in Jesus. This supports the conclusion that the first final clause in John 20:31 has an evangelistic objective.[7] This observation is important in interpreting the purpose statement, since the final clause is specifically related to the "signs" Jesus performed. The outcome of the first sign in Cana is that "his disciples believed [aorist: ἐπίστευσεν] in him" (2:11). In Jerusalem "many people believed [aorist: ἐπίστευσαν] in his name, when they saw the signs that he was doing" (2:23). Before Jesus performed the second sign in Cana, he announced that "unless you see signs and wonders you will not come to believe [aorist: πιστεύσητε]" (4:48), and then after the sign the official "believed [aorist: ἐπίστευσεν]" (4:53). When Jesus questioned the man (whom he healed of his blindness) concerning the Son of Man, the man asked, "And who is he, sir, that I may come to believe [aorist: πιστεύσω] in him?" (9:36). Before Jesus raised Lazarus from the dead,

---

[6] Note the discussion by Gordon D. Fee, "On the Text and Meaning of John 20:30–31," in *The Four Gospels 1992: Festschrift Frans Neirynck*, BETL 100, ed. Frans van Segbroeck et al. (Leuven: University Press, 1992), 2193–205; D. A. Carson, "The Purpose of the Fourth Gospel: John 20:30–31 Reconsidered," *JBL* 106 (1987): 639–51; Don A. Carson, "Syntactical and Text-Critical Observations on John 20:30–31: One More Round on the Purpose of the Fourth Gospel," *JBL* 124 (2005): 693–714. Fee's preference for the present tense and Carson's reading of the Greek syntax have been critiqued by Edward W. Klink in *The Sheep of the Fold: The Audience and Origin of the Gospel of John*, SNTSMS 141 (Cambridge: Cambridge University Press, 2007), 214–17.

[7] On the Signs Source, see the studies by Robert T. Fortna, *The Gospel of Signs: A Reconstruction of Narrative Source Underlying the Fourth-Gospel*, SNTSMS 11 (Cambridge: Cambridge University Press, 1970); and *The Fourth Gospel and Its Predecessor: From Narrative Source to Present Gospel* (Philadelphia: Polebridge, 1988). Also see the evaluation by Gilbert van Belle, *The Signs Source in the Fourth Gospel: Historical Survey and Critical Assessment of the Semeia Hypothesis*, BETL 116 (Leuven: University Press, 1994).

he exhorted Martha with the words, "If you believe [aorist: πιστεύσῃς] you will see the glory of God" (11:40). The Gospel then tells us that many Jews "believed [aorist: ἐπίστευσαν] in him" because he raised Lazarus from the dead (11:45).

In each of these instances, the Gospel uses the aorist to describe people coming to faith in Jesus as the result of his signs.[8] The content of belief concerns the identity (and work) of Jesus, which is the core christological confession of the early Christian movement, that the man Jesus is the Christ[9]—the Savior of the World (4:42) and the Son of God (1:1; 20:28).[10] In other words, we may conclude that one purpose of the Gospel according to the first final clause of the purpose statement is evangelistic; its intention is to persuade non-Christians to come to faith in Jesus.

There is more, however, in the Gospel's purpose statement. As previously mentioned, in understanding the purpose of the Gospel, most commentators have focused their attention on the interpretation of the first final clause in the purpose statement. However, in order to understand the Gospel as a whole, the second final clause may be more significant. There are several possible interpretations concerning the relationship between the two clauses. Firstly, the Gospel may have two purposes; readers must first believe in Jesus, and then they must also receive life in his name. Secondly, the two clauses may be in parallel construction, expressing more or less the same thing; the first clause is repeated in different language for emphasis. A third possibility is that there is a progression from the first to the second final clause. The Gospel has only one chief aim—that its readers may have life—but the way to receive life is through believing in Jesus. In other words, there is a logical development from believing in Jesus as the Son of God to receiving life in his name. Careful analysis of the Greek text favors this interpretation. In the Gospel of John, believing in Jesus and having life in his name incorporate two different semantic categories and are not synonymous. Furthermore, the syntax suggests a step structure, progressing from believing in Jesus to the ultimate goal of having life in his name. The second clause does not read "in order that you may have life," but "in order that *by believing* you may have life" (ἵνα πιστεύοντες ζωὴν ἔχητε). The insertion of the adverbial participle "believing" (πιστεύοντες), recalling the main verb of the first final clause, indicates the means of receiving life; the thought of the second clause builds on the first,

---

[8] The Gospel always uses the verb "to believe" (πιστεύω), never the noun "faith" (πίστις), emphasizing that belief comes through a historical process or experience. Thus, believing in Jesus means coming to Jesus (5:20; 6:35, 37, 44, 65; 7:37), receiving Jesus (1:12; 5:43), drinking the water Jesus gives (4:13–14; 6:35; 7:37), following Jesus (8:12), and loving Jesus (14:15, 21, 23; 16:27).

[9] The term "Christ" (ὁ Χριστός) is used here as elsewhere in the Gospel as a title, except for John 1:17 and 17:3 where it is used as a proper name, probably in redactional additions. On two occasions the Gospel translates the Hebrew "Messiah" (Μεσσίας for מָשִׁיחַ) by the Greek term "Christ" (1:41; 4:25), thereby identifying Jesus as the expected Jewish Messiah.

[10] The phrase "the Son of God" (ὁ υἱὸς τοῦ θεοῦ) as used in the Gospel is another christological title or designation of the Messiah, but it moves beyond traditional Jewish categories affirming the divinity of Jesus (cf. John 1:18; 5:19–27; 10:31–39; 17:1–5).

and so believing is the stepping stone to the ultimate purpose of gaining life. Therefore, the purpose of the Gospel is not only that its readers may believe, but also that they may have life.[11]

2. What Does the Gospel Mean by "Having Life"?

Since the purpose of the writing of the Gospel of John is that believers may have life, it is important to inquire exactly what the Gospel means by this new life that is to be received and experienced in Jesus' name. A casual reading reveals that the concept of life features significantly throughout the narrative; it is one of the Gospel's main themes. The noun "life" (ζωή) occurs 36 times, the verb "to live" (ζάω) occurs 17 times, and the verb "to make alive" (ζωοποιέω) occurs three times.[12] The adjective "everlasting" (αἰώνιος) is also frequently used to define the noun in the common expression "everlasting life" (ζωὴ αἰώνιος). The theme of life is introduced in the first few verses of the Gospel: the life of the universe is the Word and shines in the darkness (1:4–5). Similarly, the notion of life underlies the metaphor of the new birth in Jesus' conversation with Nicodemus, which culminates with the statement that everyone who believes in him will have life (3:16–17). In the conversation with the Samaritan woman, Jesus proclaims that he can give her "living water springing up into everlasting life" (4:13–14). In the exchange with the Jewish leaders, Jesus asserts that, like the Father, he has life in himself and that he will give life to those who believe in him (5:21–29; 6:40–51). Also in this exchange Jesus says, "I am the bread of life" (6:35, 48), the first of the seven "I am" sayings in the Gospel. Then at one of the feasts in Jerusalem, Jesus proclaims loudly that all those who thirst may come to him and drink and out of their heart will flow streams of living water (7:37–38). In the following section Jesus says that those who follow him will not walk in darkness but have the light of life (8:12). In the story of the good shepherd, Jesus says that he has come that people may have life in abundance (10:10). Before Jesus raises Lazarus from the dead, the last "I am" saying proceeds from Jesus' mouth: "I am the resurrection and the life" (11:25). In the second half of the Gospel Jesus teaches his disciples that he is "the way, the truth, and the life" (14:6), and prays that he may give everlasting life to those the Father has given him (17:1–2). Many scholars have noted the importance of the concept of life in the Gospel, and observed that the prominent place the "kingdom of God" occupies in the Synoptic Gospels is replaced by "everlasting life" in the Gospel of John.[13]

---

[11] Also see the discussion on the concept of life in Johan Ferreira, *Johannine Ecclesiology*, JSNTSup 160 (Sheffield: Sheffield Academic, 1998), 99–109.

[12] In comparison the noun ζωή occurs 7 times in Matthew, 4 times in Mark, and 5 times in Luke, whereas the verb ζάω occurs 6 times in Matthew, 3 times in Mark, and 9 times in Luke.

[13] For Leonhard Goppelt, "life" is more of a Hellenistic term than "kingdom," and hence reflects the Gospel's Hellenistic environment. See *Theology of the New Testament,* Vol. 1 (Grand Rapids: Eerdmans, 1981), 51.

It is not difficult to observe and highlight the prominence of the theme of life, or everlasting life, in the Gospel; however, it is far more challenging to ascertain what the Gospel means by the expression. The best place to start in discerning the precise content of life is most probably with the definition the Gospel provides in John 17:3: "And this is everlasting life, that they may know you, the only true God, and the one you sent, Jesus Christ." The Gospel's wording is carefully chosen and provides a clear explanation of what the concept of life entails. Firstly, we note that life is defined in terms of knowledge. The Greek word used is γινώσκω, which may refer to both intellectual perception and the process of acquiring knowledge. In the Gospel, the second meaning often features more prominently, reflecting Old Testament thought where knowledge relates to experience and activity. For example, when the Gospel says the world did not know the Word, it means that the world rejected him (1:10); Nicodemus's lack of knowledge means he has no experience of the Spirit (3:10); knowing the truth will make the disciples free (8:32); and sheep know the shepherd because they experience his care (10:14).

These examples indicate that knowledge in the Gospel of John does not refer only to intellectual understanding, but rather to subjective experience and activity.[14] Therefore, everlasting life means knowing God in the concrete experience of one's life by discovering that God is the only genuine or faithful One (τὸν μόνον ἀληθινόν). The adjective "true" (ἀληθινός) may either be understood as that which is "real," contrasting with what is false or non-existent in terms of Greek thought, or as "faithfulness," contrasting with what is unreliable in line with Old Testament theology. Whatever choice one makes, it is through experience that truth is verified. Furthermore, we note that the verb "to know" governs a double accusative—everlasting life is not only knowing God, but also the one sent, Jesus Christ. The Greek conjunction καί may be epexegetical in that it defines or qualifies the preceding statement more precisely. Everlasting life in the Gospel, then, is not just knowing that God is real or faithful, but also knowing Jesus. Indeed, it is through the believer's experience of Jesus that he or she learns that God is both real and faithful. The addition of the Greek verb "sent" (ἀπέστειλας) links the knowledge of Jesus to his historical mission in the world. The disciples, as the object of Jesus' mission, have experienced his calling, power, and grace in their lives. As the agents of Jesus' mission, they have also received the responsibility to participate in his work to evangelize, as they too are sent into the world (17:18; 20:21). In other words, everlasting life is experientially and missiologically defined. It does not consist so much of an intellectual perception of God or in a life that is just never-ending; rather, it is a life

---

[14] Note Raymond E. Brown's comment, "For John, of course, knowing God is not a purely intellectual matter but involves a life of obedience to God's commandments and of loving communion with fellow Christians (1 John 1:3; 4:8; 5:3). This is in agreement with the Hebrew use of the verb 'to know' with its connotations of immediate experience and intimacy." *The Gospel According to John: Introduction, Translation, and Notes*, Vol. 2, Anchor Bible 29a (Garden City: Doubleday, 1970), 752.

consisting of richly experiencing God and being occupied with activity in his mission to save the world.

This particular understanding of life is also seen throughout the Gospel narrative in texts that describe the abundant life that Jesus brings. For example, the first reference to life describes it as the energizing power and activity that brings positive change into the world as it shines in the darkness (1:4–5). The missiological significance of the language is unmistakable. It is this life that is given to those who believe in Jesus as they continue his mission to save the world. Even though Jesus is no longer physically present with his disciples, the light continues to shine through their witness. In the story of the Samaritan woman, the section on harvesting also emphasizes the link between evangelism and life (4:31–38). Jesus associates everlasting life with the work of mission when he says, "The reaper is receiving a reward and gathering fruit for everlasting life, so that the sower and the reaper may rejoice together" (4:36). [15] The conjunction *kai* (καί) may be interpreted as epexegetical, explaining the meaning of the reward (μισθός), and the action of the second present tense (συνάγει) may be taken as concomitant with the first (λαμβάνει). Therefore, the process of gathering the fruit is the reward of the reaper. The result of reaping, which is expressed in another present tense, is that both the sower and the reaper rejoice (χαίρῃ) in the here and now. It is not only that the reaper receives the reward of everlasting life after the mission, but everlasting life also consists in participating in the mission. Additionally, when Jesus says in John 8:12, "The one following me will never walk in darkness, but will have the light of life," it means that believers will experience the "light of life" when they follow Jesus, and not only as the final destination of their journey. Following Jesus clearly involves participating in his mission to save the world. And, finally, we may note that in John 12:24–26, life also consists of dying so that others may live, thus imitating the example of Jesus. It is only when the grain of wheat dies that it "bears much fruit." According to the context, the dying means to lose one's life to the things of the world, and follow Jesus in the way of mission.

Consequently, life is not just a soteriological term for John—it is also a decidedly missiological expression. The reader must not only become a Christian and believe that Jesus is the Christ, the Son of God, but also participate in the mission to save the world in obedience to his commission (20:21). Therefore, the purpose of the Gospel of John is eminently missiological. It is both a missionary document in terms of providing an evangelistic tract as a tool for mission, as well as a document for missionaries in terms of urging and enabling believers to engage in mission, thereby resulting in the rich experience of abundant and everlasting life.

---

[15] The metaphor of "fruit" (καρπός) in the Gospel of John is quite distinctive in comparison with Paul. In Paul it refers to Christian virtues (cf. Gal 5:21–22), whereas in the Gospel of John it refers to evangelism, i.e. making more disciples for Jesus.

3. What Does the Gospel Mean by "Seeing his Glory"?

The other major theological metaphor that the Gospel of John uses to interpret the life and mission of Jesus, in contrast to the Synoptic Gospels, is that of "glory." The noun "glory" (δόξα) occurs eighteen times in John, whereas it occurs seven times in Matthew, three times in Mark, and thirteen times in Luke. The verb "to glorify" (δοξάζω) occurs twenty-three times in the Gospel of John, whereas it occurs four times in Matthew, once in Mark, and nine times in Luke. There is not only a more pronounced frequency of the terms in the Gospel, but also a re-interpretation of their meaning with respect to the Synoptic traditions.[16]

The starting point of considering the meaning of glory in the Gospel of John must be the summative statement in the center of the Prologue (1:1–18). The ministry of Jesus is encapsulated as follows: "And the Word became flesh and tabernacled among us, and we saw his glory, glory as of the only-begotten Son from the Father, full of grace and faithfulness" (1:14). It is crucial to note here that the Gospel links Jesus' glory with the revelation of glory in the Old Testament tabernacle tradition; this relationship provides the key for understanding the concept of glory in the Gospel. The corresponding Old Testament Hebrew term is *kabod* (כבוד). It has the root meaning "to become heavy," from which the idea of honor or glory is derived. The noun has a wide semantic range, including meanings such as "wealth," "abundance," "honor," and "glory." The term occurs a few times in Genesis, but gains theological prominence in the Book of Exodus, where it is closely related to the Israelites' experience of Yahweh's grace in their deliverance from Egypt. In Exodus 14, just before the miraculous crossing of the Sea of Reeds, Yahweh tells Moses three times that he is about to gain glory through Pharaoh and the Egyptian army (Exod 14:4, 17–18). The Exodus narrative summarizes the event in terms of Yahweh's salvation and power, with the result that Israel "believed in Yahweh" (Exod 14:30–31). Following the miraculous deliverance, the narrative describes the glory of Yahweh (כב ודיהוה) appearing in the cloud with the giving of the manna in the wilderness (Exod 16:7–10), and later on Mount Sinai where Moses receives the law (Exod 24:15–18). On the mountain, Moses specifically requests Yahweh, "Show me your glory." Yahweh's response provides a carefully constructed theological interpretation of his glory, "I will cause all my goodness (טוב) to pass before you and I will proclaim before you the name of Yahweh, that is, I will be gracious (חנן) to whom I will be gracious and will show mercy (רחם) to whom I will show mercy" (Exod 33:19). Thus, the writer of Exodus interprets the glory of Yahweh in terms of his goodness, grace, and mercy. And then, finally, after the building of the tabernacle we read that "Yahweh's glory filled the tabernacle" (Exod 40:34–35; cf. Exod 29:43–46). In other words, in the Book of Exodus, "glory" is a soteriological term describing God's grace towards Israel in delivering them from the Egyptians and in dwelling among them.

---

[16] Also see the discussion on the concept of glory in Ferreira, *Johannine Ecclesiology*, 138–65.

The theme of Yahweh's glory continues to be an important *leitmotif* in the rest of the Old Testament and is developed in rich ways. When the Ark of the Covenant, the symbol of God's presence with his people, is captured, Eli's daughter-in-law names her son "Ichabod," meaning the glory has departed (1 Sam 4:19–22). But at the dedication of Solomon's temple, the glory returns and fills the temple (1 Kgs 8:10–13; cf. 1 Chr 5:13–14; 7:1–5). In the accounts in 1 Kings and 1 Chronicles, the image of glory is related to Yahweh's gracious action for his people in redemptive history. In 1 Kings, Solomon views the glory filling the temple as an indication that Yahweh has fulfilled his promise to David and his covenant "with our ancestors when he brought them out of the land of Egypt" (1 Kgs 8:14–21; 1 Chr 6:3–11)—God has kept his covenant and steadfast love (חסד) for his people (1 Kgs 8:23; 1 Chr 5:13; 6:14; 7:3). However, the exilic prophet Ezekiel has a vision of the glory of Yahweh departing from the temple and the nation, disappearing towards the east (Ezek 1:28; 8:4; 9:3; 10:4, 18–19; 11:22–23). Ezekiel's vision coincided, of course, with the destruction of the temple and the exile of Judah to Babylon. The symbolism is clear—as in the time of Eli, Israel's sin led to the forfeiture of God's grace and presence, resulting in exile. Nonetheless, the Book of Ezekiel does not finish without hope. At the end of the prophecy there is a new vision of the glory returning from the east, again filling the temple (Ezek 43:1–5; 44:4; cf. Ezek 39:21).

This hope of the glory returning to the temple is also taken up by other prophets with the additional element that not only Israel but that all nations will see it. For example, the opening vision of Second Isaiah proclaims that after God's new act of deliverance, portrayed in Exodus imagery, "the glory of Yahweh will be revealed and all people shall see it together" (Isa 40:5; Isa 59:19; 60:1–3; 66:18–19). So too, Habakkuk announces that, "the earth will be filled with the knowledge of the glory of Yahweh as the waters cover the sea" (Hab 2:14), and Haggai prophesies that God will "shake all nations" and will "fill this house with glory" (Hag 2:6–9). The glory of Yahweh is also a major metaphor in the Psalms, where it is often associated with Yahweh's acts in creation and salvation history (Ps 3:4; 21:5; 29:1–3, 9; 62:7–8; 66:2; 79:9; 102:17; 104:31; 105:1–5; 115:1; 138:5; 145:4–5, 11–12). Thus, the idea of power is often associated with God's glory (Ps 3:4; 24:7–8; 63: 2; 89:17; 145:11). However, most pronounced is the close connection between glory and God's grace (חסד) and faithfulness (אמת), the latter two terms often occurring together as a word pair (Ps 57:10–11; 85:9–10; 106: 5–7; 108:4–5; 115:1; 143:5–8). Therefore, this brief survey of the Old Testament reveals that glory features as a major soteriological motif, referring to God's gracious action in delivering and protecting his people. The motif finds its clearest expression in the glory cloud, indicative of the presence of Yahweh that fills the tabernacle and temple. However, in the prophetic writings the glory is lost, and even though there are numerous prophecies that it will return, that hope is never fulfilled in the Old Testament. This background provides the backdrop and interpretative key for the use of the concept in the Gospel of John.[17]

Against this Old Testament backdrop, the wording of the Prologue becomes at once explicable and astounding. The Greek verb "to pitch (a tent)" or "to tabernacle" (σκηνόω for the Hebrew שכן and Aramaic שכינה) recalls the Exodus story of Israel's deliverance as a revelation of the glory of God in the display of power, and more particularly in the display of God's covenant love (חסד) and faithfulness (אמת), being communicated by the Gospel of John with the Greek terms grace (χάρις) and truth (ἀλήθεια). The summary statement encapsulates the Old Testament understanding of Yahweh's glory in the Exodus, the Prophets, and the Psalms as a soteriological term describing Yahweh's grace and power in Salvation History. What is startling is that the Gospel of John portrays Jesus' ministry as the return of Yahweh's glory to his temple and people, fulfilling Old Testament prophecy. What is summarized in the Prologue is developed throughout the narrative text of the Gospel—Jesus' ministry is seen as a revelation of the glory of God. After the first sign in Cana we read that Jesus "revealed his glory, and his disciples believed in him" (2:11) just as the Israelites believed in Yahweh after the crossing of the Sea of Reeds (Exod 14:31), and so too the last sign before Jesus' death is interpreted as a revelation of glory, when Jesus says, "This illness does not lead to death; rather it is for God's glory, so that the Son of God may be glorified through it" (11:3), and when Jesus asked Martha, "Did I not tell you that if you believed, you would see the glory of God?" (11:40).

Ultimately, however, the glory of God comes to fullest manifestation in Jesus' death on the cross. Jesus' whole ministry, in fact, prepares for, leads up to, and finds fulfillment in the cross. In this respect the Gospel of John corresponds exactly with the emphasis and main point of the Gospel of Mark where all Jesus' miracles, teachings, and actions are refracted through the interpretative lens of the cross and resurrection.[18] The cross provides the definitive interpretation of the meaning of Jesus' life and teachings. In the Gospel of John, the cross is Jesus' "hour of glory," in which he will be lifted up to judge the world, cast out Satan, and draw all people to himself (John 3:15; 12:23, 27–28). Jesus' prayer, "Father, glorify your name" (12:28), and "Father, the hour has come, glorify your Son" (17:1), is the Johannine adaptation for Jesus' prayer in Gethsemane, "Abba, Father ... remove this cup from me, yet not what I will, but what you will" (Mark 14:36). The Gospel's logic is powerfully coherent: since Jesus' death on the cross is the ultimate display of God's grace and faithfulness towards his people and the world, it is indeed the greatest demonstration of God's glory. It is the "hour" that sets

---

[17] Alexander Tsutserov also relies on the Book of Exodus for defining these Johannine terms. *Glory, Grace, and Truth: Ratification of the Sinaitic Covenant according to the Gospel of John* (Eugene, OR: Pickwick, 2009).

[18] See Johan Ferreira, "The Markan Outline and Emphases," in *Content and Setting of the Gospel Tradition*, ed. Mark Harding and Alanna Nobbs (Grand Rapids: Eerdmans, 2010), 263–88.

God apart from everything and everyone else. Therefore, Jesus can say to Philip, "Whoever has seen me has seen the Father" (14:9). In other words, the Gospel's understanding of glory, steeped in Old Testament thought, is eminently soteriological.

This interpretation of Jesus' death on the cross in terms of sacrifice and as a revelation of glory already has its roots in the Old Testament. At the inauguration of Aaron's priesthood in Leviticus 9, the priests are instructed to sacrifice various animals as sin and burnt offerings before the tabernacle in order that the glory of Yahweh may appear to them (Lev 9:6–7). When they acted accordingly, the narrative concludes that "the glory of Yahweh appeared" and that "fire came out from Yahweh and consumed the burnt offering (Lev 9:22–24). Also, at the dedication of the temple after Solomon had prayed, the Chronicler records that "fire came down from heaven and consumed the burnt offering and sacrifices and the glory of Yahweh filled the temple" (2 Chr 7:1). In the imagery of the writer it may be understood that the glory cloud that filled the temple came from the smoke and fire created by the altar. This association of glory, smoke, and the altar also occur in Isaiah 6, where the prophet sees Yahweh in the temple and hears the refrain of the seraphs, "Holy, holy, holy is the LORD of hosts; the whole earth is full of his glory" (Isa 6:3). When the prophet is overcome with his own sense of impurity, he is cleansed with the coal taken from the nearby altar. Again, one may argue that the cloud that filled the temple was generated by the smoke from the altar. Significantly, the author of the Gospel of John associates Jesus' glory with Yahweh's glory in Isaiah 6 just after the glory of Jesus was linked to the cross (John 12:41; cf. 12:23, 27–28). Thus, the interpretation of Jesus' sacrifice on the cross as a revelation of glory is not altogether new in the Gospel of John. It appears that the author of the Gospel was a very careful student of the Old Testament.

There is, however, still more. Like the concept of life, glory is not only a key soteriological term in the Gospel; it is also a missiological one. Jesus' mission, which is to save the world through his suffering and death, is given to the disciples—they have to continue Jesus' mission. As such, we note that the Gospel links the glory of Jesus not just to his ministry and death, but also to the conversion of Gentiles. It is when "some Greeks" (τινες Ἕλληνες) wanted to see Jesus, that he announced, "The hour has come for the Son of Man to be glorified" (12:23). The Greeks are never again mentioned in the Johannine text, but the conversion of all people comes strongly to the fore in Jesus' words, "And I, when I am lifted up, will draw all people to myself" (12:32).[19] The significance of Jesus' words is so important that they need interpretation, "He said this to indicate the kind of death he was to die" (12:33). These themes are clearly expressed in Jesus' prayer in John 17 where Jesus glorified the Father by completing the work that the Father gave him to

---

[19] Also note the connection between "lifting up" and "glorification" in Isa 52:13. See Helen Mardaga, "The Repetitive Use of ὑψόω in the Fourth Gospel," *CBQ* 74 (2012): 101–17. The use of "lifting up" (ὑψόω) in the Gospel is an example of Johannine double entendre (cf. John 3:14; 8:28; 12:28, 32, 34).

do, which was to save the world. However, later in the prayer we learn that Jesus is now glorified in the disciples (17:10) and that he gave his glory to them (17:22). Since Jesus' glory was to complete the work of salvation, the glory given to the disciples implies that they now continue the work of salvation by being witnesses of Jesus. When Jesus prays that the disciples may see his glory (17:24), the meaning is not that he wishes that they may go to heaven, but rather that they may see the continuation and the effects of his work of salvation in the world—it is missiological. Jesus wishes that the disciples will continue his mission and see the glory of God as they carry on the divine mission through suffering and grace. Hence, the Gospel can conclude that Peter's death in the work of mission would be a glorification of God (21:19). Therefore, for the Johannine author, the Old Testament expectation that God's glory will be revealed to all nations (Num 14:21–22; Isa 40:5; 62:2; Hab 2:14) and proclaimed throughout the world (1 Chr 16:24; Ps 96:3; Isa 66:18–19) is truly fulfilled in Jesus and the mission of his disciples, but not in ways that one may have expected.[20]

4. The Two Johannine Horizons

In other words, the Gospel's two major metaphors—life and glory—are both missiologically defined. This missionary focus lies behind the overall theological framework and shapes the redaction of traditional materials in the formation of the Gospel. The Gospel works within these two hermeneutical horizons: the historical traditions concerning Jesus of Nazareth (1:45–46; 18:5–7; 19:19) and the present missionary task within the Greco-Roman world (1:29; 3:16; 20:21). The hermeneutical framework of two horizons has been applied to the Gospel by Martyn and Onuki, who emphasized the interface between the Jesus tradition and the intra-Jewish conflict experienced by the early Christian community.[21] Such a conflict is reflected in the Johannine material; however, in the final edition or form of the text, the Gospel has moved beyond these intramural concerns to embrace the wider world. The conflict with the synagogue no longer defines the spirit of the Gospel; rather the foreground has shifted to the Gentile mission. According to Martin Hengel, the Gospel has long since moved beyond the Jewish world and is now thoroughly situated within the Greco-Roman environment.[22] Jesus has indeed gone, in typical Johannine irony, to teach the Greeks (7:35).

---

[20] According to Thomas L. Brodie, "The glory in question is not something ethereal, it is found in human realities which are down-to-earth, in situations which one may not immediately think of as manifesting the divine." *The Gospel According to John: A Literary and Theological Commentary* (Oxford: Oxford University Press, 1993), 62.

[21] J. Louis Martyn, *History and Theology in the Fourth Gospel*, 2nd rev. ed. (Nashville: Abingdon, [1968] 1979); Takashi Onuki, *Gemeinde und Welt im Johannesevangelium*, WMANT 56 (Neukirchen-Vluyn: Neukirchener-Verlag, 1984).

[22] See Martin Hengel, *The Johannine Question*, 119–21; Jörg Frey, "The Diaspora Jewish Background of the Fourth Gospel," *SEÅ* 77 (2012): 169–96.

Therefore, on the one hand, the Gospel remains faithful to the historical traditions of the Jesus movement; but, on the other hand, it shapes its material to address the current needs of the Gentile mission. The Gospel takes both of these horizons seriously; one horizon supplies the background (the Jewish element) and the other the foreground (the Hellenistic element). However, there is an intermingling of these horizons in the text and one is not always able to make a clear differentiation between the two (see Figure 1). Both of these horizons are determinative for the final shape of the Gospel and, as Barrett has observed, are "fused in a unitary perspective."[23]

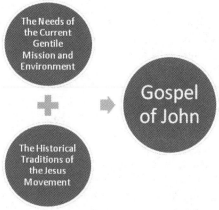

Figure 1.

The most obvious indication that the Gospel remains faithful to the traditions of the Jesus movement is its attention to historical detail that situates the life of Jesus within the contours of the Synoptic traditions and the cultural context of the land of Israel. The Jesus that the Gospel presents—the so-called "Johannine Jesus"—is the same person, does the same things, and meets the same end as the Jesus in the Synoptic Gospels. The Gospel of John clearly knows the Synoptic traditions and works within the framework established by those traditions.[24] In addition, the Gospel provides numerous

---

[23] C. K. Barrett, *The Gospel According to St John*, 2nd ed. (London: SPCK, 1978), 39.

[24] A major concern of Johannine scholarship has been trying to ascertain the most influential religious milieu for the *Sitz im Leben* of the Gospel. Three major trajectories have been proposed: 1) Hellenism (e.g., P.-H. Menoud, C. K. Barrett, C. H. Dodd, W. D. Davies); 2) Gnosticism (e.g., R. Bultmann, E. Käsemann, J. M. Robinson, L. Schottroff, R. M. Grant); and 3) Judaism (e.g., J. L. Martyn, J. A. T. Robinson, F. L. Cribbs, R. E. Brown, J. H. Charlesworth). Most scholars today situate the Gospel within a Jewish context that had close affinities with the sentiments of the Qumran Community who produced the Dead Sea Scrolls. In many ways the Dead Sea Scrolls have revolutionized our understanding of the Gospel. In light of the numerous conceptual and linguistic parallels, some historical connection is highly probable. See James H. Charlesworth, *John and the Dead Sea Scrolls* (New York: Crossroad, 1990); Mary L. Coloe and Tom Thatcher, *John, Qumran, and the Dead Sea Scrolls: Sixty Years of Discovery and Debate*, Society of Biblical Literature Early Judaism and Its Literature 32 (Atlanta: SBL, 2011). Also note Claus Westermann, *The Gospel of John in Light of the Old Testament*, trans. Siegfried S. Schatzmann (Peabody, MA: Hendrickson, 1998).

references to topographical features and cultural practices in pre-AD 70 Israel that reflect a concern for historical accuracy.[25]

The clearest indication that the Gospel's other major concern is to address the current Gentile mission is the use of Koine Greek as the medium of linguistic expression. The ordinary language of the Jewish people in the first half of the first century AD in Israel was Aramaic and Hebrew. It is not clear whether Jesus conducted his teaching ministry primarily in Aramaic or Hebrew, but it was certainly not in Greek. In other words, it is very significant that within a generation or two of Jesus' death, Greek became the major language for the propagation of the Gospel message: the intended readership of the Gospel of John was no longer Jews who spoke Aramaic or Hebrew, but Gentiles who spoke Greek. This fact is amply illustrated in the frequent explanations found in the Johannine narrative regarding the meaning of Jewish practices and Hebrew words (John 1:38, 41; 2:6, 13, 20; 4:9, 25; 9:7; 15:25; 19:13, 17, 31, 40, 42; 20:16, 24). Jewish readers, whether in Israel or in the Diaspora, would not require such explanations. In addition, as many commentators have pointed out, Jesus' enemies or the antagonists in the Gospel are generally described as "the Jews" (John 1:19; 2:18, 20; 5:10, 15–18; 6:41, 52; 7:1, 22–15; 8:22, 31, 48; 10:19, 24, 31, 33; 11:8; 12:9, 11; 13:33; 18:14, 20, 31), which is again an odd way of describing them, since Jesus, his disciples, and most people who believed in him in the Gospel were Jews. The target audience the final edition of the Gospel sought to address is clearly no longer in Palestine, nor a Jewish readership. In other words, while the historical traditions concerning Jesus provide a framework for the background of the Gospel, the foreground has now become the current Gentile mission within the Greco-Roman context. Therefore, as we will see, the Gospel often engages with Greek philosophical traditions and institutions to express its message.

5. The Johannine Outline and Style

In contrast to the Synoptics, instead of arranging its content along the motif of a journey from Galilee to Jerusalem, the Gospel of John arranges its material according to a number of integrated thematic cycles. The Gospel itself does not provide any clear demarcation between its different sections, yet there are some clues that may guide us in navigating its content. The most obvious structural feature is the Prologue at the beginning (1:1–18), followed by an Epilogue (21:1–25) after the purpose statement (20:30–31). The bulk of the narrative does not indicate an easily recognizable structural framework, but instead includes many "signs" that Jesus is the Christ, as well as extended discourses that articulate the meaning of Jesus' ministry.

It is interesting to note that this basic outline of the Johannine material corresponds with the structure for apologetic oratory as delineated by

---

[25] For example, see Urban C. von Wahlde, "Archaeology and John's Gospel," in *Jesus and Archaeology*, ed. James H. Charlesworth (Grand Rapids: Eerdmans, 2006), 523–86.

Aristotle (384–322 BC) in his treatise entitled *Rhetoric*. According to Aristotle, an apologetic speech consists of two parts: the "Statement of the Case" and the "Argument" that proves the case.[26] The Statement of the Case is also referred to as the Prologue, and Aristotle explains that within it "a foretaste of the theme is given" in order to avoid suspense and vagueness. The Argument contains "demonstrative proofs" of the main themes, which consists of two types: examples (induction) and enthymemes (syllogisms). Some speeches may also contain an introduction and an epilogue, but the two main parts are the Prologue and the Argument. In broad outline, it can be seen that the Gospel of John follows this schema as outlined by Aristotle. The Prologue of the Gospel is not just an introduction, but a summary of its major themes that states the case of the Gospel. The rest of the text is an unfolding of the case or the Argument, which proves the propositions of the Prologue. In addition, according to Aristotle's schema, the final chapter of the Gospel may be regarded as an Epilogue, which, among other things, restates the main arguments. These observations suggest that the author or final editor of the Gospel was aware of and was following these conventions of Greek oratory and literature.[27]

In his treatise entitled *Poetry*, Aristotle provides further information on the mechanics of literary discourse.[28] The most important element in the Argument or the Plot is the narration of events, where surprises, recognition scenes, and reversals in situation must feature prominently. The depiction of character, which reveals moral purpose, is secondary to the description of actions (Book 6). Other elements employed by the poet include thought, diction, spectacle, and song. Spectacle and song are self-explanatory; thought relates to statements of what is "possible and pertinent in given circumstances," whereas diction relates to the use and meaning of words.

Again, when one analyzes the content of the Gospel of John, there is a similarity with the literary features of epic poetry and tragedy as described by Aristotle. The narration of action forms the basic framework of the Johannine narrative and builds the story of Jesus around seven signs that Jesus performs in Jerusalem, Judea, and Galilee. There are numerous incidents of interaction

---

[26] Aristotle states, "A speech has two parts. You must state your case, and you must prove it" (*Rhet.* 3.13). Aristotle distinguishes between three types of oratory: political oratory, which addresses the future, forensic oratory, which addresses the past, and ceremonial oratory, which addresses the present.

[27] According to Mark W. G. Stibbe, the Gospel shows many analogies with Greco-Roman literature. *John as Story-Teller* (Cambridge: Cambridge University Press, 1992), 30. Also note the following studies which relate Greek literary conventions to the literary style of the Gospel of John. R. Alan Culpepper, "The Plot of John's Story of Jesus," *Int* 49 (1995): 347–58; Kasper Bro Larsen, *Recognition Scenes in the Gospel of John,* Biblical Interpretation Series 93 (Leiden/Boston: Brill, 2008); Jesper Tang Nielsen, "Resurrection, Recognition, Reassuring: The Function of Jesus' Resurrection in the Fourth Gospel," in *The Resurrection of Jesus in the Gospel of John,* WUNT 222, ed. Craig R. Koester and Reimund Bieringer (Tübingen: Mohr Siebeck, 2008), 177–208; Jesper Tang Nielsen, "The Narrative Structure of Glory and Glorification in the Fourth Gospel," *NTS* 56 (2010): 343–66.

[28] Aristotle distinguishes between three types of discourse: epic poetry or drama, comedy, and tragedy.

between Jesus and his disciples, opponents, and people interested in his message. Scenes of surprise, recognition, and reversal occur throughout the narrative, whereas descriptions of character and the inner feelings of the main protagonists are kept to a minimum. The presence of these literary features suggests that the Gospel has been shaped by the literary traditions of the Greco-Roman world, and is seriously engaging with the cultural institutions of its historical context. Therefore, it appears that the Gospel has a sophisticated readership in view—one familiar with Greek literary tastes and practices.[29]

Aristotle's description of the workings of rhetoric and poetry may give some guidance in discerning the overall structure and rhetorical features of the Gospel. On the basis of the discussion above, we may propose the following structure: 1) the Prologue, which states the major themes (1:1–18); 2) the Argument, which proves the themes (1:19–20:31); and 3) the Epilogue, which reiterates the main themes (21:1–25). Clearly, John 1:1–18 is a distinct section providing an overview or summary of the Gospel's main themes in elevated, almost poetic, language. Similarly, the final section of the Gospel, regarded by many commentators as a secondary conclusion after the purpose statement in John 20:30–31, also stands independently of the main narrative and highlights the disciples' ongoing task. However, in order to facilitate discussion, we may further divide the main section of the Gospel—the Argument—into three subdivisions. One perceives a change of focus after chapter 12, when Jesus turns his attention almost exclusively towards the disciples in the Farewell Discourses in chapters 13 to 17. The passion and resurrection narratives then bring the drama to a resolution. Therefore, we may propose the following outline for the Gospel:

1. The Prologue (1:1–18)
2. The Argument (1:19–20:31)
   (a) Jesus' ministry in the world (1:19–12:50)
   (b) Jesus' ministry to the disciples (13:1–17:26)
   (c) Jesus' death and resurrection (18:1–20:31)
3. The Epilogue (21:1–25)

Another difference between the Gospel of John and the Synoptics lies in the former's distinct literary style.[30] The Synoptics present Jesus' life and

---

[29] Judaism developed much sophistication in the Second Temple period and imbued the influence of the surrounding culture, especially Hellenism. See J. H. Charlesworth, "From Old to New: Paradigm Shifts concerning Judaism, the Gospel of John, Jesus, and the Advent of 'Christianity,'" in *Jesus Research: An International Symposium*, ed. James H. Charlesworth et al. (Grand Rapids: Eerdmans, 2009), 68.

[30] On reading the Gospel from a literary perspective, see R. Alan Culpepper, *Anatomy of the Fourth Gospel: A Study in Literary Design* (Philadelphia: Fortress, 1983). For more specialized studies, see Herbert Leroy, *Rätsel und Missverständnis: Ein Beitrag zur Formgeschichte des Johannesevangeliums*, BBB 30 (Bonn: Peter Hanstein Verlag, 1968); Paul D. Duke, *Irony in the Fourth Gospel* (Atlanta: John Knox, 1985); R. Alan Culpepper and Fernando F. Segovia, eds., *The Fourth Gospel from a Literary Perspective*, Semeia 53 (Atlanta: Scholars, 1991); Craig R.

teaching by means of a concise and fast running historical narrative interspersed with descriptions of miracles, disputes with opponents, pithy sayings, and parables. The Gospel of John, in contrast, places less emphasis on action; instead, it develops a number of theological themes in extended discourses that reflect the character of Greek philosophical interrogation. There is also copious use of a range of literary devices: misunderstanding, double meaning, paronomasia, irony, and symbolism occur throughout the narrative. Jesus often makes an ambiguous statement, resulting in misunderstanding and requiring further explanation. The author employs these devices not only as a means to develop the narrative, but to imply that humans often do not understand heavenly things and need revelation. Irony, where there is a contrast between appearance and reality, occurs regularly, and is a form of "silent" communication between author and reader, serving to encourage the reader to have true understanding. There is also extensive use of symbolism throughout the Gospel, which the author employs to link different spheres of reality.[31] Inherent to the Gospel's symbolic world is dualism, which places reality and behavior in a framework of opposites or contrarieties. In the Gospel, we have opposites such as above/below, light/darkness, and belief/disbelief. Finally, we may point out that another pervasive literary device is progressive parallelism. The Gospel arranges its themes in trajectories that are developed progressively and in separate parallel sections throughout the narrative until complete resolution (see Figure 2). The development of the themes of life and glory are examples of progressive parallelism in the Gospel.

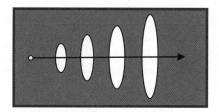

Figure 2.

5.1. The Prologue (1:1–18)

The Prologue of the Gospel of John is one of the most majestic passages in the New Testament, occupying the attention of interpreters for two millennia. We cannot be confident about the provenance or the *Vorlage* of the Prologue—however, its present form functions as a theological summary, and not just as

---

Koester, *Symbolism in the Fourth Gospel: Meaning, Mystery, Community* (Minneapolis: Fortress, 2003).

[31] Literary critics distinguish between core symbols, coordinate symbols, and subordinate symbols. Jesus, of course, is the major symbol of God. Other core symbols are light and life, with their coordinate symbols of darkness and death. Subordinate symbols of light are entities such as day, lamps, and fire; whereas for darkness we have night and blindness.

an introduction, of Jesus' life and death. It addresses two basic questions: (1) Who is Jesus? (2) What does Jesus do? The answer to these questions, and the main point of the Prologue, is that Jesus is the true revealer of God. The Prologue uses numerous christological titles and Old Testament symbolism in presenting Jesus to the reader. The content of the Prologue falls into three sections that overlap chronologically with ever-increasing magnification on Jesus as the revealer of God and the bestower of life (see Figure 3). Each section provides an overview of the ministry of Jesus, with a clear focus on the revelatory and soteriological significance of his coming. It can also be observed that the philosophical domain of the Greco-Roman environment is very much at the forefront in the Prologue. The descriptions of Jesus as Logos, Light, and Life have a closer affinity with the Greco-Roman world, as opposed to the very Jewish titles of "Messiah," the "Son of God," and the "Son of Man" in the rest of the chapter.

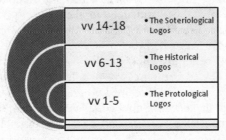

Figure 3.

The first section, verses 1 to 5, describes the preexistence of the Word, creation through the agency of the Word, and most importantly for the reader, the bestowal of life and light by the Word. The Gospel's use of Logos, or Word (λόγος), as a title for Jesus is carefully chosen. It underscores both the interpretation of Jesus' person and work in light of the Old Testament and the intent to engage with the Greco-Roman environment. With the themes of creation, darkness, light, and life the author links the ministry of Jesus with the creation account in the Book of Genesis (intertextuality), implying that the coming of Jesus has cosmic ramifications—light is dispelling darkness for the emergence of a new humanity. In the Old Testament, "word" (דבר) is the main term used to refer to God's revelation of himself in creation and in the prophetic word. Genesis 1 depicts God as creating the world through the creative act of his spoken word. In the prophets, "the word" becomes the standard designation of divine revelation. In other words, there is no doubt that the Gospel's primary intention by the use of *Logos* is to describe Jesus as the embodiment and fulfillment of the Old Testament revelatory word of God. However, the term also cannot be detached from its associated meanings in the Greco-Roman philosophical and religious environment. The term was used widely as a key concept in the Greek philosophical schools, albeit with different meanings and connotations.[32]

The Gospel of John is using the term as a point of contact to draw its Greek readers into conversation regarding the true origin and meaning of ultimate reality. Verse 3 articulates the same understanding as Gen 1:1—that the universe is not eternal but came into existence out of nothing (*creatio ex nihilo*) through the creative act of God. It therefore denies the notion of an eternal universe and materialistic positivism, and establishes the supremacy of Word and Spirit (i.e., heavenly things) above earthly things. In verses 4 and 5, the terms life, light, and darkness introduce the Gospel's soteriological and ethical themes. Verse 5 not only summarizes the ministry of Jesus, but also describes the current experience of the disciples: light is overcoming darkness.

The second section, verses 6 to 13, narrows the description to the coming of John the Baptist as a witness to Jesus, the rejection of Jesus by the world, and the acceptance of Jesus by believers. While the first section situates the ministry of Jesus against the background of protology, this section roots his ministry in the historical setting of John's activity in Bethany across the Jordan (1:28). Although John the Baptist was a great prophet and created quite a stir among the Jews, the Gospel is careful to point out that John's only significance was that he came in order to be a witness to Jesus. There is a veiled polemic directed against followers of John, who regarded him as a messianic figure.[33] The section also gives more attention to the conflict and opposition that Jesus experienced during his ministry. The use of "world" (κόσμος) has deliberate theological intent by setting Jesus' coming within a global perspective.[34] Even though Jesus' ministry was confined to the region of Israel, it has global ramifications. Verses 10 and 11 describe in ironic fashion the rejection of Jesus by the world, and more particularly by his own people, the Jews. Verses 12 and 13 describe the supernatural life and the new status as children of God received by all those who believe in Jesus. There is a deliberate contrast between these verses and the preceding ones, implying that

---

[32] In Greek philosophy the Logos was regarded as the fundamental principle underlying creation, form, and meaning. The philosopher Heracleitus (ca. 540–480 BC) regarded the Logos, which most people fail to understand, as the fundamental principle of reason underlying and sustaining the order in the universe. For the Stoics it denoted the active rational and spiritual principle by which everything exists and which permeates all reality (*anima mundi*). The first-century-AD Jewish philosopher Philo also made frequent use of the term Logos, carrying various nuances, to integrate Judaism with Greek philosophy. In Philo the Logos may represent the ideal world, the ideal human being, the agent of creation and thought, an intermediary between God and the world, and can be both transcendent and immanent.

[33] See Carl R. Kazmierski, *John the Baptist: Prophet and Evangelist* (Collegeville: Liturgical, 1996); Catherine M. Murphy, *John the Baptist: Prophet of Purity for a New Age* (Collegeville: Liturgical, 2003).

[34] The world (κόσμος) receives special prominence in the Gospel, occurring 78 times. The world is a place of hostility (16:33), does not know God (1:10; 14:17, 22; 17:25), and hates the disciples (15:18–19; 17:14); and yet the world is the object of both God's love (3:16) and Jesus' mission (1:9, 29; 10:36; 14:31; 17:18, 21, 23). Jesus came to give light (8:12; 9:5; 11:9; 12:46) and life to the world (3:17; 6:33, 51). Only in the Gospel of John is Jesus referred to as the "Savior of the World" (4:42; cf. 12:47; 1 John 4:14). Indeed, the Pharisees exclaimed in exasperation that "the world has gone after him!" (12:19).

race or ethnicity no longer defines the people of God—those who are his own—but faith in Jesus.

The third section, verses 14 to 18, highlights the revelation of glory, grace, and truth through the Word, which is nothing less than the revelation of God himself. As mentioned above, verse 14 can be considered a summary of the whole Gospel. The central idea is that divine revelation and salvation have come through Jesus Christ. The statement that "the Word became flesh" is shocking, mysterious, and wonderfully gracious all at the same time. It is the Gospel's major christological statement.[35] In general, the Greek word "flesh" (σάρξ) has a decidedly negative connotation both in Greek philosophy as well as in Pauline theology. Designating "flesh" as a mode of God's being would have been scandalous to most sophisticated readers in the first century AD, being contradictory ontological and ethical categories. The Gospel uses the term to declare the reality of the incarnation.[36] The statement affirms that there is nothing bad *per se* about the physical creation, and that Jesus became a real human being. This is, of course, a great ontological mystery. But, more importantly for the author, it shows the extent of God's love for humanity.

The Gospel's thought is steeped in Old Testament soteriological language, but it uses Greek terms to communicate its message since it is intended for an audience beyond Galilee, Samaria, and Judea. Verse 17 is a further explanation of the last phrase in verse 16, "grace upon grace" (καὶ χάριν ἀντὶ χάριτος). There is no contrast or antithesis between Moses and Jesus—rather, the idea is that more grace came through Jesus Christ.[37] Finally, verse 18 forms an *inclusio* with verse 1, and brings the thought of the Prologue to a resolution. Only Jesus has the qualifications to reveal God, since he is in the bosom of the Father and is none other than God himself. The final term that John uses to describe Jesus' revelation of God is also hugely significant. The Greek verb ἐξηγέομαι means "to explain," or more specifically in its current context "to explain by means of a narrative."[38] The explanation or the "narrative" refers to the account that we now call the Gospel of John. In other

---

[35] Most scholars agree that the Gospel has a "basic Christological interest." See R. Schnackenburg, *The Gospel According to St John*, Vol. 1 (New York: Crossroad, 1990), 154. Peculiar to Johannine Christology are the following seven "I am" sayings (ἐγώ εἰμί): 1) I am the bread of life (6:35); 2) I am the light of the world (8:12); 3) I am the gate (10:7, 9); 4) I am the good shepherd (10:11, 14); 5) I am the resurrection and the life (11:25); 6) I am the way, the truth, and the life (14:6); 7) I am the true vine (15:1). These sayings depict Christ in terms of important Old Testament salvific symbols. The expression "I am" is also used absolutely (John 8:24, 28, 58; 13:19, cf. Exod 3:14). The different images enforce the same idea, that people may have abundant and everlasting life. Therefore, the Gospel's Christology is orientated towards soteriology.

[36] We disagree with Käsemann that the Gospel espouses a docetic Christology. Rather, the Gospel presents an incarnational Christology: Jesus is presented as a real human being (John 1:14; 4:6; 11:35; 19:28).

[37] It is important to note that the Greek text contains no adversative conjunction "but" (δέ or ἀλλά). In Johannine theology Jesus fulfills the Old Testament, he does not replace it.

[38] The English expression "to exegete" is based on the etymology of this Greek word, from which we also have the noun "exegesis" (ἐξήγησις).

words, the author is saying, "If you want to know God, then read the story of Jesus." It is John's exegesis paper on God!

5.2. The Argument

(a) The Ministry of Jesus in the World (1:19–12:50)

The first section of the Argument is set within the framework of seven signs, which Jesus performs in Cana, Jerusalem, around the Sea of Galilee, and in Bethany.[39] Set against the background of the unbelief of the Jewish leaders in Jerusalem, this section not only highlights Jesus' messianic credentials but also his identity as the light and Savior of the whole world. Although the traditions and cultural context of the early Jesus movement have a formative influence on the presentation of the material, the author regularly draws his narrative into the ideological environment of the Greco-Roman world, and often points to the global significance of Jesus' ministry. For example, Jesus' "signs and wonders" (4:48) recall God's intervention for his people in the Exodus event (Deut 4:34; 6:22; 7:19; 26:8) and imply that another crucial salvific epoch has arrived with the coming of Jesus—however, the Gospel's use of the term "sign" (σημεῖον), instead of the Synoptic "miracle" (δύναμις), illustrates its propensity to contextualize the gospel message to the environs of the Greek philosophical world. The term was already used with religious connotations in the Homeric literature, but with Plato took on a new prominence when used to indicate the divine presence in the life of Socrates. Plutarch, a contemporary of the Gospel of John, devoted a whole treatise to the subject, entitled *On the Sign of Socrates*. The term was regularly used in Hellenistic religions where only the gods, particularly Zeus, were able to perform supernatural signs.[40]

Therefore, in light of this background, the signs may be interpreted to mean that Jesus was not only inaugurating a new salvific event in terms of salvation history, but also that he came from God and that his mission has divine sanction (John 3:2; 10:38). Yet, the Johannine signs go beyond both the common Jewish and Greek understandings of miracles and signs; they point to the decisive sign of the cross, which is the greatest revelation of God's glory (2:11; 11:4, 40; cf. John 2:18–19).

---

[39] The seven signs including the miracle in the Epilogue are: (i) the changing of water into wine at Cana (2:1–11); (ii) the healing of the official's son at Cana (4:46–54); (iii) the healing of the invalid at the Pool of Bethesda in Jerusalem (5:2–9); (iv) the feeding of the five thousand in Galilee (6:1–14); (v) Jesus walking on water in Galilee (6:16–21); (vi) the healing of the man born blind in Jerusalem (9:1–7); (vii) the raising of Lazarus at Bethany (11:38–44); and (viii) the miraculous catch of fish at Galilee (21:1–14).

[40] See Paul Ciholes in "The Socratic SHMEION and Johannine as Divine Manifestation," in *PRSt* 9 (1982): 251–65; C. K. Barrett, *The Gospel According to St John: An Introduction with Commentary and Notes on the Greek Text*, 76. According to Willis H. Salier, John relies more on a Hebrew background, but *semeion* is also used in judicial rhetoric in Greek and Latin authors to introduce a proof. *The Rhetorical Impact of the Sēmeia in the Gospel of John* (Tübingen: Mohr Siebeck, 2004), 34–38.

After the lofty theological language of the Prologue, the reader is introduced to the story of Jesus through the testimony of John the Baptist in historical narrative. Like the Synoptics, the Gospel of John sets the ministry of Jesus in the context of the prophetic vision of Second Isaiah, which had a global vista (Isa 40:5; 42:1; 44:5; 49:6–7, 11; 52:15; 55:4–5). John the Baptist denies that he is the Christ, or the expected Prophet, and points to Jesus as the "Lamb of God who takes away the sin of the world" (1:29). In the context of Isaiah 40:3, which introduces the message about the Suffering Servant, the Levitical imagery of the sacrificial lamb anticipates the substitutionary death of Jesus for the sin of the world that occurs at Passover.[41] In addition to dying for the sin of the world, Jesus will also baptize with the Holy Spirit, recalling the Old Testament expectation that God will create a new covenant people through the agency of his Spirit (Ezek 36:25–28).

Jesus' first disciples, Andrew, Peter, Philip, Nathaniel, and probably John (the "Beloved Disciple"), discover that Jesus is the Messiah by following him, staying with him, and observing him. The narrative emphasizes the action of "seeing" Jesus.[42] John the Baptist's confession of Jesus is predicated upon him "seeing" Jesus and the Spirit descending upon Jesus (1:32–34), and his call is for all "to see" Jesus as the Lamb of God (1:29, 36). Jesus likewise invites his first followers to "come and see" (1:39), and Philip also invites Nathaniel to "come and see" (1:46). Upon Nathaniel's confession, Jesus says that he will "see" greater things (1:50). This emphasis in the Gospel, despite the later injunction of John 20:29 on seeing and experience, may again reflect the Gospel's sensitivity to Greek philosophy, which held that understanding rests on first hand observation (cf. 1 John 1:1–2). [43] The disciples' understanding of Jesus increases according to their experience from confessing him as the "Messiah" (1:41), then as the "Prophet" (1:45), and finally as the "Son of God" and the "King of Israel" (1:49). It is also remarkable that the author presents the first disciples as coming to Jesus before Jesus performed any sign. They come to believe in Jesus through the witness of John the Baptist and by staying with him. Although the disciples see the signs and believe on account of them (2:11), their faith has a deeper foundation.

---

[41] We disagree with Forestall who says that the Gospel does not link Jesus' death with expiation or sacrifice. J. Terence Forestall, *The Word of the Cross: Salvation as Revelation in the Fourth Gospel* (Rome: Biblical Institute, 1974), 9. On atonement theology in Johannine soteriology, see Bruce H. Grigsby, "The Cross as Expiatory Sacrifice in the Fourth Gospel," *JSNT* 15 (1982): 51–80; Don A. Carson, "Adumbrations of Atonement Theology in the Fourth Gospel," *JETS* 57 (2014): 513–22.

[42] Note Dorothy Lee's insightful discussion on the use of the five senses in John. "The Gospel of John and the Five Senses," *JBL* 129 (2010): 115–27.

[43] For example, note Plato's allegory of the cave and Aristotle's correspondence theory of truth. According to Aristotle, "To say of what is that it is, or of what is not that it is not, is true" (*Metaph.* 4.7); and, "all truths are demonstrable" (*An. post.* 1.3, 1.22 [3]).

View from Khirbet Qana (Cana) looking south towards Nazareth.
Photograph by the author.

The chapter ends with a revelation of Jesus' own understanding of his identity as the "Son of Man" (1:51). The language of the angels "ascending and descending" recalls the story of Jacob at Bethel, which emphasizes the Abrahamic promise of numerous seed (Gen 28:13–14). According to Jewish tradition, it is here as the place of divine revelation where the temple was later built. But now the nexus and activity of divine revelation will shift from the temple to the person of Jesus as the "Son of Man." The expression "Son of Man" not only recalls the apocalyptic figure in the Book of Daniel, through whom God will establish his universal and everlasting kingdom that includes all nations (Dan 7:13–14), but also links the uniqueness of Jesus with his suffering and death on the cross (John 6:27, 53; 12:23; 13:31).[44] Therefore, the final christological title of the chapter is also perhaps the most revealing about Jesus' identity and work. The center of divine revelation is not just shifting to the person of Jesus, but is particularly manifested in his death on the cross, the "holiest of holies" in the new temple that he has come to build.

In chapter 2, Mary's persistent faith at a wedding in the insignificant town of Cana provides the catalyst for the start of Jesus' public ministry through the sign of changing water into wine. The narrative is filled with symbolism communicating that Jesus has come to renew Judaism and inaugurate the long expected Messianic Banquet (Hos 14:7; Amos 9:13–15; Jer 31:12; 1 En. 10:19; 2 Bar. 29:5). Some scholars have suggested that the first sign also relates to the Greek myth of Dionysus, the god of wine, showing that Jesus is far superior to Dionysus.[45] The sign reveals Jesus' identity as the Messiah and

---

[44] It is interesting to observe that the Targum Onkelos adds that "the Glory of the Lord" appeared to Jacob at the place. Bernard Grossfeld, trans. and ed., *The Targum Onqelos to Genesis* (Edinburgh: T&T Clark, 1988), 104. In Targum Neofiti, likewise, Jacob concludes, "Behold, truly, the glory of the Shekinah of the Lord—it dwells in this place." See Martin McNamara, trans. and ed., *Targum Neofiti 1, Genesis* (Edinburgh: T&T Clark, 1992), 141.

[45] Although it is likely that Greek readers would have compared the Cana sign with Dionysus as the Greek god of wine, it is hard to find evidence for the view that the Johannine sign was based on the myth of Dionysus. See Carsten Claussen, "Turning Water into Wine: Re-reading the

59

may be regarded, as with all the signs, as a scene of recognition according to Aristotle's classification. It is a proof that the revelation of God's glory has moved from the temple to rest upon Jesus (2:11). The scene then moves from the low lying Galilean Sea to the high hills of Jerusalem, where Jesus cleanses the temple in a courageous prophetic act filled with symbolism about his status and work. Jesus will ultimately demonstrate his zeal for God's house in his death on the cross, which will literally consume him (1:17). Jesus responds to the Jewish leaders' demand for a sign by pronouncing that after they have destroyed the temple, he will raise it up in three days, which the narrator interprets as referring to his resurrection (1:19–21). Although this event occurred at the end of Jesus' public ministry just before his death (cf. Mark 11:15–19), the Gospel of John places it at the beginning in order to provide a revelatory lens for viewing Jesus' ministry as a whole. He is the one who is going to rebuild the temple, that is, he is the Messiah.[46] But Jesus not only rebuilds the temple, he replaces it through his work on the cross and resurrection with his own body (2:21–22). Jesus is more than just the expected Jewish Messiah; he is the new revelation of God himself. Jesus then performs several signs in Jerusalem. Many believed in him on account of the signs, but Jesus did not entrust himself to them, indicating that their faith was problematic.

Jesus' extended conversation with a Pharisee named Nicodemus in chapter 3 stresses the need for a spiritual birth from above (ἄνωθεν) if one is to enter the kingdom of God and understand heavenly things.[47] The conversation illustrates many features of Johannine literature, including the rich use of symbolism, double meaning, misunderstanding, and *Horizontverschmelzung*. Nicodemus comes to Jesus by "night," indicating that he still lives in fear, unbelief, and spiritual darkness. Nicodemus understands Jesus' teaching regarding the new birth in physical terms, and thus takes the adverb (ἄνωθεν) to mean "again." Jesus, however, is taking about a spiritual birth from "above." The misunderstanding illustrates that humans—even religious leaders—think in worldly terms and are incapable of understanding heavenly things. The change of the personal pronoun from the singular "I" to the plural "we" in verse 11, and the difficulty in determining where Jesus' direct conversation with Nicodemus ends and the commentary by the narrator begins,

---

Miracle at the Wedding in Cana," in *Jesus Research: An International Symposium*, ed. James H. Charlesworth et al. (Grand Rapids: Eerdmans, 2009), 80–86.

[46] Early Jewish tradition also thought of the Messiah as a temple builder. See Alan R. Kerr, *The Temple of Jesus' Body: The Temple Theme in the Gospel of John*, JSNTSup 220 (Sheffield: Sheffield Academic, 2002), 67–101; Mary Coloe, *God Dwells With Us: Temple Symbolism in the Fourth Gospel* (Collegeville: Liturgical, 2001); Paul M. Hoskins, *Jesus as the Fulfillment of the Temple in the Gospel of John*, Paternoster Biblical Monographs (Carlisle: Paternoster, 2006). Also see the Dead Sea Scroll manuscript 4QFlorilegium.

[47] The Greek particle (δέ) may be interpreted in various ways; Nicodemus may be an illustration or an exception of unbelieving Jews in Jerusalem. Since Nicodemus progressively comes to know Jesus, defending (7:50) and serving him (19:39), we may take the particle as a disjunctive "but" (i.e., Nicodemus is an exception).

demonstrate that there is no fundamental difference between the teaching of the historical Jesus and the teaching of the community of believers.

The conversation with Nicodemus also contains the *leitmotif* of Johannine theology in the well-known verse, "For God so loved (ἀγαπάω) the world that he gave his only-begotten Son, that whoever believes in him should not perish but have everlasting life" (3:16). In the context of the conversation with Nicodemus, the statement interprets the meaning of the cross (3:14–15) as a revelation of God's love for the whole world (κόσμος), procuring salvation for everyone who continues to believe in Jesus. Since the only-begotten Son is most unique and the cherished one of the Father, the cross is the focal point and the clearest demonstration of the unconditional and sacrificial nature of God's love in giving his Son as a sacrifice for the sin of the world. This interpretation of love as "giving" also reflects Aristotle's emphasis that love is an activity (*Ethica eudemia*, 1237a–b and 1241b), rather than an emotion that can quickly change (*Ethica nicomachea*, 1156b).[48] The result or consequence of believing in Jesus is the gift of everlasting life, which is received already in this life.[49]

In chapter 4, a story full of surprises, there is an illustration of how a person comes to believe in Jesus and experience the new life he came to bring. It is significant for the author to point out that it is a Samaritan woman; the added detail that she came at noon suggests that she was ostracized by her community for an immoral life living with numerous men, since women would normally draw water at dawn or dusk. The narrative relates that on his return to Galilee Jesus had to pass through Samaria, which was not the normal road conservative Jews traveled, since, as the text points out, "Jews do not share things in common with Samaritans" (4:9). As in the Synoptic Gospels, the Greek impersonal verb (δεῖ) is used to underscore the divine intent behind Jesus' mission (4:4). It would have been startling for a first-century reader to note that Jesus, as a Jewish Rabbi, engages in a conversation with an immoral Samaritan woman at a waterhole defiled by Gentiles. Jesus is even prepared to drink from the woman's pitcher. However, through the conversation, which is rife with double meaning and misunderstanding, the woman progressively learns more about Jesus. She first perceives Jesus as a Jew (4:9), then he becomes a gentleman (v. 11), then she realizes that he is a prophet (4:19), and

---

[48] The frequent use of the verb ἀγαπάω and the noun ἀγαπή in the Gospel and the rest of the New Testament is significant. The most common verb in use during the first century AD for love was φιλέω; the more classical ἀγαπάω was rarely used. It appears that the New Testament authors revived a disused term for love and infused it with new meaning to describe God's love, which is unconditional, unchanging, and active.

[49] In general, it is said that the Synoptics present an imminent futuristic eschatological expectation (cf. Mark 1:15), whereas the Gospel of John has a realizing eschatology. In the Gospel of John the effects associated with the *eschaton* are already present or happening: life (3:16, 36; 5:24; 6:47); judgment (3:18–21; 12:31; 16:11); resurrection (5:25; 11:24–26); the revelation of glory (1:14; 2:11; 12:23; 17:1–5); and the "second" coming has already taken place (14:18, 28; 16:16). However, the Gospel is not consistent; future aspects remain: future resurrection (5:28–30; 6:39, 44, 54); future judgment (5:28–30; 12:48); and the future coming of Jesus (21:22).

finally she recognizes him as the Messiah (4:28–29). She believes and rushes back to her townsfolk to share her exciting discovery, forgetting her pitcher at the well (4:28). At the end of the story, we know that Jesus had to go through Samaria and meet this woman in order that the Samaritans may come to know him as the "Savior of the world" (4:42). The confession of the Samaritans proclaims the intention of the author of the Gospel: Jesus is more than just the Messiah for the Jews, he is the Savior of all humanity. The second sign that Jesus performs in Galilee relates the healing of an official's (βασιλικός) son in Capernaum while Jesus was at the village of Cana (4:46–54).[50] Jesus' healing of the son from a distance reveals his extraordinary power and results in the faith of the official and his whole household.

The recently excavated Pool of Siloam in Jerusalem.
Photograph by the author.

In chapter 5, Jesus is again in Jerusalem and heals a paralyzed man at the Pool of Bethesda, the third sign in the Gospel. Even though the healing is an extraordinary deed, its greater significance lies in what it reveals about Jesus' identity. The healing created a commotion among the Jewish leaders, since it took place on the Sabbath. Jesus' statement, "My Father is still working, and I am also working" (5:17) justifies the healing on the Sabbath and proves his identity as the Son of God. Again, Jesus is not only a miracle worker (*theios aner*), but also the Son of God. However, even though the paralyzed man received healing, he does not know who Jesus is. Jesus' encounter with the man later in the temple provides an opportunity for an increased understanding of Jesus. In chapter 6, the author takes the reader back to the "other side of the Sea of Galilee," where Jesus performs the fourth sign, the feeding of the five thousand. This is the only miracle related in all four

---

[50] Some interpreters have identified the royal official with the Gentile centurion who built the synagogue in Capernaum (cf. Luke 7:1–10).

canonical Gospels, demonstrating its importance in the early traditions of the Jesus movement. As in the Gospel of Mark, the sign in the Gospel of John is closely related to Jesus' death. The miracle occurred at the time of Passover, and in the following discourse Jesus says, "I am the living bread that came down from heaven. Whoever eats of this bread will live forever; and the bread that I will give for the life of the world is my flesh" (6:51). The result of the miracle is that the people confessed him as the Prophet (cf. Deut 18:15) who was to come into the world; however, this is an inadequate understanding of his identity. The next miracle, the fifth sign, reveals in no uncertain terms that Jesus is none other than the "I am": God himself (6:20).[51] The sixth sign occurs again in Jerusalem, but this time at the Pool of Siloam (9:1–4). The story illustrates how the blind man progressively grew in his understanding of Jesus' identity from being a miracle worker (9:11, 15), to a prophet (9:17), to the Son of Man (9:35–38), and the antagonism that faith in Jesus drew from the Pharisees. Jesus is the light of the world and he opens the eyes of the blind.

In the parable of the Good Shepherd, which occurs at the center of the Gospel's narrative, Jesus lays down the ultimate criterion for identifying the true shepherd of God's people; the good shepherd willingly lays down his life for the sheep (10:11–18). Shepherd imagery was a common metaphor in ancient cultures, used to describe the king of a nation, so the prominence of the image in the Old Testament as well as in Greek literature is not unusual.[52] In the Old Testament, God is the shepherd of his people (Gen 49:24; Ps 23:1; 28:9; 78:71; 80:1; Ezek 34:15), but the term assumes messianic connotations in the expectation of a new shepherd like David (Ezek 34:23–24). Greek literature uses the theme to describe the qualities of a true leader in providing protection and good pasture for people. However, in this parable Jesus is identified as the only true shepherd, has a much closer relationship with his "sheep," and pays the ultimate price for their preservation. In the parable Jesus knows his sheep, and his sheep recognize his voice. As the good shepherd, he lays down his life for the sheep, which is a role reversal and in stark contrast, we may note, to the Greek god of shepherds, Pan, who on occasion required human sacrifice. The Gospel emphasizes that Jesus is in total control of his life and death; no one holds power over Jesus' destiny. It also stresses that Jesus has "other sheep" that he "must bring" into the same fold (10:16), closely linking his death with the Gentile mission.[53] The new

---

[51] Schnackenburg, *The Gospel According to St John*, 2:27.

[52] On the shepherd image in the Hellenistic world, see Nicholas Cachia, *The Image of the Good Shepherd as a Source for the Spirituality of Ministerial Priesthood* (Rome: Pontificia Universit Gregoriana, 1997), 35–38. Also see Jerome H. Neyrey, "'I Am the Door' (John 10:7, 9): Jesus the Broker in the Fourth Gospel," *CBQ* 69 (2007): 271–91; Jerome H. Neyrey, "The 'Noble' Shepherd in John 10," in *The Gospel of John in Cultural and Rhetorical Perspective* (Grand Rapids: Eerdmans, 2009), 282–312. Also see Jane Heath, "Some were Saying, 'He is good' (John 7.12b)," *NTS* 56 (2010): 523–35, where it is argued that Jesus' "goodness" is linked to his willingness to die for his sheep on the cross.

[53] There is no doubt that the Old Testament expectation that God will gather his scattered people together as a shepherd gathers his sheep lies behind Jesus' words: Deut 30:3–4; Ps 106:47; Isa 11:12; 40:11; 43:5; 49:18; 54:7; 60:4; Jer 23:3; 29:14; 31:8–10; 32:37; Ezek 11:17; 20:34, 41;

sign of belonging to God's people will no longer be circumcision or the law, but recognizing Jesus as the good shepherd for all people.

The final sign before the passion, the seventh sign, reveals Jesus as the resurrection and the life, and provides the immediate context and reason for his arrest and execution. The Gospel interprets the miracle as a demonstration of God's glory. At the beginning of the story, Jesus says that the illness is "for God's glory" (11:4), and just before the resurrection of Lazarus, Jesus questions Mary, "Did I not tell you if you believed you would see the glory of God?" (11:40). Through the sign of raising Lazarus from the dead, Jesus proves that he is indeed the resurrection and the life, and that everyone who believes in him, even though they die, will live (11:25–26). Jesus' love for others prompts him not only to raise his friend Lazarus from the dead, but more importantly, to lay down his life for the salvation of the world. Jesus' strong emotional reaction to Lazarus' death goes beyond normal human behavior and can only be explained in light of the impending suffering Jesus is to experience in the events of the passion (11:33, 38; 12:27).[54] The resurrection of Lazarus, as can be imagined, caused much excitement, and brought others to believe in Jesus (11:45). When the news reached the priests and Pharisees in nearby Jerusalem, they expressed concern that matters may get out of hand and that the Romans might even come to destroy the temple. Their concern was a very real one, considering it was Passover and thousands of Jews had congregated at Jerusalem to celebrate Israel's deliverance from Egypt. Understandably, Caiaphas surmised that it was better to arrest Jesus and quickly get rid of him, rather than risking a revolt that may lead to harsh suppression. The narrator interprets Caiaphas's words as a prophecy of global mission in that Jesus was about to die "not for the nation only, but in order also to gather the dispersed children of God into one" (11:51–52).

(b) Jesus' Ministry to the Disciples (13:1–17:26)

In the second half of the Gospel, the attention shifts from Jesus' ministry in the world and conflict with the Jewish leaders to his relationship with the disciples (13:1–17:26). As such, there is not much more additional revelation in this section concerning Jesus' identity and work; instead, the emphasis is much more on the identity and work of the disciples. Jesus is preparing the community of disciples for mission in the world after his departure. In the story of the foot-washing, the author is careful to point out that the setting of the events was the festival of Passover (13:1; 18:28, 39; 19:14) in order to evoke in the mind of the reader the sacrifice of the Passover lamb and the deliverance from Egypt. The Passover provides the overall context for the events in the last days of Jesus' life, and the interpretive key for the meaning

---

28:25; 34:11–16; 36:24; 37:21; Mic 2:12–13. It is interesting to note that at times this "gathering" includes Gentiles: Ps 47:9; 102:22; Isa 43:9; 56:8; 66:18; Jer 3:17 (also cf. Hos 1:10–2:1).

[54] See Stephen Voorwinde, *Jesus' Emotions in the Fourth Gospel: Human or Divine?* (London: T&T Clark, 2005), 169–77.

of those events. His washing of the disciples' feet demonstrates his love for the disciples "to the end" (εἰς τέλος) in his commitment to fulfill the task that God had given to him. Jesus' act of love by "laying aside" (13:4; 13:37–38) his outer garment recalls his words that he will lay down his life for his sheep (10:11, 15, 17, 18).[55] Jesus' action forms the context of his new command to the disciples, "that you love one another, just as I have loved you (13:34). However, while the basis of the command is Jesus' own example, the function or purpose for the command is that of mission: "By this everyone will know that you are my disciples" (13:35). Loving one another will become one of the key means of Johannine mission.

Greek banqueting scene from the Tomb of the Leopards (480–450 BC).
Public domain.

This story also sets the context for a series of Farewell Discourses, a common literary genre employed in both Jewish and Greek literature. The genre has several characteristic features and fulfills a number of functions, but most importantly it prepares the community for life after the leader's departure.[56] In line with the main concerns of the Gospel, the section highlights the ongoing task of the disciples to continue Jesus' mission in the world. The section may be divided into three discourses which focus on particular issues.[57] The first discourse (14:1–31) deals with the departure of Jesus, the second (15:1–16:4a) addresses the need to remain faithful to his legacy, and the third (16:4b–33) highlights the revelatory work of the Spirit and the gifts of joy and peace.[58] Many commentators have interpreted the

---

[55] See David Gibson, "The Johannine Footwashing and the Death of Jesus: A Dialogue with Scholarship," *SBET* 25 (2007): 50–60; John Christopher Thomas, *Footwashing in John 13 and the Johannine Community*, JSNTSup 61 (Sheffield: JSOT, 1991), 46–50; Gail R. O'Day, "Jesus as Friend in the Gospel of John," *Int* 58 (2004): 144–57; Martin M. Culy, *Echoes of Friendship in the Gospel of John,* New Testament Monographs 30 (Sheffield: Sheffield Phoenix, 2010).

[56] For a detailed discussion and sources, see Ferreira, *Johannine Ecclesiology*, 63–66. It is particularly interesting to note Socrates' farewell speech in Plato's *Phaedo*.

[57] Some scholars have argued that the discourses reflect different occasions or specific crises in the history of the Johannine community. For example, according to John Painter, the first discourse (13:31–14:31) deals with the departure of Jesus, the second (15:1–16:4a) addresses the bitter conflict with the synagogue, and the third (16:4b–33) is directed against insularism in the community. *The Quest for the Messiah: The History, Literature and Theology of the Johannine Community* (Edinburgh: T&T Clark, 1993), 425–28.

[58] For D. Moody Smith, "A polemical situation within the synagogue … is almost certainly a significant, if not the central, milieu of the Johannine material, particularly the Fourth Gospel." *Johannine Christianity* (Columbia: University of South Carolina Press, 1984), 23.

place that Jesus was going to prepare in the first discourse as referring to heaven (14:1–4); however, it is more probable that the place (τόπος) is not an abode in heaven but a place in the new temple where Jesus is revealed to the world. After Jesus has prepared the place (through the cross), he will come again (after the resurrection) and bring his disciples to be with him in order that they may continue his mission in the world.[59] His promise to the disciples reveals that their new position is not only in heaven but also on earth: "Truly, truly, I say to you, whoever believes in me will also do the works that I do; and greater works than these will he do, because I am going to the Father" (14:12). The "greater works than these" (μείζονα τούτων) refer to the disciples' ministry, which proved to be much more successful in terms of gathering new disciples than Jesus' own. The section also highlights the work of the Holy Spirit, whom Jesus will send as another advocate and to teach the disciples more fully about his own ministry (14:25).[60]

First-century steps in Jerusalem connecting the Upper City to the Lower City.
Photograph by the author.

The concluding words of the first farewell discourse in John 14:31 have puzzled many interpreters, since the disciples do not immediately leave. Consequently the words have been taken as one of the Gospel's *aporias* (i.e., rough transitions or literary seams), showing evidence of editing. The words, "Arise, let us go from here" (ἐγείρεσθε, ἄγωμεν ἐντεῦθεν) are adopted from the tradition (cf. Mark 14:42; Matt 26:46), but are now integrated with one of the Gospel's distinctive theological themes. The sentence reminds the reader

---

[59] This is also the general interpretation of the Eastern fathers. See Brown, *The Gospel according to John*, 645.
[60] The Gospel's description of the Spirit as a "paraclete" is significant in the context of the *Sitz im Leben* of the Johannine community, as an advocate is necessary and comes to the fore when one has to defend one's position in a public hearing.

of the comment by Jesus' unbelieving brothers, "Depart from here and go into Judea, that your disciples also may see the works that you are doing" (7:3). Jesus must go from Galilee to Jerusalem, not to perform miracles, but to die on the cross; so Jesus now arises, in accordance with the command of the Father, to go to the cross. In the Passion Narrative, Jesus is led away (ἄγω) to be judged and crucified (18:13, 28; 19:4, 13), which recalls the description of the Suffering Servant in Isaiah 53:7–8 who is led like a lamb to the slaughter. The verb "to go" or "to lead" (ἄγω) is therefore persistently used to describe Jesus' journey to Jerusalem and the cross. As such, Jesus' words in John 14:31 reveal his determination to obey the Father's will, as well as his desire for the disciples to participate in his mission.[61]

In the second section of the Farewell Discourses, the parable of the vine and the branches emphasizes the need for the disciples to remain in Jesus, which specifically means to remain in his word (15:7; cf. John 8:31–32). The point of this parable is not just that the disciples continue to remain in Jesus' words (which is understandable in the context of conflict), but also that they pray and bear fruit in the work of mission. In chapter 15, the three great commandments of Johannine discipleship are in sharp focus. Firstly, the disciples need to continue to remain in Jesus; they have to receive his word, study it, and live under its authority (15:1–7). Secondly, the disciples have to love one another as Jesus loved them (15:12). And thirdly, they have to be engaged in evangelism and mission (15:8, 14–16). Jesus, as the "true vine," replaces Israel, and through the "branches"—the disciples—continues Israel's mission in the world as a light for the nations (Isa 49:6).

Jesus' language of friendship in the passage (15:14–15) again reflects the Gospel's awareness and integration of Greco-Roman sentiments within its narrative orbit. Being an esteemed social institution, the nature of friendship was a major topic of philosophical discussion in the Greco-Roman world.[62] Friendship was more than just being acquainted with others; it consisted of a deep relationship of commitment, loyalty, and love, and was regarded by many thinkers as an essential element of happiness and a necessary means of moral improvement. Friends shared common goals, were open and truthful with one another, and may even die for another—the preeminent demonstration of mutual love. In other words, Jesus' teaching on friendship is not really new; rather, what is new in the Gospel is that Jesus becomes the basis of friendship. He not only teaches the high ideals of friendship, but also demonstrates it by his life and death.[63]

---

[61] Jesus also invited his disciples to go (ἄγω) with him to raise Lazarus from the dead, which is symbolic not only of Jesus' mission but also of the disciples' mission (11:7, 15–16). Thomas's statement, "Let us go (ἄγω) and die with him," is first one of unbelief, but will become one of belief.

[62] See O'Day, "Jesus as Friend in the Gospel of John," 144–57; Culy, *Echoes of Friendship*; Takaaki Haraguchi, "Philia as Agapē: The Theme of Friendship in the Gospel of John," *AsJT* 28 (2014): 250–62.

[63] For Plato, love is the greatest demonstration of friendship; and so Achilles's death for the sake of his friend is the greatest example of true friendship (*Symp.* 179b). Aristotle also emphasizes that friends share all things in common and are willing to die for one another (*Rhet.* 1381a;

In the final section of the Farewell Discourses, Jesus completes his teaching regarding the work of the Spirit.[64] The Gospel's main teaching is that the Spirit is the "Spirit of Truth"—the Spirit of Jesus who will continue to reveal the things about Jesus to the disciples (16:12–15). It is important to note that the Evangelist ties the work and revelation of the Spirit to the earthly ministry and teachings of Jesus as recorded in the Gospel. For the Evangelist, the teaching of the Spirit will not go beyond the historical and narrative traditions of the Gospel (1 John 4:1–4).

Jesus' prayer in John 17 summarizes his work and teaching from the perspective of Johannine ecclesiology and mission. In terms of structure, it closely corresponds to the "law-court" petitionary prayer of Jewish tradition, with the divisions of address, request, and justification of the request.[65] The prayer has an apologetic purpose, justifying the existence and task of the disciples on the basis of Jesus' ministry, which culminates in the cross. The central idea of the prayer is that of glory. The first request is that the Father may glorify the Son, which, of course, is a reference to the cross of Jesus. The Son has indeed glorified the Father by completing the work the Father has given to him. In verse 10 Jesus states that he has also been glorified by the disciples. In the last section of the prayer Jesus mentions that he has given his glory to the disciples and prays that the disciples may be where he is and see his glory. The mission concerns are unmistakable, Jesus prays, "As you have sent me into the world, so I have sent them into the world" (17:18).

(c) Jesus' Death and Resurrection (18:1–20:31)

Even though the entire section covers a period of less than a week, the events of these days are of fundamental importance as they fulfill the purpose of Jesus' ministry. The passion story begins with Jesus' arrest (18:1–11) in the garden across the Kidron Valley. The words "he went out with his disciples across the Kidron Valley" link up with Jesus' command in John 14:31 and pull the disciples into the orbit of his mission as active participants. They must move beyond intra-communal love and face the hostility of the world, participating in the ministry of the cross to bring life to others. Jesus' action demonstrates his willingness to face his enemies; despite appearances, however, Jesus controls the situation. The Gospel omits Jesus' struggle at Gethsemane in order to highlight his willingness to embrace his mission to die

---

1156a; 1166a; 1167a; *Eth. nic.* 1169a). According to Cicero, life is not worth living without a friend (*Amic.* 6.20). Epictetus, a contemporary of the Gospel of John, expressed himself in the following manner, "A friend is one who loves and is loved in return, and those who think their relationship is of this character consider themselves friends" (*Diatr.* 2.7.3). Seneca, another contemporary, likewise regards dying for the other as the highest expression of true friendship (*Ep.* 9.109).

[64] Gary M. Burge, *The Anointed Community: The Holy Spirit in the Johannine Tradition* (Exeter: Paternoster, 1987).

[65] See Johan Ferreira, "The So-Called 'High Priestly Prayer' of Jesus and Ecclesiology: The Concerns of an Early Christian Community," in *Prayer and Spirituality in the Early Church*, ed. Pauline Allen et al. (Everton Park: Centre for Early Christian Studies, 1998), 15–37.

on the cross. Judas's action of bringing a detachment (σπεῖρα) of soldiers consisting of up to 600 men, along with the temple police, seems entirely out of proportion with their intent of arresting one peaceful individual, but when Jesus identifies himself as "I am he" (ἐγώ εἰμί), the whole detachment falls to the ground. The narrative therefore emphasizes Jesus' absolute power over the situation. He can escape if he so wishes, but instead willingly drinks the cup the Father has given him (18:11; cf. John 10:17–18).

The statement concerning "the cup" alludes to the famous story of Socrates's death and invites comparison with Jesus. Both are falsely accused, both stand firm in their resolve despite opportunity to escape, and both accept their destiny with courage. However, while Socrates is powerless with respect to his accusers, Jesus is always in control. One can imagine that there would have been much in-depth conversation concerning the meaning of Jesus' death compared to that of Socrates in the circle of the Johannine community. In addition, the historical detail about Malchus—a Latin name—demonstrates that Jesus not only cares for his inner group of disciples but even for those who came to arrest him.

According to the narrative, Jesus is first brought to Annas and Caiaphas before being taken to Pilate. The interrogation before these Jewish high priests comprises only six verses and lacks the formalities of a formal trial (18:19–24). The Gospel spends much more time relating Jesus' appearance before Pilate, breaking it up into seven carefully constructed scenes that oscillate between the "inside" and the "outside" of the *Praetorium* (18:28–19:24).[66] From Pilate's questioning, it can be inferred that the Jewish leaders accused Jesus of leading an insurrection against the Romans by setting himself up as a new king. However, Pilate recognizes that Jesus is accused on the basis of religious prejudice rather than political insurrection or criminality, and announces three times that Jesus is innocent (18:38; 19:4, 6). Yet, tragically, Pilate still condemns Jesus to death. The accusation on the basis of which Pilate crucified Jesus is written in the three main languages of the Roman Empire—Aramaic, Latin, and Greek—and nailed to the cross, "Jesus of Nazareth, the King of the Jews" (19:19). Jesus is proclaimed as king to the entire world; the cross is the ascent of a throne (3:15; 12:32). Jesus' final statement on the cross, "It is finished" or "It is fulfilled" (τετέλεσται; 19:30; cf. John 4:34; 5:36; 17:4) is full of theological significance for the Evangelist (John 13:1).[67] Jesus fulfills prophetic Scripture and perfectly completes the work that the Father gave him to do—he lays down his life willingly in order to take away the sin of the world. The branch of hyssop recalls the Passover

---

[66] The seven scenes are: 1) The accusation against Jesus (18:29–31); 2) Jesus' defense (18:33–38a); 3) Pilate's verdict (18:38b–40); 4) The soldiers' flogging and ridicule (19:1–3); 5) Pilate's second verdict (19:4–7); 6) Jesus' second defense (19:8–12); and 7) Jesus' sentence (19:13–16).

[67] Perhaps, the Gospel's greatest eschatological statement occurs in John 19:30, "It is finished." According to Alf Corell, *Consummatum Est: Eschatology and Church in the Gospel of St John* (London: SPCK, 1958), 107, the cry means: "(i) that the work of Jesus on earth is accomplished; (ii) that the eschatological expectations which were found in Israel and in the pagan world have now … reached their fulfillment; (iii) that the new dispensation or age has now come is in itself an anticipation of the final eschatological fulfillment."

(Exod 12:22–23); not one of his bones is broken as the perfect paschal lamb (Exod 12:46), receiving the wine indicates that he actually drank the cup that was given to him (John 18:11), and the water flowing from Jesus' side shows that his death brings life (19:34; cf. 7:37–39). Finally, as the Passion Narrative commenced with the arrest in a garden, so it closes with Jesus being buried within a new tomb in a garden (19:41).

With the discovery of the empty tomb and Jesus' appearances, the Gospel continues to develop its themes of belief overcoming unbelief and the sending of the disciples to be witnesses for Jesus. The empty tomb is discovered by Mary Magdalene, while it is still dark, early on the first day of the week.[68] She concludes that some people must have taken the body of Jesus away, possibly the Romans (as Jews would not defile themselves on the Sabbath by entering a tomb), and immediately tells Peter and "the other disciple," probably John. Upon further inspection, the two disciples both believe Mary's account that the tomb is empty and that someone has taken away Jesus' body (20:8). The comment that the disciples returned to their previous "things" (πρὸς αὐτούς) indicates that they did not connect the empty tomb with Jesus' resurrection from the dead; there was still no belief that Jesus rose. Mary, however, remains outside the tomb, grieving Jesus' death and the theft of his body, before suddenly noticing two angels in white inside the tomb. They ask her, "Woman, why are you weeping?" for her mourning was about to turn into joy (John 16:20). After she answers with the incorrect assessment that a group of people have taken the body away, Jesus himself appears and questions her. She initially mistakes him for the local gardener, but her vision is clarified when he calls her by name, "Mary." She recognizes Jesus as her teacher and embraced him, confirming the physicality of the resurrection. Whereas before she spoke (λέγει) to the disciples (20:2), she now proclaims (ἀγγέλλω) to them that she has seen the Lord (20:18).

Jesus' first resurrection appearance to the disciples occurs when they lock themselves indoors for fear of the Jews (20:19–23). The disciples' fear turns into joy when Jesus shows them convincing proofs that he is indeed alive. He then commissions them with the words, "As the Father has sent me, so I am sending you," and empowers them with the bestowal of the Holy Spirit (20:21–22), consequently fulfilling earlier prophecies concerning the creation of a new people of God (1:33; cf. Gen 2:7; Ezek 36:24–28). The second resurrection appearance occurs for the benefit of unbelieving Thomas, who was absent on the first occasion. After Thomas is convinced that Jesus is alive, he falls down and confesses that Jesus is both Lord and God (20:28). Thomas'

---

[68] Many writers have pointed out that the narration of the discovery of the empty tomb by women is significant in assessing the historicity of the account, since the testimonies of women in legal matters were not considered trustworthy in some Jewish and Greco-Roman contexts. Therefore, they have taken this as evidence that it is highly unlikely that the resurrection traditions involving women were fabrications of the early church. For Aristotle, "There is a type of manly valor; but valor in a woman, or unscrupulous cleverness is inappropriate" (*Poet.* 15.4). Also see Josephus (*A.J.* 4.219) and the Talmudic tractates, Sotah 19a; Qiddushin 82b; and Berakhot 60b.

confession serves as a climactic Christological recognition; Jesus is none other than God himself and he alone is worthy of trust, obedience, and worship. Thomas' confession may also be intended as a polemic against the emperor cult under the reign of Domitian (81–96), who attached the phrase "dominus et deus noster" (our Lord and God) to his name (Suetonius, *Dom.* 13.2).[69]

5.3. The Epilogue (21:1–25)

The final section of the Gospel, sometimes referred to as a secondary conclusion, should be regarded as an epilogue. According to Aristotle, "The Epilogue has four parts. You must (1) make the audience well-disposed towards yourself and ill-disposed towards your opponent, (2) magnify or minimize the leading facts, (3) excite the required state of emotion in your hearers, and (4) refresh their memories" (*Rhetoric*, 3.19).[70] The Gospel does not spend much time on the first and second aspects of Aristotle's explanation. There is the statement in verse 24 that the testimony of the author or the eyewitness is true and the catch of 153 big fish is extraordinary, but these details are not dramatized.[71] Rather, the author pays much more attention to remind the reader of the important themes in the Gospel. The unsuccessful labor of the disciples throughout the night, their confession that they have no fish, and Peter's awkwardness all attract the sympathy of the reader, who can easily identify with the failure of the disciples.

The emotionally charged scene between Jesus and Peter around the question of love arouses deep feelings in the reader. Jesus asks Peter three times, "Do you love me?" and three times Peter responds in the affirmative (21:15–17). The scene recalls Peter's denial of Jesus three times (John 18:15–18, 25–27). However, the Greek text reveals that the dialogue is more intricate and invites the reflection of the reader. Whereas Jesus used the verb *agapaō* (ἀγαπάω) in the first two questions, Peter responds with the term *phileō* (φιλέω), but then in the final question, Jesus changes from *agapaō* to *phileō*. Even though it seems that these verbs may be used interchangeably in the Gospel, the narrator's comment in verse 17 implies a difference. It appears that Peter, after the experience of the cross, is a very different man. Jesus is asking him if he is willing to lay down his life for his Lord, and even though he is no longer confident in his own loyalty and bravery as before (John 13:36–38), Jesus still graciously accepts his fragility. Yet, the reader knows

---

[69] See Marianne Meye Thompson, *The God of the Gospel of John* (Grand Rapids: Eerdmans, 2001), 235.

[70] *Rhet.* 3.19.

[71] Many commentators have wondered about the significance of the number 153 and have offered several ingenious solutions. One of the earliest suggestions is that the Sea of Galilee contains 153 different species of fish. Another is that the number refers to the numerical value of the Hebrew expression "I am God." Apart from the possibility that the number may simply indicate that someone actually counted the number of fish caught, the suggestion that it may recall the number of Gentiles who resided in Israel during the reign of Solomon, who also contributed to the building of the temple, is appealing (2 Chr 2:17).

that Peter laid down his life for the Lord (21:18–19). Few readers will be unaffected by the scene.[72]

Finally, while many Johannine themes surface in the details of the Epilogue, the most prominent theme in the narrative is that of mission. The location at the "Sea of Tiberias" recalls the sign of the miraculous feeding of the five thousand, which proves that Jesus is not just the Messiah for the Jews, but is the bread of God who "gives life to the world" (6:33, 51). Since the activity of fishing was commonly used as a metaphor for the evangelistic activity of Jesus' disciples, the miraculous catch of fish no doubt alludes to the fruitful mission the disciples are about to undertake. Peter's restoration is specifically intended to feed Jesus' sheep, which recalls Jesus' parable of the Good Shepherd. Since many other sheep will be added to the flock there is need for under-shepherds (1 Pet 5:1–4). Peter's restoration to pastoral ministry will climax in his own death for the sake of the ongoing mission, thereby glorifying God (20:18–19).

6. Conclusion

The Gospel of John has stimulated much reflection and debate on the significance of Jesus' life and death for the last 2000 years. It is truly remarkable that the experience, conviction, and message of a handful of ordinary Jews from Galilee, a region which to this day retains its rustic and secluded ambiance, produced a document with such sophistication and grandeur as the Gospel of John. Many books have consequently been written on aspects of the Gospel, providing new light as well as raising many questions for consideration. Although it still contains many mysteries, on the basis of the content of the Gospel itself, the following is clear: the author of the Gospel had a deep conviction that Jesus of Nazareth is unique and that his life and death hold relevance for the whole world. As such, the Gospel seeks not only to embed its message in the historical experience of Jesus, but also to relate that experience to the wider context of the Greco-Roman environment. So too, the contemporary reader cannot avoid the impact of Jesus' life and death upon history, and is invited, through the narrative of the Gospel, to "come and see." Like a diamond, it never ages, always attracts attention, and scatters light to invigorate life. There is ample scope for additional reflection and research.

---

[72] So Haraguchi, "Philia as Agapē," 257–58. Also see the re-evaluation of the scene by David Shepherd, "'Do you love me?' A Narrative-Critical Reappraisal of ἀγαπάω and φιλέω in John 21:15–17," *JBL* 129 (2010): 777–92.

Recommended Reading

Ashton, John. *Understanding the Fourth Gospel*. Oxford: Clarendon, 1991.

Barrett, C. K. *The Gospel according to St. John: An Introduction with Commentary and Notes on the Greek Text*. London: SPCK, 1955.

Brown, Raymond E. *The Gospel according to St John: Introduction, Translation, and Notes*. 2 vols. Garden City: Doubleday, 1966.

Burge, Gary M. *Interpreting the Gospel of John: A Practical Guide*. Grand Rapids: Baker, 2013.

Carson, Don A. *The Gospel according to John*. Grand Rapids: Eerdmans, 1991.

Culpepper, R. Alan. *Anatomy of the Fourth Gospel: A Study in Literary Design*. Philadelphia: Fortress, 1983.

Ferreira, Johan. *Johannine Ecclesiology*. JSNTSup 160. Sheffield: Sheffield Academic, 1998.

Keener, Craig S. *The Gospel of John: A Commentary*. 2 vols. Peabody: Hendrickson, 2003.

Kysar, Robert. *John, the Maverick Gospel*. Rev. ed. Louisville, KY: Westminster and John Knox, 1993.

Michaels, J. Ramsay. *The Gospel of John*. NICNT. Grand Rapids: Eerdmans, 2010.

Schnackenburg, Rudolf. *The Gospel according to St. John*. 3 vols. New York: Crossroad, 1990.

Voorwinde, Stephen. *Jesus' Emotions in the Fourth Gospel: Human or Divine?* London: T&T Clark, 2005.

3. Unity and Diversity in Emergent Christianity

Bradley J. Bitner

1. Early Christian Unity and Diversity

In this chapter, our focus is on the dynamic tension often characterized as unity and diversity in emergent Christianity, with particular reference to the documents of the later New Testament.[1] It is a theme as complex as it is important. By its nature we are drawn into considerations both historiographical and theological. Not only is every component of our title—"unity,"[2] "diversity,"[3] "emergent Christianity"[4]—crucial and contested; the

---

[1] Per the coverage of this volume: Acts, the Gospel of John, the so-called General (or Catholic) Epistles and Revelation. The General Epistles we concentrate on are less frequently integrated into the discussion. See Frank J. Matera, *New Testament Theology: Exploring Unity and Diversity* (Louisville: Westminster John Knox, 2007); Darian Lockett, *An Introduction to the Catholic Epistles* (London: T&T Clark, 2012).

[2] James D. G. Dunn, *Unity and Diversity in the New Testament: An Inquiry into the Character of Earliest Christianity*, 3rd edition (London: SCM 2006), 437, argues for two criteria that would render a "fundamental unity" recognizable: (1) "one on which all of Christianity was united from the beginning" and (2) one that represents "an element common to all the New Testament writings, a basic belief or practice affirmed or assumed by all the New Testament documents." Dunn's view, 437–42, is that "Easter" and "Pentecost" meet these criteria. From a different confessional angle, see Andreas J. Köstenberger and Michael J. Kruger, *The Heresy of Orthodoxy: How Contemporary Culture's Fascination with Diversity Has Reshaped Our Understanding of Early Christianity* (Wheaton: Crossway, 2010), who contend, at 233, that "Earliest Christianity ... was a largely unified movement that had coalesced around the conviction that Jesus was the Messiah and exalted Lord predicted in the Old Testament." See also Karen L. King, "Which Early Christianity?" in *The Oxford Handbook of Early Christian Studies*, ed. Susan A. Harvey and David Hunter (Oxford: Oxford University Press, 2008), 66–84, who traces methodological approaches to finding unity in the history of scholarship (especially two forms: the "ahistorical essentializing" of Harnack and the "thematic/common theological core" of Dunn). Others note an alleged "anachronistic" unity of these documents framed by the closing of the New Testament canon. See Bart D. Ehrman, *Lost Christianities: The Battles for Scripture and the Faiths We Never Knew* (Oxford: Oxford University Press, 2005).

[3] Karen L. King, "Factions, Variety, Diversity, Multiplicity: Representing Early Christian Differences for the 21st Century," *MTSR* 23 (2011): 216–37, at 216: "[S]cholars mean very different things and have quite different aims in view when they use this language." King, "Factions, Variety, Diversity, Multiplicity," 232, would also contest the "and" in our title, seeing it as a historically and ideologically illegitimate copula that reinscribes a "categorical containment of differences" on an indeterminate diversity of early Christianities.

[4] William Arnal, "The Collection and Synthesis of 'Tradition' and the Second-Century Invention of Christianity," *MTSR* 23 (2011): 193–215. Arnal argues that the shift in nomenclature from "Biblical Studies" to "New Testament Studies" to (something like) "Christian Origins" has

critical basis and cohesion, as well as the genre, authorship, and the date of each relevant text, is a matter of scholarly debate.[5] The texts themselves sit among other first and second-century documents and traditions (canonical and non-canonical) and adumbrate discussions about the limits of diversity that continued well into the fourth century. Further, the methods and models that scholars bring to the question of such unity and diversity are increasingly divergent and lead to quite different reconstructions.[6] The problem is by no means new, however. As we will see, unity and diversity at doctrinal and social levels figure prominently in the discourse strategies of our earliest Christian texts and communities.[7]

Faced with a variety of ways to analyze our topic, we will pursue the discourse strategies these later New Testament texts evince for wrestling with unity and diversity. We do so for three reasons. First, the category of discourse is increasingly employed by scholars of early Christianity in order to hold together the theological, social-historical, and rhetorical features of our texts.[8] Second, such a focus on discursive strategies aids us in the necessary task of narrowing our purview and selecting specific texts for analysis and exemplification. Finally, approaching our texts from this standpoint allows us readily to locate them within developing discourses of discernment in early Christianity, stretching from Paul to the second-century apologists and beyond. We begin by setting out examples from that spectrum as a frame for our focal texts.

1.1. Difference and Early Christian Discourses of Discernment

One early Christian text, the Didache, foregrounds the need for *critical theological and practical judgment* when it comes to recognizing the acceptable limits of diversity: "Everyone who comes in the name of the Lord

---

insufficiently reconceptualized the object of inquiry. He claims, 194, "With few exceptions (and those contested), our scholarship remains centered on the canonical writings of the New Testament, and we continue to act as though these New Testament documents represent expressions of a common—if admittedly, diverse—movement; and that as such they serve as sources for, and stand in social, historical, and/or conceptual continuity with, the ecclesiastical structures and ideologies of the second century and later."

[5] For debates concerning authorship, dates, and settings of the General Epistles examined here, the reader is pointed to essays in this and the previous two volumes as well as standard commentaries.

[6] See, for example, the very different approaches of Jonathan Z. Smith, *Drudgery Divine: On the Comparison of Early Christianities and the Religions of Late Antiquity* (London: School of Oriental and African Studies, 1990) and Larry Hurtado, "Interactive Diversity: A Proposed Model of Christian Origins," *JTS* 64 (2013): 445–62.

[7] See Stanley Stowers, "The Concept of 'Community' and the History of Early Christianity," *MTSR* 23 (2011): 238–56.

[8] Averil Cameron, *Christianity and the Rhetoric of Empire: The Development of Christian Discourse* (Berkeley: University of California Press, 1991); David Brakke, "The Early Church in North America: Late Antiquity, Theory, and the History of Christianity," *CH* 71 (2002): 473–91; Robert M. Royalty, *The Origin of Heresy: A History of Discourse in Second Temple Judaism and Early Christianity* (London: Routledge, 2013).

should be welcomed. Then, when you exercise your critical judgment [δοκιμάσαντες],⁹ you will know [γνώσεσθε] him; for you understand [σύνεσιν γὰρ ἔχετε] what is true [δεξιάν] and what is false [ἀριστεράν]."¹⁰ Especially as the Christian movement expanded and diversified, it was necessary to exercise discernment in welcoming and evaluating would-be teachers and their messages. In the Didache and other early texts, knowledge of reliable doctrine was fundamental for such discernment. In particular, a right understanding concerning the history and significance of Jesus and the form of life befitting those who believed in and ventured to teach about him was essential in order to discern, in Didache's terms, which figures were Christian (χριστιανοί) and which were to be avoided as Christmongers (χριστέμποροι; Did. 12.5; cf. 2 Tim 3:5). When, for example, did theological diversity become more than simply a matter of emphasis or phrasing; at what point did it veer into error? When, if ever, did separation or expulsion from the community become necessary? And on what basis might one make or argue for such a judgment?

The issue only grew in complexity as the Christian gospel¹¹ went into all the world and ecclesial communities¹² were formed around the Mediterranean basin. How would one recognize¹³ a Christian if one encountered her? Late in the second century, another Christian author framed the dynamics of unity and diversity in sociopolitical as well as theological terms:

> For Christians are not distinguishable from other people either by country, language, or customs [οὔτε γ οὔτε φων οὔτε ἔθεσι διακεκριμένοι]. For nowhere do they live in their own cities, speak some unusual dialect, or

---

⁹ Δοκιμάζω was a favorite early Christian verb of discernment and approval—both human and divine—related to unity and diversity within and among the early Jewish and Christian assemblies; see, e.g., Rom 2:18; 1 Cor 3:13; 11:28; 16:3; 2 Cor 13:5; Eph 5:10; Phil 1:10; 1 Thess 2:4; 5:21; 1 Tim 3:10; 1 Pet 1:7; 1 John 4:1. Cf. 1 Clem. 1.2; 42.1; Herm. Mand. 11.7 [43]. See David E. Aune, *Prophecy in Early Christianity and the Ancient Mediterranean World* (Grand Rapids: Eerdmans, 1983), 219–29.

¹⁰ Didache 12.1; cf. 11.1–12. Translation from Ehrman (LCL). The Didache is usually dated ca. AD 80–120, although some contend for a basis in even earlier oral tradition: Aaron Milavec, "When, Why, and for Whom Was the Didache Created? Insights into the Social and Historical Settings of the Didache Communities," in *Matthew and the Didache: Two Documents from the Same Jewish-Christian Milieu?* ed. H. Van de Sandt (Philadelphia: Fortress, 2005) 63–84. See also C. H. Smith, "The *Epistle of Barnabas* and the Two Ways of Teaching Authority," *VC* 68 (2014): 465–97.

¹¹ Another contested term. Still relevant: C. H. Dodd, *The Apostolic Preaching and its Developments* (London: Hodder and Stoughton, 1936), 76–78, including , 77, "[Paul] and others succeeded in reinterpreting [the Gospel] to their contemporaries in terms which made its essential relevance and truth clear to their minds ... But the attempt at reinterpretation is always in danger of becoming something quite different; that which Paul called, 'preaching another Jesus and another Gospel' [2 Cor 11:4; Gal 1:6]."

¹² Stowers, "The Concept of 'Community,'" 249: "The social complexity hidden by *community* needs to be described and explained." (italics mine).

¹³ Irenaeus famously reports that, upon encountering Polycarp in second-century Rome, Marcion asked, "Do you recognize us? (*cognoscis nos*?/ἐπιγίνωσκεις ἡμᾶς;)" to which Polycarp replied, "I do recognize (*cognosco*/ἐπιγινώσκω) you, the firstborn of Satan." Irenaeus, *Haer.* 3.3.4. See A. Rousseau and L. Doutreleau, eds., *Irénée de Lyon. Contre les hérésies. Livre III* (Paris: Cerf, 1974).

practice an uncommon lifestyle. This teaching [μάθημα] of theirs has not been discovered by the consideration [ἐπινοίᾳ] or reflection [φροντίδι] of inventive people, nor like some people do they endorse a human doctrine [δόγματος ἀνθρωπίνου]. Yet while living in both Greek and barbarian cities according to each one's lot and following local customs with respect to clothing and food and the rest of life, they demonstrate the admirable and admittedly paradoxical character of their own citizenship [τὴν κατάστασιν τῆς ἑαυτῶν πολιτείας].[14]

For Diognetus, as for other second-century Christian apologists, the language of making distinctions (διακρίνω) is placed within a broader political and cultural discourse.[15] It is predicated upon a received teaching (μάθημα) or doctrine (δόγμα) and an identifiable, if paradoxical, way of life (πολιτεία). Factors such as these required the exercise of critical discernment in the face of difference and produced a discourse that proceeds by naming, by self-examination, and by argument.[16] This discourse of discernment is also found in the New Testament, beginning with the earliest Pauline texts (e.g., 1 Thess 2:14; 5:21; Gal 6:4; 1 Cor 11:28, 29; 14:29; 16:3; 2 Cor 13:5). Two passages in particular from Paul's letters help orient us to recurrent features we will see in our later New Testament texts.

First, in 1 Cor 3:13 Paul speaks of an eschatological testing: "And the fire will test (δοκιμάσει) what sort of work each one's is." In an ecclesial context of conflict,[17] the true nature of the temple-building work done in the Corinthian assembly—that is, whether or not ministers' labor conforms to Paul's foundational proclamation about Christ—will be discerned on the day of judgment. Divinely decreed dynamics of eschatological discernment, Paul contends in 1 Cor 3:5–4:5, should thus inform the critical judgments of Corinthians within the assembly (see ἀνακρίνω in 1 Cor 4:3; κρίνετε in 1 Cor 4:5). Paul concedes a variety of ministers (1 Cor 3:5–9; 4:6) but insists upon an eschatologically-determined horizon and limit to diversity within the assembly.[18]

---

[14] Diogn. 5.1–4. Translation slightly adapted from Clayton N. Jefford, *The Epistle to Diognetus (With the Fragment of Quadratus). Introduction, Text, and Commentary.* (Oxford: Oxford University Press, 2013). Diognetus sits chronologically between Paul's statement about a heavenly *politeia* in Phil 3:20 and Augustine's argument in the *City of God*. See Denise K. Buell, *Why This New Race? Ethnic Reasoning in Early Christianity* (New York: Columbia University Press, 2005) and Benjamin H. Dunning, *Aliens and Sojourners: Self as Other in Early Christianity* (Philadelphia: University of Pennsylvania Press, 2009).

[15] Jefford, *Epistle to Diognetus*, 51–56, 220–21. Diognetus is a deliberative and apologetic example of "protreptic discourse," that is, hortatory speech aiming to attract listeners to a certain way of life.

[16] For a succinct discussion of terms and approaches, see Paul McKechnie, *The First Christian Centuries: Perspectives on the Early Church* (Leicester: Apollos, 2001), 14–20.

[17] L. L. Welborn, *Politics and Rhetoric in the Corinthian Epistles* (Macon, GA: Mercer University Press).

[18] Bradley J. Bitner, *Paul's Political Strategy in 1 Corinthians 1:1–4:6: Constitution and Covenant*, SNTSMS 163 (Cambridge: Cambridge University Press, 2015), 197–301. Cf. Benjamin A. Edsall, *Paul's Witness to Formative Early Christian Instruction*, WUNT 2:365 (Tübingen: Mohr Siebeck, 2014).

Bradley J. Bitner

Another early example of this discourse comes in Phil 1:9–10. Paul closes his thanksgiving with a prayer wish: "And this I pray, that your love may abound yet more and more in recognition [ἐπιγνώσει] and discernment [αἰσθήσει] so that you might test [δοκιμάζειν] what is distinctively important [τὰ διαφέροντα], in order that you might be pure and blameless for the day of Christ [εἰς ἡμέραν Χριστοῦ]." Once more, in an ecclesial-political context (*politeuomai*, 1:27; *politeia*, 3:20), with a view toward ethical-eschatological evaluation (1:10), and a concern for unity despite conflict (τὸ αὐτὸ φρονεῖν, 4:2), Paul invokes a discourse of discernment.

To this point we have seen that a distinct discourse developed around issues of theological and social unity and diversity in emergent Christianity. This was as true of early Pauline texts as it was of later community rule documents, such as the Didache, and apologetic texts such as Diognetus. In the present chapter, we will adopt this discourse as a category of analysis. In addition to the reasons outlined above, doing so helps us to avoid, at least initially, the pull of the orthodoxy/heresy binary that characterizes so much writing on the topic. Furthermore, the category of *discourse* encourages us to hold together textual details and theory. Commenting on the theological and historiographical problem of early Christian unity and diversity, Lewis Ayres suggests, "Approaching the question of orthodoxy at this point in the history of the field inevitably involves negotiating a complex mix of close textual study and overt theoretical reflection."[19] In the next section, we begin with the latter: theoretical reflection on proposed methods and models for approaching the problem of unity and diversity in emergent Christianity.

2. Methods and Models

Whether one endeavors to write a New Testament Theology, a history of *das Urchristentum* (i.e., an account of a more or less unified emergent Christianity),[20] or a history of divergent early Christianities (or their literatures or discourses), questions immediately arise as to which source texts to employ and how to organize the material. So much depends—especially given the synthetic nature of any attempt to capture the unity and diversity of emergent Christianity—upon the interplay between the particularities of our texts and the models with which we approach them. With regard to specifics, one realizes quickly in surveying the literature that the dating of texts, especially Acts, the Pastorals, and the General Epistles, is a central and divisive issue leading to widely varying reconstructions. Moreover, some see an emerging scriptural or canonical consciousness within the New Testament texts themselves, while others judge the canonical boundary to be arbitrary and late. With respect to the models—informed by and informing scholarly interactions with particular texts—there is a relevant history of scholarship we must

---

[19] Lewis Ayres, "Introduction," *JECS* 14 (2006): 395–98, at 398.
[20] See Stefan Alkier, *Urchristentum: Zur Geschichte und Theologie einer exegetischen Disziplin* (Tübingen: Mohr Siebeck, 1993), 175–254.

78

briefly rehearse. That is to say, before looking directly at certain aspects of unity and diversity *in the New Testament texts* we must examine unity and diversity *among the scholarly approaches to the question itself.* Doing so will help us to understand the various lines of investigation, from traditional New Testament Theologies, to Histories of Early Christianity/ies, to Histories of Early Christian Literature and Discourse. This survey will also confirm our focus on an eschatological discourse framework that integrates insights from a spectrum of contemporary studies.

2.1. New Testament Theologies

For those for whom the New Testament canon is a legitimate (or pragmatic)[21] delimitation and, importantly, for whom the New Testament corpus is an ecclesial and theological authority in contradistinction to non-canonical documents, the approach to our subject has always been that of *New Testament Theology.*[22] This is a long and living tradition stretching from Bauer[23] at the turn of the nineteenth century to major contemporary syntheses by Stuhlmacher,[24] Hahn,[25] Howard Marshall,[26] Matera,[27] and Beale.[28] Yet even among works in this vein, the principles of organization (and thus of analysis and synthesis) differ significantly.[29] Documents are variously studied in canonical, chronological, thematic, or regional order and, even if a synthesis of unity and diversity is attempted, the categories chosen are rarely the same.[30] But in nearly every case, the canonical and theological constraints on method lead to a reconstruction that brings coherence to the diversity of

[21] E.g., Georg Strecker, *Theologie des Neues Testaments* (Berlin: de Gruyter, 1996), 3–4.

[22] For histories of method, see Don A. Carson, "New Testament Theology," in *Dictionary of the Later New Testament and Its Developments*, ed. Ralph P. Martin and Peter H. Davids (Downers Grove, IL: InterVarsity, 1997), 796–814; Matera, *New Testament Theology*, xix–xxxi and Gregory K. Beale, *A New Testament Biblical Theology: The Unfolding of the Old Testament in the New* (Grand Rapids: Baker Academic, 2011), 1–25. See also Otto Merk, "Biblische Theologie II (Neues Testament)," in *Theologische Realenzyklopädie*, vol. 6, ed. H. R. Balz et al. (Berlin: de Gruyter, 1980), 455–77; Heikki Räisänen, *Beyond New Testament Theology: A Story and a Programme*, 2nd ed. (London: SCM, 2000).

[23] G. L. Bauer, *Biblische Theologie des Neuen Testaments*, 4 vols. (Leipzig: Weygrand, 1800–1802).

[24] Peter Stuhlmacher, *Biblische Theologie des Neuen Testaments*, 2 vols. (Göttingen: Vandenhoeck & Ruprecht, 1992–1999).

[25] Ferdinand Hahn, *Theologie des Neuen Testaments*, 2 vols. (Tübingen: Mohr Siebeck, 2002).

[26] I. Howard Marshall, *New Testament Theology: Many Witnesses, One Gospel* (Downers Grove, IL: InterVarsity, 2004).

[27] Matera, *New Testament Theology*.

[28] Beale, *New Testament Biblical Theology*.

[29] George B. Caird, with L. D. Hurst, *New Testament Theology* (Oxford: Clarendon, 1994), 4–26, outlines five approaches: (1) Dogmatic, (2) Chronological, (3) Kerygmatic, (4) Author-by-author, (5) Conference Table (i.e., thematic).

[30] Strecker, *Theology of the New Testament*, with six sections: (1) Pauline theology, (2) Early tradition to Gospels composition, (3) Synoptics, (4) Johannine school, (5) Deuteropaulines, (6) Catholic epistles; Matera, *New Testament Theology*, employs four sections: (1) The Synoptic Tradition, (2) The Pauline Tradition, (3) The Johannine Tradition, (4) Other Voices.

literary, social, and theological New Testament emphases by means of a unifying narrative-theological "master story" that reflects the Christocentric, Creation—Fall—Redemption—Consummation pattern of classical Christian theology.[31]

Methodologically, these New Testament theologies presuppose a theological unity that is flexible enough to embrace observable diversity. Moreover, the New Testament documents—including Acts, the Pastorals, and the General Epistles—are generally viewed as compositions of the later first century. Thus, there is a fairly tight historical unity and a clear chronological boundary perceived between the apostolic documents of the New Testament and the later "apostolic fathers." First Clement is viewed as an important transitional document dated, especially since Harnack, to the reign of Domitian (ca. AD 96).[32] These New Testament theologies operate (more or less explicitly) with a model of a unified early Church (or network of Christian communities) and lead to an opposition, promoted by the canonical documents themselves, between orthodoxy (or "proto-orthodoxy") and heresy.

2.2. Histories of Early Christianity

By contrast, after the efforts of Semler and Gabler in the late eighteenth century to decouple the study of the New Testament documents from the textual constraints of canon[33] and the framework of dogmatic theology,[34] there was a shift over the course of the nineteenth and early twentieth centuries away from analyzing unity and diversity under the rubric of *New Testament Theology* toward investigations within the paradigm of the *History of Primitive* (or *Early*) *Christianity*. Field-shaping works by Baur,[35] Wrede,[36]

---

[31] Matera, *New Testament Theology*, 427. See also Beale, *New Testament Biblical Theology*, 15–16.

[32] But see L. L. Welborn, "The Preface to 1 Clement: The Rhetorical Situation and the Traditional Date," in *Encounters with Hellenism: Studies on the First Letter of Clement*, ed. C. Breytenbach and L. L. Welborn (Leiden: Brill, 2004) 197–216. See also Christoph Markschies, "Harnack's Image of *1 Clement* and Contemporary Research," *ZAC* 18 (2013): 54–69.

[33] J. J. Semler, *Abhandlung von freier Untersuchung des Canon*, 4 vols (Halle: C. H. Hemmerde, 1771–75). On Semler, see William Baird, *History of New Testament Research, Volume 1: From Deism to Tübingen* (Minneapolis: Fortress, 1992) 117–27.

[34] J. P. Gabler, *Oratio de iusto discrimine theologiae biblicae et dogmaticae regundisque recte utriusque finibus* (1787). English translation in J. Sandys-Wunsch and L. Eldredge, "J. P. Gabler and the Distinction between Biblical and Dogmatic Theology: Translation, Commentary, and Discussion of His Originality," *SJT* 33 (1980): 133–58.

[35] Especially F. C. Baur, *Vorlesungen über neutestamentliche Theologie* (Leipzig: Fues, 1864). Cf. David Lincicum, "Ferdinand Christian Baur and Biblical Theology," *ASE* 30 (2013): 79–92. Lincicum notes, 90, Baur's concept of *Totalanschauung* ("view of the totality of early Christian history") as the result of a unifying analytic impulse despite a focus on historical and theological diversity and development.

[36] W. Wrede, *Über Aufgabe und Methode der sogenannten neutestamentlichen Theologie* (Göttingen: Vandenhoeck & Ruprecht, 1897). English translation by Robert Morgan as "The Tasks and Method of 'New Testament Theology,'" in Robert Morgan, ed., *The Nature of New Testament Theology* (London: SCM, 1973), 68–116.

Weiss,[37] and Bultmann[38] drove steadily towards a historicizing of the New Testament documents. These scholars deconstructed the canonical barrier and removed or radically reconfigured the theological framework of investigation.[39] As a result, these works rarely structured their analysis document by document in the canonical order,[40] preferring instead to reorder the material in a chronological, regional, or thematic framework.

Synthetic claims grew more modest and less normatively theological.[41] This was in keeping with a methodology that sought historical intelligibility by a thematic analysis, one that set the New Testament documents within their larger "religious" and cultural contexts,[42] that privileged diversity, and that spoke of unity (if at all) in terms of the subjective religious experience of faith.[43] Acts, the Pastorals, and the General Epistles are dated late, with significant implications for the reconstructive possibilities relative to the

---

[37] J. Weiss, *Das Urchristentum* (Göttingen: Vandenhoeck & Ruprecht, 1917). English translation by F. C. Grant, first published as *The History of Primitive Christianity*, 2 vols. (New York: Wilson-Erikson, 1937) and subsequently as *Earliest Christianity: A History of the Period A.D. 30–150*, 2 vols. (Gloucester, MA: Peter Smith, 1970).

[38] R. Bultmann, *Theology of the New Testament*, trans K. Grobel, 2 vols. (Waco: Baylor University Press, 2007). Lincicum, "Ferdinand Christian Baur and Biblical Theology," 79, places Bultmann, who focused on the *Verschiedenheit* (variety) of the New Testament documents over their *Einheit* (unity), firmly in the line of Baur.

[39] Wrede, "Task and Methods," is clear and programmatic in this respect. He contends, 102–103, "The question of the real limits of the discipline can now be taken up afresh ... it is clear that a fixed literary boundary cannot be given.... Furthermore, no exact date can be given as the boundary, such as AD 120, 130 or 150.... On particular issues, the boundary can only be decided in the course of the work. There will always be a certain elasticity in determining it."

[40] E.g., Weiss, *Earliest Christianity*, employs five major sections: (i) The Primitive Community, (ii) The Gentile Mission and Paul the Missionary, (iii) Paul the Christian and Theologian, (iv) The Missionary Congregations and the Beginnings of the Church, and (v) The Separate Areas (i.e., from Judaea westwards by Roman province to Rome); Bultmann, *Theology of the New Testament*, uses a four-part structure: (i) Presuppositions and Motifs of New Testament Theology, (ii) The Theology of Paul, (iii) Johannine Theology, and (iv) The Development toward the Ancient Church.

[41] See Bultmann, *Theology of the New Testament*, 2:237–52. Cf. Caird and Hurst, *New Testament Theology*, 4: "[T]here is no such thing as New Testament theology. It is not an entity waiting to be discovered by industrious and perspicacious scholars ... New Testament theology is nothing more than a book which some scholar chooses to write, an attempt to describe in some sort of orderly fashion what the writers of the New Testament believed."

[42] Wrede, "Task and Methods," 90, "The norms governing the presentation are therefore not the writings [nor the traditional dogmatic *loci*] but the decisive ideas, problems, and spiritual or intellectual phenomena." Further, 96, "Our procedure here is always both genetic and comparative. We are every point interested in distances, connections and effects."; and 97, "In trying to explain things we do, of course, all too often run up against gaps, so that our whole endeavour can be seen as one large fragment."

[43] E.g., Weiss, *Earliest Christianity*, 2:650, "The study of Paul in the foregoing chapters, has resulted in a picture of extraordinary variety (*ausserordentlich mannigfaltiges*) ... All this is held in unity (*zussamengehalten*) by the personal, thankful, humble consciousness of having himself experienced the grace of God.... It is in this that the man's variegated world-view (*die so bunte ... Vorstellungswelt*) and mode of thought, full of contradictions as they are (*widerspruchsvolle*), have their unifying principle (*ihre Einheit*)." Cf. *Das Urchristentum*, 511. See also Bultmann, *Theology of the New Testament*, 2:237.

Bradley J. Bitner

"earliest Christianity" of the first century.[44] Overwhelmingly, these and subsequent "histories of early Christian theology" operate with a quasi-quantum model of "deterministic chaos,"[45] a phrase coined by François Vouga that suggests a complex state resulting from an early diversity of conflicting positions and interpretations.

2.3. Heresy, Orthodoxy, and Trajectories

A third approach, and important offshoot of these *Histories of Early Christianity*, is epitomized by Walter Bauer (1934)[46] and subsequently Robinson and Koester (1971).[47] In the four decades between these seminal works, the conceptualization of the object of inquiry shifted decisively from "early Christianity" to "early Christianities." An originary diversity that resisted any analytic imposition of a unified frame quickly became the guiding presupposition. In his *Orthodoxy and Heresy in Earliest Christianity* (1971),[48] Bauer analyzed texts—overwhelmingly second-century, non-canonical documents—in two major movements: first, geographically, moving from Edessa to Rome; second, in a series of more thematic chapters, with generalizing inferences concerning the discursive strategies of "orthodoxy" and "heresy."

Bauer's approach solidified three methodological modifications, each rooted in his understanding of a "scientific approach to history" unshackled from "dogmatic" opinion.[49] First, the textual basis shifted, eliding the canonical/non-canonical distinction and giving special attention to the so-called heretical texts. "[The] New Testament," remarked Bauer, "seems to be both too unproductive and too much disputed to be able to serve as a point of departure."[50] Second, the chronological basis continued to alter, becoming in fact of much less importance. Bauer rejected "the ecclesiastical opinion as to what is early and late, original and dependent, essential and unimportant."[51] With varying degrees of argumentation, Bauer dated Acts to the time of Ignatius (ca. AD 115–120),[52] the Pastorals to the post-Marcion decades of the mid-second century,[53] and Hebrews and 1 Peter to the same time as 1

---

[44] Compare, e.g., an earlier work such as Weiss, *Earliest Christianity*, 1:1–11 with Arnal, "Second-Century Invention of Christianity."

[45] François Vouga, *Geschichte des frühen Christentums* (Tübingen and Basel: Francke, 1994), 13–20. Cf. Räisänen, *Beyond New Testament Theology*, 140–41.

[46] Walter Bauer, *Rechtgläubigkeit und Ketzerei im ältesten Christentum* (Tübingen: Mohr Siebeck, 1934).

[47] James M. Robinson and Helmut Koester, *Trajectories through Early Christianity* (Philadelphia: Fortress, 1971).

[48] Walter Bauer, *Orthodoxy and Heresy in Earliest Christianity*, trans. Robert A. Kraft et al. (Philadelphia: Fortress, 1971).

[49] Bauer, *Orthodoxy and Heresy*, xxii–xxiii.

[50] Bauer, *Orthodoxy and Heresy*, xxv.

[51] Bauer, *Orthodoxy and Heresy*, xxiv.

[52] Bauer, *Orthodoxy and Heresy*, 84.

[53] Bauer, *Orthodoxy and Heresy*, 84, 226.

Clement, at the very close of the first century.[54] Third, the geographical arrangement of the second-century, non-canonical texts provided the decisive framework for Bauer's interpretation of the New Testament documents. In terms of an embracing model for early *Christianity* (still singular in his title), Bauer did not break free of the traditional binary of orthodoxy–heresy; rather, what he accomplished was the reinscription of that opposition in reverse, privileging "heresy" and thereby making dispute, diversity, and fragmentation fundamental. This led him to exclaim, near the end of his study, "Is there anything that did not have its place alongside everything else in primitive Christianity!"[55]

Praising Bauer's work as "brilliant," Helmut Koester published an essay in 1965[56] that became the centerpiece of *Trajectories through Early Christianity*, which he co-authored with James Robinson in 1971. Building on Bauer's argument, Koester and Robinson constructed a detailed and comprehensive vision for the historical analysis of early *Christianities*.[57] What was noteworthy about their vision was that it was driven in part by new data[58] and, most importantly, that it was unambiguous in its call for a reconceptualization of the object of inquiry at the level of heuristic/analytic model.[59] Like Bauer, Koester and Robinson insisted on dissolving the canonical boundary and on including all available data on equal footing.[60] Unlike Bauer, however, they focused their attention on the "apostolic" rather than the second-century era and thus dealt more thoroughly with the New Testament documents.[61] Furthermore, they offered a compelling new model, visualized as "trajectories" within a larger (cultural) stream. The model was intended to break with the older binary between orthodoxy and heresy.[62] For Koester and Robinson, this trajectories model operated critically at the levels of genre, of geography, and of tracing the structures of conflicts.[63] Koester in particular

---

[54] Bauer, *Orthodoxy and Heresy*, 128, 240.

[55] Bauer, *Orthodoxy and Heresy*, 237 n. 13.

[56] Helmut Koester, "*GNOMAI DIAPHOROI*: The Origin and Nature of Diversification in the History of Early Christianity," *HTR* 58 (1965): 279–318.

[57] Koester, *Trajectories*, concluded, 270, "One can only speak of a 'History of Early Christian Literature.'"

[58] I.e., the Qumran and Nag Hammadi documents (including the Gospel of Thomas).

[59] In response to what they termed a "crisis of categories" facing New Testament and Early Christian studies, Robinson and Koester argued, *Trajectories*, 13–14, that the "static categories of 'background' or 'environment' or 'context' are all-embracing as well as specific [i.e., still operate with a fundamental heuristic of unity]. Their re-categorization as 'trajectories' applies both to the most embracing movement in which a whole culture is caught up, even to the history of its ontological assumptions ... and to more specific streams, such as the course of its religious understanding or the trajectory of one specific religious tradition within the wider streams of movement. Just as a fixed datum was 'located' on a spectrum or grid of static positions, so a trajectory of limited extent moves along as a variant or eddy within a broader religious or cultural current. Indeed only if the more pervasive flow is charted can the course of the specific trajectory be relevantly distinguished in its variance from that of the broader movement."

[60] Robinson and Koester, *Trajectories*, 115–19.

[61] Robinson and Koester, *Trajectories*, 119.

[62] Robinson and Koester, *Trajectories*, 8–19, 269–79.

[63] Robinson and Koester, *Trajectories*, 270–79.

has worked out this method on a large scale in publications from the 1970s to the present, structuring his analysis within the trajectories model traced thematically and geographically.[64]

2.4. From Trajectories to Discourse Strategies

Recently, Larry Hurtado has questioned the continued efficacy of the trajectories model for the study of "Christian Origins." In his essay, Hurtado sketches inadequacies—both conceptual and of detail—that he discerns in the trajectories model,[65] offering what he deems a better one, namely, "interactive diversity."[66] He argues that such a model more adequately accounts for the intense, complex, and even adversarial interaction within early Christianity while still preserving a distinct chronological and theological role for the New Testament documents and a conceptual space for "commonality," if not "unity."[67] It remains to be seen what major syntheses Hurtado or others might produce along the lines intimated in his essay, or whether his model of "interactive diversity" is conceptually vivid enough and has the explanatory power to replace the older "trajectories" model.

One final recent study deserves mention in our consideration. Robert Royalty's *The Origin of Heresy* is noteworthy because it foregrounds the discourse dynamics inherent in the study of our topic. Royalty is critical of both the traditionalist historiography of unity devolving into error, and Bauer's historiography of radical diversity, which, taken to its conclusion, (by Burton Mack, among others), "atomizes the religious movement [of early Christianity] at the moment of origin."[68] These two historiographies are ideologically distinct but, Royalty argues, both unwittingly remain methodologically in debt to Hegesippus (an early heresiologist preserved by Eusebius) and the supposed movement from original unity to subsequent diversity. The only difference becomes just how early one locates significant diversity. Rather than rejecting the old orthodoxy-heresy binary, Royalty reuses it to interrogate the discursive (i.e., political-rhetorical) strategies of early Christian texts in order to trace the history and features of heresiological discourse. He locates this discourse squarely in the New Testament texts, arguing

---

[64] Notably: *History and Literature of Early Christianity* (Berlin: de Gruyter, 1982/2000). Koester's project has been extended by scholars such as Karen King and William Arnal mentioned above. Cf. Peter Lampe, "Induction as Historiographical Tool: Methodological and Conceptual Reflections on Locally and Regionally Focused Studies," *ASE* 30 (2013): 9–20.

[65] Hurtado, "Interactive Diversity," 445–52. Hurtado's criticisms of the "trajectories" model are basically two: (i) it may oversimplify matters by suggesting "uni-linear" development (e.g., 450, a specific linking of Q and Gos. Thom. in just such a way); (ii) it may over-determine the historical data in the interest of a certain contemporary interpretive impulse (on which, he notes, 451, Koester's admirable "candor" in a 1991 essay).

[66] Hurtado, "Interactive Diversity," 452–54.

[67] Hurtado, "Interactive Diversity," 454–60.

[68] Royalty, *Origin of Heresy*, 13.

The canonical texts provide the best sources we have to study first-century Christianity from the inside, especially when so few of the non-canonical texts can be confidently dated to the first century.... It is in these earliest Christian texts adopted by the orthodox party that we find the origins of heresiology as the formative discourse of orthodox Christianity itself.[69]

Primarily on the basis of the New Testament texts, Royalty concludes that "orthodoxy was inclusive of multiple theological positions"; indeed, that *the political success of orthodoxy relates directly to its relative flexibility in the face of theological difference.*[70] Most importantly for our purposes, Royalty draws attention to a crucial and sometimes neglected feature that animated early Christian discourse about difference: eschatology. New Testament eschatology, especially in its "apocalyptic" accent, emphasizes the epoch-shifting death, resurrection, and expected return of Jesus Christ, the idea that doctrinal disagreement could be satanic or demonic, and the necessarily oppositional stance between Christians and the "world."[71] It is these eschatological dynamics, Royalty suggests, that drive early Christian heresiology and generate a discourse of difference.[72]

Although his approach is a further step in examining the question of unity and diversity as the "history of a political discourse," Royalty is not alone among interpreters in drawing attention to the eschatological framework of early Christianity in its manifold aspects. In fact, scholars representing the range of methods outlined above (New Testament Theology,[73] History of Early Christianity/ies,[74] History of Early Christian discourse[75]) have pointed in recent years to the eschatological matrix of "everything that could be said about Jesus' acts and message, his identity and salvific function."[76] We suggest that this fusion of eschatology and discourse offers us a way to find unity among the diversity of approaches to our question, for it allows us to bind the theological, social, and rhetorical elements of our texts.[77] Moreover, it offers us a productively unifying mode in which to navigate among the

---

[69] Royalty, *Origin of Heresy*, 17.

[70] Royalty, *Origin of Heresy*, 175–76.

[71] Royalty, *Origin of Heresy*, 26–27. He identifies, 167, a second strand of "quietest-imperial" eschatology in texts like 1 Peter.

[72] Royalty, *Origin of Heresy*, 26–27, 167–76.

[73] E.g., Strecker, *Theology of the New Testament*; Beale, *New Testament Biblical Theology*, especially 317–54 on the eschatological matrix of the General Epistles and Revelation.

[74] Heikki Räisänen, "Last Things First: 'Eschatology' as the First Chapter in an Overall Account of Early Christian Ideas," in *Moving Beyond New Testament Theology? Essays in Conversation with Heikki Räisänen*, ed. Todd Penner and C. Vander Stichele (Göttingen: Vandenhoeck & Ruprecht, 2005), 444–87; and Räisänen, "Towards an Alternative to New Testament Theology: Different 'paths to salvation,'" in *Aufgabe und Durchführung einer Theologie des Neuen Testaments*, ed. Cilliers Breytenbach and Jörg Frey (Tübingen: Mohr Siebeck, 2007), 175–203.

[75] Royalty, *Origin of Heresy*.

[76] Jörg Frey, "New Testament Eschatology—an Introduction: Classical Issues, Disputed Themes, and Current Perspectives," in *Eschatology of the New Testament and Some Related Documents*, ed. Jan G. van der Watt (Tübingen: Mohr Siebeck, 2011), 27.

[77] On "early Christian discourse studies," see Brakke, "The Early Church in North America," 485–91.

diversity of approaches and to engage the texts in a way that is not satisfied merely to posit an abstracted or truncated theological unity (e.g., Dunn's "minimum core" of Easter and Pentecost)[78] or a commonality located only in the diffuse social and communicative ties of interactive diversity.

For this reason, we will bring to the later New Testament documents an analytical frame that incorporates these insights and examines the texts for *discourse strategies of eschatological discernment, dispute, and (dis)approval.* Having heeded Ayres's advice in attending to overt theoretical reflection on the study of unity and diversity in this section, we now turn to a close study of selected texts and themes from the General Epistles.

3. Discourse Strategies of Eschatological Discernment in the General Epistles

The death, resurrection, ascension, and promised return of Jesus Christ precipitated an eschatological tension within emergent Christianity, a tension inscribed upon the pages of the New Testament and other early Christian documents. That tension itself is a unifying, if not uniform, field embracing the General Epistles. Our aim in this section is to trace the lineaments of the discourse strategies of discernment the authors of these texts employ in response to the interface of that eschatological horizon with a variety of first-century ecclesial situations. Our task in the final section will be to collate and compare the unities and diversities—theological, social, and rhetorical—that emerge in this discourse.

Here, however, we must ask: if such a discourse of discernment is in fact eschatologically embedded, what are its signal terms, its modes and methods of engagement? As we sample texts from Hebrews, James, Jude and 2 Peter, and 2 and 3 John, several features of this discourse strategy will appear. To begin with, just as we saw in the Pauline and later apologetic texts above, these epistles utilize a vocabulary of discernment. Terms such as διακρίνω and δοκιμάζω (and cognates), as well as other related words and concepts, are not of course unique to the New Testament documents, being found elsewhere in philosophical, political, and legal discourse.[79] The former two terms can have significant semantic overlap, centering on the sense of *examination* or *scrutiny* with a view towards *(dis)approval* or *discrimination* in matters material, moral, social, or (in our texts especially) theological.[80] Especially with διακρίνω, the sense shades perceptibly, depending on context, towards *dispute* (as in Jude 9 and 23). These terms, therefore, often signal the kind of

---

[78] See n. 2 above.

[79] Frederick W. Danker and Walter Bauer, *A Greek-English Lexicon of the New Testament and Other Early Christian Literature* (Chicago: University of Chicago Press, 2000) s.vv. διακρίνω; δοκιμάζω. See also James H. Moulton and George Milligan, *The Vocabulary of the Greek Testament* (Peabody, MA: Hendrickson, 1997), s.vv. διακρίνω; δοκιμάζω.

[80] Διακρίνω especially comes to be used of making theological distinctions in early Christian literature; see G. W. H. Lampe, *A Patristic Greek Lexicon* (Oxford: Clarendon, 1976), s.v. διακρίνω.

discourse of discernment in which we are interested; but we must not be content with mere word studies. Rather, we will attempt to situate these terms within their varied rhetorical and social contexts. In doing so, we will observe recurrent strategies of discernment intended to authorize certain interpretive approaches to the Old Testament (and some New Testament) Scriptures, to proscribe certain teachers and doctrine (especially in relation to Christology), to commend certain intellectual and ethical practices, and to sanction certain social practices within the ecclesial communities. In each of these areas, this eschatological discourse of discernment works to authorize and (dis)approve,[81] urging the hearer to reflect critically, sometimes with respect to herself and the final day of divine appearing and judgment, sometimes with respect to texts, teachers, and teaching within the assembly, and sometimes with respect to opposition from without the assembly. Always, it is constructed as a persuasive, *paraenetic* discourse, aimed variously at the purity, peace, and preservation of those for whom Jesus Christ is Lord and for whom his apostolic witnesses are authoritative.

3.1. Hebrews 5:14

But solid food is for adults, who on account of their mature state [διὰ τὴν ἕξιν] have their faculties [τὰ ἀσθητήρια] trained to distinguish [πρὸς διάκρισιν] between good and bad.

Arguably, one of the most eschatologically oriented books among the General Epistles is the so-called Epistle to the Hebrews. We begin with Hebrews, not so much because of the canonical order of the General Epistles but because in it we find a thoroughgoing eschatological exhortation that orients us to several interrelated discourse themes. With a complex, doubled "spatial/temporal," or "heavenly sanctuary/two-age" conceptual framework, the author of Hebrews employs a discourse strategy that interweaves Old Testament interpretation, Christology, and exhortation in a setting of external opposition—all with a striking eschatological urgency.[82]

At the heart of this hortatory sermonic-epistle[83] we come in 5:14 to an explicit text of discernment. Set within a larger sub-unit marked off at 5:11 and 6:12 by the term "sluggish" (νωθροί), 5:14 is framed by a concern for eschatological-moral discernment.[84] Formally, 5:13–14 comprises an imperfect chiasm whose rhetorical center of gravity is, in fact,

[81] Royalty, *Origin of Heresy,* 18.
[82] Gert J. Steyn, "The Eschatology of Hebrews: As Understood within a Cultic Setting," in van der Watt, *Eschatology of the New Testament,* 429–50. See also Scott D. Mackie, *Eschatology and Exhortation in the Epistle to the Hebrews,* WUNT 2:223 (Tübingen: Mohr Siebeck, 2007) and Kenneth L. Schenck, *Cosmology and Eschatology in Hebrews: The Settings of the Sacrifice,* SNTSMS 143 (Cambridge: Cambridge University Press, 2007).
[83] Harold W. Attridge, *Hebrews* (Minneapolis: Fortress, 1989), 13–14; Mackie, *Eschatology,* 24–25.
[84] Mackie, *Eschatology,* 54–58.

"discernment."[85] The accent of this discourse in its near context is ethical (in this case drawing a distinction between good and evil). But 5:14 clearly draws into its orbit an intellectual discernment that all who are mature ought to possess. "Discernment" here highlights by contrast the underdeveloped faculties of the addressees. It describes the capacity necessary for proper scriptural interpretation (in relation to the λόγος δυσερμήνευτος of 5:11), faithful ethical conduct (καλοῦ τε καὶ κακοῦ, 5:14), and perseverance despite external opposition.[86]

It is important to note that discernment in relation to false teaching is not directly in view here. Instead, the issue is one of spiritual and intellectual maturity.[87] Accordingly, the textual unit functions as a serious rebuke[88] in relation to hermeneutical, and especially theological, immaturity that is a threat to perseverance.[89] Working overwhelmingly from the LXX,[90] the author insists that interpretive discernment is a critically important factor enabling faithfulness. This is particularly the case with regard to the person and work of Christ in view of the Old Testament Scriptures[91] and—through Christ's ministry—the community's eschatological encounters with the powers of the coming age (6:1–5; cf. 2:1–4). It is in discerning the nature and ministry of Jesus Christ as the "great high priest," both scripturally and experientially, that divine empowerment is communicated to the faithful so that they may "hold fast the confession" (3:6, 14; 4:14; 6:11, 18–20; 10:23, 39).[92] Thus we see that the eschatological discourse of discernment in Hebrews relates on a thematic level most closely to scriptural interpretation, Christology, ethics, and perseverance.

3.2. James 2:4

And haven't you made distinctions [οὐ διεκρίθητε] among yourselves and become judges characterized by immoral decisions [κριταὶ διαλογισμῶν πονηρῶν]?

---

[85] Paul Ellingworth, *The Epistle to the Hebrews* (Grand Rapids: Eerdmans, 1993), 305.

[86] Hans Windisch, *Der Hebräerbrief*, 2nd ed. (Tübingen: Mohr Siebeck, 1931), 47–49; Attridge, *Hebrews*, 161–62.

[87] According to Ellingworth, *Hebrews*, 310, "distinguish ... here implies intellectual discernment."

[88] Windisch, *Der Hebräerbrief*, 46, "ein ernster Tadel." See also, Brent Nongbri, "A Touch of Condemnation in a Word of Exhortation: Apocalyptic Language and Graeco-Roman Rhetoric in Hebrews 6:4–12," *NovT* 45 (2003): 265–79. That the term ἕξις should be understood as "mature state" and not "practice" has been demonstrated by John A. L. Lee, "Hebrews 5:14 and Ἕξις: A History of Misunderstanding," *NovT* 39 (1997): 151–76.

[89] Mackie, *Eschatology*, contra Attridge, 161 n. 86.

[90] Attridge, *Hebrews*, 23–25. See also Radu Gheorghita, *The Role of the Septuagint in Hebrews*, WUNT 2:160 (Tübingen: Mohr Siebeck, 2003), especially 1–29.

[91] Steyn, "The Eschatology of Hebrews," 431.

[92] Ellingworth, *Hebrews*, 309–10. Attridge, *Hebrews*, 161, "The imagery here [5:14] relates in a complex way to its analogue in the author's theological and paraenetic program."

The situation is somewhat different when we come to the Epistle of James, a New Testament document with a looming "eschatological horizon,"[93] but which some have alleged has no Christology.[94] Although the eschatology of James "controls the reading of the epistle as a whole,"[95] it has its own distinctive accent, mingling wisdom (1:5–8; 3:13–18) and apocalyptic (5:8–9).[96] One might even call it a mundane eschatology,[97] providing a worldview[98]—more implicit than overt—characterized by an imminent expectation of reversal (1:9–11)[99] and *parousia* (5:7–11).[100] James holds out a Torah-wisdom recast as the "law of liberty" (1:25; 2:12),[101] a wisdom that offers consolation in the midst of suffering and testing.[102] Penner has argued that, structurally and thematically, James evinces an eschatological-paraenetic framework of divine judgment and reversal intended to bolster the faith of those who are "poor" and suffering under trial.[103]

Figuring prominently in the opening frame of 1:2–12 is the eschatological language of trial (πειρασμός), testing (δοκίμιον), wisdom (σοφία), and doubting (διακρίνω).[104] Once that discourse frame has been constructed, it is within the later passage, 2:1–13,[105] that we encounter in 2:4 a distinctive type of discrimination, one that is *condemned* with reference both to a christological confession (2:1) and Old Testament legal precedent (2:8–13).[106] According to Watson, James 2:2–4 functions within 2:1–13 as a rhetorical proof (from contrary example, γάρ, 2:2) of the condemnation of partiality

---

[93] Todd C. Penner, *The Epistle of James and Eschatology: Re-reading an Ancient Christian Letter*, JSNTSup 121 (Sheffield: Sheffield Academic, 1996); Patrick J. Hartin, "James and Eschatology," in van der Watt, *Eschatology of the New Testament*, 451–71.

[94] On this claim and a response, see J. Ramsey Michaels, "Catholic Christologies in the Catholic Epistles," in *Contours of Christology in the New Testament*, ed. Richard N. Longenecker (Grand Rapids: Eerdmans, 2005), 268–91, at 269.

[95] Penner, *James and Eschatology*, 121; Dale C. Allison, *James* (London: Bloomsbury T&T Clark, 2013), 92–94.

[96] See Richard Bauckham, *James* (London: Routledge, 1999), 29–35, at 34, "Generically, James is not an apocalypse; it is wisdom paraenesis. But an eschatological orientation is not therefore anomalous; it is to be expected in wisdom paraenesis from the first century CE."

[97] Martin Dibelius, *James*, trans. Michael A. Williams (Philadelphia: Fortress, 1976), 87. Whether this encourages a "passive piety," as Dibelius contends, 49, is debatable.

[98] Hartin, "James and Eschatology," 466. See also Peter H. Davids, *The Epistle of James* (Grand Rapids: Eerdmans, 1982), 38–39.

[99] Dibelius, *James*, 84.

[100] Davids, *James*, 181–84.

[101] Davids, *James*, 98–100.

[102] Dibelius, *James*, 84; Penner, *James and Eschatology*, 217–23.

[103] Penner, *James and Eschatology*, 119–213. A theme emphasized through repetition; so Allison, *James*, 78.

[104] On the eschatological framework of testing in other early Christian and Jewish texts, see Penner, *James and Eschatology*, 183–210. Penner draws a special thematic-rhetorical (i.e., discourse) connection between Jas 1:2–12 and 1 Pet 1:6–9 (195–98).

[105] Section breaks: 2:1, "my brothers;" 2:14, "my brothers;" 3:1, "my brothers." These differ from the transitional "my beloved brothers" of 2:5 (but see 3:10). On the diatribe-admonitory style of 2:1–13; 2:14–26; and 3:1–12, see Dibelius, *James*, 124; Allison, *James*, 88.

[106] Allison, *James*, 393.

Bradley J. Bitner

(προσωπολημψία) found in 2:1.[107] Syntactically, the improper social distinction pictured in 2:4 is the *apodosis*, in the form of a question expecting a "yes" answer (οὐ διεκρίθητε ...), that completes the conditional beginning with a *protasis* (ἐάν ...) in 2:2. Making quasi-judicial distinctions in a gathered assembly[108]—distinctions of the kind that honor a well-dressed, respectable figure (2:2)[109] over a poor, shabbily-clothed man—is evil (2:4) because it conforms to the world (1:27) rather than to either the law of liberty (2:12) or the Lord of glory (2:1). James has employed an eschatological discourse strategy that indicts those "brothers" who would (ad)judge one of their own immorally and thus fail to hold to their faith in the Lord Jesus Christ (2:1).[110]

As in Hebrews, so in James, discernment is not associated with the threat of false teaching; rather, it is directed towards the Christian assembly itself, cutting against socioeconomic, discriminatory practices found in the surrounding world (1:27). It is not judgment *per se* that is condemned, but judgment with *partiality*.[111] Counterintuitively, this eschatological discourse of distinction-making works against division and promotes an ethic, undergirded by a wisdom theology and anticipated judgment, of special care for the lowly poor (ταπεινός, πτωχός; e.g., 1:9, 27; 2:1–13; 2:14–17), and of social unity.[112] Christology is invoked (2:1), but with a much lighter touch than in Hebrews. In terms of Old Testament interpretation and application, central precepts of Torah (LXX Lev 19:18;[113] Exod 20:13–14 ‖ Deut 5:17–18) are leveraged in 2:8–13 in order to underline the absolute standard of judgment and transition to the discussion linking faith and works in 2:14–26.[114] In sum, the eschatological discourse of distinction in James appeals strongly to Torah, taps into a submerged Christology, and has a prophetic-sapiential accent all its own directed toward ethics-in-community.[115]

---

[107] Duane F. Watson, "James 2 in Light of Greco-Roman Schemes of Argumentation," *NTS* 39 (1993): 94–121, at 102–8.
[108] See especially Roy Bowen Ward, "Partiality in the Assembly: James 2:2–4," *HTR* 62 (1969): 87–97. Cf. Allison, *James*, 370–82.
[109] Who is never called "rich" (πλούσιος), unlike the "outsider" figures in 2:6–7. So Ward, "Partiality in the Assembly," 96–97.
[110] See Bauckham, *James*, 104–5.
[111] Penner, *James and Eschatology*, 238–41, builds on Ward's argument concerning judgment in assembly and considers The Community Rule from Qumran (1QS) as another text of eschatological "community instruction" with resemblance to James. Cf. Bradley J. Bitner, "Exclusion and Ethics: Contrasting Covenant Communities in 1QS V, 1–VII, 25 and 1 Cor 5:1–6:11," in *Keter Shem Tov: Essays on the Dead Sea Scrolls in Memory of Alan Crown*, ed. Shani Tzoref and Ian Young (Piscataway, NJ: Gorgias, 2013), 259–304.
[112] See Strecker, *Theology of the New Testament*, 676–82.
[113] Ward, "Partiality in the Assembly," argues Lev 19:15 is also in view. See also Allison, *James*, 394.
[114] Davids, *James*, 114–19.
[115] Penner, *James and Eschatology*, 279–81.

3.3. Jude 22–23

> Snatch some from the fire, but on those who dispute [διακρινομένους] have mercy with fear.

Although there is much we could observe regarding the distinctive and explicit eschatological discourse strategy in relation to testing and approval in 1 Peter,[116] we are compelled by constraints of space to examine next Jude and 2 Peter. These epistles are worth lingering over, for both offer us a window on our topic that is out of proportion to their relatively short length.[117]

None would dispute either the fact that these two texts are marked by a literary interrelationship, or that both manifest an obviously apocalyptic eschatology.[118] In terms of the former, most scholars see 2 Peter as directly dependent upon Jude,[119] although this involves assumptions about the authorship and dating of both documents that are too complex for us to engage with here.[120] Most important for our purposes in this chapter is the debate over what to make of the eschatology of both documents. Käsemann saw the stylized, oppositional eschatology they share as a sign that the imminent expectation of the *parousia* characterizing earliest Christianity (i.e., the Pauline epistles) was collapsing. He understood it therefore as an early symptom of a calcifying orthodoxy, which he labelled "early Catholicism."[121]

---

[116] 1 Peter 1:3–11 (and especially 6–9) is a key text in which the terminological signals include "in the last time" (ἐν καιρῷ ἐσχάτῳ, 1:5), "tested genuineness" (τὸ δοκίμιον, 1:7), and "tested through fire" (διὰ πυρὸς δὲ δοκιμαζομένου, 1:7). Strecker, *Theology of the New Testament*, 627, is among those noting the interrelation of eschatological approval and a Christology focused both on atonement and *imitatio*. The following are particularly helpful in pursuit of the eschatological discourse strategy of 1 Peter: Lauri Thurén, *Argument and Theology in 1 Peter: The Origins of Christian Paraenesis*, JSNTSup 114 (Sheffield: Sheffield Academic, 1995); Fika J. van Resburg, "The Eschatology of 1 Peter: Hope and Vindication for Visiting and Resident Strangers," in van der Watt, *Eschatology of the New Testament*, 472–92; Travis B. Williams, *Persecution in 1 Peter: Differentiating and Contextualizing Early Christian Suffering*, NovTSup 145 (Leiden: Brill, 2012); Kelly D. Liebengood, *The Eschatology of 1 Peter: Considering the Influence of Zechariah 9–14*, SNTSMS 157 (Cambridge: Cambridge University Press, 2014).

[117] For the scanty reception history of these letters, see Wolfgang Grünstäudl and Tobias Nicklas, "Searching for Evidence: The History of Reception of the Epistles of Jude and 2 Peter," in *Reading 1–2 Peter and Jude: A Resource for Students*, ed. Eric F. Mason and Troy W. Martin (Atlanta: Society of Biblical Literature, 2014), 215–28.

[118] See Jörg Frey, "Judgment on the Ungodly and the *Parousia* of Christ: Eschatology in Jude and 2 Peter," in van der Watt, *Eschatology of the New Testament*, 493–513.

[119] Michael J. Gilmour, *The Significance of Parallels between 2 Peter and Other Early Christian Literature* (Leiden: Brill, 2002), 121–22. See also Jeremy F. Hultin, "The Literary Relationships among 1 Peter, 2 Peter, and Jude," in Mason and Martin, *Reading 1–2 Peter and Jude*, 27–45.

[120] See Richard J. Bauckham, *Jude, 2 Peter* (Waco, TX: Word, 1983), 157–63; Gene L Green, "Second Peter's Use of Jude: *Imitatio* and the Sociology of Early Christianity," in *Reading Second Peter with New Eyes: Methodological Reassessments of the Letter of Second Peter*, LNTS 382, ed. Robert L. Webb and Duane F. Watson (London: T&T Clark, 2010), 1–25. For a dissenting view, skeptical of pseudonymity, see J. Daryl Charles, *Literary Strategy in the Epistle of Jude* (Scranton: University of Scranton Press, 1993).

[121] Ernst Käsemann, "An Apologia for Primitive Christian Eschatology," in Käsemann, *Essays on New Testament Themes* (London: SCM, 1964), 169–95.

This influential hypothesis has now been problematized,[122] and Strecker judges that "Jude and 2 Peter, in opposition to other Christian teachers at work in the churches in late New Testament times, advocate a fundamental orientation to apostolic beginnings, and do so on specific items of doctrinal substance."[123] This is a critical insight, especially in light of our investigation, for it recognizes that both Jude, as an apocalyptic-paraenetic tract,[124] and 2 Peter, as a testamentary epistle, situate their opposition to false teachers eschatologically;[125] both employ a similar Christology in their *paraenesis*; and both appeal in overlapping ways to scriptural authority—in its prophetic (Old Testament) and apostolic modes—in their arguments. Nevertheless, in their specific discourse strategies of dispute and discernment they diverge in certain interesting ways.

We turn first to the pervasive discourse of dispute in Jude in order to probe his strategy. Jude opens with an exhortation toward a kind of theological antagonism, urging his hearers in v. 3 to "contend (ἐπαγωνίζεσθαι)[126] for the faith once delivered to the saints." The unfolding pattern of argument is characterized by scriptural citation or allusion followed by direct polemic against opponents. These opponents are alleged (among other things) to disfigure divine grace (v. 4), to blasphemously reject authority (v. 8), to cause divisions, and to be devoid of the Spirit (v.19). In the midst of this mounting oppositional paradigm falls an *exemplum* of godly contending in v. 9.[127] Structurally, v. 9 may be seen as the central term of a chiastic narrative illustration against slander in vv. 8–10 (βλασφεμοῦσιν, v. 8; βλασφημίας, v. 9; βλασφημοῦσιν, v. 10).[128] Although the issue of the background and sources of

---

[122] Bauckham, *Jude, 2 Peter*, 8–11, 151–54; Strecker, *Theology of the New Testament*, 641–53; Frey, "Judgment on the Ungodly and the *Parousia* of Christ," 493–94.

[123] Strecker, *Theology of the New Testament*, 642.

[124] Bauckham, *Jude, 2 Peter*, 3–6, 131–35, although, at 3, he prefers "epistolary sermon" for Jude. See also Strecker, *Theology of the New Testament*, 642–43; Lutz Doering, *Ancient Jewish Letters and the Beginnings of Christian Epistolography*, WUNT 298 (Tübingen: Mohr Siebeck, 2012), 477–82.

[125] For caution against identifying the opponents over-precisely, see Michel Desjardins, "The Portrayal of the Dissidents in 2 Peter and Jude: Does It Tell Us More about the 'Godly' than the 'Ungodly?'" *JSNT* 30 (1987): 89–102. Cf. Frey, "Judgment on the Ungodly and the *Parousia* of Christ," 495–96, 507–10. But against seeing the opponents merely as rhetorical stereotypes, see Bauckham, *Jude, 2 Peter*, 11–13, 154–57. Opponents are referred to as ψευδοδιδάσκαλοι, 2 Pet 2:1; οὗτοι, 2 Pet 2:12, 17; τινες ἄνθρωποι, Jude 4; οὗτοι/τούτοι, Jude 8, 10, 11, 12, 14, 16.

[126] This New Testament *hapax* taps into a larger cultural discourse drawn from athletics and Stoic philosophy; see Bauckham, *Jude, 2 Peter*, 31–34. For the sometimes neglected political (i.e., civic) resonances of the term in the inscriptions, see especially J. H. Moulton and G. Milligan, *Vocabulary of the New Testament* (Peabody, MA: Hendrickson, 2004), s.v. ἐπαγωνίζομαι. Cf. J. N. D. Kelly, *A Commentary on the Epistles of Peter and Jude* (London: Adam & Charles Black, 1969), 246–47.

[127] This pattern is summarized by Lewis R. Donelson, *From Hebrews to Revelation: A Theological Introduction* (Louisville, KY: Westminster John Knox, 2001), 89.

[128] Robert L. Webb, "The Use of 'Story' in the Letter of Jude: Rhetorical Strategies of Jude's Narrative Episodes," *JSNT* 31 (2008): 53–87, at 59. Cf. Peter Spitaler, "Doubt or Dispute (Jude 9 and 22–23): Rereading a Special New Testament Meaning through the Lens of Internal Evidence," *Biblica* 87 (2006): 201–22, at 205–09.

the dispute over Moses' body is rather involved,[129] the strategic value of the rhetorical proof is straightforward: as the archangel Michael disputed (διακρινόμενος) with the devil, he censured him in a manner direct and yet submissive to divine judicial authority. His rebuke, in the name of the Lord Christ,[130] was restrained, eschatologically informed, and rhetorically pointed, all of which work together to cast into stark relief the reviling judgments of the false teachers.[131] According to Jude 9, both the method and the manner of dispute over theological difference matter. But for all this, v. 9 leaves somewhat vague the application of Michael's example to the current situation faced by Jude's audience. The manner of godly disputing and the degree and goal of engagement with those who have infiltrated the community is clarified only in the penultimate verses of the epistle.

It is in vv. 20–23 that Jude draws the reader to the pinnacle of his discourse, gathering together the strands of his strategy. He assumes that his readers, having been persuaded by his proofs and warned against judgment (vv. 4–19), will in fact contend for the faith (v. 3) in the near future.[132] On that basis, he proceeds to give final instructions to those who, kept by God (v. 1) and keeping the faith (v. 20), must exercise a reverent, cautious, and merciful ministry of engagement with those who dispute (v. 23).[133] The textual history of vv. 22–23 is complicated, but regardless of whether one adopts the "two-clause" or "three-clause" text, there is good reason to see a structural focus on διακρινομένους.[134] In other words, *dispute* is elevated structurally and rhetorically to prominence.

In focusing on the key term διακρινομένους, Spitaler is among those who have argued compellingly for translating the substantival participle as "those who dispute" rather than as "those who doubt," a meaning unattested in extrabiblical Greek and contested within the New Testament.[135] It is evident that the correct translation materially affects the interpretation of this final

---

[129] See Bauckham, *Jude, 2 Peter*, 65–76. Cf. Eric F. Mason, "Biblical and Nonbiblical Traditions in Jude and 2 Peter: Sources, Usage, and the Question of Canon," in Mason and Martin, *Reading 1–2 Peter and Jude*, 181–200.

[130] See Webb, "The Use of 'Story,'" 69, 72.

[131] Kelly, *A Commentary on the Epistles of Peter and Jude*, 264–66; Bauckham, *Jude, 2 Peter*, 62–64; Spitaler, "Doubt or Dispute," 207–08.

[132] Stephan J. Joubert, "Persuasion in the Letter of Jude," *JSNT* 58 (1995): 75–87, at 79–86. Webb, "The Eschatology of the Epistle of Jude," *BBR* 6 (1996): 129–51, at 149–51, notes that the rhetorical function of the discourse aims at persuading the readers to adopt a certain framework of judgment or discernment while the social function is to separate the faithful of the community from those who have crept into it.

[133] I work from the two-clause text of vv. 22–23 attested by 𝔓[72], although the following observations would not be significantly altered if one accepts the three-clause text preferred by NA[28]. For the text-critical and lexical issues related to Jude 22–23, see Bauckham, *Jude, 2 Peter*, 108–11; Charles Landon, *A Text-Critical Study of the Epistle of Jude* (Sheffield: Sheffield Academic, 1996) 131–34; Spitaler, "Doubt or Dispute," 216 n. 43.

[134] Centrally placed, either at the beginning of v. 23 or the end of v. 22, respectively. See Spitaler, "Doubt or Dispute," 216–20.

[135] Spitaler, "Doubt or Dispute," especially 201–5. See also Bauckham, *Jude, 2 Peter*, 115–17. Cf. Lampe, *A Patristic Greek Lexicon*, s.v. διακρίνω (F.) who notes the later sense of "dissent" in the Chalcedonian controversies.

admonition. If we take διακρινομένους as "those who dispute,"[136] a translation much more likely in terms of lexical semantics and context, we perceive more clearly Jude's discourse strategy: he eschatologically re-orients his hearers toward those opponents who have crept into the community.[137] The strategy of engagement Jude gave in outline with the example of the archangel Michael in v. 9 is now filled out for his recipients—they are to offer a robust response (cf. v. 3) to the disputant infiltrators. But it must be one characterized by mercy and caution, and exercised in the light cast by the eschatological fires of judgment (vv. 6–7, 22) and mercy (vv. 2, 21).[138]

If, therefore, a vigorous and vigilant charity is called for by the commands of vv. 22–23 in the context of the epistle, what are the strategic discourse assumptions that undergird such an engagement with those whose unacceptable theological and ethical diversity is causing division and moral stumbling? First, unlike in Hebrews and James, the eschatological discourse of discernment in Jude is aimed directly at false teachers. This lends a sharper tone to the epistle as it relentlessly discriminates by labelling: note well the recurring rhetorical divisions marking off the beloved "us" (vv. 1, 3, 17, 20) from the ungodly "them" (vv. 4, 8, 12, 14, 16, 19).[139] Second, by structurally alternating between exhortation and *exemplum*, Jude models an eschatological approach toward ethical and scriptural reflection. As Webb notes with regard to the tradition regarding Moses' body in v. 9, Jude appeals to scriptural narratives that are known and granted authoritative status by his readers; he then surprises them by applying *those* familiar narratives to *their* situation in a *pesher*-like manner.[140]

Further, there are repeated allusions to a significant christological framework with discourse signals such as "remind" (v. 5) and "remember" (v. 17). Such signals direct the recipients to a larger tradition constituting the "faith once delivered" (v. 3) and the apostolic teaching (v. 17).[141] The focus of Jude's Christology is on Christ's judgment as Master and Lord—past and present—and especially on his yet-to-come *parousia* as Savior (vv. 4, 6, 14–15, 21, 24–25).[142] Moreover, this eschatologically-focused Christology is set in the context of "traditional catechetical material" reflecting an allusive

---

[136] Also marked as οὕς at the beginning of v. 22 in the two-clause text; cf. οὗτοι εἰσιν, vv. 16, 19, clearly referring to the opponents of v. 4.

[137] Joubert, "Persuasion in the Letter of Jude," 85–86.

[138] Spitaler, "Doubt or Dispute," 219, "In combination, [mercy and salvation] denote the direction to which Jude summons his eschatological community: toward active engagement with the disputers who face "fire" in the dawning eschaton ... [there are therefore] eschatological implications for both disputers and faithful community members."

[139] See Webb, "The Eschatology of the Epistle of Jude," 151.

[140] Webb, "The Use of 'Story'," 66. See also Darian Lockett, "Purity and Polemic: A Reassessment of Jude's Theological World," in *Reading Jude with New Eyes: Methodological Reassessments of the Letter of Jude*, ed. Robert L. Webb and Peter H. Davids (London: T&T Clark; New York: Bloomsbury, 2009), 5–31.

[141] Bauckham, *Jude, 2 Peter*, 32–34, 102–04; Webb, "The Use of 'Story' in the Letter of Jude," 67.

[142] See Webb, "The Use of 'Story,'" 67–72.

Trinitarian theology (especially in vv. 17–21).[143] Overall, then, Jude's discourse strategy evinces a familiar yet distinctive combination of features of eschatological discernment, scriptural interpretation and application, and Christology.[144] It is a strategy aimed at guarding the faithful from error by means of a direct and wisely charitable engagement with opposition that draws clear lines between "us" and "them." A common faith (v. 3) and common meal (v. 12) bespeak the desirability of unity; however, the threat of disfigured grace (v. 4) and ungodly living (vv. 7–16) imply the real possibility that a divisive diversity (v. 19) of this kind must lead to separation.

3.4. 2 Peter 3:15–16

And consider [ἡγεῖσθε] the patience of our Lord as salvation, just as also our beloved brother Paul wrote to you according to the wisdom given to him, as he also does in all his letters [ἐν πάσαις ταῖς ἐπιστολαῖς] when he speaks in them concerning these things, in which letters there are some difficult things [δυσνόητά τινα] which the ignorant and unstable distort [οἱ ἀμαθεῖς καὶ ἀστήρικτοι στρεβλώσουσιν], as they also do the rest of the Scriptures, leading to their own destruction.

If a calibrated balance between judgment and mercy characterizes the eschatological tone of Jude, some would see the balanced tipped towards judgment in 2 Peter.[145] At one level, 2 Peter is structurally straightforward: an epistolary opening (1:1–2) and conclusion (3:18b) frame a letter body (1:3–3:18a) focused on the confirmation of the elect in their godly hope and the condemnation of false teachers with their errant and immoral deceptions.[146] The discourse strategy works explicitly against eschatological scepticism[147] and an attendant ethical libertinism: 2 Peter intends to "stir [the recipients] up by way of reminder,"[148] pointing them back to the first appearing of the Lord Jesus Christ (1:16) and assuring them of his second coming, despite apparent delay (3:4, 12).[149] His eschatological "stirring up" incorporates common elements of scriptural interpretation and Christology that we have seen in Hebrews, James, and (especially) Jude, but in a distinctive configuration.

---

[143] Bauckham, *Jude, 2 Peter*, 111–14.

[144] See Michaels, "Catholic Christologies," 282–85.

[145] Bultmann, *Theology of the New* Testament, 2:169. See the repeated language of "destruction" (ἀπωλεία; 2:3; 3:7, 16), "perish" (ἀπόλλυμι; 3:6, 9), and "coming" (παρουσία; 1:16; 3:4, 12), especially in contexts of cataclysmic judgment language.

[146] Cf. Duane F. Watson, *Invention, Arrangement, and Style: Rhetorical Criticism of Jude and 2 Peter*, SBLDS 104 (Atlanta: Scholars, 1988).

[147] 2 Peter addresses a "crisis of eschatology" according to Duane F. Watson, "The Epistolary Rhetoric of 1 Peter, 2 Peter, and Jude," in Mason and Martin, *Reading 1–2 Peter and Jude*, 47–62, at 55.

[148] See 1:13; 3:1 (διεγείρω ... ἐν ὑπομνήσει). The stated purpose of this rhetorical "stirring" is to direct the recipients back to the prophetic and apostolic Scriptures with reference to the promises of a second appearing of Christ (see 3:2).

[149] Duane F. Watson, *The Intertexture of Apocalyptic Discourse in the New Testament* (Leiden: Brill, 2003), 197–214.

This configuration emerges most clearly in 2 Peter as the flow of discourse reaches its peak in 3:14–18a (διό, v. 14; οὖν, v. 17).[150] In 2:13 and 3:9, 2 Peter has sought to deconstruct a skewed eschatological *evaluation*, expressed with the verb ἡγέομαι ("consider"), and the errant theology, ethics, and divine judgment to which such an evaluation inevitably leads. This same verb of evaluative discernment appears in 3:15 (ἡγεῖσθε). There it links a reconstructed eschatology (3:14a, 15a) with a blameless ethic (3:14b) and a Pauline eschatology (3:15b).[151] Paul's epistles are represented in 3:15–16 as themselves authoritative Scripture, though sometimes difficult (δυσνόητα) to interpret.[152] In the larger context of 2 Peter, the converse of this positive mode of discernment advocated at the rhetorical climax of the letter is to ignore or misinterpret both the Scriptures and their relation to the present moment.[153] The false teachers, and those susceptible to their destabilizing teaching, "overlook" (λανθάνω, 3:5, 8) and "twist" (στρεβλόω, 3:16) what has been divinely revealed in the Scriptures. The consequence is ungodliness, error, and destruction. By deploying such a harsh discourse of condemnation, 2 Peter hopes to warn and confirm the "beloved" in a properly eschatological comprehension of "the grace and knowledge of our Lord and Savior Jesus Christ" (3:18a).

In 2 Peter, the manner and method of engagement with false teaching is more oblique than in Jude. Although incorrect eschatological and christological assumptions are condemned with strong judgment language, the readers are not exhorted (as in Jude 22–23) to refute the false teachers themselves directly.[154] Their errant views are depicted as enticing and exploitative (2:3, 14, 18) and those susceptible to their influence are labeled ignorant and unstable (2:14; 3:16; cf. 1:12; 2:20). Rhetorically, this language works similarly to that in Jude; it draws lines between those who are within the ambit of acceptable theological diversity and those who are not. In 2 Peter, being located without this boundary is tantamount to being liable to divine judgment (2:3; 9, 17, 20; 3:7). Embracing the eschatological views espoused in 2 Peter, by contrast, ushers one toward entrance into the eternal kingdom of Christ (1:11), a new creation typified ultimately by perfect righteousness (3:13)[155] and proleptically by godly living (3:14).

In terms of discourse strategy, then, 2 Peter employs a distinctive pattern of scriptural interpretation, Christology, and ethics,[156] a pattern that to many

---

[150] See Watson, "The Epistolary Rhetoric of 1 Peter, 2 Peter, and Jude," 56, 59.
[151] Bauckham, *Jude, 2 Peter*, 330–31, thinks it more likely that a general Pauline eschatological *paraenesis* is in view rather than any specific Pauline epistle.
[152] Cf. 1 Clem. 47.1, "Take up the epistle of the blessed Paul the apostle ..."
[153] Bauckham, *Jude, 2 Peter*, 334, "It was not a question of minor doctrinal errors, but of using their misinterpretations to justify immorality."
[154] See Peter H. Davids, "Are the Others Too Other? The Issue of 'Others' in Jude and 2 Peter," Mason and Martin, *Reading 1–2 Peter and Jude: A Resource for Students*, 201–13.
[155] See Kelley Coblentz Bausch, "'Awaiting New Heavens and a New Earth': The Apocalyptic Imagination of 1–2 Peter and Jude," in Mason and Martin, *Reading 1–2 Peter and Jude*, 63–82.
[156] See Henning Paulsen, *Der zweite Petrusbrief und der Judasbrief*, KEK 12 (Göttingen: Vandenhoeck & Ruprecht, 1992), 100–101.

appears to draw on an emergent "fixed tradition of early Christian theology."[157] Strong appeals to the appropriately interpreted Scriptures frame (1:20–21; 3:15–16) and punctuate (2:4–10, 15–16; 3:2, 5–7) the confirmation/condemnation motif of the letter body. These scriptural appeals are interleaved with the Christology of 2 Peter, which has been rightly seen as focusing on revelatory knowledge.[158] The result is that repeated christological titles[159] and an emphasis on an effective and fruitful knowledge (1:8)[160] as the means to godly stability and growth in grace (3:18a) serve to ground the ethical *paraenesis* of 2 Peter in a high Christology mediated especially through the prophetic-apostolic Scriptures.

3.5. 2 John 9–11; 3 John 9–10, 12

Everyone who goes beyond [πᾶς ὁ προάγων] and does not remain in the teaching of the Christ [ἐν τ διδαχ τοῦ Χριστοῦ] does not have God; the one who remains in the teaching [ἐν τ διδαχ], he has both the Father and the Son. If someone comes to you and does not bear this teaching [τὴν διδαχὴν οὐ φέρει], do not receive him into the house and do not speak a greeting to him; for the one who speaks a greeting to him partners [κοινωνεῖ] in his evil deeds. (2 John 9–11)

I wrote something to the assembly; but the one who loves to put himself first [ὁ φιλοπρωτεύων], namely Diotrephes, does not receive us [οὐκ ἐπιδέχεται]. For this reason, if I come, I will bring to remembrance his works which he is doing, slandering us with evil words. And not being content with these neither does he receive [οὔτε ... ἐπιδέχεται] the brothers and he prevents those who want to and expels [ἐκβάλλει] them from the assembly ... Demetrius has been given testimonials [μεμαρτύρηται] by all and by the truth itself; and we also give testimonial [μαρτυροῦμεν], and you know that our testimony [ἡ μαρτυρία ἡμῶν] is true. (3 John 9–10, 12)

The eschatology of 2 and 3 John is no less shadowy than the role these brief epistles tend to play in works synthesizing the theology of the New Testament.[161] Nonetheless, especially when these letters are read

---

[157] E.g., Jerome H. Neyrey, *2 Peter, Jude* (New Haven: Yale University Press, 1994), 250. See also Theo K. Heckel, "Die Traditionsverknüpfungen des Zweiten Petrusbriefes und die Anfänge einer neutestamentlichen biblischen Theologie," in *Die bleibende Gegenwart des Evangeliums: Festschrift für Otto Merk*, ed. R. Gebauer and M. Meiser (Marburg: Elwert, 2003), 193–95.

[158] Michaels, "Catholic Christologies," 280–82.

[159] God and Savior Jesus Christ (1:1b); Lord Jesus Christ (1:14, 16); Master (2:1); Lord and Savior (3:2); Lord and Savior Jesus Christ (2:20; 3:18a). Following on from the latter in 3:18a, it is Christ himself in 3:18b to whom the concluding doxology is directed (cf. Heb 13:21; Jude 25).

[160] On the interchangeability of γνῶσις and ἐπίγνωσις in 2 Peter see Bauckham, *Jude, 2 Peter*, 337–38.

[161] Strecker, *Theology of the New Testament*, 424 and n. 2. The precise relationship of 2 and 3 John to one another and to other Johannine literature (1 John, Gospel of John, and Revelation) is vigorously debated. See especially Strecker, *Theology of the New Testament*, 419–22; Judith Lieu, *I, II, & III John: A Commentary* (Louisville: Westminster John Knox, 2008), 277.

together, with 2 John preceding and being referred to by 3 John, there is a perceptible eschatological horizon that emerges in the Presbyter's conflict with false teachers (and those who refuse to receive true teachers). It erupts most noticeably in 2 John 7–11. In this dispute, a focus on Christology and recourse to the tactics of testimonial emerge as noteworthy elements of an eschatological discourse strategy of discernment and exclusion. The setting is most likely a network of local assemblies in late-first-century Asia Minor.[162]

In 2 John 7, the dispute centers on the deception practiced by itinerant teachers who have "gone out [ἐξῆλθον] into the world" and who do not confess "the coming of Jesus Christ in the flesh" (cf. 1 John 4:1–3).[163] Their error is christological, but just how precisely? It is possible, on the basis of the present participle ἐρχόμενον ("Jesus Christ *coming* in the flesh"; contrast the perfect indicative ἐληλυθότα, 4:2), and in connection with the laconic ethical injunction of 2 John 8, to see this doctrinal error in relation to the eschatological expectation of the *parousia* of Jesus Christ and not (or not primarily) to a docetic denial of his prior incarnation.[164] Alternatively, the present aspect of "coming" in 2 John 7 may be a formulaic variation of the confession found in 1 John 4:2 and echoed elsewhere. If so, it is equivalent to "the expected Messiah," albeit with an emphasis on Christ's ongoing corporeality.[165] In any case, the one who "goes beyond" (προάγω, 2 John 9)[166] the received doctrine about Christ[167] is himself not to be received (λαμβάνω, 2 John 10), for this would imply formal association and partnership (κοινωνία, 2 John 11). Doctrine in 2 John 9–10 (διδαχή τοῦ Χριστοῦ)[168] is thus

---

[162] Strecker, *Theology of the New Testament*, 422; Paul Trebilco, *The Early Christians in Ephesus from Paul to Ignatius* (Grand Rapids: Eerdmans, 2007), 270.

[163] Whether these are figures who were "insiders" who left the community or "outsiders" described in formulaic language is debated. See Daniel R. Streett, *"They Went Out from Us": The Identity of the Opponents in First John*, BZNW 177 (Berlin: de Gruyter, 2011), 342, "less a warning about enemies within than predators without ... stock apocalyptic paraenesis..."

[164] Strecker, *Theology of the New Testament*, 425–28, who mentions, at 427, similar locutions in early Christian texts (e.g., Barn. 6:9, "the one will be manifested to you in the flesh." But see critiques of this interpretation by Hans-Josef Klauck, *Der zweite und dritte Johannesbrief* (Zürich: Neukirchener, 1992), 53–56; Gerd Lüdemann, *Heretics: The Other Side of Early Christianity* (Louisville: Westminster John Knox, 1996) 175–76; Streett, *"They Went Out from Us,"* 340–48, 360. Cf. John 1:9; 11:27; 3 John 3.

[165] So Streett, *"They Went Out from Us,"* 346–48. See also Ulrich Wilckens, *Der Sohn Gottes und seine Gemeinde: Studien zur Theologie der Johanneischen Schriften* (Göttingen: Vandenhoeck & Ruprecht, 2003), 111–12.

[166] Either in the sense of *innovation* or *departure*. See Lieu, *I, II, & III John*, 273; Streett, *"They Went Out from Us,"* 357–60. Lexically, the sense "preside" is also possible here; see Moulton-Milligan, *Vocabulary of the Greek Testament*, s.v. προάγω. In this case the meaning would be that anyone presiding in the assembly is judged by adherence to a defined christological doctrine.

[167] For plausible reconstructions of divergent Christologies in this conflict, see Larry W. Hurtado, *Lord Jesus Christ: Devotion to Jesus in Earliest Christianity* (Grand Rapids: Eerdmans, 2003), 408–26.

[168] This should be construed as an objective genitive (i.e., "the doctrine *about* the Messiah"). So Rudolf Bultmann, *A Commentary on the Johannine Epistles* (Philadelphia: Fortress, 1973), 113; Strecker, *Theology of the New Testament*, 429. See also Lüdemann, *Heretics*, 176, "In II John 7, the elder measures the heretics by a confessional formula from whose content they deviate, and

eschatological with respect to its christological emphasis, and functions as a criterion of discernment with regard to teachers to be welcomed by local assemblies. Hurtado underlines the fact that, for the assemblies involved, these doctrinal disputes were "practical problems with profound social implications."[169]

Once these facts are established from 2 John, christological conflict must then be seen as the background to the dispute with Diotrephes recorded in 3 John 9 ("I wrote something to the assembly..."). In 3 John, this ongoing tension revolves not merely around a conflict of personalities, nor around the social matter of Christian hospitality, but connects directly to the critical issue of discerning which traveling teachers ought to be formally received and listened to on account of their right doctrine (i.e., 3 John 5–8: the fellow workers who "have gone out [ἐξῆλθον] for the sake of the name").[170] That is to say, the discourse of 2 and 3 John is doubly eschatological: not only is there a *parousia*-significance to the Christology being taught in these "Johannine" communities, there is also the now familiar last-days reality of discerning which teachers ought to be welcomed. The Presbyter's "apocalyptic" discourse[171] here has in view the preservation of right doctrine at a time and in a place where teachers with very diverse Christologies roved among the Christian assemblies and the issue of criteria for receiving them had become acute (recall Did. 11.1–12 and 12.1 above at n. 11).

Indeed, some brothers associated with the Presbyter himself were sent to assemblies in the surrounding region (3 John 10). This is why, having written 2 John in order to help other ecclesial communities draw doctrinal (i.e., christologically-determined) boundaries, the Presbyter finds himself and those associated with him rebuffed by Diotrephes. As someone with ambition[172] and authority in his assembly,[173] Diotrephes refused to receive formally those sent by the Presbyter (3 John 9).[174] When some objected, he worked to have them expelled from the assembly (3 John 10). In contrast to Diotrephes, the

---

puts them in an apocalyptic system of coordinates." Judith Lieu, *The Theology of the Johannine Epistles* (Cambridge: Cambridge University Press, 1991), 94, relates 2 John 9–10 to other allusive doctrinal-creedal affirmations such as 2 Timothy 2:15; 3:14.

[169] Hurtado, *Lord Jesus Christ*, 426,

[170] See especially Lüdemann, *Heretics*, 181–83. Contra Abraham J. Malherbe, "Hospitality and Inhospitality in the Church," in *God's Christ and His People: Studies in Honour of Nils Alstrup Dahl*, ed. Jacob Jervell and Wayne Meeks (Oslo: Universitetsforlaget, 1977), 222–32. See also Margaret M. Mitchell, "'Diotrephes Does Not Receive Us': The Lexicographical and Social Context of 3 John 9–10," *JBL* 117 (1998): 299–320. Contrast the contexts of 1 John 2:19 (ἐξῆλθαν) and 4:1 (ἐξεληλύθασιν).

[171] Strecker, *Theology of the New Testament*, 425–34.

[172] ὁ φιλοπρωτεύων: Lieu, *I, II, & III John*, 273, rightly sees this term in 3 John 9 as mutually interpretive of ὁ προάγων in 2 John 9, connecting both to the issue of personality in relation to doctrine. On the associated keyword "truth" (ἀλήθεια) in 2 and 3 John, see Strecker, *Theology of the New Testament*, 429–32.

[173] On differing reconstructions of the situation, including Bauer (John vs. Cerinthian Gnostics) and Käsemann, (John as the "heretic"), see Lieu, *I, II, & III John*, 270–80.

[174] Mitchell, "'Diotrephes Does Not Receive Us,'" 318–20. See also Lieu, *I, II, and III John*, 275.

Presbyter holds up the figure of Demetrius as an exemplar. The manner in which he leverages Demetrius rhetorically is by reference to a triple testimonial (testimony from "everyone," the "truth itself," and the Presbyter ["by us"], 3 John 12).[175]

Leutzsch (followed by Klauck) has demonstrated that the language of testimonial (μαρτυρέω, μαρτυρία) in 3 John opens a window onto the social experience of these early Christian assemblies.[176] On the analogy of public assemblies of civic or other groups, these *ekklesiai* gathered semi-formally to receive information about and praise for figures—sometimes local, sometimes arrived from elsewhere—in the form of testimonials.[177] Such verbal testimonials, delivered in assembly and often recorded in written form, performed the sociopolitical function of granting credibility and honor to the one to whom they testified. In 3 John 12, Demetrius, who is likely the bearer of the Presbyter's epistle, is sent to the assembly of Diotrephes as an authorized and commended teacher of true doctrine. The assemblies reading the epistle of 3 John, therefore, are provided with a theological and sociological method for discerning whom, among varied traveling teachers, they ought to receive. Discernment and evaluation of doctrine and its teachers took place in an ecclesial (i.e., assembly) context.

While more could be said of these texts, we already see in 2 and 3 John a distinctive strategy of eschatological discernment. As in the other texts we have examined, Christology looms large, and this despite the complete absence of the messianic name from 3 John. In particular, the "coming" of Jesus Christ as "the Son of the Father" (2 John 3, 7) is a central criterion for true Christology—one that underpins a life that abides in the Father and the Son (2 John 9) and that imitates good rather than evil (3 John 11). Christology is the mainline of this discourse, whereas appeals to Scripture are absent and ethical issues are only just audible on the periphery. What is unmistakeable in 3 John is the element of *testimonial in assembly* as a feature of evaluating theological diversity among emergent Christian assemblies.

4. Distinction without Separation?

unius et indivisae substantiae (Tertullian, *Prax.* 8)

---

[175] On the possible theological significance of this triple testimonial, see Streett, *"They Went Out from Us,"* 302–3.

[176] Martin Leutzsch, *Die Bewährung der Wahrheit: der dritte Johannesbrief als Dokument urchristlichen Alltags*, BAC 16 (Trier: Wissenschaftlicher Verlag Trier, 1994); Hans-Josef Klauck, *Religion und Gesellschaft im frühen Christentum: Neutestamentliche Studien*, WUNT 152 (Tübingen: Mohr Siebeck, 2003), 232–47. Cf. Lieu, *I, II, & III John*, 280; Bradley J. Bitner, *Paul's Political Strategy*, 151–65.

[177] See Christina Kokkinia, "Letters of Roman Authorities on Local Dignitaries: The Case of Vedius Antoninus," *ZPE* 142 (2003): 197–213.

Tertullian, in his early Trinitarian theological treatise *Against Praxeas*, coined the phrase "distinction without separation."[178] As we conclude, we might retroject Tertullian's catchphrase into the first century and ask regarding the documents we have sampled in this chapter: which distinctions made a difference in the extant, canonical discourses of emergent Christianity? What kinds of difference mattered most and just how? Is there a sense in which we can say that the New Testament documents witness to substantive theological diversity yet with common features? When and in what ways did difference of certain kinds stretch early Christian assemblies to the breaking point and lead indeed to separation?

Clearly there is a striking diversity of genre, geography, social setting, rhetorical strategy, and tone perceptible in the General Epistles; this is not to mention the varied views of dating, authorship, and cultural influences visible in the respective documents and their arguments. Evident, too, in many of our texts is a vigorous discourse that surely reflects accompanying theological and social conflicts within early Christian assemblies. Plurality is clearly present at a very early stage. Nevertheless, we have also seen a remarkable commonality emerge, not least as these documents evince an approach that wrestles already with issues of unity and diversity. This commonality emerges particularly in the features of what we have characterized as a New Testament eschatological discourse of discernment.

In the first section we saw that this discourse was present from the earliest Pauline epistles through to the second-century apologists and beyond. Early Christian assemblies faced challenges of theological and social diversity from the very beginning, to a degree that complicates the Hegesippian historiography of error with its emphasis on the pristine precedence of orthodoxy.[179] We then noted the importance of the models with which we approach the texts, and briefly traced the relevant history of interpretation. That history reveals a network of assumptions, methods, and heuristic categories that significantly shape one's selection of data and ultimate synthesis. We argued that our chosen framework of an eschatological discourse of discernment provides a method (if not quite as visually suggestive a model as "trajectories") that integrates insights from a variety of classic and contemporary approaches to the question.

In turning to the texts of several General Epistles themselves, certain commonalities surfaced at the level of discourse. Four of these common elements bear summarizing as we conclude. Recurrent features of this discourse include (1) an eschatological framework governing ecclesial life,

---

[178] With reference to the distinguishable persons but indivisible substance of the Father and the Son. Adolf Harnack, *History of Dogma, vol. 1* (Eugene, OR: Wipf & Stock, 1997), 57, praised *Against Praxeas* as "the most important dogmatic treatise which the West produced previous to Augustine."

[179] Royalty, *The Origin of Heresy*. Cf. Paul A. Hartog, "From Völker to this Volume: A Trajectory of Critiques and a Final Reflection," in Hartog, ed., *Orthodoxy and Heresy in Early Christian Contexts: Reconsidering the Bauer Thesis* (Eugene, OR: Pickwick, 2015), 235–48, at 247–48, "the foundational issue is ultimately neither precedence ... nor plurality ... [but] normativity ... and the 'horizoning' of historiography."

both inward and outward facing. This framework is brought to bear with the language of discernment, distinction making, and critical reflection. Engagement with opposing views and personalities is enacted and encouraged through (2) interpreting and deploying Old Testament (and other) texts, (3) carefully selecting aspects of Christology, and (4) connecting theology to ethics, usually by means of *paraenesis*.

4.1. Eschatological Framework

Eschatology embraces the texts we examined. This framework, animated by the recollection of Jesus Christ's death, resurrection, and ascension, and the indication of his *parousia*, lies sometimes on the surface of the discourse (Hebrews), sometimes submerged (2 and 3 John), but is always pressed upon the present of the recipients. Yet, even this broad discursive commonality branches out into difference depending on the strategies of the respective documents. Hebrews has an overlapping, two-age, dual-space eschatology; James stresses a wisdom from above and the imminent reversal at the *parousia*; Jude reminds of both past and *parousia* judgments in the face of false teachers; 2 Peter enlists a similar strategy of remembrance, but to combat eschatological *ennui* and commend confidence in the *parousia*; 2 and 3 John evince an embedded eschatology of christological conflict arising from the reality of itinerant teachers with significantly varying messages. Importantly, it is the eschatological edge to this collective discourse that necessitates discernment and that works to differentiate the mature/godly from the immature/ungodly (in Hebrews and James) and to distinguish those within theological and ecclesiastical bounds from those without (in Jude, 2 Peter, 2 and 3 John).

4.2. Scriptural Interpretation and Application

Apart from 2 and 3 John, each text we examined relies significantly on methods of scriptural interpretation, conditioned by eschatological and christological horizons. The eschatology of Hebrews creates space for the ascended, intercessory, high-priestly ministry of a Melchizedekian Christ; but only those with properly trained faculties of discernment will perceive this hermeneutically sophisticated Christology. James reflects repeatedly on Torah in connection with holding rightly to faith in the Lord Jesus Christ, the Lord of glory. Jude draws upon Old Testament and intertestamental texts as well as apparently traditional catechetical material, interpretively applying *exempla* to his audience by means of simile and *pesher*. 2 Peter insists upon a literal, patient reading of the authoritative prophetic-apostolic Scriptures in light of eschatological skepticism. In every case, an eschatological exigence calls forth and conditions strategies of scriptural interpretation that give shape to the discourse of discernment.

4.3. Christological Aspects

Christology is a critical touchstone in each instance. It provides, in turn, the theological groundwork for *paraenesis* toward perseverance (Hebrews), the reference point for ecclesial ethics (Hebrews, James, Jude, 2 Peter), and the flash-point of theological and social conflict (Jude, 2 Peter, 2 and 3 John). In several instances, Christology—in its salvific-atonement or *parousia* aspects—emerges as the core of coalescing doctrine (most clearly, but not exclusively, in 2 John 9). If eschatology is the discourse frame and scriptural interpretation its mode, then Christology presents as the variegated leitmotif throughout the General Epistles.

4.4. Ethical Emphases

Ethics and exhortation overwhelmingly form the rhetorical aim of these letters. *Paraenesis*, on the basis of the other discourse elements, focuses on righteousness, purity, and blamelessness (Hebrews, James, Jude, 2 Peter), on the ethics of scriptural interpretation (Hebrews, 2 Peter), on social-ecclesial equality and impartiality (James), and on the interrelation of right doctrine and right living (Hebrews, James, 2 Peter, 2 and 3 John). In both the eschatological discourses and implied settings of these texts there is a necessity for a coherent ethics of discernment with regard to doctrine, purity, and social inclusion/exclusion.

5. Conclusion

In conclusion, we have focused on the General Epistles with a view towards the features that comprise their eschatological discourse strategies of discernment. Keeping in mind that each of these letters is in fact an example of canonized *discourse* reminds us that they combine theological, rhetorical, and social-historical aspects. As we seek to grapple with the question of unity and diversity across these levels, we do well not merely to summarize the content of these documents of emergent Christianity, but to begin by discerning and reflecting upon the commonalities and divergences of their respective discourse strategies.

Recommended Reading

Balla, Peter. *Challenges to New Testament Theology*. WUNT 2:95. Tübingen: Mohr Siebeck, 1997.

Donelson, Lewis R. *From Hebrews to Revelation: A Theological Introduction*. Louisville: Westminster John Knox, 2001.

Dunn, James D. G. *Unity and Diversity in the New Testament: An Inquiry into the Character of Earliest Christianity*. Third edition. London: SCM, 2006.

Köstenberger, Andreas J., and Michael J. Kruger. *The Heresy of Orthodoxy*. Wheaton, IL: Crossway, 2010.

Lockett, Darian. *An Introduction to the Catholic Epistles*. London: T&T Clark, 2012.

Mason, Eric F., and Troy W. Martin, *Reading 1–2 Peter and Jude: A Resource for Students*. Atlanta: Society of Biblical Literature, 2014.

McKechnie, Paul. *The First Christian Centuries: Perspectives on the Early Church.* Leicester: Apollos, 2001.

Räisänen, Heikki. *Beyond New Testament Theology*. Second edition. London: SCM, 2000.

Robinson, James M., and Helmut Koester, *Trajectories through Early Christianity.* Philadelphia: Fortress, 1971.

Royalty, Robert M. *The Origin of Heresy. A History of Discourse in Second Temple Judaism and Early Christianity*. London: Routledge, 2013.

Strecker, Georg. *Theology of the New Testament.* Berlin: de Gruyter; Louisville, KY: Westminster John Knox, 2000.

Van der Watt, Jan G. *Eschatology of the New Testament and Some Related Documents*. WUNT 2:315. Tübingen: Mohr Siebeck, 2011.

4. "Not as the Gentiles": The Ethics of the Earliest Christians

David Starling

1. The View from Above

Early in the second century AD, the Roman aristocrat Pliny the Younger, who had recently been appointed as governor of Bithynia and Pontus, wrote to the emperor Trajan with some questions that had been perplexing him about the people within the province who had been denounced to him as Christians. Having not previously participated in the prosecution of Christians, he was uncertain of how the accusations were to be dealt with, and put to the emperor a string of questions including the issue of "whether it is the mere name of Christian which is punishable, or rather the crimes [*flagitia*] associated with the name."[1]

The account of his investigations that he offers in the following paragraphs of the letter includes a description of the group's activities. These had been given to him by some former members, who had since recanted by making invocation to the gods and presenting offerings to the statue of the emperor. On the basis of their description, and the evidence of two deaconesses whom he had questioned under torture, Pliny offered his own summary impression of the movement as "nothing but a degenerate sort of cult [*nihil aliud ... quam superstitionem pravam*] carried to extravagant lengths."[2]

The language and tone of Pliny's assessment are similar to those of his friend Suetonius.[3] His *Lives of the Caesars* includes a brief reference to the fact that, under Nero, "punishment was inflicted on the Christians, a class of men given to a new and mischievous superstition [*superstitio nova ac malefica*]" (an action listed as one example among others of the ways in which "during his reign many abuses were severely punished and put

---

[1] Pliny, *Ep.* 10.96, as translated (here and in subsequent quotations) in Pliny, *Pliny: Letters and Panegyricus*, trans. Betty Radice, 2 vols., LCL (Cambridge, MA: Harvard University Press, 1969).

[2] Pliny, *Ep.* 10.96.

[3] The evidence of Pliny, *Ep.* 10.94 suggests the likelihood that Suetonius was present with Pliny in Bithynia and possibly even working on his staff at the time when Pliny was encountering the experiences that occasioned letters 96–97.

down").[4] Tacitus, similarly, in his account of how Nero had chosen the Christians in Rome to be scapegoats for the fire of AD 64, describes the Christians as "a class of men, loathed for their vices [*flagitia*]," and characterizes the movement as a "pernicious superstition [*exitiabilis superstitio*]," which—after the temporary rebuff of its founder's crucifixion— had broken out again "not merely in Judea, the home of the disease, but in the capital itself, where all things horrible or shameful in the world collect and find a vogue."[5]

Taken together, the three descriptions provide a useful snapshot of the early second-century Christian movement, as it was viewed from outside (and above) by its aristocratic Roman observers. At surface level, if we focus on their brief, bottom-line summaries, the view from all three writers is simple, consistent, and negative: all three characterize Christianity as a *superstitio*, with an array of accompanying adjectives expressing their distaste and contempt for its beliefs and practices.[6] If we dig a little deeper, however, several important questions and complexities begin to emerge.

In the first place, there is the question of the degree to which the practices and commitments of the Christians are seen to deviate from the morality of the Greco-Roman mainstream and the religious and political loyalties demanded by the empire. Both Tacitus and Pliny comment on the "vices" or "crimes" that are associated with the movement in popular opinion, but Pliny takes care to report that his own investigations have uncovered nothing of the sort: the meal that the Christians share is, according to his informants, merely "food of an ordinary, harmless kind," and the oath that they swear is nothing seditious or criminal, but quite the opposite—an oath "to abstain from theft, robbery and adultery, to commit no breach of trust and not to deny a deposit when called upon to restore it." Pliny's policy, which is endorsed in Trajan's reply, is to execute people denounced as Christians if they refuse to renounce Christ, invoke the gods, and offer reverence to the statue of the emperor. Whatever else they may be guilty of, this refusal in itself amounts (in Pliny's eyes) to a display of "stubbornness and unshakeable obstinacy" that is serious enough to be punishable by death. Nevertheless, Trajan insists, "these people must not be hunted out."[7] The threat that they pose through the contagious example of their obstinacy is real enough to warrant execution, but the more indirect threat that they represent as a source of competition for the traditional cults, while clearly a matter of concern,[8] is not deemed serious enough to warrant proactive prosecution.

---

[4] Suetonius, *Nero* 6.16, as translated (here and in subsequent quotations) in *Suetonius*, trans. John Carew Rolfe, 2 vols., LCL (Cambridge, MA: Harvard University Press, 1914), 110–11.
[5] Tacitus, *Ann.* 15.44, as translated (here and in subsequent quotations) in *Tacitus: The Histories and the Annals*, trans. Clifford H. Moore and John Jackson, 4 vols. LCL (Cambridge, MA: Harvard University Press, 1925), 282–85.
[6] See the discussion in Edwin A. Judge, "Judaism and the Rise of Christianity: A Roman Perspective," *TynBul* 45 (1994): 359–62.
[7] Pliny, *Ep.* 10.97.
[8] See the comments in the final paragraph of Pliny, *Ep.* 10.96.

A second matter of some complexity is the relationship between the teachings and practices of the Christians and the more familiar (if equally alien) teachings and practices of Judaism. Suetonius's brief description of Christianity refers explicitly to the novelty of the movement, and he offers no indication that he interprets it in relation to its Jewish roots.[9] Tacitus, on the other hand, makes it clear that he is aware of the Christian movement's Judean origins, and when he goes on to speak of the unpopularity that made the Christians such easy scapegoats, he ascribes it to their "hatred of the human race [*odio humani generis*]"—language that is strongly reminiscent of the stereotypical criticisms of Jewish "misanthropy" that can be found in his own writings and those of other Roman and Greek intellectuals.[10]

These two questions, emerging from the earliest surviving descriptions of Christianity as seen from the vantage-point of the Greco-Roman elite, work nicely as a jumping-off point for our own discussion of the ethics of the earliest Christians. If we examine the writings of the New Testament as the best surviving evidence of the view from within early Christianity,[11] how might the insiders' viewpoints confirm, complement, or contradict the outsiders' perspectives that we find in the writings of Pliny, Tacitus, and Suetonius? To what extent—according to the self-understanding of the writers and teachers within the early Christian movement—did its moral norms and political loyalties line up with those of the surrounding culture? And where they differed, how much of that difference can be explained by the movement's origins within Second Temple Judaism and the continuing ethical authority that it granted to the Old Testament Scriptures? In other words, to what extent were the ethics of the earliest Christians distinctive, when compared with the moral norms of Judaism on the one hand and Greco-Roman culture on the other?

Framing the question in this manner—as an inquiry into what was *distinctive* about the ethics of the earliest Christians—carries with it a risk of distortion that should be acknowledged and guarded against. Wayne Meeks sounds an important warning on this score:

> Those of us who want most to follow in the way of the first Christians tend to focus our attention on what was new about them. What was unique about their

---

[9] His earlier reference to the expulsion of the Jews from Rome on account of "disturbances at the instigation of Chrestus" (*Claud.* 5.25) offers no indication that he had drawn a connection between these Jewish disputes in the time of Claudius and the "Christians" who were punished under Nero. Cf. the brief comments in Judge, "Judaism and the Rise of Christianity," 361.

[10] E.g., Tacitus, *Hist.* 5.5; Cicero, *Flac.* 28.68; Diodorus Siculus, *Hist.* 34.1; Quintilian, *Inst.* 3.7.21.

[11] Strictly speaking, of course, the perspectives represented by the writers of the New Testament do not necessarily add up to "the ethics of the earliest Christians"; as will be discussed below, the circumstances that occasioned many of the texts that came to be part of the New Testament included sharp disagreements between the texts' authors and the communities to which they were written. Nevertheless, the voices that we hear in the New Testament—even when they are at their most stridently critical in the stance that they take toward their addressees—are still insiders' voices, whose perspectives can be fruitfully compared and contrasted with the outsiders' perspectives represented by writers such as Pliny, Suetonius, and Tacitus.

morality? What was the essence of their ethics? I have argued throughout this book that these questions do not represent an adequate way toward understanding. To obtain the essence of something we have to boil it down, distill, filter out; what is left is not the living thing, but a residue, an abstraction. In the second century it was the sophisticated detractors of Christianity who emphasized its newness. "Novel," wrote Tacitus, and therefore, "a superstition." Christianity's defenders insisted that it was not new at all, but as old as creation, as old as the sacred books of the Jews, its ideas familiar in the best of the Greek and Roman philosophers, its practices not dissimilar from the best of pagan ritual and life. Yet, in other contexts, they could also emphasize its differences and its novelty. In order to understand the first Christians, it is not enough either to abstract their novelties or to add up the "parallels" and "influences" from their environment. It is the patterns of the whole that we have been trying to discern.[12]

Meeks's larger task—to discern "the patterns of the whole"—is beyond the scope of this chapter. But even within the smaller ambit of our own task, it will be important to remember that the question we are exploring is not simply a yes/no question about *whether* the ethics of the early Christians were distinctive; nor, for that matter, will it be solely an attempt to identify *which* elements of their ethics were the distinctive ones, as if they were the only elements of real historical or theological significance. Our inquiry, rather, will be into the *extent* to which the early Christians' ethics were distinctive (and therefore also, by implication, the extent to which they were not): both the elements of contrast and the elements of continuity will be of interest, as will be the ways in which those dynamics of contrast and continuity are interpreted and accounted for by the New Testament writers.

2. "The Ethics" of the Earliest Christians?

Any investigation into "the ethics of the earliest Christians" raises obvious issues that need to be addressed at the outset. To begin with there is the sheer diversity of authors, audiences, and situations that the New Testament embraces; this is not a single text but a collection of texts. There is also the further question of the range of genres represented. Among the many documents contained within the New Testament, there is nothing that even comes close to offering a comprehensive code of behavior or Torah-interpretation that could be compared, for example, with the Mishnah of Rabbinic Judaism or the Qumran *Community Rule*;[13] nor do we find a systematic philosophical discussion comparable to Aristotle's *Nicomachean*

---

[12] Wayne A. Meeks, *The Moral World of the First Christians* (Philadelphia: Westminster, 1986), 161. Meeks's reference to Tacitus describing Christianity as "novel" appears to be based on a conflation of Tacitus's description with the description in Suetonius, but the essential point still stands.

[13] The Sermon on the Mount perhaps certainly offers a kind of epitome of Jesus' teaching on how the Torah is to be fulfilled by his disciples, but it is still very brief, and is structured as a selection of worked examples, not a comprehensive code.

Ethics or Philo's *On the Virtues*. Instead we find a collection of biographical and historical narratives, a series of letters (and epistolary homilies) addressed to churches and individuals, and a book of apocalyptic visions. In the face of this diversity of genres, authors, audiences, and situations, can we really speak of "the ethics" of the earliest Christians?

These issues are of no small importance, but they should not cause us to give up on our quest before we have even begun. Even when we have taken due account of their diversity, there is still an enormous amount that the New Testament documents share as common features: that they originated within communities bound together by a shared allegiance and devotion to Jesus as Messiah and Lord; that they are characterized, in almost every case, by explicit and pervasive intertextual reference to the Old Testament Scriptures, and were produced by writers who were conscious of those Scriptures' continuing authority within the communities for which they wrote; that they were written within the sociopolitical context of the first-century Roman empire; and that they all disclose, in one way or another, an interest in shaping the moral vision and ethical norms of the communities to which they are addressed. Narratives, epistles, and apocalypses, while hardly constituting an encyclopedic manual of conduct or a systematic ethical treatise, can still be deeply influential in forming a community's moral vision and articulating an account of the patterns of behavior that it celebrates as good, beautiful, and honorable.[14] And this particular collection of narratives, epistles, and apocalypses has enough in common for it to be genuinely regarded as a window (or better, perhaps, a row of windows) onto the ethics of a single movement.

Within this chapter, then, we will devote our attention to a selection of the narrative, epistolary, and apocalyptic texts of the New Testament, to explore some of the ways in which writers within the early Christian movement articulated their understanding of the ethics of the movement, and of the ways in which it contrasted or aligned with the ethics of the Jewish tradition and the Greco-Roman world.[15]

---

[14] See, for example, the discussions of narrative and ethics in Stanley Hauerwas, *A Community of Character: Toward a Constructive Christian Social Ethic* (Notre Dame: University of Notre Dame Press, 1981) and Gordon J. Wenham, *Story as Torah: Reading Old Testament Narrative Ethically* (Grand Rapids: Baker, 2004). On apocalyptic, see Ellen T. Charry, "'A Sharp, Two-Edged Sword': Pastoral Implications of Apocalyptic," in *Character and Scripture: Moral Formation, Community, and Biblical Interpretation*, ed. William P. Brown (Grand Rapids: Eerdmans, 2002).

[15] One implication of framing the question in this manner, with its focus on the "texts" and "writers" of early Christianity, is that the investigation will not include an attempt to peer back past the texts to the oral traditions that (in some cases) preceded them, or to reconstruct the ethical teachings of Jesus himself.

3. Narrative and Ethos: Luke–Acts and Matthew

Among the culture-forming narratives of earliest Christianity, the four gospels and the book of Acts have an obvious centrality and pride of place.[16] These were not the only stories that the early Christians told, but as extended narrations of the story of Jesus (in the case of the four gospels) and the post-Easter mission of the church (in the case of Acts) they had a unique role in shaping and articulating both the central commitments and the distinctive emphases of the early Christians' self-understanding. Given the focus of our enquiry in this chapter, we will concentrate on two case studies: Luke–Acts as a case study in how early Christianity related to the moral values and political arrangements of the Greco-Roman world, and Matthew's Gospel as a case study in how early Christianity related to the ethical and legal traditions of early Judaism.

The choice of these two case studies is informed, in part at least, by the different audiences for which Matthew and Luke–Acts appear to have been written and the different positions that they occupy within the (metaphorical) territory of earliest Christianity. Writers such as Richard Bauckham and Loveday Alexander have rightly stressed the interconnectedness of the various communities within whom the gospel-writers produced their respective accounts of the life of Jesus; Michael Thompson uses the image of a "holy internet" to describe the single, sprawling reading community for which the gospels were written.[17] Nevertheless, it is still true to say that each of the four gospels originated in a particular geographical and social location within the networks of earliest Christianity, and reflects the assumptions and debates of its closest context. In the case of Matthew's Gospel, the concerns of Jewish Christians and their interactions with their non-Christian Jewish neighbors are of obvious and pressing relevance; in the case of Luke–Acts, Jewish concerns are by no means absent, but—from start to finish of the story Luke narrates—they are explicitly and consistently related to the wider context of the Greco-Roman world.

3.1. *The World Turned Upside Down: Narrative, Ethics, and Empire in Luke–Acts*

Each of the four gospels, in its own way, expresses an interest in the implications of the story of the Jewish prophet Jesus for the Gentiles of his own time and beyond. It is in Luke's Gospel, however, and its sequel Acts, that we move the furthest (both literally and metaphorically) from the soil of

---

[16] On the gospels and Acts as "culture-forming narratives," see C. Kavin Rowe, *World Upside Down: Reading Acts in the Graeco-Roman Age* (Oxford: Oxford University Press, 2009) and Frances M. Young, *Biblical Exegesis and the Formation of Christian Culture* (Cambridge: Cambridge University Press, 1997).

[17] Michael B. Thompson, "The Holy Internet: Communication between Churches in the First Christian Generation," in *The Gospels for All Christians: Rethinking the Gospel Audiences*, ed. Richard Bauckham (Grand Rapids: Eerdmans, 1998), 49–70.

Judea and Galilee into the larger, surrounding world of Hellenistic culture and Roman imperial arrangements. Richard Hays makes the point vividly and memorably:

> To move from reading Mark to reading Luke is like moving from Beowulf to Milton. In both cases, the former presents a shadowy world whose bleak passion we can comprehend only in part, through a glass darkly; the latter portrays a well-lit civilized world informed by the social and literary conventions of classical antiquity. Part of Luke's literary achievement is to make the foreboding story of Jesus seem reasonable and inviting to a more cultured readership in the Hellenistic world.[18]

One obvious clue to Luke's reasons for framing of the story in this manner can be found in the preface to his Gospel (Luke 1:1–4). Whilst it would be a mistake to read the dedication to Theophilus as an indication that the book is intended *exclusively* for the dedicatee and others of a similar social station, it certainly suggests that Theophilus and his peers are *included* among the book's intended readers.[19] If Theophilus is to be reinforced in his assurance of the stability and security (ἀσφάλεια) of the things he has been taught about Jesus, then the "orderly account" provided for him by Luke will need to be one that supplies him, not only with the bare facts of what took place, but also with a basis for responding to the social stigma and political precariousness that he would have incurred by associating with the community of Jesus' followers.[20]

Given this likely dimension of Luke's purpose, it is not surprising that we find a number of points within Luke–Acts at which the moral norms and political judgments implied by the narrator coincide quite closely with those of the respectable Greco-Roman mainstream. It is Luke, for example, who preserves the fine print of the exhortations that accompanied and concretized John the Baptist's call to repentance, clarifying the extent and nature of its economic and political ramifications. John's word to tax collectors, Luke tells us, was simply that they should "collect no more than the amount prescribed for you" (Luke 3:13)—an injunction that could sit comfortably alongside the famous reminder that Tiberius himself had given to his tax-hungry governors, that he wanted his sheep "shorn, not shaven."[21] John's word to the soldiers is similar—"Do not extort money from anyone by threats or false accusation, and be satisfied with your wages" (Luke 3:14)—and corresponds closely to the terms in which Josephus (that most Hellenized of Pharisees!) describes the

---

[18] Richard B. Hays, *The Moral Vision of the New Testament: Community, Cross, New Creation: A Contemporary Introduction to New Testament Ethics* (San Francisco: Harper, 1996), 113.

[19] See the comments in Loveday Alexander, *The Preface to Luke's Gospel: Literary Convention and Social Context in Luke 1.1–4 and Acts 1.1*, SNTSMS 78 (Cambridge: Cambridge University Press, 1993), 168–86; Craig S. Keener, *Acts: An Exegetical Commentary: Introduction and 1:1—2:47* (Grand Rapids: Baker, 2012), 423–34.

[20] See Darrell L. Bock, *Luke*, 2 vols., BECNT (Grand Rapids: Baker, 1994), 15; Hays, *Moral Vision*, 113; Keener, *Acts*, 148–65, 435–58.

[21] Quoted in Suetonius, *Tib.* 3.32 and Dio Cassius, *Hist.* 57.10.5.

disciplines that he imposed on the soldiers fighting under his command.[22] The resultant summary of John's teaching would certainly have been encountered by Theophilus and his peers as a message that made serious ethical demands, but (despite the fieriness of the rhetoric) it could hardly have been taken as a call to insurrection.

A similar conclusion could be drawn from the descriptions of the Jerusalem church that Luke offers in the opening chapters of Acts (2:41–47; 4:32–37), in the wake of the apostles' preaching and the baptism of those who welcomed the message. Once again, there are obvious ethical demands that wealthy Greco-Roman readers would have found implicit in the description (particularly in the repeated emphasis on how "all who believed were together and had all things in common"; "they would sell their possessions and goods and distribute the proceeds to all, as any had need"; "no-one claimed private ownership of any possessions, but everything they owned was held in common"; and "there was not a needy person among them, for as many as owned lands or houses sold them and brought the proceeds of what they sold"), but the description would not have jarred completely with the ideals of their culture; rather, as Richard Hays suggests, it would likely have struck them as a fulfillment or extension of them:[23]

> Already in Aristotle's *Nicomachean Ethics*, it is assumed that the ideals of sharing and unity of soul between friends are truisms: "All the proverbs agree with this: 'Friends have one soul between them' and 'Friends' goods are common property.'" Thus, the Jerusalem community embodies in its life together the Greek vision of authentic friendship, not just between two people or within a small intimate circle but now exponentially expanded into the life of a community of thousands.[24]

The attractiveness of the Jerusalem church's community life is underlined by Luke's repeated claim that they "enjoyed the goodwill of all the people" (Acts 2:27; cf. 5:13 and the similar language used of Jesus in Luke 2:52). While this popular verdict functions, in part at least, as a contrast with the hostile stance of the temple authorities (e.g., Acts 5:26; cf. Luke 22:2), it also

---

[22] Josephus, *Vita* 47. Although the events described took place when he was commanding Jewish forces *against* the Romans, the account was written late in Josephus's life as an apologetic response to the criticisms of Justus of Tiberias, appealing (at least in part) to the moral and political values of the elite in Rome. For a brief summary of the argument for an elite Roman audience as the principal readership addressed by Josephus in the *Life*, see the introductory comments by Steve Mason in Flavius Josephus, *Life of Josephus* (Leiden: Brill, 2001), xix–xxi.

[23] Compare the way in which Jesus' teaching on hospitality in Luke 14:12–14 functions as an extension and radicalization of Greco-Roman moral norms, endorsing the value of the practice but exploding the conventional boundaries of friendship and reciprocity. Cf. the discussion in Brian Capper, "Reciprocity and the Ethic of Acts," in *Witness to the Gospel: The Theology of Acts*, ed. I. Howard Marshall and David G. Peterson (Grand Rapids: Eerdmans, 1998), 512–18.

[24] Hays, *Moral Vision*, 123. Of course, as Hays goes on to add, Luke's comment that "there was not a needy person among them" suggests that he would also have expected his readers to interpret the description in relation to the covenant stipulations and promises of Deuteronomy 15.

finds a powerful echo in the series of official verdicts that Luke reports, coming from the mouths of Roman officials and, in one instance, the puppet king Agrippa, declaring that the followers of Jesus are "innocent" of the various charges leveled against them (Acts 18:14–15; 19:37; 23:29; 25:25; 26:31–32). If Paul's claim to Festus is that "I have not offended … against Caesar" (25:8), then the consistent conclusion drawn by Caesar's servants throughout the book of Acts appears to be that he is correct.

But exonerating verdicts of this sort are not the only opinions of Paul and the early Christians that are reported within the pages of Acts. Side by side with these declarations of the innocence and innocuousness of the movement—and often in direct collision with them—there is another series of sharply contrary assessments reported. In Acts 16, for example, when Paul and Silas disrupt the business activities of the fortune-telling slave-girl's owners in Philippi, they find themselves dragged before the magistrates and accused of "advocat[ing] customs which it is not lawful for us Romans to accept or practice" (16:21). In Thessalonica, Paul and his companions are accused of "acting contrary to the decrees of the emperor, saying that there is another king named Jesus" (17:7). In Corinth the charge is that they are "persuading people to worship God in ways that are contrary to the law" (18:13). And in Caesarea, before the governor Felix, Paul is denounced as "a troublemaker, stirring up riots among the Jews all over the world" (24:5). In their immediate contexts, of course, all of these accusations receive swift answers in the dismissive verdicts of the officials before whom they are made. But this does not mean that their force is extinguished altogether. After all, the reader of Luke–Acts is left in little doubt of the fate that awaits Paul at the end of his long journey to Jerusalem and Rome (see Acts 9:16; 20:25, 38; 21:10–14, and the sense of tragic irony implied in 26:32), despite the repeated official declarations of his innocence. Nor is Luke sparing in the detail with which he recounts the political and economic upheaval that Paul and his companions introduce into the towns in which they preach the gospel: there is more than a grain of truth in the charge that "these people … have been turning the world upside down" (17:6).[25]

What are we to do with these two contrasting sets of judgments about the implications of early Christianity for the moral values and political arrangements of the Greco-Roman world? It is certainly not an adequate assessment of the evidence (or, for that matter, an adequate interpretation of Luke's rhetorical purpose) simply to choose one set of judgements and discard the other. C. Kavin Rowe's warnings on this score are well made:

> Scholarly readers are presented with a false choice in which they are forced to opt for one abstracted part of the narrative over another. So, for example, in light of the majority construal of Lukan politics, "I found he had done nothing deserving death" is read against and, hence, cancels out "these men … advocate customs which it is not lawful for us Romans to accept or

---

[25] See especially the analysis of Acts 14, 16, 17 and 19 in Rowe, *World Upside Down*, 17–52.

practice"—or vice versa. But the very fact that Luke included both sets of texts should warn us against being caught in pendulum hermeneutics.... The question is ... not so much whether we should believe the owners of the pythoness in Philippi who accuse Paul or the governor Festus who exonerates him, but how we can do justice to both kinds of passages within the same larger whole. "These men ... advocate customs which it is not lawful for us Romans to accept or practice" must be read together with "I found he had done nothing deserving death." The hermeneutical necessity is *to think the juxtaposition*.[26]

"Think[ing] the juxtaposition" requires something more, too, than just balancing out one set of judgements against the other. If we are to form an adequate interpretation of how Luke wishes his readers to see the relationship between the ethics and politics of Jesus' followers and those of the Greco-Roman mainstream (and, in particular, the guardians of the imperial order), these contrasting sets of statements need to be placed within the larger narrative whole that Luke has constructed. Within that larger narrative, the defining climax is the crucifixion and resurrection of Jesus, understood as the fulfillment of divine plans and purposes that continue to be worked out as Jesus' servants proclaim "repentance and forgiveness of sins ... in his name to all nations" (Luke 24:47). Read within that framework, the teachings and practices of Jesus' disciples are to be interpreted (in part at least) as extensions of the words and actions of Jesus—things said and done "in his name."[27] It is no surprise, then, that the string of exonerating verdicts that Roman officials pronounce on Paul and the early Christians in Acts has a precedent in the cluster of pronouncements that the Roman governor Pilate makes about Jesus himself (23:4, 14–15, 22), echoed in the mouth of the centurion who oversaw the crucifixion (23:47).[28] Nor is it a surprise that Paul and his companions share such a strong sense of foreboding about the eventual outcome of his journey to Rome—they, after all, know what Pilate ended up doing to the "innocent" man Jesus, despite his own repeated pronouncements that "he has done nothing to deserve death" (23:15).[29]

The connection between Jesus and the disciples who bear his name is not merely a matter of the way in which they are received by others or the fate that they endure in the end. It is also fundamental to the way in which Luke

---

[26] Rowe, *World Upside Down*, 55–56; emphasis original.

[27] Hence the language of Acts 1:1, in which the contents of Luke's former book are said to be "all that Jesus began to do and to teach" (NIV; πάντων ... ὧν ἤρξατο ὁ Ἰησοῦς ποιεῖν τε καὶ διδάσκειν), with the implication that he continues to do and to teach through his apostles. See David G. Peterson, *The Acts of the Apostles*, PNTC (Grand Rapids: Eerdmans, 2009), 102.

[28] The difference between Luke's version of the centurion's words ("Surely this was a righteous man") and the version in Mark ("Surely this man was the Son of God") presumably reflects the connection in Luke's mind between the centurion's words and the governor's.

[29] Note the way in which the believers in Acts 4 draw lines of explicit continuity between the crucifixion of Jesus under Herod and Pontius Pilate and their own persecution at the hands of the temple authorities—an interpretation (as Richard Hays points out) that makes a mess of any attempt to argue that Luke pins the blame of the crucifixion solely on the Jewish leaders and exonerates the Roman state. See Hays, *Moral Vision*, 127–28.

presents the content and motive of their own moral conduct, and the way in which it relates to the moral norms of the surrounding culture. The clearest example of this can be seen in Jesus' teaching about greatness and service, recorded by Luke in the context of Jesus' final meal with his disciples:

> A dispute also arose among them as to which one of them was to be regarded as the greatest. But he said to them, "The kings of the Gentiles Lord it over them; and those in authority over them are called benefactors. But not so with you; rather, the greatest among you must become like the youngest, and the leader like the one who serves. For who is greater, the one who is at the table or the one who serves? Is it not the one at the table? But I am among you as one who serves. (Luke 22:24–27)

Joel Green offers a neat summation of this pattern and its implications for how we are to understand the shape of the ethics that Luke wishes his readers to derive from his account:

> What is often striking about [Jesus'] instruction [in Luke's Gospel] is its orientation not to "proper behavior" per se but toward a reconstructed vision of God and the sort of world order that might reflect this vision of God.... For Luke, then, the call to discipleship is fundamentally an invitation for persons to align themselves with Jesus, and thus with God.... Jesus thus calls on people to live as he lives, in contradistinction to the agonistic, competitive form of life marked by conventional notions of honor and status typical of the larger Roman world. Behaviors that grow out of service in the kingdom of God take a different turn: Love your enemies. Do good to those who hate you. Extend hospitality to those who cannot reciprocate. Give without expectation of return.[30]

Crucial as this pattern is, the kind of "alignment" with Jesus that Luke's storyline calls for cannot, of course, be reduced to a one-dimensional summons to "live as he lives." The logic of Luke's narrative also implies, at another level, a fundamental distinction between the identity and action of Jesus himself and the identity and action of his disciples. According to the story that Luke tells, acting and speaking in Jesus' name does not mean simply following his example or continuing his work; the message that the disciples speak when they speak in Jesus' name is not only a message that announces (as Jesus had) the drawing near of God's kingdom, but also a message that announces Jesus himself as the Messiah and Lord in whom the Kingdom had drawn near (e.g., Acts 2:36; 28:31). Jesus' reminder to his disciples that "I am among you as one who serves" (Luke 22:27) derives its force, in part at least, from the identity of Jesus as the "I" in the sentence, and the way in which it is given content by the surrounding narrative: according to the larger story that Luke tells, the Jesus of his Gospel is to be known as "Lord," and the table service of Jesus in his last meal with the disciples is to

---

[30] Joel B. Green, *The Gospel of Luke*, NICNT (Grand Rapids: Eerdmans, 1997), 24.

David Starling

be understood as an anticipation of the table service of the exalted Lord in his coming kingdom (Luke 22:29; cf. 12:37).[31]

Allegiance to Jesus not only as teacher and exemplar but as *Lord* had obvious and destabilizing religio-political ramifications within the Roman imperial order. To reject the worship of the gods was to tear at the fabric of culture, and to serve and proclaim Jesus as universal Lord was inevitably to collide with the propaganda of empire.[32] The early Christian gatherings may not have been hotbeds of *flagitia* or nests of insurrection, but the message that their members proclaimed and lived by still represented a fundamental challenge to the beliefs and practices of the social order. The stories that Luke gathers together, and the overarching narrative frame in which they are placed, should leave his readers entirely unsurprised if—despite the innocence and innocuousness of their intentions; despite all the ways in which their teachings and practices found points of connection with societal norms and ideals; despite all the times when the verdict may be repeated that they have committed no crime—they find themselves becoming the cause of social unrest and the objects of official prosecution. The message of Luke's story for Theophilus and his fellow-readers is not the promise of an easy and harmonious relationship with the Greco-Roman social order; on the contrary, for all its emphasis on the innocence of Jesus and his followers (even when measured by the moral norms and legal standards of the Greco-Roman establishment) Luke–Acts still functions as a warning that "it is through many persecutions that we must enter the kingdom of God" (Acts 14:22) and an invitation for readers to brace themselves and be ready for whatever may come:

> Basic to Luke's "upside down" epistemological commitments are the conviction that there really can be only one Lord of all and the corresponding sense for the necessity of a narrative whose deep structure evidences a refusal to flinch in the face of the inevitable religio-political repercussions.[33]

Of course, the narrative that grounds such a stance is not one that begins *de novo* with the birth or baptism of Jesus. From the earliest chapters of Luke's Gospel it is made clear that the story to be told is one that took place in fulfillment of patterns and promises deeply rooted in the Old Testament narrative of God's saving involvement in the life of the nation of Israel.[34] Mary's song, for example, is not only an unmistakable echo of the ancient

---

[31] See especially the discussion of "the deity who waits on tables," in H. Douglas Buckwalter, "The Divine Saviour," in Marshall and Peterson, *Witness to the Gospel: The Theology of Acts*, 120–22, and C. Kavin Rowe, *Early Narrative Christology: The Lord in the Gospel of Luke* (Grand Rapids: Baker, 2009), 151–57.

[32] See especially Rowe, *World Upside Down*, 17–51 and Seyoon Kim, *Christ and Caesar: The Gospel and the Roman Empire in the Writings of Paul and Luke* (Grand Rapids: Eerdmans, 2008), 78–90.

[33] Rowe, *World Upside Down*, 116.

[34] See the discussion in N. T. Wright, *The New Testament and the People of God* (Minneapolis: Fortress, 1992), 378–84.

116

songs of Hannah and Miriam, but also an explicit declaration that the mercies and world-reversing judgments of God in her own time are to be interpreted as instances of divine covenant-faithfulness, "according to the promises he made to our ancestors, to Abraham and his descendants forever" (Luke 1:55). This strong note of continuity with the promises and teachings of the Old Testament continues through to the final chapters of Acts, in which Paul is depicted as declaring before Agrippa that "I stand here on trial on account of my hope in the promise of God made to my ancestors" (26:6) and insisting to the Jewish leaders in Rome that "I had done nothing against our people or the customs of our ancestors" (28:17). In the eyes of his critics, too, on more than one occasion, it is the *Jewish* identity and commitments of Paul and his friends that make them suspect and alien (Acts 16:20b; 19:34).

According to the picture that Luke paints, the points of tension between early Christianity and the Greco-Roman social order were understood by both the members of the group and its critics to be attributable to the Jewish roots of the movement and its adherence to the teachings of the Old Testament. This much can be said with some confidence, even after due allowance has been made for the obvious rhetorical reasons why the Jewish roots of early Christianity would have been stressed by Luke himself and (in various situations within his story) by the followers of Jesus and their critics. But the fact that Luke's picture also includes numerous incidences of tension between the early Christians and the local Jewish communities that they encounter suggests that the relationship between the ethics of early Christianity and the ethics of the Jewish tradition was hardly understood as one of total equivalence. To explore this relationship in greater depth and closer detail, we turn in the next section of the chapter from Luke–Acts, the early Christian narrative positioned most closely to the movement's boundary with the Greco-Roman world, to the Gospel of Matthew, the narrative positioned most closely to the movement's boundary with early Judaism.

3.2. Fulfilling the Law and the Prophets: Narrative, Ethics, and Law in Matthew's Gospel

From the earliest pages of Matthew's Gospel, it is clear that this is a telling of the story of Jesus that places a heavy emphasis on its continuities with the story of Israel and with Israel's Scriptures: the opening portion of the Gospel is described as a βίβλος γενέσεως (NRSV: "an account of the genealogy"), recalling the language of LXX Gen 2:4 and 5:1; the main character is introduced as "Jesus the Messiah, the son of David, the son of Abraham"; his genealogy is constructed as a summary of Israel's story, from Abraham to David, from David to the deportation, and from the deportation to the birth of the Messiah;[35] and in the infancy narrative that follows, almost every pericope is constructed around a citation from the Old Testament, with repeated

---

[35] See especially Jason B. Hood, *The Messiah, His Brothers, and the Nations: Matthew 1.1–17*, LNTS (London: T&T Clark, 2011); Wright, *The New Testament and the People of God*, 385.

assertions that "all this took place to fulfill what had been spoken by the Lord through the prophet" (1:22, cf. 2:15, 17, 23).

Also prominent within the Gospel are emphatic assertions of ethical continuity with the teachings of the Old Testament, including the words of Jesus quoted in Matt 5:17–19:

> Do not think that I have come to abolish the law or the prophets; I have come not to abolish but to fulfill. For truly I tell you, until heaven and earth pass away, not one letter, not one stroke of a letter, will pass from the law until all is accomplished. Therefore, whoever breaks one of the least of these commandments, and teaches others to do the same, will be called least in the kingdom of heaven; but whoever does them and teaches them will be called great in the kingdom of heaven.

There is no doubt that Matthew intends the readers of his Gospel to hear the words of Jesus as a strong endorsement of the continuing authority of the Old Testament's ethical teaching. But agreeing with the Jews of his day about the authority of Scripture is not the same as agreeing about how Scripture is to be interpreted and applied. According to Matthew, the proper interpretation of Scripture requires "a scribe who has been trained for the kingdom of heaven" (13:51), and the teachings of Jesus recorded within the Gospel included numerous and vigorous instances of interpretive disagreement between Jesus and various representatives of official Judaism.

In some cases the conversations about the interpretation and application of the law that Matthew records have a character and content that could (if taken in isolation) be interpreted as nothing more than participation in the normal patterns of halakhic dispute within a common Judaism. The conversation about divorce recorded in Matt 19:3–9, for example, can sensibly be read against the background of the well-known rabbinic dispute between Hillelites and Shammaites over the proper interpretation of Deut 24:1 (though even here Matthew's introductory comment that the conversation began with a question that was asked by "some Pharisees … to test him" locates it within a larger conflict narrative that renders such an interpretation problematic).[36]

Taken as a whole, however, the pronouncements of Jesus on the interpretation of the law suggest a hermeneutical confrontation more convulsive than merely a series of contributions to an ongoing debate within an intact interpretive community. Matthew wants his readers to remember a Jesus who contrasted "you have heard that it was said" with "but I say to you" (5:21–22, 27–28, 31–32, 33–34, 38–39, 43–44), who summoned his hearers to build their lives on his words (7:24–27) and take his yoke on their shoulders (11:29),[37] and who interacted with the tradition in such a manner that "the crowds were astounded at his teaching, for he taught them as one having

---

[36] On the background to the conversation and its function within Matthew's narrative, see Ben Witherington III, *Matthew* (Macon, GA: Smyth & Helwys, 2006), 359–66.
[37] Cf. the words that are said of personified Wisdom in Sir 6:24–30; 51:26, and of the Torah in 2 Bar. 41.3.

authority, and not as their scribes" (7:28–29).[38] Nor is Jesus remembered in Matthew's Gospel solely as a teacher of the crowds or a debater with the scribes: he is also, crucially, depicted as the founder of a community that will function as a new Israel (16:18; 19:28) and inherit Israel's calling to be "the light of the world ... a city on a hill" (5:14); within this community Jesus' teachings are undisputed and his authority unquestioned. By the end of Matthew's Gospel, at the conclusion to the book's final round of public debates between Jesus and a series of delegations from the Pharisees, Herodians, and Sadducees, it is clear that the interpretive contest between Jesus and Israel's teachers has run its course: "No one was able to give him any answer, nor from that day did anyone dare to ask him any more questions" (22:46). All that remains is—on Jesus' part—a series of dark, climactic woes (23:1–39),[39] and—on the part of the chief priests, scribes, and elders—the machinations that will lead to Jesus' arrest and crucifixion (26:2, 57; 27:1).

As the founder of an eschatological remnant community—the builder of an *ekklēsia* (16:18)—and as its authoritative interpreter of Scripture, the Jesus of Matthew's Gospel has obvious similarities with the figure of the Teacher of Righteousness as he was remembered in the literature of the Qumran community (CD I, 11; 4Q171 III, 16; 1QpHab VII, 5). There are striking similarities too, at a number of points, between the contents of the ethics taught by Jesus and the ethics taught at Qumran:

> It is clear that this [i.e., the ethic expressed in the antitheses of Matthew 5] is a perfectionist ethic, and that it is sectarian in that such requirements are expressly set over against the ordinary demands of the Torah upon everyone. In similar fashion the Essenes radicalized the commandments; indeed two of these same rules appear in their literature or reports about them—they forbade both oaths and expressions of anger toward fellows.[40]

---

[38] Another revealing indication of the extent of the rift between the community of Jesus' disciples (as it is depicted in Matthew's Gospel) and the interpretive community of official Judaism is the way in which words spoken by Jesus against the way of life practiced by the Gentiles can be recycled as criticisms of the scribes and Pharisees (e.g., the parallel between 20:26 and 23:11, or the transition from 5:34–45 to 5:46–47).

[39] In this context, Jesus' words to his disciples in 23:2–3a ("The scribes and the Pharisees sit on Moses' seat; therefore, do whatever they teach you and follow it...") make best sense when read, not as a blanket endorsement of the interpretive authority of Jesus' opponents, but as an ironic foil for the instruction that follows ("... but do not do as they do, for they do not practice what they teach"). Cf. R. T. France, *The Gospel of Matthew*, NICNT (Grand Rapids: Eerdmans, 2007), 859–60.

[40] Meeks, *Moral World*, 139, citing 1QS V, 25–26; Josephus, *B.J.* 2.135; *A.J.* 15.371. It is also worth noting the close similarities between the teachings of Jesus in Matt 18:15–17 about the resolution of grievances within the community of disciples and the requirement in 1QS VI, 1 that "no man accuse his companion before the Congregation without having admonished him in the presence of witnesses." On Jesus' command to love enemies and its parallels in the Testaments of the Twelve Patriarchs (esp. T.Gad 6:7; T.Jos. 18:2), see John Piper, *"Love Your Enemies": Jesus' Love Command in the Synoptic Gospels and in the Early Christian Paraenesis*, SNTSMS 38 (Cambridge: Cambridge University Press, 1979), 43–45.

But this sort of radicalization of the demand made by the commandments is not the sum total of the approach to Torah-interpretation that Jesus teaches and models within Matthew's Gospel. The interpretation of the law that he teaches also insists that it has a focus, in the exhortations to love God and neighbor (on which "all the Law and the Prophets" depend; 22:34–40); that some matters within it—such as its calls for justice, mercy, and faith—are "weightier" than others (23:18–24); and that those who want to interpret it rightly must read it in light of YHWH's word, given through Hosea, that "I desire mercy, not sacrifice" (9:13; 12:7): "Jesus' teaching provides a dramatic new hermeneutical filter that necessitates a rereading of everything in the Law in light of the dominant imperative of mercy. In contrast to the scribes and Pharisees, who are said to 'tie up heavy burdens, hard to bear, and lay them on the shoulders of others' (23:4), the wisdom taught by Jesus yields a very different reading of Torah."[41]

Nor is the place occupied by Jesus within the moral vision of Matthew's Gospel confined to his role as the authoritative interpreter of Scripture:

> Perhaps the most important difference [between the Gospel of Matthew and the Qumran literature] is precisely in the characteristic form of the literature produced by each group. Both produce rulebooks, reinterpretations of Scripture, exhortations, apocalypses. From Qumran, however, we have no biography, no "gospel." We do not even know the name of the Righteous Teacher … The person vanishes behind the organization he founded and the interpretations of prophecy and Torah that his followers continued. Not so the Jesus of Matthew. Mark had made his story the "gospel" itself, the proclamation of the eschatological good news. Matthew makes that story part of the grammar of Christian ethics. The commandments are not separable from the commander, the teachings from the teacher. Discipleship is "following" the person identified in the story, who, raised from the dead, goes on leading the community.[42]

For the readers of Matthew's Gospel, the calling of the disciple is "to be like the teacher" (10:25), not only by being ready to endure a fate like the teacher's fate, but also by finding a way (within the changed circumstances of the post-Easter community) to imitate the teacher's conduct.[43] The resultant ethical pattern is not merely a perpetuation of the ethics of the Old Testament,

---

[41] Hays, *Moral Vision*, 100. Hays notes the fact that the pronouncement of Hos 6:6 was also given great hermeneutical prominence in the teachings of Yohanan ben Zakkai, in the aftermath of the destruction of the Jerusalem temple, but rightly stresses the very different function that it serves within the hermeneutics of Matthew's Gospel, compared with its function in the hermeneutics of Pharisaism.

[42] Meeks, *Moral World*, 143.

[43] For a long list of instances in which the teaching of Jesus in Matthew's Gospel is echoed or exemplified in his conduct, see Jason B. Hood, *Imitating God in Christ: Recapturing a Biblical Pattern* (Downers Grove, IL: IVP Academic, 2013), 77–79. For a brief discussion of the hermeneutical implications of the location of 10:24–25 within the unique circumstances of the first disciples' commissioning for their pre-Easter mission to Israel, see Meeks, *Moral World*, 141–42.

or a variant species within the genus of Second Temple Jewish interpretations of the Torah, but a genuinely new and distinctive vision of how the law and the prophets come to be fulfilled in the life of the Messiah and his people.[44] Even here, at one of the closest points of contact between the New Testament and the world of early Judaism, the remembered story of Jesus (told as the fulfillment of the story of Israel) gives a distinctive shape and center to the early Christians' moral vision.

4. The Ethics of the Epistles: 1 Corinthians and 1 Peter

If the narrative shape of the gospels was one of the crucial and distinctive ways in which they functioned to shape the ethics of their readers, can a similar distinctiveness be found when we turn our focus from the gospels to the essentially non-narrative genre of the New Testament Epistles?

According to one influential twentieth-century school of interpretation, the answer to that question is a largely negative one. Perhaps the most outspoken proponent of this viewpoint was Martin Dibelius, whose studies of the parallels between the moral teaching of the New Testament letters and the paraenetic literature of both Hellenistic Judaism and the Greco-Roman mainstream yielded the conclusion that New Testament paraenesis was, essentially, a conventional form recycling conventional content.[45] The Epistles were, according to Dibelius, "the transmitters of [the] popular ethics of antiquity."[46] A similar judgment is made by Hans Dieter Betz, in relation to the ethical instructions in the final chapters of Galatians: "Paul does not provide the Galatians with a specifically Christian ethic. The Christian is addressed as an educated and responsible person. He is expected to do no more than would be expected of any other educated person in the Hellenistic culture of the time. In a rather conspicuous way Paul conforms to the ethical thought of his contemporaries."[47]

It is certainly true that it is not difficult to find overlaps between the moral teachings of the New Testament Epistles and the vocabulary, norms, and judgments of Hellenistic Judaism and Greco-Roman popular philosophy. Paul's advice in favor of singleness as the wise response to "the present distress" (1 Cor 7:26), for example, has striking parallels in the writings of the Cynic and Stoic philosophers,[48] and his response in 1 Cor 1:10–11 to the

---

[44] On the language of "fulfilling the law and the prophets," see especially France, *The Gospel of Matthew*, 183.

[45] See especially Martin Dibelius, *A Fresh Approach to the New Testament and Early Christian Literature* (Hertford: Nicholson & Watson, 1936), 143–44, 217–20 and the discussion in Hays, *Moral Vision*, 16–19. The term "paraenesis" refers to the form of literature that strings together lists of moral instructions, often consisting of maxims derived from popular moral philosophy.

[46] Martin Dibelius, Heinrich Greeven, and Helmut Koester, *James, a Commentary on the Epistle of James*, Hermeneia (Philadelphia: Fortress, 1976), 5.

[47] Hans Dieter Betz, *Galatians: A Commentary on Paul's Letter to the Churches in Galatia* (Philadelphia: Fortress, 1979), 292.

[48] See especially Will Deming, *Paul on Marriage and Celibacy: The Hellenistic Background of 1 Corinthians 7*, 2nd ed. (Grand Rapids: Eerdmans, 2004), 169–73.

reports of quarrels and divisions within the Corinthian church is framed in language that is noticeably similar to the standard vocabulary of Greco-Roman political ethics.[49] The string of metaphors that James employs in his teaching on self-control and the tongue in James 3:2–8 (bits and bridles; ships and rudders; fire; the taming of animals) draws on a long tradition of interconnected metaphors used to discuss the mind and the passions in Hellenistic moral philosophy.[50] Elements of the vocabulary and style of Greco-Roman ethical treatises and honorific decrees are also ostentatiously present in the summons to the readers in 2 Pet 1:3–11 to add to their faith "goodness … knowledge … self-control … endurance … godliness … mutual affection, and … love," as the outworking of a salvation that makes it possible for them to "escape from the corruption that is in the world because of lust" and "become participants of the divine nature."[51]

Despite the existence of parallels such as these (and the list of examples could, of course, be multiplied) it would be a mistake to conclude that the ethical instruction in the New Testament Epistles is nothing more than an assimilation to the popular morality of the day. Nor is it an adequate explanation of the points at which the ethics of the Epistles diverge from the popular morality of the day to attribute the differences solely to the continuing influence of Jewish tradition within early Christian morality. When the moral exhortation of the Epistles is read within the context of their larger rhetorical strategy for forming the identity and conduct of the readers, a more complex picture emerges, in which the light of the Old Testament Scriptures is refracted into the world of the readers through the interpretive lens of the basic Christian convictions about the action of God in Christ and in the sending of the Spirit. The resultant moral vision has significant overlaps with both Jewish tradition and Greco-Roman morality, but its overall shape and inner logic derive from a distinctively Christian hermeneutic. For the purposes of this chapter we will focus on two examples as case studies in the hermeneutical roots of the ethics taught in the Epistles.

4.1. Called to be Saints: Ethics and Hermeneutics in 1 Corinthians

It is clear from the very beginning of Paul's first letter to the Corinthians that he wishes his readers to understand themselves as a community whose way of life ought to contrast with that of their neighbors—according to the language of the letter's greeting, they are "the church of God that is in Corinth …

---

[49] See J. B. Lightfoot, *Notes on Epistles of St Paul from Unpublished Commentaries* (London: Macmillan, 1895), 151 (citing instances from Thucydides, Aristotle, and Polybius) and Margaret Mary Mitchell, *Paul and the Rhetoric of Reconciliation: An Exegetical Investigation of the Language and Composition of 1 Corinthians* (Tübingen: Mohr Siebeck, 1991), 68–80.
[50] See the survey of parallels and the discussion of the complexities of James's use of the traditional metaphors in Dibelius, Greeven, and Koester, *James*, 184–201.
[51] See especially Frederick W. Danker, "2 Peter 1: A Solemn Decree," *CBQ* 40 (1978): 64–82; Ben Witherington, *Letters and Homilies for Hellenized Christians*, 2 vols. (Downers Grove, IL: InterVarsity, 2007), 2:297–314.

sanctified in Christ Jesus, called to be saints" (1:2). This emphasis is pervasive throughout the letter: the wisdom that they are to learn and live by is "not a wisdom of this age or of the rulers of this age" (2:6); the Spirit they have received is "not the spirit of the world" (2:12); they are to take their disputes for judgment not to "the unrighteous" but to "the saints" (6:1); the life they once lived they are to live no longer (6:11); the spirituality they once prized is now to be replaced by a radically different pattern of worship (12:2); "good morals" must not be ruined by "bad company" (15:31).

The distinction that Paul expects between the values and conduct of the church and those of the surrounding city does not amount to a total disjunction, without any points of overlap or connection; nor does Paul describe the pattern of life his readers are called to in terms that render irrelevant the categories and symbols of conventional Greco-Roman morality. The very saying Paul quotes in 15:33 to warn against the ruinous effects of "bad company" (i.e., that of the Greco-Roman mainstream) on Christian morals is borrowed, perhaps with a touch of conscious irony, from the Greek proverbial tradition;[52] the disgracefulness of the sexual conduct that Paul describes in 5:1 is amplified by the fact that it is "of a kind that is not even found among the pagans";[53] the advice Paul gives in 11:2–16 presupposes the meaningfulness of a cultural code within which the presence or absence of a head covering could be interpreted, and a universally accessible message taught by "nature itself" to Christians and their non-Christian neighbors alike. But even here, when Paul is arguing for the maintenance of a conventional system of gender symbols and appealing to "nature" in support of his appeal, the argument is still framed by unashamedly particularist appeals to "the traditions just as I handed them on to you" (v. 2) and the "practice … [of] the churches" (v. 16). The shape of the relationship between husbands and wives that Paul wants to see symbolized within the assembly is described by analogy with the relationship between God and Christ (v. 3) and supported by multiple appeals to the Genesis creation narratives (vv. 7–12), which function as a canonical lens through which the ambiguities and complexities of "nature" are to be interpreted.[54] While Paul assumes at a number of points within the letter that there will be some overlap between the church's vision of what is

---

[52] It can also be found in the playwright Menander's comedy *Thaïs* (frag. 187).

[53] Cf. the discussion in David G. Horrell, *Solidarity and Difference: A Contemporary Reading of Paul's Ethics* (London: T&T Clark, 2005), 153–63. The NRSV translation of the phrase, quoted here, follows most of the EVV in supplying "found." The NIV11, following some commentators—e.g., Anthony C. Thiselton, *The First Epistle to the Corinthians: A Commentary on the Greek Text* (Grand Rapids: Eerdmans, 2000), 384–86—instead supplies "tolerate[d]," on the basis that incestuous liaisons like the one in Corinth were certainly found in Greco-Roman culture, but were not generally approved of. The NRSV is to be preferred as closer to the original: whilst it is unlikely that Paul is claiming this sort of incest is not *ever* found among their non-Christian neighbors, it is reasonable to allow him a little hyperbole in pointing out to the Corinthians that sexual immorality this depraved is not even part of the (normal, customary) way of life of the Greco-Roman mainstream.

[54] Cf. the discussion of the interpretive relationship between appeals to "nature" and allusions to the creation narratives in Charles Anderson, "If It's Natural, Then Do It: Creation and Ethics in 1 Corinthians," Tyndale New Testament Lecture, 2014.

"proper" (and, conversely, what is "shameful") and that of their neighbors, there is no suggestion that his advice on how Christians should see things is offered merely as a pragmatic accommodation to mainstream Greco-Roman values.

Much of the difference between the ethical perspective that Paul commends to the Corinthians and the ethics of the Greco-Roman mainstream can be attributed to the continuing role that Paul gives to the Scriptures of Israel in shaping the mind and conduct of Christian believers. In chapters 1–4, Paul's assault on the "puffed up" mindset of the aspiring elite within the Corinthian churches is undergirded by repeated appeals to Scripture, summed up in a call to "learn ... the meaning of the saying, 'Nothing beyond what is written'" (4:6).[55] While the density of explicit scriptural citations diminishes a little in chapters 5–7, the collection of advice and admonitions that Paul offers in response to the string of reports and questions about sexual conduct, financial disputes, celibacy, and marriage is still deeply informed by the stories, symbols, and commandments of Scripture.[56] The same can be said of the answer that he offers in chapters 8–10 to the Corinthians' questions about temple feasts and food offered to idols,[57] his response in chapters 11–14 to their questions about spirituality and worship,[58] and his climactic rebuttal in chapter 15 of "[those who] say there is no resurrection of the dead" (15:12).[59] A basic conviction informing all of Paul's ethical instruction is that the people of Israel were "our ancestors" (10:1), and that the scriptural accounts of God's dealings with them were "written down to instruct us" (10:11).[60]

Pervasive as its influence is, scriptural tradition alone is not enough to explain the particular shape that Paul's ethical instruction within the letter takes; equally crucial for both the method and the content of Paul's teaching is the interpretive framework within which he reads the Scriptures and applies them to the questions that he addresses. Within chapters 1–4, for example, Paul's appeals to Scripture are embedded within a reminder and exposition of "the mystery of God ... Jesus Christ, and him crucified" (2:1–2) and directed toward a summons to imitate "my ways in Christ Jesus, as I teach them

---

[55] See especially J. Ross Wagner, "'Not Beyond the Things Which are Written': A Call to Boast Only in the Lord (1 Cor 4.6)," *NTS* 44 (1998): 279–87, and David I. Starling, "'Nothing Beyond What is Written'? First Corinthians and the Hermeneutics of Early Christian *Theologia*," *JTI* 8 (2014): 51–55.
[56] See especially Brian S. Rosner, *Paul, Scripture and Ethics: A Study of 1 Corinthians 5–7* (Leiden: Brill, 1994), 177–94. For a more ambitious (but less carefully argued) proposal regarding the extent of pentateuchal influence on the language and ideas of 1 Corinthians, see Thomas L. Brodie, "The Systematic Use of the Pentateuch in 1 Corinthians," in *The Corinthian Correspondence*, ed. Reimund Bieringer (Leuven: Leuven University Press, 1996).
[57] See Starling, "Nothing Beyond What is Written?" 55–58.
[58] See Roy E. Ciampa and Brian S. Rosner, *The First Letter to the Corinthians*, PNTC (Grand Rapids: Eerdmans, 2010), 599–735.
[59] Starling, "Nothing Beyond What is Written?" 58–61.
[60] See especially Richard B. Hays, "Ecclesiology and Ethics in 1 Corinthians," *ExAud* 10 (1994): 36–41 and Richard B. Hays, *The Conversion of the Imagination: Paul as Interpreter of Israel's Scripture* (Grand Rapids: Eerdmans, 2005), 1–24.

everywhere in every church" (4:17);[61] the ethical outworking of this cross-centered interpretive framework is a frontal assault on the agonistic value-system of Greco-Roman leadership culture that is without parallel in the extant literature of Second Temple Judaism.[62] Within chapters 8–10, similarly, while the creational monotheism of the Old Testament is foundational for the "knowledge" that Paul summarizes in 8:4–6 as the starting point of the discussion, and the ethical teaching of the Torah is not forgotten in the chapters that follow (e.g., 9:9; 10:1–12), the larger shape of Paul's argument is determined not by the demands of Torah but by the pattern of the cross,[63] and focused on a summons to "be imitators of me, as I am of Christ" (11:1).[64] And at the climax of the letter, in chapter 15, Paul's urgent appeal to the Corinthians to resist "bad company" and preserve "good morals" is not so much a call to comply with the requirements of the Mosaic law as it is a summons to live in the light of the resurrection.[65] Taken as a whole, the moral vision that Paul commends to the Corinthians within the letter, while grounded in the Scriptures of the Old Testament and coinciding at a number of points with the ethics of the Greco-Roman mainstream, is explicitly and emphatically centered on the core Christian traditions concerning the death and resurrection of Jesus, which are urged upon the readers as requiring a way of life that is distinctive to the Christian community.

4.2. As Aliens and Exiles: Ethics and Hermeneutics in 1 Peter

The ethical teaching of 1 Peter, like that of 1 Corinthians, is framed as a summons to a new and distinctive way of life, befitting the readers' shared identity as a chosen, holy people. The readers are addressed as people who have been "sanctified by the spirit to be obedient to Jesus Christ" (1:2) and encouraged to view themselves as "a chosen race, a royal priesthood, a holy

---

[61] See especially Raymond Pickett, *The Cross in Corinth: The Social Significance of the Death of Jesus*, JSNTSup 143 (Sheffield: Sheffield Academic, 1997), 37–84.

[62] Note also the way in which Paul's use of the body metaphor in chapter 12 subverts the traditional uses of the *topos* within the Greco-Roman political literature; cf. Dale B. Martin, *The Corinthian Body* (New Haven: Yale University Press, 1995), 38–68. The fact that both passages within the letter are framed as an assault *against* practices and attitudes that were endemic within the church in Corinth—together with the evidence of 1 Clement, which would suggest that similar attitudes and practices were still alive and well nearly half a century later—should warn us against any facile equation between the ethical stance advocated by the writers of the New Testament and "the ethics of the earliest Christians."

[63] Note, for example, Paul's insistence in 9:20–21 that he himself is "not under the law ... but ... under Christ's law." For a useful discussion of the broader question of how the Old Testament law functions within Paul's ethical teaching, see Brian S. Rosner, *Paul and the Law: Keeping the Commandments of God*, NSBT (Downers Grove, IL: IVP Academic, 2013).

[64] Thus, the account that Paul offers in 8:7–9:27 of how the knowledge summarized in 8:4–6 is to be used in love is articulated in terms of practices and attitudes that involve becoming "a slave to all" (9:19), treating one's brother or sister as a person "for whom Christ died" (8:11), and doing all things "for the sake of the gospel" (9:23). Cf. Starling, "Nothing Beyond What is Written?" 55–56, Meeks, *Moral World*, 130–36.

[65] Starling, "Nothing Beyond What is Written?" 58–62.

nation, God's own people" (2:9). This identity, they are reminded, calls for a radical departure from the conduct and desires that characterized their pre-conversion existence: "Like obedient children, do not be conformed to the desires that you formerly had in ignorance. Instead, as he who called you is holy, be holy yourselves in all your conduct; for it is written, 'You shall be holy, for I am holy'" (1:14–16; cf. 1:18; 2:1–2; 4:3). In this respect the two letters possess obvious similarities.

But while Paul's reminders and reproaches in 1 Corinthians are directed to a church that was, in his view, dangerously comfortable within its social environment,[66] the addressees of 1 Peter are represented within the letter as occupying a starkly different situation.[67] This is a letter addressed to "exiles of the Dispersion" (1:1),[68] from a writer who is deeply conscious of the "various trials" that they are suffering (1:5), including not only the ordinary trials of life but also the particular hostility and ridicule that are directed at them because of their identity as Christians (4:16; cf. 3:17; 4:4, 14).

Within that context, the letter's ethical exhortations are frequently coupled with an explicit statement of the apologetic function that they are intended to serve: "Conduct yourselves honorably among the Gentiles, so that, though they malign you as evildoers, they may see your honorable deeds and glorify God when he comes to judge" (2:12); "for it is God's will that by doing right you should silence the ignorance of the foolish" (2:15); "wives ... accept the authority of your husbands, so that, even if some of them do not obey the word, they may be won over without a word by their wives' conduct, when they see the purity and reverence of your lives" (3:1–2); "Who will harm you if you are eager to do what is good?" (3:13); "Keep your conscience clear, so that, when you are maligned, those who abuse you for your good conduct in Christ may be put to shame" (3:16).

In some of these instances (2:13–14; 3:1) the particular pattern of behavior that is being advocated is one of submission to the various authorities of the established social order.[69] In others, however, the scope of the exhortation is

---

[66] John M. G. Barclay, "Thessalonica and Corinth: Social Contrasts in Pauline Christianity," *JSNT* 47 (1992): 56–72.

[67] See especially Karen H. Jobes, *1 Peter*, BECNT (Grand Rapids: Baker, 2005), 8–10, 42–44, and John H. Elliott, *A Home for the Homeless: A Sociological Exegesis of 1 Peter, its Situation and Strategy* (Philadelphia: Fortress, 1981).

[68] While there is every likelihood that some of the letter's recipients would have been among the many in the province who had experienced a literal geographical displacement (see Jobes, *1 Peter*, 28–41; Elliott, *A Home for the Homeless*, 24–27), the Babylon typology of 5:13 and the reference to "the time of your exile" in 1:17 (read in the light of the eschatological context established in 1:3–7, 13, 21) suggest that the exile language in 1:1 functions primarily as a metaphor for the social alienation experienced by the readers under the powers of the present age, as they wait for the salvation of the age to come.

[69] At this level of the letter's social ethics there are obvious similarities between the "reverent fear" (φόβος) counseled in 1 Peter (e.g., 1:17; 2:18; 3:2) and the typical formulations of traditional Greco-Roman moral philosophy, e.g., the summary of the social duties taught by philosophy, in Pseudo-Plutarch, *On the Education of Children*, 10: "how a man must bear himself in his relations with the gods, with his parents, with his elders, with the laws, with strangers, with those in authority, with friends, with women, with children, with servants; that one ought to reverence the gods, to honour one's parents, to respect one's elders, to be obedient

broader: believers are being exhorted to devote themselves to "honorable deeds" (2:12: καλὰ ἔργα) and to be "eager to do what is good" (3:13: τοῦ ἀγαθοῦ ζηλωταὶ γένησθε)—language that implies both abstention from private vices (2:11–12) and, where opportunity permitted, participation in acts of public benevolence (2:14).[70]

The hope expressed within the letter that the conduct of its readers will be perceived as "honorable" should not be taken as implying that the codes of honor and value that pertained within the empire of Rome are simply being absorbed uncritically into the ethics of the letter; within the moral vision of the letter, the inclusion of the shamed and suffering figure of the crucified Jesus—now risen and glorified—at the center of Christian faith and devotion (1:2, 21; 5:10, 14) has the effect of radically recalibrating the scale of values on which honor and preciousness are to be measured.[71]

This emphasis emerges as early in the letter as 1:10–11, where the readers are told that "the Spirit of Christ" testified through the prophets to "the sufferings destined for Christ and the subsequent glory." The connection between suffering and glory is expressed in 1:11 as a sequential one (τὰ εἰς Χριστὸν παθήματα καὶ τὰς μετὰ ταῦτα δόξας) but its representation takes on more complexity in 1:18–19, where the blood of Christ's crucifixion—through Roman eyes, a badge of almost unutterable shame and ugliness—is depicted as "precious" (τίμιος), in the retrospective light of the divine verdict of glorification that is referred to in verse 21. The same language of "preciousness" recurs in the following paragraph, where the crucified and resurrected Jesus is described as "a living stone, though rejected by mortals yet chosen and precious in God's sight" (2:4)—a description that is supported by a citation in verse 6 from Isa 28:16 that speaks of "a cornerstone chosen and precious," laid by God in Zion.

This representation of the crucified Christ as "chosen and precious" to God carries implications of chosenness, beauty, and preciousness for those who are associated with him—including the humble, the powerless, and the persecuted. This connection is anticipated in the opening verse of the letter, which addresses the readers as "chosen," and in 1:7, where their faith in the midst of sufferings is depicted as "more precious than gold." The link between "living stone" and "living stones" is made explicit in 2:4–5, and its

---

to the laws, to yield to those in authority, to love one's friends, to be chaste with women, to be affectionate with children, and not to be overbearing with slaves." ET: Plutarch, *Plutarch's Moralia*, trans. Frank Cole Babbitt, 14 vols., LCL (Cambridge, MA: Harvard University Press, 1927). Even in this dimension of the letter's ethics, however, there is distinctively Christian shape given to the φόβος that Christians are to demonstrate in their social relationships, and a distinctively Christian set of warrants given for why the readers are to adopt this posture. See the discussion in David I. Starling, "'She Who is in Babylon': 1 Peter and the Hermeneutics of Empire," in *Reactions to Empire: Sacred Texts in Their Socio-Political Contexts*, ed. John Anthony Dunne and Dan Batovici (Tübingen: Mohr Siebeck, 2014), 115–19.

[70] Starling, "She Who is in Babylon," 122–24, cf. Bruce W. Winter, *Seek the Welfare of the City: Christians as Benefactors and Citizens* (Grand Rapids: Eerdmans, 1994), 21–23, 26–40.

[71] The material in the following paragraphs is adapted from Starling, "She Who is in Babylon," 125–27.

implication for the "precious[ness]" of the readers is spelt out in 2:7 (reading ὑμῖν ... ἡ τιμή as referring, not to the status of Christ in the estimation of the readers, but to the status of the readers in their association with Christ).[72]

The most obvious implication that is drawn from this line of connection within the letter is for the way in which the readers are to regard the sufferings that they undergo—the pattern of "sufferings and subsequent glory" established in 1:11 recurs across the rest of the letter (4:13–16; 5:1, 10) and is extended to the sufferings and disgrace of those who "bear this name" (4:16). But suffering and persecution are not the only points at which the readers' social experience is to be interpreted and evaluated according to a scale of honor that has been recalibrated in the light of the story of Christ. Wives are told in 3:4 that "a gentle and quiet spirit" constitutes "unfading beauty" that is "very precious [πολυτελές] in God's sight,"[73] and husbands are urged to give "honor" (τιμή) to their wives (3:4) precisely on account of their weaker position. The unjust punishments experienced by slaves are depicted, not only as a matter of shame and suffering that will one day be reversed by the honor that they will share with Christ, but also as an expression of a decision on their part to defer to their masters' authority—a stance of submission and endurance that is valorized in 2:20 as carrying great honor (κλέος) in God's sight.[74] The extended citation of Isaiah 53 that follows is presented not only as an example to be imitated but also as a proof that those who do so "have God's approval" (verse 20)—presumably a conclusion drawn from the references to divine exaltation and glorification that frame the fourth servant song (Isa 52:13; 53:3–4, 12).

The fact that God is depicted within the letter, not as the private deity of Christians, but as the creator of all the world (1 Pet 2:13; 4:19) goes some way toward explaining the author's confidence that there is the possibility of a kind of commensurability between the values of the church and those of the surrounding culture.[75] If beauty, honor, and preciousness are ultimately to be measured by how things appear "in the sight of God" (2:4, 5, 20; 3:4), then the countercultural value system according to which things are measured in the letter is commended to the readers, not merely as the private morality and aesthetics of a sectarian community, but as the way things really are. What is beautiful in the sight of God is—at least in principle—discoverable as beautiful by all who have eyes to see (cf. 2:12; 3:1–2).

---

[72] Cf. Paul J. Achtemeier and Eldon Jay Epp, *1 Peter: A Commentary on First Peter*, Hermeneia (Minneapolis: Fortress, 1996), 160–61.

[73] See the comments on πολυτελές and its function within the discourse of status and honor in John H. Elliott, *1 Peter: A New Translation with Introduction and Commentary*, Anchor Bible (New York: Doubleday, 2000), 568; Barth L. Campbell, *Honor, Shame and the Rhetoric of 1 Peter*, SBLDS 160 (Atlanta: Scholars, 1998), 157.

[74] For a discussion of the heroic connotations of κλέος and its function within the lexicon of honor, see J. E. Lendon, *Empire of Honour: The Art of Government in the Roman World* (Oxford: Clarendon, 1997), 277.

[75] Miroslav Volf, "Soft Difference: Theological Reflections on the Relation between Church and Culture in 1 Peter," *ExAud* 10 (1994): 26.

5. The Ethics of the Apocalypse

Turning from the exhortation and advice-giving of the Epistles to the apocalyptic visions of the book of Revelation involves a jolting change of genre. There are obvious apocalyptic elements within the Epistles (e.g., the programmatic contrast in 1 Cor 2:6–7 between the "secret and hidden" wisdom of God and the wisdom of "the rulers of this age, who are doomed to perish," and the reminder in 1 Pet 4:7 that "the end of all things is near," which functions as a basic premise for the instruction and encouragement in the remainder of the chapter). There are also epistolary elements within the book of Revelation (e.g., the greeting in 1:4 and the letters in chapters 2–3).[76] Yet there remains an unmistakable difference between the rhetorical strategies that are employed within the two kinds of communication to shape the moral vision of their recipients and influence their patterns of behavior. The letters in Revelation 2–3 are, after all, not presented as being from John to the churches but from "him who holds the seven stars in his right hand" (2:1; cf. the similar descriptions in 2:8, 12, 18; 3:1, 7, 14) to "the angel[s]" of the various churches, and within the letters and the surrounding vision-reports there is not a trace of the kind of dialogue or argumentation to be found (for example) in Paul's correspondence with the Corinthians (e.g., 1 Cor 5:9–13; 7:1; 10:15; 15:35–49).

Hand in hand with the difference of genre between the Epistles and the Apocalypse comes a corresponding difference of perspective. Those who hear the visions described in Revelation are encouraged to interpret their world within a series of stark, opposing contrasts, with little if any explicit allowance made for the complexities and shades of gray that are encountered within the details of daily experience. Like the readers of 1 Peter they are being taught to view Rome as "Babylon" (Revelation 18–19; cf. 1 Pet 5:13), but there is nothing within the visions that functions as an equivalent to 1 Peter's balancing demands that they "honor the emperor" (2:17), "accept the authority of every human institution" (2:13), and, in their social relationships with those outside the church, "seek peace and pursue it" (3:11); one day, they are told, "the kings of the earth will bring their glory into [the new Jerusalem]" (21:24), but in the meantime they are given no encouragement to expect anything from the authorities but persecution, seduction, and pressure

---

[76] "Apocalyptic" refers properly to a particular corpus of early Jewish writings: "a genre of revelatory literature with a narrative framework, in which a revelation is mediated by an otherworldly being to a human recipient ... envisag[ing] eschatological salvation and involv[ing] a supernatural world ... intended to interpret present earthly circumstances in light of the supernatural world and of the future, and to influence both the understanding and the behavior of the audience by means of divine authority." John J. Collins, "Early Jewish Apocalypticism," in *Anchor Bible Dictionary*, ed. David Noel Freedman (New York: Doubleday, 1992), 1.282. More broadly, and by extension, the adjective "apocalyptic" can also be used with reference to the literary and theological aspects of many other texts from early Judaism and early Christianity that share an affinity of outlook with these apocalyptic writings. See the discussion of 1 Corinthians in B. J. Oropeza, "Echoes of Isaiah in the Rhetoric of Paul: New Exodus, Wisdom and the Humility of the Cross in Utopian-Apocalyptic Expectations," in *The Intertexture of Apocalyptic Discourse*, ed. Duane F. Watson (Atlanta: Scholars, 2002), 87–112.

to conform to a false, idolatrous order. Like the readers of 1 Corinthians, they are warned against fornication and idol-feasts (2:14, 20; cf. 1 Cor 10:6–22), but they are offered nothing like the careful parsing of the complexities of motive and circumstance with which Paul precedes and follows the warning in 1 Cor 8:1–13 and 10:23–33. Richard Hays's summary of the intended function of the letters to the churches in Revelation 2–3 is apt:

> The overall message of the seven letters is to call for sharper boundaries between the church and the world. Those who advocate eating idol-food apparently think that they can blend in as "normal" members of their society; perhaps some even argue that Christians can accommodate the emperor cult as a civic obligation without betraying their faith in Jesus. Against such thinking, John sounds an alarm. It is no accident that the letter to Laodicea comes as the climax of this section. There can be no compromise, John insists, and the church that thinks it can live comfortably within the empire's economic system is in spiritual danger.[77]

The book of Revelation's call for sharpened boundaries between the church and the surrounding world, and its encouragement to resist the demands of an idolatrous empire, even to the point of martyrdom, suggest obvious affinities with traditional Jewish ideologies of separation and resistance. The language that is used to describe "the synagogue[s] of Satan who say they are Jews and are not" (2:9; 3:9) suggests a situation in which the churches are being urged to be, if anything, *more* zealously committed to this ideology than are the synagogues whose members "slander" them.[78] The descriptions in 9:20–21, 21:8, and 22:15 of those who are condemned and excluded by the divine judgment draw freely on the stereotypical Jewish depictions of Gentile vices,[79] implying a substantial overlap of moral norms between John and his Jewish forebears and contemporaries.

The theopolitical vision that informs those norms is likewise one that suggests obvious parallels within Second Temple Judaism. Adela Yarbro Collins comments:

> Given a situation of persecution a variety of responses are possible. One might decide to write an apology for the Christian faith rather than an apocalypse. The fact that the author chose to write an apocalypse and one which involves such a thoroughgoing attack on the authority of Rome is an indication that he

---

[77] Hays, *Moral Vision*, 177. Cf. the similar observations in Meeks, *Moral World*, 147.

[78] On the reconstruction of the likely background to these verses, see David A. deSilva, *Seeing Things John's Way: The Rhetoric of the Book of Revelation* (Louisville, KY: Westminster John Knox, 2009), 55–58.

[79] E.g., Wisd 14:22–29; Sib. Or. 2.254–82. Note, however, the way in which the inclusion of "cowards" within the list in 21:8 operates in contrast with "those who conquer" (v. 7) to imply a specifically Christian characterization of the vice of cowardice as a failure to persevere in solidarity with the risen Jesus and his people. Cf. the discussion in Grant R. Osborne, *Revelation*, BECNT (Grand Rapids: Baker, 2002), 740–41.

shared the fundamental theological principle of the Zealots: that the kingdom of God is incompatible with the kingdom of Caesar.[80]

But the politics of Revelation is not identical in all respects with the politics of Zealotry, or even with the gentler politics of those apocalyptic texts that urge passive resistance over armed resistance; nor is the martyrdom for which it urges its readers to brace themselves identical in meaning to the martyrdoms described and commended in the Second Temple Jewish literature.[81] This is a revelation "of Jesus Christ" (1:1); the heavenly vision is one in which the throne of divine sovereignty has at its center a slaughtered lamb (5:6; 7:17); the redeemed are "those who follow the Lamb wherever he goes" (14:4), and they overcome "by the blood of the Lamb and by the word of their testimony" (12:11). This is not mere empty symbolism—the pasting of an occasional Christian icon onto an otherwise unaltered Jewish apocalyptic schema. The worship of the Lamb plays a formative role in shaping the ethics of the apocalypse. A revealing instance of this can be seen in the solemn warning of 13:10: "If you are to be taken captive, into captivity you go; if you kill with the sword with the sword you must be killed." Here, as Hays points out, the call for "the endurance and faith of the saints" is framed as a summons to follow in the steps of Jesus and in obedience to his teaching.[82]

6. Conclusion

In each of the texts surveyed within this chapter, significant overlaps have been apparent between the ethics of early Christianity and the respective ethical frameworks of the Jewish tradition and the Greco-Roman world. In some texts (e.g., Luke–Acts and 1 Peter), explicit emphasis is placed upon the points of common ground between the moral norms that shaped the behavior of the early Christians and the criteria by which their neighbors and social superiors made judgments about guilt and innocence, honor, and shame. In other texts (e.g., Matthew and Revelation), there is an obvious continuity with Jewish traditions of Torah-interpretation (in the case of Matthew) and ideologies of resistance to empire (in the case of Revelation). But in none of the texts surveyed is there a vision for the shape of the moral life that is identical with either Jewish tradition on the one hand or popular morality on

---

[80] Adela Yarbro Collins, "The Political Perspective of the Revelation to John," *JBL* 96 (1977): 252.

[81] E.g., 2 and 4 Maccabees, and As. Mos. 9.

[82] Hays, *Moral Vision*, 185, 179; cf. G. B. Caird, *A Commentary on the Revelation of St. John the Divine*, HNTC (New York: Harper & Row, 1966), 169–70. Hays (along with the translators of the NRSV) opts for the better-attested reading of 13:10b (εἴ τις ἐν μαχαίρῃ ἀποκτείνει, δεῖ αὐτὸν ἐν μαχαίρῃ ἀποκτανθῆναι) over the thinly-attested reading adopted by the UBS[4] editors (εἴ τις ἐν μαχαίρῃ ἀποκτανθῆναι αὐτὸν ἐν μαχαίρῃ ἀποκτανθῆναι), arguing that it is more likely a copyist would have altered the former reading to the latter in order to conform it to the original wording in Jeremiah than that a copyist would have altered the latter to the former under the influence of Matt 26:52.

the other; in every instance, the moral norms articulated or implied by the text show the imprint of distinctively Christian devotional practices and beliefs, centered on the story of the crucified and risen Jesus. Worship of Jesus as the risen Lord implies an allegiance to him and a commitment to his teachings that relativizes all other political authorities and ethical norms. The fact that it is the *crucified* Jesus who is confessed as Lord gives a sharp focus to the contrast between the ethics of the early Christians and those of their Jewish counterparts and of the Greco-Roman mainstream, radically challenging traditional hierarchies of status and honor, and valorizing non-retaliation, love of enemies, humble service, and the patient endurance of shameful sufferings.

The fact that the ethics of the earliest Christians were shaped by a dynamic of this sort goes a long way toward explaining the puzzled ambivalence of Pliny and his peers toward a movement that was (viewed from a distance, and from a great height) distastefully novel and potentially threatening, yet (on closer inspection) surprisingly innocent and strikingly reminiscent of its Judean roots. Their assessment of the movement is exactly the sort of response one would expect from observers in their position toward a way of life shaped by such a vision. Then, as now, authentic confession of the Christian gospel calls for a way of life that has deep roots in Old Testament tradition and obvious points of contact with the common knowledge and experience of humanity, but can never be easily comprehended by an outside observer, nor smoothly harmonized with the existing social order.

Recommended Reading

DeSilva, David Arthur. *Seeing Things John's Way: The Rhetoric of the Book of Revelation.* Louisville, KY: Westminster John Knox, 2009.

Hays, Richard B. *The Moral Vision of the New Testament: Community, Cross, New Creation: A Contemporary Introduction to New Testament Ethics.* San Francisco: Harper, 1996.

Hood, Jason B. *Imitating God in Christ: Recapturing a Biblical Pattern.* Downers Grove, IL: IVP Academic, 2013.

Horrell, David G. *Solidarity and Difference: A Contemporary Reading of Paul's Ethics.* London: T&T Clark, 2005.

Kim, Seyoon. *Christ and Caesar: The Gospel and the Roman Empire in the Writings of Paul and Luke.* Grand Rapids: Eerdmans, 2008.

Matera, Frank J. *New Testament Ethics: The Legacies of Jesus and Paul.* Louisville, KY: Westminster John Knox, 1996.

Meeks, Wayne A. *The Moral World of the First Christians.* Philadelphia: Westminster, 1986.

Pickett, Raymond. *The Cross in Corinth: The Social Significance of the Death of Jesus.* JSNTSup 143. Sheffield: Sheffield Academic, 1997.

Pregeant, Russell. *Knowing Truth, Doing Good: Engaging New Testament Ethics.* Minneapolis: Fortress, 2008.

Rowe, Christopher Kavin. *World Upside Down: Reading Acts in the Graeco-Roman Age.* Oxford: Oxford University Press, 2009.

Volf, Miroslav. "Soft Difference: Theological Reflections on the Relation between Church and Culture in 1 Peter." *ExAud* 10 (1994): 15–30.

Winter, Bruce W. *After Paul Left Corinth: The Influence of Secular Ethics and Social Change*. Grand Rapids: Eerdmans, 2001.

5. Jewish Christianity to AD 100[*]

Paul McKechnie

1. The Jerusalem Spring

When Peter spoke on the day of Pentecost, in the year when Jesus died, to a festival crowd of Jewish pilgrims to Jerusalem from everywhere,[1] the sermon, so Acts says, made a great impression on the crowd:

> Those who welcomed his message were baptized, and that day about three thousand persons were added. They devoted themselves to the apostles' teaching and fellowship, to the breaking of bread and the prayers (Acts 2:41–42).

In the previous chapter of Acts, the number of believers had been about a hundred and twenty (Acts 1:15). And although most of the three thousand new believers must have left Jerusalem when the festival was over, Peter and others went on preaching and became a distinctive element on the Jerusalem scene. At Solomon's Portico in the Temple, after the attempt by the high-priestly Annas family to investigate the incident of the man lame from birth had been brought to a standstill (Acts 3:1–4:22), they were admired but aloof (Acts 5:12–13), and "more than ever believers were added to the Lord, great numbers of both men and women" (Acts 5:14).

Gerhard Lohfink observed that at this point in Acts, Luke had picked out from what was, on balance, the negative history of the church in Jerusalem, a

---

[*] I wish to thank Professor Richard Bauckham and my hosts at Ridley Hall, Cambridge (Michaelmas Term, 2014) for discussing parts of this chapter with me, and I wish to thank an anonymous referee for valuable suggestions. None of the above should be blamed for the chapter's faults.
[1] Acts 2:9–11: "Parthians, Medes, Elamites, and residents of Mesopotamia, Judea and Cappadocia, Pontus and Asia, Phrygia and Pamphylia, Egypt and the parts of Libya belonging to Cyrene, and visitors from Rome, both Jews and proselytes, Cretans and Arabs...." I am not inclined to read "devout Jews from every nation under heaven living in Jerusalem" (Acts 2:5, ἐν Ἰερουσαλὴμ κατοικοῦντες Ἰουδαῖοι, ἄνδρες εὐλαβεῖς ἀπὸ παντὸς ἔθνους τῶν ὑπὸ τὸν οὐρανόν) as indicating that most of the people referred to were ordinarily resident in Jerusalem: James D. G. Dunn addresses this point with admirable subtlety (*Beginning from Jerusalem* [Grand Rapids and Cambridge: Eerdmans, 2009], 169) when he characterizes the crowd "not (only as) pilgrims attending the feast from abroad."

period that Lohfink called "a kind of Jerusalem spring."[2] Joseph B. Tyson cites this phrase in the course of commenting on the scholarly disagreement (which he instantiates by contrasting the views of Jacob Jervell and Jack T. Sanders) over whether Luke–Acts is a pro-Jewish or anti-Jewish text.[3] Lohfink's point, however, is to argue that Luke has narrated all this success for Jesus' followers in the first five chapters of Acts, whereas the word "church" (ἐκκλησία) appears for the first time at 5:11, in the chapter where "Luke ends the actual representation of the 'bringing-together of Israel'":[4] he sees a divergence from chapter 6 onwards.

In Luke's Gospel, more than elsewhere, it is made clear that Jesus' planning included sending his disciples to preach. He told them that repentance and forgiveness of sins should be preached to all nations, beginning from Jerusalem (Luke 24:47). Earlier, he had sent seventy of his followers to travel ahead of him to towns and places where he intended to go, to heal the sick and tell the people that the kingdom of heaven had come near them (Luke 10:1–12).[5] Not that this is the whole story: somehow when Paul reached Ephesus, years later, he found about twelve disciples who had received John's baptism but not heard of the Holy Spirit (Acts 19:4). The impact of what John and Jesus said reverberated: the Ephesus twelve were probably pilgrims who had heard John preach in Judea, as the three thousand had heard Peter at Pentecost.

The principal business of this chapter will be a concise examination of the Nazarene church in Jerusalem and the Land of Israel, together with the mission work undertaken by Jesus' family in Galilee, and further north into the province of Syria.

2. A Contested Category

From the year when Jesus died, or earlier if one counts John's disciples as effectively belonging to Jesus (it seems Paul was ready to), Jesus' Jewish followers were lively, and increasing in numbers. They referred to themselves and their movement—or others did—by using a number of terms:[6] "the Way" (also "the Way of the Lord" and "the Way of God");[7] "the saints";[8] "the

---

[2] Gerhard Lohfink, *Die Sammlung Israels: eine Untersuchung zur lukanischen Ekklesiologie* (Munich: Kösel, 1975), 55.

[3] Joseph B. Tyson, "Jews and Judaism in Luke–Acts: Reading as a Godfearer," *NTS* 41 (1995): 19–38 (19–22).

[4] Lohfink, *Sammlung Israels*, 56: "bringing-together of Israel" is my rendition of *Sammlung Israels*.

[5] Luke is the only gospel that refers to the seventy; the partial parallel passage at Matthew 10:1–14 refers to Jesus sending out [only] the Twelve with a similar brief (cf. Mark 6:7–13).

[6] See Richard Bauckham, "James and the Jerusalem Community" in *Jewish Believers in Jesus*, ed. Oskar Skarsaune and Reidar Hvalvik (Peabody, MA: Hendrickson, 2007), 55–95 (56–59).

[7] Acts 9:2, 19:9 and 23, 24:14 and 22: "this Way" at 22:4; "Way of the Lord," Acts 18:25; "Way of God," Acts 18:26. Cf. Bauckham, "James and the Jerusalem Community," 56–57.

[8] Acts 9:13, 32 and 41, 26:10, and frequent in the Pauline epistles, Hebrews and Jude: cf. Bauckham, "James and the Jerusalem Community," 57.

church of God";[9] "the disciples";[10] "the brothers and sisters";[11] "the sect of the Nazarenes" (τῆς τῶν Ναζωραίων αἱρέσεως).[12] These were the first adherents of the Jewish Christianity referred to in the title of this chapter. And yet that phrase cannot be used without analysis. Acts says that the disciples were first called "Christians" in Antioch (Acts 11:26: χρηματίσαι τε πρώτως ἐν Ἀντιοχείᾳ τοὺς μαθητὰς Χριστιανούς), and there the local context was more Gentile than Jewish. Accordingly, the phrase "Jewish Christian" is imprecise. After tracing the use of the phrase "Jewish Christian" by F. C. Baur and later scholars indebted to his analysis (which saw the character of early Christianity as coming out of a Hegelian dialectic between Pauline/Hellenistic Christianity and Petrine/Jewish Christianity),[13] John W. Marshall argues that things became worse, not better, as the phrase was adopted by English speakers: "If Jewish Christianity was a category overdetermined by Hegelian metanarrative in the treatment of F. C. Baur and his heirs," he writes, "in its move to the mainstream of English-speaking academia it became a deeply confused and prejudicial category that neither drove historical-critical analysis nor underpinned a philosophical reading of history."[14]

In a 2009 article, Daniel Boyarin took a logical step that he had stopped short of taking at the time of *Border Lines*, his 2004 book about what he calls the "partition of Judeo-Christianity." In the 2004 book he had argued that "Judaism is not the 'mother' of Christianity: they are twins, joined at the hip":[15] on each side, from the second century to the fifth, discussion and definition of heresy progressively created, as well as policed, difference between Christianity and Judaism. His essential thesis was:

> The idea of orthodoxy comes into the world some time in the second century with a group of Christian writers called "heresiologists," the anatomizers of heresy and heresies, and their Jewish counterparts, the Rabbis.... Ancient heresiologists tried to police the boundaries so as to identify and interdict

[9] Bauckham argues ("James and the Jerusalem Community," 57) that "[f]rom 1 Cor 15:9 and 1 Thess 2:14, it seems likely that this was the full form of the term originally used by the Jerusalem church."

[10] Acts 6:1–2 and 7; 9:1; 15:10 and elsewhere.

[11] Used by Jews in general of one another, as by Peter addressing the festival crowd at Acts 2:29: Ἄνδρες ἀδελφοί, which the NRSV renders as "Fellow Israelites …" Cf. Bauckham, "James and the Jerusalem Community," 58 for its application in the Jerusalem church, e.g. at Acts 6:3 and Jas 1:2.

[12] Acts 24:5, cf. Bauckham, "James and the Jerusalem Community," 58, and Ray A. Pritz, *Nazarene Jewish Christianity: from the End of the New Testament Period until its Disappearance in the Fifth Century* (Jerusalem and Leiden: Magnes and Brill, 1988), 14–17.

[13] John W. Marshall, "John's Jewish (Christian?) Apocalypse" in Matt Jackson-McCabe, *Jewish Christianity Reconsidered* (Minneapolis: Fortress, 2007), 233–56 (236); so that "Paul is not a Jewish Christian. Jewish Christianity … is a value-laden and subordinate category in an effectively racist schema of Christian development" ("John's Jewish [Christian?] Apocalypse," 237, citing Shawn Kelley, *Racializing Jesus: Race, Ideology and the Formation of Modern Biblical Scholarship* [London: Routledge, 2002]).

[14] Marshall, "John's Jewish (Christian?) Apocalypse," 241–42.

[15] Daniel Boyarin, *Border Lines: The Partition of Judaeo-Christianity* (Philadelphia: University of Pennsylvania Press, 2004), 5.

those who respected no borders, those smugglers of ideas and practices newly declared to be contraband, nomads who would not recognize the efforts to institute limits, to posit a separation between "two opposed places" and thus to clearly establish who was and who was not a "Christian," a "Jew."[16]

Against that background, his 2009 article, written in part to review Matt Jackson-McCabe's *Jewish Christianity Reconsidered* and Oskar Skarsaune and Reidar Hvalvik's *Jewish Believers in Jesus*, was in a way little more than the correction of an omission: Boyarin's proposal now is that the term "Jewish Christianity" should be abandoned altogether. The two books, he says, "exemplify for me the pitfalls of using this terminology itself, even in the hands of very critical writers indeed."[17] His core contention is that "the term 'Jewish Christianity' always functions as a term of art in a modernist heresiology"[18]—with the result that "even the most critical, modern, and best-willed usages of the term in scholarship devolve willy-nilly to heresiology."[19]

The account Boyarin gives of how the border between Christian and Jew was policed from the second century onward is subtle, though not in my view powerful enough to support the weight of the most striking propositions he seeks to derive from it—for instance, his assertion that "'Judaism' as the name of a 'religion' is a product of Christianity in its attempt to establish a separate identity."[20] And James Carleton Paget makes the shrewd point that "Jewish Christian" (and with it its German equivalent *Judenchrist*[21]) is "a neologism dating from the sixteenth century"[22]—so that any difficulties are to do with modern usage rather than being inherent in the term itself. Using a simpler criterion, Craig C. Hill observes that the Jerusalem Christians "practiced cultic veneration of Jesus, and so, on that basis, might fairly be called *Jewish Christians*."[23] Therefore, while there may be much to contest in past scholarly accounts of Jewish Christianity, the term itself can hardly merit wholesale suppression.[24] Better to be a "very critical writer indeed," in Boyarin's words,

[16] Boyarin, *Border Lines*, 2.
[17] Boyarin, "Rethinking Jewish Christianity: an Argument for Dismantling a Dubious Category (to which is Appended a Correction of my *Border Lines*)" *JQR* 99 (2009): 7–36 (8).
[18] Boyarin, "Rethinking Jewish Christianity," 7.
[19] Boyarin, "Rethinking Jewish Christianity," 8.
[20] Boyarin, "Rethinking Jewish Christianity," 11: this proposition perhaps asks for more of inverted commas than they can deliver in terms of distancing words from their ordinary meanings.
[21] James Carleton Paget cautions, however, that "'Judenchrist' is not the same as a 'Jewish Christian'" (*Jews, Christians and Jewish Christians in Antiquity* [Tübingen: Mohr Siebeck, 2010], 316).
[22] Carleton Paget, *Jews, Christians and Jewish Christians*, 2 n. 1; detailed discussion at 289–324, which is a revised version of Carleton Paget's chapter called "The Definition of the Terms *Jewish Christian* and *Jewish Christianity* in the History of Research" in Skarsaune and Hvalvik, *Jewish Believers in Jesus*, 22–54.
[23] Craig C. Hill, "The Jerusalem Church," in Matt Jackson-McCabe, *Jewish Christianity Reconsidered* (Minneapolis: Fortress, 2007), 39–56 (55).
[24] In the year when Boyarin made his case against "Jewish Christianity," Edwin K. Broadhead invested thirty-one pages of his book on the subject in defining the term (*Jewish Ways of Following Jesus: Redrawing the Religious Map of Antiquity* [Tübingen, Mohr Siebeck, 2009],

and risk disapproval from those who are persuaded by his case against "Jewish Christianity."

3. People and Events in Jerusalem and the Land of Israel

Given the multiple difficulties that have arisen over many decades from unclear definitions, therefore, it is important to state what this chapter will and will not examine. If before AD 100 there was anywhere a wholly Gentile Christian congregation, there is no extant evidence to indicate where it was: perhaps in Illyria. But even a minimalist view of the size and comparative strength of the Jewish element in Christian congregations would portray Jewish Christians (in Jacob Jervell's words) as a "mighty minority."[25] Jervell makes a case for an understanding of Jewish Christians as having "looked upon themselves as the very center of the church" and says not only that they "survived the catastrophe of the year 70" but that the "Jewish-Christian minorities are constantly setting the agenda of the church."[26]

This chapter will not, however, seek to trace the activities and influence of all Jewish Christians throughout the first-century churches across the Roman world—not because such a study would be unimportant, but in order not to duplicate the themes of other chapters in this book.[27] Paul called himself "an apostle to the Gentiles" (Rom 11:13), but within the churches in his sphere of influence, Jewish Christians were numerous and Jewish Christian preaching was influential enough at times to cause Paul deep concern. In Jerry L. Sumney's analysis, it is better to refer to Paul's opponents in 2 Corinthians as "Christ-believers who are also Jews" but to call those Paul opposes in

---

28–58). It remains to be seen whether the phrase will wither on the vine. Karen L. King in 2011 wrote that "the over-determined category of Jewish Christianity is recognized to be manifestly confused" ("Factions, Variety, Diversity, Multiplicity: Representing Early Christian Differences for the 21st Century" *MTSR* 23 [2011], 216–37 [223]), and argued (224) that "[i]t would be more accurate to speak of a variety of Christian positionalities" than of "Jewish Christianity" and other "monolithic entities."

[25] Jacob Jervell, "The Mighty Minority" *ST* 34 (1980): 13–38. On 21 Jervell writes: "In the years 70 to 100 AD we have without any doubt a clear Gentile majority—that is taken from a numerical point of view." And yet the idea of a Jewish minority and a Gentile majority in the churches, as early as the first century, remains open to question in view of Justin, *1 Apol.* 53, where Justin (writing in the 150s) says that "the Christians from among the Gentiles are both more numerous and more true than those from among the Jews and Samaritans." Not the product of a social survey, his assertion cannot be cross-referenced or checked; but presumably it reflects in some way a sense that Justin had in the mid-second century (as a Gentile from Neapolis [Nablus/Shechem] in the province of Palestine, who had taken up residence at Rome) of its being noteworthy that there were more Gentile than Jewish Christians in the churches he knew something about.

[26] Jervell, "The Mighty Minority," 26.

[27] Especially chapter 6, "The Parting of the Ways," chapter 7, "The Letter to the Hebrews," chapter 8, "Christians and Jews in Antioch," chapter 11, "Aliens and Strangers: Minority Group Rhetoric in the Later New Testament Writings," and chapter 13, "Roman Political Ideology and the Authority of First Clement."

Galatians "Jews who are also Christ-believers."[28] In Philippians, Paul is particularly angry about someone who is advocating circumcision for Gentile believers.[29] No doubt there were subtle differences in different cases. At any rate the opponents at Corinth apparently had letters of recommendation (2 Cor 3:1), perhaps from Jerusalem, possibly from someone whose name would be recognizable if it were known today. Jervell goes further in inferring a harder line from Jerusalem toward Paul's Gentile mission in the fifties than previously, so that

> many Jewish Christians opposed him. This anti-Pauline movement grew gradually stronger and reached a climax in the last ten years of Paul's active life as a missionary. Until the time of the council, or shortly before it, Paul worked seemingly undisturbed. The leading people in Jerusalem acknowledged his law-free mission among the Gentiles and accepted Barnabas and Paul as partners, Gal 2:9–10. When Paul writes his letter to the Galatians, this has changed, Gal 2:11ff. Jerusalem has now adopted a harder line, led by James, and he won Peter, Barnabas, and the other Jewish Christians over to this new course, Gal 2:11ff. That the conflict with the leaders in Jerusalem became more intense at the end of Paul's life can be seen from Rom 15,30ff. and is confirmed by Acts 21:17ff.[30]

In ascribing a role in policy and planning to the Jerusalem church, this goes further than some scholars would wish to go; and yet Sumney, while he does not follow Jervell in seeing Jerusalem as orchestrating opposition to Paul, seems to be justified in arguing that in the Corinthian case: "Paul, his rivals, and the ... church all see being Jewish as a persuasive element of a claim to authority."[31] The complex dialectic that characterized church life in the Pauline communities will not, however, be examined further in this chapter, whose principal business will be a concise examination of the Nazarene church in Jerusalem and the Land of Israel, together with the mission work undertaken by Jesus' family in Galilee, and further north into the province of Syria.

The "Jerusalem spring" in Acts ends with the death of Stephen, and Acts as a whole advances through the story of Paul's mission to the Gentiles, reaching its non-culmination at the inconclusive ending of the book, with Paul in Rome awaiting a hearing in front of the emperor.[32] Three times in the

---

[28] Jerry L. Sumney, "Paul and Christ-believing Jews Whom He Opposes," in Matt Jackson-McCabe, *Jewish Christianity Reconsidered* (Minneapolis: Fortress, 2007), 57–80 (60).

[29] Phil 3:2: "Beware of the dogs, beware of the evil workers, beware of those who mutilate the flesh!"

[30] Jervell, "The Mighty Minority," 21–22.

[31] Sumney, "Paul and Christ-believing Jews," 63.

[32] In the past I have cited Eccl 12:12 ("of making many books there is no end") to account for my unwillingness to add to debate on the date of Acts (Paul McKechnie, "Paul among the Jews," in *All Things to All Cultures*, ed. Mark Harding and Alanna Nobbs [Grand Rapids: Eerdmans, 2013], 103–23 [105])—a text which, following Adolf von Harnack's mature view (*Neue Untersuchungen zur Apostelgeschichte und zur Abfassungszeit der synoptischen Evangelien*

narrative Paul announces that he is turning to the Gentiles[33]—enough to show that Gentiles and their response to the gospel are a key theme in Acts. This fact in itself perhaps falls short of justifying Robert C. Tannehill's conclusion in his 1985 article that "[t]he story of Israel, so far as the author of Luke–Acts can tell it, is a tragic story";[34] but the same data inform Jack T. Sanders's trial and conviction of Luke, in a 1981 article, on a charge of anti-Semitism.[35]

The narrative shape of Acts, however, is not altogether affirmed by data from elsewhere—or even by internal evidence, if one treats seriously the account of many priests becoming obedient to the faith (Acts 6:7), or what James and the elders said to Paul when he visited Jerusalem, in or about AD 57: "You see … how many thousands of believers there are among the Jews, and they are all zealous for the law."[36] The Jerusalem church, then, even if not a uniquely agenda-setting organization in the fifties, was more (*pace* Jervell) than a "mighty minority." Richard Bauckham, in the detailed exposition which he contributed to Skarsaune and Hvalvik's *Jewish Believers in Jesus*, summarizes the organization's religious life (attending daily prayers in the Temple, assembling to hear the apostles teach in the outer court, meeting in smaller groups in homes, such meetings focusing on a common meal),[37] and discusses the community of goods that was practiced:[38] he argues that although evidence of other Christian groups following this model is lacking, it remains credible that "they would sell their possessions and goods and distribute the proceeds to all."[39] Their daily distribution was to do with a

---

[Leipzig: Hinrich, 1911], 64–65), I would date to 62. I do not share the outlook of the minority of scholars who see Acts as an unusually unreliable source document.

[33] Acts 13:46 (Antioch of Pisidia); 18:6 (Corinth); 28:28 (Rome): cf. Robert C. Tannehill, "Israel in Luke–Acts: a Tragic Story" *JBL* 104 (1985): 69–85, who comments (74), "a pattern is established that conveys a general impression of the way things are going. This pattern allows room for exceptions. It is not the same as a general statement about all Jews everywhere. Nevertheless, it indicates a turn in the story away from what we were led to expect by the proclamations of salvation for Israel through Jesus, Israel's messiah, in Luke 1–2."

[34] Tannehill, "Israel in Luke–Acts: a Tragic Story," 85.

[35] Jack T. Sanders, "The Parable of the Pounds and Lucan anti-Semitism," *TS* 42 (1981): 660–68, at 667: "The entire geographico-theological plan of Luke–Acts is predicated on the simple evangelical premise that the Jews rejected Jesus and that the gospel was then taken to the Gentiles, who accepted it. While such a notion is the backbone of Luke's theology, however, it is hardly reliable history. It is, in fact, so patently untrue … that we recognize it for the anti-Semitic lie that it is. Without that lie we would not have Lucan theology."

[36] Acts 21:20, taken as factual for example by Jervell ("The Mighty Minority," 29), who supposes that Luke was writing about 90, twenty years after the destruction of the Temple.

[37] Bauckham, "James and the Jerusalem Community," 61.

[38] Acts 2:44–45; 4:32–5:11.

[39] Bauckham, "James and the Jerusalem Community," 62, citing Brian Capper, "The Palestinian Cultural Context of Earliest Christian Community of Goods," in *The Book of Acts in Its Palestinian Setting*, ed. Richard Bauckham, vol. 4 of *The Book of Acts in Its First Century Setting*, ed. Bruce W. Winter (Grand Rapids: Eerdmans; Carlisle: Paternoster, 1995), 323–56. Capper notes (327–41) the Essene system whereby new members of communities, both the celibate community at Qumran and the more secular Essene communities attested by the *Damascus Document*, "mixed" their property with the community's shared assets, after a probationary period. He observes, however (341–45), that the Essene Quarter at Jerusalem was probably occupied by fewer Essenes after AD 6, when direct Roman rule of Judea commenced

shared meal,[40] which explains why the solution to the Hellenists' complaint regarding their neglected widows was to appoint "seven men of good standing, full of the Spirit and of wisdom" whose job would be to wait on tables (Acts 6:2–3).

The identity of the Hellenists *vis-à-vis* the Hebrews in connection with this incident has been a *cause célèbre* in biblical scholarship. More recent work has been skeptical of the idea (with Tübingen school roots[41]) of the Hellenists as diaspora Jews with more liberal ideas about Torah observance than Jews from the land of Israel. Language-use is the determinant for the terminology, and Hellenists were Greek-speaking Jews from the western diaspora (those from the eastern diaspora spoke Aramaic); but the supposition that a western diaspora origin determined a less strict view of Torah and Temple is by no means compelling—especially since these Hellenists in Jerusalem had chosen to make a pilgrimage there, or even to settle there permanently, actions which in many cases arose from devotion to the Temple and the Law of Moses.[42]

The seven deacons appointed after the Hellenists' complaint, Stephen, Philip, Prochorus, Nicanor, Timon, Parmenas, and Nicolaus, were all Jews with Greek names—except that Nicolaus was a proselyte (Acts 6:5). This seems to indicate that Hellenists were given responsibility for addressing the difficulties Hellenists had identified. But if conflict within the Jerusalem community had been resolved, aggression against it from outside was about to commence in earnest for the first time since the death of Jesus. Stephen was brought before the Council and stoned to death (Acts 6:8–7:60). Bauckham observes that "in every known case action against the Jerusalem church or its leaders was taken when the reigning high priest … belonged to the powerful Sadducean family of Annas (Ananus)."[43] Caiaphas, high priest when Jesus was put to death, was still in office at the time of Stephen's death; and as a result of persecution afterwards, "all except the apostles were scattered throughout the countryside of Judea and Samaria."[44]

---

(344). But he argues that "[i]n all probability some kind of Essene presence continued," and that the early church in Jerusalem from ca. 30 was located in the vicinity of the (erstwhile) Essene Quarter (349).

[40] Acts 6:1: NRSV translates "… the daily distribution of food," which as a translation gives a slightly false specificity to τῇ διακονίᾳ τῇ καθημερινῇ; but Capper stresses ("Palestinian Cultural Context," 351) that "care for the poor of the community was always associated with table-fellowship in early Christianity."

[41] Kelley (*Racializing Jesus*, 74) summarizes Baur: "These two parties split Jesus into *form* and *content*, with the Hebrews latching on to the mere form of Jesus' life while the Hellenists grasped the deeper significance of the content of Jesus' teaching."

[42] Bauckham, "James and the Jerusalem Community," 64.

[43] Bauckham, "James and the Jerusalem Community," 75.

[44] Acts 8:1: Bauckham argues that while others left Jerusalem permanently, the apostles may have been imprisoned and later released—or even have left town for safety but later returned (Bauckham, "James and the Jerusalem Community" in idem, *The Book of Acts in Its Palestinian Setting*, 415–80 [429]).

4. Peter, James, and the Jerusalem Bishops

Later, in AD 42, when (probably) Matthias son of Annas was high priest,[45] Herod Agrippa I—who had been rewarded in 41 for his support by Claudius, the new emperor,[46] with an enlargement of his client kingdom which brought Judea into it—recommenced violent action in Jerusalem against the Nazarenes, having James son of Zebedee killed, and Peter imprisoned.[47] The story of Peter's deliverance from prison occupies much of Acts 12. When, at the house of Mary the mother of John Mark, Peter has succeeded in convincing the people gathered to pray that he is the real human Peter, and in explaining how he got out of the prison, he asks them to "Tell this to James and to the believers." Next, the text adds mysteriously, "he left and went to another place."[48]

This seems to be a pointer to how James, the Lord's brother, became the leading figure in the Jerusalem community. The Twelve, at the beginning of Acts, seem to be taking charge, with Peter in a prominent role; and when Paul visited Jerusalem three years after his experience on the Damascus road (about AD 35), he stayed fifteen days with Cephas [Peter] and "did not see any other apostle except James the Lord's brother" (Gal 1:18–19)—which seems to imply that James was a person of importance in the Nazarene community by that time. Then, after fourteen years, when Paul was in Jerusalem again, he writes in Galatians that "James and Cephas and John, who were acknowledged pillars, recognized the grace that had been given to me" (Gal 2:9).

A list of "bishops of Jerusalem," preserved in Eusebius and (not in identical form) in Epiphanius, and in part in a document called the *Letter of James to Quadratus*, which exists in Armenian and in Syriac, may be able to be reinterpreted to yield information about how James's leadership of the Jerusalem church worked. Now Eusebius, writing in the fourth century, thought this list was a list of bishops who presided over the Jerusalem church one after another, as is apparent from what he says:

> The chronology of the bishops of Jerusalem I have nowhere found preserved in writing; for tradition says that they were all short lived. But I have learned

---

[45] Cf. Bauckham, "James and the Jerusalem Community," 75.

[46] Josephus's story at *A.J.* 19.236–47 is that at the time of the assassination of Gaius Caligula, Agrippa urged Claudius not to miss the chance to take charge, and managed the communications that led to the Senate recognizing him as emperor.

[47] Acts 12:1–5. Peter's arrest "pleased the Jews" (12:3), which Bauckham glosses ("James and the Jerusalem Community," 75) as meaning that Agrippa hoped to mend fences with Matthias, whose brother Theophilus he had earlier deposed as high priest.

[48] Acts 12:12–17: evidently not expecting to remain in Jerusalem to tell James personally. John Wenham argues for acceptance of the traditional view that this would be the moment when Peter first traveled to Rome (*Redating Matthew, Mark & Luke* [London: Hodder & Stoughton, 1991], 146–72), citing George Edmundson's discussion of the question (*The Church in Rome in the First Century* [London: Longmans, 1913], 42–53).

this much from writings, that until the siege of the Jews, which took place under Hadrian, there were fifteen bishops in succession there, all of whom are said to have been of Hebrew descent, and to have received the knowledge of Christ in purity, so that they were approved by those who were able to judge of such matters, and were deemed worthy of the episcopate. For their whole church consisted then of believing Hebrews who continued from the days of the apostles until the siege which took place at this time; in which siege the Jews, having again rebelled against the Romans, were conquered after severe battles.[49]

This would set the end of the time-frame at 135 when the Third Jewish War came to an end. The list given by Eusebius and Epiphanius consists of fifteen names, as here:

The Jerusalem Bishops List[50]			
			Letter of James to Quadratus[51]
	Eusebius[52]	Epiphanius[53]	Armenian	Syriac
1	Ἰάκωβος	Ἰάκωβος		
2	Συμεών	Συμεών		
3	Ἰοῦστος	Ἰούδας		
4	Ζακχαῖος	Ζαχαρίας		
5	Τωβίας	Τωβίας		
6	Βενιαμίν	Βενιαμίν		
7	Ἰωάννης	Ἰωάννης		
8	Ματθίας	Ματθίας		
9	Φίλιππος	Φίλιππος	Philip	Philip
10	Σενεκᾶς	Σενεκᾶς	Senikus	Senikus
11	Ἰοῦστος	Ἰοῦστος	Justus	Justus
12	Λευίς	Λευίς	Levi	Levi
13	Ἐφρής	Οὐαφρίς	Aphre	Aphre
14	Ἰωσήφ	Ἰωσίς		
15	Ἰούδας	Ἰούδας	Juda	

Bauckham rejects Eusebius's feeble explanation that the fifteen bishops were all short-lived.[54] He observes that Symeon son of Clopas,[55] second on

---

[49] Eusebius, *Hist. eccl.* 4.5.1–2.

[50] Table from Bauckham, *Jude and the Relatives in the Early Church* (Edinburgh: T&T Clark, 1990), 71.

[51] Translation by P. Vetter at R. van den Broek, "Der Brief des Jakobus an Quadratus und das Problem der judenchristlichen Bischöfe von Jerusalem (Eusebius, *Hist. eccl.* IV,5,1–3)," in *Text and Testimony: Essays on New Testament and Apocryphal Literature in Honour of A. F. J. Klijn*, ed. Tjitze Baarda et al. (Kampen: Kok, 1988), 56–65 (57–58).

[52] Eusebius, *Hist. eccl.* 4.5.3–4 and 5.12.1–2.

[53] Epiphanius, *Pan.* 66.19.9–20.15.

[54] Bauckham, *Jude and the Relatives*, 72.

[55] Bauckham, *Jude and the Relatives*, 16: "There is ... little room for doubt that he is the Clopas to whom Hegesippus refers, as the brother of Joseph and therefore uncle of Jesus, and the father

the list, was martyred under Trajan (98–117),[56] and infers that "the thirteen names following … can scarcely be the names of thirteen bishops in linear succession before 134."[57] In the Armenian and Syriac *Letter of James to Quadratus*, however, six of the names from the list occur—not as bishops, but described as "respected scribes of the Jews" converted to Christianity, who (at the dramatic date of the letter, which was not written at that epoch) are arguing from the Scriptures with non-Christian Jews.[58] Bauckham concludes that Justus, third in the list, was leader of the Jerusalem church between the death of Symeon and the Bar Kokhba revolt,[59] and the remaining twelve names on the list should be understood as belonging to "a college of elders who presided over the church along with James."[60]

These twelve, then, may be the elders referred to in Acts when Paul returns to Jerusalem in 57 and takes four men who are under a vow to the Temple to undergo their purification.[61] Bauckham argues for identifying Joseph/Josis and Judas with Jesus' brothers of those names;[62] John, Matthias, and Philip with three of the Twelve apostles; Levi and Zacchaeus with the people of those names in the Gospels;[63] and Justus with Joseph Barsabbas, who missed out in the drawing of lots to take Judas Iscariot's place as one of the Twelve apostles (Acts 1:23). If all these identifications are correct, eight out of twelve Jerusalem elders are known from the New Testament narrative. Their position at Jerusalem did not make it impossible for them to travel for missionary reasons, and Paul in 1 Corinthians asks if he and Barnabas are the only apostles not allowed to be accompanied by a believing wife, as "the other apostles and the brothers of the Lord and Cephas" are.[64]

5. The Council of Jerusalem

So it was that, in AD 49, some people from Judea traveled to Antioch and began to teach the brothers in the church that unless they were circumcised they could not be saved. This might have seemed in Judea to be a matter of

---

of Symeon … who succeeded James the Lord's brother in the leadership of the Jerusalem church (Hegesippus *ap.* Eusebius, *Hist. eccl.* 3:11; 3:32:6; 4:22:4)."

[56] Eusebius, *Hist. eccl.* 3.32.1–6; cf. Bauckham, *Jude and the Relatives*, 72.
[57] Bauckham, *Jude and the Relatives*, 72.
[58] Van den Broek, "Der Brief des Jakobus an Quadratus," 58.
[59] When Epiphanius reaches Justus, eleventh on his list, he notes: "Justus, bringing us to Hadrian" (*Pan.* 66.20.11); but Eusebius has two people on his list with the name of Justus, third and eleventh (Epiphanius gives the third name as Judas). There is some confusion, but Epiphanius's note may tend to confirm that a person called Justus was the (third and last) Jewish bishop of Jerusalem, until the Third Jewish War brought a catastrophe on the Jerusalem church as a whole. Cf. Bauckham, *Jude and the Relatives*, 78.
[60] Bauckham, *Jude and the Relatives*, 73: "subsequently misunderstood in the tradition as successors to James."
[61] "Paul went with us to visit James; and all the elders were present," Acts 21:18; purification of four Nazirites, attack on Paul, his rescue/arrest by a Roman tribune, Acts 21:23–33.
[62] Bauckham, *Jude and the Relatives*, 76; cf. Mark 6:3 // Matthew 13:55.
[63] Levi, Luke 5:27 // Mark 2:14; Zacchaeus, Luke 19:1–10.
[64] 1 Cor 9:5, cf. Bauckham, *Jude and the Relatives*, 57–61.

the Jerusalem-based church encouraging a proper approach to Gentile converts to the gospel of Jesus—to Gentile *Christians*, given that the word "Christian" was first used in Antioch[65]—but it was later denied that the people who came to Antioch did so under instruction from the Jerusalem leadership (Acts 15:24). The view that circumcision was necessary for Gentiles, however, ran into articulate opposition from Paul and Barnabas, and they, together with others, were deputed to go to Jerusalem and discuss the question "with the apostles and elders" (Acts 15:1–2).

Peter was back in Jerusalem, and in his contribution to the discussion he said, "You know that in the early days God made a choice among you, that I should be the one through whom the Gentiles would hear the message of the good news and become believers" (Acts 15:7). This refers to the Cornelius incident (Acts 10:1–48), and perhaps to more sustained contact with Gentiles not narrated in Acts. After the debate, a letter was written to the Antioch believers, the burden of which was to say,

> it has seemed good to the Holy Spirit and to us to impose on you no further burden than these essentials: that you abstain from what has been sacrificed to idols and from blood and from what is strangled and from fornication. If you keep yourselves from these, you will do well. Farewell (Acts 15:28–29).

The expectation was that Gentile Christians would live as those non-Israelites who lived in the land of Israel were commanded to live in Leviticus 17–18. The most striking thing about the meeting at Jerusalem, however, is how its decision was made: at the end of the debate James quotes the prophet Amos, saying "I will rebuild the dwelling of David … so that all other peoples may seek the Lord—even all the Gentiles over whom my name has been called,"[66] and then he says, "Therefore I have reached the decision that we should not trouble those Gentiles who are turning to God" (Acts 15:19). The decision was evidently his to make, even assuming that Peter was still present.

A question that the decision given at Jerusalem did not address was of table-fellowship: was it right for Jewish believers to eat with Gentiles? It was an important loose end, considering that the Jerusalem decision gave a rule about the food Gentile Christians should eat. This, then, was what was at issue in the Antioch incident, which Paul writes of in Galatians:

---

[65] Acts 11:26, "it was in Antioch that the disciples were first called 'Christians'": a category applied to them all, not only the Gentiles—so that John W. Marshall's claim that "Paul is not a Jewish Christian" (see above, n. 13) runs against the evidence.

[66] Amos 9:11–12, which has this meaning in the Septuagint (ἀναστήσω τὴν σκηνὴν Δαυιδ … ὅπως ἐκζητήσωσιν οἱ κατάλοιποι τῶν ἀνθρώπων καὶ πάντα τὰ ἔθνη, ἐφ' οὓς ἐπικέκληται τὸ ὄνομά μου ἐπ' αὐτούς). NRSV, translating from the Hebrew, says "I will raise up the booth of David … in order that they [sc. the children of Israel] may possess the remnant of Edom and all the nations who are called by my name"—which is less to do with Gentiles seeking the Lord. Bauckham writes of "a prophecy in which it was clear that Gentiles who join the messianic people of God do so precisely as Gentiles" ("James and the Jerusalem Community," 74).

When Cephas came to Antioch, I opposed him to his face, because he stood self-condemned; for until certain people came from James, he used to eat with the Gentiles. But after they came, he drew back and kept himself separate for fear of the circumcision faction. And the other Jews joined him in this hypocrisy, so that even Barnabas was led astray by their hypocrisy. But when I saw that they were not acting consistently with the truth of the gospel, I said to Cephas before them all, "If you, though a Jew, live like a Gentile and not like a Jew, how can you compel the Gentiles to live like Jews?" (Gal 2:11–14)[67]

So again at this time Cephas (Peter) complied with instructions from James,[68] incurring Paul's anger. Hill observes that this incident led to Paul being unable to win the argument and "abandoning Antioch as his missionary base";[69] he goes on to note other instances of Paul acknowledging the primacy of the Jerusalem church. To the church at Thessalonica he writes, "you, brothers and sisters, became imitators of the churches of God in Christ Jesus that are in Judea" (1 Thess 2:14). Writing to Corinth, he commends the collection for the saints, the fundraising project recommended to him at Jerusalem (Gal 2:10): the churches in Macedonia, he says, "voluntarily gave according to their means, and even beyond their means, begging us earnestly for the privilege of sharing in this ministry to the saints" (2 Cor 8:3–4), and he asks the Corinthians to contribute to relieving the poverty of the Jerusalem church, effectively on the ground that his Gentile believers were spiritual debtors to the Jerusalem believers.[70]

6. James Stoned; Symeon Takes Over

In AD 62, twenty years after the death of James son of Zebedee, another member of the Annas/Ananus family became high priest, when Joseph Cabi ben Simon was deposed. Porcius Festus, procurator of Judea, had died in office, and his successor Lucceius Albinus had not yet arrived in the province when Ananus ben Ananus had James, the Lord's brother, brought before the

---

[67] The theory that Acts 15 and Galatians 2 deal with different events I find too improbable to be worthy of further discussion here, even though at a number of points the two accounts differ.

[68] Bruce Chilton and Jacob Neusner, in *Judaism in the New Testament* (London and New York: Routledge, 1995), 100, analyze the incident in terms of "natural conservatism" reasserting itself, when (following Cephas's example) Jews and Gentiles began again to eat their meals separately. They are right to note how radical Paul's position was (and how isolated he became from "*every other Christian Jew*" [their italics] when he dug his heels in), but they disregard Peter's visit to Cornelius (Acts 10:1–48) and so omit comment on how Cephas/Peter in this story obeys James rather than relying on conclusions that he had previously reached on a similar matter ("I truly understand that God shows no partiality, but in every nation anyone who fears him and does what is right is acceptable to him," Acts 10:34–35). This is the behavior that Paul, perhaps harshly, calls "hypocrisy."

[69] Hill, "Jerusalem Church," 43.

[70] Cf. Hill, "Jerusalem Church," 44.

Council, condemned, and stoned.[71] Bauckham argues[72] that the offence of which he was found guilty must have been either being a blasphemer[73] or being a *maddiaḥ*, one who [potentially] leads astray a whole town.[74] Zeal, Bauckham surmises, led the Council members "to ignore the need to refer the matter to the governor":[75] certainly they had no right to impose a death penalty, and it is clear that it was only because a vacancy in the procuratorship coincided with the recapture of the high priesthood, by that same family of Sadducees, that those in the priesthood who were zealous opponents of James and the Nazarenes had the opportunity to put him to death. The consequence for Ananus was that when Albinus arrived and took the reins of power, he deposed him from the high priesthood, after only three months in office.[76]

Eusebius, drawing on Hegesippus, links the death of James to the fall of Jerusalem and the destruction of the Temple, as if there had not been eight years in between:

> And one of them, who was a fuller, took the club with which he beat out clothes and struck the just man on the head. And thus he suffered martyrdom. And they buried him on the spot, by the temple, and his monument still remains by the temple. He became a true witness, both to Jews and Greeks, that Jesus is the Christ. And immediately Vespasian besieged them. These things are related at length by Hegesippus, who is in agreement with Clement. James was so admirable a man and so celebrated among all for his justice, that the more sensible even of the Jews were of the opinion that this was the cause of the siege of Jerusalem, which happened to them immediately after his martyrdom for no other reason than their daring act against him.[77]

It is this confusion that leads him to narrate the succession of Symeon son of Clopas as leader of the Jerusalem church after the destruction of Jerusalem by Titus.[78]

The upshot is that it is hard to judge whether the conflict around Thebouthis ought to be dated in the sixties: Eusebius narrates unanimity around appointing Symeon, and then adds:

> But Thebouthis, because he was not made bishop, began to corrupt it [sc. the Church]. He also was sprung from the seven sects among the people, like Simon, from whom came the Simonians, and Cleobius, from whom came the

---

[71] Josephus, *A.J.* 20.197–99, cf. Eusebius, *Hist. eccl.* 2.23.8–18, who ascribes the action against James to scribes and Pharisees: Josephus's account makes it clear that Sadducees were James's leading opponents (and Acts 15:5 shows that Jerusalem believers included some Pharisees).

[72] Richard Bauckham, "For what Offence was James Put to Death?" in *James the Just and Christian Origins*, ed. Bruce Chilton and Craig A. Evans (Leiden: Brill, 1999), 199–232 (229).

[73] Cf. Lev 24:10–23.

[74] Cf. Deut 13:12–16.

[75] Bauckham, "For what Offence …?" 220.

[76] Josephus, *A.J.* 20.202–03.

[77] Eusebius, *Hist. eccl.* 2.23.18–19; Bauckham argues that "we should probably suppose Simeon to have succeeded James in 62" ("James and the Jerusalem Community," 77).

[78] Eusebius, *Hist. eccl.* 3.11.1–2.

Cleobians, and Dositheus, from whom came the Dositheans, and Gorthaeus, from whom came the Goratheni, and Masbotheus, from whom came the Masbothaeans.[79]

He continues the genealogy of heretical sects across several more lines. Thebouthis, known only from this passage, was, Bauckham infers, "the source of some schism among Palestinian Jewish Christians";[80] but elsewhere, and more convincingly, Bauckham notes the artificiality of the idea of Thebouthis belonging to all seven sects, and argues that the polemical point of the description of Thebouthis must be "to give the Gnostic heresies of his own time a pedigree which derives them from the Jewish sects which opposed Jesus."[81]

7. Ebionites

Bauckham thinks it probable that the split between Symeon and Thebouthis was doctrinal, and argues that "possibly this was the ultimate origin of the distinction between Nazarenes and Ebionites, who emerge as the two main forms of Jewish Christianity in the mid-second century."[82] The Ebionites are first mentioned as a heretical group by Irenaeus, who writes:

> Those who are called Ebionites agree that the world was made by God; but their opinions with respect to the Lord are similar to those of Cerinthus and Carpocrates. They use the Gospel according to Matthew only, and repudiate the Apostle Paul, maintaining that he was an apostate from the law. As to the prophetical writings, they endeavor to expound them in a somewhat singular manner: they practice circumcision, persevere in the observance of those customs which are enjoined by the law, and are so Judaic in their style of life, that they even adore Jerusalem as if it were the house of God.[83]

This shows the Ebionites as a Jewish Christian sect, but it is a complex source to draw on. Irenaeus wrote perhaps in the 180s, and the Latin translation (ancient but of unclear date) says that the Ebionites' view of the Lord is *not* similar to the views of Cerinthus and Carpocrates—Oskar Skarsaune argues that it is impossible to decide on purely critical grounds whether the "not" should be in the text.[84] To Origen in *Against Celsus*, written in the late 240s, it seems that in effect all Jewish Christians are Ebionites: answering Celsus's claim that Christians have "forsaken the law of their

---

[79] Eusebius, *Hist. eccl.* 4.22.5.
[80] Bauckham, "James and the Jerusalem Community," 78.
[81] Bauckham, *Jude and the Relatives*, 89.
[82] Bauckham, "James and the Jerusalem Community," 78; cf. Bauckham, *Jude and the Relatives*, 90.
[83] Irenaeus, *Haer.* 1.26.2.
[84] Oskar Skarsaune, "The Ebionites," in Skarsaune and Hvalvik, *Jewish Believers in Jesus*, 419–62 (428).

fathers" by embracing Christianity, he says that "he has not observed that the Jewish converts have not deserted the law of their fathers ... and those Jews who have received Jesus as Christ are called by the name of Ebionites."[85] Later in his book, however, Origen shows that he does know of two kinds of Ebionites, and writes of "the twofold sect of Ebionites, who either acknowledge with us that Jesus was born of a virgin, or deny this, and maintain that He was begotten like other human beings."[86]

The denial of the virgin birth was an Ebionite distinctive in doctrine, and prompted Eusebius to say that "the ancients quite properly called these men Ebionites, because they held poor and mean opinions concerning Christ."[87] Scholarly views differ on whether the Ebionites or the Nazarenes were the successors of the Jerusalem church after the destruction of the Temple, and have differed since the days of the Tübingen school: Baur viewed the Nazarenes (who accepted Paul as an apostle) as representing a later phase of Jewish Christianity, but Albrecht Ritschl argued to the contrary that an anti-Pauline Jewish Christianity was not the dominant current in the first century. The debate is summarized by Petri Luomanen,[88] who comes down on Baur's side,[89] while noting that Ray A. Pritz is on Ritschl's side in the debate.[90]

Pritz also argues that there was "a split in the Nazarene ranks around the turn of the first century,"[91] and Bauckham argues that "the low christology later adopted by the Ebionites should not be projected back on to the Jerusalem church"[92]—meaning the church up to and including the sixties. And yet whatever impact Thebouthis may have had, whether he was a proto-Ebionite (so Bauckham) or not, the second half of the century brought a greater crisis to the Jerusalem church: the First Jewish War. As Bauckham observes, the church was a prominent enough group in Jerusalem for the leaders of the Zealot-led revolt to want to know its attitude—even if not all members of the church could be expected to follow the official line.[93] Balabanski comments on the difficulties this must have caused for the Jerusalem church, who, she surmises, "shared a passivist stance which went back to Jesus himself,"[94] and which cannot have been congenial to the

[85] Origen, *Cels.* 2.1.
[86] Origen, *Cels.* 5.61, cf. Pritz, *Nazarenes*, 21–23.
[87] Eusebius, *Hist. eccl.* 3.27.1; in the Hebrew Bible, *ebion* (plural *ebionim*) means "poor": "those within the people of Israel who are the primary addressees of God's salvation" (Skarsaune, "Ebionites," 421).
[88] Petri Luomanen, "Ebionites and Nazarenes," in Matt Jackson-McCabe, *Jewish Christianity Reconsidered* (Minneapolis: Fortress, 2007), 81–118 (82).
[89] Luomanen, "Ebionites and Nazarenes," 83: "I find the Ebionites better candidates than the Nazarenes for being the successors of the Jerusalem community."
[90] Pritz, *Nazarene Jewish Christianity*, 108–10.
[91] Pritz, *Nazarene Jewish Christianity*, 108.
[92] Bauckham, "James and the Jerusalem Community," 77.
[93] Bauckham, "James and the Jerusalem Community," 78.
[94] Vicky Balabanski, *Eschatology in the Making: Matthew, Mark and the Didache* (Cambridge: Cambridge University Press, 1997), 130.

Zealots. It was under these conditions, she argues, that an oracle advising evacuating Jerusalem was received.[95]

8. Pella

Eusebius and Epiphanius both write that the Jerusalem church evacuated from Jerusalem during the First Jewish War to Pella, one of the cities of the Decapolis. Eusebius says,

> The people of the church in Jerusalem had been commanded by a revelation, vouchsafed to approved men there before the war, to leave the city and to dwell in a certain town of Perea called Pella. And when those that believed in Christ had come there from Jerusalem, then, as if the royal city of the Jews and the whole land of Judea were entirely destitute of holy men, the judgment of God at length overtook those who had committed such outrages against Christ and his apostles, and totally destroyed that generation of impious men.[96]

And in the fifth century, in his discussion of what he calls the heresy of the Nazoreans, Epiphanius writes,

> This sect of Nazoraeans is to be found in Beroea near Coelesyria, in the Decapolis near Pella, and in Bashanitis at the place called Cocabe—Khokhabe in Hebrew. For that was its place of origin, since all the disciples had settled in Pella after their remove from Jerusalem—Christ having told them to abandon Jerusalem and withdraw from it because of the siege it was about to undergo. And they settled in Peraea for this reason and, as I said, lived their lives there. It was from this that the Nazoraean sect had its origin.[97]

The two writers' agendas are different: Eusebius wishing to comment on God's judgment against unbelieving Jews, but Epiphanius aiming to explain where a deviant form of Christianity came from. Ephiphanius wrote much later, and a question arises over whether he had any factual source other than Eusebius. Vicky Balabanski summarizes the debate in her book on eschatology,[98] and it is noticeable that those who think Epiphanius had a source other than Eusebius tend also to be those who conclude that the story of the evacuation to Pella is true, whereas those who think Epiphanius drew (only) on Eusebius tend to conclude that there was no evacuation to Pella.

Pella (Tabaqat Fahl) is closer to Jerusalem than Nazareth is, but east of the Jordan, and therefore (vitally) in the Decapolis and outside the province of

---

[95] Balabanski, *Eschatology*, 130, not only meaning the revelation of which Eusebius writes (see below), but also Mark 13:14, "But when you see the desolating sacrilege set up where it ought not to be (let the reader understand), then those in Judea must flee to the mountains...."
[96] Eusebius, *Hist. eccl.* 3.5.3.
[97] Epiphanius, *Pan.* 29.7.7–8.
[98] Balabanski, *Eschatology*, 109–12.

Judea, while still being within the Land of Israel as biblically defined.[99] The Decapolis remained as a region of quasi-autonomous cities until the Romans annexed it as part of their new province of Arabia in 106. It would be rational to choose Pella as a place of exile, particularly if the decision to evacuate was made early, before the cessation of sacrifices on behalf of the emperor at the Temple, which marked the beginning of the war.[100] The pillaging of Pella, a majority-Gentile city, by Jews in 66 in the early days of the war, has sometimes cast doubt over the flight to Pella (was it practical to flee to a place which had recently been pillaged?),[101] but Pritz argues that the damage may not have made the city uninhabitable, and that there may have been a Gentile Christian community that could play host to the Jerusalem believers.[102]

Figure 1. Jerusalem, Pella, and the Decapolis.
Public Domain.

What is at issue, as Gerd Lüdemann observes, is whether the Jerusalem church (as such) perished in the First Jewish War.[103] His solution, drawing on

---

[99] Josh 13:24–31. The notion of the twelve tribes as having territories which belonged to them was familiar to biblically-informed Jews, and in the rabbinic tradition it was known that the Land of Israel was not the same as, let alone defined by, the territory described by the Romans as the "province of Judaea." See map at figure 2 on page 154.

[100] Josephus, *B.J.* 2.409.

[101] Josephus, *B.J.* 2.457–58.

[102] Pritz, *Nazarene Jewish Christianity*, 124–26, followed by Balabanski, *Eschatology*, 119.

[103] Gerd Lüdemann, *Opposition to Paul in Jewish Christianity* (Minneapolis: Fortress, 1988), 201.

Epiphanius's *Weights and Measures*, is to note that "a small church of God, in the upper room to which the disciples had gone after the ascension of the Savior from the Mount of Olives," survived and was there for Hadrian to find, "in that part of Zion which had escaped destruction":[104] "an exodus was thus dispensable," he writes optimistically,[105] shoring up his finding that there was no Pella migration. And yet he comments on the problem caused by the death of the apostles, which was addressed in the years 70–100 (on his view) by the production of the pseudonymous writings of the New Testament.[106] On this view, as he observes, the story of the Pella migration can hardly have been told first by Pella Christians trying to appear as the successors of the Jerusalem church—since such a claim would involve holding up "a view of the significance of Jerusalem Christianity that other Gentile Christian churches could hardly have shared."[107]

On balance, rejecting the (relatively slender) evidence for the Pella migration seems to cause more difficulties than it solves, and resorting to the claim that getting out of Jerusalem was impossible strains credibility.[108] The Jerusalem bishops list clearly implies a Jerusalem church after 70, and Lüdemann's argument that evacuation would have been redundant because Epiphanius thought there was a church left in the "portion of Zion which escaped destruction, together with blocks of houses in the neighborhood of Zion and the seven synagogues which alone remained standing in Zion, like solitary huts ... 'like a booth in a vineyard,'"[109] is weak. Jerusalem was largely in ruins between 70 and 135, even if a few buildings remained. It seems to be correct to adopt Bauckham's conclusion that from 70 to 135 the Jerusalem church was effectively a church in exile, east of the Jordan: "Eusebius' story," Bauckham concludes, "probably has at least some historical worth."[110]

An archaeological investigation carried out jointly in 1967 at Tabaqat Fahl by Wooster College and the University of Sydney led to findings that Robert H. Smith described as furnishing evidence of a Christian presence in Pella in the first century.[111] In the northern apse of a sixth-century Byzantine church a first-century Roman sarcophagus was found, and as Balabanski summarizes, "[t]he church seems to have been built in such a way that the grave would rest just below the paving, suggesting that the positioning was intended to venerate the remains of a very important person."[112] Evaluation of this find depends on interpretation: did the sixth-century builders construct the church

---

[104] Epiphanius, *Weights and Measures,* 14.

[105] Lüdemann, *Opposition to Paul,* 210.

[106] Lüdemann, *Opposition to Paul,* 212.

[107] Lüdemann, *Opposition to Paul,* 212.

[108] Pritz refers to multiple escapes from the siege of Jerusalem narrated by Josephus, commenting that "the cumulative picture ... is impressive in its portrayal of the continuous escape from the city by thousands" (*Nazarene Jewish Christianity*, 126).

[109] Epiphanius, *Weights and Measures,* 14.

[110] Bauckham, "James and the Jerusalem Community," 79.

[111] Robert H. Smith, *Pella of the Decapolis I: the 1967 Campaign of the College of Wooster Expedition to Pella* (Wooster: College of Wooster, 1973), 143–49.

[112] Balabanski, *Eschatology*, 118 n. 33.

as they did in the belief that they were honoring the memory of a great (first-century) saint? Possibly—but nothing was found which would have proved who it was whom they labored to commemorate; and presuming that the interpretation of the find as relating to veneration of a first-century Christian who died at Pella is correct, nothing exists to show whether the deceased's presence in Pella was accounted for by the evacuation of leading believers from Jerusalem in the late sixties.

Therefore the story of the migration to Pella remains frustratingly incomplete; and the inferences to be drawn about the ongoing influence of the Jerusalem church after 70 are by no means straightforward, either. As Bauckham tells the story, there was a substantial decrease in the prestige of the Jerusalem church, in effect right from the moment when Titus demolished the Temple. He gives three reasons: there no longer being a Christian community in Jerusalem itself; there being no annual flow of pilgrims to the Temple (hence links between Jerusalem and the diaspora being weakened); and the bishops of Jerusalem in exile being unable to hold "the same position of power and influence beyond Palestine that James had earlier had."[113] And yet the plausibility of this view as a whole rests on an overall understanding of how the New Testament was formed. If Lüdemann is right in his surmise that characteristically Jewish-Christian writings, such as, for example, Matthew, James, Hebrews, and 1 and 2 Peter were produced in the last three decades of the first century, then—regardless of the situation on the ground in Jerusalem—it might be right to think in terms of an ongoing impact made by writers who could, in broad terms, be associated with the Jerusalem community as it had been—the smile lingering on after the Cheshire cat itself melted away.

9. Beyond the Jerusalem Church

Jerusalem, however, had been only one of the concerns of Jesus' family during the first generation in which the gospel of Jesus was preached; and it appears that Roman victory in the war of 66–70 had relatively little impact on the church which had come into being as a result of their endeavors in Galilee and beyond. Paul refers in Corinthians to Jesus' brothers as traveling missionaries (1 Cor 9:5), and Sextus Julius Africanus in his *Letter to Aristides*, written in the first half of the third century, referred to the *desposynoi*,[114] so called from their connection with the Savior's family,[115]

---

[113] Bauckham, "James and the Jerusalem Community," 80.

[114] Bauckham (*Jude and the Relatives*, 61–62) glosses *desposynoi* (δεσπόσυνοι) as "those who belong to the Master," which is not exhaustive: Pollux (*Onomasticon* 3.73.3) says, "the younger master is called *desposynos* and *trophimos*," and the scholia on Euripides, *Hecuba* 99 say, "*desposynos* principally means the master's son" (Eduard Schwartz, *Scholia in Euripidem*, 2 vols. [Berlin: Reimer, 1:1887; 2:1891]). Drawing on these definitions, it would make better sense to gloss *desposynoi* as "the Lord's relatives," while also bearing in mind the idea of their being his successors.

who traveled from Nazareth and Kokhaba, Jewish villages, to the rest of the land, expounding the genealogy that they had to hand from the "Book of Days"[116] as far as they traveled.[117] The point of using the genealogy in their preaching was to explain "the messianic significance of Jesus as they understood it."[118]

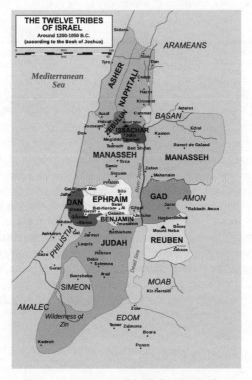

Figure 2. Territories of the Tribes per Joshua.
Public Domain.

Jesus' relatives apparently approached their ministry as wandering missionaries in the same way Jesus had approached his preaching mission: less interested in larger centers, and more inclined to spend time in rural districts and smaller centers. Jesus went to "the region of Tyre" (but apparently not into the city), and then reached Sidon (the city) before turning

[115] Bauckham argues that *desposynoi* was "a technical term for the family of Jesus which was current in the Greek usage of Palestinian Jewish Christian circles, but not elsewhere" (*Jude and the Relatives*, 361).

[116] The "Book of Days" is a reference to the biblical books of 1 and 2 Chronicles.

[117] Sextus Julius Africanus, *Ep. Arist.* v. For text, see *ANF* 6:127 and Walther Reichardt, *Die Briefe des Sextus Julius Africanus an Aristides und Origenes* (Leipzig: Hinrichs, 1909). See also Bauckham, *Jude and the Relatives*, 61.

[118] Bauckham, *Jude and the Relatives*, 363.

south again and heading for the Decapolis.[119] The *desposynoi* based their mission in small towns and villages: Nazareth, Jesus' home town, and Kokhaba. Identifying which Kokhaba they made their base is difficult because it was a common place-name. In the passage quoted above, Epiphanius identifies Kokhaba in Bashanitis (Batanea, east from the Sea of Galilee, and part of the Roman province of Syria from 53) as where the sect of Nazoreans is found;[120] but Bauckham argues that the Kokhaba that Julius Africanus had in mind is a village, now called Kaukab, to the north of Sepphoris and sixteen kilometers from Nazareth,[121] and he comments that "to associate the *desposynoi* of the first Christian generation with ... Kokhaba [in Batanea] would be most improbable."[122] His grounds for the last inference seem to be weak: in terms of distance from Nazareth, Kokhaba in Batanea would not be more remote than Sidon, which Jesus visited—and moreover, all of Batanea (Bashan) forms part of the Land of Israel as biblically defined.[123] Elsewhere, Bauckham notes how the agenda for missionary activity set in Acts 1:8 ("you will be my witnesses in Jerusalem, in all Judea and Samaria, and to the ends of the earth") "obscures the probability of missionary activity throughout Palestine from the beginning":[124] and here, arguably, "Palestine"[125] should be replaced with "the Land of Israel," because the Land of Israel was a more important idea in Jewish thought than any of the provinces or client kingdoms into which the relevant territory was divided by the Romans in the period when the *desposynoi* were itinerant preachers.[126]

There are some hints of activity outside the Land of Israel. As Bauckham says, Phoenicia, Damascus, and the Decapolis would have been "obvious places for missionary work," and one may wonder if the church at Damascus that Saul went to persecute had resulted from preaching by the relatives of Jesus[127]—but there are equally plausible speculations to hand. Another possibility should be raised, if inconclusively. Medieval chronicles say that the founder of the church at Seleuceia-Ctesiphon on the Tigris was Mari, and the names listed after him on the list of bishops are Abris, Abraham, and Ya'qub—Abris being described as "of the family and race of Joseph" the husband of Mary, and Abraham as "of the kin of James called a brother of the

---

[119] Mark 7:24 // Matt 15:21; Mark 7:31.
[120] Epiphanius, *Pan.* 29.7.7: modern Kaukab, in Syria just to the north of the border with Jordan (cf. Bauckham, *Jude and the Relatives*, 63).
[121] Bauckham, *Jude and the Relatives*, 64, where another candidate location is also mentioned: Kokhav Hayarden/Kawkab al-Hawa, a Palestinian village built within the walls of Belvoir castle, but destroyed on 21 May 1948 by the Golani Brigade in the course of Operation Gideon.
[122] Bauckham, *Jude and the Relatives*, 63.
[123] In the territory of Manasseh, cf. Josh 13:29–31.
[124] Bauckham, *Jude and the Relatives*, 66; on the following page he notes that Galilee, not mentioned elsewhere in Acts, has a successful and growing church at Acts 9:31 ("the church throughout Judea, Galilee, and Samaria had peace and was built up").
[125] A word used by Bauckham without regard to chronology, in that the province of Judea was renamed as Palestine at a later date, in 134, as part of the Roman reprisals after the Third Jewish War.
[126] See, for example, m. Kelim 1.6: "The Land of Israel is holier than all other lands."
[127] Cf. Bauckham, *Jude and the Relatives*, 68.

Lord": Bauckham argues that these obscure figures are not legendary, but that because of the large Jewish diaspora in Mesopotamia it is credible that members of Jesus' family would have traveled there to spread the gospel.[128]

Itinerant preaching did not necessarily bring with it the loss of all connection to the family's home district. Hegesippus, a second-century writer whose work, now lost, was drawn on by Eusebius, reported on the order given by Domitian (AD 81–96) to put members of the royal family of David to death. "There still survived of the family of the Lord the grandsons of Jude,"[129] Eusebius writes, and he says that informers caused them to be brought before Domitian. When he asked them if they were descendants of David, they admitted it, but when he asked them what assets and how much money they had (πόσας κτήσεις ἔχουσιν ἢ πόσων χρημάτων κυριεύουσιν), they said they were worth 9,000 denarii between them, not in cash, but because that was the value of the thirty-nine plethra of land (3.7 hectares), which they worked to support themselves and pay their taxes.[130] Questioned about Christ and his kingdom, they explained that it was a heavenly and angelic kingdom that would appear at the end of the world: Domitian after hearing all this "in no way condemned them, but despised them as men of no account," let them go, and ended his persecution against the church.[131]

It is difficult to imagine Jude's grandsons, whose names were Zoker and James,[132] being brought before Domitian—but not impossible, since Paul was brought before Nero (or at least, the end of Acts gives the reader to understand that Paul was certain to be brought into the imperial presence when it suited Nero to call him), and Zoker and James were probably of some political importance in the province of Judea. Eusebius, still drawing on Hegesippus, goes on to say that "when released they ruled the churches"—which suggests that if the churches in and around Galilee had represented a threat to Domitian, taking action against Zoker and James would have been an understandable course of action on his part. Hegesippus says that they remained alive till the time of Trajan,[133] and says the same of their kinsman Symeon son of Clopas—who was also accused of being a Davidide, though brought up before Atticus the governor (Tiberius Claudius Atticus Herodes, praetorian legate of Judea 99–102[134]) rather than the emperor himself.[135]

Rejecting Hegesippus's assertion that Symeon lived to be one hundred and twenty—the biblically defined maximum lifespan for a human being (Gen 6:3), and one that made Symeon seem to be a Moses-like figure (Deut 34:7)—Bauckham does conclude that he was "leader of the Jerusalem church and probably the most important figure in Jewish Christianity for nearly forty

[128] Bauckham, *Jude and the Relatives*, 68–70.
[129] Eusebius, *Hist. eccl.* 3.20.1.
[130] Eusebius, *Hist. eccl.* 3.20.1–2.
[131] Eusebius, *Hist. eccl.* 3.20.3–5.
[132] Sources assembled at Bauckham, *Jude and the Relatives*, 97–99.
[133] Eusebius, *Hist. eccl.* 3.20.6.
[134] E. Mary Smallwood, "Atticus, Legate of Judaea under Trajan," *JRS* 52 (1962): 131–33.
[135] Eusebius, *Hist. eccl.* 3.32.1–6.

years."[136] His appearance before Atticus shows that Symeon at the turn of the century was no longer outside Roman jurisdiction in Pella, but the hearing at which he was sentenced to death probably took place in Caesarea Maritima, the provincial capital. Symeon's crucifixion[137] at the end of the first century marks the end of this chapter, and it only remains to add that during the years of Symeon's leadership the Jerusalem church, although it survived the destruction of the Temple, became much less influential across the Christian world, while "the churches outside Palestine were growing more distant from their Palestinian roots, and ... leadership was passing from Jewish to Gentile Christians."[138]

Recommended Reading

Balabanski, Vicky. *Eschatology in the Making: Matthew, Mark and the Didache.* Cambridge: Cambridge University Press, 1997.

Bauckham, Richard. "James and the Jerusalem Community." Pages 55–95 in *Jewish Believers in Jesus.* Edited by Oskar Skarsaune and Reider Hvalvik. Peabody, MA: Hendrickson, 2007.

Bauckham, Richard. *Jude and the Relatives of Jesus in the Early Church.* Edinburgh: T&T Clark, 1990.

Boyarin, Daniel. "Rethinking Jewish Christianity: An Argument for Dismantling a Dubious Category." *JQR* 99 (2009): 7–36.

Boyarin, Daniel. *Border Lines: The Partition of Judaeo-Christianity.* Philadelphia: University of Pennsylvania Press, 2004.

Carleton Paget, James. *Jews, Christians and Jewish Christians in Antiquity.* Tübingen: Mohr Siebeck, 2010.

Jackson-McCabe, Matt, ed. *Jewish Christianity Reconsidered.* Minneapolis: Fortress, 2007.

Jervell, Jacob. "The Mighty Minority." *ST* 34 (1980): 13–38.

Lohfink, Gerhard. *Die Sammlung Israels: eine Untersuchung zur lukanischer Ekklesiologie.* Munich: Kösel, 1975.

Pritz, Ray A. *Nazarene Jewish Christianity: From the End of the New Testament Period until its Disappearance in the Fifth Century.* Jerusalem: Magnes; Leiden: Brill, 1988.

Skarsaune, Oskar, and Reidar Hvalvik, eds. *Jewish Believers in Jesus.* Peabody, MA: Hendrickson, 2007.

---

[136] Bauckham, *Jude and the Relatives*, 93.

[137] Eusebius, *Hist. eccl.* 3.32.6, "orders were given that he should be crucified."

[138] Bauckham, *Jude and the Relatives*, 93.

6. "The Parting of the Ways"

Lydia Gore-Jones and Stephen Llewelyn

According to the great commission (Matt 28:16–20) Jesus, before his ascension, charged the eleven with the task of making disciples of all nations and teaching them to keep everything that he had commanded. Within decades, the Jesus Movement had spread rapidly in the Greco-Roman world, attracting large numbers of followers of non-Jewish descent. Neither Jesus himself nor his apostles apparently intended to create a new religion, yet in hindsight it would appear that the Gentile mission was a major factor contributing to the development of a new "religion" that in time viewed its own identity as distinct from emergent Judaism. But, of course, this is to view the development from a Christian perspective.

The question of the "parting of the ways"—the expression often used to designate the phenomenon—investigates the historical separation of Christianity and Judaism from a common background to become two distinct identities: why, how, and when it happened. But before we approach the question, a number of preliminary issues need to be addressed, the first of which involves the metaphor itself.[1]

1. Metaphors, Names, Identity, and Diversity

The power of metaphor is to provide a way of thinking about something, often that is abstract, in terms that are more familiar to and evocative for us. And thus it is with the metaphor of the "parting of the ways."[2] The familiar and comfortable metaphor of the journey and its constituent elements of roads, travelers, beginnings, and ends, together with their entailments derived from

---

[1] The metaphor seems to be first adopted in 1912 in a volume edited by F. J. Foakes-Jackson, *The Parting of the Roads: Studies in the Development of Judaism and Early Christianity* (London: Edward Arnold, 1912). For a history of the concept, see Judith Lieu, "'The Parting of the Ways': Theological Construct or Historical Reality?" *JSNT* 56 (1994): 101–19. Also Adam H. Becker and Annette Yoshiko Reed, "Introduction," in *The Ways That Never Parted: Jews and Christians in Late Antiquity and the Early Middle Ages*, TSAJ 95, ed. Adam H. Becker and Annette Yoshiko Reed (Minneapolis: Fortress, 2003), 8–9.

[2] It will also be noted that the expression "parting of the ways" is sometimes prefixed by the definite article, which assumes, unless it is construed as anaphoric, that one knows the process to which it refers. This is problematic as the reference is to a linguistic construct and as already noted very little is known of the actual process.

our rich experience of them (e.g., roads have ups and downs, roads diverge, and roads converge, roads may lead the wrong way, journeys have fellow travelers) is used to explain the abstract notion of the religious divergence between Judaism and Christianity. But one must be careful in determining what exactly is mapped in the metaphor and not be led by the metaphor to assume an existent state of affairs or situation in the target domain (RELIGIOUS DIVERGENCE) based on the metaphor's source domain (JOURNEY). The metaphor should not imply that there was any one point where the roads diverged or even that there was any one cause for the divergence. The "parting of the ways" between Judaism and Christianity is not a single historical event;[3] rather the metaphor seeks to explain an indeterminate process for which the beginning is assumed (the origins of Christianity in Jewish movements of the Second Temple period) and the end is observed (two religions that sense themselves as distinct).[4]

Related to the problem of metaphor is the danger of essentialism: the idea that constitutive realities underlie what we name and that these differ between differently named objects. For example, did "Christianity" and "Judaism" as we understand the terms—as faiths, with their respective creeds, orthodoxies, and institutions—actually exist in the early centuries?[5] In this regard it is important to pay particular attention to the terms used by the ancients and the meanings intended by them.

The author of Acts tells us that the name, Christians, Χριστιανοί—(Greek)/*Christiani* (Latin)—was first used in Antioch (Acts 11:26), and it has been generally argued that this was a name applied by Gentile outsiders as a derogatory term for those who were said to follow a man called *Christos*.[6] Within a few decades it appears to have been accepted as a Christian self-designation, with its earliest attestations in the Didache (12.4; arguably dated to the late first to early second century), and the letters of Ignatius of Antioch (early second century). Ignatius is also the first on record to use the term

---

[3] James D. G. Dunn, *The Partings of the Ways Between Christianity and Judaism and Their Significance for the Character of Christianity* (London: SCM, 1991; 2006). It is for the above reason that Dunn titles his book "Partings (plural) of the Ways." In the words of Dunn, "the reason for entitling this volume, 'The *Partings* (plural) of the Ways,' was and is, of course, to make the point that the separation of Christianity from rabbinic Judaism cannot neatly be identified as taking place at a particular point in time or place, as though there was only one 'parting of the ways'" (Preface to the Second Edition, xi).

[4] The journey metaphor, like other metaphors used of the process (e.g., familial metaphors of siblings or parent and child), seeks to structure how we think about the relationship and how it changes.

[5] See a critique on the terms in Daniel Boyarin, "Semantic Differences; or, 'Judaism'/'Christianity,'" in Becker and Reed, *The Ways That Never Parted*, 65–86.

[6] This term is most probably associated with Gentile Jesus followers, although there are certain gray areas, especially in the situation of mixed members. The Jewish Christians are known as the *notzrim*, named after their Nazarene origin. In a modern analogy, Jewish Jesus-believers are known as Messianic Jews rather than Christians.

Christianismos (Christianity) in antithesis to *Ioudaismos* (Judaism; cf. Ign. *Magn.* 8.1; 10.3).[7]

The term "Jews," *Ioudaioi*, originally denoted the people from the land of Judah, a designation of a *genos* similar to the labels "Egyptians" or "Chaldeans." By the first century it had probably lost its geographical association, but its ethnic (as opposed to a strictly religious) meaning remained, used very much in opposition and contrast to Gentiles, Samaritans, Greeks, and Romans.[8] As for Judaism, the only usage of the word *Ioudaismos* by Jewish writers before the common era appears in 2 Maccabees, in which it means not a religion, but an ancestral way of life: the practices, the zeal and the loyalty associated with it that mark out the Hasmonean nation from its Hellenistic neighbors.[9] *Ioudaismos* only comes to mean Judaism as a religion in the late second century in the mind and writing of Tertullian, who uses the term in contrast to *Christianismos*.[10]

So what does it mean to be a "Christian" or a "Jew"? When it comes to a study of human identity whether as individuals or as groups, we are dealing with socially constructed features that are used to designate difference and to create a sense of belonging. Such features are neither preexistent nor do they survive independently of the social matrix that engenders them. Circumcision or Baptism, Sabbath or Sunday, Hanukkah or Christmas, Passover or Easter—these are the socially constructed practices that differentiate. What, then, is implied by the designations "Judaism" and "Christianity"? How did members of communities in the early centuries perceive their own identities as Christian or Jewish? Because of these difficulties Boyarin even goes as far as to say that "there is no non-theological or non-anachronistic way" of distinguishing the two until "institutions are in place to make and enforce that distinction." In his view, this did not occur till the fourth century. Yet even then we know very little about what members of communities at a grassroots level were actually thinking and doing.[11] Boyarin's words, of course, remind us of the importance of exercising extreme caution when applying labels; that said, it is also important

---

[7] See Tim Hegedus, "Naming Christians in Antiquity," *SR* 33 (2004): 173–90. Also Harold B. Mattingly, "The Origin of the Name *Christiani*," *JTS* 9 (1958): 26–37; Henry J. Cadbury, "Names for Christians and Christianity in Acts," in *The Beginnings of Christianity: The Acts of the Apostles*, ed. F. J. Foakes-Jackson and Kirsopp Lake (Grand Rapids: Baker, 1979), 5:371–92; Elias J. Bickerman, "The Name of Christian," *HTR* 42 (1949): 109–24, reprinted in *Studies in Jewish and Christian History*, 3:139–51 (Leiden: Brill, 1986).

[8] See Stephen G. Wilson, "'Jew' and Related Terms in the Ancient World," *SR* 33 (2004): 157–71. Also H. Lowe, "Who were the Ioudaioi?" *NovT* 18 (1976): 101–30; and Graham Harvey, *True Israel. Uses of the Names Jew, Hebrew and Israel in Ancient Jewish and Early Christian Literature* (Boston and Leiden: Brill, 2001).

[9] See Daniel Boyarin, "Rethinking Jewish Christianity: An Argument for Dismantling a Dubious Category (to which is Appended a Correction of my *Border Lines*)," *JQR* 99.1 (2009): 7–36 (8).

[10] See Steve Mason, "Jews, Judaeans, Judaizing, Judaism: Problems of Categorization in Ancient History," *JSJ* 38.4–5 (2007): 457–512 (472–76). Mason particularly comments that Tertullian's use of *Ioudaismus* "strips away all that was different in Judaean culture—its position among ancient peoples, ancestral traditions, laws and customs, constitution, aristocracy, priesthood, philosophical schools—abstracting only an impoverished belief system" (472).

[11] Boyarin, "Rethinking," 28.

to allow the early Jesus Movement within Judaism to be seen as identifiably Christian, something that can be discussed meaningfully as the beginning of Christianity despite being in its initial, fluid state.[12]

To return to the issue of identity more generally, the study of its formation in the ancient world is problematic on a number of fronts. These need to be borne in mind in assessing the soundness of any result. First, we are unable to question the subjects but must rely on the traces that are left behind by them in the historical record. Survival of such data may be selective, and thus biased. Moreover, it will require assumptions to interpret that evidence and its significance.[13] Second, identity is not mono-dimensional but constructed along a number of different social planes or vectors. We are interested in the religious vector, but there are many others of equal significance such as race, class, and sex. And even along the religious vector there are other religious traditions that may affect the nature of Jewish and Christian relations. One only has to think of the hostility that missionary activity and conversion could arouse in Greco-Roman society, and the argument that this was one of the factors that prompted Jewish communities to distance themselves from the Jesus Movement. Third, the model used to understand identity formation is based on the binary of "self" and "other": "us" and "them." As the latter reiteration of the model shows, there is a privileging of conflict and tension in its construction. In other words, insofar as we focus on the terms "Jew" and "Christian" as identity markers, we will tend to look for areas of difference, which naturally are best attested in evidence of conflict. It is therefore not surprising that much of the debate has been preoccupied with the *contra Iudaeos* literature.

Evidential, social, and geographical diversity needs also to be factored into any consideration of the issue. Literary evidence tends to represent the views of an elite authority and to reflect its norms, while archaeological and documentary evidence gives expression to the lived experience of a local community. The former tends to state the ideal and the latter to reflect actual practice. Moreover, the evidence we gather, be it textual or archaeological, is limited to specific periods and locations. Relationships between Christianity and Judaism could have been quite different in Palestine, in the western Mediterranean world, in North Africa and in the eastern Parthian (248 BC–AD 224) and Sassanid (AD 224–651) Empires; or quite diverse in different social and cultural contexts even within the same geographical location. Because of this discrepancy, Judith Lieu

---

[12] Or in D. A. Hagner's words, "If one means by them [the terms Christianity and Rabbinic Judaism] static entities, like forms of set concrete, we shall find them only later. If, on the other hand, one means emerging systems undergoing active development, yet with enough focus and fixity to make them essentially definable, then we can speak of them in the first century." See "Another Look at 'The Parting of the Ways,'" in *Earliest Christian History: History, Literature, and Theology: Essays from the Tyndale Fellowship in Honor of Martin Hengel*, ed. Michael F. Bird and Jason Maston (Tübingen: Mohr Siebeck, 2012), 381–427 (389).

[13] For example, answering such questions as "Does the use of a Jewish name in a papyrus letter imply a Jewish or Christian connection or is the question even relevant for the period concerned?" or "Is a papyrus copy of the Septuagint Jewish or Christian?" requires a number of assumptions. Indeed, in the early centuries it is quite rare to find evidence for Christianity in the papyrological evidence.

warns that "what we know about is the specific and the local," while discussions of the "parting of the ways" tend to operate "essentially with the abstract or universal conception of each religion."[14] These observations remind us of the complexity inherent to any study of ancient society. The boundary between identities can be murky and fluid, and even within their own walls Christianity and Judaism could hardly be seen as monolithic or uniform entities. Still, focus on the lived reality and experience remains a desideratum in the study of Jewish and Christian relations in the early centuries. For too long the studies have been preoccupied with the literary evidence, which is now increasingly seen as non-representative of how Jews and Christians interacted on a day-to-day basis in the cities of the Mediterranean.

Despite its limitations, the "parting of the ways" presents a workable metaphor to help us see the trajectories of two religions that shared a common origin but eventually saw themselves as fundamentally different.[15] To borrow Alexander's visual analogy (another metaphor, but this time used to structure how we think about groups with mixed identities and/or allegiances), today Christianity and Judaism can be seen as two self-contained and separate circles; but, tracing their antecedents back, in the fourth century one sees them overlapping at points (e.g., Jewish Christians or Christian Jews), and in the first few decades of the first century the circle of Christianity is entirely contained within the circle of Judaism.[16]

To slightly modify Alexander's analogy, one might speak of "Christianities" and "Judaisms" to account for diversity in the late Second Temple period, and view both as contained within the one circle.[17] It is within that same circle that the origins of what would later be known as Rabbinic Judaism are to be found. In other words, one cannot simply assume that Rabbinic Judaism is a natural continuation of Second Temple Judaism; instead, like Christianity, it developed for the most part from a form of Second Temple Judaism (i.e., Pharisaism), which gradually gained religious and political recognition in the Jewish world. Just as Christianity defined itself in opposition to Judaism, Rabbinic Judaism also established its orthodoxy over against Christianity.[18] Here one might avail oneself of yet another metaphor, that of the family, to structure how we think about the relationship between Judaism and Christianity, especially the traits

---

[14] "'The Parting of the Ways': Theological Construct or Historical Reality?" 108.

[15] For a detailed discussion of the usefulness as well as limitations of the metaphor, see Anders Klostergaard Petersen, "At the End of the Road—Reflections on a Popular Scholarly Metaphor," in Jostein Ådna, ed., *The Formation of the Early Church* (Tübingen: Mohr Siebeck, 2005), 45–72.

[16] P. S. Alexander, "The Parting of the Ways from the Perspective of Rabbinic Judaism," in *Jews and Christians: The Parting of the Ways: A.D. 70 to 135*, ed. James D. G. Dunn (Grand Rapids: Eerdmans, 1992), 1–25.

[17] According to the Jerusalem Talmud (y. Sanh. 10.6, 29c), R. Yohannan stated that "Israel did not go into exile until there were twenty-four sects of *minim*." The translation is by Martin Goodman, *Judaism in the Roman World: Collected Essays* (Leiden: Brill, 2007), 46. The number twenty-four may well be symbolic, but the saying of R. Yohannan demonstrates the reality of plurality in Judaism in the Second Temple period.

[18] Daniel Boyarin, *Border Lines: The Partition of Judeo-Christianity* (Philadelphia: University of Pennsylvania Press, 2004).

and features that are shared and those that differ. Accordingly, Judaism and Christianity can be viewed as two siblings of the same mother when a common origin is assumed, or as mother and daughter when a hierarchical relationship is assumed.[19] Clearly, an awareness of the metaphors used to describe the process is needed in order to understand the issues that they entail for the study of the topic.

2. Approaches: The Why and How Questions

Attempts to answer the question "why did the ways part?" tend to consider the issue from the perspective either of internal factors that are thought to make Judaism and Christianity incompatible, or of external factors, such as historical events, with political as well as socioeconomic significance, that led to the schism. Accordingly, there are two approaches that can and are usually taken in discussing the causes of the "parting of the ways." Interestingly, the approaches usually correlate with the types of evidence considered.

2.1. The Theological Approach

The first is what we will call the *theological approach*; it tends to focus on the literary evidence, and as this is weighted toward Christian texts which more explicitly address their position vis-à-vis the *Ioudaioi*, the appearance is given that the initiative to part is Christian. The ideas expressed in the literature are taken and analyzed with the aim of showing that the two "religions" held incongruent belief systems, and that as a result the seeds of separation were germinating already in the first century. One of the most influential works in this approach is Dunn's *Partings of the Ways* (1991, 2006), in which he identifies monotheism, election, the law, and the temple as the four pillars of Second Temple Judaism, and argues that the distinctive doctrines of Christianity in response to the four pillars pull the two religions apart in the first century.[20]

Examples of others who adopt this approach can be multiplied. To cite a few instances, Hagner considers the division to arise from the "newness of the gospel and early Christianity" and that this could not be "contained within a sect of Judaism."[21] The division occurred because of the teaching of ideas that were unacceptable and intolerable to Judaism; these were focused on the issues (pillars) of the election of Israel, the temple, the Torah, and monotheism. The process of boundary formation between Judaism and gentile Christianity found its cause in a new attitude expressed in Christianity very much from its

---

[19] Alan F. Segal uses such a metaphor in *Rebecca's Children: Judaism and Christianity in the Roman World* (Cambridge, MA: Harvard University Press, 1986). Boyarin even claims, "Judaism is not the 'mother' of Christianity; they are twins, joined at the hip" (*Border Lines*, 5).
[20] "One thought in particular has returned to me again and again during my work in preparing these chapters: Christianity began as a movement of renewal breaking through the boundaries first within and then round the Judaism of the first century" (337).
[21] Hagner, "Another Look at 'The Parting of the Ways,'" 382–83.

inception. As a further example, Stuhlmacher[22] sees the parting as arising in particular in the high Christology centered on Christ and his messianic and redemptive roles. As he observes:

> The Christology derived from Jesus' own consciousness of his messianic sending and grounded in his Passion and resurrection is the real driving force behind the separation of Jews ([and Gentiles] who do not believe in Jesus as Lord and Messiah) on the one hand and Christians on the other.[23]

Paul, writing in the first century, is seen as playing a pivotal role in preserving and clarifying this Christology, and elevating it to such "determinative doctrinal norm for the entire church" that the path the church took became irreversible unless at the cost of the gospel and the Christian faith itself.

Daniel Boyarin offers an example that draws principally, though not solely, from the Jewish sources. He argues that the concept of religion, as understood today, is the product of heresiology, in particular the attempt by Gentile Christians from the time of Justin Martyr to determine who they were by the construction of the hybrid others (Jews and heretics). At first the rabbis followed suit, as seen in their use of the rhetorical construct of *minut*, as typified in m. Sanh. 10.1, and the establishment of a *diadoche* of authorities.[24] Central from the rabbinic side in defining itself over against Christianity and the synagogue, which was an institution initially outside its control, was the discursive creation of the heresy of the Two Powers in Heaven: the idea that the Word/Wisdom was with God as expressed in John 1 and the Memra theology of the synagogues.[25] For the earlier rabbis the Word/Wisdom was identified as the Torah, which spoke with one voice.[26] However, by the time of the Babylonian Talmud that way of determining Jewish identity was rejected and "interpretative indeterminacy and endless dispute" became the norm, where the Oral Torah became "one many-voiced text with no author."[27] However, by that time both Judaism and Christianity were well-established and separate entities.[28]

---

[22] P. Stuhlmacher, "The Understanding of Christ in the Pauline School: A Sketch," in Dunn, *Jews and Christians*, 159–75.

[23] Stuhlmacher, "The Understanding of Christ," 174.

[24] Daniel Boyarin, *Border Lines*, 29–30, 58–63 and 74–86, respectively.

[25] Boyarin, *Border Lines*, 112–27. The preexistence of divine Wisdom, whether viewed as personified or as hypostatic, is widely attested in both diaspora Judaism and Palestinian Jewish traditions; to cite a few examples, see Prov 3:19; 8:22–30; Wisd 7:26; 8:4–6; Sir 24:9; 2 En. 30.8.

[26] Boyarin, *Border Lines*, 128–29.

[27] Boyarin, *Border Lines*, 156 and 196, respectively. As Boyarin comments: "the latest layer of Babylonian rabbinic literature, the finally redacted Talmud, not only rejected *homonoia* but promulgated instead a sensibility of the ultimate contingency of all truth claims" (153).

[28] Boyarin questions the use of the terms Judaism and Christianity before the fourth century based on the changed concept of *religio* (i.e., the separation between ethnos/culture and belief/cult) that took place with the official recognition of Christianity. See Boyarin, "Semantic Differences; or, 'Judaism/Christianity,'" in Becker and Reed, *The Ways That Never Parted*, 65–85, and "Rethinking Jewish Christianity: An Argument for Dismantling a Dubious Category,"

2.2. The Historical Approach

The second approach, which we call "historical," is found in attempts to trace the cause for the partition between Christianity and Judaism to significant historical events that shaped the contours of development or worked as catalysts for the final division of the two religions. The focus here is the desire to date the parting and thus provide it with an interpretive historical context. The late-first (e.g., the fall of Jerusalem and destruction of the temple—AD 70), mid-second (e.g., the Bar Kokhba revolt—AD 135) or fourth (the Christianization of the Roman Empire) centuries are crucial periods for those adopting this approach.[29]

Martin Goodman and Marius Heemstra provide two examples. Goodman[30] argues that the imposition of the *fiscus judaicus* in the aftermath of AD 70, and its evolution, especially under Nerva when its application was relaxed to only practicing Jews, did much to change the designation of *Ioudaios* from that of a member of a *gens* to that of a practitioner of a particular *religio*. By implication, it worked as a push for those worshiping in the church to part with any potential Jewish identity they might have. For those wishing to remain loyal to their Jewish identity, it further sharpened for them the division between the *religio* of the *Ioudaios* and the *religio* of others.

Heemstra[31] takes a similar point of reference; believing that the "parting of the ways" was at its core the separation between Judaism and Jewish Christians, he seeks to argue that the rigorous nature of the exaction of the Jewish tax under Domitian from AD 85, and its relaxation with changed definition under Nerva from AD 96, was a significant factor in the separation of the ways.[32] The effect of the change under Nerva was to make the definition of those subject to the

---

JQR 99.1 (2009): 7–36. At the same time he entertains a prototype theory of categorization to understand the earlier period using "definable clusters of religious features" (or indicia) with indefinable (or unclear) boundaries that "congealed" into Judaism and Christianity "via Ideological State Apparatuses and Repressive State Apparatuses" ("Semantic Differences," 77). Yet the enterprise would seem in prospect anachronistic in its use of terminology (e.g. "religious features") and irretrievably circular in its application, i.e., "membership gradience" with its "chained communion or communication" still appears to assume the "politically charged and … diachronically varying category" of "best example."

[29] Note the specific mention of AD 70 to 135, the period between the two Jewish wars against the Romans as the crucial time for the Christian and Jewish division, in the volume edited by James D. G. Dunn under the title *The Parting of the Ways*.

[30] Martin Goodman, "Diaspora Reactions to the Destruction of the Temple," in Dunn, *Jews and Christians*, 27–38. The focus here is more on the Roman and diaspora Jewish perspective. Also see his "Nerva, the *fiscus Judaicus* and the Jewish identity," *JRS* 79 (1989): 40–44.

[31] Marius Heemstra, *The Fiscus Judaicus and the Parting of the Ways*, WUNT 2.277 (Tübingen: Mohr Siebeck, 2010).

[32] Heemstra seeks to make a distinction in the descriptions of the legislation by Suetonius (*Dom.* 12.2) and Dio Cassius (*Hist.* 66.7.2) with the former reflecting that under Domitian (dated ca. AD 85, 27) and the latter that under Nerva (dated AD 96, 80–82). The argument is somewhat speculative, based on an attempt to make sense of the numismatic claim by Nerva that under him FISCI IUDAICI CALUMNIA SUBLATA, and an interpretation of New Testament literature deemed to be Jewish-Christian.

Jewish tax religious rather than ethnic in nature.[33] This had the effect of excluding Jewish Christians from the protection that Judaism offered as a *religio licita*, and thus differentiating them from Jews in Roman eyes. At roughly the same time the promulgation of the Birkat Haminim [the so-called benediction against the heretics] (ca. AD 90) further marginalized Jewish Christians. The curse had been prompted by a growing division in the synagogue caused by a number of factors, for example, different views to proselytism prompted by antagonism to conversion, the claim made by Jewish Christians to be the "true Israel," and their development of a "Christology" that placed the Messiah above the Torah.

2.3. The Sociological Approach

The examples cited above are universalizing, in the sense that they tend to diminish or undervalue considerations and evidence that complicate the process. In other words, geographical and chronological differences and variations are placed in the background. A subcategory of the historical approach addresses itself more fully to the social context within which Jews and Christians found themselves. The approach seeks to make up for the under-determination of the evidence by the use of sociological models of how certain types of societies work to fill in the gaps in that evidence.

Using this approach, Fredriksen[34] finds intimate social interactions among Jews, "pagans," and Christians of different kinds in the Mediterranean cities, despite the presence of profound animosity in their respective literatures. She sees the stridency of the polemical *contra Iudaeos* tradition (the product of the educated elite) as both a response to the degree of continued contact at the city level and an attempt to demarcate Christian identity.[35] Actual, effective segregation, she states, lies outside late antiquity, "well off into the Middle Ages."[36]

Of course it is not always possible to distinguish between approaches. For example, Robinson's[37] focus on the church at Antioch in the late first or early

[33] Heemstra, 80–82. The evidence for the religious nature of Nerva's change is slight, falling heavily on Ignatius's use of *Christianismos*, *Magn.* 9.1; 10.1, 3; *Phld.* 6.1; and *Rom.* 3.3, and John's use of the expression "the Jews."
[34] Paula Fredriksen, "What Parting of the Ways?" in Becker and Reed, *The Ways That Never Parted*, 35–63.
[35] For a similar approach see F. J. E. Boddens Hosang, *Establishing Boundaries: Christian-Jewish Relations in Early Council Texts and the Writings of Church Fathers* (Leiden: Brill, 2010): "Literary argumentation does not necessarily mean that therefore day to day contacts did not exist, or when they did, they were antagonistic" (14). Boddens Hosang speaks of "levels" at which the partings occur.
[36] She therefore concludes, "How, then, can we best respond to the question, 'When was the Parting of the Ways?' Only with the question: 'What Parting of the Ways?'" (62–63).
[37] Thomas A. Robinson, *Ignatius of Antioch and the Parting of the Ways: Early Jewish-Christian Relations* (Grand Rapids: Baker, 2009), uses the church at Antioch as a focused study; his findings appear to be the opposite of Fredriksen's. He concludes that the separation of Judaism and Christianity was a *fait accompli* before the time of Ignatius's writing to the churches. Cf. Robinson, *Ignatius of Antioch*, 148–53. His contention is based on the hostile

second century, insofar as it relies on the reading of Ignatius's letters, might be thought to fall under the theological approach; however, he uses sociological modeling to understand identity. Another work that corroborates Robinson's conclusion of an early date of separation is Stephen Spence's case study of the Roman church.[38] He likewise uses literary evidence, but applies sociological modeling to differentiate possible religious groups represented in it. However, instead of conflict and hostility between Christians and Jews as found in Antioch, he finds that the church and the synagogue in Rome went their separate ways early, and that throughout the second half of the first century the two communities virtually ignored each other. He suggests that the religious influence of Israel on the church was not the result of ongoing contact with the synagogue, but originated from its Jewish beginning and was transmitted through the church's continued use of the Septuagint and its own traditions. The debates within Christian literature are internal to the church, not juxtaposed with the synagogue in an attempt to justify the church's own position. If Spence's conclusion is accepted, it shows once again the importance of studying the "parting of the ways" by examining specific historical examples rather than abstract theological categories alone.

3. The Self-Identity of the Jesus Movement in the First Century

What caused the Jesus Movement to later part ways with Judaism? Political events such as the destruction of Jerusalem with its temple and the imposition of the Jewish tax lent impetus and accelerated the process, but they were not the root cause. Theological disputes certainly played an important role as well. The picture offered by the Gospels paints a Jesus in conflict with his fellow *Ioudaioi* in matters of practice and teaching. And for the argument here it matters little whether this was real or imposed by the evangelists in light of their own contemporary experience of a fraught relationship. However, we have indicators of its intensity in their willingness to portray the deaths of Jesus, Stephen, and James as martyrdoms. From the Christian perspective, at least, this indicates a polarization of position. That said, no matter how severe the conflict was, it remained an intramural quarrel within Judaism, as long as the Jesus followers both regarded themselves and were regarded by fellow *Ioudaioi* as Jewish. What caused the parting between Judaism and Christianity was not theological disputation, but a changing demographic caused by Gentile converts, who adopted observances and practices which, while deeply rooted in Jewish tradition, were only partial in nature. In other words, the

---

attitude expressed in the letters to Judaism and its "otherness"—an attitude he believes is "mainstream" and not just found at Antioch—and a rigid delineation of the "boundaries" of both religions. The cause of hostility is complex—Robinson paints a picture of the precarious nature of Jews in Antioch who would as a result be intolerant of "fringe groups" (139) like the Christians. His argument for citizenship appears suspect—but Robinson does note the issue of competition for converts (65–69, 111) and the acceptance of Gentiles.

[38] Stephen Spence, *The Parting of the Ways: The Roman Church as a Case Study* (Leuven: Peeters, 2004).

Lydia Gore-Jones and Stephen Llewelyn

parting might be better seen as the result of ethnic, rather than theological, divergence.

3.1. The Jewish Self-Identity of the Jesus Movement in the First Century: Galatians as an Example

Jewish identity was at the core of the quarrel within the early churches. Among the very first issues confronting the Movement was the treatment of Gentile believers. The confrontation between Paul and Peter in Antioch[39] as well as the first Jerusalem Council decree regarding the requirement of Gentile followers (Acts 15:1:31; 21:25) marked a potential challenge for the Jewish identity of the Jesus Movement, a potential that part of the church fought against, as evidenced in the epistles of Paul. Paul's letters reveal that there were serious arguments between himself and his opponents over the necessity of Torah observance. These arguments have been conventionally interpreted as theological debates over whether the Mosaic Law had been made redundant by Christ; however, the conflict is better viewed as one over the markers of Jewish identity. Circumcision, dietary law, and Sabbath keeping are the external observances that were used to delineate Jewishness. This would explain the motives of Paul's opponents in their apparent effort to contradict his teaching and to challenge his apostolic status among the Gentile churches.

The letter to the Galatians is just such a case in point. Some unnamed men had come to the Galatian churches and preached the need for the Gentile converts to be circumcised. They were likely to be Jewish Christians, as Paul described them as "the circumcised" (6:13) preaching "a different gospel" (1:6). There were also Gentile agitators among the local Galatians, against whom Paul used the strong language: "I wish those who unsettle you would castrate themselves" (5:15). What lies at the core of the strife is not a theological debate over salvation by Law or by faith, but rather whether the nascent church, now counting an increasing number of Gentiles as members, needed to maintain its Jewish identity. It is most telling when Paul says:

> It is those who want to make a good showing in the flesh that try to compel you to be circumcised—only that they may not be persecuted for the cross of Christ. Even the circumcised do not themselves obey the law, but they want you to be circumcised so that they may boast about your flesh (6:12–13, NRSV).[40]

---

[39] Galatians 2:11–17. Did Paul win the argument? Craig C. Hill speculates that Paul lost the argument and consequently had to abandon Antioch as his missionary base. See "The Jerusalem Church" in *Jewish Christianity Reconsidered*, ed. Matt Jackson-McCabe (Minneapolis: Fortress, 2007), 39–56 (43). However, this episode in Galatians 1–2 is part of a series of arguments in support of Paul's authority. It would augment his position and make sense only if he won over Peter. Either way, the episode shows that Gentile members of the church would always pose a problem for the church to remain a Jewish sect.

[40] NRSV is used for all NT quotations in this chapter.

These men seemed to be under great external pressure to have Gentile converts circumcised. Who would have "persecuted" them if they failed to comply? Was it the leadership of the Jewish Christian church in Jerusalem, or was it instead Jewish authorities who had put the Jerusalem church under severe pressure? Either way, it demonstrated that the Movement's leadership felt the need to legitimate its members as Jewish. If the pressure and persecution came from Jewish authorities, it is apparent that what was of concern was not the personal significance of Jesus, but Torah observance among the church's Gentile members.

Did Paul, by opposing the demands placed upon Gentile converts, intend to surrender the Jewish identity of the churches? For after all, he famously said that "in Christ Jesus neither circumcision nor uncircumcision counts for anything" (5:6), and that

> there is no longer Jew or Greek, there is no longer slave or free, there is no longer male and female; for all of you are now in Christ Jesus (3:28).

One should note, however, that it is not only the ethnic difference that Paul's words seem to want to eliminate, but also that of social status and gender. Was he intentionally trying to cast off the Jewish identity of the Jesus Movement? We think not. Paul genuinely believed that he was living in the end time ushered in by the resurrection of the Christ. As such he urged believers to remain in the state they were already in, be it their marital or social status, or condition as circumcised or uncircumcised, as "the time is short"; that is, the end is near (1 Cor 7:8–31). His insistence on Gentiles remaining Gentiles was not motivated by a desire to see a non-Jewish church, or even to create a religion different from Judaism, but rather, it should be seen in the light of the fulfillment of the Isaianic vision that the Gentiles would turn in the future to worship the one true God (Isa 2:2; 11:10; 49:6; 55:5; 60:3). He saw his own ministry among the Gentiles as a role to fulfill that vision. It would have been important, then, that the Gentile converts remain Gentiles. This wish of Paul's apparently ran contrary to that of his opponents, to whom a legitimate Jewish identity was paramount.

3.2. The Jewish Self-Identity of the Church by the End of the First Century: Johannine Literature as an Example

Not only do the Pauline epistles in the middle of the first century AD betray evidence of a concern in certain quarters for a continued Jewish identity, the Johannine literature produced around the end of the first century (John, 1–3 John and Revelation) also shows how the Jesus Movement recognized itself as representing the Jewish nation. The literature was written in a background of mutual hostility between the Johannine community and other Jews; a separation between John's church and the synagogue had already occurred (John 9:22; 16:2). Issues and concerns of this background were projected onto the life events of Jesus. The argument between the believers and other Jews centered on the person of Jesus, his authority and messiahship. While other Jews called themselves disciples of Moses, John's community argued for the higher authority of Jesus (John 9:28–29; 1:17; 6:32–33). The claim about Jesus being the Messiah and Son of God was rejected by other Jews (3:10–11; 8:12–18; 5:22, 36–38). The correct way of interpreting scriptures was also debated (5:39–40), as well as the question of who are truly Abraham's children (8:31–47). The latter is reminiscent of Paul's argument on who are the sons of Abraham (Galatians 3; Romans 4). The dispute over who has the right to claim Abraham as their ancestor indicates that both John's group and its rival vied to be seen as the true representative of the Abrahamic promise. Such fierce debates seriously split the community. Repeatedly, one is told that people were divided because of Jesus; some deserted him, many put their faith in him, and many would not believe in him (6:60–66; 7:25–27; 7:43; 8:30; 10:19; 10:42; 12:11; 12:37; 12:42).

Scholarship that attributes the "parting of the ways" to theological debates, especially those of a christological nature, is correct only to the extent that such debates caused serious conflicts and division in their communities; the theological differences did not create a "Christian" identity, for the church represented in the Johannine literature refused to relinquish its Jewish identity. They certainly did not think of themselves as branching out to start something new; rather, they saw themselves as the true heirs of the tradition, the remnant of Israel, while the others erred and cut themselves off from it. 1 John states,

> Children, it is the last hour! As you have heard that antichrist is coming, so now many antichrists have come. From this we know that it is the last hour. They went out from us, but they did not belong to us; for if they had belonged to us, they would have remained with us. But by going out they made it plain that none of them belongs to us (2:18–19).

The antichrists are those who denied that Jesus is the Christ (2:20–21); in other words, the *Ioudaioi* who did not believe in Jesus. 1 John clearly identifies its own community as the true Israel "in the last hour" (2:18).

Not only did the Johannine literature make the claim that its community was the true Israel, it also confirmed this Israel to be truly Jewish. In his rhetoric against the synagogue, John the prophet calls the opponents of the churches of Smyrna and Philadelphia "those … who say they are Jews and are not" (Rev 2:9; 3:9). Wilson suggests that "those who say they are Jews and are not" are Gentiles who observed Jewish practices, or Gentile Christian Judaizers. Otherwise, he states, it would be hardly convincing for the author to deny the Jewishness of the Jews "when they so manifestly were Jews," for although "a general claim to Israel's heritage is common … most other Christians are at pains to distance themselves from 'Jews.'"[41] But here the words "those who say they are Jews and are not" are polemical, similar to the words John put in Jesus'

---

[41] Stephen G. Wilson, *Related Strangers: Jews and Christians, 70–170 C.E.* (Minneapolis: Fortress, 1995), 162–63.

mouth when he denied that Abraham was their father, saying, "you are from your father the devil" (8:39–44). John's words make perfect sense if "sons of Abraham," "Israel," and "Jews" are equally important identities for the author. Besides, any Gentile Judaizers who left the church to join the synagogue would have been absorbed into that community, unlikely to be a separate force strong enough to cause ructions in the church. As for distancing themselves from the synagogue, that would have been a later stance of Gentile churches. Here the author of Revelation is indeed claiming the title of Israel and by inference also that of *Ioudaios*. In other words, the "Israel" self-identity of the Jesus Movement in Johannine literature embraces the ethnic component of the term as well.[42] This is in sharp contrast to the later outlook of Justin Martyr in his discourse on the Christian Church as the true Israel. Justin claims for the Church the heritage of true Israel, but happily leaves the label of *Ioudaioi* to its opponent, represented by the synagogue; instead, he envisages the uncircumcised as "a people," "a proper nation," and differentiated from the *Ioudaioi*.[43]

In the second century, therefore, the Gentile churches forfeited any identity associated with the title *Ioudaios*, but kept that identity associated with the designation Israel.[44] This new identity was not due to any escalated theological debate, although such debate would further widen the schism; rather, it happened as a result of the changed demographic, as non-Jewish membership in the churches increased and as the influence and authority of their Jewish leaderships waned. The time at which the transition occurred, no doubt, differed from place to place.

4. Christians in Roman Eyes in the First Century

The Christians (or some of them at least) may have tried to identify themselves as *Ioudaioi*, but did they appear to be Jewish to external observers such as the Romans? From when did the Romans begin to see the *Christianoi* as distinct from the *Ioudaioi*, not simply one among many sects among Judaism?

4.1. Roman Encounters with Christians before AD 70

Roman understanding of the origin of Christianity and its connection with Judaism was a developing process that was in line with the spread of Christianity among Gentiles in the Mediterranean world. Early Roman encounters with Christianity show that identity was judged not on theological

---

[42] Note that even for Paul, "Israel" also refers to his compatriots of Jewish descent, when he says that "the gifts and the call of God are irrevocable" (Rom 11:29) and that "all Israel will be saved" (Rom 11:26).

[43] Justin Martyr, *Dial.* 123:1–2.

[44] This, of course, should not be taken as a sweeping statement; situations could have been vastly different in various locales.

differences but by a definition of ethnicity, which in antiquity was closely entwined with an ancestral way of life. In other words, belief was simply not a criterion; instead the Romans applied the rule of *ethnos*. Some Christians were Jews in their eyes, but others were not Jews but persons who had simply turned their backs on their own ancestral ways and followed the Jewish "superstition." Thus the Romans dealt with the Jewish and non-Jewish Christians accordingly.

When the Jesus Movement initially remained an internal Jewish phenomenon, Romans on the whole adopted the usual policy of letting the Jews decide their own affairs as long as public order was maintained. In the portrayal of Acts, Paul and his companions followed a pattern of targeting Jewish synagogues first and then the Gentiles.[45] Wherever they went, fierce debates and even violent turmoil were stirred up in the local synagogues. Sometimes the case was taken to the local Roman authorities. In Thessalonica, for example, the Jews dragged Paul's host Jason to the city officials to have them stopped (Acts 17:1–9). In another case in Corinth, Paul was brought to the court of the Roman proconsul Gallio with the charge of perverting the law (Acts 18:1–17). In the first case, those being accused were let go after paying a bond, whereas in the second, Gallio simply refused to judge such a matter, which he deemed an internal Jewish affair concerning their own law (18:15–17).[46] It seems that at this stage the Romans were both largely unaware of the existence of the Jesus Movement and unconcerned about what they saw as an internal issue as long as public order was maintained.

Such internal strife even reached Rome. Suetonius tells us that the emperor Claudius expelled Jews from Rome because of the unrest provoked by a certain *Chrestus* among them. This event is dated to AD 49 by general consensus.[47] Most scholars are convinced that the turmoil was caused by the arrival in Rome of disciples of Jesus and their activities in the Jewish communities there. Christians were among the Jews who were expelled. This event is corroborated by Luke, who speaks about Paul's meeting in Corinth with Aquila, "a Jew," and his wife Priscilla, who left Rome because of the order of Claudius (Acts 18:2). The Romans in this incident did not draw any distinction between the *Ioudaioi* and *Christianoi*.

---

[45] The portrayal of Acts appears consistent with Paul's statement that salvation was "to the Jew first and also to the Greek" (Rom 1:16).

[46] Acts reports, "Gallio said to the Jews, 'If it were a matter of crime or serious villainy, I would be justified in accepting the complaint of you Jews; but since it is a matter of questions about words and names and your own law, see to it yourselves; I do not wish to be a judge of these matters.' And he dismissed them from the tribunal" (18:14–16).

[47] The problem is Suetonius (*Claud.* 25.4) does not indicate the year, but the fifth century writer Orosius (*Adversus paganos* 7.6.15) assigned it to 49. Yet Dio Cassius, *Hist.* 60.6.6 places the only order by Claudius with respect to the Jews to 41, and Tacitus's *Annals* does not register any edict against the Jews in 49. The common opinion is that there were two edicts from Claudius, the first in 41, prohibiting the Jews from meeting together, and the second in 49, which contained the order of expulsion from Rome on account of the disturbances caused by *Chrestus*. See more detailed discussion in Giorgio Jossa, *Jews or Christians? The Followers of Jesus in Search of Their Own Identity*, WUNT 202 (Tübingen: Mohr Siebeck, 2006), 127–28.

Yet fifteen years later (64), a new event showed the situation quite differently. In the aftermath of the disastrous fire in Rome, Nero, in order to clear himself from suspicion, singled out the Christians as his scapegoats. The famous passage from Tacitus is worth quoting:

> Therefore to scotch the rumour, Nero substituted as culprits, and punished with the utmost refinements of cruelty a class of men, loathed for their vices, whom the crowd styled Christians. Christus, the founder of the name, had undergone the death penalty in the reign of Tiberius, by sentence of the procurator Pontius Pilatus, and the pernicious superstition was checked for a moment, only to break out once more, not merely in Judea, the home of the disease, but in the capital itself, where all things horrible or shameful in the world collect and find a vogue.[48]

Tacitus was writing approximately half a century after the event, and it is believed that, as a Roman senator, he had access to the Roman senate's records.[49] It is not clear to what extent Tacitus was dependent on his source in this account or whether it was entirely his own reconstruction; however, the fact that the "Christians" were singled out for the crime indicates that they had an identity which was discernable to both the Roman authorities and the general public.

If we are to trust Tacitus' account, how can one explain the changed Roman understanding of Christians within such a short period of time? Between Claudius and Nero, the number of Christians increased in Roman urban centers, with the dominant proportion arguably being Gentiles. In 49, under Claudius, the conflicts that arose after the arrival of the disciples of Jesus occurred largely within the Jewish community and trouble was contained within it. Hence the order of Claudius targeted Jews in general, with no differentiation made whether they were Christian Jews. Indeed, Luke (Acts 18:2) particularly mentions that the expelled Christian Aquila was "a Jew." The situation, however, was drastically different later. According to Acts, when Paul arrived in Rome and asked to see the Jewish leaders there, the latter admitted that they had heard of the "bad" reputation of the Nazarene sect (i.e., Jewish Christians as per later Jewish usage), but knew virtually nothing about their views and were eager to find out from Paul (Acts 28:17–28). This supports Spence's conclusion that the church and the synagogue went separate ways early in Rome, and virtually ignored each other in the second half of the century.[50] The reason for this separation and mutual disinterest was that the Christian church in Rome after the period of expulsion grew to be a Gentile phenomenon in the main, despite the fact that it contained Jewish members who were likely to be in

---

[48] *Ann.* 15.44.2–3, trans. J. Jackson, LCL, in *Greek and Latin Authors on Jews and Judaism*, ed. Menahem Stern, vol. 2 (Jerusalem: Israel Academy of Sciences and Humanities, 1980), 88–89.

[49] See *The Annals by Tacitus*, translated with introduction and notes by A. J. Woodman (Indianapolis: Hackett, 2004), x–xx, in particular xiv–xv.

[50] Spence, *The Parting of the Ways: The Roman Church as a Case Study*.

leadership roles.[51] Despite its origin in Judaism, clearly neither the Roman authorities nor the general public recognized them as Jewish, but as those styled "Christians" by the populace, and distinct enough to become Nero's target in 64.

4.2. *Christian Identity and the* Fiscus Judaicus *after AD 70*

This distinction between Christians and Jews in Roman perspective became further sharpened through the administration of the Jewish Tax after the Roman crushing of the first Jewish rebellion and the destruction of the Jerusalem Temple in AD 70. The tax itself did not cause the separation of the ways; yet it reinforced a yardstick that further clarified for Jews, Christians, and Romans alike what constituted Jewishness.

After his destruction of the Jerusalem Temple, Vespasian imposed an annual tax of two *denarii* on all Jews to replace the former Jewish Temple Tax. The new tax would now go to the rebuilding of the temple of Jupiter Capitoline in Rome instead.[52] How would the Roman authority identify those eligible for the tax? The synagogue, as the focal point of each Jewish community in a specific town or city and playing multiple roles as a center of communal observance and authority, would be the most important source both of information about those liable to the tax and of those assigned to collect it. Indeed, Philo and Josephus testify the function of the synagogue in the collection of the temple tax prior to AD 70.[53] This would naturally exclude anyone who was not part of the Jewish community—that is, those under the authority of the synagogue as recognized by Rome.

During the reign of Vespasian's second son, Domitian (81–96), however, additional measures were introduced:

Besides other taxes, that on the Jews was levied with the utmost vigour, and those were prosecuted who without publicly acknowledging that faith yet lived as Jews, as well as those who concealed their origin and did not pay the tribute levied upon their people. I recall being present in my youth when the person of a man ninety years old was examined before the procurator and a very crowded court, to see whether he was circumcised.[54]

Domitian's excessive policy expanded the definition of Jew to include those who "without publicly acknowledging that faith yet lived as Jews" and those who "concealed their origin." It is generally agreed that Domitian's victims would include Jewish proselytes, Jewish apostates and Jewish Christians, but it has been debated whether Gentile Christians would also fall

---

[51] See Paul's greetings to church leaders at the end of Romans.
[52] Josephus, *B.J.* 7.218; Dio Cassius, *Hist.* 66.7.2.
[53] Philo, *Spec.* 1.77–78; *Legat.* 156–57, 291, 312–16; Josephus, *A.J.* 16.167–70. On the importance of the synagogue in the collection of the Jewish tax, see Heemstra, *The Fiscus Judaicus and the Parting of the Ways*, 22–23.
[54] Suetonius, *Dom.* 12.1–2.

within its scope.[55] The circumcision test in the account of Suetonius, however, indicates that it was those who were ethnically Jews but no longer associated with Jewish practice who were targeted. As Thompson points out, Gentiles who adopted Jewish ways could not have been given legal recognition by a tax,[56] and as a matter of fact many of them, particularly those holding high offices or social status, laid themselves open to prosecution for "atheism." Executions of those on a charge of atheism "who drifted into Jewish ways" are indeed recorded by Dio Cassius. Domitian condemned many to death for just such a crime, including his relative, Flavius Clemens the consul, while others were deprived of their property, and Flavius Clemens's wife Domitilla, also a relative of the emperor, was banished.[57] Christians who refused the sporadic demands of the imperial cult and were put to death should probably also be understood in this context (Rev 13:15; 20:4). It seems, therefore, that under Domitian, what defined one's "Jewishness" was his or her ethnic origin, with the result that Gentile Christians were not considered Jewish and thus did not enjoy the protection afforded by legitimate religion. In other words, the distinction was not religiously but ethnically based.

In AD 96 Domitian's successor, Nerva, removed the excesses imposed by Domitian, and advertised his reform by the issue of coins that bear the legend "*fisci Iudaici calumnia sublata*" (to commemorate the suppression of wrongful accusations in regard to the Jewish tax).[58] Nerva not only corrected "wrongful accusations" but redefined the legal concept of "Jew." Who would now be counted as Jewish and subject to the tax? According to Heemstra, Nerva's decision is reflected in the report on the Jewish Tax by Dio Cassius, written in the third century, which specifies "the Jews who continued to observe their ancestral customs."[59] In Goodman's words, this would mean those who "declared themselves as Jews—that is, if they carried on their Jewish customs *professi*."[60] This change of definition of Jewishness from an external criterion (i.e., ethnicity) to an individual's practice would have had a significant impact on the identity of Jewish Christians, who had been caught between loyalty to ancestral practices and rejection by the larger Jewish community for being *minim* (heretics).

In summary, the Romans in the first century drew a distinction between Jews and Christians, not along religious lines, but by their ethnic identities. This

---

[55] For a summary of previous scholarship and detailed discussion, see Heemstra, *Fiscus Judaicus*, 32–63.

[56] Lloyd A. Thompson, "Domitian and the Jewish Tax," *Historia* 31 (1982): 329–42; also Martin Goodman, "Nerva, the Fiscus Judaicus and Jewish Identity," 41.

[57] Dio Cassius, *Hist.* 67.14.1–3.

[58] Harold Mattingly, *Coins of the Roman Empire in the British Museum, Volume III* (London: Trustees of the British Museum, 1936), 15, 17, 19. Trans. L. A. Thompson, "Domitian and the Jewish Tax," 329.

[59] Heemstra, *Fiscus Judaicus*, 80. Dio Cassius, *Hist.* 66.7.2 reports, "Thus was Jerusalem destroyed on the very day of Saturn, the day which even now the Jews reverence most. From that time forth it was ordered that the Jews who continued to observe their ancestral customs should pay an annual tribute of two *denarii* to Jupiter Capitolinus." Trans. E. Cary, LCL, in Stern, *Greek and Latin Authors*, 2:375.

[60] "Nerva, the Fiscus Judaicus and Jewish Identity," 41–42.

they did as the Jesus Movement increasingly expanded its mission—and thus, membership—beyond the synagogue to include Gentiles, although the distinction may not always have been obvious in the case of churches of mixed ethnic origin, and particularly within Jewish Christian communities. It is from the second century that both Christian and Roman literary sources begin to show no hesitation about the followers of Jesus.[61] "Christian" became a natural choice for self-identification in the language of the Didache (12.4) and Ignatius of Antioch (Ign. *Magn.* 10.1; Ign. *Rom.* 3.3), who even coined the term "Christianity" as opposed to the Jewish and Gentile ways of life (Ign. *Phld.* 6.1). Similarly, Pliny the Younger and Trajan[62] "spoke with the same ease of trials against the Christians, without making any reference to their relationship with the Jews."[63] In their eyes, "humanity seems to be divided into Romans, Jews and Christians."[64] Yet the "parting" was not yet complete, for interactions between Jews and Christians persisted, and their identities continued to evolve. But most importantly, there were communities that belonged to both "ways": the Jewish Christians.

5. Jewish Christians or Christian Jews and the Birkat Haminim

The above discussion has operated largely on a binary distinction between Jew and Christian with little account given to the presence of "hybrid" groups, the so-called Jewish Christians.[65] However, in recent decades they have increasingly become an important element in the discussion of the "parting of the ways." Even if it is granted that the Gentile church established a separate identity at an early stage, for Jewish Christians (or Christian Jews) the story seems more complex. The existence of such groups blurred the otherwise seemingly clear borders between church and synagogue. For example, Alexander[66] focuses on the presence of Jewish Christians and evidence for attempts to exclude them from the synagogues (in particular by the inclusion of the Birkat Haminim in the eighteen benedictions), to supervise what could be read in synagogues, and to curtail social contact and commensality with them.

As to the Birkat Haminim in particular, there have been a number of recent studies that impinge upon the present debate, especially as it concerns Jewish Christianity. But again the evidence is indeterminate in and of itself without

---

[61] Jossa, *Jews or Christians?* 143.

[62] Pliny the Younger, *Ep.* 10.96.1 and 10.97.1.

[63] Jossa, *Jews or Christians?* 144.

[64] Jossa, *Jews or Christians?* 144.

[65] For a critique of the term "Jewish Christianity" see Boyarin, "Rethinking Jewish Christianity: An Argument for Dismantling a Dubious Category," *JQR* 99.1 (2009): 7–36. For Boyarin Jewish Christianity is the product of heresiological discourse which sought to create the hybrid other opposed to orthodoxy.

[66] P. S. Alexander, "'The Parting of the Ways' from the Perspective of Rabbinic Judaism," in Dunn, *Jews and Christians*, 1–25.

attendant assumptions. The problems in the evidence can be viewed from both Jewish and Christian perspectives.

5.1. The Jewish Side

The first problem to be encountered is that the earliest extant versions of the text of the curse are from the Cairo Genizah (eighth to ninth centuries AD) with much of the tradition before then assumed to be oral and thus fluid in nature.[67] The earliest reference to the Birkat Haminim in rabbinic literature, though its text is not given, is in the Tosefta (t. Ber. 3.25, after mid-third century). The limited evidence and the effect that methodology and presuppositions have on the outcome of any investigation have led Ruth Langer to declare recently: "We can neither fully reconstruct what motivated the institution of the *Birkat HaMinim* nor can we know its original text, if there was one."[68] A number of issues are involved here:

(a) The Evolving and Composite Nature of the Benedictions

The baraita at b. Ber. 28b–29a records two items of tradition: (1) that the curse against the *minim* (no mention of *notzrim*) was fixed (תקן)[69] at Yavneh under R. Gamaliel;[70] and (2) that R. Judah cites the authority of Rav (third-century *Amora*) that one who errs (טעה) in reciting the Birkat Haminim is removed (העלה) under suspicion (חוש) lest he be a *min* (חיישינן שמא מין).[71] But the discussion is late and more generally interested in accounting for the discrepancy between the actual number of blessings, and the number implied by the name Shemoneh Esreh, i.e. Eighteen Benedictions.[72] The text of the latter still appears to be fluid, and discussion as to where error might occur, and thus need correction, is divergent in the traditions of the Amoraic period.[73]

---

[67] See b. Ber. 28b and Simeon ha-Paquli's forgetting how he had fixed the Twelfth Benediction. On the logic of the ordering of the benedictions and the placing of the Birkat Haminim see b. Meg. 17b and y. Ber. 2.3, 4b–5a. On the extant MSS see Uri Ehrlich and Ruth Langer, "The Earliest Texts of the *Birkat Haminim*," *HUCA* 76 (2005): 63–112 and Ruth Langer, *Cursing the Christians? A History of the Birkat HaMinim* (Oxford: Oxford University Press, 2012), 187–95.

[68] Langer, *Cursing the Christians?* 16. On the possible later date for its promulgation see 35–36. She notes that the Hadrianic persecution stops the reading of the Torah and reciting of the *Shema* but is silent on the benediction, which is odd given the content of the Birkat Haminim.

[69] What "fixed" actually means is unclear. Wording was not fixed. It is suggested that it might refer to either subject matter or its order, but again this also does not appear to be "fixed."

[70] Cf. also y. Ber. 4.3, which assumes that some did not say the Birkat Haminim, thereby counting 17 rather than 18 benedictions.

[71] Cf. discussion in Yaakov Y. Teppler, *Birkat HaMinim: Jews and Christians in Conflict in the Ancient World* (Tübingen: Mohr Siebeck, 2007), 74.

[72] T. Ber. 3.25 speaks of insertions in the Shemoneh Esreh presumably to maintain the prescribed number of elements.

[73] Langer, *Cursing the Christians?* 18–26. The idea that only the recitation of the Birkat Haminim carries the risk of removal is not shared by m. Ber. 5.3 and y. Ber. 5.3, 9c.

(b) The Name Birkat Haminim

The earliest evidence (Jerusalem Talmud) for the title of the Twelfth Benediction is its closing phrase "who humbles the arrogant," though it does in places assume that *minim* are named in it.[74] The earliest evidence (Babylonian Talmud) for the title is thus late.

(c) The Reference of the Term Minim

It is now generally accepted that the term *minim* refers not specifically to Christians but to Jews whose actions do not conform to a prescribed norm.[75] The curse, insofar as it used only this term, would thus not be aimed at Gentile Christians; however, Jewish Christians would certainly fall within its scope.[76] The curse thus either acted as a "filter," allowing the synagogue to identify *minim* by their errant recitations of the Birkat Haminim, and then to remove them (but presumably only by the precentor); or it functioned as self-censorship, with those unable to say it leaving of their own accord, though again here there is a problem that individuals, in cursing the *minim* as unspecified, would not necessarily think that they were naming themselves.[77] In other words, the concept of *minut* (heresy, if that is the best term) is just too ill-defined to permit a clear determination of who was intended. No doubt the curse might have included Jewish Christians, but it cannot be seen as solely

---

[74] Teppler, *Birkat HaMinim*, 66–67, 134, 136.

[75] For the sorts of action and words considered "heretical," see m. Meg. 4.8–9, m. Sanh. 10.1 (it does not use the term *minim*), t. Sanh. 12.5. For rules prohibiting community with *minim* see t. Hull. 2.20–24 (cited below). Note the emphasis on action rather than belief, though the point is somewhat moot given that what one says may render one a *min*. Of course, the use of such a term as "norm" is potentially anachronistic when applied to the early centuries when the extent of authority exercised by rabbinic institutions is very much questioned.

[76] Reuven Kimelman, "*Birkat hamminim* and the Lack of Evidence for an Anti-Christian Jewish Prayer in Late Antiquity," in *Jewish and Christian Self-Definition, vol. 2. Aspects of Judaism in the Graeco-Roman Period*, ed. E. P. Sanders et al. (London: SCM, 1981), 228–32, argues that a more general reference in the term *minim* to refer to Gentiles is an amoraic development in Babylonia. In Palestine, however, the term could include Jewish Christians. Shaye J. D. Cohen, "The Significance of Yavneh: Pharisees, Rabbis, and the End of Jewish Sectarianism," *HUCA* 55 (1984): 28–36, oddly proposes the loss of sectarianism after AD 70 and the institution of a rabbinic acceptance or toleration of diversity, i.e., "not exclusivity but elasticity" (29). Such a view leaves the *minim* as sectarians who failed to adopt the "orthodox" principle of toleration and to accept the will of the majority; even so they are denounced but not expelled. For a counter argument see Martin Goodman, "The Function of Minim in Early Rabbinic Judaism," in *Judaism in the Roman World. Collected Essays*, (Leiden: Brill 2007), 163–73. He offers the definition that "heretics are those who (in the eyes of others) break the covenant by willful misinterpretation of its meaning" (165) and argues that the rabbis did develop the concept of heresy but were content to leave the concept vague. Such persons were simply to be ignored and avoided.

[77] So Kimelman, "*Birkat hamminim*," 227. Cf. also Steven T. Katz, "Issues in the Separation of Judaism and Christianity after 70 C.E.: A Reconsideration," *JBL* 103 (1984): 51 and 74–76. Langer, *Cursing the Christians?* 5, 8, 36–37, notes its use as a preemptive curse and boundary marker to "promote compliance and social cohesions" but also observes that there is no evidence that this was its purpose till later Midrash Tunhuma.

directed at them.[78] It is important here also to distinguish between the
rabbinical motivation for the promulgation of the curse and the Gentile
Christian response to it, as it is a matter of perspective. In other words, the
curse may not have had Christians in view (i.e., it may have been intentionally
directed only at sectarian Jews) but in cursing the *minim*, including the Jewish
Christians, the larger group felt implicated.[79]

(d) The Date and Reference of the Term Notzrim

Though the Genizah fragments attest a cursing of the *notzrim* (Nazarenes) and
minim, it is unclear whether the former term was original to the curse.
Kimelman, who frames his argument against a general reference to Christians
in the Birkat Haminim, sees the term as a later addition (or replacement,
perhaps, for "apostates" or "informers") but the argument is largely one from
silence: based on word order one would have expected the benediction to be
named Birkat Hanotzrim; John's Gospel speaks of exclusion from the
synagogue but does not associate it with prayers or curses; Justin believes that
the cursing occurs after prayer; neither John nor Justin speak of an exclusion
or cursing of Christians in general.[80] Based on Epiphanius, Kimelman
concludes that *notzrim* refers not to the Christians but the Jewish sect of
Nazareans, but he does not consider Tertullian, *Marc.* 4.8.1. Tertullian either
rightly or wrongly believed[81] that the Jews called Christians Nazarenes:
Nazaraeus vocari habebat secundum prophetiam Christus creatoris. Unde et

---

[78] Recently Teppler, *Birkat HaMinim,* has argued contra to the consensus view that the *minim* in
the earliest rabbinic texts refers to Christians generally, i.e. both Jewish and pagan believers
(154–64). He holds that before the Bar Kokhba revolt (in the Yavnian period) Christianity was
still seen as an internal phenomenon by the rabbis. After that period and the promulgation of the
Birkat Haminim, the Christians (Jewish and pagan) were considered outsiders. See 237–95. His
view, however, is problematic on a number of fronts. For example, he accepts the ascription by
b. Ber. 28b–29a that the text was composed at Yavneh at the behest of Gamaliel II, though he is
hesitant about an authorship by Shemuel haQatan (preferring a consensus of rabbis), and
believes that the council at Yavneh was recognized by Rome and Jews generally. See 114, 130–
31, 143, 147. Teppler is also forced to construct the opponents as Christians from an
interpretation of texts that do not name them specifically, for example, as the objects of bans and
restrictions (e.g., m. Hull. 2.9 and the later "Books of the Minim" rulings) and as *minim* in the
"Two Powers" debate (m. Sanh. 4.5, m. Meg. 4.9 and m. Ber. 5.3). See 189–229 and 298–347.
There is little consideration given to the possibility that the texts envisage alternative opponents,
and a rather monolithic construction of the texts is assumed.
[79] I agree with Teppler, *Birkat HaMinim,* 354–57, who recognizes the rhetorical nature of the
Christian response and believes it a "mistake to expect revelations of expertise" (357).
[80] Kimelman, 232–40. In "At the Crossroads: Tannaitic Perspectives on the Jewish-Christian
Schism," in Sanders et al., *Jewish and Christian Self-Definition,* 2:149–55, Lawrence Schiffman
sees the curse as directed at Jewish Christians when instituted at Yavneh, while *notserim* was
added later when the curse was extended to include all Christians. Katz, "Issues in the
Separation of Judaism and Christianity after 70 C.E," 62, 65–66 and 72–74, also questions that
Jewish Christians were a paramount issue for early Judaism. Katz considers the reference to
Nazarenes a later addition. Cf. Joel Marcus, "*Birkat hamminim* Revisited," *NTS* 55.4 (2009):
523–51, who argues for an early date of the curse naming the Nazarenes as well as the *minim*.
[81] In citing Lam 4:7 Tertullian appears either to confuse or interpret Nazarite (*nezirim*) and
Nazarene (*notzrim*)

ipso nomine nos Iudaei Nazarenos appellant per eum [the Creator's Christ according to prophecy had to be called a Nazarene. Whence also by the very name the Jews call us Nazarenes on his account]. Teppler also believes that *notzrim* is late, added some time from the late fourth century AD (as evidenced by Epiphanius and Jerome) when in his view the term *minim* had come to refer less specifically to Christians.[82] In rabbinic literature *notzrim* does not occur till the Amoraic period (first attested in Jerusalem Talmud) and one must wait till after the Babylonian Talmud for it to become a term of abuse. A contrary view is expressed by Ehrlich and Langer.[83] They believe that both terms (Nazareans and *minim*) were added at the same time to the Birkat Haminim and were probably original to it. They note that Nazareans is consistently placed before *minim* in Genizah fragments and possibly removed later under self-censorship.

(e) How Effective was a Curse

Under (c) above problems with self-censorship have already been noted. Indeed, it is argued that other measures may have been sufficient to achieve the objective. Here texts such as Tosefta Hullin 2.20c–21 play an important part:

> For they have stated, "The act of slaughter of a *min* [is routinely deemed to be for the purposes of] idolatry [m. Hull. 2.7E]. Their bread [is deemed] the bread of Samaritans, and their wine is deemed wine used for idolatrous purposes, and their produce is deemed wholly untithed, and their books are deemed magical books, and their children are *mamzerin*. People are not to sell anything to them or buy anything from them. And they do not take wives from them or give children to them. And they do not teach their sons a craft. And they do not seek assistance from them, either financial assistance or medical assistance."[84]

If the Tosefta ruling was enforced, it is difficult to see what added authority the Birkat Haminim would bring to the marginalization of the *minim* in Jewish society. Of course, viewed from a purely institutionalised perspective it may have provided a useful vehicle by which to advertise through regular prayer their ostracism or, as has been suggested, it may have been a means of identity-demarcation by naming the "other," albeit in an ill-defined manner.

---

[82] For Teppler the pairing of *notzrim* and *minim* in the Genizah texts is not a redundancy as the *minim* were now viewed as a Jewish sect, i.e., the Karaites. For Teppler's discussion more generally, see 28–58.

[83] Ehrlich and Langer, *HUCA* 76 (2005): 96–97.

[84] Cited from Tzvee Zahavy and Jacob Neusner, *How the Halakhah Unfolds: Hullin in the Mishnah, Tosefta, and Bavli* (Lanham, MD: University Press of America 2010), 38.

5.2. The Christian Side

Christian texts are said to offer the earliest evidence, though indirect and assumed, for the promulgation of the Birkat Haminim. Two issues arise here. First is whether one can assume a normative value for these texts. How representative are they? Opposing voices suggest that they are rhetorical in nature and the arguments of the elite. Indeed, the stridency of the *contra Iudaeos* literature can equally be read as a response to the continued association between Jews and Christians and attractiveness of the synagogue. At the same time as questions arise over the normative value of the Christian texts, doubt also arises over the influence and authority of the rabbis to enforce adherence to their views in this period. Indeed, the council of Yavneh is seen by some as a social construct read back into the earlier period by later rabbis.[85]

The second issue concerns the precision or lack of it in New Testament and patristic texts. What exactly is meant by John's use of *aposynagogos* (9:22; 12:42 and 16:2)?[86] For John the reason for exclusion appears to have been christological, but as Kloppenborg points out, the term tends to be used by the excluding party and envisages "temporary, disciplinary exclusion" against those who display behavioral deviance or group disloyalty.[87] Of course, it should be observed that the term need not refer to exclusion from the synagogue as we conceive it today but to exclusion from communal assembly howsoever this was conceived. More particularly, Justin Martyr[88] speaks of the Jews cursing Christians in the synagogues. However, there is disagreement about the specificity of Justin's evidence (e.g., Justin believes that the cursing occurs after prayer and thus cannot be used as evidence for the synagogue prayer) with some opting for the less ambiguous statements of Epiphanius (*Pan.* 29.9.1)[89] and Jerome to argue that the Birkat Haminim had only become anti-Christian in the late fourth or early fifth centuries.[90] But do we expect too great a degree of exactitude in Justin? As Horbury observes:

---

[85] See, for example, Boyarin, *Border Lines*, 48–49. As he observes (68): "The aroma of legend hovers over this entire account."

[86] Dale C. Allison Jr., "Blessing God and Cursing People: James 3:9–10," *JBL* 130 (2011): 397–405, finds an unlikely reference to the Birkat Haminim in the blessing and cursing allusion in James.

[87] John S. Kloppenborg, "Disaffiliation in Associations and the ἀποσυναγωγός," *HTS* 67.1 (2011)—accessed online at: http://www.hts.org.za/index.php/HTS/article/view/962/html. Kloppenborg sees John's high Christology as a retrospective rationalization for expulsion rather than its cause; the latter probably arose from some behavioral deviance such as clique formation that claimed a "special knowledge of the divine" and constituted themselves as a "fictive family."

[88] Justin Martyr, *Dial.* 16.4, 47.4 and 96.2. Cf. also *Dial.* 137.2, 138.1.

[89] Frank Williams, *The Panarion of Epiphanius of Salamis*, Book 1 (Sects 1–46), (Leiden: Brill 2009), 130: "Yet to the Jews they are very much enemies. Not only do Jewish people bear hatred against them; they even stand up at dawn, at midday, and toward evening, three times a day when they recite their prayers in the synagogues, and curse and anathematize them—saying three times a day, 'God curse the Nazoraeans.'"

[90] Langer, *Cursing the Christians?* 30–33. On the basis of Epiphanius, *Pan.* 29.9, and Jerome, *Comm. Isa.* [on Isaiah 5:18–19], passim, which mention Nazarenes (like the Genizah text) and

Justin, the first non-Jewish witness who directly alleges a synagogue curse, was right in supposing that Christians, both Jewish and Gentile, were cursed in synagogue. The curse, one of a number of measures against emergent Christianity, was a form of the benediction of the *minim*. This malediction on heretics was approved at Jamnia under Gamaliel II and incorporated in the Tefillah, which at this time was gaining in importance as a bond of Jewish unity. The wording of the benediction was variable, and no surviving text can be assumed to reproduce a specimen form of the Jamnian prayer. As has often been noted, it could apply to heretics other than Christians; but the impression of Jewish opposition given by Christian sources from Paul to Justin, confirmed by the scattered but hostile references to Christianity in early rabbinic literature, suggests that Christians were prominently in view at the time of the benediction's approval.[91]

6. Conclusion

A major problem with the theological approach is the existence of divergence within early Judaic and Jesus movements and the difficulty in determining the complex factors that contribute to communal identity. In other words, communities can exist with divergence in beliefs, but at what point does this manifest as separation? And even the term "separation" is metaphorical, expressing in terms of space what is fundamentally a social relationship. Also, insofar as this approach rests on the reading of the literature produced by Christianity and to a lesser extent by Judaism,[92] the problem of contextualizing that literature to determine whether it is in fact descriptive or even representative arises. Do John's references to expulsion on the grounds of Christology reflect what actually happened in the past of his community? Does the *contra Iudaeos* literature reflect the attitude of the churches and their members more generally? Does the *haggadah* of Rabbi Eliezer that even a *bath qol* (divine voice) can establish an interpretation of the Torah bear the representative weight it is sometimes given?

The historical approach, as we have already seen, faces the dilemma of insufficient evidence and thus its under-determination. In this situation such events as: (1) the destruction of the temple;[93] (2) its aftermath with key roles being played by the council at Yavneh (and associated promulgation of the

---

the practice of reciting the benediction three times in synagogues, Langer concludes by the late fourth to early fifth century the Birkat Haminim had become explicitly anti-Christian.

[91] William Horbury, "The Benediction of the Minim and Early Jewish-Christian Controversy," *JTS* 33.1 (1982): 59–60. He accepts the evidence in the *baraita* recorded at b. Ber. 28b–29a, and has argued for an early date for the curse on the basis of a convergence of evidence from both Christian and Jewish sources as well as to the need to "illuminate" the complaint.

[92] One might note in passing the risk of circularity entailed in the classification of literature as Christian or Jewish because of who later claimed it within their corpus.

[93] See for example, Lawrence Schiffman, "At the Crossroads: Tannaitic Perspectives on the Jewish-Christian Schism," 115–56, esp. 148–49 and 155–56, who credits the need for unity within Judaism in the post-destruction era and growth in the number of Gentile Christians as determining factors.

Birkat Haminim) and *fiscus judaicus*; (3) the Bar Kokhba revolt; or (4) Christianization of the Roman empire with its attendant legislation from the fourth century, take on a disproportionate role in focusing discussion. Alternatively the approach might use sociological modeling to offer an interpretative structure to what little data there is. Either way, the approach fails to properly take into consideration the disparate nature of the communities scattered across the Mediterranean and beyond.

Needless to say, given the complexity of the problem and our limited sources, any discussion of the "parting of the ways" would have to be by nature a simplification, a generalization of certain aspects from a long historical process. Within the first century of the Jesus Movement, however, the ethnic identity of believers was a determining factor in shaping the self-identity of the churches, as well as the perceptions of the Romans and the Jewish populations. The ways eventually parted with the gradual disappearance of Jewish Christian communities; Christianity remained (and still is) a Judaic religion, but would no longer be Jewish.

Recommended Reading

Becker, Adam H., and Annette Yoshiko Reed, eds. *The Ways that Never Parted: Jews and Christians in Late Antiquity and the Early Middle Ages.* TSAJ 95. Tübingen: Mohr Siebeck, 2003.

Boyarin, Daniel. *Border Lines: The Partition of Judeo-Christianity.* Philadelphia: University of Pennsylvania Press, 2004.

Dunn, James D. G. *The Partings of the Ways between Christianity and Judaism and Their Significance for the Character of Christianity.* Second edition. London: SCM, 2006.

Dunn, James D. G., ed. *Jews and Christians—The Parting of the Ways, A.D. 70 to 135: The Second Durham-Tübingen Research Symposium on Earliest Christianity and Judaism, Durham, September, 1989.* Grand Rapids: Eerdmans, 1992.

Goodman, Martin. "Nerva, the *Fiscus Judaicus*, and Jewish Identity." *JRS* 79 (1989): 40–44.

Hagner, D. A. "Another Look at 'The Parting of the Ways.'" Pages 381–427 in *Earliest Christian History: History, Literature, and Theology: Essays from the Tyndale Fellowship in Honor of Martin Hengel.* Edited by Michael F. Bird and Jason Maston. Tübingen: Mohr Siebeck, 2012.

Heemtra, Marius. *The Fiscus Judaicus and the Parting of the Ways.* WUNT 2.277. Tübingen: Mohr Siebeck, 2010.

Jossa, Giorgio. *Jews or Christians? The Followers of Jesus in Search of Their Own Identity.* Translated by Molly Rogers. WUNT 202. Tübingen: Mohr Siebeck, 2006.

Lieu, Judith. *Neither Jew nor Greek? Constructing Early Christianity.* New York: T&T Clark, 2002.

Robinson, Thomas A. *Ignatius of Antioch and the Parting of the Ways: Early Jewish-Christian Relations.* Peabody, MA: Hendrickson, 2009.

Spence, Stephen. *The Parting of the Ways: the Roman Church as a Case Study.* Interdisciplinary Studies in Ancient Culture and Religion 5. Leuven: Peeters, 2004.

Wilson, Stephen G. *Related Strangers: Jews and Christians, 70–170 C.E.* Minneapolis: Fortress, 1995.

7. The Letter to the Hebrews

Ian K. Smith

The letter to the Hebrews must rank among the most enigmatic of the books of the New Testament. Though usually referred to as a letter, it is in fact a sermon (a "word of exhortation," Heb 13:22) that is addressed to a group of Christians who were experiencing intense opposition (10:32–34) and were tempted to "fall away" (3:12). Beyond this, however, there appears to be little agreement. Debates abound about its authorship, the location and situation of the addressees, the nature of the crisis, the meaning of "fall away," the date of composition, the literary genre and theological distinctives.

1. Authorship

The anonymity of the text most probably emanates from its genre; letters began with the designation of the author whereas sermons did not. The author appears to be a man, as is seen by a self-reference using a masculine participle in 11:32 (διηγούμενον, telling).[1] He was a master of Greek rhetoric. He states several theses throughout the sermon and develops his argument by dependence on the Old Testament and on Second Temple practices. It is a very well-crafted work. This can be seen by the opening sentence (1:1–4), with its alliteration of the letter π, which sets the argument for the entire discourse. The author's literary prowess can be seen in the use of metaphors: "a ship missing the harbor (2:1), an anchor gripping the seabed (6:19), a double-edged sword that penetrates and divides the inmost faculties of the soul (4:12), a wrestler hopelessly exposed in a headlock (4:13), fields richly watered by rain and producing useful crops or worthless weeds (6:7–8)."[2] Allusions to the Greek translation of the Hebrew Bible (LXX) and to Second Temple practices and literature abound. From all this, the author points out the superiority of the new covenant to the old. His conclusions go beyond

---

[1] Perhaps the author presents as a man? Adolf von Harnack postulated that the author of Hebrews was the Priscilla mentioned in Acts 18:2, 18, 26; Rom 16:3; 2 Tim 4:19. See his "Probabilia über die Adresse und den Verfasser des Hebräerbriefes," *ZNW* 1 (1900): 16–41. The English translation is available in Lee Anna Starr, *The Bible Status of Woman* (Zarephath, NJ: Pillar of Fire, 1926, reprinted 1955), 392–415. Note also Ruth Hoppin, *Priscilla's Letter: Finding the Author of the Epistle to the Hebrews* (Fort Bragg, CA: Lost Coast, 1997, 2009).

[2] William L. Lane, *Hebrews 1–8*, WBC 47 (Nashville: Thomas Nelson, 1991), xlix.

theological propositions as he provides encouragement, admonition, and pastoral direction to his addressees. But who was he?

One of the earliest suggestions is that Paul was the author of Hebrews. The oldest extant manuscript that preserves the letter for us, the Chester Beatty Papyrus (early third century AD), places it among the Pauline letters immediately after Romans. In the great codices of the fourth and fifth centuries (Vaticanus [B], Sinaiticus [א] and Alexandrinus [A]), Hebrews is placed after Paul's letters to churches and prior to his letters to individuals. Early Alexandrian scholars such as Clement (AD 150–215) and Origen (AD 182–254) tell us through Eusebius of Pauline authorship. Eusebius preserves Origen's complete statement, which reads: "But as for myself, if I were to state my own opinion, I should say that the thoughts are the apostle's, but that the style and composition belong to one who called to mind the apostle's teaching and, as it were, made short notes of what this master said."[3] Origen does not speculate about the identity of this scribe. The tradition of Pauline authorship was more extensively held in the East than in the West.

Greater doubt has been cast over Pauline authorship in the West. The earliest known reference to Hebrews appears in a Western text, 1 Clement, written from Rome around the end of the first century.[4] Other early texts, prior to the fourth century, such as the Muratorian Canon and the writings of Irenaeus and Hippolytus of Rome, all agree that Paul was not the author.[5] It was not until the time of Jerome (AD 347–420) and Augustine (AD 354–430) that Pauline authorship started to be accepted in the West. Jerome, conscious that many denied Pauline authorship, said it does not matter who authored the work as it is "honored daily by being read in the churches."[6]

The writer of Hebrews appears to be a member of the Pauline circle due to the reference to "our brother Timothy" (13:23). It is unlikely, however, that Paul himself wrote the letter. In Heb 2:3 the author does not number himself among those who received the message of the gospel directly from the Lord. He states, "it was declared at first by the Lord, and then it was attested to us by those who heard." This stands in contradistinction to Paul's clear statement that he did not depend on anyone for his knowledge of the gospel: "For I did not receive it from any man, nor was I taught it, but I received it through a revelation of Jesus Christ" (Gal 1:12). Furthermore, the sophistication of the literary, syntactical, and grammatical finesse of Hebrews far exceeds that of Pauline writing. Theological emphases of Hebrews differ from those of Paul. The High Priesthood of Christ, a major theme of Hebrews, is absent from Pauline letters. Similarly, Hebrews portrays Christ's work in terms of

---

[3] Eusebius, *Hist. eccl.* 6.25.13.

[4] 1 Clement is normally dated at AD 96. Some scholars date it in the early second century, but none dates it beyond AD 140. See Laurence L. Welborn, "The Preface to *1 Clement*: The Rhetorical Situation and the Traditional Date," in *Encounters with Hellenism: Studies in the First Letter of Clement*, AGJU 53, ed. Cilliers Breytenbach and Laurence L. Welborn (Leiden: Brill, 2004), 201.

[5] Don A. Carson, Douglas J. Moo, and Leon Morris, *An Introduction to the New Testament* (Grand Rapids: Zondervan, 1992), 395.

[6] Jerome, *Epist.* 129.3.

185

cleansing, sanctifying, and perfecting. These are concepts that are foreign to the Pauline corpus. Several emphases common in Paul's letters are absent in Hebrews such as union with Christ, justification by faith, the contrast between grace and works, the tension between flesh and spirit. The resurrection, which is so prominent in Paul (and also in Lucan writings), is only mentioned in Heb 13:20. For these reasons, Pauline authorship is unlikely, although some, such as David Alan Black,[7] still argue for it.

Other members of the Pauline circle have been suggested as the author. Luke received his information about Jesus from eyewitnesses (Luke 1:1–4; cf. Heb 2:3) and writes in a similar sophisticated style. Clement of Alexandria suggested that Luke translated an original Hebrew version written by Paul.[8] A modern proponent of Lucan authorship is David Allen, who points out linguistic similarities between Lucan writings and Hebrews: just over 67% of Hebrews' vocabulary is also found in Luke–Acts. Only Acts and Hebrews among New Testament writings call Jesus ἀρχηγός ("pioneer": Acts 3:15; 5:31; Heb 2:10; 12:2). He also argues that there are 49 words unique to Luke and Hebrews (but, it could also be argued that there are 56 words unique to Hebrews and to Pauline writings).[9]

Another contender is Apollos, who was also a member of the Pauline circle. This theory is mainly fueled by Luke's description of Apollos as ἀνὴρ λόγιος ... δυνατὸς ὢν ἐν ταῖς γραφαῖς (an eloquent man ... competent in the Scriptures: Acts 18:24). Despite Martin Luther's acceptance of this theory,[10] the absence of an early tradition is a serious problem. The only other serious contender is Barnabas, but the arguments are even more tenuous. He was part of the Pauline circle, and Tertullian (AD 160–220) argues for this theory. Barnabas was a Levite (Acts 4:36) and would have known the temple ritual intimately; he is called a "son of encouragement" (υἱὸς παρακλήσεως: Acts 4:36) and Hebrews is "a word of consolation/encouragement" (τοῦ λόγου τῆς παρακλήσεως: Heb 13:22). Such data falls far short of concluding the authorship debate. In short, Origen can sum up the argument with his famous statement, "But who wrote the epistle, in truth God knows."[11]

The destination of the letter provides a bit more clarity. The letter concludes with a greeting from οἱ ἀπὸ τῆς Ἰταλίας (those from Italy: 13:24). This greeting could refer to people living in Italy, or people away from Italy sending greetings back home. On balance the latter seems more probable, and is adopted by the ESV (those who come from Italy) hence the letter is addressed to Christians living in Rome. A similar reference to those "from Italy" (ἀπὸ τῆς Ἰταλίας) is found in Acts 18:2 where the phrase refers to

[7] David Alan Black, "Who Wrote Hebrews? The Internal and External Evidence Re-examined," *Faith and Mission* 18 (2001): 3–26. Black argues that Paul dictated the letter to Luke, to whom he gave significant latitude in expression.
[8] Eusebius, *Hist. eccl.* 6.14.2
[9] David Allen, "The Authorship of Hebrews: The Lukan Proposal," *Faith and Mission* 18 (2001): 27–40.
[10] For more information on Luther's suggestion of Apollos see Donald Guthrie, *New Testament Introduction: Hebrews to Revelation* (London: Tyndale, 1962), 21 n. 3.
[11] Eusebius, *Hist. eccl.* 6.25.14.

Aquila and Priscilla who were in Corinth, having left Italy because of the Emperor Claudius's expulsion of the Jews from Rome (ca. AD 49). Furthermore, assuming a Roman provenance for Colossians and Philemon,[12] we can conclude from Col 1:1 and Phlm 1 that Timothy was known in Rome (cf. Heb 13:23).

2. Recipients

The destination of Rome is confirmed by several references throughout the letter. The recipients appear to live in a city due to the author's insistence that "here we have no lasting city" (13:14), as well as by the range of pastoral concerns reflected in chapter 13, such as, "show hospitality to strangers" (v. 2), the warning "do not be led away by diverse and strange teachings" (v. 9), and identification with those who suffered in prison (v. 3).[13] Similarly, the allusion to the readers' generosity (6:10–11; 10:33–34) is consistent with what we know of the character of Roman Christianity.[14] The sufferings endured by the Christians shortly after they came to faith (10:32–34) could suggest the events surrounding Claudius's expulsion (ca. AD 49). Additional support for the premise that the recipients of the letter lived in Rome comes to us from 1 Clement, a letter with such striking parallels to Hebrews that it appears to be literarily dependent at a number of junctures (e.g., 1 Clem. 36.1–6/Heb 1:3–13; 1 Clem. 9:4/Heb 11:7; 1 Clem. 12:1/Heb 11:31).[15] Although the situation of the readers cannot be proven, what we know of the Jewish community and the house churches in Rome (see Rom 16:3–5, 10, 11, 14, 15) also helps to strengthen the Roman hypothesis.

It would appear that the recipients of Hebrews have an association with a Hellenistic synagogue within Rome, as the sermonic style of Hebrews is similar to examples of Jewish-Hellenistic preaching.[16] When comparing

---

[12] See Ian K. Smith, "The Later Pauline Letters: Ephesians, Philippians, Colossians," in *All Things to All Cultures*, ed. M. Harding and A. Nobbs (Grand Rapids: Eerdmans, 2013), 302–27 (308–12).

[13] For more detail see Lane, *Hebrews 1–8*, liii.

[14] Note the Greeting of Ign. *Rom.*; Eusebius, *Hist. eccl.* 4.23.10.

[15] "This is the way, beloved, in which we found our salvation, Jesus Christ, the high priest of our offerings, the defender and helper of our weakness. Through him we fix our gaze on the heights of Heaven, through him we see the reflection of his faultless and lofty countenance, through him the eyes of our hearts were opened, through him our foolish and darkened understanding blossoms towards the light, through him the Master willed that we should taste the immortal knowledge; 'who, being the brightness of his majesty is by so much greater than angels as he hath inherited a more excellent name.' For it is written thus 'Who maketh his angels spirits, and his ministers a flame of fire.' But of the son the Master said thus 'Thou art my son: today have I begotten thee. Ask of me, and I will give thee the heathen for thine inheritance, and the ends of the earth for thy possession.' And again he says to him 'Sit thou on my right hand until I make thine enemies a footstool of thy feet.' Who then are the enemies? Those who are wicked and oppose his will." (1 Clem. 36.1–6, trans. Kirsopp Lake).

[16] The classic study of Jewish-Hellenistic and early Christian homily forms from about the time of the first century is Hartwig Thyen, *Der Stil des judisch-hellenistischen Homilie* (Göttingen: Vandenhoek & Ruprecht, 1955). For a summary of Thyen's argument in English, see J. Swetnam, "On the Literary Genre of the 'Epistle' to the Hebrews," *NovT* 11 (1969): 261–69.

Hebrews with Stephen's speech in Acts 7 and with Paul's synagogue preaching in Acts 13:16–41,[17] authoritative Old Testament examples are in each case given either as scriptural quotations or allusions, including biblical characters such as Moses, or Old Testament events such as the wilderness wanderings. This retelling of Israel's history is now interpreted through the lens of messianic fulfillment in Jesus, which leads to conclusions and exhortations. This structure creates a pattern of thesis and paraenesis and affirms continuity between the Old and New Testaments.

The author's assumption of the audience's familiarity with the text of the Old Testament shows a community more familiar with the Septuagint (LXX) than with the Hebrew Bible. Where there are differences between the LXX and the Hebrew Bible, Hebrews follows the LXX. An example of this can be seen in Heb 2:2 where the writer alludes to angels as the heavenly mediators of the Mosaic covenant. There is no indication in Exodus 19 and 20 that angels were present at the giving of the law. In Deut 33:2, however, Moses declares that God came from "ten thousands of holy ones," which the LXX renders, ἐκ δεξιῶν αὐτοῦ ἄγγελοι μετ᾽ αὐτοῦ (angels were with him at his right hand: cf. Ps 68:17). This belief in angels as mediators of the law had gained acceptance some time prior to the first century, and had spread among Hellenistic Jews (cf. Acts 7:38, 53; Gal 3:19; Josephus *A.J.* 15.136). Other clues to Hellenistic Judaism occur throughout the letter. These include seeing the Son of God in categories of divine wisdom,[18] the references to Moses (2:2; 9:13; 10:28; 12:25; cf. Philo, *Mos.* 2.66–186; *Her.* 182), and the repeated comparison of Moses and Jesus (3:1–6; 8:3–5; 12:18–29; 13:20).

We conclude, therefore, that the letter was written by a member of the Pauline circle, probably not Paul, to Christians in Rome who were connected to one of the Jewish synagogues in that city. As will be noted below, these recipients were facing a crisis. It is at this point that the dating of the letter becomes important in order to identify the exact nature of the crisis.

3. Dating

Hebrews could not have been written prior to the crucifixion of Jesus (ca. AD 30) and it is unlikely that it was written prior to AD 50 due to the many references that indicate elapsed time. In 2:3, we read that the addressees belong to at least the second generation of Christians; similarly, the writer expects further progress "by this time" (5:12). The recipients are called to

Thyen compares texts such as Philo's Commentary on Genesis; 1 Clement; 4 Maccabees; James; portions of 1 and 3 Maccabees; Stephen's speech in Acts 7; the Didache 1–6. Thyen's conclusions have been challenged by Helmut Koester, *Introduction to the New Testament: History and Literature of Early Christianity* (Berlin: de Gruyter, 1982), 2:273, and Karl Donfried, *The Setting of Second Clement in Early Christianity*, NovTSup 38 (Leiden: Brill, 1974), 26, who dismiss such form-critical analysis as vague and ambiguous, since we know comparatively little about synagogue homilies, however the genre identification *sermon* sticks.

[17] See Lawrence Wills, "The Form of the Sermon in Hellenistic Judaism and Early Christianity," *HTR* 77 (1984): 277–99, who sees Acts 13 as a paradigmatic synagogue sermon.

[18] Lane, *Hebrews 1–8*, liv.

remember "the former days" when the light of the gospel shone into their lives (10:32), and they are urged to remember their leaders who first spoke the word of God to them (13:7). Furthermore, we can deduce that Hebrews is written before the close of the first century. It is referred to in 1 Clement (esp. 36.1–6),[19] which is dated around AD 96.[20] Moreover, it is likely that the letter was written prior to the destruction of the Second Temple in AD 70. Although Hebrews is primarily concerned with the Levitical rituals of the tabernacle, and has no direct reference to the temple *per se*, these practices became the basis for later temple rituals. It would appear that such practices were continuing at the time of writing, as Heb 10:2 implies that the Levitical sacrifices had not yet ceased.[21]

4. Situation

If this deduction of a Roman destination and a timeframe of AD 50–70 is correct, there are two main Jewish and/or Christian persecutions in Rome within this period. The latter of these two persecutions was that inflicted under Nero in AD 64, when many Christians lost their lives. The Roman historian, Tacitus, says of this persecution,

> They were put to death with exquisite cruelty, and to their sufferings Nero added mockery and derision. Some were covered with the skins of wild beasts, and left to be devoured by dogs; others were nailed to the cross; numbers were burnt alive; and many, covered over with inflammable matter, were lighted up, when the day declined, to serve as torches during the night.[22]

This would be an unlikely backdrop for Hebrews, in which the author says of the recipients, "in your struggle against sin you have not resisted to the point of shedding your blood" (12:4). The former of the two persecutions happened in AD 49 when the Emperor Claudius expelled Jews or Jewish Christians from Rome. Suetonius informs us that these Jews were expelled because "they were constantly indulging in riots at the instigation of Chrestus" (*Iudaeos impulsore Chresto assidue tumultuantis Roma expulit*),[23] a name that was not uncommon among Romans. It is plausible that "Chrestus" is a reference to "Christ,"[24] and the disturbance arose in Roman Jewish

---

[19] Note footnote 15 (above).

[20] For more detail about the dating of 1 Clement see Donald A. Hagner, *The Use of the Old and New Testaments in Clement of Rome* (Leiden: Brill, 1973); Paul Ellingworth, "Hebrews and 1 Clement: Literary Dependence or Common Tradition," *BZ* 23 (1979): 437–40.

[21] See Peter T. O'Brien, *The Letter to the Hebrews* (Grand Rapids: Eerdmans; Nottingham: Apollos, 2010), 18–19.

[22] Tacitus, *Ann.* 15.44.6 in Tacitus, *The Annals* (London: J. M. Dent & Sons; New York: E. P. Dutton and Co., 1908), 487; note also 1 Clem. 6.2.

[23] Suetonius, *Claud.* 25.4.

[24] O'Brien, *Hebrews*, 17; Craig R. Koester, *The Dwelling of God: The Tabernacle in the Old Testament, Intertestamental Jewish Literature, and the New Testament* (Washington: Catholic Biblical Association of America, 1989), 51 n. 108.

synagogues because some Jews were claiming that Jesus of Nazareth is the Christ. Hints of this abuse can be found in 10:32, "But recall the former days when after you were enlightened, you endured a hard struggle with suffering." The expulsion may be seen in the reference to the faithful exiles on the earth seeking a homeland and a better country (11:13–16) and to the fact that Christians do not have a city that lasts (13:14).[25] It is a likely hypothesis that the earlier trials referred to in Hebrews are the days of Claudius's expulsion of the Jews.

The Jews expelled by Claudius returned to Rome on Nero's accession to the throne in AD 54, which would place the writing of Hebrews after this date. Furthermore, because the author is concerned that the letter's recipients persevere in their Christian faith (3:1; 4:14; 10:23) in the context of a larger society that does not accept Christ (3:7–4:11; 10:32–39; 12:1–13), it would appear the letter is written at a time of mounting persecution. By the time the letter is written, some had already defected from the faith (10:25) even though they had not yet suffered to the point of shedding blood (12:4). This would conform well to the growing opposition to Christians in the days leading up to Nero's massacre of them in AD 64, a time when Tacitus points out that Christians were hated within Roman society.[26] If this reconstruction is correct, the date of authorship can be narrowed to between AD 54 and 64, and most likely in the early 60s due to the rising tide or opposition.

This reconstruction is important as it shows the nature of the dilemma. Whereas the expulsion of Jews in AD 49 would have included Christians, at a time when Rome could not distinguish between the two groups,[27] in the lead-up to the Neronian persecutions of AD 64 the distinction between Christians and Jews was more apparent. In the wake of the great fire of Rome (18 and 19 July AD 64), Tacitus notes that Romans searched for a scapegoat in the light of the rumors that Nero was responsible for the fire. In order to deflect blame, Nero targeted Christians, who were thrown to dogs or crucified or burned.[28] In the years of growing hostility immediately prior to AD 64, the temptation for Jewish Christians was to revert to Judaism in order to avoid persecution. In the light of this reconstruction, we can appreciate that apostasy in Hebrews is not the threat that Christians would no longer believe in God and become atheists; apostasy meant that Jewish Christians would deny the Christ and revert to the practices of Judaism. This understanding of apostasy helps us to understand the repeated reference to the superiority of the new covenant over the old covenant, the word κρείττων (better) appearing 13 times in the epistle (Heb 1:4; 6:9; 7:7, 19, 22; 8:6 [twice]; 9:23; 10:34; 11:16, 35, 40 12:24). That which is better is not just the state of an individual believer, but the state of Israel under Christ when compared with Israel outside of Christ. This situation for Jewish Christians, and the comparison between Israel under Christ and

---

[25] Koester, *The Dwelling of God*, 52.
[26] Tacitus, *Ann.* 15.44.
[27] See James D. G. Dunn, *The Partings of the Ways: Between Christianity and Judaism and their Significance for the Character of Christianity* (London: SCM, 2006).
[28] Tacitus *Ann.* 15.44.

Israel outside of Christ, helps us to understand much of the teaching of the letter, in particular the warning passages concerning apostasy, to which we now turn our attention.

5. Warning Passages

The warning passages in Hebrews have occasioned significant disquiet, particularly among Christians who believe in the Calvinist doctrine of the preservation and perseverance of the saints, which asserts that God will preserve all Christians to the end and that none will fall away. An example of this teaching can be seen in the Westminster Confession of Faith, which states: "They whom God hath accepted in his Beloved, effectually called, and sanctified by his Spirit, can neither totally nor finally fall away from the state of grace, but shall persevere therein to the end, and be eternally saved."[29] The Westminster Confession cites the following scriptural support for this view: Phil 1:6; 2 Pet 1:10; John 10:28, 29; 1 John 3:9; 1 Pet 1:5, 9. The task of harmonizing this doctrine with Hebrews' teaching on apostasy has raised several attempts at resolving the tension. Some, such as Thomas Schreiner, argue that the warnings are a *means* by which God keeps his elect; those who are truly saved always heed the warnings, and it is precisely by heeding the warnings that they are preserved until the end.[30] This explanation, however, raises another question, namely, if these passages are giving a warning of what is an impossible event, what is the purpose of such a warning? Other scholars have divided Christians between those who belong to the visible church and those who belong to the invisible church; only members of the invisible church will persevere, and the reason one knows they are part of the invisible church is by their perseverance. This argument, in different forms, has been common among Calvinists due to this interpretation by John Calvin, by the influential Puritan John Owen, and by more modern advocates such as Roger Nicole and Wayne Grudem.[31] The argument is true, but is circular at best.

It is at this point that our understanding of the setting of the addressees of the letter becomes important. If our reconstruction is correct, the author is not talking about the recipients becoming atheists; the issue is a reversion to Judaism in the lead-up to the persecution of Christians in Rome. In this light, the warning passages, although addressed to Jewish Christians, are not descriptions of Christians but of Israel's rejection of Christ in the days of the new covenant. The recipients are warned against returning to the continual pattern of Israel's history: a pattern of repeated faithlessness to God's covenantal blessings. There are five such warning passages (2:1–4; 3:12–4:13;

---

[29] *The Westminster Confession of Faith* (Glasgow: Free Presbyterian Publications, 2003), 17.1 (73).
[30] See Thomas R. Schreiner and Ardel B. Caneday, *The Race Set Before Us: A Biblical Theology of Perseverance and Assurance* (Downers Grove, IL: InterVarsity, 2001), 193–213.
[31] See Schreiner and Caneday, *The Race Set Before Us*, 195–96, for references to scholars' works.

5:11–6:8; 10:26–31; 12:13b–17, 25–29), each of which grounds its exhortation in an application of Old Testament Scripture. Of these passages, the most controversial is 5:11–6:8 as it talks about the impossibility of restoration for those who have fallen away (6:4–6). These verses raise not only significant pastoral questions, but also introduce exegetical questions, as Scripture is replete with examples of those who have been restored after having fallen, even to the point of denying Christ (e.g., Peter: John 21:15–29). Other questions also abound within this passage, such as why Christians would leave the elementary doctrines of Christ (6:1). Surely, Christians do not move on from the basic truths of the Christian faith! Furthermore, if the recipients have the need for someone to teach them the basics of Christian doctrine (5:12), why then, two verses later, are they instructed to leave these basic teachings behind (6:1)? Such questions are answered when we understand that our author is pointing to Old Testament history as an expression of Israel outside of Christ. As long as Israel refuses to acknowledge what has happened in "these last days" (1:2) in the ministry of the Christ, "there no longer remains a sacrifice for sins" (10:26). The crucifixion has happened and will not be repeated. Hence, as has already been noted, the retelling of Israel's history in Hebrews creates a pattern of thesis and paraenesis. We turn our attention to an exegesis of relevant sections of this controversial passage to explain this more carefully. A very helpful and much neglected article was published in the *Westminster Theological Journal* in 1976 by the Australian Biblical scholar, Noel Weeks, which points to a way of reading the warning passages as describing the situation of Israel outside of Christ.[32] More recently, Dave Mathewson has argued for an Old Testament background for the warning passage in Heb 6:4–6. He states, "much misunderstanding of this section of Hebrews stems from a failure to appreciate its OT matrix."[33]

Our author begins this warning passage in 5:12 (παλιν χρειαν ἐχετε του διδασκειν ὑμας τινα τα στοιχεια της ἀρχης των λογιων του θεου—text deliberately unaccented), which is normally understood to mean that the letter's recipients need someone to teach them again the basic principles of the oracles of God. Unfortunately this translation may not bring out the intent of the original Greek. The word "someone" is a translation of τινα. The accentuation of this word makes a significant difference to the meaning: if it is accented τίνα (interrogative pronoun = "what are"), the translation would be, as in the Douay Rheims Bible, "you have need to be taught again *what are* the first elements of the words of God" (emphasis mine). Most English translations, however, follow τινα (indefinite pronoun = "someone") resulting in translations as in the ESV: "you need *someone* to teach you again the basic principles of the oracles of God (emphasis mine). This preference for the

---

[32] Noel Weeks, "Admonition and Error in Hebrews," *WTJ* 39.1 (1976): 72–80. This paper is also indebted to an unpublished Master of Divinity project by Ross Carruthers, "An Exegetical Analysis of the Greek Text of Hebrews 5:11–6:8" (Sydney: Australian College of Theology, 2013).

[33] Dave Mathewson, "Reading Heb 6:4–6 in light of the Old Testament," *WTJ* 61.2 (1999): 210.

indefinite pronoun is surprising, as the textual data seems to favor τίνα.[34] If this accentuation is correct, the readers need to be taught again *what are* the basic elements of the oracles of God, namely the Old Testament. It is these basics that have been left behind by the Jewish Christian recipients of the letter.

In Heb 6:1 the author points out that the letter's recipients have left behind Old Testament teaching. Again we are not served well by our English translations. The Greek uses ἀφέντες, which is an aorist participle meaning "having left behind." Unfortunately, most English translations do not bring out the force of this aorist participle as they assume that the author is referring to leaving behind basic Christian doctrine. Most translations give ἀφέντες a present hortatory force: "let us leave the elementary doctrine of Christ and go on to maturity" (ESV), "let us leave the elementary teaching about Christ.... (NIV84), "let us move beyond...." (NIV11). This is not only an unusual translation of an aorist participle, but it also raises the question of whether a Christian should ever leave behind or move beyond basic Christian doctrine.

If our understanding of Heb 5:12 is correct, however, and the author is referring to having left behind Old Testament teaching, the normal meaning of the aorist participle makes more sense. Hebrews 6:1 is not a plea to leave behind rudimentary New Testament teaching; it is a statement addressed to Jewish Christians of having left behind foundational Old Testament oracles.[35] A more literal (and better) translation of Hebrews 6:1 is, "Having left behind the beginning of the teaching about Christ, let us be carried along to maturity not laying again a foundation of repentance...." Note that the author includes himself among those addressed—this is not for those who have given up the Christian faith, it is for all those who have moved on from the Old Testament in the light of the ministry of the Christ. This translation is confirmed as the author goes on to outline the Old Testament teachings that have been left behind in Heb 6:1–2.

Each of the foundational teachings mentioned in 6:1–2 could refer to the Old Testament. The first thing from which these Christians have moved on is "repentance from dead works" (μετανοίας ἀπὸ νεκρῶν ἔργων: 6:1). The only other New Testament occurrence of νεκρῶν ἔργων (dead works) is in Heb 9:14, where the author brings these works into close contrast with Old Testament rituals (cf. Heb 9:13); hence the expression appears to refer to the works of the Levitical sacrificial system. Similarly, "faith towards God" (πίστεως ἐπὶ θεόν: 6:1) is not unique to believers of the New Testament. Old Testament faith is a theme that is developed in Hebrews 11, with its focus being in a forward direction as "the assurance of things hoped for, the conviction of things not seen" (Heb 11:1). Such faith finds its fulfillment in

---

[34] UBS[5] gives a {c} rating between τινά and τίνα and τινα and *omit. The Greek New Testament* edited by Barbara Aland et al., eds., fifth revised edition (Stuttgart: Deutsche Bibelgesellschaft/American Bible Society/United Bible Societies, 2014), 727.

[35] See F. F. Bruce, *Commentary on the Epistle to the Hebrews: The English Text with Introduction, Exposition and Notes* (London: Marshall, Morgan & Scott, 1965), 112–13.

the coming of the Christ.[36] Similarly, instructions about washings (βαπτισμῶν διδαχῆς: 6:2) is not a reference to New Testament baptism as is reflected in several English translations (KJV, NIV84, NRSV), but a reference to ritual washings that were part of Old Testament purification rites (e.g., ESV, NIV11, HCSB). The same word (βαπτισμός) is used in Heb 9:10 and Mark 7:4 with reference to purification rites. Furthermore, βαπτισμῶν is plural; the New Testament knows nothing of plural Christian baptisms.[37] Similarly, the other foundational beliefs found in 6:1, 2 all find expression in the Old Testament, whether the laying on of hands (e.g., Gen 48:14, 17; Exod 29:10, 15, 19; Lev 1:4; 3:2, 8, 13; 4:4, 15, 24, 29, 33; 8:14, 18, 22; 16:21; Num 8:10, 12; 27:18, 23; Deut 34:9; 2 Chron 29:23), resurrection (e.g., Ps 49:15; Dan 12:1–3; Isa 26:19; Job 19:25–26; Ezek 37:1–14) or judgment (e.g., Pss 1:5; 36:6; 51:4; 75:5; 110:6; Isa 26:8,9; Dan 7:26–27; 12:2). These Old Testament, and sometimes priestly, images help us to understand the corrective to apostasy being a better appreciation of the priestly work of Christ (Heb 4:14–16; 5:1–9), a key theme of Hebrews to which we will turn shortly. There is, therefore, no reason to see Heb 6:1–2 as referring to New Testament Christian experience; it refers to the practices of Old Testament Israel the recipients have left behind in the wake of the coming of the Messiah.[38]

With this background of Heb 6:1–2, it is easier to understand the most controversial of the warning passages in Heb 6:4–6, which talks about the impossibility of restoration for those who have fallen away. An understanding of this passage as referring to lapsed Christians has caused significant disquiet for exegetical, theological, and pastoral reasons. Exegetically, it seems to be inconsistent with what is taught in other parts of Scripture. At one level the Bible is a repeated story of the restoration of the lapsed: whether Jonah, King David, the apostle Peter, or the Prodigal Son. Theologically, it causes significant issues for those who are committed to the doctrine of the perseverance of the saints. Pastorally, it raises the question in the light of the universality of sin: to what degree does a believer need to lapse before they are beyond repentance? The premise for each of these issues is the understanding that our author is referring to lapsed Christians. However, if our exegesis of 6:1–2 is correct, this passage is talking of the apostasy of Israel outside of Christ, whose history is that of repeated rebellion that comes to a climax in their rejection of the Christ. As long as Israel continues to reject Jesus, the Messiah, there is no road of restoration. Hebrews 6:4–6 does not refer to the Christian who has fallen away but to the story of Old Testament Israel and her continual apostasy.[39]

Hebrews 6:4–6 forms an *inclusio* with ἀδύνατον (impossible) introducing the *inclusio* in v. 4 and πάλιν ἀνακαινίζειν εἰς μετάνοιαν (to restore again to repentance) concluding it in v. 6. Due to an understanding of this passage

---

[36] See Steve M. Baugh, "The Cloud of Witnesses in Hebrews 11," *WTJ* 68 (2006): 113–32.

[37] Weeks, "Admonition and Error in Hebrews," 76 n. 8.

[38] Weeks, "Admonition and Error in Hebrews," 74–75. See also Carruthers, "An Exegetical Analysis of the Greek Text of Hebrews 5:11–6:8."

[39] Weeks, "Admonition and Error in Hebrews," 76–78.

referring to lapsed Christians, many New Testament exegetes have sought to soften the force of ἀδύνατον (impossible). Some have suggested that it be read as "impossible for humans but possible for God,"[40] or a moral, societal, or psychological impossibility.[41] Such accommodations are not a true reflection of the word ἀδύνατον which is "forceful and emphatic."[42] The author of Hebrews uses the word on three other occasions to point out that it is impossible for God to lie (6:18), for the blood of bulls and goats to take away sins (10:4), and to please God apart from faith (11:6). "The expression clearly means that something cannot happen."[43] The center of the *inclusio* in 6:4–6 defines who it is who cannot be restored, by giving five accusative participles, all governed by the one definite article: τούς (the). This, therefore, refers to one group of people described in five different ways. It is our contention that each of these participles does not refer to New Testament Christians, but as with the descriptions in 6:1–2, the participles of vv. 4–6 each refer to Old Testament Israel.

The first participial phrase, ἅπαξ φωτισθέντας (once enlightened: Heb 6:4), need not refer to Christians enlightened by the gospel despite the similarity with the same expression in 10:32, which appears to refer to the enlightenment at the beginning of the Christian life. The concept of enlightenment is also found in the Old Testament (e.g., Judg 13:8; 2 Kgs 12:2 [2 Kgs 12:3 LXX]; Ps 119:130 [118:30 LXX]; Isa 60:1, 19; Mic 7:8). Nehemiah refers to the pillar of fire that illuminated the way for the Israelites through the Exodus from Egypt (Neh 9:12, 19; cf. Exod 13:21).[44] This enlightenment of Israel, however, has now been eclipsed by the rejection of Israel's Messiah (John 1:9–11), which culminates in Jesus' crucifixion.[45]

Similarly, the second participial phrase, γευσαμένους τε τῆς δωρεᾶς ἐπουρανίου (having tasted the heavenly gift: Heb 6:4) could refer to Israel with particular reference to the Exodus generation. The verb γεύομαι (taste) in the New Testament normally refers to full participation, hence it is not a

---

[40] Bruce states, "Those who have shared the covenant privileges of the people of God, and then deliberately renounced them, are the most difficult persons of all to reclaim to faith. It is indeed impossible to reclaim them, says our author. We know, of course, that nothing of this sort is ultimately impossible for the grace of God, but as a matter of human experience the reclamation of such people is, practically speaking, impossible." Bruce, *Hebrews*, 118.

[41] Spicq as cited in John C. McCullough, "Some Recent Developments in Research on the Epistle to the Hebrews" *IBS* 3 (1981): 40. Similarly, seeing the impossibility through the lens of patron/client relationships, in that the client does not "expect to begin to be able to begin the journey to God's inheritance again" (David A. deSilva, "Hebrews 6:4–8: A Socio-Rhetorical Investigation [Part 1]," *TynBul* 50.1 [1999]: 50), but it "may not reveal the ultimate condition of the benefactor's mind" (David A. deSilva, "Hebrews 6:4–8: A Socio-Rhetorical Investigation [Part 2]," *TynBul* 50.2 [1999]: 235), ultimately softens the meaning of ἀδύνατον.

[42] Harold W. Attridge, *The Epistle to the Hebrews: A Commentary on the Epistle to the Hebrews* (Philadelphia: Fortress, 1989), 167.

[43] O'Brien, *Hebrews*, 219.

[44] Weeks, "Admonition and Error in Hebrews," 78; Attridge, *Hebrews*, 169 n. 43.

[45] See Roger Nicole, "Some Comments on Hebrews 6:4–6 and the Doctrine of the Perseverance of God with the Saints," in *Current Issues in Biblical and Patristic Interpretation*, ed. Gerald Hawthorne (Grand Rapids: Eerdmans, 1975), 360.

Ian K. Smith

partial acceptance; six of the fifteen occurrences in the New Testament refer to tasting death (Matt 16:28; Mark 9:1; Luke 9:27; 14:24; John 8:52; Heb 2:9). It is unlikely, therefore, that "the writer describes those who belong only outwardly to the covenant community,"[46] having tasted but not fully consumed. The manna provided to the Israelites en route from Egypt to the Promised Land is described as a heavenly gift (Pss 78:24 [77:24 LXX]; 105:40 [104:40 LXX]; Neh 9:15, 20), which was tasted (Exod 16:31; Num 11:8; Deut 8:3) and appears to be a more plausible referent for this heavenly gift.[47]

The third participial phrase, μετόχους γενηθέντας πνεύματος ἁγίου (having become partakers of the Holy Spirit: Heb 6:4) is traditionally seen as a reference to Christians, who are partakers of the Spirit (e.g., Rom 8:9). While not denying that New Testament Christians have received the Spirit, part of the wilderness experience of the children of Israel was the reception of God's Spirit. In Num 11:16–29 God assures Moses that he will not need to carry the burden of the people alone (Num 11:17), and God will take the Spirit that is upon Moses and place it upon the seventy elders of Israel (Num 11:17, 25). Similarly Isaiah recites what God did in the days of Moses, "who put in the midst of them his Holy Spirit" (Isa 63:11).[48] Other passages which refer to the Holy Spirit as a companion empowering the people of God in the Old Testament can be found with reference to the Exodus generation (Exod 35:30–31; Neh 9:20, 30). This activity of the Spirit, however, does not lead to Old Testament Israel recognizing her Messiah, as is pointed out by Stephen in Acts 7:51, where the Jews of the time of Jesus are seen in a trajectory from their forefathers when they are described as "You stiff-necked people, uncircumcised in heart and ears, you always resist the Holy Spirit. As your fathers did, so do you."[49]

The fourth participle, γευσαμένους (having tasted), has two objects: καλὸν ... θεοῦ ῥῆμα (the word of God is good)[50] and δυνάμεις τε μέλλοντος αἰῶνος (and powers of the coming age: Heb 6:5). The first object (the word of God is good) finds many antecedents in the Old Testament; more specifically, the adjective καλός (good, beautiful) is found in relation to God's word in passages such as Deut 1:14; Josh 21:45; 23:14, 15; Prov 16:24; Zech 1:13.[51] The second object (the powers of the coming age) helps us to see how the Old Testament is clearly in the mind of the author. If he were addressing Christians, this coming age would be a reference to Christ's second coming. This does not accord with the overall teaching of Hebrews,[52] which sees the coming of Christ as issuing in the "last days" (1:2) and the sacrifice of Christ

---

[46] See Michael Horton, _The Christian Faith: A Systematic Theology for Pilgrims on the Way_ (Grand Rapids: Zondervan, 2011), 683.
[47] Weeks, "Admonition and Error in Hebrews," 78.
[48] Mathewson, "Reading Heb 6:4–6 in light of the Old Testament," 217.
[49] Bruce, _Hebrews_, 145 n. 38.
[50] See C. F. D. Moule, _An Idiom Book of New Testament Greek_ (Cambridge: Cambridge University, 1963), 36.
[51] See Attridge, _Hebrews_, 170.
[52] Weeks, "Admonition and Error in Hebrews," 78–79.

as happening at the end of the ages (9:26: ἐπὶ συντελείᾳ τῶν αἰώνων, at the end of the ages). The power of the age to come has been tasted by Israel, but this day has now come with the ministry of Jesus, the Messiah. As any reader of the Old Testament knows, the wilderness wanderings were times both of the demonstration of God's power and of an exhibition of Israel's apostasy. This apostasy finds many expressions in the Old Testament, but its greatest manifestation is not until the New Testament, at the crucifixion of Jesus, Israel's Messiah. It is to this climactic point that the author moves with the final participle. Israel, who has (1) been enlightened, (2) tasted the heavenly gift, (3) partaken of the Holy Spirit, and (4) tasted both the word of God that is good and the coming age (the age of the Messiah), has now (5) in the age of that Messiah, performed her greatest act of apostasy in the crucifixion of Jesus, the Messiah.

The final and climactic participle, still governed by τούς (the), is παραπεσόντας, which comes from παραπίπτω, meaning, "fail to follow through on a commitment."[53] We could therefore translate the aorist participle παραπεσόντας as "having acted unfaithfully." Although παραπίπτω only occurs here in the New Testament, it appears five times in Ezekiel (14:13; 15:8; 18:24; 20:27) as a translation of מַעַל (*ma'al*), which has the connotation of acting unfaithfully.

It would appear, therefore, that Heb 6:4–6 is not talking of Christians falling away from the faith,[54] or of the New Testament church members who were not truly Christians.[55] This passage refers to the covenant unfaithfulness of Old Testament Israel that climaxed with the crucifixion of the Messiah. Hence, as Weeks points out, the argument of Hebrews is "against those who stressed their continuity with Israel, [to whom] it had to be pointed out that this was not a glorious lineage."[56]

This interpretation, of Israel outside of Christ being the referent of the warning passages, is strengthened by the reason given for the impossibility of renewal again to repentance (πάλιν ἀνακαινίζειν εἰς μετάνοιαν, again to renew to repentance: Heb 6:6). The history of the Old Testament Israel is a repeated story of renewal to repentance. This repentance is now impossible again (πάλιν) in the wake of the crucifixion of the Son of God; no further sacrifice for sins remains (cf. Heb 10:26). Unfortunately, most English translations render ἀνασταυροῦντας in Heb 6:6 as "crucifying again": "they are crucifying once again the Son of God to their own harm and holding him up to contempt" (ESV) or "they are crucifying the Son of God all over again and subjecting him to public disgrace" (NIV84). The reference to recrucifixion has

---

[53] *BDAG*, 770.

[54] E.g., I. Howard Marshall, *Kept by the Power of God: A Study of Perseverance and Falling Away* (Minneapolis: Bethany House Publishers, 1969), 138–52.

[55] E.g., Wayne Grudem, "Perseverance of the Saints: A Case Study from Hebrews 6:4–6 and Other Warning Passages in Hebrews," in *The Grace of God and the Bondage of the Will*, ed. Thomas R. Schreiner and Bruce A. Ware (Grand Rapids: Baker, 1995), 133–82; Nicole, "Some Comments on Hebrews 6:4–6," 355–64.

[56] Weeks, "Admonition and Error in Hebrews," 74.

influenced many exegetes to believe that the passage refers to apostate Christians, as a second crucifixion would logically happen after the first crucifixion.[57] This translation is unfortunate for various reasons. Firstly, how many people were crucified more than once? Capital punishment is normally only executed once! For this obvious reason we have no examples of ἀνασταυρόω referring to recrucifixion in extant Greek literature. Secondly, the ἀνα- prefix can mean "up" as well as "again." With Koine Greek's tendency to use prepositions with verbs, it would appear that the ἀνα- prefix is used to intensify the meaning of crucifixion that happened in the lifting up of the condemned. Thirdly, this understanding of ἀνασταυρόω can be found in the writings of Josephus, who uses ἀνασταυρόω twenty-six times across three works, in each case meaning "crucify" or "impale."[58] The simple σταυρόω is used only four times.[59] The compound word is therefore Josephus's normal word for "crucify." It should be concluded that ἀνασταυρόω is speaking of Jesus' crucifixion. "What is referred to here is not a figurative re-crucifixion by apostate Christians; rather, it is the original crucifixion of the Lord by those who were recipients of all the blessings which came to Israel by Moses."[60] In the light of the original readers of the letter being tempted to revert to Judaism, the author reminds them that it is impossible to renew Judaism while it continues to despise the Son of God. Old Testament apostasy has culminated in the crucifixion of Christ. As long as the readers see the Old Testament revelation "as being on the same level as the new"[61] they will not appreciate the significance of the ministry of the Christ, and therefore the possibility of repentance will not be present. The Messiah has come, and from this point in salvation history, repentance is made available only through the crucifixion of Christ. As long as Jews (or indeed anyone) continue to be the perpetrators of crucifixion, rather than the recipients, there remains no other means of salvation. It is impossible for Israel outside of Christ to be renewed to repentance.

The other warning passages in Hebrews can also be seen as describing the situation of Israel outside of Christ, rather than the plight of the individual New Testament believer. The first warning passage (Heb 2:1–4) begins with the warning "lest we drift away" (μήποτε παραρυῶμεν: 2:1) and then 2:2–4 reinforces the comparison between the Mosaic covenant and the New Covenant. The basis for the warning is the fact that the Mosaic covenant was given by angels (δι᾽ ἀγγέλων, through angels: 2:2),[62] but the new covenant

---

[57] Weeks, "Admonition and Error in Hebrews," 79; Carruthers, "An Exegetical Analysis of the Greek Text of Hebrews 5:11–6:8."

[58] *A Complete Concordance to Flavius Josephus*, vol. 1, ed. Karl Heinrich Rengstorf (Leiden, Boston: Brill, 2002), 109.

[59] *A Complete Concordance to Flavius Josephus*, vol. 2, ed. Karl Heinrich Rengstorf (Leiden, Boston: Brill, 2002), 1736.

[60] Weeks, "Admonition and Error in Hebrews," 79.

[61] Weeks, "Admonition and Error in Hebrews," 77.

[62] As has already been noted, in Second Temple Judaism there is a tradition that the law was mediated through angels at Mount Sinai based on the LXX's translation of Deut 33:2, which

was mediated through the Lord (διὰ τοῦ κυρίου, through the Lord: 2:3). Furthermore, the reference to "signs and wonders" in 2:4 depicts the "miraculous events surrounding the Exodus."[63] This passage is clearly a comparison between the history of Israel in the Old Testament and the new revelation that has come through Christ. Should the readers of Hebrews, being Jewish Christians, drift away, πῶς ἡμεῖς ἐκφευξόμεθα τηλικαύτης ἀμελήσαντες σωτηρίας (how shall we escape having neglected so great a salvation: 2:3)? The greatness of the salvation is grounded in the mediator of the covenant. It is again a warning addressed to Jewish Christians about the peril of reverting to Judaism, mediated by angels, for now, in the time of the new covenant, salvation is only found through the Lord, Jesus Christ.

Similarly, the second warning passage (Heb 3:12–4:13) is also addressed to the situation of Israel outside of Christ based on an application of Psalm 95. In Heb 3:12–19 the focus falls on the exclusion of the Exodus generation from entering God's rest because of their unbelief and rebellion. In Heb 4:1–11, this truth from Israel's history is applied to the Christian community, who like their forebears experience the tension between peril and promise. They are exhorted to hold fast to the good news that came to them (4:2) lest they forsake entry into God's rest by reverting to Judaism.

Another warning passage is found in Heb 10:26–31. It is summarized well in 10:26: "if we go on sinning deliberately after receiving the knowledge of the truth, there no longer remains a sacrifice for sin." The reason given for this in 10:28–29 is again expressed in a comparison between Moses and Christ. If disobedience to the Mosaic Law led to execution (10:28; cf. Deut 17:6) how much more serious is the issue of disobedience to Christ and how much greater is the punishment for a person who spurns Christ (v. 29). This does not mean that a repentant person cannot return, but such a person can only return on the basis of the crucifixion of Christ; no further sacrifice for sin is available. Again, our author is talking about the state of Israel outside of Christ. Similarly in the final warning in Heb 12:14–29, the superiority of Jesus is shown against a rich tapestry of Old Testament allusions. The message is clear: "do not refuse him...." (Heb 12:25).

From the above we can see that the teaching of Hebrews is not concerned with the impossibility of a prodigal child returning, but of the hopelessness of the situation for the Jew outside of Christ. Apostasy in Hebrews is not exactly the same situation as often occurs in modern churches, where a church member appears to "give up on God altogether"; apostasy in Hebrews means that a person has ceased to believe in the fulfillment of Old Testament promises in Jesus, the Christ. The warning that the recipients of the letter need to heed is that, in the wake of the coming of the Christ, there is now no salvation for Israel outside of Christ. If our reconstruction to this point is

---

says ἐκ δεξιῶν αὐτοῦ ἄγγελοι μετ᾽ αὐτοῦ (at his right hand angels with him). See also Jubilees 2.2.

[63] Mathewson, "Reading Heb 6:4–6 in light of the Old Testament," 219. Rengstorf states, "When the OT speaks of God's signs and wonders ... the reference is almost always to the leading of the people out of Egypt by Moses." Karl Heinrich Rengstorf, "σημεῖον," *TDNT* 7:217.

accurate then the message is that the Jewish Christians of Rome needed to stand firm in their profession of Jesus as they face rising persecutions, which are directed particularly at Christians. A reversion to their former days of Judaism may avert Roman persecution, but it will incite the wrath of God. Their only eternal refuge is in Jesus.

6. Old Testament and Christology

In the light of this reconstruction, we can more easily understand the author's use of the Old Testament and its emphasis on Christology. The readers need to realize that the coming of the Christ is central to Old Testament teaching and has been fulfilled in Jesus. Old Testament quotations and allusions abound throughout Hebrews, although there is no common agreement to the number. Longenecker suggests there are 38 quotations, Caird finds only 29, Spicq identifies 36 and Michel 32. Lane finds 31 explicit quotations and 4 more implicit quotations, a minimum of 37 allusions, 19 instances of Old Testament material summaries, and 13 more where a biblical name or topic is cited without reference to a specific context.[64] With the exception of Heb 4:7 and 9:20, Old Testament citations are presented anonymously. In twenty of the Old Testament citations, God is the grammatical subject in the context (1:5a, 5b, 6, 7, 8–9, 10–12, 13; 4:4; 5:5, 6; 6:14; 7:17, 21; 8:5, 8–12; 10:30a, 30b, 37–38; 12:26; 13:5); four quotations are assigned to the Son (2:12, 13a, 13b; 10:5–7) and five are attributed to the Holy Spirit (3:7b–11; 4:3, 5; 10:15–17).[65] In the light of the reconstruction of the situation of the letter as being addressed to Jewish Christians, the repeated Old Testament teaching is clear: there is an expected Messiah and our author affirms that Jesus is he.

The author, in his use of Old Testament expectation, focuses particularly upon the Psalms. With the exception of 2 Sam 7:14, Deut 32:43 (LXX), and Isa 8:17–18, which are introduced as direct messianic prophecies, "all the biblical portions used to explicate the nature of the person of Christ are drawn entirely from the Psalms."[66] The most frequently cited Psalm in reference to the person of Christ is Psalm 110, especially vv. 1 and 4, which mentions the Old Testament priest, Melchizedek. The author of Hebrews uses this figure to point out to his readers the superiority of the priesthood of Jesus to that of the line of Levi.[67] The extended discussion of Melchizedek, introduced in Heb 5:6 and unpacked in 7:1–28, is a unique christological emphasis of Hebrews and suggests the author's and readers' appreciation of this Jewish tradition. It is helpful to trace this tradition at this point.

---

[64] Lane, *Hebrews*, cxvi.

[65] At points it is difficult to tell whether a reference is applied to God or to the Holy Spirit (esp. 4:3, 5 and 10:15–17).

[66] Richard N. Longenecker, *Biblical Exegesis in the Apostolic Period* (Carlisle: Paternoster, 1975), 167.

[67] O. Palmer Robertson, *The Israel of God* (Phillipsburg, NJ: Presbyterian & Reformed, 2000), 53–84.

Melchizedek is an enigmatic figure who appears only twice in the Old Testament and then in Hebrews. His name means "king of righteousness." He first appears in Gen 14:17–20, after Abram defeats Kedorlaomer. Abram is met by the king of Sodom and Melchizedek, the king of Salem (=Jerusalem, cf. Ps 76:2) and a priest of God Most High. Melchizedek brings out bread and wine and utters a blessing, after which Abram gives Melchizedek a tenth of everything, or vice versa; the Hebrew is ambiguous (Gen 14:20). Melchizedek then disappears from the narrative. The other Old Testament appearance of Melchizedek is in Ps 110:4 in which the Davidic King is said to be "a priest forever after the order of Melchizedek." The inference is that because Melchizedek was both king and priest in Jerusalem, these two roles are subsumed in the Davidic king.

From the above it is easy to see why the author of Hebrews focuses on Melchizedek, who is both a priest and a king simultaneously, as being a type of Jesus. It also helps to explain why Psalm 110 is the most cited Old Testament passage in the New Testament.[68] The Christology of Hebrews brings together these two roles: priest and king. This combination is seen from the beginning of the book, with the priestly image of Christ having made "purification for sins" being combined with the royal image of having "sat down at the right hand of the Majesty on high" (Heb 1:3). The dual roles continue through the letter to the benediction in Heb 13:20–21, with the reference to Jesus as the resurrected "great shepherd of the sheep" (a common royal image in the Old Testament) and the "blood of the eternal covenant" (cultic imagery).

This reference to Melchizedek with the two roles of priest and king finds expression in several non-biblical texts from Second Temple Judaism. He is an important figure in the Dead Sea Scrolls (note 11Q13) and reference is made to him in 2 Enoch, which is an extension of the Enoch legend.[69] The 2 Enoch account is concerned with the antediluvian priesthood, coming to its climax with Melchizedek who is assumed to Heaven where he is guarded until after the flood. In 2 Enoch 68–73 is found the story of Melchizedek's birth. Melchizedek's father is Nir, the grandson of Methuselah and the brother of Noah. Nir's wife, Sothonim, is found to be pregnant in her old age. As she has not recently slept with her husband, Nir shuns her until it is revealed to him that the conception is by a supernatural cause. When the time for the birth comes, Sothonim dies, but the baby emerges from her dead body fully clothed and with the body of a three year old, with the badge of priesthood on his chest. The child even speaks and blesses the Lord. Later he is carried away by

---

[68] See Don A. Carson, "Getting Excited about Melchizedek," in *The Scriptures Testify about Me: Jesus and the Gospel in the Old Testament*, ed. Don A. Carson (Wheaton, IL: Crossway, 2013), 145–74.

[69] See Dale C. Allison Jr., "Melchizedek," in *Dictionary of the Later New Testament and its Development*, ed. Ralph P. Martin and Peter H. Davids (Downers Grove, IL/Leicester: InterVarsity, 1997), 729–31, which also mentions other extrabiblical references such as 2 Enoch. As 2 Enoch refers to the temple, it appears to have been composed (even if an earlier redaction) by AD 70.

an angel of the Lord to Paradise so he will not be destroyed in Noah's flood. The above references show not only a development in the Melchizedek legend beyond that which is contained in the Old Testament, but evidence that Melchizedek was an important character in Second Temple Judaism.

The writer of Hebrews aligns Jesus' priesthood with that of Melchizedek in three ways: Melchizedek's lack of genealogy, which suggests immortality (7:3); Melchizedek's reception of tithes, which suggests his superiority to Abram, as the inferior pays the superior (7:4–6); Melchizedek's blessing of Abram which shows his superiority to Abram, as the inferior is blessed by the superior (7:6, 7). This typological argument proves Melchizedek to be greater than the Levites, the descendants of Abraham. Much of this argument is dependent on extrabiblical sources, for example, Melchizedek being referred to as "king of righteousness" (Heb 7:2 cf. Josephus, *A.J.* 1.180 and the targums of Gen 14:18); "king of peace" (Gen 14:18, Salem = peace: Heb 7:2, cf. Philo, *Leg.* 3.79) and his reception of tithes rather than vice versa (Heb 7:4, cf. 1QapGen XXII, 17; Josephus, *A.J.* 1.181). Without father or mother or genealogy may reflect the Dead Sea Scrolls—of Melchizedek being a heavenly being (11Q13)—which also relates to the aforementioned 2 Enoch legend.[70]

The question for us is, how does this relate to the issue of apostasy in Hebrews? Clearly the priesthood of Jesus being greater than that of Levi is a good antidote for those who would seek to revert to Judaism. Jesus' priesthood arises in the likeness (ὁμοιότης, likeness: 4:15; 7:15) of Melchizedek, who has become a priest, not according to a legal requirement of bodily descent, but by the power of an indestructible life (7:15). For the author, Melchizedek and Christ are priests continually (εἰς τὸν αἰῶνα, into eternity: 7:24).[71] Since Aaron's priesthood was founded on an external system of rules and regulations, his days as priest were numbered; they commenced with an initiatory rite and were terminated by death. Jesus' priesthood, however, is "better," securing a "better hope" (7:19, 22). The priest-king Melchizedek of Genesis 14 is like Jesus in that his priesthood is based on character and rooted in the eternal will of God rather than in outward human ordinances. With the superiority of the priesthood of Melchizedek established, our author can compare the priesthood of Christ to that of Aaron. This is central to his argument, as it is to these Aaronic practices that apostates will return.

The author highlights the fact that the Aaronic priests were chosen from among men and appointed by God (5:1; 8:3) to serve in the earthly sanctuary. Particular emphasis is placed on the rituals of the Day of Atonement, when an animal was killed and its blood was brought into the holy of holies by the high priest (9:7) in order that the people of Israel might have access to God (4:16; 7:18–28; 10:1, 19, 22). In a similar but superior way Jesus has entered the

---

[70] Paul J. Kobelski, *Melchizedek and Melchiresa*, CBQMS 10 (Washington: Catholic Biblical Association of America, 1981).

[71] Fred L. Horton, *The Melchizedek Tradition*, SNTSMS 30 (Cambridge: Cambridge University Press, 1976).

"greater and more perfect tent (not made with hands, that is, not of this creation)" (9:11) and into "the holy place, not by means of the blood of goats and calves but by means of his own blood, thus securing an eternal redemption" (9:12). When the readers recognize the superiority of Christ's priesthood, the Old Testament is seen for what it is—a copy and shadow (8:5). The readers of Hebrews are in danger of lapsing back into the shadow, rather than benefiting from the full substance of the sacrificial ministry of Christ on their behalf. Unlike the Aaronic priests, Christ is "a priest forever" (5:6; 7:15–17, 21) because he now always lives and is able for all time to save those who approach God through him (7:23–28, esp. 7:25). The old covenant priesthood was valuable in its day in that it pointed the way forward to Christ's priesthood; but now, when the Christ has come, its function is fulfilled. The New Testament believer is not to fall away into Old Testament religion, for outside of Christ, there is now no salvation. Christ is shown to be the mediator of a new covenant better than that represented by the Old Testament law (Heb 8:1–13); Christ's death establishes this new covenant (Heb 9:15–22) by providing for it the superior and permanently effective sacrifice (Heb 9:23–10:18); the blessings of the new covenant are greater than blessings associated with the revelation at Sinai (12:18–29). This superiority all rests on the work of Jesus, the "founder and perfecter of our faith" (Heb 12:2) whose patient endurance within suffering can be an encouragement for Christians in their trials (Heb 12:5–13).

The author not only explains the function of Christ's work as priest and king, he also shows the result of this work, which is to secure the eschatological hopes of Israel. The recipients of the letter are reminded to have faith in what God will do (11:1) even if current circumstances appear to be hopeless. The fact that the Christ has come and inaugurated the last days (1:2) is testimony to God's faithfulness in keeping his word. The catena of Scripture in Heb 1:5–13 reminds the reader of the fulfillment of God's promises concerning the Messiah that has been effected in the first advent of Jesus (Heb 5:5; 8:1; 10:12–13; 12:2). Likewise the ideal Adam's reign as "the Son of Man" portrayed in Psalm 8 was never completely realized in the Old Testament period, but now is applied to Christ (Heb 2:6–9). Christ has done what the first Adam and Israel, the corporate Adam, failed to achieve.[72] He has brought about a new age.

7. Perfection

Christ's qualification to achieve all that Old Israel failed to achieve is expressed in terms of "perfection" (2:10; 5:9; 7:28).[73] Although the Son existed prior to the incarnation (1:2, 3), it is through his earthly life that "he

---

[72] For the notion of Israel as a corporate Adam see N. T. Wright, *Climax of the Covenant: Christ and the Law in Pauline Theology* (Minneapolis: Fortress, 1991), 21–26.

[73] David G. Peterson, "Perfection: Achieved and Experienced," in *The Perfect Saviour: Key Themes in Hebrews*, ed. Jonathan Griffiths (Nottingham: Inter-Varsity, 2012), 125.

learned obedience through what he suffered" (5:8). This does not mean that there was *moral* imperfection in Jesus; rather the humanity that he assumed was not already perfected as it suffered from the effects of sin. The incarnate Jesus felt the force of temptation (4:15), and was susceptible to death (2:14, 15) and to trepidation in the face of death (5:7). He thereby experienced that which the preexistent Son could not experience. In the light of these sufferings, Jesus learnt obedience (5:8, 9), was perfected (2:10; 5:9; 7:28), and became the source of perfection for others (10:14; 11:40; 12:23). The final reference to Jesus attaining perfection in 7:28 comes in the context of his resurrection, ascension, and heavenly session, by which he was exalted above the heavens (7:26) and made a priest forever, after the order of Melchizedek (7:17).[74] He thereby became the mediator between humanity and God and is always able to make intercession (7:25).[75] Jesus therefore is both the one who is fully in solidarity with humans, sharing their sufferings, and yet simultaneously is separated from actual sin and in solidarity with divine holiness.[76]

The perfecting of believers was not possible through the Levitical priesthood (7:11, 19; 9:9; 10:1). The institutions of the Old Testament, to which some were tempted to return—whether priesthood, law, sacrifice or tabernacle/temple—did not bring about ultimate access, for "the law made nothing perfect" (7:19).[77] The perfecting of Jesus is required for believers to "draw near to God" (7:19) "by the power of an indestructible life" (7:16), a reference to the resurrection/ascension.[78] This concept of perfecting believers is unpacked in chapters 8–10. Jesus experienced and conquered the effects of the fall through obedience. These effects included temptation, fear, and death; this means that not only is he qualified to draw near to God, but believers may also draw near, having been perfected through his obedience. Christians therefore have already drawn near (12:22) to God and are members of the heavenly assembly (12:23) because they have come to God through Jesus, "the mediator of a new covenant" (12:24). They are able to worship and to serve God (9:14; 10:2; 12:28) with a cleansed conscience (9:9; 10:2, 22; 13:18) and they are invited to follow Jesus through suffering to the Father's presence (12:2), to offer acceptable worship (12:28–29), and to live holy, loving, and obedient lives (13:1–16).[79] Such worship is seen in every sphere of the believers' lives and is based on the perfecting work of Christ.[80] Such a life is a participation in the life of the eschatological reality of the "last days" (1:2).

---

[74] Peterson, "Perfection: Achieved and Experienced," 135.

[75] David G. Peterson, *Hebrews and Perfection: An Examination of the Concept of Perfection in the 'Epistle to the Hebrews'* (Cambridge: Cambridge University Press, 1982), 114–16.

[76] Andrew T. Lincoln, *Hebrews: A Guide* (London: T&T Clark, 2006), 88–89.

[77] Peterson, "Perfection: Achieved and Experienced," 137.

[78] Peterson, "Perfection: Achieved and Experienced," 135.

[79] Peterson, "Perfection: Achieved and Experienced," 140–41.

[80] David G. Peterson, *Engaging with God: A Biblical Theology of Worship* (Leicester: Apollos, 1992), 241–46.

8. Eschatology

This eschatological teaching of Hebrews does not just look at Old Testament fulfillment in the ministry of Jesus, but it also reminds the readers that what Christ has begun will come to its final consummation. He will lead his people to their completed salvation (Heb 2:10; 5:8, 9, 14; 6:1; 7:11, 19, 28; 9:9; 10:1, 14; 11:40; 12:2).[81] Christ has decisively defeated the power of the Devil and of death (Heb 2:14), a reality not expected to occur until the eschatological new creation; Christ's mission "to put away sin by the sacrifice of himself" is an event taking place "at the end of the ages" (Heb 9:26; cf. Heb 10:10, 12, 14). Thus Jeremiah's prophecy of a new covenant is beginning to be fulfilled, a point underscored as Hebrews quotes Jer 31:31–34 with the concluding words, "I will be merciful toward their iniquities, and I will remember their sins no more" (Heb 8:8–12; cf. Heb 10:16–17). Christ's sacrifice of himself inaugurates the eschatological temple (9:8, 23) into which we can now enter with confidence (10:19ff).[82] Jesus himself is the forerunner (6:20), and it is precisely because he has passed through the veil (6:20; 10:20) and entered now into the holy place in the city of God that Christians can be confident (10:22) that in due course they shall reach the city that is to come (13:14). It is in Christ that Jesus' followers have already "come to Mount Zion and to the city of the living God, the heavenly Jerusalem" (Heb 12:22). In a related image, Hebrews speaks of Christ's priestly work of sacrificing himself as inaugurating the eschatological temple (9:8, 23). Finally the author of Hebrews mentions the resurrection of Christ (Heb 13:20), a hallmark of the arrival of the last age.

Many of these images, which speak of heavenly realities (esp. Heb 12:14–24), raise questions about how the future habitation of Christians conform to the wider biblical teaching of new Heavens and a new Earth (Isa 65:17; 66:22; 2 Pet 3:13; Rev 21:1), and that the heavenly Jerusalem comes down to Earth (Rev 21:1–8). However, Hebrews does not diverge from this biblical teaching. When our author lists among the inhabitants of the heavenly Jerusalem "the spirits of the righteous made perfect" (12:23), this conforms to the Pauline teaching of Christians who are awaiting their bodies at the resurrection (e.g., 2 Cor 5:1–8; Phil 1:23–24). Similarly, in Hebrews, the resurrection of Jesus (13:20) is more than just the release of the soul to a heavenly dwelling. Physicality is important. The incarnation is emphasized, in which Jesus shared flesh and blood, became like his brothers in every respect (2:14, 17; 4:15), and suffered and died (2:9, 10, 18; 5:7, 8). As high priest, Jesus does not leave his creaturely humanity behind. Therefore in similar ways to how the rest of the New Testament affirms the eschatological hope of a transformed cosmos (1 Thess 1:10; 4:14–17; Phil 3:20, 21; Matt 24:29–31; 25:31–46; Rev 22:1–7, 20), Hebrews also emphasizes a second coming of the Christ who appeared

---

[81] See Moisés Silva, "Perfection and Eschatology in Hebrews," *WTJ* 39 (1976–1977): 60–71.

[82] Hebrews, however, does not make mention of the temple in Jerusalem: it focuses on the tabernacle that Moses built in the desert. See David Gooding, "The Tabernacle: No Museum Piece," in Griffiths, *The Perfect Saviour*, 69–88.

"at the end of the ages" (9:26) to remove sin once for all, and who will appear a second time to complete the salvation of those who eagerly await him (9:26–28). That day is approaching (10:25); the one who is coming will not delay (10:36, 37). This is the coming from Heaven that will be the realization of Christ's cosmic inheritance (1:2), the completion of salvation through the subjection to him of the world to come (2:5–8).[83]

These eschatological images, already inaugurated in the coming of Christ, remind the readers of God's faithfulness to complete what has been promised. Amidst the troubles that the original readers of the Epistle were experiencing, the author reminds Christians that in this life there is no abiding city; they seek the city that is to come (13:14). Insofar as Jesus' followers have already tasted the powers of the age to come (6:5), their eternal inheritance is secure. The repeated reference to "rest" is a reference to the final consummation, a promise that "remains" and has not yet been fulfilled (Heb 3:6, 14; 4:1, 6, 9, 10; cf. 11:16). Furthermore, in light of the current atrocities that believers experience, the readers are reminded of the reward for perseverance in the coming age (6:11–12, 17–18; 9:15; 10:23, 34–35; 11:39) and the judgment for apostates (6:2; 9:27; 10:27–31, 36–38; 12:25–29; 13:4). The Promised Land is what the true believers will receive at the eschaton (11:9–16; 13:14). God will raise them from the dead that they might participate in this final inheritance (11:35, cf. 6:20), which is indestructible (12:27–28) and eternal. Hence readers should not be lax about these exhortations because the day is near (10:25).[84]

9. Conclusion

We conclude, therefore, that Hebrews is a sermon addressed to Jewish Christians who, in the light of rising persecution in Rome, were tempted to revert to Judaism. Hebrews points out that in the light of the ministry of Christ and the better covenant that he brings, such a reversion would not only incur the wrath of God but it would also leave these Jews beyond hope as long as they continued in their rejection of Jesus, the Christ. The continual rebellion of Israel throughout its Old Testament history has reached its culmination in the crucifixion of Jesus, the Messiah. No further messiah will come. No other means of salvation is offered. As with their forebears who left Egypt for the Promised Land, the recipients of this letter must also persevere, trusting in the promises of God, to enter the promised rest. The means of perseverance is through faith in Jesus, their representative, mediator, defender, perfecter, and champion as High Priest and King in the order of Melchizedek.

---

[83] Lincoln, *Hebrews: A Guide*, 96–97.

[84] See George W. MacRae, "Heavenly Temple and Eschatology in the Letter to the Hebrews," *Semeia* 12 (1978): 179–99 and Clyde Woods, "Eschatological Motifs in the Epistle to the Hebrews," in *The Last Things: Essays Presented to W. B. West Jr.*, ed. Jack P. Lewis (Austin, TX: Sweet, 1972), 140–51.

Recommended Reading

Cockerill, Gareth Lee. *The Epistle to the Hebrews.* Grand Rapids: Eerdmans, 2012.

Griffiths, Jonathan, ed. *The Perfect Saviour: Key Themes in Hebrews*. Nottingham: Inter-Varsity, 2012.

Horton, Fred L. *The Melchizedek Tradition: A Critical Examination of the Sources to the Fifth Century AD and in the Epistle to the Hebrews*. Cambridge: Cambridge University Press, 1976.

Lane, William L. *Hebrews 1–8*. WBC 47. Nashville: Thomas Nelson, 1991.
Hebrews 9–13. WBC 47B. Nashville: Thomas Nelson, 1991.

Lincoln, Andrew T. *Hebrews: A Guide*. London: T&T Clark, 2006.

McKelvey, R. J. *Pioneer and Priest: Jesus Christ in the Epistle to the Hebrews*. Eugene, OR: Pickwick, 2013.

McKnight, Edgar V., and Christopher Church. *Hebrews–James*. Macon, GA: Smyth & Helwys, 2004.

O'Brien, Peter T. *The Letter to the Hebrews*. Grand Rapids: Eerdmans; Nottingham: Apollos, 2010.

Olyott, Stuart. *I Wish Someone Would Explain Hebrews to Me!* Edinburgh: Banner of Truth, 2010.

Phillips, Richard D. *Hebrews*. Phillipsburg, NJ: Presbyterian & Reformed, 2006.

Thompson, James W. *Hebrews.* Grand Rapids: Baker, 2008.

Trotter, Andrew H. *Interpreting the Epistle to the Hebrews*. Grand Rapids: Baker, 1997.

8. Christians and Jews in Antioch

Edward Bridge

Antioch has a special place in the New Testament. It was the city in which Gentiles were first converted to Christianity in large numbers (Acts 11:19–21), apparently without any requirement for them to observe the Mosaic laws (Acts 15:1; Gal 2:1–14; implied in Acts 11:22–24), and was the city from which the first known organized mission to Gentiles originated. It was the city that became the base for Paul and Barnabas's teaching ministry (Acts 11:29; 13:1) and Paul's three missionary journeys (Acts 13:1–3; Acts 14:26–28; 15:35–41; 18:22–23). In later centuries, Antioch became a major center for Christianity and, from the fourth century AD, competed with Alexandria in Egypt as the center of Christian theological thought.

Other chapters in this volume deal with the place of Antioch in the spread of Christianity and in Christian life in relation to society around it: Chris Forbes, "The Acts of the Apostles as a Source for Studying Early Christianity"; Paul McKechnie, "Jewish Christianity to AD 100"; Brad Bitner, "Unity and Diversity in Emergent Christianity"; and Lydia Gore-Jones and Stephen Llewelyn, "The Parting of the Ways." The current chapter focuses on the presence of Christians and Jews in Antioch and their interaction with each other as far as can be ascertained from the New Testament and other ancient sources such as the Didache and the letters of Ignatius. A history of the city will be given, followed by a description of the Jewish community there, the rise of the Christian community, and finally Jewish-Christian relations in Antioch.

1. Antioch in the Ancient World

1.1. Antioch as a Major City in the New Testament Period

In the New Testament period, or just at the beginning of it, Antioch was recognized as the third or fourth largest city in the Roman Empire.[1] It was certainly the largest city in the Roman province of Syria. Antioch was a cosmopolitan city. It has been described as a meeting point of "the Greek and the Oriental civilizations, filled with orientalized Greeks and Hellenized

---

[1] Strabo, *Geogr.* 16.2.5 (fourth largest city); Josephus, *B.J.* 3.29 (the third city of the empire).

Orientals."[2] The religious situation was diverse. Greco-Roman deities were worshiped alongside Syrian deities, and mystery cults were present. Antioch was the capital of the province of Syria and also a major commercial center. Consequently, travelers came from all places for commercial, religious, and political reasons, which added to the cosmopolitan nature of the city. Jews were present in large numbers. From this, Downey can claim that Antioch "was well prepared for Christianity," and "Antioch was one of the places that was receptive to the new teaching."[3] How did this come about?

1.2. Ancient Sources

For a large and important city in antiquity, Antioch suffers from a surprising paucity of extant writings in which it is mentioned, and especially a lack of extant histories of the city. The earliest extant history of the city is that by Libanius, a well-known teacher in the second half of the fourth century AD. The most comprehensive extant history is that of Ioannes Malalas, *Chronographia*, written in the sixth century AD. Other key literary sources for Antioch are John Chrysostom, a former pupil of Libanius, and Evagrius's *Historia ecclesiastica* (late sixth century AD). Antioch is also mentioned incidentally in Strabo's *Geographica*, Tacitus's *Historiae* and *Annales*, some letters of Cicero, 1–2 Maccabees, and Josephus's *Antiquitates judaicae* (*Jewish Antiquities*) and *Bellum judaicum* (*Jewish War*). All references are in connection with events of importance to the respective authors. First, Second and Four Maccabees and the writings of Josephus also refer to the Jewish community in Antioch and some of its affairs. The letters of Ignatius hint at Christian life in Antioch very early in the second century AD. Archaeological excavations of Antioch were conducted in 1932–39. These provide confirmation of a number of buildings in the city and the city's expansion over time. Coins and mosaics that were found reveal something of the political and cultural life of the city. This archaeological work was hampered by the continuing inhabitation of the site, the reuse of materials for building, the burning of marble for lime, and the problem of silt deposits up to ten meters thick in many places.[4]

---

[2] Glanville Downey, *A History of Antioch in Syria from Seleucus to the Arab Conquests* (Princeton: Princeton University Press, 1961), 272, Cf. Libanius, *Orationes* 11, fourth century AD, in which it is said that if a person went to the market place of Antioch, they "will sample every city,… so many people from each place…" (cited in Thomas A. Robinson, *Ignatius of Antioch and the Parting of the Ways: Early Jewish-Christian Relations* (Grand Rapids: Baker, 2009), 15.

[3] Downey, *History*, 272. Cf. Irina Levinskaya, *The Book of Acts in Its Diaspora Setting*, vol. 5 of *The Book of Acts in Its First Century Setting*, ed. Bruce W. Winter (Grand Rapids: Eerdmans; Carlisle: Paternoster, 1996), 135, from the perspective of Gentiles being attracted to the synagogue.

[4] For a comprehensive listing of ancient sources on, or which mention, Antioch, see Downey, *History*, 24–45. Non-extant works that cover Antioch or Syria are also listed (35–37). For artifacts: see Frederick W. Norris, "Artifacts from Antioch," in *Social History of the Matthean Community*, ed. David L. Balch (Minneapolis: Fortress, 1991), 248–58, which gives a

Edward Bridge

The literary sources, especially Malalas's *Chronographia* and Libanius's *Antiochicus* (= *Oration* 11), suffer from uncritical dependence on their sources and a bias to promote Antioch. The *Antiochicus* is an encomium of Antioch; and Malalas, despite his coverage of all periods of Antioch's history, shows poor knowledge of history, frequently pretends to have used his sources first hand, and the extant text of *Chronographia* suffers from being an epitome of the original. For the early Roman period, he may have used local records, but even for this period he narrates events that occurred years apart as simultaneous events, especially imperial visits and building programs.[5] First, Second and Fourth Maccabees and Josephus suffer from bias toward the Jews and a consequent exaggeration of their status and importance in Antioch.[6]

The combination of extant ancient sources and their biases and problems means that the fourth to sixth centuries AD are the best and most accurately covered. The early Roman imperial period (first centuries BC and AD) is also covered well, but the Hellenistic period is poorly covered. The Books of the Maccabees and Josephus, however, give some details from 167 BC onwards.

With regard to scholarship on Antioch, the first monograph written was Carl Otfried Müller's *Antiquitates Antiochenae*, published in 1839,[7] and based entirely on ancient literary sources. Despite its limitations, Downey comments that it is still a valuable work and the basis of all subsequent study on Antioch, including his.[8] The development of photography and then the opening up of travel to Syria in the 1890s allowed further study of Antioch to be undertaken, which saw the publication of inscriptions, artifacts and sculpture in the early twentieth century, and stimulated the publication of then-new editions of the works of Malalas and Libanius. This culminated in the archaeological excavations, already noted, led by Princeton University in 1932–39, and the publication of the field reports.[9]

---

convenient description and discussion. The paucity of ancient sources mentioning Antioch is symptomatic of the general paucity of ancient sources that deal with or mention the Seleucid kingdom. See, e.g., Charles Edson, "*Imperium Macedonium*: The Seleucid empire and the Literary evidence," *CP* 53 (1953): 153–70 (153). Edson comments that "literary sources are late and sparse," and there is "relatively little documentary evidence" extant, a situation still true sixty years after Edson's article was published.

[5] Downey, *History*, 38–41.

[6] See, e.g., Downey, *History*, 49, 107, 123. See also Carl H. Kraeling, "The Jewish Community in Antioch," *JBL* 52 (1932): 131–32.

[7] Carl Otfried Müller, *Antiquitates Antiochenae* (Göttingen: Libraria Dieterichiana, 1839).

[8] Downey, *History*, 4, 44.

[9] See Downey, *History*, 44–45, for details of the most important publications. For recent editions and translations of Libanius's *Orations*, see Lieve van Hoof, ed., *Libanius: A Critical Edition* (Cambridge: Cambridge University Press, 2014). For *Antiochicus* (*Oration* 11), see 331–32 and references. For a recent edition of Malalas's *Chronographia*, see Ioannis Malalae, *Chronographia*, Corpus fontium historiae Byzantinae 35, ed. Ioannes Thurn (Berlin: Walter de Gruyter, 2000); and for an English translation, see Elizabeth Jeffreys et al., trans., *The Chronicle of John Malalas: A Translation*, Byzantina Australiensia 4 (Melbourne: Australian Association for Byzantine Studies/University of Sydney, 1986).

1.3. History of Antioch

Any history of Antioch is dependent on Malalas's *Chronographia*, despite its limitations.[10] Of the modern scholars, Glanville Downey's *History of Antioch* is now the standard work. It is itself a critical use of the writings of Malalas and Libanius, with the addition of other ancient sources and the findings of the 1930s archaeological excavations.[11] Downey's work is yet to be superseded, due to the lack of additional archaeological study of Antioch and the lack of new extant ancient literary sources on Antioch. The brief history of Antioch presented here is dependent on Downey's *History*, and focuses on the city rather than the history of the politics of the Seleucid and Roman periods. The aim is to set the scene for later discussion and to show that Antioch was a large and cosmopolitan city.

Antioch-on-the-Orontes was one of four Hellenistic cities founded in 300 BC by Seleucus Nicator I, after he gained northern Syria as a result of the settlement following the wars of the *Didachoi* (330–301 BC). The other cities were Seleucia Pieria (on the mouth of the Orontes), Apamea/Pella (inland on the upper Orontes, to the south east of Antioch), and Laodicea (south of Antioch, on the coast). These four cities controlled trade routes from the coast to the inland. Antioch and Apamea also controlled the important inland north–south trade route between Mesopotamia (and also Anatolia) and Palestine, and so to Egypt. This trade route ran through the Amuq Plain and along the upper Orontes, east of the Lebanon and Anti-Lebanon mountains.[12] In relation to the territory covered in the expanded Seleucid Empire, Antioch and Seleucia-in-Pieria were the most centrally located cities.

Antioch and Seleucia-in-Pieria were founded in locations without existing cities, and where the population was largely Aramaic/Syrian. However, there is evidence of Greeks trading in villages near the site of Seleucia Pieria, and the idea of a Hellenistic city in this region was not novel to Seleucus I. His defeated rival, Antigonus, had already started building a Hellenistic city (Antigonia) near where Antioch was located, and Antigonus may have also had his capital at or near Seleucia Pieria. Seleucus I dismantled Antigonia, brought that city's *Tyche* (the goddess governing the prosperity of a city) to Antioch, and, in addition to his own Greco-Macedonian settlers, resettled in Antioch a number of Athenians who had been settled by Antigonus in

---

[10] E.g., Magnus Zetterholm, "Antioch (Syria)," in *The Eerdmans Dictionary of Early Judaism*, ed. John J. Collins and Daniel C. Harlow (Grand Rapids: Eerdmans, 2010), 336–38 (336), who cites Malalas frequently, though is clearly dependent also on Downey's *History*.

[11] Noted, e.g., by Thomas A. Robinson, *Ignatius of Antioch and the Parting of the Ways: Early Jewish-Christian Relations* (Grand Rapids: Baker, 2009), 8 n. 25; and John D. Grainger, *The Cities of Seleukid Syria* (Oxford: Clarendon, 1990), 3–6.

[12] For a detailed description of the geography, see Robyn Tracey, "Syria," in *The Book of Acts in Its Graeco-Roman Setting*, ed. David W. J. Gill and Conrad Gempf (Grand Rapids: Eerdmans, 1994), vol. 2 of Winter, *The Book of Acts in Its First Century Setting*, 223–78 (224–32). Cf. the older work, Edwyn Robert Bevan, *The House of Seleucus, vol. I* (London: Routledge & Kegan Paul, repr. 1966 [1902]), 206–22, whose descriptions of the geography of Syria are unaffected by the large increase in human activity and settlement in the region in the last century.

Antigonia.[13] What Seleucus I and Antigonus before him were attempting to do was not new. The region of Antioch, the Amuq Plain to its east, and the north–south trade route from Mesopotamia to Egypt had all long been thought worthy of control by external powers, going back to the Bronze Age. In the Bronze Age, a local kingdom based at Alalakh in the Amuq plain was frequently subject to external powers including the Hittites.[14] From the Iron II period onwards (ca. 900–600 BC), external powers (e.g., Assyria and Babylon) engaged in frequent deportations of the local peoples.[15] Antigonus and Seleucus I were in effect repopulating the area, but with colonists from Greece and Macedon. This continued the tradition of external control over the region, except that now the external peoples migrated into the region and ultimately ruled from this region.[16]

Despite the gradual contraction of the Seleucid Empire over time,[17] Antioch grew in size and importance. It became the capital of Syria sometime after Seleucus I's death (in 281 BC), though Grainger argues this happened in 188 BC, during the time of Antiochus III.[18] The city was expanded sometime in the 230s BC, then again in 223–163 BC, especially during the reigns of Antiochus III (223–187 BC) and Antiochus IV (175–163 BC).[19] Despite the

---

[13] See Downey, *History*, 46–51, 60–61.

[14] See Charles Leonard Woolley, *A Forgotten Kingdom* (London: Penguin, 1953) for brief details, see D. J. Wiseman, "Alalah," in *The New Bible Dictionary*, ed. D. R. W. Wood and I. Howard Marshall (Leicester: Inter-Varsity, 1996), 23–24; H. H. Hardy II, "Alalakh," in *Lexham Bible Dictionary*, ed. John D. Barry and Lazarus Wentz (Bellingham, WA: Lexham, 2012–2015) electronic publication; Edward J. Bridge, "Amuq Plain," in *Lexham Bible Dictionary*.

[15] Grainger, *Cities*, 7; Peter M. M. G. Akkermans and Glenn M. Schwarz, *The Archaeology of Syria: From Complex Hunter-Gatherers to Early Urban Societies (ca. 16,000–300 BC)* (Cambridge World Archaeology; Cambridge: Cambridge University Press, 2003), 379, 384. Akkermans and Schwarz also note the problem that material evidence for the well-known "historical record" of mass deportations from Syria "is difficult to validate" (379).

[16] For detail, see Getzel M. Cohen, *The Seleucid Colonies: Studies in Founding, Administration, and Organization*, Historia 30 (Wiesbaden: Franz Steiner, 1978). Getzel argues most cities the Seleucids established were initially military colonies (see, e.g., 4), designed "to assure a Seleucid presence" (25; this includes civilian colonies), and initially composed of a homogenous Greco-Macedonian population (41) who were given, or had the right of use of, land for farming purposes (45–71). See also the briefer summary in Susan Sherwin-White and Amélie Kuhrt, *From Samarkhand to Sardis: A New Approach to the Seleucid Empire* (London: Duckworth, 1993), 20–21. Sherwin-White and Kuhrt (20–28) also argue that with the colonization policy was a change in the administration practice of the monarchy: centralizing where possible; the use of family names for the new colonies and cities; deliberately using co-regencies with the king and successor-designate each responsible for certain areas of rule; and creating a dynastic era and mythology. Cf. Bevan: "It was in the Orontes that the life of Seleucid Syria pulsed most strongly" (209); and Greco-Roman artifacts from inland Syria witness to a large population in the Hellenistic-Roman period (217). See also Edson, "*Imperium Macedonium*," 165, who notes from ancient sources that "Syria, or the Syrian area largely defined, held a special position within the empire."

[17] Celts invaded central Asia Minor in 275 BC; Parthia progressively made gains in the east from 247 BC onwards; the kingdom of Pergamum controlled the whole of Asia Minor (and subjugated the Celts) in 230 BC. See, e.g., Robinson, *Ignatius*, 11; and Grainger, *Cities*, 123–24.

[18] Grainger, *Cities*, 122. Downey, *History*, 87, notes, from numismatic evidence, that Ephesos, a city elsewhere in Syria, also served as a capital alongside Antioch (58 n. 23).

[19] Mentioned in Strabo, *Geogr.* 16.2.4.

paucity of ancient evidence, there are indications that Antioch was a cultural and intellectual center. During Antiochus III's reign, a library is mentioned along with well-known poets and philosophers who were active in the city.[20] Livy and Strabo also record Antiochus IV's expansion of the city; that is, these expansions and the grandeur that went with them had become well-known. Despite the weakening of the Seleucid dynasty after Antiochus IV's death due to near-constant fighting by claimants for the throne, Cicero could write that during Antiochus VIII's reign (121–96 BC), Antioch was "a renowned and populous city, the seat of brilliant scholarship and artistic refinement."[21]

When Syria came under the control of the Romans in 64 BC, Antioch remained the capital of the now province of Syria due to its size, former status as the Seleucid capital, and centrality for communications.[22] Its nearness to the Parthian border also meant troops would be stationed near the city before they engaged in warfare with Parthia. However, it was not until the time of Augustus that Antioch began to prosper as a capital, helped by Syria's frontier status with Parthia and Antioch's control of the trade routes to the border.[23] The city was further expanded by benefactors such as Herod the Great, probably as a result of the visits of Augustus to Antioch in 31–30 and 20 BC. Malalas reports much building activity during the reign of Tiberius, but Downey critiques this to suggest most of it was started earlier, and argues that Tiberius, at the most, only completed some outstanding projects.[24] In AD 43/44, Claudius established an Olympic Games—though not long afterwards, a severe famine occurred and then a severe earthquake.[25] Antioch's importance as a city became prominent from AD 69, the Year of the Four Emperors when, because of the three or four legions regularly stationed in Antioch, the legate of Syria could wield numbers and therefore have support if he wished to contest the imperial seat or offer his support for an imperial contender, as Mucianus did in support of Vespasian.[26] Towards the end of the New Testament period, ancient sources mention the activity of philosophers,[27] and Domitian engaged in some building activities. Trajan also engaged in building activities in the city, but it is difficult to know if these projects were started before the devastating earthquake of AD 115, during which he himself was hurt, or were rebuilding activities after the earthquake. The persecution of

---

[20] Downey, *History*, 94.

[21] Cicero, *Arch.* 3. See also Pausanias, *Descr.* 8.33.3.

[22] See discussion in Tracey, "Syria," 237–39, on the vagueness of the terms used by Josephus (*B.J.* 3.29) and Tacitus (*Hist.* 2.78) and in the municipal coinage. Tracey eventually concludes that Antioch was the capital of the Roman province of Syria, but for some reason, Tacitus deliberately uses vague language.

[23] Downey, *History*, 163–65, 170.

[24] Downey, *History*, 169–85. A fire in AD 23 or 24 may be the cause of some of the building program attributed to Tiberius (185).

[25] Downey, *History*, 195–97. On 195, Downey claims that the Olympic Games at Antioch "became celebrated throughout the Roman world," but does not provide evidence for this claim.

[26] Downey, *History*, 202. Cf. Tracey, "Syria," 244.

[27] Pliny, *Ep.* 1.10; 3.11; Philostratus, *Vit. Apoll.* 6.38.

Christians at Antioch, which led to Ignatius's martyrdom, may have been due to them being accused in connection with the earthquake.[28]

Even though the few extant ancient sources focus on political events and rulers' building activities, there is enough evidence to show that Antioch, at least from 200 BC onwards, was a center of cultural and intellectual activity. Its steady increase in population and therefore size, despite the problems of the late Seleucid Empire and then the Roman civil wars, meant that by the time of Acts 11 (early 40s AD), it was an attractive target for Christian missionary work, and a wealthy-enough center for those who became Christians to then support missionary activity elsewhere. Later Christians tapped into the intellectual and cultural climate of the city to make the city a key center of theological thought.

2. Jews in Antioch

2.1. Ancient Sources

As with Antioch as a whole, ancient sources mentioning the Jewish community in Antioch are very meager. The majority of references are found in Josephus (*Antiquitates judaicae, Bellum judaicum, Contra Apionem*) and in 1–2 Maccabees. These ancient writings focus on Jews in Judaea and write with an obvious bias to Jews. Events concerning Jews in Antioch are only incidental. The time period covered is also limited. First and Second Maccabees cover only part of the late Hellenistic period. Josephus, in addition to the late Hellenistic period, covers events concerning Jews in the Roman period to AD 71. This is useful for our purposes, but the incidental nature of the coverage is a problem. Except for one or two remarks, Josephus does not describe Jewish life in Antioch, how the community was organized, and the level of their adherence to the Mosaic Law. Scholars have to rely on later sources (e.g., Chrysostom, *Adversus Judaeos*) for relevant information. Scholars also use both Josephus and Philo (e.g., *Legatio ad Gaium*) on the Jews' situation in Egypt, and extrapolate to the Antiochene situation. A comment by Josephus allows such an extrapolation. In AD 71, Titus, when requested by the citizens of Antioch to expel the Jews from Antioch and rescind their privileges, had a copy of the Jewish privileges in Alexandria displayed publicly in Antioch instead (Josephus, *B.J.* 7.96–111; *A.J.* 12.121–24). That is, according to Josephus, Jewish privileges in Antioch and Alexandria were the same. From this, scholars suggest the two communities were organized similarly. Rabbinic writings make the occasional comment about Jews in Antioch, but these are very sparse, and most do not refer to the first century AD.

With regard to scholarship on the Jewish community in Antioch, the primary writing is Kraeling's 1932 article, "The Jewish Community in

---

[28] Downey, *History*, 211–15. Trajan was in Antioch at the time because he had just annexed Mesopotamia from Parthia (213).

Antioch."[29] Kraeling gives an exhaustive treatment of the Jewish community using all extant ancient sources, including Rabbinic. In the absence of further recently discovered epigraphic evidence concerning Jews in Antioch, Kraeling's article remains the most detailed study. Consequently, all scholarly publications on Jews in Antioch since 1932 are dependent to some extent on Kraeling's article, and mostly differ in how much detail is presented and in interpretations on some matters. Of these, Downey (esp. 107–11, 122–26) and Levinskaya (128–35) contain the most extensive information (but see also Meeks and Wilken).[30] However, they predominately focus on the situation during the reign of Antiochus IV and immediately afterwards, and the Roman period from AD 40–71, following (naturally) the coverage of the ancient sources.[31] Barclay also gives considerable detail about the Jews in Antioch, but this is set in discussion about diaspora Jews in wider Syria, including the Phoenician coast and the Hellenistic cities in Palestine.[32] In contrast, Robinson departs from reliance on Kraeling to discuss extensively the size of the Antiochene Jewish community, the Jews' status, privileges, practices, and so on.[33] This discussion is thorough and interacts with an extensive range of scholars, but focuses on the time of Ignatius. Despite this narrow focus, Robinson's publication complements well Kraeling's article. Articles in dictionaries and encyclopedias tend to give only very brief details. Of these, the best is Zetterholm's entry on Antioch in *Eerdmans Dictionary of Early Judaism*.[34]

The following summary is naturally dependent on Kraeling and Robinson. It is designed to provide brief details of the Jewish community in Antioch to set the background before discussing Jewish–Christian relations in Antioch.

2.2. The Jewish Community in Antioch

Josephus claims that Seleucus I settled Jews in Antioch from the time of its founding (*A.J.* 12.119; *C. Ap.* 2.39) as a result of their involvement in the wars of Seleucus (*A.J.* 12.119). This is not disputed by scholarship, partly because Josephus (in *C. Ap.* 1.192, 200) quotes Hecataeus of Abdera saying Jews served in the armies of Alexander the Great.[35] Further, evidence from the Elephantine Papyri indicates that Jews were soldiers for their overlords in the

---

[29] Kraeling, "Jewish Community," 130–60.
[30] Wayne A. Meeks, and Robert L. Wilken, *Jews and Christians in Antioch*, SBLSBS (Missoula: Scholars, 1978), 1–13.
[31] Downey, *History*, 107–11, 122–26; Levinskaya, *Book of Acts*, 127–35. However, scattered throughout Downey's work are comments about Jews in Antioch where the ancient sources (citing Kraeling's use of them) make reference.
[32] John M. G. Barclay, *Jews in the Mediterranean Diaspora: From Alexander to Trajan (323 BCE–117 CE)* (Edinburgh: T&T Clark, 1999), 243–58.
[33] Robinson, *Ignatius*, 18–39.
[34] Zetterholm, "Antioch (Syria)," 336–38.
[35] See Kraeling, "Jewish Community," 131–32.

Persian period.[36] It can be inferred therefore that Jews served as soldiers long before the Hellenistic period.

Josephus also claims that Jews were afforded πολίτευμα, by which he understood full citizenship, since Antioch's foundation (*A.J.* 12.119; *C. Ap.* 2.39). This is disputed by scholarship, as is it understood that πολίτευμα would entail obligations to worship the city's gods,[37] Josephus's use of πολίτευμα is an attempt to claim that the Jews in Antioch had a high standing in the wider community, and that this high standing in Antioch had always been the case. The same tendency is found in the Rabbinic writings, in which the claim is made that Antioch is the same city as biblical Hamath and Riblah, and that the Jewish Great Sanhedrin met with King Nebuchadnezzar of Babylon at Daphne.[38] This claim is clearly legendary, since it contains two anachronisms: Antioch did not exist in the sixth century BC, and "Sanhedrin" is a Hellenistic term.

However, 1 Macc 4:9–10 implies that Jews in Antioch in Antiochus IV's time did have some form of citizenship, since it narrates that Jason, a leading Jew in Jerusalem, offered money to Antiochus IV so that Jews in Jerusalem could have the same. Josephus also claims that the successors of Antiochus IV also granted civic privileges similar to that of the Greeks (*B.J.* 7.44). From this evidence, and also the situation in Alexandria, Kraeling concludes that the Jews in Antioch "were organized as a separate πολίτευμα within the local community." This gave considerable religious and legal freedom, though not necessarily representation in the βουλή. Ancient sources such as Chrysostom, *Adv. Jud.* 1.3 [uses πολιτεία] and the Jerusalem Talmud (y. Sanh. 3, 21a) support this conclusion. Downey agrees with this conclusion, and Levinskaya agrees with both Kraeling and Downey.[39] In contrast, Barclay denies that Jews had any citizenship-like status prior to Antiochus III's reign.

The internal organization of the Jewish community in Antioch is hard to determine. The earliest reference to any office holder in the community is in AD 69, in Josephus (*B.J.* 7.47). This is the office of ἄρχων, which Chrysostom affirms continued into his time (*Adv. Jud.* 5.3). Consequently, one has to look in ancient sources that refer to Jews outside of Antioch and assume that Jews in Antioch organized themselves similarly to Jews in other cities. Consequently, Kraeling assumes the Jews in Antioch had πρεσβύτεροι (elders) for leaders, one of which was a προστάτης (a presiding officer), assisted by ἄρχοντες, who were members of a council "with special executive

---

[36] See especially Aramaic Papyri no. 30 in A. Cowley, *Aramaic Papyri of the Fifth Century B.C.* (Oxford: Clarendon, 1923), 108–19 in which the Jewish leaders claim they had settled at Yeb (Elephantine), a fortress, prior to the rule of Cambyses (d. 522 BC). That Yeb is a fortress suggests the Jewish community there was a military colony. After Cambyses conquered Egypt, Yeb became a border post for the Persian province of Egypt.
[37] E.g., Downey, *History*, 80, 107, cf. 115; Kraeling, "Jewish Community," 137; Barclay, *Jews*, 245 n. 29.
[38] Y. Seqal. 6, 50a; cited in Kraeling, "Jewish Community," 131–32.
[39] Kraeling, "Jewish Community," 138; Downey, *History*, 107. Levinskaya, *Book of Acts*, 128. Barclay, *Jews*, 245 n. 29.

obligations."[40] Paul and Barnabas's appointment of πρεσβύτεροι (elders) as leaders in the new churches of southern Galatia (Acts 16:23) suggests that Jewish communities there were also led by elders, and so provides additional suggestion that the Jews in Antioch were led similarly.

Ancient sources from different periods indicate that Jewish community in Antioch was diverse. Most texts are later than AD 100, but nevertheless indicate occupations Jews may have had prior to that time. Josephus, the earliest source, implies that some Jews were precious metal workers in the time of Antiochus IV (*B.J.* 7.45). Later texts indicate that Jews were merchants and shop keepers (b. Ketub. 67a; Chrysostom, *Hom. Rom.* 12:20) and farmers (t. Demai 2.1; y. Hor. 3, 48a).[41] No doubt there were wealthy Jews who sought political or social influence. In sum, Jews in Antioch were like any other people in a given region: diverse in occupation and livelihood.

The size of the Jewish community in Antioch is uncertain. Kraeling guesses at 65,000 Jews in Antioch for a city of 500,000 people in the Roman period, based on proportional figures of the Jewish population in Alexandria and Josephus's comment that Jews were present in the province of Syria in large numbers (*B.J.* 7.43).[42] Zetterholm reports estimates by scholars that Jews made up five to ten percent of the population.[43] This is a lower estimate than Kraeling's, assuming Antioch's total population was 500,000 in the first century AD. Whatever the exact figures were, especially for the first century AD, later Jewish writings indicate that Antioch was the "big city" for Palestinian and Babylonian Jews. The phrase, *as large as Antioch*, appears in y. Ta'an. 3, 66d; Semahot 2, 12; t. Erub. 4 (3), 13; y. Erub. 5, 22d.[44] Certainly the Jewish community was significant enough in 170 BC for the high priest Onias to flee to Daphne for sanctuary, and for his subsequent murder to provoke reaction from Jews living in Antioch (2 Macc 4:32–38).[45] The excavations of Antioch in the 1930s did not uncover areas identifiable as Jewish residential districts or synagogues, but the ancient sources suggest Jews lived in Antioch proper, in Daphne (an inference from 2 Macc 4:33–34), and in the plain to the east (y. Demai 2, 6b; y. Hor. 3, 48a).[46] Kraeling also argues that those Jews who lived in Antioch proper lived in the eastern part of the city, on the basis of where Herod the Great engaged in his building programs and the later early church traditions of sites connected with the apostles.[47] Schwemer and Hengel summarize the evidence to say Jews lived in

---

[40] Kraeling, "Jewish Community," 137.

[41] Citations from Kraeling, "Jewish Community," 133.

[42] Kraeling, "Jewish Community," 136.

[43] Zetterholm, "Antioch (Syria)," 336.

[44] Kraeling, "Jewish Community," 132; cf. the general comment in Downey, *History*, 108.

[45] Barclay, *Jews*, 248. The assumption is that 2 Macc 4:32–38 has reported the incident accurately.

[46] Kraeling, "Jewish Community," 140–43.

[47] Kraeling, "Jewish Community," 144–45. By using the Christian traditions of apostles being connected with sites in Antioch, Kraeling infers that the earliest Christians in Antioch were predominately Jewish.

many parts of Antioch, unlike in Alexandria and Rome, where they lived in separate neighborhoods.[48]

2.3. Jewish Relations with Others in Antioch

Because of the incidental nature of the references to Jews in Antioch in the ancient sources, there is little information on how well Jews interacted with other peoples in the city. For the early Hellenistic period, there is no information at all. Josephus makes the comment that during the time of Antiochus I (281/0–261 BC), it became "safe for Jews to dwell" in Antioch (*B.J.* 7.43). From this, Kraeling argues that Jews were hardly distinguishable from native Syrians before then and were "unprivileged and unprotected."[49] It is most likely true that Jews were initially unprivileged and unprotected, given that Antioch was founded as a Greco-Macedonian city.[50] However, it is unlikely that they were indistinguishable from others because of their aniconic monotheism and visibly unique customs such as the Sabbath, circumcision, and food laws, regardless of the extent to which these were observed. Jews in the late Roman Republic and early Empire were noted for these and other customs, and frequently derided for them,[51] so it can be assumed the same was the case for Jews in Antioch.

The possible bringing of Jewish captives from Judaea to Antioch during the rule of Antiochus IV (175–163 BC)[52] may have caused ill feeling between Jews and others in Antioch at the time.[53] Josephus, however, only reports tensions between Jews and others first appearing in the time of Demetrius II (145–139 BC) when Demetrius II used Jewish mercenaries to put down a rebellion of Antiochenes (*A.J.* 13.135–42; cf. 1 Macc 11:45–47). As already noted above, it appears that Antiochus IV's successors improved the status of Jews in the community (Josephus *B.J.* 7.44). It would seem that Demetrius II thought Jews, including those outside of Antioch, were loyal to him. There is

---

[48] Martin Hengel and Anna Maria Schwemer, *Paulus zwischen Damaskus und Antiochien: Die unbekannten Jahre des Apostels*, WUNT 108 (Tübingen: Mohr Siebeck, 2006), 300; Anna Maria Schwemer, "Paulus in Antiochien," *BZ* 199 (1998): 161–80; also Anna Maria Schwemer, trans. Diana Raysz, "The First Christians in Syria," in *Earliest Christian History: History, Literature, and Theology: Essays from the Tyndale Fellowship in Honor of Martin Hengel*, WUNT 320, ed. Michael F. Bird and Jason Maston (Tübingen: Mohr Siebeck, 2012), 429–56 (438).

[49] Kraeling, "Jewish Community," 145–46.

[50] But see discussion above on Jews as a πολίτευμα in Antioch.

[51] See the many citations from ancient writers in Molly Whittaker, *Jews and Christians: Graeco-Roman Views*, Cambridge Commentaries on Writings of the Jewish and Christian World 200 BC to 200 AD (Cambridge: Cambridge University Press, 1984), 63–85; and Louis H. Feldman and Meyer Reinhold, eds., *Jewish Life and Thought among Greeks and Romans* (Edinburgh: T&T Clark, 1996), 361–86.

[52] 1 Macc 1:32, and Josephus, *A.J.* 12.251, report the capture, but do not say where the captives went.

[53] So Kraeling, "Jewish Community," 146, followed by Downey, *History*, 109. See also Barclay, *Jews*, 246–48, who, however, focuses on Jew–Greek tensions in Judaea and nearby during the expansion phase of the Hasmonaean kingdom. However, he concedes (249) that we cannot tell if Jew–Gentile relations in distant cities such as Antioch were affected.

also the possibility that Jews sided with Parthia in the war between Antiochus and Parthia, and even attacked Antioch.[54] However, Josephus reports that by the time Alexander Jannaeus was ruling Judaea (103–76 BC), tension between Jews and others in Antioch had increased to such an extent that Jews could not be recruited to serve in the Syrian army (*B.J.* 1.88). It then appears that relations improved. Josephus observes that the numbers of Jews increased, and infers that their wealth also increased. This is reflected in the ability of members of the Jewish community to send votive offerings to Jerusalem (*B.J.* 7.44–45). We also note that Jewish Christians were able to send money to Jerusalem in ca. AD 40 for famine relief (Acts 11:27–30). Josephus (*B.J.* 7.45; cf. 2.463, 559–61) and Acts (6:5; 11:20) record Gentiles being attracted to Judaism and Christianity respectively. On the other hand, Jews across Syria were also influenced by Hellenistic culture. This is most in evidence in 4 Macc 17:7–10, which depicts Jews entertaining ideas of making frescoes that were to depict the trials of the Maccabaean martyrs.[55]

Jew–Gentile relations in Antioch changed for the worse in AD 40 when a pogrom erupted against the Jews as a result of factional rivalry at the circus (Malalas, *Chron.* 244.15–245.1). At the same time, Gaius Caligula ordered a statue of himself to be erected in the Jerusalem Temple (Josephus, *A.J.* 18.261–309). The Antiochene Jews would have been aware of this edict, since it was the legate in Antioch who was charged with carrying out Gaius's order, but Josephus's narrative focuses on the efforts of Jews in Judaea and Galilee, Petronius the legate, and Herod Agrippa I to have Gaius rescind his order.[56] Tension again erupted in AD 66–70 in connection with the Jewish war in Galilee and Judaea. It appears that two key incidents occurred, of which one was an extensive fire in the city. Accusations against the Jews were led by one Antiochus, the apostate son of a Jewish ἄρχων. The result was that many Jews were killed (Josephus, *B.J.* 2.462–63, 479; 7.46–52, 54–60). When Titus arrived in AD 70 or 71 after the Jews in Jerusalem had been defeated, he refused to rescind Jewish privileges (Josephus, *B.J.* 7.96–111; *A.J.* 12.121–24), but did humiliate them by permitting some spoils from Palestine to be set up in public in Antioch (Malalas, *Chron.* 260.21–261.12).[57] From this, Kraeling argues, "it would appear that the [Jewish community] had lost its self-assertiveness, had ceased to play a significant part in the eyes of others,

---

[54] Downey, *History*, 126.

[55] Kraeling, "Jewish Community," 148, argues that 4 Maccabees was written in Antioch. See, e.g., Eric M. Meyers and Mark A. Chancey, *Alexander to Constantine: Archaeology of the Land of the Bible*, AYBRL 3 (New Haven: Yale University Press, 2012), who argue on the basis of archaeological evidence that Jews in the Eastern Mediterranean were happy to use "pagan" pictures and motifs in artwork and mosaics, yet remained theologically conservative. See especially chapter 10 onwards.

[56] Kraeling, "Jewish Community," 148–49; Downey, *History*, 192–94. Both Kraeling and Downey discount the claim of Malalas that the high priest in Jerusalem sent 30,000 Jews to assist the Jews in Antioch (*Chron.* 245). At about the same time, there was a pogrom involving Jews in Alexandria during the visit of Herod Agrippa 1 in AD 38. It is likely the Jews in Antioch were aware of this (Downey, *History*, 194).

[57] See Kraeling, "Jewish Community," 148–52; Downey, *History*, 206.

Edward Bridge

and was effectively thrust back upon itself."[58] This statement is too strong. Kraeling himself notes that some Christians in Antioch were sympathetic to the Jews. This is evidenced in Ignatius's letters (*Magn.* 8.1–2; 10.3; *Phld.* 6.1) and the practice of many Christians in Antioch celebrating Easter on the date of the Jewish Passover.[59] Certainly, the Jewish community in Antioch lost prestige, and most likely their wealth also, evidenced in y. Hor. 3, 48a, but rabbis visiting the city indicate that the community remained in touch with Jews elsewhere in the world.

3. The Christian Community in Antioch

3.1. Beginnings of the Christian Community in Antioch

The beginnings of Christianity in Antioch are only narrated in the Book of Acts. The information is minimal, but well known.[60] According to Acts, Christianity was first preached in Antioch by Christian Jews who fled from the persecution that started with the martyrdom of Stephen and was led by Saul (Paul) (Acts 11:19; see 8:1, 4; 9:1–2; 22:4; 26:9–12). Only Jews were initially evangelized, but sometime later, *some men of Cyprus and Cyrene* also spoke *to the Hellenists* (Ἑλληνιστάς), with success (11:20–21). Ἑλληνιστής has long been assumed to refer to Gentiles, supported by a textual tradition that has *Greeks* (Ἕλληνας: e.g., $\mathfrak{P}^{47}$, $\aleph^2$, A, D*).[61] On hearing about this, the church in Jerusalem sent Barnabas to investigate (11:22). Barnabas evidently affirmed what was happening and brought Saul to assist (11:23–26). After this, Acts narrates a few events that involve the Christians in Antioch: a famine relief effort (11:27–30) for Christians in Jerusalem; Paul's first missionary journey, which started from Antioch (13:1–3; 14:26–27); a dispute about Gentile believers in Antioch needing to observe the Mosaic Law, which resulted in a meeting in Jerusalem of the church (15:1–35); and Paul's second and third missionary journeys, both of which also started from Antioch (Acts 15:36–40; 18:22–23). There is silence then in the extant earliest Christian literature, except for the letters of Ignatius. In these, Ignatius focuses on his own personal situation of impending martyrdom, but mentions some sort of trouble in Antioch, which is apparently resolved while he is on his way to Rome, along with his now well-known complaint about Christians being interested in Jewish things (Ign. *Magn.* 8.1–2; 10.3; *Phld.* 6.1). The next mention of Christianity in Antioch is in the brief accounts of early bishops of

[58] Kraeling, "Jewish Community," 152–53.
[59] Kraeling, "Jewish Community," 154–55. It took an edict of the Synod of Antioch in AD 341 to stop this practice.
[60] For a fuller discussion on the account of the spread of Christianity in Acts, see "The Acts of the Apostles as a Source for Studying Early Christianity," by Chris Forbes, in this volume. For Antioch specifically, see Robinson, *Ignatius*, 70–71 for a convenient list of references; also David L. Eastman, "Paul: An Outline of his Life," in *All Things to All Cultures: Paul among Jews, Greeks, and Romans*, ed. Mark Harding and Alanna Nobbs (Grand Rapids: Eerdmans, 2013), 34–56 (52).
[61] Hengel and Schwemer, *Paulus*, 238 n. 958 accept Ἕλληνας.

220

Antioch by Eusebius (*Hist. eccl.* 3.22; 4.20; *Chronicon* 261, 268).[62] Eusebius also mentions the letters of Ignatius (*Hist. eccl.* 3.36). Polycarp (d. AD 155–166) mentions Ignatius in *Phil.* 9.1 and 13.1–2, but says nothing about Christianity in Antioch.

The purpose of the discussion below is not to scrutinize the historicity or otherwise of Acts, or the relation of Paul's autobiographical narrative about his conversion and interactions with the Jerusalem church in Galatians 1 and 2 versus the narrative in Acts 9, 11, 13, and 15. These are extensively discussed in the commentaries and scholarly literature.[63] The multi-volume series, *The Book of Acts in its First Century Setting*, has done much to show the usability of Acts for historical study.[64] We will focus on four things in this section of this chapter: the arrival of Christianity in Antioch; the people who made up the early Christian community in Antioch; Acts' portrayal of Jewish–Christian relations in Antioch; and the witness of the Gospel of Matthew and the Didache to Jewish–Christian relations in Antioch. The specific situation of Christian–Jewish relations in the time of Ignatius is dealt with by Gore-Jones and Llewelyn in their chapter in this volume ("The Parting of the Ways").

As Eastman has recently pointed out well in relation to a chronology of Paul's life and ministry,[65] dates of key events in the expansion of the early church as portrayed in the New Testament can be difficult to determine. An especially problematic date is when Christianity first arrived in Antioch. As just noted, Acts 11:19–20 indicates that Christianity arrived in Antioch with Jewish Christians who fled the persecution in connection with Stephen. A plausible argument can be made that these Christians were the "Hellenist" Jews associated with Stephen.[66] A date at about the time of Paul's

---

[62] For a still-useful critical discussion on Eusebius's lists of bishops, see C. H. Turner, "The Early Episcopal Lists," *JTS* 1 (1899-1900): 181–200, 529–53; 18 (1916–1917): 103–34. The references to the bishops of Antioch (along with those in Rome, Jerusalem, and Alexandria) are found in Book 2 of *Chronicon*. This was translated into Latin by Jerome and now serves as the primary extant source for Book 2 (see, e.g., Jerome, *Chronicle*, ed. and trans. Roger Pearse and others [2005]. http://www.tertullian.org/fathers/jerome_chronicle_03_part2.htm). In sections 261 and 268 of *Chronicle* and in *Hist. eccl.* 3.36, Eusebius claims that Ignatius became the second bishop of Antioch in the thirteenth year of Nero, that is, AD 68, after Euodius, who was appointed bishop in Antioch in AD 44. Both Eusebius and Origen (*Hom Luc. 6*) claim Peter first oversaw the church in Antioch, but Origen does not mention Euodius.

[63] For a recent and thorough discussion, see Eastman, "Paul," 34–45.

[64] Published by Eerdmans, 1993–96. Thus far in the two books edited by Mark Harding and Alanna Nobbs, to which this volume will be added, only one chapter has dealt with Acts. This is Paul McKechnie's "Paul among the Jews," in Harding and Nobbs, *All Things to All Cultures*, 103–24. McKechnie does not discuss the critical questions about Acts, choosing instead to focus on how Acts portrays Paul's interaction with Jews in his life and missionary work. The first chapter of this volume, "The Acts of the Apostles as a Source for Studying Early Christianity," by Chris Forbes, goes some way to addressing this lack of focus on Acts.

[65] Eastman, "Paul," 34–56. See also Loveday C. A. Alexander, "Chronology of Paul," in *Dictionary of Paul and his Letters*, ed. G. F. Hawthorne, R. P. Martin, and D. G. Reid (Leicester: Inter-Varsity, 1993), 115–23.

[66] Schwemer, "First Christians," 433–39; Cf. Mark Harding, "The Gospels and Second Temple Judaism," in *The Content and Setting of the Gospel Tradition*, ed. Mark Harding and Alanna Nobbs (Grand Rapids; Eerdmans, 2010), 127–54 (153).

conversion/call becomes reasonable, though it is possible that the persecution continued for some time after his conversion. However, it is also possible that Christianity arrived in Antioch before Paul's conversion/call, but after Stephen's martyrdom. Many scholars date Paul's conversion/call at AD 33/34,[67] so a date of AD 34 or at the latest AD 36 is reasonable for when Christianity first arrived in Antioch.[68] Acts 11 does not indicate if the same group of believers traveled through Phoenicia, or if there were a number of groups, some of whom targeted Antioch early. Acts also does not give any time frame for when the Ἑλληνιστάς in Antioch were first evangelized, and then when "a great number became believers and turned to the Lord" (v. 21). The Acts narrative (vv. 22–26) is terse: the Jerusalem church heard about the conversions; sent Barnabas; Barnabas approved what was happening; then searched for Paul; and brought Paul to Antioch. Paul's time frame (Gal 1:21 and 2:1) of fourteen years when he was in the regions of Syria and Cilicia before he went to Jerusalem for a second visit, combined with Acts 11:26, which says Paul and Barnabas spent an entire year teaching the church at Antioch, suggests a long period of time elapsed. Despite the debate on the correlation of Galatians 1–2 with Acts 11–15, most scholars understand Paul's second visit to Jerusalem in Gal 2:1 to be the famine relief visit of Acts 11:27–30 and 12:25.[69] This is generally dated to AD 48, which means Paul arrived in Antioch in AD 47. If Paul's first missionary journey is included in this time period, then the arrival of Christianity in Antioch and Paul's arrival will have occurred much closer together.

No matter exactly when Christianity arrived in Antioch, it is safe to say that it arrived a few years before the pogrom of AD 40 and the Caligula statue incident. From Acts 11:19, Jews were first evangelized, and presumably large numbers of them accepted the message of the gospel. Given that Jewish–Gentile relations may have soured from AD 40 onwards,[70] it seems reasonable that the initial Ἑλληνιστάς, most likely Gentiles, interested in Christianity,[71] would have shown that interest when Jews were not being harassed.[72] It is most likely that non-Jews initially saw Christianity as a sect of Judaism, but after the Caligula statue debacle began to see Christianity as different from

---

[67] See the chart in Eastman, "Paul," 52. In addition to the scholars surveyed by Eastman, note also Alexander, "Chronology of Paul," 122–23.

[68] Schwemer ("First Christians," 434) places the occurrence "not longer than the three years that Paul was in Damascus and Arabia," and settles for AD 36.

[69] Many scholars argue against this. For a recent example, see A. J. M. Wedderburn, *A History of the First Christians* (London: T&T Clark, 2004). On this matter, see again Eastman, "Paul," 34–56; and Alexander, "Chronology of Paul," 115–23. Eastman, "Paul," 50, in his chart on the correlation of Acts and Paul's letters for events in Paul's life, correlates Gal 2:1–10 with Acts 15, and does not include Acts 11:27–30 in his discussion. For a recent defense of Gal 2:1 equating with Acts 11:27–30, see Schwemer, "First Christians," 443–44. See also the brief comments in Paul W. Barnett, "Appendix 1: Paul in the Book of Acts," in Harding and Nobbs, *All Things to All Cultures*, 392–95, who also defends the correlation of Gal 2:1–10 with Acts 11:27–30.

[70] Especially if Malalas's account of Jewish reprisals (*Chron.* 245) contains any truth.

[71] Cf. Hengel and Schwemer, *Paulus*, 101–39. See also Harding, "The Gospels," 153 n. 89.

[72] Cf. Downey, *History*, 192–97.

Judaism.[73] In contrast, Robinson argues from Acts 11:26, in which the invention of the name *Christian* (Χριστιανóς) is narrated, and also from Acts 15 and Gal 2:11–14, that Jews in Antioch from the start had trouble perceiving Christianity as part of Judaism.[74] This may have been the case, but it is safer to assume that most people in Antioch would have seen Christianity initially as a sect of Judaism until something happened to show that Christians were different.[75] In Antioch, the identification of Christians as different from Jews clearly happened early, unless the author of Acts has read back the title *Christian* to the 40s. Yet, despite the debacle in AD 40, which is not mentioned in Acts, Acts 11 implies the Christian community continued to grow. This is evidenced by the need to have Paul (Saul) there and also by Christians having enough wealth to send funds to Jerusalem for the relief of (Jewish) Christians in the AD 48 famine.[76] That is, people continued to see Christianity as attractive, no matter what the standing of Jews was in Antioch after AD 40.

3.2. The People in the Christian Community in Antioch

The make-up of the Christian community in Antioch is only recorded in scant detail in Acts. Clearly both Jews and Gentiles were converted (Acts 11:19–20). At the time of Paul's first missionary journey, the named leaders in Acts 13:1 are Jewish Christians.[77] When the leadership changed to Gentile Christian leadership is unknown, and not indicated in the New Testament. In his *Chronicon* 261 and 268, Eusebius claims that a certain Euodius, apparently a Gentile, was appointed as bishop of Antioch in AD 44.[78] Certainly, by the time of Ignatius's letters, the church can be classified as "Gentile," given his criticism of Christians interested in Jewish things (Ign. *Magn.* 10.3; *Phld.* 6.1).

Scholarship tends to argue that the first Gentile converts in any of the cities in the Eastern Roman Empire came from the ranks of proselytes (προσήλυτος), "God-fearers" (ὁ φοβούμενος [τòν θεόν]), and "God-worshippers" (ὁ σεβόμενος [τòν θεόν]); terms that are used in Acts.[79] This is the case with Cornelius, a centurion based at Caesarea, and the first Gentile to be recorded as converting to Christianity. He is designated in Acts 10:2 and

---

[73] Schwemer, "First Christians," 441. Schwemer also argues that Christians in Antioch were able to keep themselves separate from both sides of the conflict.

[74] Robinson, *Ignatius*, 68, 88.

[75] E.g., the Neronian persecution of Christians in Rome.

[76] Cf. Schwemer, "First Christians," 441; Kraeling, "Jewish community," 147.

[77] For the argument that Barnabas was the most important leader (he is first in the list) and Paul (Saul) was the most junior leader (he is last in the list), see Hengel and Schwemer, *Paulus*, 334–35; summarized in Schwemer, "First Christians," 442.

[78] See n. 62 above.

[79] προσήλυτος is used in Acts 2:11; 6:5; 13:43; and also Matt 23:15 (there are no references in the Apostolic Fathers; see Robinson, *Ignatius*, 40 n. 3). The term ὁ φοβούμενος [τòν θεόν] is used in Acts 10:2, 22, 35; 13:16, 26, while ὁ σεβόμενος [τòν θεόν] is used in Acts 13:43, 50; 16:14; 17:4, 17; 18:7.

22 as one who feared God (ὁ φοβούμενος τὸν θεόν). The use of the three terms in the narratives of the Pauline mission encourages the understanding that most, if not all, of the initial Gentile converts to Christianity were people who had had some prior attraction to Judaism; and that such people, proselytes included, saw in Christianity a relaxation of Jewish law observance. But Robinson argues against this. He concedes that initially "God-fearers" and "God-worshippers" may have been interested in Christianity, but only for the first few generations.[80] With regard to proselytes, Robinson notes the paucity of references to them (only in Acts 2:11 and 6:5 and 13:43) and the portrayal of proselytes as hostile to Christianity in both Matt 23:15 and in the second century AD (Justin Martyr, *Dial.* 122–23; Tertullian, *Adv. Jud.* 1.1) to argue that proselytes most likely remained firmly attached to Judaism, no matter how Jews viewed them (and how they viewed themselves). On this argument, even if proselytes were among the initial converts to Christianity, it is likely that once Christianity was perceived to be distinct from the Jewish community, proselytes would be less likely to convert, since they had made the decision to be fully identified with Jews in the eyes of wider society and would know what Christians believed.[81] Still, Robinson's argument allows for proselytes and God-fearers to be a significant proportion of converts to Christianity for most of the New Testament period.

It is assumed that the make-up of Christians in Antioch would be the same as for other cities in the Pauline mission. As noted above, Acts 13:1 indicates Jewish Christians were the initial leaders of the church. Despite Robinson's argument about the composition of Christians in Antioch being part of a larger argument that suggests Gentiles saw Christianity as a conduit to Judaism,[82] which is what he understands Ignatius to refer to in *Magn.* 8.1–2; 10.3 and *Phld.* 6.1, it is likely that as the decades went on, Christianity drew its converts from "pagan" Gentiles rather than Gentiles interested in Judaism. This is supported by Ignatius's lack of use of the term προσήλυτος in his letters. When exactly "pagan" Antiochene Gentiles started to become the majority of people converted to Christianity will never be known (Eusebius's date for Euodius becoming bishop of Antioch is disputed), but it can be

---

[80] Robinson, *Ignatius*, 40–68.

[81] Robinson, *Ignatius*, 42–51.

[82] Robinson, *Ignatius*, 65–69. For a similar argument for the "agitators" in Galatia, see Greg W. Forbes, "The Letter to the Galatians," in Harding and Nobbs, *All Things to All Cultures*, 248 and n. 18. Here, the argument is in terms of "completing the gospel" rather than having the new Gentile believers in Jesus convert to Judaism. However, the end result is that the Gentile believers would be living culturally as Jews. See also Robert Jewett, "The Agitators and the Galatian Congregation," *NTS* 17 (1971): 198–212. The arguments summarized by Forbes, and Jewett's argument, are all based on the assumption of Christian–Jewish tension in Jerusalem/Judaea, which caused Jewish Christians to travel to both Antioch and Galatia and exert pressure on Gentile converts in those regions. Ben Witherington III, *Grace in Galatia: A Commentary on Paul's Letter to the Galatians* (Grand Rapids: Eerdmans, 1998) 43, 448–49 takes an alternative view: the agitators in Galatia were local Christians who wanted approval from the Jews in their area.

assumed that at about the same time, the leadership of the church in Antioch also began to be dominated by Gentiles.

4. Christian–Jewish Relationships in Antioch

4.1. Direct Witness in the New Testament

The relationship between Jews and Christians in Antioch up to the time of Ignatius is difficult to determine. The New Testament itself gives no clear evidence of tension in the community. Tension between Christians and Jews in Antioch can only be inferred if: the Gospel of Matthew is thought to have been written in Antioch, or at least in Syria, and its critical stance to Jews and Judaism reflects the circumstances of its writing; the controversy in Antioch as reported in Acts 15 and Gal 2:11–14 involved or spilled over into the Jewish community there;[83] and the negative comments about *Judaizers* and Judaism in Ignatius's letters (*Magn.* 8.1–2; 10.3 and *Phld.* 6.1) and Did. 8.1–2 reflect tensions between the two communities rather than the authors of these works polemicizing against the attractiveness of Judaism.

The New Testament's narration of tension between Christians and Jews focuses on Jerusalem (Acts 6:8–8:3; 9:1; 11:19) and the Pauline mission, narrated for the cities of southern Galatia, Thessalonica, Berea, Corinth, and Ephesus (Acts 13–14; 16–19). Paul's arrest and eventual journey to Rome (Acts 21–28) is also a result of Jewish opposition to his ministry (cf. Rom 15:31). The letters to the seven churches in Revelation 2–3 also suggest Jewish opposition to Christians. The majority of scholars understand the Gospel of John to reflect a situation of Jewish opposition to Christianity.[84] The references in Acts show that the author does not shy away from narrating Jewish hostility to the earliest Christians, but it is noteworthy that he does not mention any hostility to Christians by Jews in Antioch.

Such silence is in contrast to Robinson's argument, noted above, that the controversy in Antioch represented an implied tension between the Jewish community and the Christian community on identity.[85] Further, the author of Acts, had he chosen to do so, could have mentioned the Caligula statue crisis and the AD 40 pogrom against the Jews, and how those events affected Christians in Antioch. For whatever reason, these two events were not important for the author of Acts. The same might be said for Jewish–Christian tension in Antioch, if there was any.

---

[83] E.g., Robinson, *Ignatius*, 72, 148. Witherington, *Grace*, 43, 448–49. The problem with this argument is that there is no supporting evidence. Robinson, for example, has to argue that the author of Acts has chosen not to narrate any response to the Acts 15 situation by the wider Jewish community in Antioch, and to assume (but not uncritically) the possibility that the Gospel of Matthew and the Didache were written in Antioch or, at least, in Syria. See discussion below.

[84] See, e.g., Johan Ferreira, "The Johannine Purpose and Outline," in the present volume.

[85] Robinson, *Ignatius*, 68, 88. Robinson is too dismissive of Acts' record of Christian–Jewish relations in Antioch.

The situation narrated by Paul in Gal 2:11–13 is not tension between Jews and Christians in Antioch, but tension *between* Christians on the matter of observing the Mosaic law. The people who apparently advocated that non-Jewish Christians should observe the law had not come from Antioch, but from outside—from Jerusalem (Gal 2:11). This is the same scenario as presented in Acts 15:1–2. More widely, the New Testament (Phil 3:2–3; Gal 3:1–5; 5:2–12; 6:12; and the Pastoral Letters) presents evidence of a similar situation of persons advocating that non-Jewish Christians should observe the law.[86] From such evidence, especially Gal 2:1–14, and also the Gospel of Matthew and Didache, Zetterholm argues that "the main problem within the early Jesus movement probably had very little, if anything, to do with Jewish views of the validity of the Torah for Jesus-believing Jews, but rather concerned the relations between Jews and non-Jews within the movement."[87] This is an overstatement, since, as shown above by Acts, the Gospel of John, Rom 15:31 and Revelation 2–3, there was clearly opposition to Christianity by Jews in the New Testament period. Christians had to respond to that as well as to their own internal disputes on the role of the Mosaic Law for Gentile believers. The problem with Zetterholm's argument is that he has not considered the witness of Acts, nor the Johannine material. The Johannine material can be understandably omitted by Zetterholm because of the general consensus that it originated from Asia Minor, but Zetterholm's argument is too broad to be applied solely to Antioch, Syria, and Judaea/Galilee.

We conclude that the New Testament's direct witness is that there was *no* tension between Jews and Christians in Antioch prior to AD 66. Instead, the impression is that relations between the two groups were good enough that Christian preaching had great success, though Acts 11:21 focuses on the response of Gentiles (the Ἑλληνιστάς). It can be assumed, along with Schwemer, that the success of Christian preaching to both God-fearers and pagan Gentiles would have aroused the concern of the Jewish community in Antioch,[88] but if there was any concern and action by Jews, the New Testament does not provide evidence of it. Instead, as Kraeling points out, Judaism remained attractive to Antiochene Christians for some centuries. This is evidenced by Ignatius's polemic against Christians interested in Jewish things; the continued celebration of Easter on the date of the Jewish Passover

[86] See the commentaries. For a recent discussion on the identity of Paul's opponents in Galatia, see Forbes, "Galatians," 246–49; and for the false teachers in the Pastoral Epistles, see Mark Harding, "The Pastoral Epistles," in Harding and Nobbs, *All Things to All Cultures*, 328–52 (342–43). See also n. 82 above. Paul's language in Galatians indicates that the opponents came from outside Galatia (this can also be inferred for Phil 3:2–3); whereas the language in the Pastoral Epistles indicates the "Jewish" teaching was indigenous to the regions to which the letters were sent.
[87] Magnus Zetterholm, "The Didache, Matthew, James—and Paul: Reconstructing the Historical Developments in Antioch," in *Matthew, James, and Didache*, SBL Symposium Series 45, ed. Huub van de Sandt and Jürgen K. Zangenburg (Atlanta: Society of Biblical Literature, 2008), 73–90 (81).
[88] Schwemer, "First Christians," 440. Schwemer suggests this would be due to the loss of Jewish members to the Christian movement along with the loss of Gentile benefaction to the Jewish community.

despite legislation against this practice that was passed at the Synod of Antioch in AD 341; and the veneration of the Maccabaean martyrs by Christians. Kraeling notes that only in the fifth century AD did relations between Jews and Christians sour enough to discourage such practices by Christians.[89] This witness by the New Testament and the meager evidence from subsequent centuries parallels Josephus's constant claims that people in Antioch and other cities in Syria were attracted to Judaism (*B.J.* 2.463, 559–61; 7.45; cf. *B.J.* 2.267, 287; *A.J.* 20.178), despite the periodic tensions between Jews and others that he describes and which have been summarized above. It seems then, from the double witness by the New Testament and Josephus, that however the Jews in Antioch conducted themselves, observed the Mosaic laws, and maintained their identity and were seen as distinct from wider society, it was done in such a way that Gentiles were generally attracted to them, including those who had become Christians.

What, then, leads scholars to argue that there was Christian–Jewish tension in Antioch in the first decades of Christianity?

4.2. The Gospel of Matthew

Generally, it is the strong polemic against Jews in general, and the Pharisees in particular, in the Gospel according to Matthew that informs the consensus that there was Christian–Jewish tension in Antioch in the early decades of Christianity. This relies on the argument that Matthew was written in Antioch, or somewhere in Syria. In addition is the argument that the Didache also was written in Antioch or Syria.

All four Gospels report opposition to Jesus by his fellow Jews, most notably the Pharisees and scribes but also, when Jesus is in Jerusalem in the week leading up to his death, the priests at the temple. The Gospel of John speaks of an undefined group or groups called *the Jews*. It is this opposition that resulted in the arrest of Jesus, his trial, and his eventual crucifixion by the Romans. However, it is the Gospel of Matthew that has the most negative view of Jewish leaders. The Gospel of Mark has Jesus saying that the scribe who asked him about the greatest commandment (Mark 12:28–34) is *not far from the kingdom of God* (v. 34). Despite the sustained opposition of Pharisees, *the Jews*, and others in John, Nicodemus—a Pharisee—follows Jesus (John 3:1–15; 7:50–51; 19:39). In John 12:42, the Evangelist remarks that a number of leaders in Jerusalem (ἐκ τῶν ἀρχόντων πολλοί) *believed in* Jesus, but in secret.[90] The Gospel of Luke—despite, as in Mark and Matthew, narrating the

---

[89] Kraeling, "Jewish Community," 154–55 and footnotes; citing the First Canon of the Synod of Antioch, AD 341, and the Syrian Calendar of Christian Saints.

[90] The NIV and NASB translate John 9:40 to infer some Pharisees were also followers of Jesus (ἐκ τῶν Φαρισαίων ... οἱ μετ' αὐτοῦ ὄντες). Such translation assumes μετά means "with" as in "in association with." Most commentators, however, understand the clause ἐκ τῶν Φαρισαίων ... οἱ μετ' αὐτοῦ ὄντες to refer to Pharisees who were listening to Jesus' dialogue with the blind man and then Jesus' final statement in John 9:35–39 (e.g., NRSV) rather than actually being followers of Jesus (so NRSV, ESV).

Edward Bridge

Pharisees and scribes' opposition to various activities of Jesus, especially in connection with the Sabbath (reflected also in John 5 and 9), and having six "woes" proclaimed against them (Luke 11:42–52)—narrates Jesus being invited to eat with Pharisees on three occasions (Luke 7:36; 11:37; 14:1). In Acts, both priests (6:7) and Pharisees (15:5) believe in Jesus.

In the Gospel of Matthew, there is no indication that Pharisees, scribes, or the leaders in Jerusalem were positive toward Jesus. Joseph of Arimathea's status as a member of the Sanhedrin is omitted (contrast Mark 15:43 and Luke 23:50–51), which allows the Jewish leadership to be seen in a thoroughly negative light. The "woes" against the scribes and Pharisees are given more extensive treatment in Matthew (Matthew 23) than in Luke (Luke 11:42–52). The question about the greatest commandment in Matt 22:34–40 is narrated as being asked by a "lawyer" from the Pharisees, and there is no further narrative after Jesus gives his reply.[91] Jesus' question to an unspecified audience about whose son is the Messiah (Mark 12:35–37; Luke 19:41–44) is directed to the Pharisees in Matt 22:41–46. Pharisees are also narrated as being with other leadership groups in Jerusalem and also active in Jerusalem (Matt 22:45; 27:62), which is in contrast to Luke and Mark.[92] That is, the Jewish leaders— Pharisees, scribes, lawyers, Sanhedrin, and others—are portrayed as consistently hostile to Jesus.[93]

Consequently, scholarship on the Gospel of Matthew generally concludes that it was written for Christians who were in tension with the Jewish community. In addition, many argue that Matthew's readership was Jewish-Christian, yet engaged in mission to Gentiles. This is argued on the basis of, for example: the ongoing validity of the law (Matt 5:17–20; cf. 24:20); the "fulfillment" quotations from the Scriptures; Jewish customs are not explained

[91] In the parallel in Luke 10:25–28, a short dialogue immediately occurs between the *lawyer* and Jesus on the practical application of the answer, which includes the Parable of the Good Samaritan (vv. 29–37).
[92] Cf. the Gospel of John, in which the Pharisees are also portrayed as active in Jerusalem and involved in the Jewish leadership. Compare also Acts 5:33–39, in which Gamaliel, said to be a Pharisee (v. 34), is a member of the Sanhedrin, and gives advice that is accepted by the Sanhedrin.
[93] Cf. Anthony J. Saldarini, *Matthew's Christian-Jewish Community*, Chicago Studies in the History of Judaism (Chicago and London: University of Chicago Press, 1994), 195. In this summary statement, Saldarini notes that in the scene of Jesus' trial before Pilate, only Jesus' opponents are condemned, not the people as a whole (Matt 27:20–25). This argument needs to be nuanced, since the same situation occurs in the scene in Mark 15:6–15. Luke depicts the crowds playing a part in condemning Jesus (Luke 23:13–25), but when Jesus has been crucified, Luke, unlike Matt 27:39 and Mark 15:29, does not mention the crowd mocking Jesus but merely watching (Luke 23:35). That is, following the two-source hypothesis, Matthew has followed Mark's account of Jesus' trial before Pilate without substantial alteration, which Saldarini has not noted. See also, Francois P. Viljoen, "Matthew, the Church and Anti-Semitism," in *The Gospel of Matthew at the Crossroads of Early Christianity*, BETL 243, ed. Donald Senior (Leuven: Peeters, 2011), 665–82 (682); and Wim Weren, "The History and Social Setting of the Matthean Community," in *Matthew and the Didache: Two Documents from the Same Jewish-Christian Milieu?* ed. Huub van de Sandt (Assen: Royal Van Gorcum, 2005), 51–62 (59). Timothy J. Harris, "Distinctive Features of the Gospels," in Harding and Nobbs, *Content and Setting*, 308, notes that "the leaders are undeveloped as characters."

(contrary to Mark); the inclusion of Gentiles in Jesus' genealogy (1:3–6); the narration of the visit of the Magi in 2:1–12; and references to Jesus and the disciples' ministry being worldwide (e.g., 5:13–16; 13:38; and 28:20).[94] To this can be added evidence that Matthew was the most used of the canonical Gospels in Jewish Christianity.[95]

The next stage in the argument that there was Christian–Jewish tension in Antioch in the first decades of Christianity requires the proposal that the Gospel of Matthew was written in Antioch, or in northern Syria. This proposal was popularized by Streeter in 1924,[96] and remains dominant in scholarship. The provenance of Matthew is discussed in all major commentaries and New Testament introductions. For the purposes of the present chapter, the following are used either singly, all together, or some together, to argue for the Gospel's origin in Antioch or northern Syria:

1. The mention of *Syria* in Matt 4:24, which suggests the author's location was in Syria. Contrast the mention of *Tyre and Sidon* in Mark 3:8 and Luke 6:17.
2. The name of the coin in Matt 17:27, "stater." It was a coin minted only in Antioch and Damascus.
3. The "stolen body" story in Matt 28:15. This story was still current at the time of writing. Such a story would be more familiar to Jews in Palestine/Syria than elsewhere.
4. The apparent use of Matthew by Ignatius, bishop of Antioch. Ign. *Eph.* 19.1–3 refers to the star the wise men saw when Jesus was an infant (Matt 2:2, 9); Ign. *Smyrn.* 1.1 contains the clause, *all righteousness might be fulfilled*, an apparent citation of Jesus' words in Matt 3:15 to John the Baptist (*to fulfill all righteousness*);[97] and Ign. *Pol.* 2.2 (*be wise as a serpent in all things*

---

[94] Some representative commentators are: Craig A. Evans, *Matthew*, NCBC (Cambridge: Cambridge University Press, 2012), 6–7; Dale C. Allison Jr., ed., *Matthew: A Shorter Commentary* (London and New York: T&T Clark, 2004), xiii; Craig S. Keener, *Matthew*, IVPNTC (Downers Grove, IL: InterVarsity, 1997), 33–35; Leon L. Morris, *The Gospel According to Matthew*, Pillar (Grand Rapids: Eerdmans, 1992), 3. See also Ulrich Luz, "Matthew the Evangelist: A Jewish Christian at the Crossroads," in *Studies in Matthew*, trans. Rosemary Selle (Grand Rapids: Eerdmans, 2005 [1991]), 3–17 (7–14); Alan F. Segal, "Matthew's Jewish Voice," in *Social History of the Matthean Community*, ed. David L. Balch (Minneapolis: Fortress, 1991) 3–37; Saldarini, *Matthew's Christian-Jewish Community*; Viljoen, "Matthew," 665–82; Weren, "History," 51–62. Contrast Christopher Tuckett, "Matthew: The Social and Historical Context—Jewish Christian and/or Gentile?" in Senior, *The Gospel of Matthew*, 99–129, who argues that Matthew's readers did not observe important Jewish identity markers such as the Sabbath and the food laws. However, Tuckett concedes that there was tension between Matthew's readers and the synagogue and that "Jewishness" was important for the readers.

[95] Luz, "Matthew," 11. Luz cites the *Gospel of the Nazarenes*, the *Gospel of the Ebionites* ("especially close to Matthew"), the pseudo-Clementine letters, the *Didaskalia* and the Jewish-Christian Gnostic *Apocalypse of Peter* from Nag Hammadi. See also Saldarini, *Matthew's Christian-Jewish Community*, 24.

[96] B. H. Streeter, *The Four Gospels* (London: Macmillan, 1924), 500–523.

[97] Πληρωθῇ πᾶσα δικαιοσύνη in *Smyr.* 1.1; πληρῶσαι πᾶσαν δικαιοσύνην in Matt 3:15.

and always pure as the dove) paraphrases Matt 10:16 (*be as wise as serpents and innocent as doves*; NRSV). The argument is that Ignatius is the earliest unambiguous witness to the Gospel of Matthew, and so adds to the argument that not only was the Gospel known there, but it originated from Antioch or at least somewhere nearby in Syria.[98]

In addition to the above are arguments that Antioch had large Jewish and Christian communities; the Christian community was engaged in outreach to non-Jews as evidenced by Acts (as discussed above); and the Gospel of Matthew was written to believers faced with possible exclusion from the synagogues with the promulgation of the Birkat Haminim by the Jewish council at Jamnia. Obviously, counter-arguments are marshaled against the Antioch provenance of Matthew.[99]

In recent years, many scholars have been hesitant to commit themselves to a specific region or city as the provenance for Matthew.[100] Thus, Forbes can write "Matthew's Gospel *may* have been written in Antioch in north Syria," and Donald Senior comments that the Gospel's origins may be on some "axis" from "northern Galilee to Antioch."[101] It is only scholars who advocate Matthew's origin in Antioch or north Syria who can then argue that there was

---

[98] See, Robert M. Grant, *After the New Testament* (Minneapolis: Fortress, 1967), 37–54.

[99] See, e.g., Benedict T. Viviano OP, "Where was the Gospel according to St. Matthew Written?" *CBQ* 41 (1979): 533–46; reprinted in *Matthew and his World: The Gospel of the Open Jewish Christians: Studies in Biblical Theology*, NTOA 61 (Fribourg: Academic, 2007), 9–23. Viviano argues for Caesarea, but in an additional note at the end of the reprinted argument as a response to criticism of his earlier article, he notes the plausibility of Syria, either north or south. Note also Weren, "History," 51–62 (southern Syria); Segal, "Matthew's Jewish Voice," 3–37 (southern Syria or Galilee); Luz, "Matthew," 3–17 (southern Syria); Ben Witherington III, *Matthew*, Smyth & Helwys Bible Commentary (Macon, GA: Smyth & Helwys, 2006), 22–28 (Capernaum). In his arguments against Streeter's proposal, Viviano does not deal with Streeter's positive argument for Antioch, only Streeter's negative arguments for a Palestinian provenance (Viviano, "Where was the Gospel according to St. Matthew Written?" 9–10). I have not chosen to list commentators and scholars who argue for or assume Antioch as the place of writing for Matthew because this is the majority view and they are dependent on the points listed in this chapter.

[100] Note the commentators listed in n. 94 above, Allison, *Shorter*, xiii; Morris, *Matthew*, 11–12 (Antioch, but is hesitant). Some other commentators are: Charles H. Talbert, *Matthew*, Paideia CNT (Grand Rapids: Baker, 2010), 4; R. T. France, *Matthew: An Introduction and Commentary*, TNTC 1 (Leicester: InterVarsity; Grand Rapids: Eerdmans, 1985), 27–28; Robert H. Gundry, *Matthew: A Commentary on his Handbook for a Mixed Church under Persecution* (Grand Rapids: Eerdmans, 1994), 609 (Antioch, but, like Morris, hesitant). See also Huub van de Sandt, "Matthew and the Didache," in *Matthew and his Christian Contemporaries*, LNTS 333, ed. David C. Sim and Boris Repschinski (London: T&T Clark, 2008), 123–38, who does not speculate on the provenance of Matthew and the Didache, though acknowledges the Jewishness of both documents.

[101] Chris Forbes, "The Historical Jesus," in Harding and Nobbs, *Content and Setting*, 231–62 (236); Donald Senior, "Matthew at the Crossroads of Early Christianity: An Introductory Assessment," in Senior, *The Gospel of Matthew*, xiii–xxviii (xxviii). Cf. Craig S. Keener, *Matthew*, 33.

Christian–Jewish tension in Antioch.[102] However, southern Syria seems to be gaining acceptance, argued on the persistent theme of Pharisaic opposition to Jesus in the Gospel; the mention of *Syria* in Matt 4:24; and a late dating for Matthew which allows for the sentiment of the effects of the Birkat Haminim to be felt throughout Galilee/southern Syria at the time of the Gospel's writing.[103] Consequently, this hesitancy of many scholars and the apparent increasing consensus for a provenance in southern Syria dampens an automatic acceptance that Matthew witnesses to Christian–Jewish tension in Antioch. In this case, the witness of Acts is affirmed: there was no Christian–Jewish tension in Antioch.

4.3. Didache

As noted, the argument that there was Christian–Jewish tension in Antioch implies that the Didache also originated in Antioch.[104] Many scholars argue that the Didache was written for the same community as the Gospel of Matthew.[105] The Didache shows strong affinity with Matthew, with its mention of the Lord's Prayer (Did. 8.2; Matt 6:5–13), the Trinitarian baptismal formula (Did. 7.1; Matt 20:19), itinerant teachers and apostles (Didache 11–13; Matt 7:15–23; 10:5–15, 40–42; 24:11, 24), community discipline (Did. 15.3; Matt 18:15–17), and various themes from Matthew 5–7 found in 1.3–2.1.[106] As for Matthew, it appears the Didache was written for a

---

[102] Most notably, Zetterholm, "The Didache, Matthew, James—and Paul," 73–90 (but in the context of intra-Christian tension in Antioch); and Robinson, *Ignatius*, 20, 64.

[103] See the scholars listed in n. 99 above: Weren, Segal, Luz, and Viviano in his additional note to the reprint of his 1979 article ("Where was the Gospel according to St. Matthew Written?" reprinted in *Matthew and his World*, 22–23). See also Evans, *Matthew*, 5–6 (but does not specify north or south Syria). For the dating of the Gospel of Matthew, most scholars assume or argue for a date of AD 80 onwards, or at least after 70 (see the scholars listed in the footnotes above). Conservative commentators, by contrast, argue for a pre-AD 70 date. See, e.g., Knox Chamblin, *Matthew, Volume 1: Chapters 1–13*, Mentor Commentary (Fearn: Mentor [Christian Focus Publications], 2010), 161–68; Morris, *Matthew*, 8–11; Evans, *Matthew*, 5; France, 28–30 (hesitant). Talbert, *Matthew*, 4, is undecided; and Keener, *Matthew*, 34, argues for late AD 70s.

[104] For arguments, see, e.g., Jonathan Draper, "Torah and Troublesome Apostles in the Didache Community," *NovT* 33 (1991): 347–72; and "The Apostolic Fathers: The Didache," *ExpTim* 117 (2006): 177–81; Michelle Slee, *The Church in Antioch in the First Century CE: Communion and Conflict*, JSNTSup 244 (London: Sheffield University Press, 2003), 54–76; and Clayton N. Jefford, "Social Locators as a Bridge between the Didache and Matthew," in *Trajectories through the New Testament and the Apostolic Fathers*, ed. A. Gregory and C. Tuckett (Oxford: Oxford University Press, 2005), 256–64. Zetterholm, "The Didache, Matthew, James—and Paul," 73–90, assumes Draper's arguments for the provenance of Didache.

[105] E.g., Slee, *The Church in Antioch*, 118–55; Draper, "Torah and Troublesome Apostles," 347–72; Zetterholm, "The Didache, Matthew, James—and Paul," 73–90. Contra Joseph Verheyden, "Jewish Christianity, A State of Affairs: Affinities and Differences with Respect to Matthew, James, and the Didache," in *Matthew, James, and Didache*, SBL Symposium Series 45, ed. Huub van de Sandt and Jürgen K. Zangenburg (Atlanta: Society of Biblical Literature, 2008), 123–35, who argues that the audiences of Matthew and the Didache were independent of, but in communication with, each other.

[106] Van de Sandt, "Matthew and the Didache," 123. Van de Sandt also notes allusions between Didache and teaching shared between Matthew and Luke. For the absence of allusions or

Jewish-Christian audience (e.g., the prayer in 10.6, "Hosanna to the God of David"; and the comment in chapter 13 that true prophets are the audience's "high priests" and tithes are given to them). Yet this community is differentiated from the Jewish community. This is especially evident in Did. 8.1–2, in which the Jewish practice of fasting on Wednesdays and Saturdays is criticized and alternative days proposed. The affinities with Matthew and the Jewish-Christian flavor of the Didache suggest that it "may even have emanated from the same geographical, social and cultural setting as Matthew."[107] Therefore, if the Gospel of Matthew was written in Antioch, then the likelihood of the Didache being written in Antioch also becomes high.

However, the origins of the Didache are less certain than for Matthew. Generally, Syria-Palestine is argued for, but not necessarily Antioch.[108] Yet, the Didache was used by early Christian writers from Egypt (mentioned by Athanasius, and cited by Didymus the Blind), and a fragment of an early copy of the Didache has also been found in Egypt, which indicates that the Didache was widely used in Egypt and soon after its composition.[109] Consequently, a number of scholars do not commit themselves to identifying the provenance of the Didache.[110] The dating, once commonly accepted to be the mid-second century AD, is now placed at the end of the first century AD, or at the end of the first decade of the second century AD at the latest. The reason for the change is that scholars now take seriously the Jewish flavor of the Didache, its witness to a twofold leadership structure of bishops and deacons (Did. 8.1) rather than Ignatius's threefold leadership structure of bishops, elders, and deacons, and the existence of traveling apostles and prophets (Didache 11–13) alongside a local leadership.[111] Some scholars, however, argue that Didache was composed early, in fact earlier than Matthew, strongly influencing not

citations of the rest of the now-canonical New Testament books in the Didache, see Christopher Tuckett, "The Didache and the Writings that later became the New Testament," in *The Reception of the New Testament in the Apostolic Fathers*, ed. Andrew Gregory and Christopher Tuckett (Oxford: Oxford University Press, 2005), 83–127.

[107] Van de Sandt, "Matthew and the Didache," 124. For arguments, see, e.g., the essays in *Matthew and the Didache: Two Documents from the Same Jewish-Christian Milieu?* ed. H. van de Sandt (Assen: Royal van Gorcum, 2005); and in Jonathan A. Draper, ed., *The Didache in Modern Research* (Leiden: Brill, 1996).

[108] E.g., Kurt Niederwimmer, *The Didache*, Hermeneia (Minneapolis: Fortress, 1998); W. Rordorf and A. Tuilier, *La Doctrine des douze apôtres (Didache): Introduction, texte, traduction*, 2nd ed., SC 248 (Paris: Cerf, 1998).

[109] Robert A. Kraft, *Barnabas and the Didache: The Apostolic Fathers,* Vol. 3 (New York: Nelson, 1965), and "Didache," in *Anchor Bible Dictionary*, ed. David Noel Freedman (New York: Doubleday, 1992), 2:197–98, argues for Egypt on the basis of the patristic evidence.

[110] Most notably, the editors of the two major critical editions and translations of the Didache: Bart D. Ehrman, ed. and trans., *The Apostolic Fathers,* Volume 1, LCL (Cambridge, MA/London: Harvard University Press, 2003), 411–12; Michael W. Holmes, ed. and trans., *The Apostolic Fathers: Greek Texts and English Translations*, 3rd ed. (Grand Rapids: Baker, 2007), 338. Both editors note the reference to *mountains* in the Eucharistic prayer in Did. 9.4, which suggests a setting in Syria rather than Egypt for at least some parts of the text. However, for the final form of the text, both editors comment that it could have been put together anywhere.

[111] See the summary in Holmes, *Apostolic Fathers*, 338–39.

only their argument for continuing Jewish–Christian tension in Antioch but also Matthew's use of the Didache as a source.[112] However, it is more common for scholars to argue that the Didache was written later than Matthew. It is suggested that Matthew's polemic implies a situation of tension (see discussion above), yet the Didache presupposes that the tension with Jewish communities has abated.[113] In addition, some scholars argue that Matthew and the Didache drew upon a common source.[114] Regardless of which document was written first, since the two documents are now recognized as having been written only a few decades apart, wherever Matthew was written the Didache may have been written in the same or a nearby location.

4.4. The Witness of Matthew and the Didache

It would seem therefore that it is difficult to use both the Gospel of Matthew and the Didache to determine the presence of Christian–Jewish tension in Antioch. The primary sticking point is the lack of consensus on the provenance of both documents. However, even if both documents originated in Antioch, Matthew contains an antagonistic portrayal of the Jewish leadership in Judaea and Galilee, whereas the Didache is only criticizing readers who wish to observe certain known Jewish customs (*Did.* 8.1–2). From this, it can be argued that Matthew is in tension with the wider Jewish community, but the Didache deals with a situation where members of its intended readership are in contact with Jews and wish to practice some of their customs.[115] That is, there is no tension between Christians and Jews, only criticism of Christians who wish to take up Jewish practices. If both documents did originate from the same region, then an explanation is required: either the respective audiences of Matthew and the Didache are different communities, each with a different relationship with the Jewish community in their location (so Verheyden), or they are the same community but in different periods of its history (so Draper, Zetterholm, Slee, Tuckett, Robinson).

Similarly, Ignatius's comments against Jews (*Magn.* 8.1–2; 10.3; *Phld.* 6.1), need not be interpreted as indicating the presence of tension between the church and the Jewish community in Antioch. As already noted, Kraeling argues from Ignatius's letters that some Christians in Antioch were

---

[112] See, for example, Draper, "Torah and Troublesome Apostles," 347–72.

[113] See, for example, Verheyden, "Jewish Christianity," 123–35; van der Sandt, "Matthew and the Didache," 123–28; Tuckett, "The Didache and the Writings," 83–127.

[114] See, for example, van der Sandt, "Matthew and the Didache," 124; Rordorf and A. Tuilier, *La Doctrine*, 91, 232.

[115] E.g., Ehrman, *Apostolic Fathers I*, 409; Zetterholm, "The Didache, Matthew, James—and Paul," 86–89; Verheyden, "Jewish Christianity," 132; Robinson, *Ignatius*, 161 (n. 116), 232, 235 (this fits with Robinson's thesis that Christians found Judaism attractive, and Ignatius attempted to curb it). Cf. van der Sandt, "Matthew and Didache," 134–37 (*Did.* 6.2–3 presupposes Gentile converts to Christianity who do not need to observe many of the Jewish laws).

Edward Bridge

sympathetic to the Jews.[116] Others argue that Ignatius is polemically engaged with Christians who adopt Jewish practices.[117] Noteworthy is Robinson who, despite his sustained argument that there was Jewish–Christian tension in Antioch from the beginning of the church, says, "Ignatius distinguishes sharply between Christianity and Judaism but recounts no particular clash between the two groups."[118]

In effect, Ignatius intends to make the Christian community identifiably different from the Jewish community. This puts him in a tradition going back to Paul, a view argued very sharply by Bibliowicz.[119] In contrast is an argument, now old but still current, that Ignatius directs his comments at Judaizers within the church: believers in Jesus who advocate the observance of the Jewish law by all Christians.[120] That is, Ignatius continues a debate since Paul's time (see, e.g., Acts 15 and Gal 2:1–14) on the role of the Jewish law with regard to Gentile believers.

5. Christians and Jews in Antioch

In conclusion, it would appear that Christians and Jews had amicable relations in Antioch. Acts does not narrate hostility between the two groups, yet narrates hostility between Jews and Christians elsewhere in the eastern Roman Empire, including Jerusalem. The absence of any narration of tension in Antioch could be due to the author's purposes in writing Acts, but it should nevertheless be considered worthy of discussion. It can be assumed that Jews disliked people converting to Christianity, and may have attempted to cause some trouble for the Christian community. But if this occurred, it was not extensive enough to be noteworthy. The next clear witness of Christian–Jewish relations in Antioch is Ignatius, but current scholarship is divided on whether in *Magn.* 8.1–2; 10.3 and *Phld.* 6.1 Ignatius is simply criticizing members of the church for adopting Jewish practices, or whether he is criticizing Judaizers within the church. If the latter, then Ignatius is part of a tradition of thought that encouraged a clear break between the church and Judaism.

The evidence of the Gospel of Matthew and Didache on Christian–Jewish relations in Antioch is problematic. The provenance of both texts cannot be identified with Antioch with any certainty. The Didache is even less securely tied to Antioch than Matthew. A number of scholars argue persuasively that

---

[116] Kraeling, "Jewish Community," 152–55. See Section 3.2 above.
[117] Meeks and Wilken, 19–20; Schwemer, "First Christians," 439 n. 38.
[118] Robinson, *Ignatius*, 146.
[119] Abel Mordechai Bibliowicz, *Jews and Gentiles in the Early Jesus Movement* (New York: Palgrave Macmillan, 2013). Robinson thinks similarly, but is irenic in his language.
[120] Slee, *The Church in Antioch*, 54–76, 118–28; Zetterholm, "Historical Developments," 73–90. See also Ehrman, *Apostolic Fathers*, 1:206; Holmes, *Apostolic Fathers*, 167. Ehrman cites Cyril Richardson, *The Christianity of Ignatius of Antioch* (New York: Columbia University Press, 1935); Virginia Corwin, *St. Ignatius and Christianity in Antioch* (New Haven: Yale University Press, 1960); and Paul J. Donohue, "Jewish Christianity in the Letters of Ignatius of Antioch," *VC* 32 (1978): 81–93.

234

Matthew was written in Galilee or southern Syria. As is the case for Ignatius, the Didache can be interpreted as the author's criticizing members of his community for adopting Jewish practices, or as criticizing Judaizers in his community, rather than mounting a polemic against Jews. Therefore, if the Didache was written in Antioch, then it evidences a lack of tension between Christians and Jews sometime before Ignatius became bishop. If the Gospel of Matthew was written in Antioch, it presents a problem, since it indicates a Christian community or communities that are in tension with the Jewish community. If Matthew was written in Antioch, then it was most likely written in a period when tension between Christians and Jews had emerged, yet it has to be early enough for the Antioch Christian community to be Jewish in character. The same applies to the Didache. The period of time leading up to the Jewish War of AD 66–70, when Jews were in tension with the wider community, is one possibility. Another is sometime after AD 75, when the *birkat hamminim* had been developed, but this requires that the rabbinic account of the Council of Jamnia actually happened and that the *birkat hamminim* was taken to Antioch quickly and then became immediately accepted in the Jewish community there.[121]

The continuing disagreement about the provenance of both Matthew and the Didache raises questions over the use of the two texts to assist discussion about the relationship between Christians and Jews in Antioch. The fact that the Didache can be interpreted as a witness against Christian–Jewish tension puts a further brake on using the text to indicate Christian–Jewish tension in Antioch, even if that city is its provenance. Therefore, arguments *for* tension such as those by Draper and Slee, which use Matthew, the Didache, and the letters of Ignatius, though plausible in their entirety,[122] become seriously weakened. Therefore we conclude that Christians and Jews in Antioch had generally amicable relations up to the time of Ignatius. If there was tension between the two groups, it would appear that it was not serious enough to dampen enthusiasm by Christians in Antioch for adopting Jewish practices, an enthusiasm that remained for some centuries. Ignatius, therefore (and the Didache, if written in Antioch), simply complains about enthusiasm for Jewish practices, and is part of a tradition that sought to render the Christian community in Antioch identifiably different from the Jewish community

---

[121] See Saldarini, *Matthew's Christian-Jewish Community*, for a persuasive argument, accepted by a number of scholars, that it took some centuries for Rabbinic teaching to gain the ascendancy in Judaism and become dominant in Jewish communities in antiquity. This is also the thesis of Meyers and Chancey, *Alexander to Constantine*, for which they use Sepphoris as their key example (chapter 10).

[122] Draper ("Torah and Troublesome Apostles") uses an interpretative method known as the "hypothetico-deductive method." This method, developed by Dagfinn Føllesdal, works by postulating a series of connected hypotheses. The individual hypotheses are individually not confirmed as true, but the deduced consequences from the sequence are verified if they "correspond to our experiences and with our other well-supported beliefs" (Zetterholm, "The Didache, Matthew, James—and Paul," 75–76 [76]). Zetterholm uses the same approach, but to argue for continuing tension within the Christian community in Antioch over the role of the Jewish law, rather than for Christian-Jewish tension.

there, thus testifying to a parting of the ways between Christianity and Judaism that occurred long before his time.[123]

Recommended Reading

Downey, Glanville. *A History of Antioch in Syria from Seleucus to the Arab Conquests*. Princeton: Princeton University Press, 1961.

Grainger, John D. *The Cities of Seleukid Syria*. Oxford: Clarendon, 1990.

Hengel, Martin, and Anna Maria Schwemer. *Paulus zwischen Damaskus und Antiochien: Die unbekannten Jahre des Apostels*. WUNT 108. Tübingen: Mohr Siebeck, 2006.

Kraeling, Carl H. "The Jewish Community in Antioch." *JBL* 52 (1932): 130–160.

Levinskaya, Irina. *The Book of Acts in its Diaspora Setting*. Vol. 5 of *The Book of Acts in Its First Century Setting*. Edited by Bruce W. Winter. Grand Rapids: Eerdmans, 1996.

Meeks, W. A., and R. J. Wilken. *Jews and Christians in Antioch*. SBLSBS. Missoula, MT: Scholars, 1978.

Robinson, Thomas A. *Ignatius of Antioch and the Parting of the Ways: Early Jewish-Christian Relations*. Grand Rapids: Baker, 2009.

Schwemer, Anna Maria. "The First Christians in Syria." Translated by Diana Raysz. Pages 429–56 in *Earliest Christian History: History, Literature, and Theology: Essays from the Tyndale Fellowship in Honor of Martin Hengel*. WUNT 320. Edited by Michael F. Bird and Jason Maston. Tübingen: Mohr Siebeck, 2012.

Senior, Donald, ed. *The Gospel of Matthew at the Crossroads of Early Christianity*. BETL 243; Leuven: Peeters, 2011.

Slee, Michelle. *The Church in Antioch in the First Century CE: Communion and Conflict*. JSNTSup 244. London: Sheffield University Press, 2003.

Van de Sandt, Huub, ed. *Matthew and the Didache: Two Documents from the Same Jewish-Christian Milieu?* Assen: Royal Van Gorcum, 2005.

Zetterholm, Magnus, "The Didache, Matthew, James—and Paul: Reconstructing the Historical Developments in Antioch." Pages 73–90 in *Matthew, James, and Didache*. SBL Symposium Series 45. Edited by Huub van de Sandt and Jürgen K. Zangenburg. Atlanta: Society of Biblical Literature, 2008.

---

[123] Both Robinson and Bibliowicz argue that the "parting of the ways" began with Paul. See Gore-Jones and Llewelyn, "The Parting of the Ways," in this volume, for the variety of perspectives on this topic.

9. Divine Imperial Cultic Activities and the Early Church

Bruce W. Winter

The fastest growing religious movement in the first century was not Christianity. It was the imperial cult that spread like wildfire in both the East and West of Rome's vast empire. "The diffusion of the cult of Augustus (BC 27–AD 14) and of other members of his family in Asia Minor and throughout the Greek East from the beginning of the empire was rapid, indeed almost instantaneous."[1]

"Rome's main export to the empire was the cult of the emperors... It appealed to Augustus, as it did to later emperors, as a way of focusing the loyalty of provincials on the imperial persona."[2] Tertullian, the second-century Christian apologist, noted that the emperor became known as "the god of the Romans" (*Romanorum deus*).[3]

In official city calendars a number of "no work" high and holy days were specifically set aside for the worship of the emperor so that all in its cities could venerate him as a god and express their loyalty and thankfulness for the divine "Roman peace" (*pax romana*) he had bestowed on them.[4]

Imperial cult temples in the East were erected in the heart of the city in the most dominant position overlooking the city center where all commerce, civic administration, and law courts were situated. Not only was the temple in the hub of city life, but it was also host to festive and entertainment activities held in its theaters and stadiums.[5]

Official imperial decrees issued by emperors to cities and provinces began with their divine titles, some of which were also used of Jesus in the New Testament. Emperors themselves are seen to have played a highly significant cultic role as the high priest for the whole empire, interceding with the gods for its safety and material blessings.

---

[1] Stephen Mitchell, *Anatolia: Land, Men, and Gods in Asia Minor: The Celts and the Impact of Roman Rule*, 2 vols. (Oxford: Clarendon, 1993), 1:100.

[2] Peter Garnsey and Richard Saller, *The Roman Empire: Economy, Society and Culture* (London: Duckworth, 1987), 164, 165.

[3] Tertullian, *Apologeticus* 24.9.

[4] *Corpus Inscriptionum Latinarum*, 10, 8375.

[5] For evidence from Galatia, see *Orientis Graeci Inscriptiones Selectae*, 33.

To profile the nature of imperial cult veneration, a number of important inscriptions will be cited in this chapter, containing the official titles of emperors and also official coins bearing imperial images. The purpose is that like first-century recipients in the Roman Empire, the reader can construct the nature of imperial cultic activities. Scheid in his chapter "Epigraphy and Roman Religion" has stated that these were essential in their day and can be now used as a tool to understand the nature of the cult of emperor worship:

> The study of Roman religion cannot do without epigraphy any more than it can do without archaeology. No one neglects the literary sources, obviously, but it is essential to recognize that without direct documentation... [it is] very fragmentary, imprecise and burdened with the lumber of the scholars of Antiquity.[6]

How would the first Christians cope with Rome's expectation that all were expected to render to Caesar the things that are God's as the standard expression of their loyalty to Rome's rule, given the contrary ruling of Jesus of the strict divide (Mark 14:17)? Mitchell concludes:

> One cannot avoid the impression that the obstacle which stood in the way of the progress of Christianity, and the force which would have drawn new adherents back to conformity with the prevailing paganism, was the public worship of the emperors ... where Christians could not (if they wanted to) conceal their beliefs and activities from their fellows.[7]

In this chapter it is proposed (1) to profile imperial cultic activities, (2) to record the divine titles used by emperors in the official decrees promulgated from Rome, (3) to show how the Jews were able to adapt to this phenomenon within the parameters of their own sacrificial system, and (4) to explore some of the first Christians' responses to this inescapable reality, as recorded in the New Testament.[8] The persecution of Christians from Nero to Hadrian (AD 54–138) and the punishment of Christians in the cities in Revelation are discussed in chapters 10 and 12 respectively of this book.

---

[6] John Scheid, "Epigraphy and Roman Religion," in *Epigraphy and the Historical Sciences*, Proceedings of the British Academy 177, ed. John Davies and John Wilkers (Oxford and New York: Oxford University Press, 2012), 37. See also Angelos Chaniotis's comment, "Ancient inscriptions offer us material which has never been fully exploited." He argues this with respect to the "emotional dimensions of oral communication" but his point has wider application in this sub–discipline of ancient history, "Listening to the Stones: Orality and Emotions in Ancient Inscriptions," in Davies and Wilkers, *Epigraphy and the Historical Sciences*, 303 (no. 177).
[7] Mitchell, *Anatolia: Land, Men and Gods*, 2:10.
[8] For a more extensive discussion see my *Divine Honours for the Caesars: The First Christians' Response* (Grand Rapids: Eerdmans, 2015).

1. Imperial Cultic Activities

One of the features often overlooked in discussion of the imperial cult is the way it was skillfully combined with very popular activities in the city. It also helps explain why it spread so rapidly throughout the Latin West and the Greek East of the Roman Empire.

1.1. Imperial Cultic Celebrations Combined with Other Spectacles

In the Province of Galatia in the Augustan era, "the festival at Ancyra is explicitly stated to have been held at the imperial temple; horse races were run there and the other spectacles, gladiatorial and animal fights, competitions, sacrifices and feasts, may also have taken place nearby."[9] Feasts connected with the cultic activities may have been restricted to certain classes of citizens, but that would not be the case with spectacles and others public events.

An inscription from this province of Galatia records the variety and intensity of such festivities and helps us understand this.

> The Galatians who sacrificed to the divine Augustus and divine Roma ... son of King Brigatus, gave a public feast and provided olive oil for four months; he presented spectacles and 30 pairs of gladiators and gave a beast-hunt with bulls and wild beasts. Rufus gave a public feast and presented spectacles and a beast-hunt.
>
> In the governorship of Metilius. Pylaemenes, son of King Amyntas, twice gave a public feast and twice presented spectacles and presented games with athletes, chariots and race-horses. Likewise a bull-fight and a beast-hunt. He gave oil to the city. He offered up young animals where the temple of Augustus is situated and the festival and horse racing takes place. Albiorix, son of Ateporix, gave a public feast and dedicated two statues, of Caesar and of Julia Augusta. Amyntas, son of Gaezatodiastes, twice gave a public feast and sacrificed a hecatomb and presented public spectacles and gave corn rations at the rate of 5 *modii* ... of Diognetus. Albiorix, son of Ateporix, for the second time gave a public feast.
>
> In the governorship of Fronto. Metrodorus, son of Menemachus and the natural son of Dorylaus, gave a public feast and provided olive oil for four months. Musaeus, son of Articnus, gave a public feast ... son of Seleucus, gave a public feast and provided oil for four months. Pylaemenes, son of King Amyntas, gave a public feast for the three tribes[10] and at Ancyra sacrificed a hecatomb and presented spectacles and a procession; likewise, a bull-fight and bull-fighters and 50 pairs of gladiators. He provided oil for the three tribes for the whole year and presented a wild beast-fight.[11]

---

[9] Simon R. F. Price, *Rituals and Power: The Imperial Cult and Asia Minor* (Cambridge: Cambridge University Press, 1984), 109.

[10] The three tribes made up the Galatians: the Tolistobogii, Tectosages, and Trocmi.

[11] *Inscriptiones Graecae ad res Romanas*, IV, 1756.

Fishwick concludes: "The end result was that sacrifices became more and more a pretext for a good meal, religious anniversaries simply an occasion for a free dinner when one might indulge oneself in over-eating and over-drinking" and "inscriptions and papyri confirm that games and banquets were a staple appurtenance of major festivals of the imperial cult throughout the empire."[12]

Mitchell notes, "It is clear that gladiatorial games reached the East.... The vast majority of gladiatorial inscriptions are linked with the imperial cult, and in most cases the responsibility for mounting gladiatorial fights lay with the high priests."[13]

Price also observes, "The gladiatorial games and animal fights, which spread from Rome and became very popular in the Greek world under the empire, were put on almost exclusively in connection with the imperial cult."[14] As a result, "when a high priest organized gladiatorial games, he was acclaimed by the crowd and responded by further munificence ... the spectacle, especially of the gladiators, caused the greatest astonishment and even incredulity as roses and gifts were thrown into the amphitheater where the variety of the gladiators' arms was wondered at" and "at the provincial level, imperial choirs are only known ... in the provincial cult of Asia."[15]

It also emerges from reading official inscriptions that it is more accurate to refer to imperial cultic activities and not "the" imperial cult. Hillard rightly argued that we should not speak of *the* imperial cult, but imperial *cults*.[16] The reason for this is that loyal citizens prayed to and participated in sacrifices to the gods for the emperor's safety, and did the same to the emperor as a divine being, seeking the continued blessing on and safety of the empire. Furthermore he had a liturgical role as the *pontifex maximus*, literally the "greatest bridge builder," that was rendered in Greek as "the high priest" (ὁ ἀρχιερεύς). He was the link between the empire and the gods, sacrificing to them and interceding to them for the peace of the empire.

These three cultic activities to, for, and by the ruling emperor are recorded in one inscription from the city of Sardis where later a Christian community would be established (Rev 3:1–6). The occasion was when one of Augustus's adopted sons, Gaius, whom he appointed as his successor, received the traditional garment of manhood, the *toga virilis*.

---

[12] Duncan Fishwick, *Imperial Cult in the Latin West: Studies in the Ruler Cult in the Western Provinces* (Leiden: Brill, 1991), II.1, 585, 587–88.

[13] Mitchell, *Anatolia: Land, Men, and Gods in Asia Minor*, 1:110.

[14] Price, *Rituals and Power: The Imperial Cult and Asia Minor*, 89.

[15] Price, *Rituals and Power: The Imperial Cult and Asia Minor*, 116, 88.

[16] Tom W. Hillard, "Vespasian's Death-Bed Attitude to His Impending Deification," in *Religion in the Ancient World: New Themes and Approaches*, ed. Matthew Dillon (Amsterdam: Hakkert, 1996), 197–98.

1.2. Prayers to Augustus

The decree reads:

> Since Gaius Iulius Caesar, the eldest of the sons of Augustus, has put on the
> *toga* most earnestly prayed for (and) radiant with every decoration, in place of
> the one with purple border, and there is joy among all men to see [by this
> event] the prayers that have been awakened everywhere to Augustus on behalf
> of his sons (lines 7–10).[17]

Firstly, the decree specifically stated there had been "prayers to Augustus
for his sons" (τῷ Σεβαστῷ τὰς ὑπὲρ τῶν παίδων εὐχάς: line 9). The other
adopted son was Lucius Caesar. Both were were his nominated heirs, but were
killed in battles before he died. He was succeeded by Tiberius in AD 14.

The date on which Gaius assumed the toga in 5 BC was also to be
incorporated into cities' imperial calendars and celebrated annually, just as it
had been for Augustus when he assumed the *toga virilis*. According to the
Calendar of Cumae in Italy (AD 4–14), it would be celebrated on 18
October.[18] This milestone in the life of an heir of Augustus was now a fixed
imperial high and holy day in that city.

1.3. Sacrificing to the Gods for the Divine Augustus and his Family

Secondly, in Sardis the *strategoi*—officials appointed annually—were to offer
up sacrifices to the gods, but this celebration would not involve just a few
cultic officials.

> Our city on the occasion of such a great good fortune has ruled that the day
> which completed his transition from boy to manhood to be a holy day, on
> which each year all our people in their brightest clothing shall wear wreaths,
> and [on which] sacrifices shall be performed by the *strategoi* of the year to the
> gods [τοῖς θεοῖς], and prayers shall be offered through the sacred heralds for
> his [i.e., Gaius's] safety [ὑπὲρ τῆς σωτηρίας], and [on which] his image shall
> be jointly consecrated and set up in his father's temple, and on that [day] on
> which our city received the glad tidings [εὐαγγελίσθη] and this decree was
> passed, on that day too wreaths shall be worn and most splendid sacrifices
> performed to the gods [θυσίας τοῖς θεοῖς]. (lines 10–15).

In Sardis there would also be "prayers offered through the sacred heralds
for his [Gaius'] safety" (ὑπὲρ τῆς σωτηρίας: lines 11–12). The Sardians had
officially resolved that the statue of Gaius would be "jointly consecrated and

---

[17] *IGRom.* 4:1756, lines 7–10. This is not an isolated celebration as it was also observed in
Messene in Achaea in the same period and imperial cultic celebrations were extended to all
leading cities in the province including Corinth, *Supplementum Epigraphicum Graecum* (1968)
XXIII, 206.
[18] *Corpus Inscriptionum Latinarum* 10:8375. Fishwick, *The Imperial Cult in the Latin West*,
II.1.490.

set up in his father's temple" (τῷ τοῦ πατρὸς ἐνιδρύοντας ναῷ), that is, the temple of Augustus (lines 13–14). The city authorities "ruled all were to wear wreaths" (ἔκρινεν ... στεφανηφορεῖν ἅπαντας: line 11). This was to be done not only when his statue was to be consecrated in the temple dedicated to his father, but also on the anniversary of Gaius's rite of passage to manhood. The resolution clause of the inscription stipulated "this decree was passed, on that day too wreaths shall be worn" (lines 14–15).

Furthermore, there were to be annual sacrifices—"most splendid sacrifices performed to the gods" (θυσίας τοῖς θεοῖς ἐκπρεπεστάτας ἐπιτελέσαι: line 15)—when the statue of Gaius was consecrated in the temple of Augustus (lines 13–14). As well, coins of Sardis recording the divinity of the imperial family were later minted in the time of Nero, with the inscription "Nero Caesar" and the "goddess Octavia," portraying a bust of her with a wreath made out of ears of corn.[19] Gaius was also fêted in "the Games of the Imperial Family in Sardis" with "Gaius Caesar (victor) in the Isthmian boys stadion-race" in ca. AD 5.[20]

1.4. Augustus, the High Priest of the Roman Empire

Augustus's response to the Sardinian embassy is recorded in a decree in the same inscription referring to his role as high priest.

> Imperator Caesar, son of a god [θεοῦ υἱός], Augustus, high priest [ἀρχιερεύς], holder of the tribunician power for the nineteenth time [5 BC] to the Sardinian magistrates, Council and People, greetings. Your envoys, Iollas [son] of Metrodores and Menogenes [son] of Isidoros [grandson] of Menogenes, met with me in Rome and gave me the decree from you by means of which you disclosed what had been decreed by you concerning yourselves and rejoiced with me at the translation to manhood of the elder of my sons. (lines 23–27)

Not only did Augustus in this decree refer to his role as the high priest of his empire, but he also officially endorsed the activities in Sardis when a delegation from there came to Rome for an audience with him to convey their loyalty to one of two of his appointed successors, Gaius, the other being Lucius. Both would be subsequently killed in battle before Augustus himself died in AD 14.[21]

---

[19] Andrew Burnett, Michael Amandry and Pere Pau Ripollès, *Roman Provincial Coinage: From the Death of Caesar to the Death of Vitellius (44 B.C.–A.D. 69)* (London: British Museum Press; Paris: Bibliothèque nationale de France, 1998), nos. 2997-3001.

[20] *Sylloge Inscriptionum Graecarum*[3], 1065.

[21] See the inscription from the same era from Messene in the province of Achaea of which Corinth was the capital, *SEG* (1968) XXIII, 206 and for discussion of this see my chapter "Honours to, for and by the Caesars and Reciprocal Benefits," *Divine Honours for the Caesars: the First Christians' Responses*, ch. 3.

2. Divine Titles Used by and of Roman Emperors and Jesus

In official imperial decrees, many emanating from emperors, the titles were traditionally used by and of them, namely "a son of a god," "savior," "god manifest" and "lord of all the world." The following inscriptions record divine titles and similar titles used by and of Jesus in the New Testament.

2.1. Son of God and the Son of God

In late 39 or early 38 BC, in the Roman East, Augustus himself wrote to the Magistrates, the Council, and the People of Ephesus beginning with his titles, "Imperator Caesar, son of god Julius" (Αὐτοκράτωρ Καῖσαρ θεοῦ Ἰουλίου υἱός).[22]

In Egypt an official inscription recorded the dedication of a porch that began with a reference to "Imperator Caesar Zeus the Liberator, god, son of a god, Augustus" in AD 1.[23] Coins in Thessalonica were struck showing the crowned head of Julius Caesar with the inscription "god" (θεός), and on the reverse the bare head of Augustus and the word "Thessalonica."[24]

It was not only Augustus and his contemporaries who used the term but also his successors, who were not always natural-born sons of their predecessor. Latin inscriptions recording the names of emperors indicate that they were either a son, or a grandson or great-grandson of a god. One begins with Augustus as "son of a god" (the god being Julius Caesar). Gaius Caesar and Lucius Caesar, his nominated successors, are both called "grandson of a god" and Tiberius who succeeded him is likewise called "grandson of a god." Germanicus was a "great-grandson of a god."[25]

A bilingual inscription from Cyrene in the time of Nero clearly traces his "ancestry" back to Augustus and provides evidence of the equivalent terms in Latin and Greek.

> Nero Claudius Caesar Augustus Germanicus, son of the divine Claudius [*divi Claudi f.*, θεοῦ Κλαυδίου υἱός] grandson of Germanicus Caesar, great-grandson of Tiberius Caesar Augustus great-great-grandson of the divine Augustus [*divi Augusti*, θεοῦ Σεβαστοῦ], *pontifex maximus* [ἀρχιερεύς], with tribunician power, imperator, consul...[26]

---

[22] Joyce Reynolds, *Aphrodisias and Rome*, The Society for the Promotion of Roman Studies (Hertford: Stephen Austin, 1982), no. 12, line 1. See also the letter from Augustus describing himself as "imperator Caesar, son of the god Julius" to the city of Mylasa in 31 BC. *SIG*³, 768: αὐτοκράτωρ = *imperator* and *dictator*.

[23] *Orientis Graeci Inscriptiones Selectae*, 659.

[24] *Roman Provincial Coins*, nos. 1554–55.

[25] *Inscriptones Latinae Selectae*, 107, cited Robin Seager, *Tiberius* (London: Methuen, 1972), 46–47.

[26] For this bilingual inscription of Nero see Martin Percival Charlesworth, "Nero," *Documents Illustrating the Reigns of Claudius & Nero* (Cambridge: Cambridge University Press, 1939), no. 4.

The phrases "a son of a god," "son of the divine," or "the son of greatest of the gods" (i.e., a deceased emperor) would be heard and understood differently in the first century, as would the term "god." The important point is that extant evidence shows that these official designations of the imperial rulers enjoyed wide currency in the Roman East.

Was Jesus accused of claiming to be equal with, or a competitor of, the reigning emperor Tiberius as "a son of a god"? During his trial as recorded in John 19:1–16 and after ordering his scourging, Pilate declared before the crowd, "See, I am bringing him out to you that you may know that I find no fault in him." The chief priests and the officers immediately responded, calling for his crucifixion on the grounds "that he made himself a son of a god" (ὅτι υἱὸν θεοῦ ἑαυτὸν ἐποίησεν; John 19:7).

After further interrogation of Jesus away from the crowd, Pilate sought to release him and it was then that the Jews confronted the Roman governor. They retaliated. "If you release this man, you are not Caesar's friend" (οὐκ εἶ φίλος τοῦ Καίσαρος: 19:12). While there are no extant inscriptions nor literary evidence that Pilate had this important honorary title of a "friend of Caesar" conferred by Tiberius, he was a close associate and a loyal official, and substantial extant evidence exists of leading Roman officials bearing this title.[27]

The accusers reminded Pilate, who was on his annual assize in Jerusalem, of his judicial role, as governor, to punish breaches of Roman law, that "everyone who makes himself a king opposes Caesar" (πᾶς ὁ βασιλέα ἑαυτὸν ποιῶν ἀντιλέγει τῷ Καίσαρι). Later when the governor ironically announced "Behold your king," they again asserted their total loyalty to Rome by declaring "we have no king but Caesar" (19:15).

It is significant that the chief priests' and Jewish officials' case rested on their assertion, not that Jesus called himself "the Son of the God" as attested in John's gospel, but that he was said to have made himself a rival of Tiberius—hence their claim of the present divine emperor as "a son of a god' (υἱὸν θεοῦ), both of which were recorded without the article before either of the nouns. The Jewish officials would be aware of the claims of Tiberius, and his title "a son of a god." Theirs was the appropriate charge of sedition or treason to bring against Jesus in that he was a self-made rival of Tiberius. The implication was that Pilate could be guilty of "treason" (*maiestas*) by reason of guilt by association if he set him free.[28]

At the crucifixion of Jesus, the Jews who had heard of his comment about the destruction of the temple taunted him and are recorded repeating his claim, "If you are a son of a god [εἰ υἱὸς εἶ τοῦ θεοῦ], come down from the cross" (Matt 27:40). At the same time others report the claim of Jesus, "He trusts in

---

[27] For a list of extant Caesar's Friends see John A. Crook, *Consilium Principis: Imperial Councils and Counsellors from Augustus to Diocletian* (Cambridge: Cambridge University Press, 1955), 148–90.

[28] Treason "was the political crime *par excellence*," according to John A. Crook, *Law and Life of Rome, 90 B.C.–A.D. 212*, Aspects of Greek and Roman Life (Ithaca, NY: Cornell University Press, 1967), 269.

God who should deliver him, for He said, 'I am a son of a god'" (εἶπεν γὰρ ὅτι θεοῦ εἰμι υἱός: Matt 27:43). It is a surprise, but not out of character in terms of cultural usage, immediately after the death of Jesus the New Testament records a Roman centurion declaring literally, "Truly this man was a son of a god" (οὗτος ὁ ἄνθρωπος υἱὸς θεοῦ ἦν: Matt 27:54; Mark 15:39). He was reading into the superscription not only his Roman understanding of divinity from the headpiece, "King of the Jews," that was placed at Pilate's insistence, but also the nature of the way he died. It is interesting to see the absence of the definite article with respect to "son" and "God" recorded here *verbatim*.

There was a critical linguistic subtlety, the implications of which would not be lost on the first Christians. Compared with the Greek speaking Roman East, Christians inserted the article when using certain terms, so that Jesus was "the" son of "the" God. At the same time the New Testament records non-Christians, including Jews, using the terms "a son" and "a god" as shown above.

John writes his Gospel with the specific intention "that you might believe that Jesus is the Messiah, "the Son of the God [ὁ υἱὸς τοῦ θεοῦ], and believing you might have life through His name" (John 20:31). John the Baptist had already declared emphatically, "I have seen and have borne witness that this is 'the' Son of God" (ὁ υἱὸς τοῦ θεοῦ: 1:34). In John's Gospel the phrase "the only begotten [μονογενής] God in the bosom of the Father" (1:14) distances the title even further from "a son of a god" officially used of emperors. The New International Version translates the phrase as "the one and only Son of God" (1:14, 18, 3:16, 18).

The Jewish high priest is recorded as questioning Jesus, "Tell us if you are the Messiah, the Son of the God" (εἰ σὺ εἶ ὁ χριστὸς ὁ υἱὸς τοῦ θεοῦ: Matt 26:63). "God" and "the Son of the God" were terms used specifically of Jesus by Christians; they could not in all good conscience call the reigning emperor "a son of a god." Christians did not use the official phrase "son of god" of Jesus but always added the definite article "the" (ὁ), so that he was declared "*the* Son of *the* God"—the only God. The term "Messiah" indicated the role of king. When Pilate said of Jesus "Behold your king," the chief priests instantly declared "We have no king but Caesar" (John 19:14–55).

These titles put the early Christians on an inevitable ideological clash with their compatriots, whose polytheistic view of divinity could readily incorporate the concept of the reigning Caesar as "a god, a son of a god," with men who became gods and some of whom were posthumously awarded perpetual divinity.[29]

---

[29] See David Wardle, "*Deus* or *divus*: The Genesis of Roman Terminology for Deified Emperors and a Philosopher's Contribution," in *Philosophy and Power in the Graeco-Roman World: Essays in Honour of Miriam Griffin*, ed. Gillian Clark and Tessa Rajak (Oxford: Oxford University Press, 2002), 181–209.

2.2. The Savior and God Manifest

An official inscription from Halicarnassus in Turkey, involving surrounding cities, had declared Augustus to be "savior of the common race of man" (σωτῆρα τοῦ κοινοῦ ἀνθρώπων γένος).[30] The title, "the savior of all humankind" (τὸν πάντων ἀνθρώνων σωτῆρα), was also later inscribed on the plinth of a statue of Claudius.[31] It was written of Claudius that he was "the most divine Caesar and truly our savior" (τοῦ θειοτάτου Καίσαρος καὶ ὡς ἀληθῶς σωτῆρος ἡμῶν).[32]

Later an Alexandrian coin AD 62–63 with Nero's head on the obverse side declared on the reverse side he was "the savior of the world" (ὁ σωτὴρ τῆς οἰκουμένης).[33] This was an equivalent title used of Jesus (ὁ σωτὴρ τοῦ κόσμου: John 4:42). An earlier inscription of AD 37 refers to the emperor, Gaius (AD 37–41), indicating that he was now ruling with the "great gods" (τηλικούτων θεῶν).[34] The "appearing of the great God and Savior of ours, Jesus Christ" (τοῦ μεγάλου θεοῦ καὶ σωτῆρος ἡμῶν), was seen as the foundation for every Christian's future hope (Tit 2:13).

In Arneae, Lycia and Aezani, Phrygia, references were made to Claudius as "god manifest, and savior of our people" (θεὸν ἐπιφανῆ σωτῆρα καὶ τοῦ ἡμετέρου δήμου) and "divine savior and benefactor...god manifest" (θεοῦ σωτῆρος καὶ εὐεργέται ... θεοῦ ἐπιγανοῦς).[35] In a papyrus from Oxyrhynchus announcing the death of Claudius and Nero's succession, the former was officially declared to be "god manifest" (ἐνφανὴς θεός).[36] Jesus was confessed by early Christians to be "God manifest in the flesh" (θεός ὃς ἐφανερώθη) (see 1 Tim 3:16).

The same papyrus continues: "and the expectation and hope of the world [ὁ δὲ τῆς οἰκουμένης καὶ προσδοκηθεὶς καὶ ἐλπισθείς] has been declared emperor [αὐτοκράτωρ], the good *genius* of the world [ἀγαθὸς δαίμων δὲ τῆς οἰκουμένης] and the source of all good things [ἀρχὴ ὢν μέγιστε πάντων], Nero has been declared Caesar [Νέρων Καῖσαρ ἀποδέδεικται]."[37] The confidence of the early community of believers was "Christ in you, the hope of glory" (Col 1:17), and that "all things were made through him [Christ] and without him nothing was made that was created" (John 1:3). Colossians 1:27

---

[30] Gustav Hirschfeld, ed., *Collection of Ancient Greek Inscriptions in the British Museum*, Part IV, Section I (Oxford: Clarendon, 1893), no. 894.

[31] E. Mary Smallwood, *Documents Illustrating the Principates of Gaius, Claudius and Nero* (Cambridge: Cambridge University Press, 1967) no. 135, lines 21–22 (AD 52–53).

[32] *IGRom.* 1:1118, lines 34–35 (5 April, AD 54).

[33] *Roman Provincial Coins*, 5271E.

[34] *IGRom.* 1:145, line 9.

[35] *Tituli Asiae Minoris*, II, 760 and *IGRom.* 4:584. In the former inscription the full titles of Britannicus are spelt out, "Tiberius Claudius Caesar Britannicus, son of Imperator Tiberius Claudius Caesar Augustus," This is followed by the titles of Claudius, including "god manifest." In the case of the latter the formal construction used throughout the inscription of the sponsor of the imperial games of Augustus Claudius and the temple officer (νεωκόρος) of Zeus and of Claudius, the phrase "god manifest" refers to Claudius and not Britannicus.

[36] *Oxyrhynchus Papyrus*, 1021, lines 2–3.

[37] *Oxyrhynchus Papyrus*, 1021, lines 5–13.

states that in Christ "all things hold together." Again these affirmations starkly conflicted with the claims of and for the Caesars.

2.3. The Lord of All the World and Lord

An official civic inscription records Nero's presence in Corinth at the Isthmian Games on 29 November AD 67, where Epaminondas, the high priest of the Achaean provincial imperial cult, declared him to be "the Lord of all the world" (ὁ τοῦ παντὸς κόσμου κύριος).[38] Christians confessed another as the Lord of the world, and believed that all humanity would one day bow and acknowledge that this title rightly belonged to Jesus, who alone was God incarnate (Phil 2:10–11).

It was later that Domitian (AD 81–96) insisted that he be addressed in person as both "Lord and God."[39] Much earlier, the apostle Thomas is recorded as addressing Jesus in a post-resurrection experience as "my Lord and my God" (ὁ κύριος μου καὶ ὁ θεός μου: John 20:28). On the other hand, Corinthian Christians could not endorse imperial titles because of their "creed"—"But for us there is one God, the Father … and one Lord, Jesus Christ" (1 Cor 8:6).

A combination of titles could be used of the emperor, as in the case of an inscription to Augustus in Eleusis, a city located between Athens and Corinth. He was called "Imperator Caesar, son of god, Julius, his savior and benefactor" (Αὐτοκράτορα Καίσαρα θεοῦ Ἰουλίου υἱὸν τὸν α[ὐ]τοῦ σωτῆρα καὶ εὐεργέτην).[40]

The convention associated with ancient rulers of the Greek and Hellenistic eras had been to give "appropriate" titles and veneration that were of "equal honors to the gods" (ἰσόθεοι τιμαί). Rome's imperial gods and goddesses could be assimilated into the existing local pantheon for provincials in the Roman East, especially when they prayed to their gods for the emperor as part of the imperial cultic activities.[41] The precedent for this is said to have stretched back to Philip and Alexander the Great.[42]

In Ephesus "the initiates" of Dionysus described the placing of a statue of the second-century emperor, Hadrian, alongside that of a divinity as "sharing the throne of Dionysus" (σύνφρονον τῷ Διονύσῳ).[43] Such a liaison would not have been possible for the Christian movement, with its roots in Judaism. For them the initial commandment in the Mosaic law—"you shall have no other gods alongside me" (Exod 20:2)—was binding, and against monolatry, which

---

[38] *Sylloge Inscriptionum Graecarum*³ no. 814, line 26.

[39] Suetonius, *Dom.* 13.

[40] James Henry Oliver, *Greek Constitutions of Early Roman Emperors from Inscriptions and Papyri* (Philadelphia: American Philosophical Society, 1989), 26.

[41] For helpful discussion see Duncan Fishwick, "*Isotheoi Timai*," *Imperial Cult in the Latin West* (Leiden: Brill, 1993²), I.1, ch. III.

[42] Ernest A. Fredricksmeyer, "On the Background of the Ruler Cult," *Ancient Macedonian Studies in Honor of Charles F. Edson* (Institute for Balkan Studies, Thessaloniki, 1981), 145–56 (154).

[43] *Supplementum Epigraphicum Graecum*, xxvi, 1272 = I.Eph. 275.

is the worship of one god without denying the existence of other gods. They could never entertain the concept, as these Ephesians did, of any imperial gods "sharing" the throne of God because of their firm belief that there was only one God and Father; any others were not divine (1 Cor 8:6; Eph 4:6).

At the end of the New Testament *corpus* in the Book of the Revelation, the term "throne" (θρόνος) occurs forty-seven times and its rightful occupancy by God and the Lamb is a central concern of its author. There is one reference to the throne of the beast and a kingdom (16:10). For the first Christians the concept of a throne that could be shared by divine reigning and deceased emperors with God and Jesus, the Lamb of God, was impossible, and any attempts to do so would be a sign of apostasy.

3. Jewish Responses: Adopt, Adapt and Abstain

How did the Jews react to the imperial cult phenomena? There were three responses up to the time of the destruction of their temple in AD 70. In the time of Augustus an actual imperial cult temple was built in their kingdom, which was part of the Roman Empire. In the long term the Jews adapted to Rome rule, expressing their loyalty with a daily sacrifice for the safety of the emperor in their own temple in Jerusalem until they abstained in AD 66. This was a signal to Rome of their revolt against its rule. It followed with a war that lasted four years and resulted in the total destruction of their one and only temple where sacrifices could legitimately be offered.

3.1. Herod the Great's Adopting the Imperial Cult Veneration

Herod the Great, who was the king of the Jews until his death in 4 BC, constructed a Roman imperial cult when he built the great city of Caesarea Maritima as his center. As in other cities in the East outside of the Jewish kingdom, he also constructed an imperial cult temple there that dominated the city, being built on the highest location. While Caesarea Maritima was in the Samaritan region, it was still within the borders of his Jewish kingdom. In doing this Herod would certainly have been seen to be acting with blatant duplicity and blasphemy by orthodox Jews of his day.[44]

Later in Philo of Alexandria's time (25 BC–AD 50) this temple continued to function as an imperial cultic site. He recorded the Jews' appeal to Pontius Pilate, the governor of Judea, to "take down the shields at once and have them transferred from the capital [Jerusalem] to Caesarea on the coast [Maritima] surnamed Augusta ... to be set up in the temple of Augustus and so they were."[45]

---

[44] For a full discussion of the enormous building projects of Herod the Great see Duane W. Roller, "Catalogue of Herod's Building Program," *The Building Program of Herod the Great* (Berkeley: University of California Press, 1998), 125–238, 259–60.
[45] Philo, *Legat.* 305.

Furthermore in Caesarea Maritima itself an inscription records the Roman governor further promoting imperial cultic worship in the time of Jesus. It records "Pontius Pilate, the prefect of Judea, erected an altar dedicated to Tiberius," who succeeded Augustus.[46]

3.2. The Jews' Adaptation within the Parameters of their Faith

Rutgers made an important distinction in *The Hidden Heritage of Diaspora Judaism*: "Jews did not adopt non-Jewish ways, but they adapted such elements for their own purposes. They integrated foreign elements into their own way of life," having noted in the commencement of his monograph "and perhaps, to a very limited extent, even religiously."[47] Josephus (AD 37–ca. 100) explained:

> For them [Roman Emperors] we also offer perpetual sacrifices [*continua sacrificia*] ... we perform these ceremonies daily, at the expense of the whole Jewish community, but while we offer no other such sacrifices out of our common expenses ... yet we do this as a peculiar honor to the emperors and to them alone, while we do the same to no other individual.[48]

The Jewish arrangement had satisfied Rome in that they were undertaking cultic activities as a sign of their imperial loyalty that recognized Rome's suzerainty over their kingdom. At the same time their adaptation meant Jews did not have to compromise their cultic traditions by offering sacrifices to the emperor's statue, as did the rest of the empire, and thereby overtly participate in an idolatrous cultic activity. Within the parameters of their own sacrificial system in the Jerusalem temple, a Jewish priest offered up a daily sacrifice to his God for the emperor's safety.

Is there evidence of the Jewish honoring of the emperor in the synagogues of the Diaspora? Inscriptions in Jewish synagogues not only in Judaea but also Kadyoun, Ostia, and Intercisa have the prayer addressed "to the Eternal God for the safety of emperor" (*Deo Aeterno pro salute Augusti*) but of course never to the emperor.[49]

---

[46] See the recent discussion by Joan E. Taylor "Pontius Pilate and the Imperial Cult in Roman Judaea," *NTS* 52 (2006): 555–82 especially 564–65.

[47] Leonard V. Rutgers, *The Hidden Heritage of Diaspora Judaism* (Leuven: Peeters, 1998), 227 and Robert S. Dutch, "The Greek Gymnasium and the Corinthian Christians," *The Educated Elite in 1 Corinthians: Education and Community Conflict in Graeco-Roman Context* (London: T&T Clark, 2005), 147–67 both discuss Jews in the Diaspora participating in first-century education.

[48] Josephus, *C. Ap.* 2.77.

[49] M. Pucci Ben Zeev, *Jewish Rights in the Roman World: Texts and Studies in Ancient Judaism* (Tübingen: Mohr Siebeck), 1998), 472.

3.3. The Jews Abstain as the Sign of Rebellion Against Rome

Miriam Pucci Ben Zeev notes: "According to Josephus, the suspension of the sacrifice [in the temple in Jerusalem] for the well-being of the emperor was the first tangible sign of the incipient rebellion against Roman rule in 66 CE."[50] The Jewish revolt ultimately saw the utter destruction of Jerusalem after a horrendous and prolonged siege by the Roman army. Josephus records:

> Eleazar, son of Ananias the high-priest, a very daring youth, then holding the position of captain, persuaded those who officiated in the Temple services to accept no gift or sacrifice from a foreigner. This action laid the foundation of the war with the Romans; for the sacrifices offered on behalf of that nation and the emperor were in consequence rejected.[51]

Their refusal to offer sacrifice for the safety of the emperor sent a very clear signal to Rome of Jewish abandonment of the long-standing and imperially-endorsed act expressing their loyalty. The Jews were in revolt against Rome, the consequences of which resulted in the prolonged four-year war with the siege of Jerusalem and the destruction of the temple in Jerusalem, the very heart of its sacrifices and liturgical practices.

4. Diverse Christian Responses

If this is how the monotheistic Jews coped with the challenge of loyalty to the emperor, how did the first Christians respond in the cities in the Roman East where imperial cultic activities thrived as an integral part of civic life? They also rejected all idolatry but, uniquely, had no sacrificial rituals. Garnsey and Saller assert that, on the basis of their beliefs, "Christians invited persecution by their denial of the gods of Rome."[52]

4.1. Thessalonians Turned from Idols to Serve the True and Living God

From the very beginning of Paul's mission in Thessalonica, there some of the Jews and a great many of the Greek God-fearers from the local synagogue, along with a number of "leading women" in the city, became Christians as a result of Paul's proclaiming the suffering Jesus as the Messiah. The loss felt by the members of the synagogue resulted in them stirring up the "rabble," and a riot ensued (Acts 17:2–5).

Before city authorities, they made the allegations that Jason and some of the other Christians had associated with known Jewish revolutionaries. They alleged of Paul and Silas, who had actually been sent by Jerusalem Council to Syria (Acts 15:22): "these men who have turned the world upside down have

---

[50] Pucci Ben Zeev, *Jewish Rights*, 472.
[51] Josephus, *B.J.* 2.409.
[52] "Religion," Garnsey and Saller, *The Roman Empire*, 174.

come here" (Acts 17:6). There had been a group of Jewish revolutionaries whom Claudius had specifically warned against associating with. His official edict threatened

> not to invite in as allies or approve of [μηδὲ ἐπάγεσθαι ἢ προσίεσθαι][53] Jews who come down the river from Syria or Egypt, a proceeding which will compel me to conceive serious suspicions; otherwise I will by all means take vengeance on them as fermenters of what is a general plague infesting the whole world.[54]

It was alleged that "Jason has received them" (Acts 17:7). He was guilty of "treason" (*maiestas*) by reason of guilt by association with Paul and Silas, and those who associated with Jason were also culpable.[55] Luke records the crime; they alleged these converts were "plotting" or "acting against the decrees of Caesar" (τῶν δογμάτων Καίσαρος πράσσουσιν).[56] The charge is further explained. They were "saying there is another king, Jesus" (βασιλέα ἕτερον λέγοντες εἶναι Ἰησοῦν). Paul and Silas had declared in the synagogue that "Jesus is the Messiah" (Acts 17:3). The charge by the Jews was therefore not unwarranted, given the messianic claim of Jesus' kingship.

It was not one decree but a plurality of "the decrees of Caesar" (τῶν δογμάτων Καίσαρος) that Luke notes. Can this mean all of Caesar's decrees? Scholarly discussion has assumed that the accusers had a specific legal decree or a set of decrees in mind.[57] More recently this interpretation has been questioned, and an alternative proposed that the decrees had to do with the law concerning regulation of associations that were seen as hotbeds of sedition.[58] It is certainly well-documented that since the time of Augustus, his successors legislated to curtail the politicization of associations by restricting their registered monthly meetings. The same legislation specifically permitted Jews to hold weekly meetings. Subsequent Julio-Claudian emperors also addressed similar problems regarding unruly and disloyal associations.[59]

---

[53] The verbs ἐπάγεσθαι used to denote to "bring in, invite as aiders or allies" and προσείσθαι used in the passive "to be like," i.e., identify with, approve.

[54] *Greek Papyri in the British Museum*, VI, 1912, lines 96–99.

[55] Treason "was the political crime *par excellence*," according to Crook, *Law and Life of Rome*, 69.

[56] The verb has a number of meanings, i.e., "plotting" or "passing over," with the latter meaning "only found in the present" according to Liddell & Scott. Also ἀπέναντι "against" with the genitive "opposite" with Liddell & Scott also citing Acts 17:7. A clear rejection of the decrees is implied.

[57] Edwin A. Judge, "The Decrees of Caesar in Thessalonica," in *The First Christians in the Roman World: Augustan and New Testament Essays*, ed. James R. Harrison (Tübingen: Mohr Siebeck, 2008), ch. 32.

[58] Justin K. Hardin, "Decrees and Drachmas at Thessalonica: An Illegal Assembly in Jason's House (Acts 17.1–10a)," *NTS* 52.1 (2006): 29–49.

[59] For a summary of Julio-Claudian emperors' responses to associations, see my "Roman Law and Society in Romans 12–15," in *Rome in the Bible and the Early Church*, ed. Peter Oakes (Carlisle: Paternoster; Grand Rapids: Baker, 2002), 71–74.

However, it was a long-standing legal and literary convention to begin official imperial decrees by indicating the emperor's name followed by his titles. One common convention of such decrees was that all used the term "a god" followed by the phrase "a son of a god."[60] They then added "*imperator*"—the Latin term for the Greek equivalent was αὐτοκράτωρ that is rendered in the English as "emperor," i.e., "king."[61] Hence to declare there was another king was to reject the jurisdiction of all the imperial decrees that governed them and this was a treasonable offence.

What legal processes were involved? Normally such allegations would have come within the remit of the criminal jurisdiction of the provincial governor. While "Thessalonica was the residence of the imperial procurator of the province,"[62] in AD 44 Claudius had introduced changes in both Achaea and Macedonia in the jurisdiction of the magistrates who were now "entrusted [with] various judicial cases that the consuls had previously tried."[63]

It is also important to note that Thessalonica under the Romans had been awarded the special status of "a free city" (*civitas libera*), as was Athens. As a result it was not under the jurisdiction of the Roman governor of the province in the way that others cities were.[64] Therefore it was within the remit of its most senior officials to act in a legal capacity. This may well explain the immediate move by the politarchs when they heard that Paul and Silas were alleged to be Jewish revolutionaries who "have turned this world upside down" (Acts 17:6). Claudius had given a warning to the Alexandrians of the draconian action that he would take against those who associated with them.[65] For these leading Thessalonian officials the best course of action was to get them out of their privileged city lest somehow their presence might forfeit the most privileged status that Rome could confer on a leading city.

Their solution was the "taking the surety" (λαβόντα τὸ ἱκανόν) of Jason and the others (Acts 17:9). Under the section "Criminal Proceedings" in the *Digesta*, the Roman legal code, "the surety was given if the reputation of the persons were such that they would not be expected to break their word as a matter of honor."[66] An earlier inscription from the city of Messene in the neighboring province of Achaea in southern Greece used the same legal terms in an inscription as Luke did (λαβόντα τὸ ἱκανόν).[67]

---

[60] Prior to Paul's coming coins minted in Thessalonica had shown the crowned head of Julius Caesar with the inscription "god" (θεός) and on the reverse side the bare head of Augustus with the word "Thessalonica," *Roman Provincial Coins*, 1554–55.

[61] For a bilingual imperial decree in Latin and Greek, see Charlesworth, "Nero," no. 4.

[62] Pantelis M. Nigdelis, "A New *Procurator Augusti* in the Province of Macedonia," *GRBS* 52 (2012): 198–207 [207].

[63] Dio Cassius, *Hist.* 60.24.3.

[64] Andrew Lintott, *Imperium Romanum: Politics and Administration* (London: Routledge, 1993), 36–41 for a discussion of a "free city" under the Romans. Of the concern regarding the possible loss of status or some other penalty imposed by the governor of the province for riotous behavior, see Acts 19:35–41 esp. v. 40.

[65] *Greek Papyri in the British Museum*, 1912, lines 96–99

[66] *Dig.* 48.3.1.

[67] *Sylloge Epigraphicum Graecum*, 41.332, line 19.

Paul later records the widespread report, from Christians elsewhere in the provinces of Macedonia and Achaea, of the nature of Thessalonian Christians' conversion and one result—"they had turned to god from idols in order to serve the true and living God and to wait for his Son from heaven" (1 Thess 1:9). That was a blatant rejection of the giving of honors to statues of the divine Claudius as "a son of a god."

In 2 Thessalonians 2:4 there is a reference to one described as "a man of lawlessness who opposes and exalts himself against every so-called god or object of worship and takes its seat in the temple of God, proclaiming himself to be god" about whom Paul had warned them. To whom it refers is uncertain but an inscription records that Claudius had been declared "the most divine Caesar and truly our savior" (τοῦ θειοτάτου Καίσαρος καὶ ὡς ἀληθῶς σωτῆρος ἡμῶν).[68]

4.2. Corinthian Christians' Exemption (but Some Later Participated)

In Corinth there was initially a legal decision given in the Province of Achaea when the Jews laid a charge before its governor, Gallio, the brother of Seneca the Younger, both of whom their father had sent to Rome for legal training. The latter was the personal tutor of Nero and then his personal advisor on becoming emperor. Gallio subsequently would return to Rome and be appointed Nero's herald.[69] The formal charge the Jews brought against Paul "is persuading people to worship God contrary to the law" (Acts 18:13).

The legal expertise of Gallio is shown in that after the Jews presented their case and Paul was about to make his initial defense, he stepped in and ruled that there was no case for the accused to answer. "If it were a matter of wrong-doing or a vicious crime, O Jews, I would have reason in accepting your complaint." He ruled, in effect, that the charges in their petition were over "a matter of questions about words and names and your law" (Acts 18:15). The case was therefore dismissed. For Paul and all the Corinthian Christians the implication was that they had not committed a felony against Roman law, as they were part of the Jewish faith. This meant that just as Jews were exempted from imperial cultic celebrations, so too were the first Christians. It is important to register that this ruling applied only to those in the Province of Achaea over which Gallio exercised legal and other responsibilities.

Soon after Paul left Corinth there was a major development in imperial cultic activities. This prestigious Roman colony became the center for annual, week-long, provincial imperial cultic celebrations presided over by a provincial imperial high priest for life, appointed by Rome. It is recorded in an important inscription in Corinth:

---

[68] *IGRom.* 1:1118, lines 34–35.
[69] For evidence see my "Rehabilitating Gallio and His Judgement in Acts 18:14–15," *TynBul* 57.2 (2002): 164–66.

Gaius Julius Spartiaticus, son of Laco, grandson of Eurycles, of the Fabian tribe, procurator of Caesar and the Augusta Agrippina, military tribune, decorated with the public horse by the deified Claudius, *flamen* of the Deified Julius, magistrate of the fifth year twice, president of the Isthmian and Caesarean Sebastean games, high priest for life of the Augustan house, the first of the Achaeans to hold this office on account of his excellence and unsparing and most lavish generosity both to the divine family [*domus divina*] and to our colony: the tribesmen of the Calpurnian tribe [set up this statue] for their patron.[70]

Traditionally the one who held the federal high priesthood had to be "the most distinguished available candidate of the day," for it was "the summit of a man's career" in the East.[71] Here is evidence that Spartiaticus was the first to hold this office and that the provincial cult began in the early months of Nero's reign between late AD 54 and early AD 55.[72]

Some Corinthian Christians of social status possessed the right to participate in an important feature of the imperial cultic activities. They elected to attend its prestigious dinners, reclining at tables especially laid out in the precincts of the imperial cult temple. This concerned other Christians and was one the urgent issues that they raised with Paul in a letter to him, seeking his apostolic ruling on such a crucial issue (1 Cor 8:1, 4).

Those Christians who reclined at the imperial cult dinner had rationalized their participation on the grounds that "we know that an idol is nothing and that there is no God but one," Paul records (1 Cor 8:4). They did so on the grounds of their civic right—"this right of yours" (ἡ ἐξουσία ὑμῶν αὕτη: 8:9).

Paul's deep concern was that "if any one sees you reclining at table" (κατακείμενον: 8:10) the exercising of "this right of yours" (ἡ ἐξουσία ὑμῶν αὕτη: 8:9) can become a stumbling block to other Christians (8:9) that leads to their apostasy (8:11).

The actual festive celebration can be further identified as an imperial cultic one as in this era attendees drank a toast to the divine *genius* of Roman emperors past and present. Fishwick shows in relation to his discussion of the imperial cult that the Latin term, *genius,* is rendered in Greek as δαίμων and in this context refers to the emperors past and present.[73]

Paul later warned Christians: "you cannot drink of the cup of the Lord and the cup of the *genii* [emperors]. You cannot partake of the table of the Lord

---

[70] L. Ross Taylor and A. B. West, "The Euryclids in Latin Inscriptions from Corinth," *AJA* XXX (1926): 393–400 and revised in 1931 by West, *Corinth*, VIII.2 no. 68 and E. Mary Smallwood, *Documents Illustrating the Principates of Gaius, Claudius, and Nero* (Cambridge: Cambridge University Press, 1967), no. 264.

[71] Duncan Fishwick, *Provincial Cult: Imperial Cult in the Latin West* (Leiden: Brill, 2002), III.2.306. See also Antony N. Spawforth, "Corinth, Argos, and the Imperial Cult: A Reconsideration of Pseudo-Julian, Letters 198," *Hesperia* 63.2 (1994): 219.

[72] Fishwick, *Provincial Cult*, 218.

[73] Fishwick, *Provincial Cult*, 218.

and the table of *genii*" (10:21).[74] So at the prestigious imperial cult festival some Christians are reclining at tables especially assembled for the occasion in the imperial cult temple precincts and drinking a "toast" to the divine imperial spirits.

Paul deemed it necessary to engage in extended arguments (8:1–11:1) in order to persuade those Corinthian Christians who had justified their participation. They had to flee idolatry by ceasing to participate in the annual provincial imperial cult feasts held in this capital of the Roman province of Achaea (10:14; 10:31–11:1).

4.3. Galatian Christians' Strategy to Adopt a Jewish Identity[75]

It is important to note that only at the end of Paul's letter to the Galatians does he expose the motive of those who are compelling Gentile Christians in that province to undergo the Jewish rite of circumcision. He preceded this with a summary of what every Galatian Christian had to do—"So then, as we have opportunity let us do good to everyone, especially those who are of the household of faith" (6:10).[76]

Paul then declared that by contrast, and in order to give Christians a recognized public identity as Jews, they are "compelling you [Gentile converts] to undergo circumcision." He declares that they were doing this for one reason—"only in order that they might may not be persecuted for the cross of Christ" (μόνον ἵνα τῷ σταυρῷ τοῦ Χριστοῦ μὴ διώκωνται: 6:12).

Circumcision was repugnant in Greek and the Roman eyes because of the importance of the male's foreskin as a sign of the beauty of the body. It was seen as an "iconographic representation of male excellence."[77] Therefore forcing someone else to be circumcised became a criminal offence of castration under Roman law.[78]

---

[74] Traditionally the transliterated term *daimon* in Greek has been translated in the New Testament as "demon," except where it occurs in Acts 17:18. There the cognate is given its non-Jewish meaning of "divinities"—Paul appeared to those Athenians who heard him there to be "a preacher of foreign divinities" (δαιμονίων).

[75] For a response to my "The Imperial Cult and the Early Christians in Pisidian Antioch (Acts 13 and Galatians 6)," in *Actes du 1er congrès international sur Antioche de Pisidie*, ed. Thomas Drew-Bear, Mehmet Tashalan, and Christine M. Thomas (Lyon: Université Lumière-Lyon, 2002), 67–75 see Alexander V. Prokhorov, "Taking the Jews out of the Equation: Galatians 6:12–17 as a Summons to Cease Evading Persecution," *JNTS* 36.2 (2013): 172–88. The article includes a section, "Suggested Improvements to Winter's Theory," 180–84, arguing it was "not a Jewish Christian and Gentile Christian conflict but an 'intra-Gentile' conflict that revolved around the Roman imperial cult veneration and their fomenting the Galatian Christians' crisis." For my subsequent discussion of critiques see "Avoiding Divine Honours: Some Galatian Christians' Strategy," in *Divine Honours for the Caesars: The First Christians' Responses* (Grand Rapids: Eerdmans, 2015), ch. 9.

[76] As a summary of discussions in Greek with the use of the two particles "so then" (ἄρα οὖν) see Margaret Thrall, *Greek Particles in the New Testament* (Leiden: Brill, 1962), 10–11.

[77] Frederick M. Hodges, "The Ideal *Prepuse* in the Ancient Greece and Rome: Male Genital Aesthetics and their Relation to *Lipodermos*, Circumcision, Foreskin Restoration and the *Kynodesme*," *Bulletin of the History of Medicine* 75 (2001): 375–405 (376 and 405).

[78] See Justinian, *Dig.* 48.8.11 and for a discussion see E. Mary Smallwood, "The Legislation of

Because of this, compelling arguments had to have been mounted in favor of male Gentile Christians in Galatia capitulating by undergoing circumcision, thus presenting themselves with a key identity marker of a Jew and also observing Jewish laws and traditions—hence the series of arguments by Paul in his letter to the Galatians (1:6–6:10).

The outcome being promised by these promoters of circumcision was a good social identity, even though it is often, but incorrectly, rendered as "show in the flesh" (εὐπροσωπῆσαι ἐν σαρκί: 6:12).[79] Whether the perpetrators of this move were Jewish Christians or Gentile converts is not central to this discussion,[80] but identifying their motivation is important in seeking to understand their actions.

Given the evidence of the imperial cultic activities and their central place in city life in Galatia (see section 1 [i] above) and that Jews in the Diaspora, including proselytes, were exempt from any involvement in imperial cultic activities on the high and holy days of the annual calendar (see section 1 [ii] above), it is understandable why some Galatian Christians mounted strong and, in some cases, compelling arguments for the same public identity to be had by all Galatian Christians.

Therefore the Jewish umbrella was a safe haven, an easy escape route from any persecution for the failure to express divine honors for the reigning emperor as their Galatian compatriots did in the imperial cult temples. The culmination of Paul's letter is his declaration that his sole boast is the crucified Christ and not any Jewish identity, given the emphasis on the new creation of Christ (6:14). He gives a benediction on those who focus on this and not on a Jewish identity for all Galatian Christians (6:16).

4.4. Past Multiple and Pending Sufferings in the Letter to the Hebrews

A first-century reader of the letter to the Hebrews might well be arrested by the fact that its author commences with the perpetual divinity of Jesus (Heb 1:2–3) and devotes a substantial section to his ongoing role as the great high priest (4:1–8:1). The Roman Senate awarded perpetual divinity to some deceased Julio-Claudian emperors, while during their reign all held the office of high priest.

The author also records that already the recipients "had endured much conflict of sufferings" (πολλὴν ἄθλησιν ὑπεμείνατε παθημάτων: 10:32). The term "conflict" (ἄθλησις) in this context evokes a combative image appropriately borrowed not only from their sporting contests but also linked to

---

Hadrian and Antonius Pius against Circumcision," *Latomus* 18 (1959): 347.

[79] For an important discussion of the evidence of this Greek civic term πρόσωπον and its Latin equivalent *persona* in the first century as a central social identity marker, see V. Henry T. Nguyen, "Social Identity and Persona," in *Christian Identity in Corinth: A Comparative Study of 2 Corinthians, Epictetus and Valerius Maximus*, WUNT 2.243 (Tübingen: Mohr Siebeck, 2008), ch. 2 and 117–18 for its legal/social status as *persona* in Gal 6:12.

[80] Note the discussion in Prokhorov, "Taking the Jews out of the Equation."

warfare.[81] When that had happened they had not cut and run, and they must not do so now. The punishments they endured after they were first "enlightened" by the gospel have been succinctly catalogued in 10:32–34.

(a) Verbal Public Abuse in the Theater

The letter notes that "on the one hand" there had been "public exposure" in the one place where this sort of thing happened in the ancient world—the theater. The term θεατρίζω used here means "to put on stage," "to publicly expose" (10:33). The verb in the passive indicates what had happened to them. In Liddell & Scott's *Greek-English Dictionary*, this verb is rendered as "to be made a show of," "held up to shame." It actually cites Heb 10:33 in the literary sources as an appropriate example.[82] A hostile audience had assembled in the theater hurling "insulting abuses" at these Christians and other criminals at the commencement of their punishments.

(b) Public Scourging

The recipients had experienced not only "verbal abuses [ὀνειδιμοῖς] in this public setting but also physical punishments [τε καὶ θλίψεσιν]," that is, public floggings (10:33). Philo of Alexandria records a similar process overseen by the Prefect of Egypt in his day.

> He arranged a splendid procession to send through the middle of the market-place of a body of old men prisoners, with their hands bound, some with thongs and others with iron chains, whom he led in this plight into the theater, a most miserable spectacle, and incongruous with the occasion. And then he commanded them all to stand in front of their enemies, who were sitting down, to make their disgrace the more conspicuous, and ordered them all to be stripped of their clothes and scourged with stripes, in a way that only the most wicked of malefactors are usually treated, and they were flogged with such severity that some of them the moment they were carried out died of their

---

[81] Zahra Newby, *Athletics in the Ancient World* (London: Bristol Classical, 2006), 93. Games were aggressive and even trainers sometimes beat their team with whips, see the vase painting, 72, Plate 14. Liddell & Scott, *Classical Greek-English Lexicon* records the term means "contest," "combat," especially of athletes, Polybius, *Hist.* 5.64.6, *SIG* 1073.24 (Olympia), *IG* 14.1102 "in the athletic competitions." They also cite the metaphorical use of this word in Heb 10:32 to refer generally to a "struggle," or "trial."

[82] For the use of this term "expose to public shame" see Polybius, *Hist.* 11.8.7. For a cognate θεατρίζω "make a public show of," Polybius, *Hist.* 3.91.10. Contra N. Clayton Croy, *Endurance in Suffering: Hebrews 12.1–13 in its Rhetorical, Religious and Philosophical Context*, SNTSMS 98 (Cambridge: Cambridge University Press, 1998), 163, who argues that the rarity of this word thwarts a more precise definition. Paul also used the cognate θέατρον, as he invites them to "follow" him and other apostles where traditionally convicted criminals were humiliated before their public execution as entertainment of the citizens in the theater, cf. 1 Cor 4:9. See V. Henry Nguyen, "The Identification of Paul's Spectacle of Death Metaphor in 1 Corinthians 4:9," *NTS* 53 (2007): 489–501 for a helpful discussion of this text.

wounds, while others were rendered so ill for a long time that their recovery was despaired of.[83]

This account by Philo of how Aulus Avillus Flaccus, the Prefect from AD 32–38, humiliated Alexandrian Jews in a public "spectacle" in the city's theater records this "show" (θέα) had been carefully staged as part of the day's entertainment for the citizens. "The first of the public spectacles" (θεαμάτων) were the physical punishments of naked Jews "in the middle of the orchestra." These lasted "from the morning to the third or fourth hour." Then they were dragged off from the theater to their execution. He recounts derisively "and after this beautiful 'exhibition' came the dancers, and the buffoons, and the flute-players, and all the other diversions of the theatrical contests."[84]

Philo recorded this to be "the custom that only the most wicked of criminals are treated with" (αἷς ἔθος τοὺς κακούγων πονηροτάτους προπηλακίζεσθαι).[85] Some of the early Christian converts had been similarly ill-treated. Hebrews 10:33 refers to some having experienced public abuse and physical beatings—official forms of punishment officially inflicted on Christians and others as well who had been convicted of indictable offences under the law—and some having been partners with those so treated.

(c) Imprisonment

Their humiliation in the theater was followed by incarceration. 10:33 makes reference to "fellow" (κοινωνοί) prisoners. These Christians "also became partners with those treated thus" [τοῦτο δὲ κοινωνοὶ τῶν οὕτως ἀναστρεφομένοι γενηθέντες: 10:33b],[86] "and for those in bonds you had compassion" [καὶ γὰρ τοῖς δεσμίοις συνεπαθήσατε: 10:34]. Later the writer tells them they had to remember those still in bonds (μιμνήσκεσθαι τῶν δεσμίων) "as bound with them" [συνδεδεμένοι] who are ill-treated [τῶν κακουχουμένων: 13:3], who suffered "abuse and afflictions."

---

[83] Philo, *Flacc.* 74–75. For recent discussions of *In Flaccum* (*Against Flaccus*) see Per Bilde, "Philo as a Polemist and a Political Apologist: An Investigation of his Two Historical Treatises Against Flaccus and The Embassy to Gaius," in *Alexandria A Cultural and Religious Melting Pot*, Aarhus Studies in Mediterranean Antiquity 9, ed. George Hinge and Jens A. Krasilinikoff (Aarhus: Aarhus University Press, 2010), 97–114 and Daniel R. Swartz, "Philo and Josephus on the violence in Alexandria in 38 C.E.," SPhiloA 24 (2012), 149–66.

[84] Philo, *Flacc.* 84–85, Josephus, *C. Ap.* 1.43 also succinctly records how these same Jews were physically punished in the theater and then put to death.

[85] Philo, *Flacc.* 75.

[86] Friedrich Blass and Albert Debrunner, *A Greek Grammar of the New Testament and Other Early Christian Literature*, English Translation Robert W. Funk (Cambridge: Cambridge University Press; Chicago: University of Chicago Press, 1961), §290 (5), 151, "'τοῦτο δέ ... but also' is also adverbial," actually citing Heb 10:33.

(d) The Confiscation of their Possessions

Another blow had occurred at the time of their incarceration: "the seizure of your possessions" (τὴν ἁρπαγὴν τῶν ὑπαρχόντων ἡμῶν: 10:34b). Liddell & Scott equates ὕπραξις "like τὰ ὑπάρχοντα" and actually cite Heb 10:34 as an example of "substance, property," that is, "possessions." The concept of "seizure" is also reflected in the cognate "to seize" (ἁρπάζω). It was used of the sequestration of property through the due process of the law.[87] The context is clear that it was an official confiscation of their property.

Yet in spite of this substantial loss they had amazingly accepted all this "with joy." This response was determined by their awareness "of a better possession and an abiding one" (10:34). They drew a distinction between what had been theirs then and what they would ultimately have—"a great reward" (μεγάλη μισθαποδοσία: 10:35).

At the time of writing, these Christians had served their jail sentence because of the reference to imprisonment that occurred "in former days." Their incarceration had another positive result. "They had sympathy" [συνεπαθήσατε] with others also imprisoned with them. Today that would be described as "empathy." There is the command "you must call to remembrance [ἀναμιμνήσκεσθαι] how you endured such a great conflict of sufferings" (10:32). Their past sufferings were by no means being trivialized or indeed minimized in the letter.

Aubert draws attention to harsher punishments in Roman criminal law in the time of Nero.[88] He also notes, "Roman magistrates had acquired some leeway in the interpretation of the law." They also blurred the punishments of different penalties for different social classes. This trend, he concludes, was a "discrepancy or congruence, between the theory and the practice in Roman criminal law."[89]

Under the subheading of "Harsher Punishments," Aubert also notes, "Legislators devised new and harsher penalties, such as hard labor, mandatory exile and deportation to an island."[90]

Roman governors had not always followed the letter of the law, even though its proper administration was their responsibility.[91] This legal paradigm shift helps explain not only the multiple punishments Christians had experienced but also the temptation to apostasy because of a further and much feared punishment addressed at the conclusion of the letter.

---

[87] Liddell & Scott note the use of the verb ὑπάρχω is "frequently in neuter plural participle [form], ἡ ὑπάρχουσα οὐσι [refers to] possessions, resources." They cite as an example Isocrates, *Demon.* 28, τὴν ὑπάρχουσαν οὐσίαν.

[88] Jean-Jacques Aubert, "A Double Standard in Roman Criminal Law? The Death Penalty and Social Structure in Late Republic and Early Roman Empire," in Jean-Jacques Aubert and Boudewijn Sirks, eds., *Speculum Ivris: Roman Law as a Reflection of Social and Economic Life in Antiquity* (Ann Arbor: University of Michigan Press, 2002), 94–133 (103).

[89] Aubert, "A Double Standard in Roman Criminal Law?" 94–133 (106).

[90] Aubert, "A Double Standard in Roman Criminal Law?" 94–133 (103).

[91] Crook, *Law and Life of Rome*, 274 citing *Dig.* 48.19 fragments 8, 9 and 35. See also Paul's delay, Acts 24:26–27.

(e) Now Facing the Dire Penalty of Exile and its Misery

Two phrases were used to describe exile in the letter to the Hebrews: "outside the camp" and "outside the gate" (13:11–14). Just as under the Jewish law sacrifices for sin were burnt outside the camp [κατακαίεται ἔξω τῆς παρεμβολῆς], so also Jesus had "suffered outside the gate [of the city] [ἔξω τῆς πύλης ἔπαθεν] but his punishment was in order to sanctify the people through his own blood" (13:12).

The title of Williams's monograph, *The Curse of Exile*, discusses the ignominy, loneliness, harshness, and other losses experienced in exile by Ovid (43 BC–AD 17) who in his *Ibis* and *Ex Ponto* bears eloquent witness to his own experiences.[92] Claassen, in *Displaced Persons*, also discusses the emotional feelings and terrible deprivation felt by a wider group of people in Roman society in her chapter, "The Horror of Isolation."[93]

Claassan shows that it was abhorred because of the places of desolation that were chosen for such punishment. There was the deprivation suffered from adverse climatic conditions, no access to fertile land for producing good food, and the lack of clean water.[94] It carried with it the possibility of not being able to return, as exile could be permanent. Exile under Roman law was to a distant place, to an island or "to the most desert part" of a province, to cite the Roman legal code.[95] Crook has shown going into exile was "an accepted way of avoiding the [death] penalty."[96] Garnsey notes that the verb "to be cast out" (ἐκβάλλω) was used to describe being banished, with φυγάς being the legal term for "exile."[97]

Ovid is a good example of this experience. He managed to offend Augustus in one of his poems and, for an additional reason not disclosed, Augustus exiled him ca. AD 1 to Tomis, an isolated place on the Black Sea coast, where he remained until his death in AD 12.[98]

Exile also involved the loss of citizenship and all property.[99] In Roman law the loss of property was not a consequence for the lesser punishment of "relegation" (*relegatio*). However it was prescribed for the more serious offence of "exile" (*exsul*).[100] Thus, incurring relegation meant that a person was usually banished for a limited time, but exile was permanent.

---

[92] Gareth D. Williams, *The Curse of Exile: A Study of Ovid's Ibis*. Some of his chapter headings succinctly reflect the emotional feelings and the psychological effects on those banished, "Needing to Scream: Restraint and Self-abandon in the *Ibis*," "The *Ibis* in context: Melancholy, Mania and Exile" and "Cruel Pleasure: Mystery and Meaning in the *Ibis*-catalogue," chs. 2, 4, and 5.

[93] Jo-Marie Claassen, "The Horror of Isolation," in *Displaced Persons: The Literature of Exile from Cicero to Boethius* (London: Duckworth, 1999), ch. 7.

[94] Claassen, "The Horror of Isolation."

[95] Justinian, *Dig.* 48.22.7.9.

[96] Crook, *Law and Life of Rome*, 272.

[97] Peter Garnsey, *Social Status and Legal Privilege in the Roman Empire* (Oxford: Clarendon, 1970), 111–21.

[98] Ovid, *Trist.* II, 131–32.

[99] Garnsey, *Social Status and Legal Privilege*, 111–21.

[100] Herbert F. Jolowicz, *Historical Introduction to the Study of Roman Law* (Cambridge:

The writer of the letter prescribes the following remedy to help the Christians mentioned here face the future. They must not turn their backs on the dire prospect of exile and thus experience the even greater "penalty" of spiritual apostasy. "So now let us go forth to him outside the camp and bear the abuse he [Jesus] endured" (13:13). The term τοίνυν indicates the steps they were to take, while "abuse" (ὀνειδισμός) is the same word already used of public verbal abuse endured in their first imprisonment (10:33).

(f) Ongoing Endurance with Christ as their Example

The first reason given for further endurance was that Christ himself suffered "outside the gate" to secure the sanctification of God's people through the cost of shedding his own blood in Jerusalem (13:12). They were also reminded of another reason for enduring—"for we have here no abiding city but we are seeking the one that is to come" (13:14). Both reasons are intended to provide help in ameliorating the dark thought of the impending suffering of exile.

This explains further the statement already made in 10:34 that they have "a better possession and abiding one." It contradicted the propaganda that the everlasting city was the "eternal Rome" (Roma Aeterna) that boasted of its permanence. Other empires and cities had come and gone, but the power and permanence of heaven could never be superseded.

The exhortation to these Christians is that they should not make the worst decision ever by "throwing away our confidence, which had a great reward" (10:35). They should weigh up the guaranteed eternal security awaiting them in heaven with the "temporary" nature of exile (10:34).

The writer does not minimize the fact that the time immediately ahead would be very difficult. Hence he uses the present tense, "For you have need of endurance [ὑπομονῆς γὰρ ἔχετε χρείαν]" (10:36). The term ὑπομονή referred to the capacity to hold on in adverse circumstances, to survive, and even thrive.[101] They were reminded that there was a "great reward" awaiting them in the future. The incentive for continuing to endure was "so that you may do the will of God and receive what is promised" (10:36). Tenacity was needed to persist in doing God's will and thereby receive his reward.

The remedy was the anticipation of the "great reward" and also the eschatological promise that there was a secure end in sight. The author cites from the Old Testament prophets—"For yet a little while, and the coming one shall come and not delay" (10:37).[102] The view of the imminent messianic

---

Cambridge University Press, 1932), 408–9.

[101] For example, it was used to describe a tree surviving in very adverse conditions such as growing on a rocky cliff face; see Theophrastus, *Caus. plant.* 5.16.3.

[102] For a helpful treatment of the texts gathered from Isa 26:10 and Hab 2:3b see Peter T. O'Brien, *The Letter to the Hebrews* (Grand Rapids: Eerdmans; Nottingham: Apollos, 2010), 389–92.

return was in direct opposition to the first-century philosophical view of the eternity of the world and the propaganda concerning its eternal city, Rome.[103]

These Christians faced a choice to live in the light of the promised return of Christ "and my righteous one shall live by faith" (10:38a) or abandon their faith because they could not bear to face any more adversity.

They were warned that if they retreated from the faith, God's blessing would not be with them—"if he shrinks back, my soul will have no pleasure in him" (10:38b) is the grave warning cited from Hab 2:3–4. The writer hastens to add with emphasis "and we ourselves are not those who shrink back for destruction." His use of "destruction" [ἀπώλεια] as a synonymous concept for apostasy indicates how dire the consequences would be. Because of this he affirms, "but we are those who have faith and preserve their souls" (10:39).

A definition of real "faith" is provided—"the assurance of things hoped for, the certainty of things not seen" (11:1). Then follows the well-known long "homily" on what perseverance meant for some of God's people from the past who had lived by faith, listing many examples of trust and endurance with sometimes fatal consequences (11:4–40).

The writer uses the image of an athlete who runs a challenging race in a stadium while being watched by a huge crowd—"so great a cloud of witnesses" (12:1). Like competing athletes, Christians have metaphorically to strip down, laying aside "every weight" (ὄγκον). This term can refer literally to "weight" or can be used of "trouble" that weighs a person down.[104] In this case it is a burden they can rightly abandon. They must also "shed the sin that clings so closely." Just as athletes traditionally discarded all their clothes to run their race unencumbered,[105] so too must Christians cast aside these hindrances.

The analogy continues. Greek marathon runners had to stay the arduous course. Christians "must run with endurance" in order to finish the race (12:1). The term "endurance" was previously used in 10:36 where comparable sufferings had to be "endured," difficult as that was (10:32). Total focus on the finishing line was essential for athletes to complete the course. Christians then, must "look to Jesus" to do so. This verb ἀφοράω means "to look away from all others at one person."[106] Thus the use of this powerful athletic imagery illustrated how the Christians were to run their life's race without being distracted by their present difficult circumstances. Their total concentration was to reach the finishing line (12:1).

Another focus of their attention was the sacrifice of Jesus on the cross, which also provided a paradigm for them in their present situation. Knowing

---

[103] Philo of Alexandria in his *De aeternitate mundi* (*The Eternity of the World*) argues on the basis of the ancient Greek philosophy.

[104] See Liddell & Scott s.v. ὄγκος II for this metaphorical use.

[105] The abandoning of the loincloth in athletics enabled runners to participate unencumbered by tying up the foreskin. Pausanias, *Descr.* 1.44.1 attributes this originally to Orsippos at the Olympic Games in 720 BC who "intentionally let the loincloth slip off him, realizing that a naked man can run more easily than one with it on." For a discussion of other ancient sources that attribute this convention to others, see Newby, *Athletics in the Ancient World*, 71–72, 93.

[106] Herodotus, *Hist.* 8.35, line 9.

the ultimate "joy" awaiting him, Jesus poured scorn on the humiliating shame experienced at his crucifixion. He did this as "the founder and perfector [τελειωτής] of our faith." The word "perfector" was chosen as it refers to one who brings something to a successful conclusion. Jesus looked beyond his humiliating death knowing he would secure his inheritance: the place of permanent honor and power at the right hand of God (12:2).

When these Christians had been in prison, their focus on the future resulted in joy even when they had had their possessions confiscated. They knew their long-term inheritance was all-important (10:34–35). It paralleled the "joy" Jesus anticipated as the result of his sacrifice, which enabled him to endure suffering (12:2). However the writer, aware of their fragility, admonishes them not to grow weary or faint-hearted in running this spiritual race with its lasting prize.[107] Their present struggles are in no way comparable to those suffered by Jesus because they "have not yet resisted to the point of shedding your blood" (12:3–4).

(g) Fortified to Face Exile

The prelude in Heb 12:3–6 to the quotation of Prov 3:11–12 is the requirement to consider the endurance of Christ that led to the shedding of his blood; it was not leading to capital punishment in their case, but rather exile. Furthermore, their suffering was not a sign of divine disapproval, but the assurance of their divine filial relationship. Suffering or adversity was certainly not seen in this way in the first century. Liebeschuetz notes that there is "an abundant evidence that the Romans were even obsessively convinced of the need to placate the gods" and Christians potentially faced charges of treason.[108] Although painful, these Christians were exhorted to see it is as beneficial. It was part of their sanctification that would produce "the peaceful fruits of righteousness by those who are trained by it" (12:7–11).

The letter also records the encouraging news of Timothy's release from prison, so the recipients who had shared the same experience would undoubtedly have rejoiced on learning of this (13:23).

The extended discussion of suffering in Heb 10:32–12:13 concludes with a final exhortation to the Christians to take responsibility, pull themselves together, and run on the straight path. "Therefore lifting up your drooping hands and strengthening your knees you must make straight paths for your feet in order that what is lame may not be put out of joint but rather be healed" (12:12–13). Those who felt downhearted and disorientated because of impending suffering are called upon to get themselves back on track and continue to endure to the completion of their earthly race. As Attridge notes of

---

[107] Prizes for races won at the Games at Olympia and Delphi were "simple crowns of vegetation," crowns of celery in Isthmia, and monetary rewards in the Capitoline Games instituted in AD 86, where winners were given "a simple wreath, apparently of oak leaves." See Newby, *Athletics in the Ancient World*, 37, 41.

[108] J. H. W. G. Liebeschuetz, *Continuity and Change in Roman Religion* (Oxford: Clarendon, 1979), 3, 78.

this whole section on suffering, "The exhortation to faithful endurance built on athletic imagery and the proverbial understanding of suffering as educative discipline thus closes on a positive note."[109]

The writer finally ends with this appeal by way of an imperative. "I exhort you, brothers, you must listen patiently to my word of exhortation." This is his succinct summary of the overall intention of his letter (13:22). Its bottom line is to persevere in the face of impending suffering, which Mitchell describes as "the overwhelming pressure to conform [to imperial cultic activities] imposed by the institutions of his city and the activities of his neighbors."[110] This involved exile.

After using the evocative image of "suffering outside the camp" as the instruction for the difficult and lonely path of exile, they are exhorted to "go to him" (13:12–13). The thought of Christ's presence with them would ameliorate the fear of being alone, suffering in an isolated place; a punishment so greatly dreaded in the Roman world. Their high priest was indeed empathetic, given what and where he suffered, and would therefore give his timely assistance and grace to help them cope (4:16). Having outlined all this, the only credible option for the Christians addressed here was to have a heavenly perspective and conclude that they have no option but to go "to him outside the camp and bear the abuse he endured" (13:13).

The giving of divine honors to the Caesars was the official way in the Roman Empire of publicly expressing personal loyalty to the divine Caesars and, except for the Jewish cultic alternative, was an unavoidable reality facing these Christians. Chapter 12 of this volume, "The Book of Revelation," explores the persecution of Christians in Asia Minor for their refusal to participate in the Roman imperial cults, and that book's prophetic call for them to "worship, witness, and wait in the midst of violence."

Recommended Reading

Aubert, Jean-Jacques. "A Double Standard in Roman Criminal Law? The Death Penalty and Social Structure in Late Republic and Early Roman Empire." Pages 94–133 in *Speculum Ivris: Roman Law as a Reflection of Social and Economic Life in Antiquity*. Edited by Jean-Jacques Aubert and Boudewijn Sirks. Ann Arbor: University of Michigan Press, 2002.

Garnsey, Peter. *Social Status and Legal Privilege in the Roman Empire*. Oxford: Clarendon, 1970.

Garnsey Peter, and Richard Saller. "Religion." Chapter 11 in *The Roman Empire: Economy, Society and Culture*. London: Oakland: University of California, 2015.

Gradel, Ittai. "The Emperor's Genius as a State Cult." Chapter 7 in *Emperor Worship and Roman Religion*. Oxford Classical Monographs. Oxford: Clarendon, 2002.

Nguyen, V. Henry T. "Social Identity and Persona." In *Christian Identity in Corinth: A Comparative Study of 2 Corinthians, Epictetus and Valerius Maximus*. WUNT 2.243. Tübingen: Mohr Siebeck, 2008.

---

[109] Harold W. Attridge, *A Commentary on the Epistle to the Hebrews* (Philadelphia: Fortress, 1989), 365.
[110] Mitchell, *Anatolia*, II:10.

Price, Simon R. F. *Rituals and Power: The Imperial Cult and Asia Minor*. Cambridge: Cambridge University Press, 1984.

Roller, Duane W. *The Building Program of Herod the Great.* Berkeley: University of California Press, 1998.

Scheid, John. "Epigraphy and Roman Religion." Chapter 3 in *Epigraphy and the Historical Sciences*, Proceedings of the British Academy no. 177. Edited by John Davies and John Wilkers. Oxford; New York: Oxford University Press, 2012.

Taylor, Joan E. "Pontius Pilate and the Imperial Cult in Roman Judaea." *New Testament Studies* 52 (2006): 555–82.

Winter, Bruce W. "Rehabilitating Gallio and His Judgement in Acts 18:14–15." *TynBul* 57.2 (2002): 161–84.

Winter, Bruce W. *Divine Honours for the Caesars: the First Christians' Responses*. Grand Rapids: Eerdmans, 2015.

10. The Persecution of Christians from Nero to Hadrian

James R. Harrison

The persecution of Christians has become hot property in academic circles once again with the publication of Candida Moss's 2013 book The Myth of Persecution: How Early Christians Invented a Story of Martyrdom.[1] At one level, interest in the persecution of the early believers and their successors has never waned. The popular book of the English historian and martyrologist, John Foxe (1517–1587), has been in print and read continuously since its original 1568 publication.[2] However, the provocative thesis of Moss, beyond the scope of this chapter to investigate, has grabbed the attention of the popular media and has posed the question anew regarding the motivations for the persecution of the early Christians, the extent of its occurrence under the Roman empire, and the veracity of the later Christian martyrological accounts. Moss argues that Christians "were very rarely the victims of imperial persecution."[3] In many respects, Moss has revived the famous critique of the Christian persecutions by the Roman historian, Edward Gibbon (1737–1794).[4] Nevertheless, the dominant perception of Christian piety, as depicted by Hollywood (e.g., Quo Vadis, 1951) is that the early Christians hid in the catacombs to escape persecution and lived in constant fear that they would be thrown to the lions.

So how did this widespread idea of Christian "martyrdom" under persecution emerge? The Christian martyrdom accounts, Moss proposes, were based upon the Greco-Roman and Jewish martyr traditions. From the very

---

[1] Candida Moss, *The Myth of Persecution: How Early Christians Invented a Story of Martyrdom* (New York: HarperOne, 2013).

[2] John Foxe, *Foxe's Christian Martyrs of the World: The Story of the Advance of Christianity* (Philadelphia: Charles Foster Publishing, 1908 [orig. 1563]).

[3] Moss, *The Myth of Persecution*, 161.

[4] Edward Gibbon (*History of the Decline and Fall of the Roman Empire*, Volume 1 [London: Folio Edition, 1983; orig. 1776, chapters 15 and 16) famously argued that opposition guaranteed the success of Christianity. Opposition inspired its converts to an enthusiastic, but, in Gibbon's view, grotesque pursuit of martyrdom, resulting in the Christians provoking the Roman emperors through their excessive display of intolerant zeal, which itself was modeled on Jewish precedents. Notwithstanding, the Roman persecution of Christians was limited and sporadic, with many long periods of peace occurring throughout the empire. Since only 2000 Christians were killed at the height of the crisis, the elaborate accounts of Eusebius and Lactantius detailing the sufferings of the Christian martyrs are inventions. For discussion, see Charlotte Roberts, *Edward Gibbon and the Shape of History* (Oxford: Oxford University Press, 2014), 74–83.

beginning the pietistic stories of Christian martyrs were fabricated, not only by the original authors who altered them, but also by later editors who reshaped the tales for their apologetic purposes. In sum, the "myth" of a heavily persecuted church is a post-Constantinian construct, with the Christian historian Eusebius being the chief promoter of this pious fiction. Moss concludes that the "narrative of persecution and suffering developed to justify and support the institutions of orthodoxy."[5] Although the conclusions of Moss regarding the limited, local, and sporadic nature of Roman persecution of Christians under the empire, as well as the tendentiousness of the later martyrdom accounts, have long since been accepted by historians, to dismiss the entire tradition of the persecution of the early Christians as a carefully constructed myth is surely an overstatement.

This chapter will review the extensive scholarship on the persecution of the early Christians, spanning the late nineteenth century to the present. From there we will discuss the nature of our primary sources, Christian and non-Christian, and then investigate Roman attitudes towards foreign cults and Judaism within the empire as a backdrop to imperial attitudes towards the Christian "sect." The persecution of Christians from the time of Nero to Hadrian will be subjected to a source-based analysis, with a view to answering the following questions. When did the Romans discern that the early Christians were a troublesome sect distinct from Judaism and worthy of their concern? What precipitated the persecution of believers under Nero and how did the early Christians react to it? Was there a persecution of Christians under Domitian and was the discipleship of believers in this period, as presented in the New Testament, costly or compromised in its allegiance? Was an empire-wide edict ever issued against Christians? If not, what strategies did Pliny, Trajan, and Hadrian devise in handling the Christian "problem," and why? Who is driving the accusations against the Christians and for what reasons? Did the Roman rulers ever evince a protective attitude towards Christians in the legal process? What contribution do the New Testament writings make to our understanding of the period of AD 50–100, given the absence of any Roman sources on the persecution of Christians from that time?

It will be argued that the confession of the name Christianus is the litmus test for Roman authorities for determining the guilt of Christians in legal process. However, the reasons why the early Christians were persecuted are many and varied, locally induced rather than state sponsored, precipitated in many instances by Christian social distinctiveness, with the general populace being as much involved in the accusatory process as the Roman authorities.

---

[5] Moss, *The Myth of Persecution*, 245.

1. Research on the Persecution of the First Christians in the Roman World

1.1. Scholarship from Mommsen to Cook: Interpretative Issues Regarding the Persecution of Christians

After the celebrated foray of the Roman historian Edward Gibbon, noted above (n. 4), the pioneering monographs of Theodor Mommsen and Paul Allard mark the starting point for the modern investigation of the persecution of Christians. Mommsen overturned the common assumption in nineteenth-century scholarship that the Christian persecutions were based upon a Roman law or an edict emanating from the time of Nero onwards.[6] Mommsen argued that the real basis for decisions regarding the fate of the Christians was not the edicts of Roman law but rather the discretionary right of Roman officials to intercede in administrative affairs (ius coercitionis).[7] By contrast, in a massive project of sustained research, Allard wrote five volumes on the persecution of Christians up to the triumph of the church under Constantine, his research being characterized by a mastery of the ancient sources (literary and documentary), as well as a minute knowledge of the archaeology of the catacombs.[8] Allard's main thesis was that the Roman authorities unjustly persecuted the Christians, being motivated by a fanatical hatred of the "third race." In the case of the Neronian persecution (AD 64), he also posits that the Jews had instigated the accusation against the Roman believers in the capital,[9] an assertion for which (as I will argue) there is no convincing evidence, and a position, as we will see, that is regularly proposed in subsequent scholarship.

In the 1950s and 1960s three towering scholars dominated the discussion of the persecution of Christians in the Roman world: namely, the ancient historians

---

[6] Theodor Mommsen, Römisches Strafrecht (Leipzig: Duncker & Humblot, 1899; repr., Komm. für Alte Geschichte u. Epigraphik d. Dt. Archäolog. Inst. [München: C. H. Beck, 1982]), 575–80. Since the focus of this essay is upon Christians among Romans, tensions between Jews and Christians will not be discussed. See Claudia J. Setzer, Jewish Responses to Early Christians: History and Polemics, 30–150 CE (Minneapolis: Augsburg Fortress, 1994).

[7] See Jakob Engberg, Impulsore Chresto: Opposition to Christianity in the Roman Empire c. 50–250 AD (Frankfurt am Main: Peter Lang, 2007), 73, for a nuancing of Mommsen's position.

[8] Paul Allard, Histoire des persécutions pendant les deux premiers siècles d'après les documents archéologiques (Paris: V. Lecoffre, 1885); Histoire des persécutions pendant la première moitié du troisième siècle (Septime Sévère, Maximin, Dèce) d'après les documents archéologiques (Paris: V. Lecoffre, 1886); Dernières persécutions du troisième siècle (Gallus, Valérien, Aurélien) d'après les documents archéologiques (Paris: V. Lecoffre, 1887); La persécution de Dioclétien et le triomphe de l'église (Paris: V. Lecoffre, 1890, 2 Vols.). For the later period, see also Henri Grégoire, Les persecutions dans l'empire romain (Bruxelles: Palais des Académies, 1964).

[9] Allard, Histoire des persécutions pendant les deux premiers siècles, 42–44. Similarly, Adolf von Harnack, The Mission and Expansion of Christianity in the First Three Centuries, 2nd ed. (London: Williams and Norgate, 1908), 58: "Unless the evidence is misleading, they [the Jews] instigated the Neronic outburst against the Christians; and as a rule, whenever bloody persecutions are afoot in later days, the Jews are either in the background or the foreground (the synagogues being dubbed by Tertullian 'fontes persecutionum'). By a sort of instinct they felt that Gentile Christianity, though apparently it was no concern of theirs, was their peculiar foe."

A. N. Sherwin-White, G. E. M. de Ste. Croix and T. D. Barnes.[10] The incisive exchanges between Sherwin-White and Ste. Croix in particular have withstood the test of time and remain a highpoint in the history of research, with the arguments of Ste. Croix still holding the scholarly sway in the modern literature. In his famous 1952 article, Sherwin-White proposed that prior to the empire-wide edicts of persecution promulgated by the emperor Decius (AD 250), the early Christians were persecuted because of their contumacia ("obstinacy") in refusing the governor's command to render homage to the Roman cult. Thus, as Sherwin-White concludes from Pliny's correspondence from Bithynia with Trajan (Pliny, Ep. 10.96), it was not because their name (nomen) as "Christians," their past crimes (flagitia), or an imperial edict, that believers were executed, but rather because of their obstinate refusal to carry out the governor's command to offer up incense. He also noted the evidence that the Roman proconsul offered the Sicilian martyrs the opportunity of returning to the mos maiorum ("customs of the ancestors") in terms of the worship of the gods (Musurillo, The Acts of the Christian Martyrs, §6).[11] In response, Ste. Croix argued that the unrelenting monotheistic exclusivism of the early Christians was the real issue, potentially provoking the wrath of the Roman deities and thereby jeopardizing the pax deorum ("peace of the gods") with the Roman state. The so-called incense test, Ste. Croix observes, was not a test for Christians but rather a test of sincerity for those who denied that they were still Christians or that they had ever been Christians. While the contumacia of the early Christians made the Roman officials irate, it was not the primary concern of the Romans. In the mindset of the general Bithynian populace, even the economic threats to the local communities posed by the decline of the pagan sacrificial system paled in comparison to the much more dangerous dishonoring of the Roman gods by the Christian believers.[12]

In a rejoinder to Ste. Croix, Sherwin-White argues that Ste. Croix's analysis is correct for the period following the persecutions of the Christians at Lyons (AD 177: Eusebius, Hist. eccl. 5.1–2) under Marcus Aurelius.[13] But, in the earlier period from Nero to Hadrian, the Roman officials believed that the early Christians were immersed in wicked acts (scelera), evil deeds (maleficia), and shameful actions (flagitia),[14] with rumors of immorality (such as incest) and cannibalism widespread.[15] Sherwin-White proposes that their contumacia led

---

[10] The articles of G. E. M. de Ste. Croix have been collected in Christian Persecution, Martyrdom and Orthodoxy (Oxford: Oxford University Press, 2006), with 105–52 devoted to his seminal discussion of the reasons for the persecution of the Christians.

[11] A. N. Sherwin-White, "The Early Persecutions and Roman Law Again," JTS 3.2 (1952): 199–213. See Herbert Musurillo, The Acts of the Christian Martyrs: Introduction, Texts and Translations (Oxford: Clarendon, 1972), §6.

[12] Ste. Croix, Christian Persecution, Martyrdom and Orthodoxy, 105–45. Originally, G. E. M. de Ste. Croix, "Why Were the Early Christians Persecuted?" PaP 26 (1963): 6–38.

[13] A. N. Sherwin-White, "Why Were the Early Christians Persecuted?—An Amendment," PaP 27 (1964): 23–27. See Musurillo, The Acts of the Christian Martyrs, §5.

[14] Ste. Croix, Christian Persecution, Martyrdom and Orthodoxy, 145–52. Originally, G. E. M. de Ste. Croix, "Why Were the Early Christians Persecuted?—A Rejoinder," PaP 27 (1964): 28–33.

[15] See Stephen Benko, Pagan Rome and the Early Christians (Bloomington/Indianapolis: Indiana University Press, 1984), 54–78; Bart Wagemakers, "Incest, Infanticide, and Cannibalism: Anti-

ultimately to the Christians being viewed as an ungodly threat to the pax deorum after AD 177, when the charge of flagitia began to drop out of our sources and shifted to the charge of ungodliness. In response, Ste. Croix asserts that the real issue for the Roman authorities in the earlier sources (Pliny, Suetonius, Tacitus) was the superstitio ("superstition") of the early Christians.[16] In short, the Christians abandoned "their national duty of sacrifice to the Roman gods."[17] Last, Barnes, along with Sherwin-White and Ste. Croix, denies that there was ever a Neronian edict against Christians, and over against most modern historians, rejects the suggestion that this was the first paradigmatic action taken against Christians in the empire.[18] An important innovation in Barnes's study was his extended consideration of why local populaces were willing to become the accusers of believers—an important revision of the "ruler-based" approach characterizing previous and ensuing scholarship.[19]

Another outstanding contribution to martyrdom and persecution from the 1960s is the monograph of the eminent church historian W. H. C. Frend.[20] He brings the New Testament evidence more clearly into the foreground in his discussion of the persecution of the first Christians in the Roman and Jewish world[21] and his monograph remains an authoritative coverage for the period spanning the Julio-Claudian rulers to the Great Persecution. Frend's emphasis, however, is more upon martyrdom than persecution. He argues that Neoplatonist influences in Egypt led to a rejection of voluntary martyrdom as a means of salvation in the East, whereas the Jewish Maccabean tradition led inexorably to the deaths of the Donatist martyrs in the West.[22] Frend suggests several reasons for the persecution of Christians: public opinion, the attitude of local Roman governors towards illegal collegia, and, in the later period, the policy of the Roman ruler himself.[23] Like many scholars before him, Frend implicates the Jews in the accusation of Christians before Nero in AD 64.[24]

Christian Imputations in the Roman Empire," *GR* 57.2 (2010): 337–54. More generally, Robert Louis Wilken, *The Christians as the Romans Saw Them*, 2nd ed. (New Haven/London: Yale University Press, 2003).

[16] By using the derogatory term superstitio, which implied in Roman minds cultic irregularity, Roman authors deemed the first believers to be a threat to the "common good." The "good" was summed up in the ancient national tradition of Rome and its continuance was scrupulously maintained through its official cult. See Edwin A. Judge, The First Christians in the Roman World: Augustan and New Testament Essays (Tübingen: Mohr Siebeck, 2008), 434.

[17] Judge, The First Christians, 436.

[18] T. D. Barnes, "Legislation against the Christians," JRS 58.1–2 (1968): 32–50.

[19] Barnes, "Legislation," 44–50.

[20] W. H. C. Frend, Martyrdom and Persecution in the Early Church: A Study in the Conflict from the Maccabees to Donatus (Cambridge: James Clarke, 2008 [orig. 1965]).

[21] Frend, Martyrdom, 151–213.

[22] Frend, Martyrdom, 569. On Eastern (especially Egyptian) theologies of martyrdom, see 351–58. On the impact of Maccabean exempla and Christian martyrdom in the East and West, see 20–22. On the Donatist theology of martyrdom, see 353–59. On divergent views regarding voluntary martyrdom in the East, see 288–94, 357–58.

[23] Frend, Martyrdom, 162–63, 220–22, 489–521.

[24] Frend, Martyrdom, 164 writes: "On this reading of the evidence, the persecution represented a triumph for the orthodox Jews, who were able through evidence at Court, to shift the odium of the outbreak to the hated schismatics, the Christian synagogue. This they hoped to destroy at a single

Also, in line with Grégoire (see n. 8 above), Frend minimizes the number of Christians killed in the persecutions, asserting that the number killed in the first two generations of early Christianity (AD 64–135) could be "counted on the fingers of one hand."[25] Last, as Millar notes, Frend misconceives the nature of the imperial cult in thinking that Christians were charged with the refusal to worship the Roman ruler.[26] The reality was that the imperial cult included a plethora of deities, Roman and indigenous, and it was the wholesale Christian dismissal of all these deities, including the ruler as one of the deities in the Greek East, that provoked persecution.[27]

In 1983, Sordi put forward the argument that the Roman emperors benevolently tried to shield Christians from popular and senatorial prejudice, with the sole exception of Nero and Domitian, both of whom, in a striking departure from Roman convention, promoted a "theocratic and oriental form of domination."[28] Moreover, in contrast to the vast majority of scholars, Sordi gives credence to (what in the majority view are) discredited apologetic and hagiographic traditions, including Tertullian's claim that Tiberius had asked the Senate to vote on an imperial request to make Jesus a god of the Roman Pantheon (Apol. 5.2).[29] However, Sordi is one of the few scholars who discuss in depth the interim period leading up to the Neronian persecution,[30] adeptly analyzing the New Testament evidence. A solid case is mounted for the existence of a Domitianic persecution that still carries argumentative force today,[31] notwithstanding the incisive challenge of Thompson subsequently.[32] The volte-face of the Flavian and Antonine rulers is soundly treated,[33] with Sordi arguing that "none of the emperors before Decius believed that the Christians represented any kind of threat to the state," with the exception of the savage persecution of Nero and Domitian.[34]

---

tremendous blow." For a critique of Frend's overemphasis on the role of the Jews in the persecutions (Frend, Martyrdom, 158, 164, 192, 251, 259–60, 272, 323, 334), see Fergus Millar, "Review: W. H. C. Frend, Martyrdom and Persecution in the Early Church," (JRS 56.1–2 [1966]: 233–34).

[25] Frend, Martyrdom, 181.

[26] Julian Bennett (Trajan Optimus Princeps: A Life and Times [Routledge: London and New York, 1997], 123) lapses into the same mistake.

[27] Fergus Millar, "Review: W. H. C Frend," 235.

[28] Marta Sordi, The Christians and the Roman Empire (Norman: University of Oklahoma Press, 1986 [Italian orig. 1983]), 24, 29.

[29] Sordi, The Christians and the Roman Empire, 17–20. On the "utter implausibility" of Tertullian's story, see Barnes, "Legislation," 32–33. It is extremely unlikely that Tiberius would have accorded the early Christians the same legal status as the Jews (religio licita) when the Roman prefect Pilate had recently crucified its founder as a dangerous messianic pretender.

[30] Sordi, The Christians and the Roman Empire, 23–37.

[31] Sordi, The Christians and the Roman Empire, 43–53.

[32] Leonard L. Thompson, The Book of Revelation: Apocalypse and Empire (rpt. Oxford: Oxford University Press, 1990; repr. 1997).

[33] Sordi, The Christians and the Roman Empire, 55–78.

[34] Sordi, The Christians and the Roman Empire, 194.

In 1989, Keresztes published two volumes on the relationship between Rome and the Christians.[35] Like Sherwin-White before him,[36] Keresztes brings the evidence of Acts into full play,[37] discussing Paul's encounters with Roman officials and their clients, though, disappointingly, without considering the force of Luke's own political apologia in his presentation of imperial and early Christian relations.[38] In terms of the Neronic persecution, Keresztes considers the "incendiarism" charge made against the Christians to be a dramatic device employed by Tacitus as a writer of history. It is much more likely that an anti-Christian lobby, which Keresztes identifies as Jewish,[39] accused believers in Rome of not worshipping the gods of Rome.[40] He treats Domitian's (alleged) persecution of Christians fairly conventionally, considering Favius Clemens and his wife Domitilla to be proselytes to Judaism rather than Christian converts,[41] while asserting that the prior persecution of Christians mentioned by Pliny is clearly Domitianic.[42] Moreover, as far as Trajan was concerned, the very name of "Christian," without any mention of flagitia, was sufficient for the execution of confessors of the faith,[43] with Keresztes positing, over against the vast majority of scholars, that Nero must have declared Christianity a capital crime somewhere between AD 64 and 68.[44] Last, Keresztes argues that the Rescript of the fair-minded Hadrian was as "unnecessary as Trajan's Rescript," with Christians being tried "according to the common law procedure."[45]

In the early twenty-first century, the monographs of Spence (2004), Engberg (2007), and Cook (2010) touch on the persecution of Christians from particular perspectives.[46] Spence investigates the "parting of the ways" between Jews and Christians, suggesting that it took place very early in Rome. The already

---

[35] Paul Keresztes, Imperial Rome and the Christians from Herod the Great to about 200 AD, Volume 1 (Lanham/New York/London: University Press of America, 1989); Imperial Rome and the Christians: From the Severi to Constantine the Great, Volume 2 (Lanham, MD: University Press of America, 1989). See also Paul Keresztes, "The Imperial Roman Government and the Christian Church I: From Nero to the Severi," ANRWII.23.1 (1979): 247–315; "The Imperial Roman Government and the Christian Church II. From Gallienus to the Great Persecution," ANRW II.23.1 (1979): 375–86.

[36] A. N. Sherwin-White, Roman Society and the Roman Law in the New Testament (Oxford: Clarendon, 1963), 48–70, 99–119.

[37] Keresztes, Imperial Rome and the Christians, 45–66.

[38] See Paul W. Walaskay, "And So We Came to Rome": The Political Perspective of St Luke (Cambridge: Cambridge University Press, 1983). C. Kavin Rowe, World Upside Down: Reading Acts in the Graeco-Roman Age (Oxford: Oxford University Press, 2010), 91–137.

[39] Keresztes (Imperial Rome and the Christians, 77) proposes that the Jews were "moved by jealousy and envy" over the early Christian missionary success and alerted Nero to their threat.

[40] Keresztes, Imperial Rome and the Christians, 72–74.

[41] Keresztes, Imperial Rome and the Christians, 87–95.

[42] Keresztes, Imperial Rome and the Christians, 97–98. On the social location of the Roman Christians, see James S. Jeffers, Conflict at Rome: Social Order and Hierarchy in Early Christianity (Minneapolis: Fortress, 1991), 12–35.

[43] Keresztes, Imperial Rome and the Christians, 109–10.

[44] Keresztes, Imperial Rome and the Christians, 119.

[45] Keresztes, Imperial Rome and the Christians, 128–29.

[46] John Granger Cook, Roman Attitudes Toward the Christians from Claudius to Hadrian (Tübingen: Mohr Siebeck, 2010); Stephen Spence, Parting of the Ways: The Roman Church as a Case Study (Leuven: Peeters, 2004).

existing tensions between the two groups were aggravated by the expulsion of the Jews from Rome under Claudius (AD 49) arising from Christian proselytizing (i.e., Suetonius's enigmatic and much disputed "impulsore Chresto" phrase) and these increasing tensions are reflected in Paul's Epistle to the Romans. [47] In a masterful discussion of the Claudian expulsion and the persecution of believers under Nero, Domitian, and Trajan,[48] Spence argues that the early separation between Jews and Christians at Rome—or, as I would describe the phenomenon, the emergence of an increasingly distinctive social and eschatological profile on the part of the early Roman Christians—is demonstrated by Nero and the Roman populace being able to identify the Christians as a "separate group" to be persecuted only seven years after Paul wrote Romans.[49]

By contrast, Engberg highlights how modern scholars have sidelined the earlier New Testament evidence regarding persecution in preference for the later evidence of the Roman authors (Pliny, Suetonius, Tacitus).[50] Engberg helpfully distils the motives of the Roman authorities, as enunciated in modern scholarship,[51] in persecuting Christians; but, inexplicably, he bypasses the reign of Domitian in discussing the Roman evidence. In brief, Engberg argues that Roman provincial authorities (e.g., Acts 18:12–17; Phil 1:12–19) and several emperors persecuted Christians because of their worship of Christ instead of other Roman gods. In the view of the Romans, this superstitious and ungodly behavior threatened the pax deorum and, consequently, the welfare of the empire, though the Roman rulers were more reactive than proactive in dealing with the Christians. But, from AD 110–150, Christians met realistic (based on objective information), xenophobic (based on selective and biased information), and chimerical (based on non-empirical information) hostility.[52]

Finally, in an outstanding monograph characterized by intensive and incisive study of the ancient sources, Cook looks at the experience of the early Christians under Roman rule, spanning the reigns of Claudius to Hadrian, from the perspective of the Romans themselves. On central issues, Cook (a) leaves ambiguous the question whether Suetonius's "Chrestus" should be identified with Christ in discussing the expulsion of the Jews from Rome in AD 49;[53] (b) agrees with the scholarly consensus there was no specific Neronian decree against Christians;[54] (c) argues that Domitian did not persecute Christians, proposing instead that this proposal emanates from the anti-imperial apologetic

---

[47] Spence (Parting of the Ways, 352) views the early tensions in the Roman church prior to AD 49 from a sociological perspective: "For some, those whose primary community was Jewish, the church was initially a Jewish sect; for others, whose primary community was Greco-Roman, the church was an Eastern cult."

[48] Spence, Parting of the Ways, 65–171.

[49] Spence, Parting of the Ways, 127–29.

[50] Engberg, Impulsore Chresto, 45–79, 81–117.

[51] Engberg, Impulsore Chresto, 74–79.

[52] Engberg, Impulsore Chresto, 30–32, 333.

[53] Cook, Roman Attitudes, 27–28.

[54] Cook, Roman Attitudes, 95–97.

of later Christian authors;[55] (d) concludes that Christians were persecuted for the name only under Trajan;[56] and (e) posits that Hadrian's Rescript largely follows the guidelines of Trajan.[57]

In sum, the debate on the reasons for the persecution of Christians remains a quagmire, still dominated by the debates of the giants of the past (Sherwin-White, Ste. Croix, Barnes, Frend), and supplemented by incisive contributions in this century, but with no real resolution regarding the central interpretative questions. One of the obstacles we face is the problematic nature of our primary sources, Roman and Christian. We turn now to modern scholarly discussion of the evidence for persecution in the New Testament and the methodological issues raised in relation to our Roman sources.

1.2. Methodological Considerations: The Nature of Our Christian and Roman Sources

A series of monographs and articles have addressed the issue of persecution and martyrdom in the writings of New Testament.[58] These works have been largely theological, though several monographs and articles on 1 Peter, for example, have been exemplary in situating the persecution of the recipients of the letter against the backdrop of Roman Anatolia and Pliny's investigation of the Christians at Bithynia.[59] Generally speaking, there has been a failure to bring

---

[55] Cook, Roman Attitudes, 117, 121–31.

[56] Cook, Roman Attitudes, 166–68.

[57] Cook, Roman Attitudes, 265–80.

[58] Douglas R. A. Hare, The Theme of Jewish Persecution of Christians in the Gospel according to St Matthew (Cambridge: Cambridge University Press, 1967); William Horbury and Brian McNeil, Suffering and Martyrdom in the New Testament: Studies Presented to G. M. Styler (Cambridge: Cambridge University Press, 1981); John S. Pobee, Persecution and Martyrdom in the Theology of Paul (Sheffield: JSOT, 1985); Scott Cunningham "Through Many Tribulations": The Theology of Persecution in Luke–Acts (Sheffield: Sheffield Academic, 1997). On Christian and Greco-Roman martyrdom more generally, see Hans von Campenhausen, Die Idee des Martyriums in der alten Kirche (Göttingen: Vandenhoeck & Ruprecht, 1936), not seen by me; Frend, Martyrdom and Persecution, 1965; Arthur J. Droge and James D. Tabor, A Noble Death: Suicide and Martyrdom Among the Christians and Jews in Antiquity (San Francisco: HarperSanFrancisco, 1992); Glen W. Bowersock, Martyrdom and Rome (Cambridge: Cambridge University Press, 1995); Daniel Boyarin, Dying for God: Martyrdom and the Making of Christianity and Judaism (Stanford: Stanford University Press, 1999); J. Leemans, ed., Martyrdom and Persecution in Late Antique Christianity: Festschrift Boudewijn Dehandschutter (Leuven: Uitgeverij Peeters, 2011); Jakob Engberg et al., eds., Contextualising Early Christian Martyrdom (New York: Peter Lang, 2011); Paul Middelton, Martyrdom: A Guide for the Perplexed (London: T&T Clark, 2011); Candida R. Moss, The Other Christs: Imitating Jesus in Ancient Christian Ideologies of Martyrdom (Oxford: Oxford University Press, 2010); Ancient Christian Martyrdom: Diverse Practices, Theologies, and Traditions (New Haven: Yale University Press, 2012); The Myth of Persecution. For the definitive collection of martyr sources, all postdating the reign of Hadrian, see Musurillo, The Acts of the Christian Martyrs.

[59] F. G. Downing, "Pliny's Prosecution of Christians: Revelation and 1 Peter," JSNT 34 (1988): 105–23; Cook, Roman Attitudes, 240–46; David G. Horrell, Becoming Christian: Essays on 1 Peter and the Making of Christian Identity (London: Bloomsbury, 2013), 164–210; Travis B. Williams, Persecution in 1 Peter: Differentiating and Contextualizing Early Christian Suffering (Leiden: Brill, 2012), 63–130; "Suffering from a Critical Oversight," CurBS 10.2 (2012): 275–92.

the New Testament documents into dialogue with the later Roman and Jewish sources for a richer understanding of the historical, social, and ideological perspectives regarding persecution.[60] This is methodologically necessary because, as Engberg and Novak note, there are no Roman sources referring to Christians in the crucial period of AD 50–100.[61] Too often the result has been that the later non-Christian sources are given priority of place in academic discussion of the persecutions of believers at the expense of the earlier Christian materials, presumably because of the exhortatory, pastoral, and theological concerns of the latter.[62]

But the sparseness and lateness of the Roman evidence, its enigmatic brevity on occasion, and the polemical nature of its rhetoric, poses an equally challenging set of interpretative problems for scholars. The Roman evidence postdates the New Testament period, reflecting the social and religious concerns of the Flavian era as much as the personal biases of the aristocratic Roman writers themselves (Pliny, Suetonius, Tacitus). [63] Is it a case of anachronism to read back the attitudes of these later Flavian authors into our Christian first-century texts, without sufficient methodological caution, in explaining why the Romans persecuted the early Christians? It needs to be demonstrated that there is some continuity in the Roman reactions towards Jews and Christians spanning the earlier periods of the Julio-Claudians and the later period of the Flavian rulers, with attention being paid to the Latin terminology used to denigrate foreign cults and Jewish associations.[64] What so provoked the

---

[60] Pace, Hare, The Theme of Jewish Persecution, passim; Spence, The Parting of the Ways, passim.

[61] Engberg, Impulsore Chresto, 45; Ralph M. Novak, Christianity and the Roman Empire: Background Texts (Harrisburg: Trinity Press International, 2001), 51.

[62] Engberg (Impulsore Chresto, 82–83) argues that scholars dismiss the New Testament texts without any reason, preferring the later texts of Tacitus, Suetonius, Tertullian, Dio Cassius, and Eusebius. Where Christian texts are occasionally introduced into scholarly discussions of persecution, Engberg notes, they are the later texts of Acts and Revelation, bypassing thereby the letters of Paul—all of which (omitting the disputed Pastorals) predate AD 64—even though the apostle mentions the threat of imperial authorities and opposition to his message.

[63] Novak, Christianity and the Roman Empire, 51–52 writes: "Moreover, the relatively contemporary sources on Christianity in the first century C.E. did not explicitly address why Christians were unpopular, except for the statements of Tacitus and Suetonius that Christians deserved punishment for their 'hatred of mankind' and 'mischievous superstition.' However, these statements may reflect the attitudes of second-century Romans being read back into the first-century events."

[64] See Salvatore Calderone, "Superstitio," ANRW I.2 (1972): 377–96; Denise Grodzynski, "Superstitio," REA (1974): 36–60; Morton Smith, "De Superstitione," in Plutarch's Theological Writings and Early Christian Writings, ed. Hans Dieter Betz (Leiden: Brill, 1975), 1–35; L. F. Janssen, "'Superstitio' and the Persecution of Christians," VC 3 (1979): 131–59; Dieter Lührmann, "Superstitio—die Beurteilung des frühen Christentums," TZ 42 (1986): 193–213; Michele R. Salzman, "'Superstitio' in the Codes Theodosianus and the Persecution of Pagans," VC 41 (1987): 172–88; Agnes A. Nagy, "'Superstitio' et 'coniuratio,'" Numen 49 (2002): 178–92; Dale B. Martin, Inventing Superstition: From the Hippocratics to the Christians (London/Cambridge, MA: Harvard University Press, 2004); Richard Gordon, "Superstitio, Superstition and Religious Repression in the Late Roman Republic and Principate (100 BCE–300 CE)," Past and Present Supplement 3 (2008): 72–94. See also Joseph J. Walsh, "On Christian Atheism," VC 45 (1991): 255–77. On Roman religion, see Mary Beard et al., eds., Religions of Rome Volume 1: A History. Volume 2: A Sourcebook (Cambridge: Cambridge University Press, 1998); Ittai Gradel, Emperor

concern of the local Roman authorities, in diverse places and times throughout the empire, about the nature and activities of the Christian associations?

Additionally, there remains the difficulty of reconstructing the precise date and context of the early Christian writings and, in some cases, the further difficulty of penetrating the political apologia that their writings present to their audiences. In the case of the book of Acts, for example, is Luke presenting an apology on behalf of the church to Rome (apologia pro ecclesia), or is he more interested in presenting an apology on behalf of the Roman government to the church (apologia pro imperio), or are such polarizations too simplistic or misconceived?[65] What do we make of Paul's conservative attitude towards the Roman authorities espoused in Rom 13:1–7 (cf. 1 Tim 2:1–2; 1 Pet 2:13–17)?[66] Was the apostle tragically deceived or naïve regarding the nature of Roman rule, given the subsequent tragedy of AD 64 for believers at Rome? And how do we reconcile this conservative streak with the scathing denunciation of Roman rule in John's apocalypse? Last, we also need to remember that the works of later Christian apologists and historians (Tertullian, Eusebius) are also caught up in the polemics of their own age. Again, caution is required in using their evidence to reconstruct the earlier period.

In sum, there needs to be a more discerning approach in handling the intersection of the earlier first-century Christian sources with the later Roman second-century sources, with a clear recognition of the agendas animating both traditions, their occasional nature, and their limitations of evidence. There also needs to be a renewed appreciation of the contribution that the contemporaneous Christian sources from the first-century make to our understanding regarding the reasons for persecution of believers. At the outset we need to investigate Roman perceptions of foreign cults and the associations of the Jews.

2. Background: The Romans and Religious Cults

2.1. Roman Perceptions of Foreign Cults

We need to be clear about how Romans regarded the interrelationship between "religion" (religio) and the gods. For the Romans, religio referred to "the traditional honors paid to the gods by the state."[67] Thus correct cultic ritual,[68]

Worship and Roman Religion (Oxford: Clarendon, 2002); John Scheid, An Introduction to Roman Religion (Bloomington: Indiana University Press, 2003; Fr. orig. 1998); James B. Rives, Religion in the Roman Empire (Oxford/Malden: Blackwell, 2007); Jörg Rüpke, Religion of the Romans (Cambridge: Polity, 2007; Ger. orig. 2001); Clifford Ando, The Matter of the Gods: Religion and the Roman Empire (Berkeley: University of California Press, 2008); Judge, The First Christians, 404–9, 597–618, 619–68, esp. 650–62.

[65] See Walaskay, "And So We Came to Rome."

[66] James R. Harrison, Paul and the Imperial Authorities, WUNT 273 (Tübingen: Mohr Siebeck, 2011), 271–323.

[67] Beard, Religions of Rome, volume 1, 216.

[68] In his tractate De Religione, Valerius Maximus cites seventeen Roman exempla of groups and individuals who uphold cultic and ceremonial piety (Facta et Dicta Memorabilia 1.1.1b–15).

accompanied by the appropriate norms of behavior in worship, was paramount if the reciprocal relationship between the gods and the state was to be fostered and maintained (Pliny, Pan. 74.5: "This city … has always shown its devotion to religion and earned through piety the gracious favor of the gods"). The gods bestowed benefits upon those who rendered them their due,[69] but the gods were also dangerous enemies to those who had violated or ignored, intentionally or unintentionally, the cultic protocols. Consequently, Cicero advocates a scrupulous commitment to the mos maiorum ("customs of the ancestors") in matters of religio,[70] rejecting any introduction of new or foreign rites in public or sacred spaces on the part of private citizens:

> Let no one have gods separately; nor let them cultivate in private new [*novos*] and strange gods *unless publicly summoned*…. What follows concerns not only religion, but the general order of the state; namely, the prohibition which restrains private individuals from offering sacrifices *without the superintendence of the public ministers of religion*.[71]

The later jurists Paulus (fl. second/third century AD) and Modestinus (ca. AD 250) legislated deportation or death for those introducing "new kinds of worship" (novas sectas) or sponsoring the "superstitious fear of a deity" (superstitione numinis),[72] with the allocation of the punishment category depending on the social rank of the accused.[73] Even in the case of the imperial cult, the traditional Roman gods are prominently enlisted in the (not fully preserved) prayer of Valleius Paterculus for Tiberius's rule of empire:

> O Jupiter Capitolinus, and Thou, founder and preserver of the Roman name, Mars Gradivus, and Vesta, guardian of the perpetual fire, and whatsoever deity has raised this mighty mass of the Roman Empire to the world's highest peak: You I pray and invoke with public voice. Guard, preserve, protect this state of affairs, this peace, this ruler, and when he has reached the final station, fixed as the boundary to human life, grant him, at as late a date as possible, to have as successors men who are strong enough to bear upon their shoulders the burden of this empire of the whole earth, as bravely as we have seen it born by this Prince; and grant that the counsels of all citizens, if they are good…[74]

---

[69] Scheid (An Introduction to Roman Religion, 173) writes: "The only religious 'belief' for Romans consisted in the knowledge that the gods were benevolent partners of mortals in the management of the world and that the prescribed rituals represented the rightly expected counterpart to the help offered by the immortals." See also Wilken, The Christians, 48–67.

[70] Addressing Balbus the Stoic, Cicero (Nat. d. 3.6) says: "You are a philosopher, and I ought to receive from you a proof of your religion (religionis), whereas I must believe the word of our ancestors (maioribus) even without proof."

[71] Cicero, De legibus 2.8, 12; cf. Livy, Hist. 25.1; Dio Cassius, Hist. 52.35.3–6; 52.36. On Cicero's ideal Roman religio, see De legibus 2.19–22.

[72] Respectively, Paulus, Senten. 5.21.2; Modestinus, Digest 48.19.30.

[73] For discussion, see Simeon L. Guterman, Religious Toleration and Persecution (London: Aiglon, 1951), 29–34.

[74] The annual protocols of the priestly college of the Arval brethren at imperial Rome reveal the centrality of the traditional Roman gods for the continued blessing of the state and its ruler. In

It would be a mistake, however, to think that Rome was not hospitable at all to deities and cults from abroad, as the increasing momentum in the process of assimilation of foreign deities from the third century BC onwards amply demonstrates.[75] The Roman Senate, on behalf of the state, could admit the deity of a conquered city to the Pantheon or introduce a new deity for various reasons,[76] distinguishing between di novensiles (newly admitted gods) and di indigetes (old gods). Notwithstanding, any variation to traditional religious policy was unusual for the highly conservative senators.[77] Suspicion would increasingly greet any cults introduced from the East, and elsewhere, that the Senate had not publicly endorsed.[78]

The emergence of hardened Roman attitudes on the issue by the second century BC is best illustrated by the senatus consultum (186 BC) against the orgies associated with the Bacchanalian cult in Rome (CIL I. 2. 581),[79] the narrative of which, and its dramatic consequences for foreign cults, are recorded by Livy (Hist. 39.8.3–9.1).[80] Space restrictions prevent us from discussing the involvement of Romans in such cults and the complex and controverted reasons

---

thirty Arval brethren inscriptions spanning the Julio-Claudian period (21/20 BC–AD 66), no matter what sacrifices are offered to the ruler and the members of his house, Jupiter is always prioritized as the chief deity to be honored, along with sacrifices being offered to other Roman gods and hypostasized virtues. For full detail, see Harrison, Paul and the Imperial Authorities, 34 n. 157.

[75] Barnes, "Legislation," 50. Erich S. Gruen, Studies in Greek Culture and Roman Policy (Berkeley/Los Angeles: University of California Press, 1990), 39; Eric Orlin, Foreign Cults in Rome: Creating a Roman Empire (Oxford: Oxford university Press, 2010), 58–75.

[76] See Guterman, Religious Toleration and Persecution, 27–28. Guterman observes: "It was assumed in all cases that the god, by being admitted to Rome, lost his former nationality and became strictly Roman" (28). Additionally, see Sarolta A. Takács, "Politics and Religion in the Bacchanalian Affair of 186 BCE," HSCP 100 (2000): 301–10, esp. 302.

[77] James C. Walters (Ethnic Issues in Paul's Letter to the Romans: Changing Self-Definitions in Earliest Roman Christianity [Valley Forge, PA: Trinity Press International, 1993], 41) observes: "However, as foreign cults became more common and their practices more apparent, the Romans became increasingly troubled about the effects of these cults on traditional Roman religion." During the empire, as Walters further notes, no new deities were added until the introduction of Isis and Serapis under Caracalla (AD 188–217).

[78] During a plague at Rome (430–427 BC), "a horde of superstitions, mostly foreign [pleraque externa], took possession of their minds [superstitione animi], as the class of men who find their profit in superstition-ridden souls introduced strange sacrificial rites [novos ritus sacrificandi] into their homes, pretending to be seers." These "outlandish and unfamiliar sacrifices" were offered up to appease the divine anger. The praetors of Rome intervened quickly, insisting that "Roman gods should be worshipped, nor in any but the ancestral way" (Livy, Hist. 4.30.9–10). Note the incident involving religio externa ("foreign religion") during the Hannibalic war in 213 BC (Livy, Hist. 25.1.6–12), similar to the Bacchanalia (187 BC), which is discussed below. See also George La Piana, "Foreign Groups in Ancient Rome," HTR 20 (1927): 183–403.

[79] For a translation, see Frederick C. Grant, Ancient Roman Religion (New York: Liberal Arts Express, 1957), 54–56.

[80] See Richard A. Bauman, "The Suppression of the Bacchanals: Five Questions," Historia 39.3 (1990): 334–48; Gruen, Studies in Greek Culture, 34–78; P. G. Walsh, "Making a Drama out of a Crisis: Livy on the Bacchanalia," GR 43 (1996): 188–203; Takács, "Politics and Religion"; Sarah Limoges, "Expansionism or Fear: The Underlying Reasons for the Bacchanalia Affair of 186 BC," Hirundo 7 (2009): 77–92; Orlin, Foreign Cults in Rome, 162–91; Matthias Riedl, "The Containment of Dionysios: Religion and Politics in the Bacchanalia Affair of 186 BCE," International Political Anthropology 5.2 (2012): 113–33.

for the Senate's reaction, but Livy's rendering of the consul Postumius's speech spotlights the strong Roman conservatism regarding foreign rites. The political implication of suppressing the Bacchanalian affair by edict is inextricably entwined with the public affairs relating to the gods. There are genuine risks for the civic health of Rome and its citizens if the prohibition against the Bacchanalia is not handled scrupulously and cautiously within the traditions of the Senate, pontiffs, and soothsayers (Livy, Hist. 39.16.6–10; cf. Dionysius of Halicarnassus, Ant. rom. 2.19):

> Nothing is more deceptive in its appearance than a depraved religion [prava religio]. When the agency of the gods [deorum numen] is made an excuse for criminal acts, there comes into the mind the fear that in punishing human misconduct [frauds humanae] we may be doing violence to something of divine sanction [divini iuris aliquid] that is mixed up with the offences. But you are freed from such religion by countless decisions of the pontiffs, resolutions of the Senate, and, for good measure, responses of the soothsayers …. I have thought it right to give you this warning, so that no superstition [superstitio] may agitate your minds when you observe us suppressing the Bacchanalia and breaking up these criminal gatherings.

Clearly the notion of superstitio, when contrasted with religio in our texts, was reserved for any cult that was un-Roman and, concomitantly, not approved by the Senate for assimilation.[81] Thus superstitio represented a threat to the social and religious fabric of the body politic. Postumius emphasizes that the ban against such "criminal gatherings" was not so much directed against a particular form of the worship of Bacchus, but rather was aimed against (what was in the estimation of the Senate) a non-beneficent and alien god as far as Rome's destiny goes: namely, Bacchus himself.[82] "Degraded and alien rites [pravae et externae religions]" arouse crime and lust, whereas worship, prayer and veneration arise from ancestral institutions for the benefit of the state (Livy, Hist. 39.15.3–4).

In other words, the state sacrificial rituals were increasingly to command the attention of Romans over against the illegitimate "ceremonies imported from abroad [externo ritu]" (Livy 39.16.9) from the second century BC onwards. Consequently, Augustus highlighted in the Res Gestae his meticulous attention to the Roman gods (8.1; 19.1–2; 20.1, 3–4; 24.1–2) and to the great priestly colleges (7.3).[83] Fear of foreign cults continued well into the early imperial period if Tacitus's evidence is representative: these cults were permeating the households of Roman magnates (Tacitus, Ann. 14.44.3); Claudius denounced the present indolence regarding the traditional haruspices because of the progress of "alien superstitions" (11.15.1: externae superstitiones); the Roman matron,

---

[81] See Martin, Inventing Superstition, 130–35.

[82] Riedl, "The Containment of Dionysios," 119.

[83] Note Augustus's attitude to foreign cults endorsed by the Senate: Suetonius, Aug. 93: "Augustus showed great respect towards all ancient and long established foreign rites, but despised the rest."

Pomponia Graecina, wrongly identified as a Christian by some scholars,[84] was charged in ca. AD 57 with "superstitionis externae rea" (13.32.2: alien superstition).[85] But where do the "alien" associations of the Jews fit into this spectrum?

2.2. Roman Perceptions of the Jews and their Associations

Julius Caesar's charter of Jewish rights (Josephus, A.J. 14.190–264; 16.162–73), which formalized and legalized the ad hoc local arrangements and the unwritten convention of a quasi-religious liberty for Jews throughout the empire,[86] conferred upon Judaism the status of a religio licita. Augustus reaffirmed this status (Philo, Legat. 156–58; cf. 311–17), with Jews being free to gather in thiasoi ("associations," i.e., synagogues) for Sabbath and festival observance, as well as being able to enjoy autonomy in communal affairs and having exemption from military service. Not an insignificant number of Jews in Rome had become Roman citizens,[87] if the evidence of their participation in the monthly doles is indicative (Philo, Legat. 158).

Notwithstanding these privileges, Jews still faced periodic expulsions from Rome under the Julio-Claudian rulers and, more generally, racial stereotyping.[88] In AD 19, Tiberius expelled the Jews, along with adherents to the Egyptian cults, from Rome (Josephus, A.J. 18.81–84; Tacitus, Ann. 2.85; Suetonius, Tib. 36; Dio Cassius, Hist. 57.18.5a). As Walters notes, the coupling of Jews with Egyptians indicates that these expulsions "were not isolated events but indicative of a more aggressive approach to the problem of foreign cults under Tiberius."[89] The language used by the non-Jewish authors is equally revealing. Tacitus (Ann. 2.85) describes "the proscription of the Egyptian and Jewish rites" as necessary in order to deal "with those infected with that superstition [superstitione infecta]."

---

[84] For a cautious assessment, see Peter Lampe, From Paul to Valentinus: Christians at Rome in the First Two Centuries (Minneapolis: Fortress, 2003; Ger. orig. 1989), 196–97.

[85] Ronald Syme, Tacitus: Volume 1 (Oxford: Oxford University Press, 1958), 532: "Alien religions represented a double danger—the aristocracy weakened, the lower classes a prey to fanatics and false prophets."

[86] See E. Mary Smallwood, The Jews under Roman Rule (Leiden: Brill, 1976), 134–36; Leonard V. Rutgers, "Roman Policy Towards the Jews: Expulsions from the City of Rome during the First Century CE," in Judaism and Christianity in First-Century Rome, ed. Karl P. Donfried and Peter Richardson (Grand Rapids: Eerdmans, 1998), 93–116; Judge, The First Christians, 431–41.

[87] On the socialization of Jews in ancient Rome, see Harry Joshua Leon, The Jews of Ancient Rome (Philadelphia: Jewish Publication Society of America, 1960); Walters, Ethnic Issues, 28–40.

[88] For stereotypes of the Jewish Sabbath, see the ancient authors cited in Menahem Stern, Greek and Latin Authors on Jews and Judaism. Vol. 1: From Herodotus to Plutarch. Vol. 2: From Tacitus to Simplicius (Jerusalem: The Israel Academy of Sciences and Humanities, 1976): Vol. 1 §§129, 141, 142, 143, 188, 190, 239, 255, 258; Vol. 2 §301. Food laws: Vol. 1 §§176, 196, 253, 258; Vol. 2 §§298, 303. Circumcision: Vol. 1 §§129, 146, 176, 194, 240; Vol. 2 §§301, 320. Proselytism: Vol. 1 §127. Prayer house: Vol. 2 §297. Veneration of ass's head: Vol. 1 §§170, 247; Vol. 2 §281.

[89] Walters, Ethic Issues, 46.

The connection of Judaism in the estimation of Romans with illicit Egyptian cults, to momentarily digress, is reinforced by Juvenal's satire on women devotees of the eastern religions, probably written in the reign of Hadrian. In his sarcastic portrait of the Jewess, Juvenal lampoons the avarice that underlies her prophetic practices (i.e., dreams), while mocking from a Roman perspective distinctive Jewish mores and institutions (i.e., Mosaic law, high priesthood):

> No sooner has this fellow gone his way than a palsied trembling Jewess, leaving her basket and her bundle of hay, comes begging at her secret ear. She is an interpreter of the laws of Solyma [i.e., Jerusalem], a high priestess of the woods, a faithful messenger of the highest heaven. She too fills her hand, but more sparingly; for a Jew will sell you whatever dreams you prefer for even a small coin.

In the case of Suetonius (Tib. 36), the Roman biographer mentions that Tiberius overrode Jewish immunity from military service, "whereas the others of that same race or of similar beliefs [similia sectantes] he banished from the city." Dio Cassius (Hist. 57.18.5a), by contrast, underscores the fear of the large numbers of Jews in Tiberian Rome and the widespread concern about their proselytizing activities ("and were converting many of the natives to their ways").

Leaving aside for later discussion Suetonius's controversial text about the expulsion of the Jews from Rome under Claudius (AD 49: Suetonius, Claud. 25.4; Acts 18:2), Claudius reveals his nuanced attitude to Jews in a papyrus letter (10 November, AD 41) addressing the tensions between Greeks and Jews in Alexandria (CPJ II. 153). There Claudius asks the Alexandrians to behave gently and humanely towards the Jews and not to dishonor any of their traditional practices (CPJ II. 153 Col. 4 lines 82–84), allowing them to observe their customs "as they did under the deified Augustus" (CPJ II. 153 Col. 5 lines 86–87). But the Jews, as non-citizens, are "not to try to insinuate themselves into the games" at Alexandria (CPJ II. 153 Col. 5 lines 92–93), access to which they were legally excluded (CPJ II. 153 Col. 5 line 95: "in a city which is not their own"). Further, to invite additional Jews from nearby Syria or southern Egypt to the city would arouse Claudius's suspicions and force the ruler to proceed against them "as fomenting a common plague for the whole world" (CPJ II. 153 Col. 5 lines 99–100: καθάπερ κοινήν τεινα τῆς οἰκουμένης νόσον ἐξεγείροντας). Here we have strong anti-Jewish language from a Claudian document pre-dating the earliest New Testament documents by a decade.

In sum, the derogatory Roman language of sectarian belief, superstition, and contagion reflects the spiteful and propagandist caricature of the Jewish nation found elsewhere in Tacitus (Hist. 5.4–5). It is worth noting that even the status of religio licita did not protect the Jews at Rome and in the diaspora from the Roman paranoia about foreign cults or from expulsions from the city in the first century. Although Romans gave Judaism grudging respect because of its antiquity, with Gentiles converting to the faith in the first and second century

AD,[90] the popular social stereotypes of Jews nevertheless persisted among the wider Gentile populace. Last, Martin has astutely observed that Tacitus (see Ann. 15.44) has transferred to the early Christians the "typical Roman depictions of foreign religions that were perceived as a threat by the Romans."[91] There is little doubt about the social and political anxiety aroused by the early Christians if the polemical language in the Latin authors or Greek papyri is sufficiently indicative.

But how and when did the Romans differentiate the Christians as a group distinctive from the Jewish community? What clues do we get from the Roman and Christian sources as to why believers in the diaspora and at Rome would be considered as likely candidates for persecution before AD 64?

3. The Early Christians before AD 64: The Dangers of an Emerging Social Distinctiveness in Regard to Persecution

New Testament scholars are reticent to posit a clear separation between early Christianity and the synagogues at Rome prior to AD 64, asserting on the basis of the evidence in Acts that the Roman authorities did not clearly distinguish between Christ-followers and the Jews at such an early stage (e.g., Acts 18:14–15; 23:29; 25:18–25, esp. vv. 19–20a; pace 24:22). Moreover, before the Sanhedrin and Roman authorities, Paul, as depicted by Luke, strategically emphasizes the continuity of the Christian faith with the faith of Israel (Acts 23:6, 9; 24:10–21, esp. vv. 14–16), in order, it might be argued, to locate the early church as a Jewish sect (24:14a) sitting under the protection of Judaism as a religio licita. In other words, the early Christians promoted and maintained a socially quiescent posture before the Roman authorities.

However, such a conclusion is not convincing for several reasons. First, Spence rightly argues that Nero and the Roman populace had already identified the early Christians as a separate group well before AD 64 (see n. 47 above). Second, the status of religio licita did not necessarily protect first-century Jews from expulsions from Rome (AD 19, 49), or, for that matter, from the suspicion of local Greeks at Alexandria (AD 41: CPJ II. 153), or, earlier, from anti-Jewish mob violence in the same city (AD 38: Philo, Flacc. 10).[92] So why would Paul resort to such an unlikely political strategy?[93] As it was, the apostle had to

[90] See Michele Murray, *Playing a Jewish Game: Gentile Christian Judaizing in the First and Second Centuries CE* (Ontario: Canadian Corporation for Studies in Religion, 2004), 11–27.
[91] Martin, Inventing Superstition, 3.
[92] See Peter Willem van der Horst, Philo of Alexandria: Philo's Flaccus. The First Pogrom. Introduction, Translation and Commentary (Leiden/Boston: Brill, 2003).
[93] It is more likely that the Judaizing opponents at Galatia were trying to avoid persecution from the local imperial authorities by emphasizing the Jewish distinctive of circumcision (Gal 5:11–12), with a view to seeking the protection of Judaism as a religio licita. See Justin K. Hardin, Galatians and the Imperial Cult: A Critical Analysis of the First-Century Social Context of Paul's Letter (Tübingen: Mohr Siebeck, 2008), 110–14. However, Paul, in jettisoning the Jewish food and purity laws (Gal 2:11–21) and the boundary marker of circumcision (5:1–14), removed any possibility of the legal protection afforded by Judaism for his Gentile converts in Galatia, thereby distinguishing believers, to some degree, in Roman minds from the more familiar Jewish

appeal to Caesar for justice anyway (Acts 25:10–12, 21; 26:32). Third, if Luke was intending to demonstrate that the early Christians were not politically dangerous to the Romans, he has definitely not established his case. Significantly, even though Pilate declared Jesus innocent three times in Luke (23:13–22), an affirmation unique among the Gospels, the Romans, when pressured by a particularly vociferous opposition, were nevertheless willing to dispose of a perceived "troublemaker" in order to ensure the public peace, thereby ingratiating themselves with the local elites and the indigenous population. There is too much countervailing evidence indicating that early believers were a socially and politically provocative group (e.g., Acts 5:29; 16:20–21; 17:6–7; 19:23–41). [94] Luke's unflattering portrait of imperial power—illustrated by Christ's critique of the imperial rulers (Luke 22:25–26) and amplified by Luke's cavalcade of corrupt Roman officials and violent Herodian clients of the ruler (Luke 9:7–9; 13:1–2, 32; 23:1–25; Acts 2:23–24; 4:27–28; 10:39; 12:1–3, 20–23; 24:26–27; 25:9; 26:24–28)—would arouse Roman disquiet rather than diminish it. Fourth, one must come to grips with the delicate balance of Luke's political and social apologia, as Rowe has argued. [95] Although the early Christians were not political rebels against Roman rule (as were Barabbas [Luke 23:19], Judas the Galilean [Acts 5:37], and the Egyptian prophet [21:38]), [96] they were a countercultural movement challenging the traditional values and practices of antiquity. [97] In other words, they were socially distinctive from the beginning, even if it took their opponents a while to recognize publicly the full import of the early Christian threat to traditional values. In this regard, we have to recognize the continuing impact of the dominical saying of Jesus (Mark 12:16–17). While believers were to render obedience to Caesar and the lesser civil authorities in society, this was always performed within the strict parameters of rendering ultimate allegiance to God and his messianic King (Acts 5:29; 17:7). This new allegiance was pneumatically experienced (Acts 2:17–36; 11:19–26) in a radical social and ethnic upending (8:4–17, 26–40; 10:1–11:18; 11:20; 15:1–15), in other-centered body life (2:42–47; 4:32–37), and in the missionary outreach of Christ's "Kingdom" community (Luke 8:1–3; 10:1–17; Acts 1:8; 9:15; 13:46–47; 28:31). [98]

Several events demonstrate the emerging social distinctiveness of the early believers at Rome and in the wider diaspora—and, consequently, their increasing subjection to Roman scrutiny—well before AD 64. This would

---

communities. That being said, the capacity of Roman officials to adjudicate on the intricacies of Jewish and Christian disagreements over the Mosaic Law and the status of Christ was limited (Acts 25:18–21; 26:24). This is where the general label of superstitio becomes a useful "clarion call" for Romans in handling the perceived threat of foreign cults, including Christianity, entering Rome.

[94] Martin, Inventing Superstition, 135–39.

[95] Rowe, World Upside Down, passim.

[96] Rowe, World Upside Down, 55–89.

[97] Rowe, World Upside Down, `17–51.

[98] On the unusualness of the concept of "mission" in the ancient world, see Rowe, World Upside Down, 91–137.

eventually expose them to persecution. The first significant event in the diaspora was when outsiders first called the early believers Χριστιανοί at Antioch (Acts 11:26). This carefully chosen language of political partisanship, conveyed by the Latin suffix -ianus, expressed the mild contempt of either the Roman administration, army, or business community in the capitol of Syria because of (presumably) the highly successful proselytizing activities of this new "foreign cult" (Acts 11:24, 28a). [99] The Herodian elite picked up the pejorative term in late-fifties Caesarea (Acts 26:28: Χριστιανόν) and by AD 64 the general populace of Rome dismissively styled believers as Χριστιανοί (Tacitus, Ann. 15.44: "whom the crowd styled 'Christians'" [vulgus Christianos appellabat]). The political categorization of the followers of "the Way" as the Χριστιανοί by their opponents, therefore, was the inevitable Roman response to the negatively perceived profile of a rapidly expanding foreign cult.

The evidence pertaining to Claudius's expulsion of the Jews from Rome in AD 49 (Suetonius, Claud. 25.4; Acts 18:2; cf. Orosius, Seven Books of History Against the Pagans 5.6) poses a series of ambiguities and hotly disputed questions concerning the emerging social disinctiveness of believers at Rome. Suetonius's words are cryptic: "Since the Jews constantly made disturbances at the instigation of Chrestus (impulsore Chresto quodam), he expelled them from Rome." [100] It has been asserted by many scholars that "Chrestus" is a reference to "Christus," given the confusion of Christ's name with "Chrestus" in antiquity (though, significantly, Suetonius spells the name Christiani correctly elsewhere in Nero, 16.2). [101] If this scenario is the case, then either (a) the disturbances caused by the proselytizing activities of the Christians at Rome are in view here, or (b) the common messianic expectations of the Jews have led to civic disturbances. [102]

Either way, these disturbances resulted in Claudius conducting what was probably a representative expulsion of the Jews, including Jewish-Christian believers, from Rome. Much hangs on this interpretation for the exegesis of Romans 14:1–15:11. [103] The ecclesial tensions over food and calendar laws are proposed to be the inevitable result of Jewish believers returning to predominantly Gentile house churches in Rome after Claudius's death in AD

---

[99] Judge, The First Christians, 609–12; Rowe, World Upside Down, 129–35, 154–56. As evidence for Χριστιανοί denoting political partisanship, Judge notes that the Latin term Augustiani had been coined in Nero's reign as a name for the young knights commissioned to applaud at his triumphs (Suetonius, Nero 25.1; Tacitus, Ann. 14.15.5; cf. "Herodians": Matt 22:16; cf. Mark 12:13; 3:6). Smallwood (The Jews under Roman Rule, 212) comments that the Christians "indulged in the undesirable activity of proselytism with much greater energy and enthusiasm than did traditional Judaism," thereby incurring the "grave suspicion" of the Romans.

[100] Dio Cassius's mention of Claudius's ban upon the meetings of Jews in Rome (Hist. 60.6.6), effected without expelling any Jews from the city, must refer to an earlier edict at the inception of Claudius's reign (AD 41). See Smallwood, The Jews under Roman Rule, 213–15; Engberg, Impulsore Chresto, 92–96; Cook, Roman Attitudes, 25–27.

[101] Tertullian, Apol. 3.5.

[102] See Spence, The Parting of the Ways, 100–107; Engberg, Impulsore Chresto, 99–104; Cook, Roman Attitudes toward the Christians, 14–25.

[103] See Mark Reasoner, The Strong and the Weak: Romans 14:1–15:13 in Context (Cambridge: Cambridge University Press, 1999).

54. During the period of AD 49–54, therefore, the Gentile majority in the Roman house churches would have either separated from the synagogues very early on,[104] or have experienced increased tensions with the Jews because of the recent events, or have developed an increasingly Gentile profile in the absence of Jewish believers, which would have further differentiated Roman believers as a "foreign cult" from the religio licita of Judaism. This early "separation" between the Roman believers and the Roman synagogues explains why the Roman Jews knew so little about the Χριστιανοί at Rome (Acts 28:21–22), other than, significantly, that this sect (28:22: περὶ μὲν γὰρ τῆς αἱρέσις) was spoken against everywhere.[105] In sum, Nero's choice of Christians as scapegoats would have been a relatively easy decision given their increasing social distinctiveness in comparison to the Jewish community.[106]

However, if the disturbances among the Jews were not triggered by Christian proselytizing, but rather by the divisive activities of an unknown luminary in Rome called Chrestus, as several scholars have argued,[107] then the "disturbances" are merely the product of an intramural dispute within the Jewish community. No Jewish believers would have been subject to expulsion from Rome and (presumably) Priscilla and Aquila were not Christian converts when they left the city (Acts 18:2),[108] with the result that the Roman house churches remained a mixed community of Jewish and Gentile believers living together in the city, but with the routine cultural, ethnic, and nomistic tensions arising from such close interaction (Rom 14:1–15:11). In this alternate scenario, we have to ask when this mixed Christian community became sufficiently distinctive from the Jewish community at Rome before AD 64 for them to be likely prospects for persecution.

I have argued elsewhere that the pivotal issue was the arrival of Paul's gospel at Rome in his Epistle to the Romans (ca. AD 57). Paul's prophetic, apocalyptic, eschatological, and teleological gospel challenged the Julio-Claudian propaganda about the ruler's status; the apostle's alternate set of social relations in the Body of Christ inverted the hierarchical and elitist society of

---

[104] Sordi (The Christians and the Roman Empire, 28) writes: "The Christian community kept itself at a distance from the local synagogue (at least until 56) despite the number of Jewish Christians among its members."

[105] Spence, The Parting of the Ways, 112–15.

[106] Note, however, Fisk's warning (Bruce N. Fisk, "Synagogue Influence and Scriptural Knowledge among the Christians at Rome," in As It Is Written: Studying Paul's Use of Scripture, ed. Stanley E. Porter and Christopher D. Stanley [Atlanta: Society of Biblical Literature, 2008], 171) about not exaggerating the effects of the expulsion of the Jews (AD 49) in relation to subsequent relations between Jews and Gentiles at Rome, including the house churches: "With so much focus on the expulsion, it is tempting to exaggerate signs of ethnic resentment, schism and social distance and, perhaps, to miss signs of overlap, Jew–Gentile interaction and positive Jewish influence on early Roman Christianity. Correspondingly, without the conceit of Claudius's edict dominating the skyline, we are in a better position to see possible signs of the influence that Rome's Jewish community—its synagogues, leadership and practice—had on the Jesus movement." Contra Spence, The Parting of the Ways, 116.

[107] For the scholarly literature, see Harrison, Paul and the Imperial Authorities, 17 n. 75.

[108] Fisk, "Synagogue Influence," 162 n. 18; contra Smallwood, The Jews under Roman Rule, 211–12.

Augustus's Res Gestae; and his theology of "indebtedness" pinpricked the triumphal Roman attitudes towards the barbarian and the enemy.[109] The Epistle challenged the Body of Christ at Rome to live out in the Spirit the socially and spiritually transforming implications of Paul's gospel. With prophetic prescience, the apostle warned his Roman readers about the possibility of persecution and of their potential death by the ruler's sword if they did not honor and obey him appropriately (Rom 8:35; 13:4).

Intriguingly, if the epistle to the Hebrews is addressed to the Romans living in the capital,[110] we are witnessing here the beginnings of the persecution of the believers through imprisonment and the confiscation of their property (Heb 10:34), though so far without the shedding of blood in martyrdom (12:4). Was Hebrews dispatched at the outset of the persecution in Neronian Rome, when the first arrests had just been made, before the real bloodletting began? Or is this an earlier outbreak of local mob-violence at Rome, unknown to us but after Paul had sent Romans in the mid-to late-fifties, similar to that which had erupted at Alexandria (Philo, Flacc. 10), with the magistrates condoning illegal acts against an increasingly hated group?[111] Either way, the writer's concentration on the eternal high priesthood of the risen Christ in heaven (Heb 2:17–18; 3:1; 4:14–16; 5:1–10; 6:20; 7:20–25, 26–28; 9:11–28; 10:11–13) stood opposed to the earthly priesthood of Nero, who, as Pontifex Maximus, mediated between the idolatrous gods and the Roman state in suppressing superstitio. Therefore, believers need not fear that their current imprisonment and property confiscation, or, potentially, their future death, somehow pointed to the ultimate triumph of the Roman ruler and his gods. Rather the "eternal" city of Rome was a passing "side-show" in comparison to the "heavenly city" prepared by God for his saints, past and present (Heb 11:10, 16, 26, 39; 12:22–24). Because its resurrected priest, appointed "in the order of Melchizedek" (Heb 5:4–6), has triumphed over sin and death (7:15–17; cf. 10:11–18), there was nothing to fear (13:6).

It is now time to discuss the motivations for Nero's persecution of the Christians. What evidence is there for Roman Jews being informers in this process, as many modern authors have asserted? Did Nero institute an empire-wide decree against believers, as Tertullian claims? What pressures were brought to bear by the general populace, if any?

---

[109] Harrison, Paul and the Imperial Authorities, 97–323; "Augustan Rome and the Body of Christ: A Comparison of the Social Vision of the Res Gestae and Paul's Letter to the Romans," HTR 106.1 (2013): 1–36; "Paul's 'Indebtedness' to the Barbarian (Rom 1:14) in Latin West Perspective," NovT 55 (2013): 311–48. See also Judge, The First Christians, 437–40.

[110] See Stephen Muir, "The Anti-Imperial Rhetoric of Hebrews 1:3: χαρακτήρ as a 'Double-Edged' Sword," in A Cloud of Witnesses: The Theology of Hebrews in Its Ancient Contexts, ed. Richard J. Bauckham et al. (London/New York: T&T Clark, 2008), 170–88; Jason A. Whitlark, Resisting Empire: Rethinking the Purpose to the Letter to "the Hebrews" (London: Bloomsbury T&T Clarke, 2014).

[111] Peter T. O'Brien, The Letter to the Hebrews (Grand Rapids: Eerdmans, 2010), 385–86.

4. Nero and the Christians

In Annals 15.44,[112] Tacitus, writing ca. AD 115–117, describes Nero's actions against the Roman believers in this manner:

> But neither human help, nor imperial munificence, nor all the modes of placating Heaven, could stifle scandal or dispel the belief that the fire had taken place by order. Therefore, to scotch the rumor, Nero substituted as culprits, and punished with the utmost refinements of cruelty, a class of men, loathed for their vices [*quos per flagitia invisos*], whom the crowd styled Christians [*vulgus Christianos appellabat*]. Christus, the founder of the name, had undergone the death penalty in the reign of Tiberius, by sentence of the procurator Pontius Pilatus, and the pernicious superstition [*exitiabilis superstitio*] was checked for a moment, only to break out once more, not merely in Judaea, the home of the disease [*originem eius mali*], but in the capital itself, where all things horrible and shameful [*undique atrocia aut pudenda*] in the world collect and find a vogue. First, then, the confessed members of the sect were arrested; next, on their disclosures, vast numbers were convicted, not so much on the count of arson as for hatred of the human race [*odio humani generis*]. And derision [*ludibria*] accompanied their end: they were covered with wild beast's skins and torn to death by dogs; or they were fastened on crosses, and when daylight failed were burned to serve as lamps by night. Nero had offered his gardens for the spectacle...[113]

Several questions emerge from this passage and its scholarly interpretation. First, is Tacitus's link between the charge of incendiarism and Nero's persecution of the Christians correct, or, as Kereztses proposes (see n. 39 above), is it merely a piece of dramatic rhetoric? We must realize that Tacitus himself is uncertain regarding Nero's involvement in the fire of Rome (Ann. 15.38: "whether due to chance or to the malice of the sovereign is uncertain"). Whether the popular belief that Nero was the author of the fire was legally incriminating enough to force the ruler to nominate the Christians as scapegoats is a moot question. Griffin's expert review of the jaundiced Roman evidence, for example, rules Nero out as the culprit.[114] Conversely, our other non-

---

[112] See also Suetonius, Nero 16.2, 38; Dio Cassius, Hist. 52.16–18; Pliny [The Elder], Nat. 17.1.5; Seneca, Oct. 831–34.

[113] For a masterly analysis of the passage, see Cook, Roman Attitudes, 38–83. On Nero as the first persecutor of the church, see Melito (Eusebius, Hist. eccl. 4.26.9), Tertullian (Nat. 1.7.13–14; Apol. 5.1), and Lactanctius (Mort. 11.2). On the deaths of Peter and Paul at Rome, see 1 Clem. 5.1–7 (cf. Phil 1:20; 2:17; 2 Tim 2:9; 4:6–7; 1 Pet 4:12–19). For the deaths of other Roman believers, see 1 Clem. 6.1–4. On Peter's martyrdom, see Richard J. Bauckham, "The Martyrdom of Peter in Early Christian Literature," ANRW 2.26.1 (1992): 539–95. On the martyr cult of Paul, see David L. Eastman, Paul the Martyr: The Cult of the Apostle in the Latin West (Atlanta: SBL, 2011). James S. Jeffers (Conflict at Rome: Social Order and Hierarchy in Early Christianity [Minneapolis: Fortress, 1991], 17) estimates that the mid-first-century size of the Roman church, from whom "vast numbers were convicted" (Tacitus, Ann. 15.44), was 1000–1500 persons. Additionally, see Keresztes, Imperial Rome and the Christians, 78–82.

[114] Miriam T. Griffin, Nero: The End of a Dynasty (New Haven: Yale University Press, 1984), 132.

Christian sources (e.g., Suetonius, Dio Cassius, Pliny [The Elder]) do not convict the Christians with the charge in any way, attributing the blame entirely to the incendiarism of Nero. Further, as Kereztses notes, not one anti-Christian polemicist mentions the charge of incendiarism, a telling omission, and only one Christian source repeats the charge—Eusebius, but, significantly, without linking it to Nero (Chronicle, 2.29; Hist. eccl. 2.25.1–8).[115]

Second, if the "incendiarism" charge is a Tacitean rhetorical flourish for dramatic effect, why then did Nero choose to persecute the Christians? And what influence did the masses exercise in his decision? The context of our passage, cited above, is important. Tacitus tells us that Nero, prior to persecuting the Christians, tried to deal with the outbreak of the fire by religious ceremonies designed to appease the wrathful deity: consultation of the Sibylline books, public prayers, ritual banquets, and all-night vigils (Ann. 15.44). Nero acted exactly how the head of the Julio-Claudian state, as the Pontifex Maximus, should have in such circumstances. When these measures failed, the next question for the Pontifex Maximus to ask was obvious: what foreign cult groups in Rome, by virtue of their non-compliance with the mos maiorum, had provoked the divine wrath, and how should they be handled in resolving this crisis? To be sure, the Jews could equally have been chosen for persecution because, in Roman perception, they hated mankind (Tacitus, Hist. 5.5: hostile odium), possessed base and abominable customs (5.5: sinistra foeda), and showed their depravity by their obstinate persistence (5.5: pravitate valuere), to name several of the crimes in the savage cavalcade of Tacitus. Indeed, as we have noted, Tacitus transferred to the early Christians the rhetoric of denigration reserved for the Jews and other foreign cults: namely, the language of contagion, superstition and misanthropy. But the Jews were a well-known people group and the antiquity of their cult was grudgingly admired, even if their critics mocked its origins and (alleged) "ass" worship (e.g., Josephus, Ag Ap. 2.9; Suidas, s.v. Δαμόκριτος; Plutarch, Quaest. conv. 4.5; Tacitus, Hist. 5.3).

So why were the Christians chosen instead as scapegoats? The answer must lie in their increasingly distinctive profile in late fifties and early sixties Neronian Rome, notwithstanding the political quietism of the Christians (Rom 13:1–7; cf. 1 Tim 2:1–2; 1 Pet 2:13–17). Their distinctive traits included their social relations within their communities; their separatism from idolatrous cultural immersion (Tacitus's odio humani generis);[116] their rapid growth through proselytizing; their threat to the cultural and religious status quo; and the ideological challenge posed by Jesus and Paul's eschatological gospel to the imperial propaganda. The real pressure that was levered invisibly upon Nero, more than the misconceived opinion of the masses that he was an incendiary, was the increasing public hatred of the Christianoi at Rome who, in the view of

---

[115] Sordi, The Christians and the Roman Empire, 72.
[116] According to Keresztes (Imperial Rome and the Christians, 70), the phrase was associated with misanthropia, which, in a Ciceronian context, denotes "dereliction of one's duties towards the community of men, a separation from the rest of society." Thus, applied to Jews and Christians, Tacitus's phrase underscores that they "evinced hostility and aversion towards all others."

the masses, were caught up in an immoral superstitio ("a class of men, loathed for their vices [flagitia], whom the crowd styled Christians"). The time for the Roman ruler as Imperator and Pontifex Maximus had come to act decisively against "the new and mischievous superstition" (Suetonius, Nero 16.2: superstitionis novae ac maleficae).[117]

Our third question emerges from our survey of modern scholarship on persecution of Christians, previously discussed. Did the Jews from the synagogues living in the capital place pressure on Nero to persecute the Roman believers (see nn. 9, 24, 39 above)? Alternatively, did they remind Nero to bypass the Jewish population in Rome as far as punishment went because "the sophisticated circles of the emperor's court sympathized with Judaism"?[118] The alleged role of Poppaea, a Jewish sympathizer (Josephus, A.J. 20: "God fearing" [θεοσεβής]; Vita 16), features prominently here, but, as Cook correctly responds, Tacitus makes no mention of her alleged role.[119] We do not have any evidence for the involvement of Jewish sympathizers or representatives from the Roman synagogues—whom, incidentally, Acts presents as respectful before Paul (28:17–28)—other than the assertions of modern scholars. Last, Clement's (possible) insinuation that Jewish (Jewish-Christian?) jealousy and envy were the driving factor behind the persecutions at Rome (1 Clem. 4.7–13; 5.2; 6.1–3) must be dismissed because 1 Clement 4–6 is "a rhetorical passage, not a historical one."[120]

Fourth, what evidence is there for an empire-wide decree against the first Christian believers? Frend has proposed that there may have been conceivably a senatus consultum against the Roman Christians, as had been the case in the Bacchanalian episode (186 BC), but no trace of such a document has been found.[121] Our other Roman sources know nothing of such an edict, including the skilled Roman lawyer and governor, Pliny the Younger. If it had existed, any copies of the decree would have been excised under Nero's damnatio memoriae.[122] The much later Christian sources are our only evidence for such a decree: (a) the reference of Tertullian (fl. AD 200) regarding the institutum

---

[117] David Shotter, Nero, 2nd ed. (London: Routledge, 1997), 60 writes: "Nero's attack did not represent persecution of Christians for their faith, but rather the punishment of people seen as criminals for a range of assumed misdeeds, perhaps as an expiatory offering to the gods whose anger was supposedly symbolized by the fire." Conversely, Jeffers (Conflict at Rome, 17) speculates: "Popular Christian eschatology looked for the imminent destruction of the world by fire. Some Christians, then, might have openly welcomed the fire as the sign of the end." If so, this would have generated further Roman suspicion (cf. 2 Pet 3:7–12).

[118] For the latter suggestion, see Jürgen Malitz, Nero (London: Blackwell, 2005; Ger. orig. 1999), 70.

[119] Cook, Roman Attitudes, 44–45.

[120] Spence, Parting of the Ways, 135. Bauckham ("The Martyrdom of Peter," 561–62) argues that Clement is providing a homiletic reflection on "jealousy" and "envy," but without being specific regarding the perpetrators of the persecution.

[121] Frend, Martyrdom and Persecution, 44.

[122] Paul McKechnie, The First Christian Centuries: Perspectives on the Early Christian Church (Leicester: Apollos, 2001), 62.

James R. Harrison

Neronianum;[123] (b) Eusebius (AD 260–339) regarding Nero being "the first of
the emperors to be pointed out as a foe of divine religion" (Hist. eccl. 2.25); and
(c) Sulpicius Severus (AD 363–425) regarding Neronian "laws enacted" and
"edicts ... posted" (Chron. 2.3). That Sulpicius Severus uses the plural ("laws,"
"edicts") demonstrates that he is not speaking of a specific senatus
consultum.[124] Tertullian's famous "institutum Neronianum", as Barnes reminds
us,[125] denotes "the habit or practice of persecution, not its judicial basis." Thus,
given the highly polemical tone of our later Christian writings, we should not
expect legal precision in their language that would confirm the possibility of an
edict.

What hints do we get from the New Testament about Nero's proscriptions
against the Christians? The claim is frequently made that there is no direct
mention of the Neronic persecution. It has been argued, however, that an
allusion to the "disclosures" of the Christians arrested in the capital (Tacitus,
Ann. 15.44), leading to further arrests of believers and subsequent martyrdom,
is found in the Markan apocalypse (Mark 13:12a: "brother will betray brother
to death"; cf. 13:9–11).[126] This presumes, of course, that the destination of
Mark's Gospel is Rome (ca. AD 64–69).[127] Further, the author of 1 Peter, in an
emotionally intense passage inculcating perseverance under persecution (4:12–
19), warns his diaspora audience (1:1) that the time has come for judgment to
begin with the household of God (4:17a–18), passing on to them at the end of
the epistle the greetings of their sister church in Rome ("Babylon": 5:13; cf.
Rev 17:1–6, 18; 18:1–24). The warning is fraught with eschatological urgency
and poses the question whether 1 Peter is better dated to the aftermath of the
Neronian persecution than the later Flavian period, as has been recently
proposed (n. 59 above). The author of 1 Peter, I propose, alludes in a subtle
manner to the costly discipleship of the Roman believers living in the capital,
while exhorting believers in the diaspora to remain faithful to God no matter
what. What evidence is there for this proposal?

Believers, the author reminds his auditors, are being presently reproached
"for the name of Christ" (1 Pet 4:14: ἐν ὀνόματι Χριστοῦ) and suffer "as a
Christian" (4:16: ὡς Χριστιανός). This reflects the social opprobrium of the
Roman crowd (vulgus) towards believers living in the capital (Tacitus, Ann.
15.44) and which, unbeknown to the author, would face believers in Bithynia
in the early second century AD, and, if Pliny the Younger is right, even earlier
in that region. But the author of 1 Peter overturns the dishonor by referring to
the joyous hope of the eschatological revelation of Christ's glory (4:13: ἐν τῇ
ἀποκαλύψει τῆς δόξης) and, in the present, by mentioning the Spirit of glory
and of God resting upon the believer (4:14b: τὸ τῆς δόξης καὶ τὸ τοῦ θεοῦ

---

[123] Tertullian, Nat. 1.7.9: "although every other institution which existed under Nero has been
destroyed"; Apol. 5: "the first to rage with the imperial sword against this school."
[124] Williams, Persecution in 1 Peter, 221.
[125] Barnes, "Legislation," 35.
[126] Clifton C. Black, Mark: Images of an Apostolic Interpreter (Columbia: University of South
Carolina Press, 1994), 224–50.
[127] See Martin Hengel, Studies in the Gospel of Mark (London: SCM, 1985).

πνεῦμα).[128] Thus, Ste. Croix's claim that the name Χριστιανός was the focus of Roman persecution of believers has real cogency (cf. Tertullian, Apol. 1.4; 2.3, 10–11, 13, 19; 3:5; 44.2).[129] Additionally, the reference in 1 Peter 4:12 to the "fiery ordeal" (τῇ ἐν ὑμῖν πυρώσει πρὸς πειρασμόν; cf. 1:7: διὰ πυρός) facing diaspora believers does "double duty" in terms of exhortation, recalling not only the great fire at Rome which precipitated the persecution of Roman believers, but also highlighting the terrible fate of some believers being burned alive as lamps in Nero's gardens (Ann. 15.44). Last, the reference to the flagitia ("vices") of Roman believers (Ann. 15.44) may have recalled the author's warning against being an evildoer (1 Pet 4:15: κακοποιός). The author catalogues the evils that Christians should avoid (4:15: murderers, thieves, evildoers, meddlers), knowing very well that, ironically, this is precisely how the Roman crowd had come to perceive the Christians in the capital (cf. 1 Pet 4:4), with tragic results.[130] But, once again, the dishonor of Christians is overturned by the author's exhortation: "do not consider it a disgrace [μὴ αἰσχυνέσθω], but glorify [δοξαζέτω] God because you bear this name" (1 Pet 4:16). The disdain (ludibria) that the Roman Christians (Ann. 15.44) experienced must not unsettle diaspora believers (cf. 1 Pet 3:16): rather they must count, like their Roman brothers in Christ at the capital, the cost of discipleship and continue to do good (1 Pet 4:19; cf. 3:14, 16–17).

In our next section we turn to what has increasingly become a controversial area of scholarship. What evidence exists for a Domitianic persecution of Christians and how does it relate, if at all, to our New Testament documents? What other martyrdoms occurred in this period?

5. From Nero's Death to the Reign of Domitian: Costly or Compromised Discipleship for Believers?

5.1. Domitian—A Persecutor of Christians?: The Roman Evidence

There is no explicit Roman evidence that Domitian persecuted Christians. However, several pieces of evidence are co-opted by scholars to support this conclusion. First, Suetonius's account of the murder of prominent senators (Dom. 10.2), including ex-consuls, for revolution and trivial charges is well known. A key text for the Domitianic persecution of Christians is the execution of Flavius Clemens, the cousin of Domitian, and his wife Flavia Domitilla. Several scholars identify them as Christians because they were charged with "atheism" and "Jewish ways." As Dio Cassius (Hist. 67.14.1–3; cf. Suetonius, Dom. 15.2) writes:

---

[128] Note James's martyrdom in Jerusalem in the province of Judaea (AD 62) under the High Priest Ananus during the procuratorship of Albinus (Josephus, A.J. 20.200).

[129] Ste. Croix, Christian Persecution, Martyrdom and Orthodoxy, 110–11, 146, 148–49, 152, 199–200. See also Benko, Pagan Rome and the Early Christians, 1–29.

[130] Cook, Roman Attitudes, 48; Sordi, The Christians and the Roman Empire, 32–33. On allegations of Christian ritual murder, see Wilken, The Christians, 18.

And the same year Domitian slew, along with many others, Flavius Clemens the consul, although he was a cousin and had to wife Flavia Domitilla, who was also a relative of the emperor's. The charge brought against them both was that of atheism [ἀθεότητος], a charge on which many others who drifted into Jewish ways [εἰς τὰ τῶν Ἰουδαίων] were condemned. Some of these were put to death, and the rest were at least deprived of their property. Domitilla was merely banished to Pandateria.

Second, Domitian's harsher tax policy towards those who, without "professing" Jewry, nevertheless "lived a Jewish life" and concealed their ancestry, clearly refers to Jewish tax-evaders (Suetonius, Dom. 12.2). Possibly these included Jewish Christians, because believers considered themselves exempt from a Jewish tax.[131] Third, the absolutist rule of Domitian, perceived as problematic by Christians, is seen in his demand to be called "Lord and God" (Suetonius, Dom. 13.2; Dio Cassius, Hist. 67.13.4; 67.4.7; Pliny [the Younger], Ep. 33.3–4) in a manner reminiscent of Caligula (Suetonius, Cal. 22.1–3 [22.1: "Let there be one Lord, one King"]). It is sometimes argued that John's Gospel, traditionally dated to Domitian's reign, is polemically slanted against this claim in its heightened emphasis on Jesus' divinity, well-illustrated by Thomas's confession before the risen Christ (20:28: "My Lord and my God" [Ὁ κύριός μου καὶ ὁ θεός μου]).[132] Fourth, Pliny possibly implies that there had been proceedings against Christians in AD 90–112 (Pliny, Ep. 10.9.1, 6–7). How do we respond to this catalogue of evidence, supposedly pointing to a Domitianic persecution of Christians? Does its cumulative impact convince?

The charge of "atheism" and "Jewish ways" against Flavia Domitilla and her husband does not necessarily point to Christian conversion but more likely refers to the accused becoming proselytes.[133] Conversion to Judaism was now viewed with even greater suspicion after the rebellion of AD 66–70, and in popular belief anxiety about the Jews was compounded by the threat posed to the mos maiorum on account of their proselytizing.[134] The catacomb evidence appealed to corroborate that Domitilla was the founder of a "Christian dynasty" only commences toward the end of the second century AD and, notwithstanding the (unsubstantiated) confidence that Jeffers places in a family oral tradition spanning the generations, the proposal must be disregarded.[135] Clearly Domitian's tax policy was aimed at Jewish tax-evaders rather than at the religious and social

---

[131] Smallwood, The Jews Under Roman Rule, 376–77. Judge (The First Christians, 441) comments on Matt 17:24–27 (cf. Rom 13:7) in relation to the Christian payment of the Jewish tax: "Why did Christians not take this as their cue to pay the Jewish tax (which had switched the old temple-tax to the rebuilding of the temple Jupiter Capitolinus)? It would have spared them two centuries of misunderstandings and haphazard persecution."

[132] See Richard J. Cassidy, John's Gospel in New Perspective: Christology and the Realities of Roman Power (Maryknoll: Orbis 1992); John and Empire: Initial Explorations (London: T&T Clark, 2008).

[133] Lampe (From Paul to Valentinus, 198–205) argues that Flavia Domitilla is a Christian.

[134] Harry J. Leon, The Jews of Ancient Rome (Philadelphia: Jewish Publication of America, 1960), 252.

[135] Jeffers, Conflict at Rome, 62.

activities of the Christians. As it was, Domitian's successor, Nerva, minted a series of coins (BM Coins, Rom. Emp. III 15, 17, 19) with the legend FISCI IVDAICI COLVMNIA SVBLATA ("Jewish Tax Misrepresentation Removed"), thereby overturning the legal abuse that had occurred when some non-Jews were forced to pay the tax unjustly.[136] While Domitian may have unofficially accepted the court flattery of "Lord and God,"[137] there is no numismatic or inscriptional evidence corroborating Domitian's claim to the title.[138] Last, we do not know anything about the context of the persecutions predating Pliny: significantly, the governor does not implicate Domitian or appeal to his policy as a precedent for handling the Christians in Bithynia.

5.2. Domitian, the Book of Revelation, and the Later Christian Evidence

The explicit evidence for Domitian being a persecutor of believers emanates from later Christian tradition. At a general level, Eusebius states that, after having banished and put to death many of the notable men of Rome, Domitian "finally showed himself the successor of Nero's campaign of hostility to God," being "the second to promote persecution against us, though his father, Vespasian, had planned no evil against us" (Hist. eccl. 3.17). Tertullian (Apol. 5.4) speaks of a limited persecution under Domitian: "Domitian, too, who was a good deal of a Nero in cruelty, attempted it; but, being in some degree human, he soon stopped what had begun, and restored those he had banished." In 1 Clem. 1.1, Clement of Rome (d. ca. AD 99) points to "the sudden and repeated misfortunes and calamities that have befallen us." Lactantius (ca. AD 250–325) refers to an unnamed tyrant after Nero, but mention of his *damnatio memoriae* identifies the ruler as Domitian (Mort. 3.2–3). Little else is said that is informative:[139] theological polemic rather than sober history marks the commentary (e.g., Mort. 3.1–2: "impious hands" stretched "against the Lord"; "spurred on by the prompting of demons," etc.).

More specifically, Hegesippus (ca. AD 110–180), cited by Eusebius (Hist. eccl. 3.19.5), elaborates that Domitian did not "condemn them at all, but despised them as simple folk [ὡς εὐτελῶν καταφρονήσαντα], released them, and decreed an end to the persecution to the church." The "Flavia Domitilla" tradition (Dio Cassius, Hist. 67.14.1–3) is modified and expanded by Eusebius. Domitilla becomes the "niece" as opposed to the "wife" of Flavius Clemens and she is identified as a Christian (Hist. eccl. 3.18.34): "banished with many others to the island of Pontia as a testimony to Christ" (AD 96). Last, Melito of Sardis (Hist. eccl. 4.26.9), in a letter written to Marcus Aurelius (AD 161–180) and cited by Eusebius (Hist. eccl. 4.26.9), says that Nero and Domitian slandered Christian teaching, fostering thereby "the unreasonable custom of

---

[136] John D. Grainger, Nerva and the Roman Succession Crisis of AD 96–99 (London: Routledge, 2003), 53. See Smallwood, The Jews Under Roman Rule, 377–78.

[137] Brian W. Jones, The Emperor Domitian (London: Routledge, 1992), 109; Gradel, Emperor Worship and Roman Religion, 160, 190–91, 227–28, 260.

[138] Thompson, The Book of Revelation, 105.

[139] J. L. Creed, Lactantius De mortibus persecutorum (Oxford: Clarendon, 1984), 83.

falsely accusing Christians." However, Melito further claims that Trajan and Hadrian wrote rebukes to any who dared to take "new measures against the Christians," with Hadrian and his son, Marcus Aurelius, writing to the proconsul Fundanus, the governor of Asia, on the issue (Hist. eccl. 4.26.10).

Again, how reliable is the later Christian evidence for a Domitianic persecution? At the very least, if there was a persecution inaugurated by Domitian, it was temporary. We have already commented on the unlikelihood of Flavia Domitilla being a Christian, even if she is so championed by Eusebius.[140] Further, as Barnes has argued, it was more likely at this time that the "problem" of the Christians would come first to the notice of a provincial governor rather than the Roman ruler in the capital.[141] This is the case with the investigation of the Christians by Pliny the Younger, discussed below, and also, as we have seen, with the unilateral actions of the governor of Asia, Fundanus, against Christians, requiring imperial intervention. Moreover, the Christian evidence is characterized by strong polemic and it is difficult to avoid the impression that the most popularly-hated rulers in Rome, Nero and Domitian, were further demonized in later Christian tradition as "anti-Christs" and credited, in Domitian's case, with persecutions for which there is little evidence.

But surely the book of Revelation points to a Domitianic persecution in the early nineties?[142] For example, there is the mention of the martyrdom of Antipas at Pergamum (Rev 2:13). The dragon (Satan) gives the Roman ruler (or the Empire), "the beast out of the sea," its power (13:2–4), and encourages it to attack the church (13:7). Last, the provincial governor of Asia, "the beast out of the earth,"[143] decides to kill those who did not submit to the imperial cult (13:15–17; cf. 2:10–13; 6:9–10; 16:6; 17:6; 18:24; 20:4). But a Domitianic dating for Revelation is not thereby assured: Robinson has made a convincing case for the Apocalypse being written in ca. AD 69.[144] Furthermore, while some of the Asian churches suffer martyrdom and privation because of the pressures of the imperial cult and pagan culture (Rev 2:8–11; 3:7–13), the fundamental issue for several of the other late first-century churches in Asia Minor is cultural accommodation (Rev 2:1–7; 2:12–17; 2:18–29).[145] Some of the congregations, especially Sardis and Laodicea, were not facing martyrdom because they

---

[140] Barnes, "Legislation," 36, comments: "The temptation for later Christians to see in Flavia Domitilla a sympathy for, or adherence to, Christianity was irresistible: even the executed consul Flavius Clemens eventually became a Christian."
[141] Barnes, "Legislation," 48.
[142] J. Nelson Kraybill, Imperial Cult and Commerce in John's Apocalypse (Sheffield: Sheffield Academic, 1996); Apocalypse and Allegiance: Worship, Politics and Devotion in the Book of Revelation (Grand Rapids: Brazos, 2010); Judge, The First Christians, 424–26.
[143] Simon R. F. Price (Rituals and Power: The Roman Imperial Cult in Asia Minor [Cambridge: Cambridge University Press, 1984], 197–98) argues that the "beast out of the earth" is the High Priest of Ephesus, supervising the cult of Domitian in the city.
[144] John A. T. Robinson, Redating the New Testament (London: SCM, 1976), 221–53; J. Christian Wilson, "The Problem of the Domitianic Date of Revelation," NTS 39.4 (1993): 587–605; Thompson, The Book of Revelation, passim.
[145] Mark B. Stephens, Annihilation or Renewal? The Meaning and Function of New Creation in the Book of Revelation (Tübingen: Mohr Siebeck, 2011), 152–54, 261–62.

"appear to have made peace with the wider culture" (Rev 3:1b, 17).[146] Thus John underscores that believers must not participate "in compromising acts of allegiance to persons or institutions not under the Lordship of God and the Lamb."[147]

In conclusion, as Creed states, "the evidence certainly indicates that the church was exposed to harassment during the last decade of the first century, but is far from establishing that there was a systematic persecution."[148] What difference did the rescripts of Trajan and Nero make to the fate of Christians under imperial rule?

6. Trajan, Hadrian, and the Christians

In AD 111 the provincial governor of Bithynia-Pontus, Pliny the Younger, wrote to the Roman ruler, Trajan, regarding the difficulty he faced in never having been present at an "examination of Christians" (Ep. 10.96.1: cognitionibus de Christianis). Pliny knew nothing about the punishments that had been meted out to believers in the past, the grounds for commencing an investigation, and the extent to which the investigation should be pursued (Ep. 10.96.1–2). We do not know the location and time of these formal trials (cogitio) against Christians (is Pliny referring to Bithynia-Pontus or elsewhere?), but clearly they had been presided over by an official with imperium ("power"), helped by a consilium (advisory "council": cf. Ep. 6.31).[149] But several pressing issues were forcing the hand of the new Bithynian governor. The charges against the Christians were becoming more widespread and varied. There were high numbers of the accused, male and female, from every age and class (Ep. 10.96.4). Anonymous pamphleteers were circulating the names of the accused (Ep. 10.96.5) and informers were providing further names (10.96.6). Clearly, popular hatred for the Christians at Bithynia was spiraling out of control, though we must not discount the self-serving motives of some of the informers.

The reasons for this intense loathing, as articulated by Pliny, were economic, cultic, and contagious. The sale of sacrificial meat was substantially reduced with the dramatic decline in temple attendance due to the increasing conversions to Christianity (Ep. 10.96.10);[150] the sacred rites in the deserted temples were barely performed, thereby violating the region's contract with its protecting deities (10.96.10); and, last, not only were cities infected by this wretched cult (superstitionis istius contagion pervagata est) but also the

---

[146] Stephens, Annihilation, 153.

[147] Kraybill, Apocalypse and Allegiance, 45.

[148] Creed, Lactantius De mortibus persecutorum, 84. Smallwood (The Jews under Roman Rule, 381) writes: "The tradition grows steadily stronger with time, but even when the meager evidence is elaborated into a full-scale persecution, the Church Fathers find few concrete instances of Christian sufferings to provide verisimilitude."

[149] Betty Radice, Pliny Letters Books 8–10 Panegyricus (Cambridge, MA: Harvard University Press, 1969), 285 n. 2.

[150] See Cook, Roman Attitudes, 222–27.

hinterlands of the cities—towns, villages, and rural districts (10.96.9). The popular fear, resentment, and paranoia generated by the rapid progress of the Christian movement are readily apparent in Pliny's account. The book of Acts recounts a similar rising popular anxiety over the advent of early Christianity, underscoring the financial losses to prophetic practitioners, magicians, and local cultic craftsmen (Acts 16:19; 19:20, 23–25, 36), as well as its affront to the Roman mos maiorum (16:20–21; 17:5–6) and powerful indigenous deities (19:26–28, 34). Thus the traditional practice of religio at Bithynia was being violated by this superstitio.

Pliny is also writing because he is uncertain (a) whether the retraction of Christian belief ensures automatic pardon, or (b) whether such retraction avails nothing in mitigating punishment, and (c) whether the profession of the mere name of Christianus is punishable, or (d) whether attention should be paid to the crimes (flagitia) popularly associated with the name (Ep. 10.96.2). In formalizing a legal process in the absence of any law declaring Christianity a capital crime,[151] Pliny had devised a comprehensive test for those who denied that they were or ever had been Christians: namely, (a) the repetition of a formula of invocation, devised by the governor himself, before the cult statues of the gods; (b) the offer of incense and wine before the statue of Trajan (cf. Suetonius, Aug. 35.3), and (c) the reviling of the name of Christ (Ep. 10.96.5).

Pliny recounts the investigatory process he undertook with those who had admitted culpability to the charge of being Christians but who had subsequently denied it (Ep. 10.96.3–4). The process is entirely transparent. The threefold repetition of the central investigatory question—the confession of the name of Christ alone is the litmus test of guilt leading to execution—is designed to encourage the accused not to aggravate their crime by further stubbornness and obstinacy. Any retraction of the name of Christ by the accused in this interrogatory process, presumably, would be tested for its genuineness by the tests outlined above.[152] As Pliny explains:

> For the moment this is the line I have taken with all persons brought before me on the charge of being Christians [*Christiani*]. I have asked them in person if they are Christians [*Christiani*], and if they admit it, I repeat the question a second and a third time, with the warning of the punishment awaiting them. If they persist, I order them to be led away for execution; for, whatever the nature of their admission, I am convinced that their stubbornness [*pertinaciam*] and unshakeable obstinacy [*inflexibilem obstinationem*] ought not to go unpunished. There have been others similarly fanatical who are Roman citizens. I have entered them on the list of persons to be sent to Rome for trial.[153]

---

[151] Barnes, "Legislation," 36.

[152] Trajan, in his response to Pliny on the issue (Ep. 10.97), is entirely clear on the issue: "in the case of anyone who denies that he is a Christian, and makes it clear that he is not by offering prayers to our gods, he is to be pardoned as a result of his repentance however his past conduct may be."

[153] Barnes, "Legislation," 36 observes that non-citizens convicted of Christianity were executed on the spot, whereas guilty citizens were sent to Rome for punishment.

But, as noted, Pliny also had to determine whether there were any *flagitia* associated with the confession of the name of Christ. Significantly, as we see from Pliny's letter below (Ep. 10.96.7–8), none were found. But a probing of the popular caricatures of Christians emerges from Pliny's investigation. Pliny's telling comment that Christians took "food of an ordinary, harmless kind" and were not guilty of "adultery" echoes prominent stereotypes of Christians: namely, that they practiced cannibalism and sexual immorality.[154] The rites of a depraved *superstitio* over against traditional Roman *religio* are also indicated by the reference to the verses chanted to Christ as if to a god (quasi deo).[155] As Benko notes, Livy's description of the Bacchanalia (186 BC) has perhaps colored Pliny's understanding of Christians.[156] Pliny sums up the results of his investigation thus:

> They also declared that the sum total of their guilt or error amounted to no more than this: they had met regularly before dawn on a fixed day to chant verses alternatively among themselves in honor of Christ as if to a god [*quasi deo*], and to bind themselves by oath, not for any criminal purpose, but to abstain from theft, robbery and adultery, to commit no breach of trust and not to deny a deposit when called upon to restore it. After this ceremony it had been their custom to disperse and reassemble later to take food of an ordinary, harmless kind; but they had in fact given up this practice since my edict, issued on your instructions, which banned all political societies [*hetaerias*]. This made me decide it was all the more necessary to extract the truth by torture from two slave women, whom they call deaconesses. I found nothing but a degenerate sort of cult carried to extravagant lengths [*superstitionem pravam et immodicam*].

Significantly, Pliny's edict against political societies, issued upon Trajan's instructions, includes the *Christianoi* as a group because, as Trajan reminded Pliny on another occasion (Ep. 10.34), "it is societies [hetaeriae] like these which have been responsible for the political disturbances in your province, particularly in its cities."[157] Notwithstanding, in his response to Pliny's letter, Trajan advises his governor that there is "no fixed formula" in handling

---

[154] Benko, Pagan Rome and the Early Christians, 70–72; Wilken, The Christians, 17–21. Contra, Cook, Roman Attitudes, 213–14. Note, however the important methodological caution of Wilken (The Christians, 21 [original emphasis]): "it must be noted—indeed emphasized—that the accusations of promiscuity and ritual murder appear only in Christian authors. They are not present in the writings of the pagan critics of Christianity." Wilken (The Christians, 21–22 n. 11) helpfully adds: "It may be that the omission is insignificant and due to the fragmentary transmission of the writings of pagan critics, but it may also be that serious critics had more important things to say against Christianity." Additionally, the Christian authors may simply be reporting the slurs of the common populace, in whose circles the educated pagan critics did not normally move.

[155] See Cook, Roman Attitudes, 201–6. While the antiphonal singing or chanting of the early Christians was not "completely alien to a Roman" (202), worshipping quasi deo a criminal crucified by the Romans almost a century ago would have appeared unconventional and threatening politically even to the methodical and measured Pliny. Surely it violated traditional religio?

[156] Benko, Pagan Rome and the Early Christians, 11; Wilken, The Christians, 17.

[157] See Cook, Roman Attitudes, 214–15.

investigations. If the charge is proven, the accused is to be punished. He also endorses pardon for those who recant and offer "prayers to our gods"—exactly the endorsement of the Roman Pantheon that one would expect from the Roman Pontifex Maximus. But Christians, significantly, were not to be hunted out, and "pamphlets circulated anonymously must play no part in any accusation."

Finally, Hadrian's rescript to Minucius Fundanus, proconsul of Asia in AD 122/123, is found in two versions, one from Justin (1 Apol. 68.3–10), the other from Rufinus (Hist. 4.9.1), who, arguably, had sources additional to those found in Eusebius (Hist. eccl. 4.9).[158] Hadrian follows the policy of Trajan, making no change to the legal position previously enunciated. The Roman ruler allows provincials to make accusations against Christians in open court, but not on the basis of "opinions or mere outcries" (Eusebius, Hist. eccl. 4.9). Indeed, Hadrian's rescript demonstrates, to some extent, a "protective attitude towards the Christians."[159] Hadrian strongly resists the evil perpetrated by informers in the legal process because they use accusations as a pretext for blackmail (Justin, 1 Apol. 68.6.7, 10). Thus Hadrian strengthens the penalties against such duplicitous accusers: "By Hercules, if anyone brings the matter forward for the purpose of blackmail, investigate strenuously and be careful to inflict penalties adequate to the crime" (Eusebius, Hist. eccl. 4.9). Unlike Pliny's letter to Trajan, however, Hadrian's rescript affords us no insight into the motives of the locals for opposing Christianity.[160]

7. Conclusion

We have seen that the confession of the name Christianus is the litmus test for determining the guilt of accused Christians facing the Roman authorities. Notwithstanding, other issues aggravate the "problem," over and above the proverbial stubbornness and obstinacy of believers, for the Roman ruler and his provincial governors. The authorities needed to investigate the presence of flagitia, even if they were ultimately disproved, accompanying the fundamental charge. The challenge of handling appropriately the accusations of anonymous pamphleteers and informers had to be addressed. There was also the necessity to respond to widespread anxiety about the increasing public profile of the Christianoi. It was also imperative in the interrogation process to explore—if our later Christian sources can be trusted on the issue (see n. 154 above)—the lurid stereotypes of Christian morality and, equally, the unconventional social relations and separatism of believers articulated in the New Testament.

In this regard, ancient historians have to give greater recognition to the New Testament documents for the light they throw on these issues, either by way of explaining partially the reasons for the hostile reactions to the Christian communities, or appreciating how the early Christians countered their

---

[158] See Cook, Roman Attitudes, 261–62 for English translations.
[159] Alessandro Galimberti, "Hadrian, Eleusis, and the Beginning of Christian Apologetics," in Hadrian and the Christians, ed. Marco Rizzo (Berlin: de Gruyter, 2010), 82.
[160] Engberg, Impulsore Chresto, 214.

opponents' polemic regarding their punishment, or locating in the corpus subtle allusions to contemporary persecutions (e.g., Mark 13:9–12; 1 Pet 4:12–19). The absence of any Roman writings on the first-century persecutions before the early second century AD makes the New Testament writers vital contemporaneous witnesses. The plethora of issues to which the Roman authorities had to respond, and which invisibly pressured them to act, must be acknowledged for a nuanced understanding of the persecutions. Surprisingly, the Roman rulers and their provincial governors could respond in ways that afforded believers limited protection in the face of informers. Largely, the problem was first drawn to the attention of the governor well before the Roman ruler intervened (if at all). Therefore the notion of Roman rulers issuing empire-wide edicts against believers in our period is misconceived. The responses are more ad hoc, negotiated if required with the ruler and his consilium, but mostly worked out in the absence of prior imperial legislation by the governor himself. But this represents an entirely ruler-based approach to the early persecutions and it inevitably creates its own methodological blind spots. There are other equally-valuable perspectives that must be considered.

We have emphasized the importance of the Roman ideology and practice of religio as the continuous invisible influence across the generations shaping both popular and authority-based reactions. The fear of superstitio, based around foreign cults and their violations of the mos maiorum and Rome's reciprocal contract with the gods, features prominently. Therefore, a proper appreciation of this ideological background helps us to understand Nero's persecution of the Christians as the appropriate response of Rome's Pontifex Maximus in assuaging perceived divine wrath, as opposed to the ruler being motivated by popular perceptions of his complicity in the fire at Rome. It also helps us to see why Paul's eschatological, prophetic, and teleological gospel exposed the Roman Christians to further political scrutiny in the capital as they worked out its social, ethical, and communal implications. Further, the accompanying Latin language of contagion, misanthropy, and political association, to cite a few examples from our Roman texts, spans the generations: the Romans apply this terminology equally to Jews and Christians. In this context, the increasingly prominent profile of the early believers, and their countercultural attitudes and praxis, would inevitably provoke irrational fears and paranoia. This was the case irrespective of the politically quietist stance taken by the early believers, in contrast to the tragic Jewish revolts during our period (AD 60–70, 132–135). Last, the reactions of the general populace in the persecutions need to be taken more seriously. As the book of Acts reminds us, the threat to the local economy, the mos maiorum and the indigenous cults posed by the early Christians thrusts the irate members of eastern Mediterranean cities onto the historical stage as zealous opponents of the Christians. Our elitist Roman sources do not capture this element of the early persecutions as effectively as the Christian writers in the New Testament.

Recommended Reading

Barnes, Timothy D. "Legislation against the Christians." JRS 58.1–2 (1968): 32–50.

Benko, Stephen. Pagan Rome and the Early Christians. Bloomington, IN: Indiana University Press, 1984.

Cook, John Granger. Roman Attitudes Toward the Christians from Claudius to Hadrian. Tübingen: Mohr Siebeck, 2010.

Engberg, Jakob. Impulsore Chresto: Opposition to Christianity in the Roman Empire c. 50–250 AD. Frankfurt am Main: Peter Lang, 2007.

Frend, W. H. C. Martyrdom and Persecution in the Early Church: A Study in the Conflict from the Maccabees to Donatus. Cambridge: James Clarke, 2008.

Keresztes, Paul. "The Imperial Roman Government and the Christian Church I: From Nero to the Severi." *ARNW* 23.1: 247–315. Part 2, Principat, 23.1. Edited by Hildegard Temporini and Wolfgang Haase. New York: de Gruyter, 1979.

Moss, Candida. *The Myth of Persecution: How Early Christians Invented a Story of Martyrdom*. New York: HarperOne, 2013.

Rizzo, Marco, ed. Hadrian and the Christians. New York: de Gruyter, 2010.

Sherwin-White, A. N. "The Early Persecutions and Roman Law Again." JTS 3.2 (1952): 199–213.

Sordi, Marta. The Christians and the Roman Empire. Norman, OK: University of Oklahoma Press, 1986.

Spence, Stephen. Parting of the Ways: The Roman Church as a Case Study. Leuven: Peeters, 2004.

Ste. Croix, G. E. M. de. Christian Persecution, Martyrdom and Orthodoxy. Oxford: Oxford University Press, 2006.

Wilken, Robert Louis. The Christians as the Romans Saw Them. 2nd ed. New Haven/London: Yale University Press, 2003.

11. Aliens and Strangers: Minority Group Rhetoric in the Later New Testament Writings

Tim MacBride

For any minority group to survive in the face of pressure from the dominant culture to conform, certain strategies need to be adopted. Otherwise, over time, the minority group will cease to exist. The group needs to legitimate its reasons for being different from the majority, to insulate itself from the disapproval of outsiders, and to forge a strong sense of identity that prioritizes group membership above participation in the wider society. In short, a minority group needs to create an alternative world view and to articulate it to both insiders and outsiders. The kind of discourse this gives rise to is often called *minority group rhetoric*[1]—the persuasive speech and writing that seeks to define, legitimate, and insulate a given subculture against the cultural majority.

The various documents contained in the New Testament are essentially minority group rhetoric. That is, they were addressed to people who were different from the majority due to their distinctive beliefs and practices: some doubly so, if they were diaspora Jews (already a minority in the Greco-Roman empire) who had become followers of Jesus. Moreover, many of the New Testament documents have an obvious concern to persuade their addressees to resist the pressure to conform.[2] This pressure was not just the threat of physical persecution, but also the more mundane struggle of being "different" in a world that expected conformity.

In this chapter we will seek to read four such New Testament writings through this lens: 1 Peter, Hebrews, 1 John, and Revelation. Drawing together some of the findings of scholars who have employed theories from the social sciences, we will produce an overview of minority group strategies used in New Testament texts. We will then focus on each of the four texts in turn to see how understanding them as minority group rhetoric helps us appreciate not only their content, but also how they were intended to function within the communities to which they were addressed.

---

[1] See Richard Andrews, *A Theory of Contemporary Rhetoric* (New York: Routledge, 2014), 59–61; Robert Wallace Winslow, *The Emergence of Deviant Minorities, Social Problems and Social Change*, Social Problems Series (San Ramon, CA: Consensus Publishers, 1972), preface.

[2] David A. deSilva, *Honor, Patronage, Kinship & Purity: Unlocking New Testament Culture* (Downers Grove, IL: InterVarsity, 2000), 50.

Tim MacBride

This is, of course, not the only lens through which these texts can be viewed; nor is it suggested that these texts can be reduced simply to a set of generic rhetorical strategies independent of the theology they espouse. Rather, the New Testament writers—convinced that the good news of Jesus Christ necessitates the formation of a new community, which lives out the values of the kingdom he proclaimed in a manner that is both different from, yet attractive to the world around it—seek to nurture such a community by employing many of the strategies common to minority groups, within a consciously Christian framework.[3]

For twenty-first century believers this is no mere academic exercise if we understand ourselves as a minority group, facing daily pressure to conform to our own dominant culture. By understanding the intended function of these ancient minority group texts, we will allow them to speak and to function afresh within our own communities of faith.

1. The Background: Identity and Honor in the First Century

This presumes, of course, that being in a minority group is actually a problem, or a difficulty to overcome. In present day Western culture this is masked somewhat by an individualistic mindset and a general rhetoric that encourages people to "be themselves." Despite this, most people still feel pressure from society to conform to certain behavioral norms, and many struggle with self-esteem as they measure themselves against others or the unrealistic ideals promoted by advertising. Moreover, members of ethnic and cultural minority groups continue to feel isolated from mainstream society and often cluster together for support. This is because we derive our sense of self at least partly from others: their behavior, and their attitude towards us.

This was all the more so in the first-century world. In his influential essay entitled "The First-Century Personality" Bruce Malina describes the ancient Mediterranean sense of self as being essentially "dyadic" or "collectivistic." That is, ancient Mediterranean people "perceive themselves and form their self-image in terms of what others perceive and feed back to them."[4] Such people are guided not primarily by an internal sense of right and wrong, but by the attitudes of their reference group of others. This is reflected in the etymology of the Greek and Latin words for "conscience" (συνείδησις and *conscientia* respectively) being literally "with-knowledge." A person of conscience is thus originally someone who derives "with" others their knowledge of what are appropriate attitudes and behavior, and has to some extent internalized what others think and say about them.[5]

---

[3] Note the similarities with how Paul, for example, employs strategies common to the rhetoric of reconciliation, yet with a Christian "twist" in Philemon, and appeals to patronage conventions in light of God as patron in Philippians (4:10–20).
[4] Bruce J. Malina, *The New Testament World: Insights from Cultural Anthropology*, 3rd ed. (Louisville, KY: Westminster John Knox, 2001), 62.
[5] Malina, *The New Testament World*, 58–59.

The outworking of such an other-focused sense of self is a society based on honor and shame. Those who do what is right or "normal," as defined by the majority, are praised as being honorable, while those who deviate are censured as being shameful. In such a culture, the pursuit of honor (for oneself and one's family) is considered axiomatic,[6] and a supreme good: above health, wealth, and even life itself.[7] Most significantly for our purposes, honor is derived from the attitudes of the wider society or group to which an individual belongs.[8]

This quite naturally raises difficulties when a person belongs to a group that has a definition of what is honorable that differs from that of the wider society. In fact, significant social conflict occurs when groups disagree over what is honorable.[9] This conflict can be seen in the attitudes and actions of the dominant culture in seeking to shame back into conformity those who deviate, and in the response of the minority culture in either acquiescing (thereby ceasing to exist) or responding with strategies designed to maintain the group's sense of honor despite outsiders' disapproval. Diaspora Jews faced this situation if they chose to live by Torah, inviting contempt from the Gentile majority culture but maintaining honor within the minority Jewish culture. Many Jewish writings of the period encouraged their readers to make the "right" choice.[10] A similar situation was experienced—even invited—by Greco-Roman philosophical schools such as the Cynics, who often adopted unconventional lifestyles in order to demonstrate their deliberate rejection of other people as a source of identity and honor.[11]

This was also the place in which first-century followers of Jesus found themselves, often challenged on two fronts. On one front, Jewish believers were seen as dishonorable by their fellow Jews for reasons such as Jesus' shameful death on a cross, his reinterpretation of Torah (especially his radical statements on Sabbath, the Temple, and food laws), and the influx of Gentiles into the church without requiring circumcision or Torah obedience.[12] On the other front, Greco-Roman society considered Christians to be dishonorable not only because of Jesus' shameful death, but also because of their rejection of the gods and emperor worship. Devotion to the gods, although largely superficial, was woven into the fabric of society, so that non-participation was viewed as a rejection of an important part of the majority culture and a threat

---

[6] See Seneca, *Ben.* 4.16.2: "All our arguments start from this settled point, that honor is pursued for no reason except because it is honor."

[7] See Isocrates, *Demon.* 43: "Strive by all means to live in security, but if ever it falls to your lot to face the dangers of battle, seek to preserve your life, but with honor and not with disgrace; for death is the sentence which fate has passed on all mankind, but to die nobly is the special honor which nature has reserved for the good."

[8] deSilva, *Honor, Patronage*, 25.

[9] Halvor Moxnes, "Honor and Shame," in *The Social Sciences and New Testament Interpretation*, ed. Richard L. Rohrbaugh (Peabody, MA: Hendrickson, 1996), 26–27.

[10] deSilva, *Honor, Patronage*, 39.

[11] Alain De Botton, *Status Anxiety* (London: Hamish Hamilton, 2004), 119–20.

[12] deSilva, *Honor, Patronage*, 48–49.

to the gods' continuing favor.[13] Likewise, the Christians' non-participation in the emperor cult at various times—along with their rhetoric of a greater ruler who will one day rule over all earthly powers—was seen as a threat to the Roman peace and an affront to the emperors as guardians of stability and bringers of prosperity.[14] In short, the fledgling church was a minority group, under pressure from all sides to abandon its distinctiveness and conform.

2. The Tension: Distinctive Yet Attractive

For the church not to conform to this pressure required strategies to maintain its distinctiveness in the eyes of both members and outsiders. In his pioneering work on the development of religious minority groups, Bryan Wilson has shown that such a group has two options: isolation or insulation. The former is the more straightforward, but is not an option for what he terms a "conversionist sect" such as early Christianity.[15] This is because of its founder's command to go and make disciples, which necessarily involves contact with and openness to the wider society.

For this reason we see two tendencies within the rhetoric of such groups, the first of which is an instinct to draw a boundary between the group and the rest of society, described by Wilson thus:

> If the sect is to persist as an organization it must not only separate its members from the world, but must also maintain the dissimilarity of its values from those of the secular society. Its members must not normally be allowed to accept the values of the status system of the external world. The sect must see itself as marginal to the wider society ... [and] the consciousness of the inapplicability of the standards of the outside world must be retained.... Status must be status within the sect, and this should be the only group to which the status-conscious individual makes reference.[16]

The second tendency is a concern to make this boundary permeable, minimizing the obstacles for an outsider to become an insider. This is not an easy task, Wilson notes, as "the social status of its members may radically affect its prospect of winning recruits."[17] The group will often seek to overcome this by portraying their distinctive values and behaviors in attractive terms, with the ultimate aim of winning over outsiders by their very distinctiveness.[18] In 1 Peter, for example, Spörri notes a pervasive juxtaposition of "total separation from the essence and behavior of the world"

---

[13] See, for example, Isocrates, *Demon.* 13; Plutarch, *Mor.* 1125E. A fuller discussion can be found in Ramsay MacMullen, *Paganism in the Roman Empire* (New Haven: Yale University Press, 1981), 40, 62–73.
[14] deSilva, *Honor, Patronage*, 45–48.
[15] Bryan R. Wilson, "An Analysis of Sect Development," *ASR* 24 (1959): 3–15 (10).
[16] Wilson, "Sect Development," 12–13.
[17] Wilson, "Sect Development," 13.
[18] John H. Elliott, *A Home for the Homeless: A Social-Scientific Criticism of 1 Peter, Its Situation and Strategy* (Philadelphia: Fortress, 1990), 108.

with a call to "solidarity with the world through [the doing of good and suffering] with the goal of winning people for God."[19]

Thus there is an inherent tension in the rhetorical strategies of such a group as it seeks to be separate from the world while at the same time making converts. Group members are, as Green observes, "bicultural, living between two worlds, with the one a source of tension with the other."[20] The group needs to remain both distinctive *from* the world yet attractive *to* the world, which is a difficult balance to maintain. Wilson concludes, "for each sect there must be a position of optimal tension, where any greater degree of hostility against the world portends direct conflict, and any less suggests accommodation to worldly values."[21]

3. Minority Group Strategies

This leads to our focus on the strategies used by the New Testament writers to create and maintain these strong-yet-permeable boundaries. The following discussion seeks to build on the work of pioneers like Malina, Elliott, deSilva, and others, presenting the rhetorical strategies used by minority groups in the form of answers to five key questions:[22]

1. Approval: whose opinions do we care about?
2. Disapproval: whose opinions can we ignore?
3. Identity: who are we?
4. Practice: how do we live?
5. Worldview: how do we see the world?

Only a small number of biblical examples will be given as these concepts are introduced because they provide the framework that we will use in our subsequent investigation of the minority group rhetoric in 1 Peter, Hebrews, 1 John, and Revelation.

---

[19] Theophil Spörri, *Der Gemeindegedanke im ersten Petrusbrief* (Gütersloh: C. Bertelsman, 1925), 245 translated by John H. Elliott in his *A Home for the Homeless*, 109.

[20] Joel B. Green, *1 Peter*, The Two Horizons New Testament Commentary (Grand Rapids: Eerdmans, 2007), 288.

[21] Wilson, "Sect Development," 12.

[22] These questions have been used in preference to the three components of Tajfel's social identity theory—namely, cognitive, evaluative, and emotional—for two reasons: the focus is on the *rhetorical strategies* used to form social identity rather than the identity itself; and these questions have been formulated through an analysis of the rhetorical strategies found in the New Testament itself, rather than through imposing an existing social model on the biblical texts. However, there are, obviously, strong connections between the two models. See Henri Tajfel, "Interindividual Behavior and Intergroup Behavior," in *Differentiation between Social Groups: Studies in the Social Psychology of Intergroup Relations,* ed. Henri Tajfel (London: Academic, 1978), 28–29, and Philip F. Esler, "An Outline of Social Identity Theory," in *T&T Clark Handbook to Social Identity in the New Testament,* ed. J. Brian Tucker and Coleman A. Baker (London: Bloomsbury, 2014), 17.

3.1. Approval: Whose Opinions Do We Care About?

As noted above, for a culture in which notions of identity and honor were derived from the opinion of others, it was not sufficient for a minority group simply to demand that members ignore the disapproval of the outside world and proudly march to the beat of their own drum. Instead, the collection of significant others to which members looked in order to know what values and behaviors were honorable—which deSilva terms the "court of reputation"— needed to be redefined.[23] The wider society had to be removed from this court of reputation, which could well have included parents, other family members, friends, and for Jewish believers, the synagogue community. In its place stood the two primary sources for a believer's identity and honor: God and his people.

In contrast with the temporal judgments of human society, God's judgments count for eternity. This is one reason the New Testament texts maintain a strong focus on eschatological judgment and highlight how God's values are different from those of society.[24] A person can live by either set of values, but not both; a choice must be made between rival courts of reputation.

To help maintain the resolve to live according to God's values, the community of faith is presented as another reference group for one's sense of honor. They are "the most visible and, in many senses, the most available reflection of God's estimation of the individual,"[25] which is one reason the New Testament authors are keen to nurture such a community. For a person from a collectivist culture, the existence of other people who share the often countercultural values of God is essential to survival. Not only is the community an embodied reflection of these alternative values, it also provides a place where solidarity and encouragement can be found for those suffering acute rejection by the dominant culture (e.g., Heb 10:24–25; 13:1–3).

Ultimately, of course, it is not the community that has the authority to draw the group boundaries, but God. Indeed, his sovereignty provides not only the reason he should be at the center of a person's court of reputation but also the reassurance of eventual vindication. The New Testament writers present God as not only the one who is about to judge his world, but also the one who cares about his people enough to vindicate them at the appointed time in the future, and the one who has the power to sustain them in the meantime.[26]

Seeking the approval of God (and his people) rather than the approval of the wider society is thus presented as being *advantageous*, at least in the long

---

[23] deSilva, *Honor, Patronage*, 40.

[24] deSilva, *Honor, Patronage*, 55–58.

[25] deSilva, *Honor, Patronage*, 58–59.

[26] John H. Elliott, "The Jewish Messianic Movement: From Faction to Sect," in *Modelling Early Christianity: Social-Scientific Studies of the New Testament in Its Context*, ed. Philip Francis Esler (London: Routledge, 1995), 88.

term. This is the fundamental character of deliberative discourse:[27] it seeks to persuade people to adopt certain values and behaviors because they are to their advantage.[28] Frequently, this involves presenting a greater advantage in the future as opposed to a lesser advantage in the immediate present.[29] Much of the New Testament is deliberative in nature, urging its audience to endure temporary disadvantage in this life in order to gain eternal advantage in the age to come (1 Pet 1:4–6; Heb 11:26; 12:2; 1 John 2:17).

3.2. Disapproval: Whose Opinions Can We Ignore?

Although redefining the court of reputation acts in a positive way to insulate group members from the external pressure to conform, it cannot entirely prevent them from hearing the messages of disapproval from the dominant culture. Therefore, there must also be a negative counterpoint, providing a reinterpretation of this disapproval by outsiders, giving reasons it can be ignored.

At a most basic level, outsiders are portrayed as being ignorant of group values and the group narrative, and their conduct is depicted as dishonorable (1 Pet 4:4).[30] Thus their disapproval is recast as no bad thing; it is in fact a kind of validation because it is evidence that group members are *not* ignorant and dishonorable.[31] Ultimately, the outsiders who shame the group will themselves be shamed, in a "divine reversal."[32] Therefore, disapproval is to be expected and should be seen in a positive light (1 Pet 4:13–16; cf. Acts 5:41).

Moreover, the fact that group members are pre-warned to expect it means that when this disapproval occurs it further reinforces the group's narrative.[33] When New Testament authors tell their members in advance not to be "surprised" when they are shamed by society (1 Pet 4:12; 1 John 3:13; following the example of Jesus' Farewell Discourse, John 15:18–25), the subsequent fulfillment of these predictions vindicates the authors and gives power to the other rhetorical strategies they employ to reinterpret disapproval.

---

[27] The three species, or *genera*, of Greco-Roman rhetoric were forensic (which grew out of the law courts and focused on proving or disproving allegations about the past), epideictic (which accompanied civic occasions and sought to praise those who were worthy of honor in the present), and deliberative (which arose out of the city councils and attempted to persuade hearers to adopt a future course of action based on advantage).

[28] Aristotle, *Rhet.* 1.3.5; Margaret M. Mitchell, *Paul and the Rhetoric of Reconciliation* (Louisville, KY: Westminster John Knox, 1993), 27.

[29] Quintilian, *Inst.* 3.8.34–35.

[30] deSilva, *Honor, Patronage*, 62–63.

[31] We still see this strategy in use today: Fred Phelps, founder of Westboro Baptist Church, saw validation in the disapproval he received, saying "I must be doing something right…. I got every organized and unorganized group in the United States saying they want to kill me." Dugan Arnett, "Fred Phelps, Founder of Anti-Gay Westboro Baptist Church, Dies at 84," *The Sydney Morning Herald*, 21 March 2014.

[32] John H. Elliott, "Disgraced Yet Graced: The Gospel According to 1 Peter in the Key of Honor and Shame," *BTB* 24 (1995): 172.

[33] Wayne A. Meeks, *The First Urban Christians: The Social World of the Apostle Paul* (New Haven: Yale University Press, 1983), 96.

Having been forewarned, opposition can thus make the group's resolve stronger.

Disapproval can also be seen as an opportunity to display loyalty. It is relatively easy to declare allegiance to the group when to do so involves little cost; the presence of opposition provides a chance for group members to display the strength of their faith (1 Pet 1:6–7).[34] For this reason we see the life of the minority group recast as a struggle, or an athletic contest, where suffering is "an opportunity to manifest the virtues of courage and endurance."[35] It seems the sentiment "when the going gets tough, the tough get going" is not restricted to our own era.

Linked with this is the opportunity disapproval brings for group members to imitate Jesus in his enduring of shame, which is a uniquely *Christian* strategy.[36] This is a significant New Testament theme and will surface in each of the texts to be examined later: Peter describes this as "participation" in the sufferings of Christ (1 Pet 4:13); the writer to the Hebrews presents Jesus as our paradigm in not only enduring but *despising* the shame of outsiders (Heb 12:2), urging us to join him in his disgrace outside the camp (Heb 13:3);[37] and John repeatedly casts the persecution of the church as an imitation of the suffering Jesus endured prior to his vindication (Rev 11:8). Thus disapproval is imitation of Christ, and therefore should be seen as (perversely) honorable.

Conflict that arises from disapproval can, if handled correctly by group leaders, have a net positive effect on the group. More than a century ago, Georg Simmel noted how conflict can set up group boundaries and establish group values, forcing groups to tighten their structures and be less tolerant of deviation.[38] More recently, Coser has shown how conflict can strengthen a minority group, as it "contributes to the establishment and reaffirmation of the identity of the group and maintains its boundaries against the surrounding social world."[39] As Elliott notes, this is because conflict provides an opportunity for the group to clarify and reaffirm "those features of the group which make it distinctive, superior and motivated by a common 'cause.'"[40] It also provides the backdrop of a "negative reference group" which further enhances group values.[41] Thus opposition and disapproval does not *automatically* result in a pressure to conform; rather, it can serve to enhance the group's resolve to be different by reminding the group of the reasons for its distinctiveness.[42] Carrier concludes, "persecution will at times weaken affiliation to a religious group, but it can also confirm and reinforce the bonds

---

[34] Elliott, "Disgraced Yet Graced," 172.

[35] deSilva, *Honor, Patronage*, 68.

[36] Elliott, "Disgraced Yet Graced," 172.

[37] deSilva, *Honor, Patronage*, 64–65. deSilva points out that it is not only Jesus who functions as such a paradigm, but the "heroes of the faith" listed in Hebrews 11.

[38] Georg Simmel, "The Sociology of Conflict: 1," *AJS* 9 (1903): 490–525, summarized in Elliott, *A Home for the Homeless*, 113.

[39] Lewis A. Coser, *The Functions of Social Conflict* (Glencoe, IL: Free, 1956), 38.

[40] Elliott, *A Home for the Homeless*, 116.

[41] Coser, *The Functions of Social Conflict*, 95.

[42] Elliott, *A Home for the Homeless*, 114.

between the persecuted faithful."[43] The rhetorical strategies used by minority groups seek to harness the power of opposition for the latter.

Conflict can also promote unity within the group, inspiring renewed cooperation in the face of opposition and making members more accepting of internal discipline.[44] As Harnack observed, "conflict with another group leads to the mobilization of the energies of group members and hence to increased cohesion of the group."[45] This is why some groups will even exaggerate the threat from without, and seek out such threats as a means for control and cohesion.[46] Although New Testament authors do not go this far, they do at times present the threat in its strongest possible terms.

Finally, conflict also provides evangelistic opportunities as, according to Coser, it "binds antagonists," drawing them into interaction with one another. He adds, "The stranger may become familiar through one's struggle with him."[47] Elliott concludes from this that minority group rhetoric such as that encountered in 1 Peter encouraged struggle and resistance not purely for the purposes of insulating the group against the disapproval of outsiders, but "as a necessary prerequisite for an effective missionary enterprise."[48] The values and behaviors that caused the group to be shameful in the eyes of the dominant culture thus produced the kind of conflict that led both parties into dialogue and a place where the minority could influence members of the majority. Disapproval, therefore, was not necessarily a bad thing.

3.3. Identity: Who Are We?

Throughout the preceding discussion it has become evident that a shared group identity is a significant factor in a group's survival. Therefore, much of the group's rhetoric is directed to this question of "who we are." At a foundational level, this involves creating a group consciousness, using language that promotes solidarity such as kinship terms, and the "body" imagery of Greek polity appropriated by Paul (Rom 12:4–8; 1 Cor 12:12–31), reflecting the writers' theological convictions about the church. Group consciousness is also reinforced by referring to common rituals (e.g., baptism, in 1 Cor 10:17), common symbols (the cross, and the story of a crucified-yet-risen Messiah), and promoting regular contact (for instance, the numerous greetings contained in the New Testament letters). Group members are also described as having privileged knowledge (e.g., 1 Pet 1:12) that comes through a special revelation by the Spirit (1 Cor 2:6–16).[49]

---

[43] Herv Carrier, *The Sociology of Religious Belonging* (New York: Herder & Herder, 1965), 218.

[44] Simmel via Caplow, cited in Elliott, *A Home for the Homeless*, 113.

[45] Adolf von Harnack, *The Mission and Expansion of Christianity in the First Three Centuries*, trans. James Moffatt, The Cloister Library (New York: Harper, 1962), 95.

[46] Coser, *The Functions of Social Conflict*, 106.

[47] Coser, *The Functions of Social Conflict*, 121–23.

[48] Elliott, *A Home for the Homeless*, 117.

[49] Elliott, "The Jewish Messianic Movement," 80–84; Meeks, *The First Urban Christians*, 85–93.

This privileged status is heightened by frequent claims to exclusivity, often expressed in terms of being God's "elect" and "holy ones," and the beneficiaries of God's reversal of social status. Election implies a status superior to those on the outside, and is an effective strategy to promote allegiance to the group over against society. According to Wilson's study of sect development, "the more fully the sect sees itself as a chosen remnant, the more fully will it offer resistance…. Such resistance is more likely to be successful, however, if the sect has an aristocratic ethic concerning salvation—if it sees itself as a chosen elect."[50] This can be seen in how God encouraged Israel, itself a minority group, to see itself as a "royal priesthood" (Exod 19:6), a description that is then appropriated by Peter to describe the church (1 Pet 2:9).

More broadly, group members are reminded that they are part of a much larger group than their own visible community, being members of a worldwide movement of other such "elect" groups (1 Pet 1:11; 5:13; 2 John 13), as well as belonging to an eschatological multitude too numerous to count (Rev 7:9).[51]

However, the group's relationship with the parent group from which it defected is a different story. Typically, the parent body is seen as being responsible for the rift; in the case of the early church, the Jews are seen as the ones who rejected Jesus and expelled Jewish Christians from the synagogues (1 Thess 2:14–15). In contrast, the minority is depicted as being in continuity with the "true" form of the parent religion (1 Pet 2:9; Rev 2:9), and the symbols and promises of the parent group are appropriated as belonging to the minority.[52]

3.4. Practice: How Do We Live?

Flowing out of group identity are the more tangible expressions of group values and behavior. These must be reinforced, and opposite behaviors deterred,[53] thus championing a unique culture with clear boundaries not only as an outworking of gospel values, but in practical terms to ensure the group's very survival.[54] In other words, a distinctly *Christian* culture needed to be molded and promoted.

In the first instance, this involved a lifestyle consistent with Christ's teachings. It meant the avoidance of idolatry or being associated with idolatry (1 John 5:21), and the sexual immorality with which idolatry was so often associated (1 Pet 4:3; Rev 2:14).[55] Further, it meant not conforming to the Greco-Roman value system, rejecting the way in which the world judged on the basis of wealth, status, and outward appearance (1 Cor 3:3; 1 Tim 2:8; Jas

---

[50] Wilson, "Sect Development," 13.

[51] Meeks, *The First Urban Christians*, 107.

[52] Elliott, "The Jewish Messianic Movement," 84–85.

[53] deSilva, *Honor, Patronage*, 41.

[54] Meeks, *The First Urban Christians*, 84.

[55] Meeks, *The First Urban Christians*, 91.

2:1–4). Moreover, it required Christians to reject the wider society's struggle for honor in the eyes of others, instead trusting that God would ultimately honor them (1 Pet 4:15).[56] In contrast, the Christian community embraced the countercultural values championed and exemplified by Jesus. It led, as Elliott argues, to "the reordering of internal social roles, relations and criteria of status," which showed special favor to the powerless, and promoted an ethic of mutual submission.[57] Loving, serving, and forgiving one another were paramount.[58] Indeed, according to the Johannine tradition, the overriding characteristic of the Christian minority was to be love for one another (John 13:35; 2 John 5; and possibly Rev 2:4).

This behavior was intended to be in sharp contrast with the wider society. Not only did it ensure a distinctive identity and purpose for the minority group itself, but much of it was seen as potentially winsome to outsiders. Conduct consistent with the group's beliefs was seen to elicit respect from some in the majority culture (1 Pet 2:15; 3:16), and possibly even as a means of winning some over (1 Pet 3:1–2, 15).[59]

The means by which this behavior was promoted was not merely restricted to direct commands or exhortations (such as we find in, e.g., 1 Peter 4; 1 John 2; Hebrews 13). One of the three kinds of Greco-Roman oratory, known as *epideictic*, sought to praise and honor people who exemplified the values and behaviors that were considered honorable by the wider society. The purpose of such rhetoric was to reinforce these values and behaviors among the hearers, and encourage them to pursue them all the more in emulation of those being praised.[60] As well as the obvious example of Christ (1 Pet 2:21; Heb 12:2; 1 John 4:11; Rev 11:8), numerous others are highlighted in this way, including the cloud of witnesses in Hebrews 11, the addressees themselves in former days (Heb 10:32–35; Rev 2:3, 13), along with faithful witnesses such as Antipas (Rev 2:13), the martyrs under the altar (Rev 6:9), and the "blameless" ones who refuse to worship the beast (Rev 14:1–5). This use of praiseworthy examples to encourage adherence to group values and behavior will be seen in more detail below in our investigation of each of the New Testament documents.

3.5. Worldview: How Do We See the World?

A minority group that seeks approval in a different court of reputation and understands its identity as an "elect" people with distinct values and behaviors would naturally see the world in a different way from the rest of society. Minority group rhetoric thus seeks to amplify this tendency by painting this

---

[56] deSilva, *Honor, Patronage*, 74–76.

[57] Elliott, "The Jewish Messianic Movement," 87.

[58] deSilva, *Honor, Patronage*, 79.

[59] Elliott, "The Jewish Messianic Movement," 85.

[60] George A. Kennedy, *A New History of Classical Rhetoric* (Princeton: Princeton University Press, 1994), 4. See also Gerald Hauser, "Aristotle on Epideictic: The Formation of Public Morality," *RSQ* 29 (1999): 5.

worldview using special symbols and stories.[61] Elliott describes it as a "symbolic universe integrating values, goals, norms, patterns of belief and behavior and supplying ultimate (divine) legitimation for the sect's self-understanding, interests, program and strategies."[62] In the later New Testament documents, this includes the appropriation of the story of Israel as an elect nation of priests in 1 Peter, the Johannine symbolic world of starkly-defined opposites like light/darkness and children of God/the devil, and of course the sublime, fantastical, and subversive view of the cosmos revealed to John on Patmos.

A more detailed discussion on each of these will be provided later in the chapter, but as Green points out, the rhetorical strategy being employed here is an attempt to take ownership of the narrative, the lexicon, and the social conventions.[63] The minority group's story can be cast not in terms of deviance from the majority culture, but in adherence to a different story (e.g., Israel's in 1 Peter; God's in Revelation). The meaning of words can be recast, so that, for example, "Lord" refers to Jesus, not the emperor (1 Pet 2:13), and "fear" is not anxious dread of a capricious despot but reverent respect for a sovereign Creator (2:17).[64] Similarly, as already discussed above, the determinant of what is honorable and what is shameful is not the opinion of the majority culture but of the one who is truly in charge of the world. Thus the depiction of an alternative worldview can be a rhetorically offensive weapon, changing the way the contest is perceived in the minds of group members and robbing the opposing arguments of some of their power.

4. The Later New Testament Writings

We have so far constructed a framework with which to analyze New Testament writings as minority group rhetoric, looking at how they deal with issues of approval and disapproval, how they shape and maintain a distinctive identity and behavior, and how they paint an alternative worldview from that of the dominant culture. We will now focus on each of our selected New Testament documents in turn to see how they employ the strategies outlined above.

4.1. 1 Peter

First Peter is significant in this regard as it *consciously* addresses a minority group *as a minority group*. Witherington goes as far as to claim it as "the only New Testament document that systematically addresses the issue of Christians

---

[61] Meeks, *The First Urban Christians*, 93.
[62] Elliott, "The Jewish Messianic Movement," 88.
[63] Green, *1 Peter*, 284–88.
[64] Green, *1 Peter*, 287.

being resident aliens within the macrostructures of the larger society."[65] Indeed, the letter explicitly addresses the audience as "foreigners" and "exiles" (1:1, 17; 2:11), reflecting their alienation from mainstream society and minority group status. It frequently raises the topic of opposition and mistreatment by the majority and stresses the difference in values and behaviors between the group and the rest of society. That much is clear. However, the precise nature of their minority status has occasioned much debate: were they predominantly Jewish or Gentile believers, and was their alienation as much sociological as it was theological?

(a) Aliens and Strangers

One of the key discussions centers on the terms πάροικος and παρεπίδημος (2:11) that Peter uses to describe his audience. Elliott's extensive study has shown how these terms were commonly used. Πάροικος (1:17) refers to someone living "outside the household"—a person permanently residing as an outsider in a foreign land.[66] It was used in the LXX and post-exilic literature to refer to Jews living in exile.[67] Likewise, παρεπίδημος refers to an outsider temporarily living in an area,[68] and in the letter opening it is connected with the word *diaspora* (1:1), which is the technical term for the Jewish peoples scattered throughout the Mediterranean. Although the terms are similar, πάροικος emphasizes the lack of citizenship status, while παρεπίδημος stresses the transitory nature of the residence.[69] The central question is, then, in what way are Peter's audience πάροικοι and παρεπίδημοι?

Traditionally,[70] this language has often been spiritualized and therefore made generally applicable to all believers. Victor Furnish notes, "Christians are the elect of God and thus only temporarily resident in the present world.... [This] makes clear their status as 'resident aliens' so long as they remain in the world."[71] Peter Davids observes that God's people are "living outside their native land, which is not Jerusalem or Palestine but the heavenly city.... That their life on earth is temporary and that they do not belong is underlined by the use of 'sojourners' ... they are pilgrims, foreigners, those who belong to heaven."[72]

Whilst this *may* be a legitimate contemporary application, to see its original meaning in purely spiritual terms imports a foreign Pauline concept

---

[65] Ben Witherington III, *Letters and Homilies for Hellenized Christians, Volume 2: A Socio-Rhetorical Commentary on 1–2 Peter* (Downers Grove, IL: IVP Academic, 2007), 23.

[66] Elliott, *A Home for the Homeless*, 48.

[67] Witherington, *Letters and Homilies for Hellenized Christians, Volume 2,* 24. See 1 Chr 29:15; Ps 119:19; Jdt 5:7–10; Wis 19:10; 1 Esd 5:7; 2 Esd 8:35.

[68] Elliott, *A Home for the Homeless*, 48.

[69] Edward Gordon Selwyn, *The First Epistle of St. Peter* (London: Macmillan, 1946), 118.

[70] Note, however, John Calvin, *The Epistle of Paul the Apostle to the Hebrews, and the First and Second Epistles of St. Peter* (Grand Rapids: Eerdmans, 1963), 230.

[71] Victor P. Furnish, "Elect Sojourners in Christ," *PSTJ* 28 (1975): 3–4.

[72] Peter H. Davids, *The First Epistle of Peter*, The New International Commentary on the New Testament (Grand Rapids: Eerdmans, 1990), 46.

(Phil 3:20) as there is no suggestion in Peter's letter that *heaven* is the source of the believer's true citizenship. It also neglects the socioeconomic usage of the words to refer to foreigners who did not own land or have citizenship rights, as well as the LXX usage to refer to exiled Jews (noting the explicit address of actual cities in the *diaspora* in 1:1).[73] In other words, Peter's audience did not live out their lives merely *as though* they were outsiders; rather, they *were* outsiders in a very real way.

This leads to the question of whether the minority group being addressed was of primarily Jewish or Gentile background. Most contemporary scholars see the audience as predominantly Gentile believers, given that they once "lived in ignorance" (1:14) and were "not a people" (2:10), and that some of the descriptions of their past behavior sound decidedly pagan, such as "living in debauchery, lust, drunkenness, orgies, carousing and detestable idolatry" (4:3).[74] However, the "Israel in exile" language discussed above points more to a Jewish audience, particularly as the letter frequently applies imagery and terminology used of Israel in the Old Testament to the recipients (e.g., "elect," "royal priesthood," "people of God," etc.). They are also described as living among the ἔθνη (the term used by Jews to refer to non-Jewish peoples, i.e., Gentiles).[75]

In attempting to draw together the competing evidence, Witherington has argued for a thoroughly-Hellenized Jewish audience (with perhaps some Gentile God-fearers).[76] This makes sense of the Jewish terminology discussed above, and their Hellenization (particularly of the upper classes) accounts for the past "Gentile-like" behavior referred to in, for example, 4:3.[77] In this reading, the recipients are a double minority, not only being resident aliens by virtue of their Jewishness, but because they also no longer fit in with Gentile society.[78]

Green has offered an alternative harmonization by suggesting that Peter is writing to a mixed, but predominantly Gentile, audience, without much interest in their ethnic background. A key theme is his identification of Israel and the church, and he thus writes to the people of God who are, theologically, "Israel," regardless of ethnicity.[79] Gentiles, then, share in Israel's "resident alien" status when they become a part of the people of God, and so become part of that minority group.

Despite the foregoing diversity, we can draw some basic conclusions about Peter's audience. It is clear that they were in some way alienated from the majority culture. The primary cause of this was their membership of the

---

[73] Witherington, *Letters and Homilies for Hellenized Christians, Volume 2*, 65.

[74] Davids, *The First Epistle of Peter*, 8.

[75] Witherington, *Letters and Homilies for Hellenized Christians, Volume 2*, 24–25.

[76] Witherington, *Letters and Homilies for Hellenized Christians, Volume 2*, 36.

[77] Witherington, *Letters and Homilies for Hellenized Christians, Volume 2*, 30. Witherington's view stands or falls on this point, depending on whether it can be demonstrated that some Jews were sufficiently Hellenized for them to participate in the elements of civic life (e.g., idol food, cultic festivals) that were incompatible with their monotheistic beliefs.

[78] Witherington, *Letters and Homilies for Hellenized Christians, Volume 2*, 37.

[79] Green, *1 Peter*, 6.

Christ-following minority group; the values and behaviors required by this new allegiance meant that they were no longer able to be "at home" in the wider society. This had very real social consequences, seen in the repeated references to suffering for "doing good" and to being "self-controlled" in resisting the corrupting influences of the world.[80] Peter also casts this alienation in terms of Israel's experience in exile; the people of God (whether Jews or Gentiles) are still living as outsiders, away from their homeland. Finally, it is not of mere passing consequence that Peter describes them as an alienated minority; it is the purpose of his letter to address them *as a minority group* and to encourage them to remain as such in the face of opposition.[81] It is to this rhetorical strategy that we now turn.

(b) Rhetorical Strategy of 1 Peter

A striking feature of the epistle, right from the opening greeting, is the use of Israel imagery and terminology to describe the recipients, for example: "elect exiles scattered" (1:1); having an imperishable "inheritance" (1:3); the Levitical call to holiness as a defining characteristic (1:15–16); Israel's special identity as "a chosen people, a royal priesthood" (2:9); and the restored remnant envisaged by Hosea (2:10) and other Old Testament texts. Peter also appropriates Israel's narrative for his audience, depicting them as the fulfillment of the prophetic hope (1:10–12), and claims two stories from Israel's history, Sarah (3:5–6) and Noah (3:20–21). What is the intended rhetorical effect of all this?

If Peter's audience is predominantly Jewish then this is a clear case of a minority group appropriating the language, symbols, and narrative of the parent group. It claims to be the true remnant of the people of God, which stands to inherit the promises made to Israel and to fulfill her purpose in the world (2:9). It stands in continuity with the "sojourners" of Scripture: Abraham (Gen 23:4), Isaac, Jacob, Moses, and the exiles in Babylon (from where Peter metaphorically writes, 5:13). Even if the audience is mostly Gentile, the rhetoric at the very least seeks to define their new identity "by inscribing them into the world of Israel's Scriptures and the record of God's relationship with his chosen people."[82] Having left the narrative of their own culture, they have been engrafted into a different one that promises great benefits.

Indeed, Peter goes to great lengths to impress upon the addressees the benefits of group membership. Particularly for those who have jeopardized their earthly inheritance as a result of following Jesus, there is the promise of

---

[80] Green rightly cautions against an either/or approach to the question of metaphorical or non-metaphorical intention (*1 Peter*, 16.)

[81] Witherington concludes that the rhetorical function "is to encourage the sense of alienation from the macroculture and thereby aid the integration with the microculture of early Christianity. Their dual identity is that they are resident aliens in the Roman Empire, but they are 'in Christ' in God's kingdom!" (*Letters and Homilies for Hellenized Christians, Volume 2*, 24–25.)

[82] Green, *1 Peter*, 15.

an even greater, imperishable one (1:4). The end result is a far greater salvation than any emperor[83] could give (1:9)—nothing less than immortality (1:23). Perseverance in the group, despite the cost, will ultimately lead to vindication by God (5:6).

It is God who should be at the center of the audience's court of reputation. Although there is disapproval from outsiders (2:12; 3:14; 4:4, 14), God's approval is what counts. Therefore they should follow Jesus' example (2:21) who "entrusted himself to him who judges justly" (2:23), and wait for God to "exalt" them in due time (5:6). This is intensified by regular references to a coming judgment (1:13, 17; 2:12), or "inspection visit" (ἐπισκοπή, 2:12). This impending crisis will bring good for the obedient minority addressed by Peter (1:5; 3:12; 5:6) but disaster for the rebellious majority (3:12; 4:17) who will "have to give account to him who is ready to judge the living and the dead" (4:5).

In the meantime, Peter warns his audience to expect suffering and rejection by the majority. After all, the group identity is to be outcasts who are not "at home" in the world (1:1, 17). This should be expected because the group lives by different values and is heading toward a different destiny; suffering should not come as a surprise:

> Dear friends, do not be surprised at the fiery ordeal that has come on you to test you, as though something strange were happening to you. (4:12)

Suffering should be viewed positively, as an opportunity to display loyalty to God:

> These have come so that the proven genuineness of your faith … may result in praise, glory and honor. (1:7)

It is, in fact, following in the footsteps of the group founder, who is the paradigm for suffering rejection by the majority:

> As you come to him, the living Stone—rejected by humans but chosen by God and precious to him—*you also*, like living stones… (2:4–5a)

> To this you were called, because Christ suffered for you, *leaving you an example*, that you should follow in his steps. (2:21)

> Therefore, *since* Christ suffered in his body, *arm yourselves* also with the same attitude, because whoever suffers in the body is done with sin. (4:1)

---

[83] The emperor was often worshiped as a "savior" who brought peace. See Ben Witherington III, *Friendship and Finances in Philippi: The Letter of Paul to the Philippians* (Valley Forge, PA: Trinity Press International, 1994), 99–100. See P. Collart, "Inscriptions de Philippes," *BCH* 57 (1933): 340–41; Frederick W. Danker, *Benefactor: Epigraphic Study of a Graeco-Roman and New Testament Semantic Field* (St. Louis: Clayton Publishing House, 1982), 398–99.

Just as suffering was a precursor to glory for Christ, so it will be for group members:

> But rejoice inasmuch as you participate in the sufferings of Christ, *so that you may be overjoyed* when his glory is revealed. (4:13)

> For Christ also suffered once for sins, the righteous for the unrighteous, to bring you to God. He was put to death in the body *but made alive in the Spirit.* (3:18)

Despite suffering the shame of the majority culture, the group member who remains loyal to the group "will never be put to shame" (2:6). Suffering is only dishonorable if it is deserved (2:20; 4:15). Peter redefines it as honorable if, like Jesus, it is innocent suffering (2:6, 19; 3:14, 17; 4:14, 16). Thus he seeks to insulate his audience against shaming and rejection by the majority culture, redefining it as something to be expected and to be viewed as noble, bringing ultimate advantage despite temporal disadvantage.

Peter also addresses group values and behavior, defining how the minority group should live in contrast with the majority culture. Several times he appeals to the cardinal virtue of temperance (1:13; 4:7; 5:8), casting their different behavioral standard as an honorable achievement rather than a shameful deviation. It is also honorable in being the appropriate, just response to a gracious benefactor:

> As obedient children, do not conform to the evil desires you had when you lived in ignorance... (18) *For* you know that ... you were redeemed ... (19) with the precious blood of Christ, a lamb without blemish or defect. (20) He was chosen before the creation of the world, but was revealed in these last times *for your sake.* (1:14, 18–20)

> To this you were called, *because* Christ suffered for you.... (2:21)

Above all, the group should be characterized by love for one another (1:22; 4:8). This is not only a defining characteristic, but is also a way of strengthening group solidarity and insulating members against external pressure. Indeed, Peter encourages all kinds of community-strengthening behavior (2:1; 3:8; 4:9–11), and promotes group discipline by urging submission to leaders (5:5) and godly leadership consistent with group values (5:2–4). Further, he reminds them that they belong to a wider minority group throughout the world that also shares in their suffering (5:9, 13).

By contrast, the behavior of the outside majority is described as dishonorable, and is cast in pejorative terms: "evil desires ... in ignorance" (1:14); "empty way of life" (1:18), "destined" to stumble (2:8); "detestable idolatry ... reckless, wild living" (4:3–4). Their destiny is judgment (4:5). This provides a reason for the disapproval of outsiders: their conduct shows that they are ignorant, evil, dishonorable, and heading for destruction—so their opinions can safely be ignored.

317

However, the attitude towards the majority culture is not entirely negative. Peter balances the need to insulate group members with the mandate to be attractive to outsiders. Group behavior is not simply for the benefit of the group; it should in some way be attractive to outsiders (2:12; 3:1–2, 15), or at the very least, silence outsiders and vindicate the group so that outsiders are the ones "shamed" (2:12, 15; 3:16). He urges his audience to be wise, only being different where the gospel demands it; in all other situations they are to be exemplary members of society (2:13–14, 17–18; 3:1–4). When confrontation does occur, it should be seen as an opportunity to live out group values in full view of society (3:9, 14–15).

The epistle, then, employs typical minority group strategies within the unique framework of Christian belief. Firstly, it redefines the court of reputation to place God at the center, and provides ways of reinterpreting disapproval from outsiders. Secondly, group identity is affirmed, being depicted as a special, "chosen" people, appropriating the language of the parent group (Israel), thereby claiming to be the true heirs of its promises. Finally, group values and behavior are defined in ways that both promote group cohesion and identity as well as seek to be winsome to outsiders.

4.2. Hebrews

It is clear that the recipients of the letter "to the Hebrews" were a minority group that was in danger of "drifting away" (2:1), "turning away" (3:12), or "shrinking back" (10:39) from being loyal to Jesus. Less clear is *to what* they are turning, and *why*.

(a) Those Who Shrink Back

Often connected to this question is the debate over the ethnic background of the audience—traditionally viewed as Jewish—hence the title, "to the Hebrews," which goes back to the last quarter of the second century, if not earlier. This is largely due to pervasive use of the Jewish Scriptures and its rabbinic methods of argumentation.[84] More recently, commentators have pointed out that this may say more about the author than the recipients.[85] They note Paul's assumption in, for example, Galatians and Romans, that Gentile converts are familiar with the Hebrew Scriptures and have an interest in

---

[84] William L. Lane, *Hebrews 1–8*, Word Biblical Commentary (Dallas: Word, 1991), liv. This is supported by Morrison's more recent study of enthymemes in Hebrews, in which he demonstrates that their unstated but implied premises fit clearly within a Jewish worldview; see Michael Morrison, *Enthymemes in Hebrews* (2010), Kindle edition, loc. 2187–95.

[85] However, it must say *something* about the recipients' ability to understand Old Testament references and Jewish argumentation, otherwise the writer would be "a poor communicator." See Luke Timothy Johnson, *Hebrews: A Commentary*, 1st ed. (Louisville, KY: Westminster John Knox, 2006), 34.

understanding how Gentile believers are part of the story of Israel.[86] This makes it difficult to identify with any confidence whether the audience was of a Jewish or Gentile background.

However, this is not necessarily the same question as determining to which alternative to Christianity they were being attracted, if any. It is unlikely that "pagan" religion per se was the cause of their wavering, since there are no warnings against idolatry.[87] More plausible is Judaism, given the frequent comparisons highlighting the superiority of Jesus and the new covenant over anything the old covenant had to offer. This could involve Jewish believers being tempted for both social and theological reasons to return to the faith of their community, or even Gentiles considering "taking shelter in the 'camp' of Judaism."[88] Yet Thompson correctly notes that the letter does not appear to be intended as a polemic against Judaism;[89] there is no mention of any desire to return to it per se (merely to "shrink back" from following Jesus) and only once is there an explicit mention of the need to correct doctrine (13:9, and perhaps in 6:1).[90] The lack of reference to specific threats "suggests that the author is more concerned with the community's abandonment of the faith than with any alternative they might take."[91] It seems best, then, to agree with Johnson that it is more a case of the audience being tempted to abandon their loyalty to Jesus rather than the attraction of Judaism itself:

> Above all, can we determine whether the Christian hearers are being positively drawn to something else, or are reacting negatively to their own experience? The evidence tilts towards disaffection because of negative experience rather than apostasy because of a stronger attraction…. It may well be, however, that the Jewish cult—either as a new attraction or as a return—gains in attraction because of the negative consequences of commitment to Jesus as Messiah.[92]

This then leads to the question of *why* they were disaffected with following Jesus. It has already been argued that it is unlikely to have been because of an attraction *to* Judaism for theological or sociological reasons. Some have suggested that "moral lethargy" is the problem;[93] whilst it may be a factor, this ignores the frequent references to suffering and social pressure (e.g., 12:4; 13:13).[94] The looming threat of persecution hinted at in 12:4 ("you have not yet resisted to the point of shedding your blood") may well contribute, but is

[86] David A. deSilva, *Perseverance in Gratitude: A Socio-Rhetorical Commentary on the Epistle "to the Hebrews"* (Grand Rapids: Eerdmans, 2000), 2–7.
[87] Craig R. Koester, *Hebrews: A New Translation with Introduction and Commentary*, 1st ed., The Anchor Bible (New York: Doubleday, 2001), 48.
[88] Koester, *Hebrews*, 72. See also F. F. Bruce, *The Epistle to the Hebrews*, rev. ed., The New International Commentary on the New Testament (Grand Rapids: Eerdmans, 1990), 382.
[89] James Thompson, *Hebrews* (Grand Rapids: Baker Academic, 2008), 20.
[90] Thompson, *Hebrews*, 8.
[91] Thompson, *Hebrews*, 10.
[92] Johnson, *Hebrews*, 36.
[93] Thomas E. Schmidt, "Moral Lethargy and the Epistle to the Hebrews," *WTJ* 54 (1992): 167.
[94] Gareth Lee Cockerill, *The Epistle to the Hebrews*, The New International Commentary on the New Testament (Grand Rapids: Eerdmans, 2012), 118 n. 8.

not pervasive enough to be the full explanation, especially since they have previously "endured in a great conflict full of suffering" (10:32). It is more likely the experience of *marginalization* that provides the primary impetus away from remaining loyal to Christ, especially since the exemplars cited are those who embraced marginalization in order to gain something of greater value (Abraham in 11:8–22; Moses in 11:24–26; Jesus in 12:2 and 13:12).[95]

Koester notes from the text three phases in the community's history. The first phase involved proclamation and conversion, confirmed by the activity of the Holy Spirit (2:3–4), involving repentance from dead works (6:1).[96] This led to a second phase, consisting of social and physical persecution as a result:

> Remember those earlier days after you had received the light, when you endured in a great conflict full of suffering. Sometimes you were publicly exposed to insult and persecution; at other times you stood side by side with those who were so treated. You suffered along with those in prison and joyfully accepted the confiscation of your property, because you knew that you yourselves had better and lasting possessions. (10:32–34)

The intention of this persecution would have been to pressure them into giving up their beliefs and marginalize those who persisted. However, the writer notes that they endured it "joyfully" and were unashamed to be identified with those so persecuted (also 6:10). It actually served to "galvanize solidarity within the Christian community."[97]

At the time of writing, however, the community had entered a third phase in which they were faced with ongoing shame (13:13) and some were still imprisoned (13:3).[98] In relation to the wider society, they were set to remain on the outer, reflected in the description of the patriarchs as "foreigners and strangers" (ξένοι and παρεπίδημοι, 11:13) and the people of God as desert wanderers, not at home in the world (11:38). After the original leaders had died (13:7), the second generation began to see "the dissonance between the Christian claim and the reality they experience, for they do not see the world in subjection to Christ."[99] The question then became: *is following Jesus worth the loss of honor in the wider community?* As deSilva notes, this desire for honor had resurfaced over time, leading to "a reluctance on the part of some to identify with the members of a marginal, low-status group, which would undermine their own status in society."[100] Therefore some had started to withdraw from associating with the group (10:25) and ceased to show solidarity with those being persecuted (10:34). In other words, the recipients

---

[95] deSilva, *Perseverance in Gratitude*, 18.

[96] Koester, *Hebrews*, 64–66.

[97] Koester, *Hebrews*, 70.

[98] Koester, *Hebrews*, 71–72.

[99] Thompson, *Hebrews*, 9.

[100] David A. deSilva, "Despising Shame: A Cultural-Anthropological Investigation of the Epistle to the Hebrews," *JBL* 113 (1994): 400.

of the epistle were growing tired of being marginalized, and were in danger of leaving the minority group.

(b) Those Who Have Faith

In response to this situation, the author adopts a similar strategy to the writer of 1 Peter, reframing the debate in terms of eternal rather than temporal benefits.[101] This yields new answers to the questions of whose opinion counts and what kind of behavior is truly honorable.

Although the approval of society might be of temporal advantage, God is presented as the one who gives access to eternal benefits. Therefore he must be at the center of one's court of reputation. Indeed, the author begins by setting the present crisis within the story of the Creator God who has spoken throughout history (1:1–2), and the one who is now (as then) calling his people to obedience (4:7). If God's people were punished in the past for being disobedient, the audience should not expect to escape punishment if they ignore God (2:2–3). Numerous times the author seeks to evoke fear, a well-attested rhetorical strategy.[102] Those who fall away and are unfruitful are in danger of being cursed and burned (6:8); apostates can expect judgment and fire (10:27), for "it is a dreadful thing to fall into the hands of the living God" (10:31). Even Moses, on seeing God at Mount Sinai, trembled with fear (12:21). Although the audience may fear the shame of their community and so be tempted to shrink back from being identified with Christ, their fear of the living God ought to be greater.[103]

By contrast, those who do remain loyal should have confidence to stand before God (4:16), confidence that his approval is more important than that of human beings (13:6), and confidence that he will faithfully deliver on his promises (10:23; 11:11).[104] Conversely, the faithful God deserves faithful people. Drawing on the language of patronage,[105] the author paints God as a benefactor who brings great favor (χάρις, 1:9; 4:16) to whom gratitude (χάρις, 12:28) is owed; indeed, to spurn the gift is the height of ingratitude, subjecting his Son to disgrace all over again (6:6), trampling him underfoot, as it were, and insulting the Spirit of grace (χάρις, 10:29).

Many of the examples given are of God's people in the past who remained loyal to God even though that cost them worldly status, because they had in view the greater benefits God could bring. The patriarchs lived as outsiders in a foreign land because they looked forward to God's promised blessing (11:9). Moses "chose to be mistreated along with the people of God" and shunned "the treasures of Egypt" because he had his eternal reward in view;

---

[101] deSilva, *Perseverance in Gratitude*, 58.
[102] Aristotle, *Rhet.* 2.5.1; Quintilian, *Inst.* 6.2.20; Cicero, *De or.* 2.185; cf. Anders Eriksson, "Fear of Eternal Damnation: *Pathos* Appeal in 1 Corinthians 15 and 16," in *Paul and Pathos*, ed. Thomas H. Olbricht and Jerry L. Sumney (Atlanta: Society of Biblical Literature, 2001): 115-26.
[103] Koester, *Hebrews*, 90.
[104] Koester, *Hebrews*, 91.
[105] See deSilva, *Perseverance in Gratitude*, 59–64.

this stands in contrast with Esau, who sold his "inheritance" for temporal gain (12:16). Rahab (11:31) went "outside the camp" (Josh 6:23, cf. Heb 13:13)[106] of her own people in order to experience God's blessing. Jesus, of course, is the ultimate example of such faithfulness, enduring the shame of the cross for the sake of future glory (12:2). Likewise, the audience is urged to persevere in faithful gratitude, being inspired by this "cloud of witnesses" (12:1), by Christ himself, and even by the example of their own community in the recent past (10:32, "Remember those earlier days...").[107] Indeed, these witnesses function as an alternative court of reputation.[108] Furthermore, as with Jesus and the other heroes of the faith, giving up temporal honor will result in an eternal inheritance that "cannot be shaken" (12:28).

In sum, the author provides his audience with an alternative court of reputation and an alternative understanding of what is truly honorable. He responds to their shame of being marginalized and dishonored by society

> by holding up before the congregation an alternative system of honor—one familiar to them, but with regard to which they require reinforcement—which carries with it the promise of greater and lasting reward for those honored according to its standards. The author seeks to persuade the congregation to disregard the society's evaluation of honor and dishonor and to continue confidently in Christian identity and associations as a means of satisfying their desire for honor.[109]

As well as providing this positive alternative, the writer also seeks to *insulate* the audience against the disapproval of the majority culture. They are encouraged to see this hardship as God's discipline, and therefore a sign that they belong to God's people (12:7–8).[110] It is cast as a struggle, using the imagery of athletic contest in which the "cloud of witnesses" is in the stadium cheering them on (12:1–2),[111] thus appealing to the cardinal virtue of courage. Further, they are urged to cultivate a nurturing community[112] that meets regularly to encourage one another (10:25) and to provide a counterbalance to the shaming messages from the majority culture. They are to support those suffering the most (13:3), to take responsibility for one other's endurance (12:15), and to treat fellow group members as kin (13:1). In this way they will ensure that although many have been rejected by their communities and families of origin, they will have, as Thompson notes, "a new family in the

---

[106] Carl Mosser, "Rahab Outside the Camp," in *The Epistle to the Hebrews and Christian Theology*, ed. Richard J. Bauckham et al. (Grand Rapids: Eerdmans, 2009), 397.
[107] John Chrysostom, commenting on this verse, says: "Powerful is the exhortation from deeds already done: for he who begins a work ought to go forward and add to it.... And he who encourages, does thus especially encourage them from their own example" (cited in deSilva, *Perseverance in Gratitude*, 357).
[108] deSilva, *Perseverance in Gratitude*, 68.
[109] deSilva, "Despising Shame," 400.
[110] Thompson, *Hebrews*, 255.
[111] Thompson, *Hebrews*, 256. See also deSilva, *Perseverance in Gratitude*, 361–64.
[112] deSilva, *Perseverance in Gratitude*, 68–69.

community of faith that shares their confidence in the alternative reality, providing support to them in time of need."[113]

In terms of group *identity,* the author uses the symbols of the parent group (Judaism) to show the superiority of the benefits brought through Christ.[114] He is greater than angels (1:4), who (in Hellenistic Jewish thought) were mediators of the old covenant (2:1), as well as Moses (3:3), through whom *Torah* was given, and the Levitical priesthood, being a priest of a higher order (7:11). The tabernacle at which he serves is a heavenly one (8:2), of which the earthly sanctuary is a mere copy (8:5), and his once-for-all sacrifice surpasses the repeated offerings made by priests (10:11–12).[115] At no point does this become polemic;[116] the old covenant is not seen negatively, but as a shadow of something greater (10:1). In fact, a common rhetorical technique was to praise someone by comparing it to someone else highly esteemed, and show them to be even greater.[117] Here, the old covenant is not so much a negative foil as a great act of revelation by God that has been surpassed by an even greater act of revelation (1:1–2). It reinforces the Christian minority group's identity by showing it to be at every point superior to the parent group.[118] Moreover, "he has made Jesus and true faith so attractive that it would be shameful to turn back now or defect and stirring to carry on with the beliefs and behaviors they have already embraced."[119]

In essence, the writer presents an alternative worldview in which the focus is not on the temporal, visible world (which will one day be shaken) but on that which is unseen and eternal.[120] Thompson puts it well:

> For people whose own world is shattered by disappointment and alienation from the world around them, the author offers an alternative reality that does not belong to the material world and is superior to the values of the dominant culture.... Believers can live as strangers without seeing the ultimate triumph of God if they are able to see beyond the realities of this world.[121]

4.3. 1 John

The first epistle of John is a slightly different example of minority group rhetoric in that it seeks to insulate its audience on two fronts. Not only are they are a minority group seeking to resist conformity to the majority culture; at the same time they are dealing with a schism *within* the group, in which

---

[113] Thompson, *Hebrews*, 20.
[114] Koester, *Hebrews*, 77.
[115] Johnson, *Hebrews*, 32.
[116] Thompson, *Hebrews*, 20. Cockerill, *The Epistle to the Hebrews*, 20–21.
[117] Anaximenes, *Rhet. Alex.* 1.3.
[118] deSilva, *Perseverance in Gratitude*, 5.
[119] Ben Witherington III, *Letters and Homilies for Jewish Christians: A Socio-Rhetorical Commentary on Hebrews, James and Jude* (Downers Grove, IL: IVP Academic, 2007), 49.
[120] Koester, *Hebrews*, 78. may be correct in seeing this also as an appropriation of the Greco-Roman symbolic world, transforming not just Judaism but Platonism.
[121] Thompson, *Hebrews*, 20.

former members have "gone out" from them due to doctrinal and (therefore?) behavioral issues. The focus is on the redrawing of group boundaries in the wake of the schism.

Older commentaries on 1 John tended to focus on trying to identify the secessionist group, particularly focusing on its doctrinal differences.[122] However, this is difficult due to the fact that the epistle is not addressed to the secessionists at all, and contains very little in the way of argument against their teaching. Instead, it is addressed to those who had *not* been led astray by their false teaching.[123] Therefore it is not a polemic against the content of the teaching but an exercise in damage control, reaffirming the group's identity and integrity. Witherington points out, "if these secessionists have gone out, then our author is neither answering nor debating them in this sermon; rather, he is rather trying to heal his congregation(s) and do damage control after the fact."[124] Similarly, Brown concludes that "1 John was written to preserve an interpretation of the schism ... for insiders rather than to convince outsiders."[125]

Witherington rightly cautions against simplistic mirror reading, as the contrasts set up by the author are not necessarily reflective of the opponents' position.[126] As Trebilco argues, in 1 John 2:3–5 the author uses the phrases "we know," "the one who says," and "anyone who keeps" without any indication of a change of referent.[127] Further, Griffith has shown that Greek rhetoric commonly used these phrases ("if we say... if anyone says...") to advance one's argument against hypothetical objections, without necessarily having actual opponents in mind.[128] So we should not read 1 John as polemical rhetoric; rather, as Griffith observes, "foundational convictions are simply restated and commonly held values are reinforced, as a means of strengthening group identity and cohesion in the light of changed circumstances."[129] Thus when it comes to viewing the epistle through the lens of minority group rhetoric, the precise identity of the secessionists is less relevant. What *is* significant is the way in which the author seeks to rebuild the community in the aftermath of their departure. This makes the message

---

[122] Some examples include Raymond E. Brown, *The Epistles of John*, 1st ed. (Garden City, NY: Doubleday, 1982); C. H. Dodd, *The Johannine Epistles* (London: Hodder & Stoughton, 1946); I. Howard Marshall, *The Epistles of John* (Grand Rapids: Eerdmans, 1978); John R. W. Stott, *The Letters of John: An Introduction and Commentary* (Nottingham: IVP, 2009).

[123] Duane F. Watson, "Amplification Techniques in 1 John: The Interaction of Rhetorical Style and Invention," *JSNT* 51 (1993): 118.

[124] Ben Witherington III, *Letters and Homilies for Hellenized Christians, Volume 1: A Socio-Rhetorical Commentary on Titus, 1–2 Timothy and 1–3 John* (Downers Grove, IL: IVP Academic, 2006), 428.

[125] Brown, *The Epistles of John*, 91.

[126] Witherington, *Letters and Homilies for Hellenized Christians, Volume 1*, 428.

[127] Paul R. Trebilco, *The Early Christians in Ephesus from Paul to Ignatius*, WUNT (Tübingen: Mohr Siebeck, 2004), 280.

[128] Terry Griffith, "A Non-Polemical Reading of 1 John: Sin, Christology and the Limits of Johannine Christology," *TynBul* 49 (1998): 258–60.

[129] Griffith, "A Non-Polemical Reading of 1 John," 254.

more readily applicable to other cases of schism in groups of believers, regardless of the precise cause.

Fundamentally, the rhetorical strategy of 1 John is *epideictic*.[130] Kennedy highlights the fact that epideictic did not advance new ideas, but reaffirmed already accepted truth; it was "thus an important feature of cultural or group cohesion."[131] We see this in 1 John:

> 1:1 That which was from the beginning…
> 2:7 I am not writing you a new command…
> 2:21 I do not write to you because you do not know the truth, but because you do know it…

The aim is to increase adherence to already held group values[132] in the wake of the secessionists' departure. Painter and Harrington conclude, "From the beginning the author is attempting to nurture the bonds of community and to reassert the values that have bound the community together prior to the schism. Seen as a response to schism, 1 John readily fits the category of epideictic rhetoric."[133]

A key feature of epideictic discourse is the notion of honor. John encourages his audience to continue seeking their honor from God rather than the wider world (which is hostile to God and his people, see 3:13–14), especially in light of the fact that God is coming to judge:

> And now, dear children, continue in him, so that when he appears we may be confident and *unashamed* before him *at his coming*. (2:28)

Expressions such as "this is the last hour" (2:18) and "when Christ appears" (3:2) heighten the urgency of the message and the importance of being "unashamed" when he visits in judgment.

However, it is not just God who occupies the group's court of reputation; it is also one another. John seeks to strengthen the community bond in this discourse, seen in his frequent use of kinship language (2:1,8,14; 5:21) and constant urging to "love one another" (3:23). He also arouses emotion using the rhetoric of praise and blame, contrasting his faithful audience with the unfaithful ones who have gone out from among them. In 2:12–14 he praises his audience because they know God and have overcome evil. By contrast, in 2:18–27 he gives a negative summation of the secessionists' character. Watson classifies this as "an extended proof from pathos, the arousing of audience emotion for or against the issue and people involved."[134] This is

---

[130] See Duane F. Watson, "An Epideictic Strategy for Increasing Adherence to Community Values: 1 John 1:1–2:9." In *Proceedings: Eastern Great Lakes and Midwest Biblical Societies* 11 (1991): 144–45, for arguments that 1 John is epideictic.

[131] George A. Kennedy, "The Genres of Rhetoric," in *Handbook of Classical Rhetoric in the Hellenistic Period: 330 B.C.–A.D. 400*, ed. Stanley E. Porter (Boston: Brill, 2001), 45.

[132] Watson, "Amplification Techniques," 118–19.

[133] John Painter and Daniel J. Harrington, *1, 2, and 3 John* (Collegeville: Liturgical, 2002), 87.

[134] Watson, "Epideictic Strategy," 149.

achieved largely through describing the secessionists in pejorative language;[135] they are described as "antichrists" (2:18, perhaps picking up Jesus' use of the term "false Christs" in Mark 13:22) and "false prophets" (4:1) who are "of the devil" (4:3), as well as "liars" who "deny" group beliefs (2:22) and "lead astray" group members (2:26; 3:7). Indeed, their apostasy leads to death (5:16). Witherington rightly points out that this language is not used *against* the secessionists, as they are not addressed in the epistle at all, rather, it is used

> to help those remaining to let them go and focus once more on their own spiritual well-being and belief system. It is meant to ensure that the community stops losing members and that none that remain are tempted to embrace the beliefs and behavior of the departed. This homily, then, is not about directly attacking or debating with opponents. It does not seek to delineate their views or refute them with detailed arguments.[136]

Further, a clear delineation between "us" and "them" is frequently employed. In a classic sectarian strategy, the fact that the secessionists "went out" is advanced as a sign that they did not "belong to us" (2:19). They showed by their opposition that they did not belong to the group, and therefore they do not belong to God, nor do they have his approval (4:6). By contrast, they may well have a greater degree of acceptance by the majority culture because they have more in common with "the world" than with "us":

> They are from the world and therefore speak from the viewpoint of the world, and the world listens to them. (4:5)

The secessionists are thus redefined as belonging to the majority culture. The effect is to join the two fronts of the battle: rhetorical strategies to insulate against rejection and disapproval by the majority culture can be applied with equal force to those who have abandoned the group. By leaving, the secessionists show that they belong to the wider world that opposes the group; thus opposition should be expected (3:13) because the world is evil (2:16) and under control of the devil (5:19), and they oppose out of ignorance (3:14).

As well as this negative portrayal of both sources of opposition, John also seeks to reassure his audience post-schism that they are indeed in the right (3:19). As Witherington suggests, "healing is needed, reassurance must be offered, and reasons to continue to embrace the fundamental values must be given because eternal life for the members of the community hangs in the balance."[137] John does this by linking group behavior with that of its founder; if they want to be confident that God will vindicate them, they should look no further than whether or not they display the character of his Son:

---

[135] Watson, "Amplification Techniques," 121.

[136] Witherington, *Letters and Homilies for Hellenized Christians, Volume 1,* 432.

[137] Witherington, *Letters and Homilies for Hellenized Christians, Volume 1,* 131.

This is how love is made complete among us so that we will have *confidence* on the day of judgment: In this world we are like Jesus. (4:17)

In fact, confidence is the explicit reason John gives for writing:

I write these things to you who believe in the name of the Son of God *so that you may know* that you have eternal life. (5:13)

This "eternal life" is the key benefit of belonging to the group (2:25; 5:12). Similarly to Peter and the writer to the Hebrews, John reframes the debate from having a temporal to an eternal focus:

The world and its desires pass away, but whoever does the will of God lives forever. (2:17)

Those who reject being guided by the world and its desires in favor of seeking honor from God are the ones who will be vindicated (5:4). Indeed, they have special status as the children of God (3:2), and privileged knowledge (2:20, 27; 5:20). John's audience, then, can be confident of their advantage both now and into eternity if they remain true to the group values.

This, of course, entails certain behavior that is essential to the group's identity, described metaphorically as "walking in the light" (1:6) and more concretely as "keeping his commands" (2:3). Specifically, the behavior of the group should follow the behavior of the group founder, Jesus, since "whoever claims to live in him must live *as Jesus did*" (2:6) and "all who have this hope in him purify themselves, *just as he is pure*" (3:3; see also 2:29; 3:6, 9, 16; 4:12). By contrast, group membership requires the rejection of the majority culture's values; they are not to "love the world or anything in the world" (2:15), and in the closing command are told, "keep yourselves from idols" (5:21).

Although general obedience to the teachings of Jesus is in view, the author's particular area of focus is on group behavior that promotes solidarity and love for other members in a practical way (3:18). This behavior serves to make group identity concrete, and strengthens group boundaries:

John is concerned to underline what is appropriate behavior within the community. The image of light and darkness, the concept of truth and falsehood, and the experience of forgiveness and loving one another within the circle of the fellowship of believers, all combine to strengthen the sense of community, and to define its limits.[138]

This ideal of practical love for one another is phrased not merely as an exhortation but also as a command (3:23; 4:21), and is grounded in the character and example of the God who demonstrated his love in sending his son as an atoning sacrifice (4:7–12).

---

[138] Griffith, "A Non-Polemical Reading of 1 John," 261.

This supreme act of love is seen as the defining symbol of the group (4:11). Griffiths observes that the atoning blood of Christ as celebrated in the Lord's Supper—along with the signs of baptism and the receiving of the Holy Spirit (5:8)—are the unique symbols that set the audience apart from Judaism and the Greco-Roman world. "They provide symbols and shared experiences that strengthen their separate identity as believers in Messiah Jesus. These symbols are the sociological analogue of their Christological beliefs."[139]

Thus 1 John is an address to a minority group to insulate them against the twin threats of the influence of the majority culture and the departure of some from the group. It redefines the secessionists as belonging, ultimately, to the majority culture, shoring up the boundaries of the group. Orthodox, apostolic Christology is affirmed, and the audience is exhorted and commanded to live out the behavioral implications of that Christology, in part in order to further strengthen group solidarity. The end result is a reaffirmation of the confidence that group membership is worth the cost, in light of the eternal benefits that they alone will receive.

4.4. Revelation

To give even an adequate treatment of the rhetorical strategy of Revelation would require at least an entire chapter of its own, if not a book. Yet to omit it entirely from our discussion is not possible, since out of all of the New Testament documents it is arguably the most consciously focused on the minority–majority dynamic. It is also the supreme example of the fifth strategy outlined above: that of creating an alternative worldview for its audience. Through the genre of apocalyptic, the author opens a door to the heavens (4:1) and *reveals* the true nature of things from a divine perspective—a way of seeing things that stands in stark contrast to the worldview espoused by Rome and the imperial cult. For a fuller treatment, the reader is referred to David deSilva's insightful tour of the rhetoric of Revelation, *Seeing Things John's Way*.[140] Here we can present just a brief summary of some of the most important strategies used by the author.

Traditionally, Revelation was seen as being written to believers in Asia Minor during a time of severe persecution, probably under Emperor Domitian. This was because persecution tends to produce apocalyptic literature, and there are references to martyrdom and persecution throughout the work.[141] More recently, Thompson's study has rehabilitated the picture of Domitian somewhat, demonstrating that the main negative sources about him are biased.[142] This led Thompson to suggest actual persecution was not part of the

---

[139] Griffith, "A Non-Polemical Reading of 1 John," 272.

[140] David A. deSilva, *Seeing Things John's Way: The Rhetoric of the Book of Revelation* (Louisville, KY: Westminster John Knox, 2009).

[141] Noted in Adela Yarbro Collins, *Crisis and Catharsis: The Power of the Apocalypse* (Philadelphia: Westminster, 1984), 104 and deSilva, *Seeing Things John's Way*, 50.

[142] Leonard L. Thompson, *The Book of Revelation: Apocalypse and Empire* (New York: Oxford University Press, 1990).

scenario being faced by the audience, and that any sense of conflict is something John encourages in his audience, being "a part of his vision in the world."[143] Most subsequent commentators have rejected this extreme, seeing at least an imminent threat of significant imperial persecution.[144] However, the focus has rightly shifted toward viewing the main threat as more sociological than physical. The picture is one that includes tensions between church and synagogue, between Christians and pagan society, and between rich and poor.[145] Christians were possibly coming out from under the protection of being seen as a sect of Judaism, so faced disapproval and sanction for non-participation in the imperial cult.[146] There was also pressure to participate in Roman social life such as the trade guilds (necessary to practice one's trade) with their annual feasts to patron deities, eating in idol temples (which functioned as social hubs for the upper classes), and other elements of civic religion.[147] Revelation calls on them to resist temptation for compromise, and maintain faithfulness to Christian community and Christ—in other words, it is minority group rhetoric.

The strategies employed are of two kinds: deliberative and epideictic. As deSilva observes:

> Revelation both gives advice and presents models of behavior. That is, it pursues both deliberative goals (seeking to shape the ongoing behavior of the hearers in specific ways in regard to specific circumstances or settings) and epideictic goals (seeking to praise and censure particular figures with the aim of reinforcing or shaping the values of the Christian groups John addresses).[148]

The most obvious deliberative strategies appear in the letters to the seven churches, in which two courses of action are contrasted, together with their respective consequences. Those who remain true to group values (who "overcome"—note the language of contest) will experience eternal reward, while those who give in to conformity with the surrounding culture will have their lampstand removed.

> By means of these literary techniques and contrasting images, John articulates a worldview that establishes alternatives and then forces choices between them. This is highly significant in light of the rival agendas among the churches, most notably the agendas of Jezebel and of the Nicolaitans, whose position seems to envision Christians coexisting alongside and within Roman

---

[143] Thompson, *Apocalypse and Empire*, 174.
[144] Gregory K. Beale, *The Book of Revelation: A Commentary on the Greek Text* (Grand Rapids: Eerdmans, 1999), 12–15; Grant R. Osborne, *Revelation* (Grand Rapids: Baker Academic, 2002), 10–12; Thomas B. Slater, "On the Social Setting of the Revelation to John," *NTS* 44.2 (1998): 254–55; Ben Witherington III, *Revelation* (Cambridge: Cambridge University Press, 2003), 8.
[145] Adela Yarbro Collins, *Crisis and Catharsis*, 84–107.
[146] Grant R. Osborne, *Revelation* (Grand Rapids: Baker Academic, 2002), 11.
[147] deSilva, *Seeing Things John's Way*, 47–48.
[148] deSilva, *Seeing Things John's Way*, 231.

imperialism and its legitimation mechanisms. John doggedly rends asunder what Jezebel would join together.[149]

This theme of different destinies plays out in the rest of the Apocalypse. All those who oppose God end up experiencing destruction—whether they be the symbolic trinity of beast, false prophet, and antichrist (19:20) or those humans who refuse to repent of their idolatry and sorcery (9:20–21). This is contrasted with the glorious future for those who overcome, depicted as a perfectly-restored creation in chapters 21–22. As with the other documents we have surveyed, John repositions the debate, focusing on the crisis of "the end." Avoiding destruction there is thus depicted as being more important than the present, lesser crises of local persecution or fitting in with society's cultic and economic regimes.[150]

In service of this is the arousal of *pathos* (the stronger emotions), and in particular, fear. God is portrayed as a judge to be feared, one who is already at work meting out judgment on an increasing scale—one quarter (6:8), then one third (8:7–12), and finally the whole earth (ch. 16). The graphic details of the judgment scenes (e.g., 14:20) again serve to evoke fear of the dreadful consequences of worshiping the beast,[151] putting the temporal consequences of *not* worshiping in clear perspective.

At the heart of Revelation's rhetoric, however, is the epideictic strategy of praise and blame. In the apocalyptic genre powerful symbols are employed, which by their very nature can depict their referents as honorable or shameful; as good or evil. The depictions of God on his throne (4:2) and Christ as a rider on a white horse (19:11, white being symbolic of victory) send a clear message about who is in charge and who will win in the end. Likewise, the descriptions of faithful martyrs being given white robes (6:11) and the 144,000 sealed with the name of God as a sign of ownership and protection (7:1–8; 14:1) convey to the embattled Christian minority an assurance of victory and belonging.

By contrast, the symbols describing those opposed to God subvert the rhetoric of the Roman Empire. The emperor is not the divine son of the gods who brings peace,[152] but a blasphemous beast who does the work of Satan (13:1–8). The imperial cult is not the voluntary expression of gratitude to a benevolent benefactor, but a deception and imposition on the populace (13:11–18). The famed *Pax Romana,* or Roman peace, for which the emperors were worshiped, should really be seen as a war waged against God's people (13:7; 11:7). Rome itself is not the eternal city of beauty, bringing in a golden age for the benefit of the nations, as was the rhetoric of the goddess *Roma Aeterna*—she is merely a cheap whore drunk with power, whose luxurious lifestyle comes from riding the beast (the emperor's military power) at the

---

[149] deSilva, *Seeing Things John's Way*, 114.
[150] deSilva, *Seeing Things John's Way*, 112.
[151] deSilva, *Seeing Things John's Way*, 219.
[152] Epictetus, *Diatr.* 3.13.9: "Caesar has obtained for us a profound peace."

expense of the conquered peoples (17:1–6). The only thing eternal about Rome will be the smoke of her destruction (19:3).[153]

It is not just the symbols themselves that can tell a story, but also their spatial arrangement. John provides his audience with an alternative map of the cosmos, with God on his throne at the top, and the abyss at the bottom.[154] In chapter four, everything is depicted as being "in order," with God at the center, on his throne, being worshiped by all. In chapter six, the vision begins to show a world "out of order" with the rest of creation; although the Greco-Roman world saw Jewish and Christian monotheism as a cause of disorder, here the problem is identified as idolatry and polytheism (9:20–21). In light of the world John paints, idol worshipers—not Christians—are the deviant minority,[155] and unless they conform to the rest of the created order their destiny is destruction.

The symbolic world described so vividly by John is written to encourage loyalty to God and his people, even if it means being seen as *dis*-loyal to the wider culture, in particular, the Roman Empire. Although Rome may appear imposing and all-encompassing, when set alongside the rest of the cosmos it is nothing more than a rebellious aberration. Although the Emperor may seem to be a great power to be feared, he is nothing more than a jumped-up pretender in a toga with garden clippings on his head. God is the true ruler, and it is his wrath that should be feared. John thus redefines the minority group as being—from God's perspective—aligned with the majority. It is Rome that is out of step with the created order.

5. Conclusion

In this chapter we have seen how an understanding of minority group rhetoric can provide one useful lens through which the New Testament documents can be viewed, in order to understand their function within the community of the first readers. Although the examples chosen here represent some of the more *consciously* minority-focused texts, given the social situation of first-century Christians the insights gained here can still be helpful in understanding the rhetorical function of the rest of the New Testament documents.

This study also has utility beyond simply understanding how the message was heard by its original audience; it can also be suggestive of application lines in contemporary contexts. For example, our reading of 1 Peter 2–3 can transcend the cultural specifics of master–slave and husband–wife relationships and be seen as an exhortation to live *attractively different* lives which, even in the face of opposition and hostility from the majority culture, yield at least a grudging respect, and possibly more. Our use of Hebrews need not be limited to abstract theological discussions about Christ in relation to angels, Melchizedek, and the temple cult, but as a way of employing

---

[153] Beale, *The Book of Revelation*, 929.
[154] deSilva, *Seeing Things John's Way*, 94.
[155] deSilva, *Seeing Things John's Way*, 99.

theological reflection to bolster our trust in and loyalty to Jesus, and to guard against the seduction of the wider culture. We will hear with greater urgency John's message of loving one another when we see it as the way in which we both survive as a minority and express our identity as followers of Jesus. The Apocalypse will speak to us with far greater power when we scour it, not for signs of our geopolitical future, but for the way in which it critiques our present, subverting the attractiveness of a wider culture that dares set itself up in defiance of God and his just rule.

While this minority group approach would most quickly find a home among persecuted believers today, to limit it to such contexts is to miss much of the point. The attraction of the dominant culture is not necessarily felt most strongly at the point of a sword; indeed, two thousand years of martyrdom has shown that obvious, physical threats often serve to strengthen faith and increase the resolve of the Christian minority. More insidious is the social pressure that, over time, seeks to shame minorities back into conformity. This may involve rejection by family, friends, and other members of one's court of reputation; it also includes the steady erosion of respect for Christian belief in academic circles and in the media. In the secularized West, true followers of Jesus have always been a minority, yet in recent decades we have seen an increase in hostility, condescension, and disrespect. In this climate, followers of Christ need to learn afresh how to "despise shame" and instead go to our savior outside the camp and bear the disgrace he bore, with the promise of final vindication.

Recommended Reading

deSilva, David A. *Honor, Patronage, Kinship & Purity: Unlocking New Testament Culture*. Downers Grove, IL: InterVarsity Press, 2000.

deSilva, David A. *Perseverance in Gratitude: A Socio-Rhetorical Commentary on the Epistle "to the Hebrews."* Grand Rapids: Eerdmans, 2000.

deSilva, David A. *Seeing Things John's Way: The Rhetoric of the Book of Revelation*. Louisville: Westminster John Knox, 2009.

Elliott, John H. *A Home for the Homeless: A Social-Scientific Criticism of 1 Peter, Its Situation and Strategy*. Philadelphia: Fortress, 1990.

Green, Joel B. *1 Peter*. The Two Horizons New Testament Commentary. Grand Rapids: Eerdmans, 2007.

Malina, Bruce J. *The New Testament World: Insights from Cultural Anthropology*. 3rd ed. Louisville, KY: Westminster John Knox, 2001.

Thompson, Leonard L. *The Book of Revelation: Apocalypse and Empire*. New York: Oxford University Press, 1990.

Tucker, Brian J., and Coleman A. Baker, eds. *T&T Clark Handbook to Social Identity in the New Testament*. London: Bloomsbury, 2014.

Wilson, Bryan R. "An Analysis of Sect Development." *ASR* 24 (1959): 3–15.

Witherington, Ben, III. *Letters and Homilies for Hellenized Christians, Volume 1: A Socio-Rhetorical Commentary on Titus, 1–2 Timothy and 1–3 John*. Downers Grove, IL: IVP Academic, 2006.

Witherington, Ben, III. *Letters and Homilies for Hellenized Christians, Volume 2: A Socio-Rhetorical Commentary on 1–2 Peter*. Downers Grove, IL: IVP Academic, 2007.

Witherington, Ben, III. *Letters and Homilies for Jewish Christians: A Socio-Rhetorical Commentary on Hebrews, James and Jude*. Downers Grove, IL: IVP Academic, 2007.

Yarbro Collins, Adela. *Crisis and Catharsis: The Power of the Apocalypse*. 1st ed. Philadelphia: Westminster, 1984.

12. The Book of Revelation: A Call to Worship, Witness, and Wait in the Midst of Violence

Murray J. Smith

The book of Revelation speaks to Christian believers living in a violent world. In the first century, the dominance of Rome in the Mediterranean had been achieved through bloody military conquest. It was sustained by a combination of military force, economic exploitation, and cultural imperialism. The violence of imperial Rome can be overstated, but Rome was, in many respects, a brutal regime. The Roman historian Tacitus recognized that the much vaunted *pax romana* ("Roman peace") of the first century was only a "peace with bloodshed."[1] The practices of crucifying criminals,[2] decimating weak or disobedient units in the army,[3] and entertaining the masses with the blood-sport of *venationes* (beast-fights)[4] and gladiatorial contests,[5] all indicate a society in which violence was a widely accepted means of social control.[6] The book of Revelation speaks to Christian believers who not only lived in this world, but who faced persecution, violence, and even death for their devotion to the Lord Jesus Christ. The purpose of this chapter is to explore the Christian response to violence envisioned by the book. My thesis is that the book of Revelation functions as a prophetic call to Christian believers to respond to violence not with further violence, but by *worshiping* the one true God, by bearing *witness* to his work in Jesus Christ, and by *waiting* patiently for his final victory in the world. Part 1 provides a brief orientation to the book of Revelation. Part 2 sketches the origins and nature of the persecution of Christians within the Roman world, with specific reference to the Roman imperial cults and the province of Asia. Part 3 explores the book's prophetic call to worship, witness, and wait.

---

[1] Tacitus, *Ann.* 1.9–10.
[2] See esp. Martin Hengel, *Crucifixion in the Ancient World and the Folly of the Message of the Cross* (London: SCM, 1977), chs. 4–10.
[3] Suetonius, *Aug.* 24.2; Suetonius, *Cal.* 48.1; *Galb.* 12.2; Tacitus, *Ann.* 3.21.
[4] Nicholas Purcell, "Venationes," in *OCD*, ed. Simon Hornblower and Antony Spawforth (Oxford: Oxford University Press, 2003), 1586.
[5] See John P. Balsdon and Andrew W. Lintott, "Gladiators," in *OCD*, 637–38.
[6] Cicero, *Tusc.* 2.41 and Pliny the Younger, *Pan.* 33.1 both criticized the blood-sport of the arena, but did not consider this a problem if the gladiators were condemned criminals.

1. The Book of Revelation

The book of Revelation is an "unveiling" or "disclosure" (1:1: ἀποκάλυψις) of the creator God's purposes for his world. The book was most likely written by John, the son of Zebedee, brother of James, and apostle of Jesus (1:1, 4, 9),[7] from the island of Patmos (1:9), toward the end of the reign of the emperor Domitian (ca. AD 81–96).[8] The book is an *apocalyptic prophecy* in the form of a *circular letter* to the seven churches of Asia (1:4, 11; 2:1–3:22).[9] As an *apocalypse* (1:1), Revelation claims to be the word of the risen Lord Jesus himself,[10] given via an angel, through John,[11] to reveal the view from God's

---

[7] The author of the book identifies himself for his readers simply as "John" (1:1, 4, 9; 22:8), who is God's "slave" (1:1), "your brother and partner," and a "witness" for Christ who is in exile on the island of Patmos (1:9). The probability that this John is the apostle, the son of Zebedee, is suggested by: (i) the early and widespread testimony of early Christian writers, who identify the author of Revelation as "John, one of the apostles of Christ" (Justin, *Dial.* 81.4; cf. *Apocryphon of John* 1.7–8; 1.30–2.16; Irenaeus, *Haer.* 3.11.1; 3.16.5, 8; 5.30.3; Clement of Alexandria, *Quis div.* 42; Hippolytus, *Antichr.* 35–36; Origen, *Comm. Jo.* 2.41–42; Victorinus, *In Apoc.* 11.1; Muratorian canon); (ii) the significant stylistic, thematic, and terminological similarities between Revelation and the Gospel and letters of John. For a defense of this view, see esp. Robert H. Mounce, *The Book of Revelation*, rev. ed., NICNT (Grand Rapids: Eerdmans, 1998), 8–15; Grant R. Osborne, *Revelation*, BECNT (Grand Rapids: Baker, 2002), 2–6. For the connections with the Gospels and letters of John, see C. G. Ozanne, "The Language of the Apocalypse," *TynB* 16 (1965): 3–9; Stephen S. Smalley, "John's Revelation and John's Community," *BJRL* 69 (1987): 549–71. Alternatively, it is argued that Revelation was written by: (i) "John the Elder," one of Jesus' Palestinian disciples and a member of the broader apostolic circle (see esp. John J. Gunther, "The Elder John, Author of Revelation," *JSNT* 11 (1981): 3–20); (ii) "an early Christian prophet" named John (e.g., Craig R. Koester, *Revelation: A New Translation with Introduction and Commentary*, AB 38A (New Haven: Yale University Press, 2014), 68–69). The view that Revelation was written by someone using "John" as a pseudonym is now widely discounted.

[8] A strong minority of scholars advocate for a date in the 60s AD, prior to the destruction of the Jerusalem temple. See esp. J. B. Lightfoot, *Biblical Essays* (London: Macmillan, 1893), 52; F. J. A. Hort, *The Apocalypse of John I–III* (London: Macmillan, 1908), x; John A. T. Robinson, *Redating the New Testament* (London: SCM, 1976), 221–53; Christopher Rowland, *The Open Heaven: A Study of Apocalyptic in Judaism and Early Christianity* (New York: Crossroad, 1982), 403–13; J. Christian Wilson, "The Problem of the Domitianic Date of Revelation," *NTS* 39 (1993): 587–605. For a date in the reign of Domitian, see: H. B. Swete, *The Apocalypse of St. John*, 3rd ed. (London: Macmillan, 1911), xcix–cvi; I. T. Beckwith, *The Apocalypse of John* (New York: Macmillan, 1919), 197–208; R. H. Charles, *A Critical and Exegetical Commentary on the Revelation of St. John*, 2 vols. (Edinburgh,: T&T Clark, 1920), 1:xci–xcvii; A. Y. Collins, "Dating the Apocalypse of John," *BFER* 26 (1981): 33–45; Gregory K. Beale, *The Book of Revelation: A Commentary on the Greek Text*, NIGTC (Grand Rapids: Eerdmans, 1999), 4–27; Koester, *Revelation*, 71–79. For a mediating position, that the book was initially composed following the Neronian persecution in the AD 60s but given its final shape at the time of Trajan, see Martin Hengel, *The Johannine Question*, trans. J. Bowden (London: SCM, 1989), 80–81; cf. David E. Aune, *Revelation 1–5*, WBC (Dallas: Word, 1997), lviii.

[9] On the genre and its implications, see esp. Richard J. Bauckham, *The Theology of the Book of Revelation* (Cambridge: Cambridge University Press, 1993), 1–22.

[10] The Greek phrase Ἀποκάλυψις Ἰησοῦ Χριστοῦ could be understood as a subjective genitive (Jesus Christ as the one who made the revelation) or an objective genitive (Jesus Christ as the content of the revelation). Since Revelation 1:1 continues that God gave this revelation to Jesus "to show to his servants," it seems most likely that it should be understood as a subjective genitive: Jesus is the revealer of the vision.

heavenly throne-room, showing reality in true perspective, so that its recipients may rightly understand the world, and conduct themselves accordingly (1:1–3).[12] As a *prophecy* (1:1–3, 10–19; 4:1–2; 17:1–3; 21:9–10; 22:6–7, 10, 18, 19), Revelation places itself in the tradition of the Old Testament prophets (10:7–11; 19:10; 22:6, 9), and shows how their promises of God's universal kingdom on earth have begun to reach fulfillment in the life, death, and resurrection of Jesus Christ.[13] As a *circular letter* (1:4–5, 11; 22:16, 21), Revelation addresses the seven churches of the Roman province of Asia in seven individual letters (2:1–3:22), which are connected in a range of ways to John's initial vision-commission (1:9–20), to each other (2:1–3:22), and to the book's major vision (4:1–22:5). The letters address the particular challenges facing each of the churches,[14] while calling all of them together to engage in the eschatological battle described in the book's central vision, confident of the victory God has won in Christ.[15]

Revelation, then, provides the view from God's eternal throne. The book's claim is that the Lord Jesus himself has opened the door of heaven (4:1) and revealed to his servant John (1:1) the true nature of reality, so that the book's auditors might see through the false worldviews of non-Christian Judaism and the Greco-Roman world and learn to live faithfully as they wait for God's final victory.[16] The book addresses "the seven churches that are in Asia" (1:4) who had faced, were facing, and were about to face, violent persecution for their devotion to the Lord Jesus. Its primary purpose is to comfort and encourage such believers with the knowledge that "the Lord God Almighty" reigns (4:8; 11:17), and that his victory over evil—in Christ's death and resurrection—will soon be worked out in all its fullness. Christian believers, therefore, must resist compromise with the world around them, and instead *worship* the one true God, bear *witness* to his victory in Christ, and patiently *wait* for its final outworking in the world.

In what follows, I examine, in Part 2, Roman rule, the Roman imperial cults, and the persecution of Christians in Asia in the first century, before turning, in Part 3, to Revelation's response to this persecution.

---

[11] This revelation primarily takes the form of a "vision" (9:17: ὅρασις), which John "heard and saw" (22:8) and which he has, at divine command, written down (1:3, 11, 19; 2:1, 8, 12, 18; 3:1, 7, 14; 14:13; 19:9; 21:5).

[12] For recent discussion of the genre of "apocalypse," see esp. John J. Collins, "What is Apocalyptic Literature?" in *The Oxford Handbook of Apocalyptic Literature*, ed. John J. Collins, Oxford Handbooks (New York: Oxford University Press, 2014), 1–16.

[13] Bauckham, *Theology*, 145: the process of "interpreting Jesus Christ in the light of the Old Testament and the Old Testament in the light of Jesus Christ" climaxes in John's new prophetic revelation.

[14] See esp. Colin J. Hemer, *The Letters to the Seven Churches of Asia in Their Local Setting*, JSNTSup 11 (Sheffield: JSOT, 1986).

[15] The symbolism of *seven* churches indicates that the seven letters address the church at large, in its *totality*, as the body of believers throughout the whole world. See esp. Bauckham, *Theology*, 15, 125, 213.

[16] For an insightful analysis of Revelation's rhetorical strategy, see David A. deSilva, *Seeing Things John's Way: The Rhetoric of the Book of Revelation* (Louisville, KY: Westminster John Knox, 2009).

2. A Hostile World: Roman Rule, the Roman Imperial Cults, and the Persecution of Christians in Asia in the First Century

2.1. Roman Rule and the Roman Imperial Cults

The principate of Octavian (= Augustus; 27 BC–AD 14) marks the transition from the Roman Republic to the Roman Empire. Among many new developments, Augustus oversaw the remarkable rise of "imperial cults" in which worship was directed not only to Rome, as previously, but to the person of the *princeps* (later emperor) himself. These "imperial cults" are best understood as the range of ways in which people honored the Roman emperors—and members of their families—with titles and practices traditionally reserved for gods and goddesses.[17] Roman citizens and provincials honored the emperors by constructing temples, appointing priesthoods, offering sacrifices, celebrating games, holding festivals, instituting choirs, and in other related activities.

Older scholarship tended to view these imperial cults as a political tool, in the guise of religion, that served to unify the provinces with Rome.[18] More recent approaches have nuanced this view, emphasizing the way in which the rituals and symbols of the cults served to define the emperor's central role in the cosmic, political, economic, and social order by integrating the emperor into the established patterns of life in the Greco-Roman world.[19] Crucially, the emperor—who was recognized as both human and divine—came to be seen as the one who connected heaven and earth. The imperial order, with the emperor at its head, was the "guarantor and mediator of the favor of the

---

[17] For an excellent review of the literature on the Roman imperial cult and the book of Revelation to 2010, see Michael Naylor, "The Roman Imperial Cult and Revelation," *CurBR* 8.2 (2010): 207–39 (208). Important contributions since 2010 include: Anthea Portier-Young, *Apocalypse against Empire: Theologies of Resistance in Early Judaism* (Grand Rapids: Eerdmans, 2011); Richard B. Hays and Stefan Alkier, *Revelation and the Politics of Apocalyptic Interpretation* (Waco, TX: Baylor University Press, 2012); Bruce W. Winter, *Divine Honours for the Caesars: The First Christians' Responses* (Grand Rapids: Eerdmans, 2015), esp. 286–306.

[18] See, especially, the influential works of Arthur Darby Nock, "Notes on Ruler-Cult, I–IV," *JHS* 48.1 (1928): 21–43; "ΣΥΝΝΑΟΣ ΘΕΟΣ," *HSCP* 41 (1930): 1–62; *Conversion: The Old and the New in Religion from Alexander the Great to Augustine of Hippo* (London: Oxford University Press, 1933), esp. 229: "By the time of Claudius it [ruler worship] was an outward sign of loyalty which involved little sentiment"; "The Emperor's Divine *Comes*," *JRS* 37, no. 1/2 (1947): 102–16; *Essays on Religion and the Ancient World*, 2 vols. (Cambridge, MA: Harvard University Press, 1972); "Religious Developments from the Close of the Republic to the Death of Nero," in *The Cambridge Ancient History*, ed. I. E. S. Edwards (Cambridge: Cambridge University Press, 1970/75), 10:465–511; esp. 481–82; cf. also M. P. Charlesworth, "Some Observations on Ruler-Cult, Especially in Rome," *HTR* 28.1 (1935): 5–44.

[19] See especially, with different emphases, Keith Hopkins, *Conquerors and Slaves*, Sociological Studies in Roman History (Cambridge: Cambridge University Press, 1978), 197–242; Simon R. F. Price, *Rituals and Power: The Roman Imperial Cult in Asia Minor* (Cambridge: Cambridge University Press, 1984); Steven J. Friesen, *Twice Neokoros: Ephesus, Asia and the Cult of the Flavian Imperial Family*, Religions in the Graeco-Roman World (Leiden: Brill, 1993).

gods."[20] The imperial cults, therefore, which focused on the worship of the emperors, did not displace the traditional worship of gods and goddesses. They provided a crucial point of integration between the newly established cosmic order and the traditional life and worship of the cities across the empire.[21]

There was, however, no single, monolithic, centrally-established "imperial cult" during the first century. It is now increasingly recognized that the initiative in worshiping the Roman emperors was, by and large, taken by local elites, who sought to integrate their cities with the Roman world and ingratiate themselves with their Roman overlords. Emperor worship developed, therefore, in different ways across the empire.[22] In particular, the imperial cults took a different form in Rome, where only deceased emperors were officially honored as divine, and in the provinces, where the living emperor could officially be worshiped as a god.[23]

In the city of Rome, the Roman Senate honored worthy emperors, after their deaths, with a ceremony of *apotheosis* or divinization, subsequent to which the deceased emperor was considered to dwell among the gods in the region of the stars.[24] This practice began as early as 42 BC, when the Roman Senate, responding to the initiative of Octavian and his fellow *triumvirs*, posthumously deified Julius Caesar as *Divus Iulius* ("divine Julius"). It was confirmed in 29 BC when Octavian, Julius Caesar's adopted son, dedicated a temple to his deified father in the Roman forum.[25] The longstanding Roman opposition to monarchy, however, meant that Octavian was careful to manage the honors offered to him during his lifetime. In 27 BC he accepted the honorific titles *Princeps civitatis* ("first citizen") and *Augustus* ("revered one"), but made no claims to royal or divine status. The more prudent of the Roman emperors in the first century followed suit.[26] Nevertheless, Augustus was able to use the divinization of his adoptive father to present himself, on

---

[20] John M. G. Barclay, *Pauline Churches and Diaspora Jews*, WUNT 275 (T bingen: Mohr Siebeck, 2011), 355–56.

[21] For this understanding of the imperial cults, see esp. Price, *Rituals and Power*, 239–48.

[22] Cf. Mogens H. Hansen and Simon R. F. Price, "Ruler-Cult: II. Roman," in *OCD*, 1338–39.

[23] Dio Cassius, *Hist.* 51.20.

[24] Cicero, *Phil.* 1.13; 2.110; Pliny, *Pan.* 10.4; 24.5; 89.2; Manilius, *Astron.* 1.799–804; Herodian, *Hist.* 4.2. For discussion, see esp. Simon R. F. Price, "Noble Funeral to Divine Cult: The Consecration of Roman Emperors," in *Rituals of Royalty: Power and Ceremonial in Traditional Societies*, ed. David Cannadine and Simon R. F. Price (Cambridge: Cambridge University Press, 1987), 56–105; Larry J. Kreitzer, "Apotheosis of the Roman Emperor," *BA* 53.4 (1990): 210–17; *Striking New Images: Roman Imperial Coinage and the New Testament World*, JSNTSup 134 (Sheffield: Sheffield Academic, 1996), 69–98.

[25] Suetonius, *Jul.* 88.1; Pliny the Elder, *Nat.* 2.93–94. Cf. Hansen and Price, "Ruler-Cult: II. Roman," 1338.

[26] Cf. Arnaldo Momigliano, "How Roman Emperors Became Gods," *American Scholar* 55 (1986): 181–93 (187): "Generally speaking, the emperor had to approve, to limit, and occasionally to refuse ruler-cult. He had to be worshiped, and yet he had to remain a man in order to live on social terms with the Roman aristocracy of which he was supposed to be the 'Princeps.'" Momigliano summarizes the situation by saying that during his lifetime, the Roman emperor of the first century was "more of a god in his absence than in his presence."

his coins and inscriptions, as *divi filius* ("son of the divinity").[27] And certainly, after his death, Augustus was also divinized, and widely believed, by virtue of his *apotheosis*, to be ruling the world from the heavens, in the presence of his father.[28]

In the years that followed, the honor of divinization was officially only granted posthumously, and was never automatic.[29] In the first century, it was paid to Claudius (AD 41–54),[30] Vespasian (AD 69–79),[31] and Titus (AD 79–81),[32] but not to Tiberius (AD 14–37), Gaius Caligula (AD 37–41), Nero (AD 54–68), or Domitian (AD 81–96). This official reserve, however, did not stop at least some sections of the general populace in Rome, and in towns across Italy, from honoring living Roman emperors as divine.[33] It also did not stop some of the more audacious emperors from making exalted claims for themselves, even during their lifetimes, and even in the city of Rome. In the middle of the century, Gaius Caligula sought royal and even divine status for himself in Rome as well as in the provinces.[34] And forty years later, at the time when Revelation was being written, Domitian audaciously styled himself "our lord and god,"[35] minted coins that show him enthroned as "father of the gods,"[36] and filled Rome with his statues, even demanding that he be worshiped as a god, by sacrifice, in the capital itself.[37] In the first century, however, such claims remained—in the city of Rome—the exception rather than the rule.

---

[27] For the Roman emperors as "son of god," see esp. Michael Peppard, *The Son of God in the Roman World: Divine Sonship in Its Social and Political Context* (New York: Oxford University Press, 2011). For Augustus, see Lily Ross Taylor, *The Divinity of the Roman Emperor*, Philological monographs (Middletown, CT: American Philological Association, 1931), 142–80. For Nero as "son of God," see Miriam T. Griffin, *Nero: The End of a Dynasty* (New Haven: Yale University Press, 1984), 98.

[28] For the *apotheosis* and heavenly rule of Augustus, see: Suetonius, *Aug.* 100.4; Tacitus, *Ann.* 1.10; Dio Cassius, *Hist.* 41.9; Seneca, *Apocolocyntosis* 1, 10; *Oct.* 477–91, 504–33; *Clem.* 1.10.3–1.11.4; Manilius, *Astron.* 1.7–10, 384–86, 800–803, 915–16, 925–26; 4.551–52, 932–35; *Insc. lat. sel.* 137.

[29] Price, "Noble Funeral," 56–105 (57) notes that between Augustus and Constantine, a total of thirty-six of the sixty emperors, as well as twenty-seven of their family members, underwent *apotheosis* and received the title *divus* ("divine").

[30] Suetonius, *Claud.* 45; Dio Cassius, *Hist.* 61.35.1–4.

[31] Herodian, *Hist.* 4.2.

[32] Suetonius, *Dom.* 2; cf. Herodian, *Hist.* 4.2. Note also the Temple to Vespasian, which Titus began building in the Roman forum (AD 79), and which Domitian completed and dedicated to his father and brother (ca. AD 87).

[33] See esp. Ittai Gradel, *Emperor Worship and Roman Religion*, Oxford Classical Monographs (Oxford: Oxford University Press, 2002).

[34] Suetonius, *Cal.* 22; cf. also Josephus, *A.J.* 18.261–62; *B.J.* 2.184–87; Philo, *Legat.* 184–96, 346–48.

[35] Suetonius, *Dom.* 13; Cf. Ruurd R. Nauta, *Poetry for Patrons: Literary Communication in the Age of Domitian*, Mnemosyne, bibliotheca classica Batava Supplementum (Leiden; Boston: Brill, 2002), 383 who demonstrates that "lord" and "god' were applied to Domitian by his contemporaries.

[36] Aline Abaecherli, "Imperial Symbols on Certain Flavian Coins," *CP* 30 (1935): 131–40.

[37] Suetonius, *Dom.* 13; Dio Cassius, *Hist.* 67.4; cf. 8.1; Pliny, *Pan.* 52.1, 7. Cf. Statius, *Silvae* 5.2.170 who designates Domitian *deus praesens* ("present deity").

In the provinces, things were different: provincials were granted official permission, from the beginning, to worship living emperors.[38] In the Greek East this practice had deep roots in the long established Hellenistic ruler-cults, in which living rulers were granted divine honors.[39] Thus, for Roman intellectuals, like Tacitus, the honor paid to the emperor was a *Graeco adulatio* ("Greek adulation");[40] and for Jews, like Philo, it was a "barbaric custom."[41] Already during his lifetime, Augustus allowed local elites to honor him (and Rome) by constructing temples, erecting cult statues, establishing a range of associated activities (games, priesthoods, processions, sacrifices), and by attributing to him titles and qualities traditionally directed to the gods and goddesses.[42] No less than sixty-six temples were dedicated to the divine Augustus in the first century, either alone or in conjunction with the goddess *Roma* or other figures.[43] For our purposes, it is particularly significant that these imperial cults developed first and fastest in the Greek East, including in the province of Asia. Indeed, the evidence indicates that "the diffusion of the cult of Augustus and of other members of his family in Asia Minor and throughout the Greek East from the beginning of the empire was rapid, indeed almost instantaneous."[44]

2.2. Roman Imperial Cults in Asia in the First Century

In the first century, the Roman Empire dominated the political landscape of Asia Minor. The Roman armies had defeated the Seleucid King Antiochus III, who ruled the region, in 189 BC, and Rome had taken direct control of Asia in 133 BC when Attalus III of Pergamum bequeathed his kingdom to the Romans. From this point onwards, loyalty to Rome became part and parcel of

---

[38] Elias J. Bickermann, "Consecratio," in *Le culte des souverains dans l'empire romain*, ed. Willem den Boer (Geneva: Fondation Hardt, 1972), 1–37 (9–10).

[39] Price, *Rituals and Power*, 29–30, 52, argues that the Greek ruler cults can be at least partly explained as a means by which Greek cities made sense of the unprecedented power wielded by the Greek monarchs in the Hellenistic period.

[40] Tacitus, *Ann.* 6.18. For discussion, see Glen W. Bowerstock, "Greek Intellectuals and the Imperial Cult in the Second Century A.D.," in *Le Culte des souverains dans l'Empire Romain. 7 expos s suivis de discussions*, ed. Elias J. Bickerman and Willem den Boer, Entretiens sur l'antiquit classique (Vandœuvres-Gen ve: Fondation Hardt; Francke, Berne: D positaire pour la Suisse, 1973), 179–212.

[41] Philo, *Legat.* 116: Philo denounces the fact that, at the time of Gaius, some people had "even introduced the barbaric custom [τὸ βαρβαρικὸν ἔθος] into Italy of falling down in adoration [τὴν προσκύνησιν] before him [= the Roman emperor]."

[42] See Hansen and Price, "Ruler-Cult: II. Roman," 1338–39: from the time of Augustus onwards living Roman emperors were accommodated within the established Olympian pantheon and "granted temples and cult statues, priests and processions, sacrifices and games."

[43] For the details, see Heidi Hänlein-Schäfer, *Veneratio Augusti: Eine Studie zu den Tempeln des ersten römischen Kaisers.*, Archaeologica (Rome: Bretschneider, 1985). While fewer temples were dedicated to Augustus's immediate successors, there were many cults which gave generic honor to "the emperors." Price, *Rituals and Power*, 57–58 argues that this demonstrates that Augustus' "charisma" had been effectively institutionalized.

[44] Stephen Mitchell, *Anatolia: Land, Men, and Gods in Asia Minor*, 2 vols. (Oxford: Clarendon, 1993), 1:100.

life in Asia Minor. Indeed, even as early as 195 BC, Smyrna had become the first city in the region to erect a temple to the goddess Roma.[45] It was in the first century BC, however, during the principate of Augustus, that imperial cults specifically directed to the worship of the emperor began to develop. Indeed, the loyalty of Asia to the Roman emperors from Augustus onwards may be gauged by the Council of Asia's decree, in 9 BC, that the region's calendar would henceforth be measured from "the birthday of the god (Augustus)." That date, it declared, "was the beginning for the world of the glad tidings (εὐαγγέλια = gospels) that have come to men through him." The Calendar Decree goes on to announce that Augustus by his "appearance" (ἐπιφάνεια) as "savior" (σωτήρ) had brought "peace" (εἰρήνη) and "hope" (ἐλπίδα) to the known world.[46]

The imperial cults in the provinces primarily took three forms. First, provincial councils established official provincial cults with the approval of the Roman Senate and the emperor.[47] Leading cities vied with each other for the privilege of hosting a temple to the emperor, and those cities granted permission to establish an imperial cult boasted the title νεωκόρος ("temple caretaker").[48] At these centers, the cult generally followed the Roman custom of reserving the title θεός ("god") for deceased emperors who had been officially deified by the Senate.[49]

The first city in Asia to formally establish a Roman imperial cult of this kind was Pergamum. In 29 BC Augustus granted the Council of Asia permission to build a temple in the city "to himself and the City of Rome."[50] Although Pergamum lost to Ephesus its status as the leading city of the region during the course of the first century,[51] it remained the center of the Roman

---

[45] Tacitus, *Ann.* 4.56.

[46] For the full text, see *OGIS* 2:458. For a translation, see V. Ehrenberg and A. H. M. Jones, eds., *Documents Illustrating the Reigns of Augustus and Tiberius*, 2nd ed. (Oxford: Clarendon, 1976) § 98b. For further examples, see G. A. Deissmann, *Light from the Ancient East* (Grand Rapids: Baker, 1978), 366–67; trans. of *Licht vom Osten* (Tübingen: J. C. B. Mohr, 1908); Ehrenberg and Jones, *Documents*, nos. 14, 38, 41, 98, 99.

[47] For discussion and the primary evidence, see esp. Steven J. Friesen, *Imperial Cults and the Apocalypse of John* (Oxford: Oxford University Press, 2001), 25–55.

[48] For discussion, see esp. Friesen, *Twice Neokoros*, 50–75. The term originally referred to a temple official who assisted the priests and priestesses in their work. During the first century it came to be applied to cities which "took care" of the temples of the imperial cult.

[49] Friesen, *Twice Neokoros*, 22–23. See *IGRom.* 1:55–56; 4:1756.

[50] Tacitus, *Ann.* 4.37; cf. Dio Cassius, *Hist.* 51.20.6 records that following Octavian's victory at the battle of Actium (31 BC), the *koinon* (provincial council) of Asia requested, in 29 BC, permission to establish in Pergamum a cult for Rome and Octavian. The inscriptions and coins universally identify this temple as the "Temple of Rome and Augustus" (the honorific title granted Octavian in 27 BC). Two early bronze coins depict in the temple a statue of Augustus in military garb with a spear in his right hand—from AD 4–5: *BM Coins, Rom. Emp. (Mysia)* 139, #242, pl. 28; from AD 29–35: *BM Coins, Rom. Emp. (Mysia)* 140, #256, pl. 28). Two later silver coins depict in the temple a statue of Roma crowning Augustus—from the time of Claudius: *BM Coins, Rom. Emp.* 1.196, #228, pl. 34; from the time of Vespasian: *BM Coins, Rom. Emp.* 2.94, #449, pl. 43. For discussion, see especially Friesen, *Twice Neokoros*, 7–15.

[51] David S. Potter, "Pergamum," in *ABD*, ed. D. N. Freedman (New York: Doubleday, 1992), 5:228–30 (230).

Murray J. Smith

imperial cult in the province.[52] In addition to the temple of Rome and Augustus, Pergamum was granted the right to hold sacred games in honor of the emperor,[53] and to establish an imperial choir of "hymn singers," drawn from local elites with hereditary membership, which gathered at regular festivals throughout the year "to sing hymns in honor of Roma and Augustus on behalf of the province of Asia."[54] In the middle of the first century the Council of Asia decreed that Pergamum should host an annual festival to "Sebastos Tiberius Caesar god."[55] And not long after Revelation was written, the construction of a new temple to the Roman emperor Trajan (AD 98–117; ca. AD 113), the Traianeum, prominently situated at the top of the Pergamene acropolis, provides a clear indication of the trajectory towards which the imperial cult in Pergamum was headed in the latter part of the first century.[56] The construction of this temple allowed the city to boast that it was "twice temple-warden" (νεωκόρος)—the center of devotion to Caesar in the whole province of Asia.[57]

Not to be outdone, the city of Smyrna, in AD 23, requested—and was granted—the right to build a temple "to Tiberius, to his mother (Livia), and to the Senate."[58] This was an unusual move, since no other province in the empire had two temples to the emperor at this time, and Tiberius was forced to explain his actions to the Senate.[59] Several cities vied for the honor of hosting the temple, but eventually Smyrna was chosen. The construction of this temple gave Smyrna the coveted title, together with Pergamum, of "temple warden" (νεωκόρος). In the course of time the city was granted the right to build two further temples to Roman emperors under Hadrian (AD 117–138) and Caracalla (AD 211–217).[60]

In the same way, towards the end of the first century, the Council of Asia established a third temple for the imperial cult, at Ephesus, in honor of the

---

[52] Antony Spawforth and Charlotte Rouech , "Pergamum," in *OCD*, 1138; cf. Pliny, *Nat.* 5.126, writing in AD 77, who describes Pergamum as "the most famous place of Asia."
[53] *IGRom.* 4:1064 = *SIG* 3:1065 (Kos, reign of Caligula); *IGRom.* 4:498 (Pergamum).
[54] Price, *Rituals and Power*, 118. See: *I. Ephesos* Ia 18d 11–19; *I. Pergamon* 374.
[55] *IGRom.* 4:1608c = *I.Eph.* VII 2, 3801 (restored) records the decree of the Asian assembly which provides for an annual festival in Pergamum (translation from *Rituals and Power*, 105): "Since one should each year make clear display of one's piety and of all holy, fitting intentions towards the imperial house, the choir of all Asia, gathering at Pergamum on the most holy birthday of Sebastos Tiberius Caesar god, performs a task that contributes greatly to the glory of Sebastos in hymning the imperial house and performing sacrifices to the Sebastan gods and conducting festivals and feasts."
[56] Indeed, Price, *Rituals and Power*, 252–53 provides a catalogue of Imperial Temples and shrines in Asia Minor that shows that by the end of the early second century Pergamum boasted not only the temple to Rome and Augustus, but also the Temple of Zeus Philios and Trajan, and an Imperial Room in the Asclepieum. See also an inscription from the time of Hadrian that shows the cult continued well into the second century (*IGRom.* 4:353).
[57] For a comprehensive survey of the evidence from Pergamum, see Helmut Koester, *Pergamon Citadel of the Gods: Archaeological Record, Literary Description, and Religious Development*, HTS 46 (Harrisburg, PA: Trinity Press International, 1998).
[58] Tacitus, *Ann.* 4.15.
[59] Tacitus, *Ann.* 4.55–56.
[60] Price, *Rituals and Power*, 258–59.

emperor Titus.[61] This temple is attested in thirteen inscriptions from AD 89–90, and is more properly known as the "the Temple of the Sebastoi" (ναὸς τῶν Σεβαστῶν), a title that reflects what became the common practice of referring to the reigning emperor as "god Sebastos" (σεβαστός = *Augustus* = "Revered One"), and the members of the imperial family as "Sebastoi gods" ("revered gods").[62]

In addition to these formally established provincial cults, a second form of imperial cult, known as municipal or civic cults, were often established on local authority, following local customs.[63] These cults were freer in the divine honors paid to living emperors. In Asia in the first century, there were municipal or civic sanctuaries of this kind at Ephesus, Thyatira, Laodicea, and Aphrodisias. In Ephesus, for example, while the worship at the great temple of Artemis continued to dominate the civic landscape, as early as AD 15, the "Association of Roman Citizens" (*conventus Civium Romanorum*) erected, in the city's "State Agora," a temple in honor of "Divine Caesar" (*Divus Caesar*) and the "goddess Roma" (*Dea Roma*). While these institutions did not have the formal recognition of the Roman Senate, they were often established by the leading families or groups in the city, were well integrated with the city's main institutions, and played an important role in civic life.

Finally, in addition to the official provincial cults, and the municipal or civic cults, private imperial cults were established, throughout the course of the first century, in a range of unofficial locations, including among the guilds and in private households.[64] These private cults provided a means for professional associations and family groups to honor the emperor in their own way. In Smyrna, for example, there was a group called the "Caesarists" who offered sacrifices for the emperors as "revered gods" and held banquets in their honor.[65] And in Ephesus, at the time of Domitian, the worship of the goddess Demeter also included mysteries and sacrifices to the emperor.[66]

Imperial cults were, therefore, a major feature of life in the cities of Asia during the first century. Loyal citizens of the empire participated in the cults as part and parcel of their daily life. By burning incense, offering sacrifice and joining in public festivals and processions, they declared that "Caesar is Lord." In the ordinary course of life, therefore, Christian believers faced pressure to demonstrate their loyalty to the divinely established cosmic and

---

[61] It used to be thought the cult was established for Domitian. Steven J. Friesen, "Ephesus: Key to a Vision in Revelation," *BAR* 19 (1993): 24–37 notes, however, that further examination of the colossus erected at Ephesus has revealed that it depicted Titus (AD 79–81) rather than Domitian (AD 81–96).

[62] *I. Ephesos* 2.233, lines 9–10. Cf. *I. Ephesos* 2.232, 232a, 233, 234, 235, 237, 238, 239, 240, 241, 242; 5.1498; 6.2048. For discussion, see esp. Friesen, *Twice Neokoros*, 29–49. For a comprehensive survey of the evidence from Ephesus, see Helmut Koester, *Ephesos Metropolis of Asia: An Interdisciplinary Approach to Its Archaeology, Religion, and Culture*, HTS 41 (Valley Forge, PA: Trinity Press International, 1995); cf. Jerome Murphy-O'Connor, *St. Paul's Ephesus: Texts and Archaeology* (Collegeville, MN: Liturgical, 2008).

[63] For discussion and primary evidence, see esp. Friesen, *Imperial Cults*, 56–103.

[64] See esp. Friesen, *Imperial Cults*, 104–21.

[65] *IGRom.* 4:1348.

[66] *I.Eph.* 213.

social order, not only as members of the civic community, but also in their professional guilds and in their households. Refusal to participate was conspicuous and costly. It was both religious impiety and political disloyalty; both "atheism" and "treason."[67] It threatened the entire cosmic and social order. It was "hatred of the human race."[68] The fundamental and irreconcilable clash between the basic Christian conviction that Jesus is Lord and participation in the imperial cults, therefore, meant that it was only a matter of time before the early Christians came into conflict with the supporters of Roman rule in Asia.

2.3. Roman Imperial Cults and the Persecution of Christians in the First Century

The persecution of Christians in the first century must be carefully understood. The scholarship has rightly emphasized that there is no evidence for an empire-wide, state-sponsored persecution of Christians in this period, whether under Domitian or otherwise.[69] That came later, but not until the emperor Decius (AD 249–51).[70] Indeed, prior to Nero's persecution of Christians in Rome in the mid-sixties AD and the Jewish War of AD 66–70, Roman authorities tended to treat Christians as a subset of the Jews, with the effect that Christians benefitted from the *mos maiorum* granted to Jews (i.e., the right to live according to ancestral custom). This included exemption from participation in Roman religious observance, including the imperial cults.[71]

---

[67] Justin, *1 Apol.* 6: "Hence we are called atheists. And we confess that we are atheists, so far as gods of this sort are concerned, but not with respect to the most true God"; Tertullian, *Apol.* 24.1: Christians face "the accusation of treason most of all against Roman religion."

[68] Tacitus, *Ann.* 15.44. Tacitus refers to the charges against Christians at the time of the Neronian persecution in Rome. He does not make direct reference to Christian non-participation in imperial cults. There is no doubt, however, that such non-participation was widely viewed in these terms.

[69] It was once widely suggested that the emperor Domitian (AD 81–96) sponsored an empire-wide persecution of Christians. Leonard L. Thompson, *The Book of Revelation: Apocalypse and Empire* (New York: Oxford University Press, 1990) demonstrated that the evidence cannot sustain this view, but overstated the case in his attempted rehabilitation of Domitian. For a balanced assessment, see esp. Beale, *Revelation*, 12–15; cf. T. B. Slater, "On the Social Setting of the Revelation to John," *NTS* 44.2 (1998): 232–56 (254–55); Naylor, "Imperial Cult," 226–27: "it has generally been accepted in recent years that a full-blown, empire-wide persecution directed against Christians under Domitian is unlikely."

[70] See esp. G. E. M. de Ste. Croix, "Why Were the early Christians Persecuted?" *Past and Present* 26 (1963): 6–38, esp. 6–7: "We know of no persecution by the Roman government until 64, and there was no general persecution until that of Decius. Between 64 and 250 there were only isolated, local persecutions; and even if the total number of victims was quite considerable (as I think it probably was), most individual outbreaks must usually have been quite brief."

[71] For the *mos maiorum*, see esp. Tacitus, *Hist.* 5.5 and Josephus, *A.J.* 16.163. See discussion in O. F. Robinson, *The Criminal Law of Ancient Rome* (Baltimore: Johns Hopkins University Press, 1995), 97. For the inclusion of Christians under the Jewish umbrella, including exemption from participation in the imperial cult, see B. W. Winter, "Gallio's Ruling on the Legal Status of Early Christianity," *TynBul* 50 (1999): 213–24. Winter argues convincingly that Gallio's ruling (Acts 18:12–17) effectively recognized Christians as a "party" within Judaism and thus granted Christians in the province of Achaea exemption from participation in the cult.

There is, however, plenty of evidence for sporadic, localized persecution of Christians across the empire from the very beginning. This is clear in the earliest Christian texts, including the Gospels,[72] the book of Acts,[73] the Letters of Paul,[74] the Letters of Peter,[75] and others,[76] all of which provide consistent evidence of Christians facing persecution.

The pattern of these persecutions seems, at first, to have taken the form of Jewish opponents persecuting Christians, and/or "stirring up" non-Jews to persecute Christians, and/or denouncing Christians to Roman authorities, with more or less success in prosecuting the case.[77] Jewish accusations against Christians were not, for the most part, directed at Christian non-participation in Greco-Roman religion or the imperial cults, but focused on the claim that Christians were distorting Jewish traditions and practices, and disturbing the peace.[78]

There is, however, also early evidence of non-Jews actively joining in the "hatred" of Christians,[79] and of persecution of Christians for their refusal to properly honor Caesar as Lord. As early as AD 49 Paul can speak of the Thessalonian believers suffering persecution at the hands of their "own countrymen" (1 Thess 2:14: ὑπὸ τῶν ἰδίων συμφυλετῶν). According to the book of Acts, this persecution began with the Jewish accusation against Paul and his companions that Christians were refusing to properly honor Caesar by declaring that "there is another king, Jesus" (Acts 17:6–7).[80] The book of Acts, further, reports that on at least two occasions, in Philippi and in Ephesus, non-Jews initiated the persecution of Christians because of a perceived threat to the worship of the Greco-Roman gods and to the Roman

---

[72] In the Gospels, Jesus repeatedly predicts the persecution of his followers: Matt 5:11, 44; 10:23; 23:34; 24:9–12; Mark 10:30; 13:9–13; Luke 21:12–19; John 15:20; 16:2; cf. 9:22; 12:42.

[73] In the book of Acts, the apostles and other believers face repeated persecution in diverse geographical locations: (i) In Jerusalem: Acts 4:1–22; 5:17–42; 6:8–7:1; 7:54–60; 8:1–3 (cf. Acts 22:4–5, 7–8, 19–20; 26:9–12, 14–15; 1 Tim 1:13); 12:1–5, 11; 21:27, 31 (cf. 23:27; 26:21); 22:2, 10, 22–24; 23:5–6, 9, 12–15, 21, 30; 24:27; 25:3; 25:6–26:32; (ii) In Pisidian Antioch: Acts 13:50; (iii) In Iconium: Acts 14:5; (iv) In Lystra: Acts 14:19; (v) In Philippi: Acts 16:19–24, 37; (vi) In Thessalonica: Acts 17:5–9; (vii) In Berea: Acts 17:13–14; (viii) In Athens: Acts 17:32; (ix) In Corinth: Acts 18:6, 12; 20:3; (x) In Ephesus: Acts 19:9–10, 23–41; (xi) In Rome: Acts 28:20, 22. See also the general principle: Acts 14:22; cf. 6:9; 15:26; 20:11, 13, 19, 23; 21:11–13.

[74] Rom 8:35; 2 Cor 1:8; 6:4; 12:10; 1 Thess 1:6; 3:2–7; 2 Thess 1:4, 6; 2 Tim 3:11.

[75] 1 Pet 1:7; 3:13–17; 4:12–19.

[76] Heb 10:33–34.

[77] Acts 4:1–22; 5:17–42; 6:8–7:1; 7:54–60; 8:1–3 (cf. Acts 22:4–5, 7–8, 19–20; 26:9–12, 14–15; 1 Tim 1:13); 12:1–5, 11; 13:45, 50; 14:2–7, 19; 17:5–9, 13–14; 18:6, 12; 19:9–10; 20:3, 11, 19; 21:27, 31; 22:2, 10, 22–24; 23:5–6, 9, 12–15, 21, 27, 30; 25:3; 25:6–26:32; 1 Thess 2:14–16; Mart. Pol. 12:1–2; 13:1; Tertullian, *Scorp.* 10; cf. Justin, *Dial.* 16, 47, and 96, who reports the synagogue practice of pronouncing curses on Christians.

[78] Acts 18:12–17; 24:1–9.

[79] Matt 24:9; Mark 13:13; Lk 21:17; Acts 13:50; 14:5, 19; 17:5–9.

[80] Acts 17:5–9; cf. anticipations in Luke 23:1–5; John 19:2, 12–16. For discussion of the persecution of Christians in Thessalonica, see Murray J. Smith, "The Thessalonian Correspondence," in *All Things to All Cultures: Paul among Jews, Greeks and Romans*, ed. Mark Harding and Alanna Nobbs (Grand Rapids: Eerdmans, 2013), 269–301 (275–77).

way of life.[81] Christian non-participation in imperial cults is not explicitly given as the reason for the persecution in either case. Nevertheless, given that the imperial cults were "a major part of the web of power that formed the fabric of society," any attempt to advocate "customs unlawful for us Romans to accept or practice" (Acts 16:21) would have been perceived as a threat to the Roman imperial order.[82] In the same way, Tacitus's account of Nero's persecution of Christians following the fire of Rome in AD 64–65 does not explicitly highlight Christian non-participation in imperial cults. Nevertheless, his description of Christianity as a "mischievous superstition," characterized by a range of "hideous and shameful ... abominations," including "hatred against humankind," suggests that Nero singled out the "immense multitude" of Christians because they were perceived as a threat to the imperial order.[83] And certainly, Pliny's letter to the emperor Trajan in AD 110 makes it clear that Christian non-participation in the imperial cult was at issue.[84] Pliny reports to Trajan how he had allowed those denounced as "Christians" the opportunity to repudiate Christ and to demonstrate their loyalty by offering "prayer with incense and wine *to your image*." Pliny further reports that many Christians had accepted this invitation: "they all *worshiped your image* and the statues of the gods, and cursed Christ."[85] Indeed, a range of evidence from later in the second century confirms this trajectory: Christians were required to demonstrate their loyalty to the emperor by making sacrifices to him and by declaring that "Caesar is Lord";[86] many refused to do so, and were persecuted as a result.[87]

Taken together, this evidence explains well why Christians faced sporadic and localized persecution from the supporters of Roman authority in the first century: (i) the Christian proclamation of Jesus as the Jewish "Messiah" resulted in discord within the Jewish community and so threatened the peace; (ii) the Christians' exclusive devotion to the one God of Israel, the "Father," as he had revealed himself in his "Son," the "Lord Jesus Christ," cut against the polytheistic practices that bound the Greco-Roman world together, and; (iii) Christian refusal to worship the emperor as "Lord" was a shocking failure to honor the one who guaranteed and mediated the favor of the gods, and who embodied in himself the power, prosperity, and peace of the empire.

---

[81] Acts 16:19–24, 37; 19:23–41; cf. Acts 17:32.

[82] Simon R. F. Price, "Ritual and Power," in *Paul and Empire: Religion and Power in Roman Imperial Society*, ed. Richard A. Horsley (Harrisburg, PA: Trinity Press International, 1997), 71.

[83] Tacitus, *Ann.* 15.44; cf. 1 Clem. 1.1 in which Clement of Rome speaks of "the sudden and repeated misfortunes and reverses that have happened to us" (διὰ τὰς αἰφνιδίους καὶ ἐπαλλήλους γενομένας ἡμῖν συμφορὰς καὶ περιπτώσεις).

[84] Pliny, *Ep.* 10.96.

[85] Note, however, that in his reply Trajan instructs Pliny to not seek out the Christians, but to respond when accusations are brought to him against them (Pliny, *Ep.* 10.97).

[86] Mart. Pol. 8.1–12.2; cf. Tertullian, *Apol.* 34.1 who states clearly: "For my part, I am willing to give the emperor this designation ["Lord"], but in the common acceptation of the word, and when I am not forced to call him Lord as in God's place."

[87] Tertullian, *Apol.* 10 (ca. AD 197) reports the common charge as follows: "You do not worship the gods," you say; "and you do not offer sacrifices for the emperors" (*deus non colitis et pro imperatoribus sacrificia non penditis*); cf. Minucius Felix, *Oct.* 5–10; Origen, *Cels.* 8.55–67.

2.4. Roman Imperial Cults and the Persecution of Christians in the Book of Revelation

In this context, it is no surprise that when we turn to the book of Revelation, we find good evidence of Christians facing persecution for their refusal to participate in Roman imperial cults. Revelation opens with numerous indications that the Christians it addresses have suffered—or are about to suffer—violent persecution. John introduces himself as "your brother and partner in the tribulation (ἐν τῇ θλίψει) and the kingdom and the patient endurance that are in Jesus" (1:9). The risen Lord, in his letter to the church of Pergamum, speaks of "Antipas my faithful witness, who was killed among you" (2:13). The book's central vision includes a picture of "the souls of those who had been slain for the word of God and for the witness they had borne" (6:9–10).[88] And the great multitude depicted in 7:9 are described as "the ones coming out of the great tribulation" (7:14: οἱ ἐρχόμενοι ἐκ τῆς θλίψεως τῆς μεγάλης). Moreover, as the book reaches its climax, this focus on Christians suffering persecution is significantly intensified by repeated references to the "blood" (τὸ αἷμα) of God's people. We read of "the blood of the saints and prophets" (16:6), "the blood of the saints, the blood of the martyrs of Jesus" (17:6), "the blood of prophets and of saints" (18:24), and "the blood of his servants" (19:2). There are, finally, also "those who had been beheaded for the testimony of Jesus and for the word of God" (20:4).[89]

Revelation lays responsibility for this bloodshed squarely at the feet of a transcendent evil power, identified as "Satan" or the "devil" and pictured as the "dragon," which is at work through evil human empire, variously pictured as the "beast from the sea," the "beast from the land," the "prostitute," and the "great city." Indeed, Revelation makes it clear that Christians are engaged in nothing less than a spiritual war in which these powers are presented as the enemies of God and his people. "The dragon ... makes war" (12:17: ποιῆσαι πόλεμον; cf. 12:7; 16:13–14) and the "beast ... makes war" against God and the Lamb and the saints (11:7: ποιήσει ... πόλεμον; 13:7: ποιῆσαι πόλεμον; 19:19: ποιῆσαι τὸν πόλεμον; cf. 13:4; 16:14; 17:14). Similarly, "the beast" will "make war on" (ποιήσει ... πόλεμον) and "conquer" (νικήσει) and "kill" (ἀποκτενεῖ) God's "two witnesses" (11:7–8). The "great prostitute," which is "the great city" (17:18), for its part, is "drunk with the blood of the saints, the blood of the martyrs of Jesus" (17:6; cf. 18:21, 24; 19:2). She is judged because "in her was found the blood of the prophets and of saints, and of all

---

[88] Theodor Zahn, *Introduction to the New Testament Vol 2*, trans. M. W. Jacobus (Edinburgh: T&T Clark, 1909), 165–73, 409–10 argues that Rev 6:9–10 refers to Neronian persecution.

[89] Roman law distinguished between two forms of the death penalty, which were variously applied depending on the nature of the offense and *dignitas* (status) of the offender. Members of the lower classes (later called *humiliores*) were subjected to severe forms of execution known as the *summum supplicium* (burning alive, crucifixion, exposure to wild animals); members of the upper classes (later called *honestiores*) were either exiled or, if executed, beheaded (*capite puniri*). The verb πελεκίζω at Revelation 20:4 means to "behead with an axe" and probably indicates that the Christian believers so executed belonged to the upper classes. See David E. Aune, *Revelation 17–22*, WBC (Dallas: Word, 1998), 1085–88.

who have been slain on earth" (18:21, 24). And, in the end, "the great multitude in heaven" praise God whose "judgments are true and just" because he has "avenged on her [the great prostitute] the blood of his servants" (19:2). Certainly, Revelation includes evidence of Christians suffering persecution at the hands of Jewish opponents, and in more general terms. In what follows, however, I demonstrate that key passages in Revelation 2–3, 13–14 and 17–18 present the transcendent evil power of "Satan" (the "dragon"), at work through the Roman Empire and its local supporters (the two "beasts" and the "prostitute" or "great city"), as the primary source of Christian suffering in late first century Asia.[90]

(a) The Lord's Royal Edicts to his Suffering Churches (Revelation 2–3)

To begin with, the seven letters of Revelation 2–3 suggest that Revelation addresses Christians suffering persecution because of their refusal to participate in some of Asia's imperial cults. The letters present themselves, beginning with their opening form of address (τάδε λέγει: "thus speaks"), as "royal edicts" from the risen Lord Jesus, "the ruler of kings on earth" (1:5), and "the King of kings and the Lord of lords" (17:14; 19:16).[91] They are each designed to comfort Christians facing persecution, while also warning them against compromise with the world. The references to persecution in these letters are, in some cases, quite general in nature, and concern the need for "patient endurance" (2:3, 19; 3:10) in the face of "the hour of trial that is coming on the whole world" (3:10). Similarly, some of the warnings they contain are directed generally against participation in "sexual immorality" and "idol worship" (2:14, 20, 24; cf. 3:4), which fit well in a context in which Christians faced pressure to participate in imperial cults, but can also be understood as more general references to the difficulties faced by Christians making their way in the Greco-Roman world (cf. Acts 15:28–29).

In three of the letters, however, the Lord Jesus speaks more directly into the situation of Christians facing pressure to participate in Roman imperial cults. First, the Lord's "royal edict" to Smyrna acknowledges the "slander of those who say that they are Jews and are not, but are a synagogue of Satan" (2:9; cf. 3:9), and immediately prophesies that the Smyrneans are "about to suffer" because "the devil is about to throw some of you into prison, that you may be tested, and for ten days you will have tribulation" (2:10). The gravity of this "tribulation" is evident in the exhortation which follows: "Be faithful unto death, and I will give you the crown of life" (2:10). It is difficult to be certain about the precise situation, but given Smyrna's role as a center of the

---

[90] Cf. Price, *Rituals and Power*, 197–98 effectively argues that Revelation is best understood as a response to the increased pressure on the Christian communities following from the establishment of the provincial cult of Domitian at Ephesus (but cf. n. 61 above).

[91] This opening form of address simultaneously evokes the Lord God of Israel's address to his people through the prophets, and the form of address chosen by the Persian kings in their royal edicts, which was also taken up in various analogous ways in the Roman imperial edicts of the first century. For the details, see Aune, *Revelation 1–5*, 141; Beale, *Revelation*, 229.

imperial cult in Asia, the close connection between "Satan" and Roman imperial cults later in Revelation (see below), and the threat of "imprisonment" and even "death"—which only the legitimate authority in the city could achieve—it seems quite likely that the letter speaks into a situation in which Jews were denouncing Christians to Roman-sponsored authorities for their failure to participate in the imperial cults.[92]

Second, the Lord's "royal edict" to Pergamum carries four distinctive features that suggest it addresses Christian non-participation in the imperial cults of that city (2:12–17). To begin with, it is significant that Pergamum is singled out from among the seven churches as the place "where Satan's throne is ... where Satan dwells" (2:13).[93] The letters indicate that Satan is active elsewhere (2:9, 24; 3:9), but "the throne of Satan" (ὁ θρόνος τοῦ Σατανᾶ) is in Pergamum. There may have been various reasons for this designation.[94] The strong connection made between Satan and Roman emperor worship later in the book (see below), however, suggests that Pergamum was the "throne of Satan" especially because it was the first center of Roman imperial cults in all of Asia.[95] Further, sandwiched between these references to "Satan's throne," the letter to Pergamum contains the first and only reference to a named Christian martyr in the book (2:13). The Lord commends the church in Pergamum because "you hold fast to my name" (καὶ κρατεῖς τὸ ὄνομά μου) and "did not deny my faith" (καὶ οὐκ ἠρνήσω τὴν πίστιν μου) even in the days of Antipas my faithful witness, who was killed among you" (Ἀντιπᾶς ὁ μάρτυς μου ὁ πιστός μου).[96] While the details remain opaque, it seems that the Lord here refers to a past period (the "days of x"), when the church in Pergamum did not yield to pressure to deny the "name" and the "faith" of the Lord Jesus by participation in the imperial cults, and that Antipas, presumably a prominent member, suffered the ultimate consequence.[97] Moreover, the

---

[92] Cf. Beale, *Revelation*, 240.

[93] Note the *inclusio* created in this verse by the repetition of the particle ὅπου with the verb κατοικέω which first has the church and then Satan as its subject. This *inclusio* emphasizes the stark reality for the church in Pergamum: where the church dwells, Satan dwells also.

[94] The designation may include reference to: (i) the Temple of Zeus "the Savior" (σωτήρ), which had statues of giants with serpents' legs; (ii) the Temple of Asclepius, whose symbol was a serpent, and who promised "healing" or "salvation" (σωτηρία)—and even resurrection life—to his devotees; (iii) the temple of Athena the "Victory-bearer" (νικήφορος), the city's presiding deity; (iv) the throne-like shape of the acropolis itself. For discussion and bibliography, see esp. Aune, *Revelation 1–5*, 183–84. See also Steven J. Friesen, "Satan's Throne, Imperial Cults and the Social Settings of Revelation," *JSNT* 27.3 (2005): 351–73.

[95] Mounce, *Revelation*, 96–97 makes the interesting suggestion, based on Revelation 13:2 and 16:10 that, just "as Rome had become the center of Satan's activity in the West ... so Pergamum had become his 'throne' in the East."

[96] Just as Israel was called to bear the Lord's name before the nations (Exod 20:7), so the church in Pergamum, as the new Israel and the new humanity (5:9–10), is to bear the name of the Lord Jesus in the midst of an unbelieving world (cf. Matt 28:19). This involves the open confession of Christ as Lord in a world where doing so invites persecution and even death.

[97] So Hans-Joseph Klauck, "Das Sendschreiben nach Pergamon und der Kaiserkult in der Johannesoffenbarung," *Bib* 73 (1992): 153–82; Mounce, *Revelation*, 97; cf. Gerhard A. Krodel, *Revelation*, Augsburg Commentary on the New Testament (Minneapolis: Augsburg, 1989), 114

Murray J. Smith

letter contains the second of two references to an enigmatic group identified as the "Nicolaitans" (τῶν Νικολαϊτῶν), who are here connected with "sexual immorality" and "idol worship" (2:14–15 and note οὕτως; cf. 2:6). The identity of this group remains uncertain, but the Greek name, when transliterated into Hebrew, gives the numerical value 666, which then suggests a close association between this group and the second "beast" and the "false prophet" in 13:11–18, and thus with the imperial cult (see below).[98] Finally, the Lord Jesus presents himself in this letter as "the one who has the sharp two-edged sword [τὴν ῥομφαίαν τὴν δίστομον τὴν ὀξεῖα] in his mouth" (2:12; cf. 2:16; 1:16; 19:15, 25). In doing so he employs an image that has its roots in the Scriptures of Israel (Isa 11:4;[99] cf. Isa 30:27–28, 33; 49:2; Ps 32:6; Pss. Sol. 17.24; 2 Thess 2:8), but which speaks with polemical daring into the Roman world, where the Roman emperor carried a sword or dagger as a symbol of his office, and the Roman governor exercised the *ius gladii*, or "right of the sword," in his province (Rom 13:4).[100] This striking polemical engagement with Roman imperial rule, precisely at the point where "Satan has his throne," where a deviant group is advocating "sexual immorality" and "idol worship," and where at least one Christian has been killed, strongly suggests that the imperial cults of Pergamum, and Christian non-participation in them, are at issue. The Lord Jesus, then, in speaking of himself as "him who has the sharp two-edged sword," comforts the church in Pergamum by announcing that his throne is higher than that of the emperor or his governor, and by implying that his sword of justice will be exercised against the enemies of his people (cf. 19:15, 25).[101]

Third, more briefly, the risen Lord Jesus, in his "royal edict" to the church in Thyatira (2:18–29), speaks of himself as the "Son of God" (2:18). This is the only occurrence of the title in the book. The title, of course, has obvious roots in the biblical understanding of Israel, and especially of David, as "son of God" (Exod 4:22; 2 Sam 7:13–14; Ps 2:7). It also speaks, however, with polemical force into a world where the Roman emperors, from Augustus onwards, regularly presented themselves as "son of God."[102] It is significant, then, that Thyatira had, sometime before 2 BC, established a civic cult in honor of Rome and Augustus, and that the city was famous for its purple cloth, favored by the emperors (Acts 16:14).[103] In this context, the references

who notes that there is no evidence that Christians were persecuted for failure to participate in the other cults.

[98] Michael Topham, "Hanniqola῾īt s," *ExpTim* 98 (1986): 44–45.

[99] The allusion here is confirmed by the use of Isaiah 11:2 at Rev 1:4b.

[100] Tacitus, *Hist.* 3.68; Suetonius, *Galb.* 11; Dio Cassius, *Hist.* 42.37.

[101] Mark W. Wilson, *Revelation*, ZIBBC (Grand Rapids: Zondervan, 2007), 268 suggests that the enigmatic reference to the "white stone" which the Lord promises to give "to the one who conquers" (2:17) may be a further polemical reference to Roman power since the Asian Calendar Decree of 9 BC was inscribed on white stones (see n. 46 above).

[102] See n. 27 above.

[103] See E. M. Blaiklock, "Thyatira," *ZPEB* 5:743–44; Robert North, "Thyatira," *ISBE* 4:846; Everett C. Blake and Anna G. Edmonds, *Biblical Sites in Turkey* (Istanbul: Redhouse, 1996), 131–33.

350

in the letter to a false prophetess, identified as "Jezebel" (2:20), who seduced Christians to "practice sexual immorality and to eat food sacrificed to idols" (2:20), and whose teaching is associated with "Satan" (2:24), are best understood not merely as general references to the pressure faced by Christians to conform to Greco-Roman religion, but more specifically to the pressure they faced to participate in the city's Roman imperial cults.

(b) The Dragon and the Beasts (Revelation 12–13)

Revelation 12–13 further develops these connections between the activity of "Satan" or "the Devil" and evil human empire, suggests that Rome is the contemporary manifestation of this evil empire, and identifies this complex as the primary source of the persecution of Christians. Revelation 12 introduces a "great dragon" (12:3, 9: δράκων μέγας; 12:9: ὁ δράκων ὁ μέγας) and identifies this dragon as "that ancient serpent, who is called the devil and Satan, the deceiver of the whole world" (12:9: ὁ ὄφις ὁ ἀρχαῖος, ὁ καλούμενος Διάβολος καὶ ὁ Σατανᾶς, ὁ πλανῶν τὴν οἰκουμένην ὅλην; cf. 20:2, 7, 10). The "great dragon" is clearly an evil transcendent being.[104] At the same time, the description of Satan in these terms hints that the "dragon" is to work out its evil purposes in the world through human empire. The only occurrence of the phrase "the great dragon" in the LXX is found in Ezekiel's vision of "Pharaoh the great dragon" (Ezek 29:3: Φαραω τὸν δράκοντα τὸν μέγαν),[105] and the Scriptures of Israel consistently employ the image of the "dragon" (תנין = δράκων) to speak of foreign powers that oppress God's people.[106] Later Jewish literature follows this trajectory,[107] and even applies the image to Rome.[108] Strikingly, the Sibylline Oracles at one point identify the Roman emperor Nero as "a terrible snake" (δεινὸς ὄφις).[109] Thus, while the "great

---

[104] The roots of the image, of course, go back to the foundation narrative of the Hebrew Scriptures and the "serpent" of the Garden of Eden (Gen 3:1, 2, 4: ὁ ὄφις). The term "Satan" is a transliteration of the Hebrew שטן = adversary (e.g., 1 Kgs 11:14 for Hadad the Edomite as a "satan" the LORD raised up against Solomon). The OT has a few references to "satan" as the transcendent adversary of God and his people (Job 1–2; 1 Chr 21:1; Zech 3:1–2), but it was Jesus' encounter with "the Satan" that more fully revealed the character of this transcendent evil being (see Mark 1:13 and Matt 4:1–11 where "the satan" is also described as "the devil/slanderer" (ὁ διάβολος) and "the tempter" (ὁ πειράζων)). "Satan" appears throughout Revelation (2:9, 13 [x2], 24; 3:9; 12:9; 20:2, 7).

[105] Cf. Beale, *Revelation*, 633.

[106] Egypt and Pharaoh: Ps 74:13–14; 87:4; 89:10; Isa 30:7; 51:9; Ezek 29:3; 32:2–3; Hab 3:8–15; Nebuchadnezzar: Jer 51:34.

[107] Tg. Isa. 27:1 interprets Isaiah's prophecy of God's victory over the "dragon" as a reference to God's victory over "the king who became great" and uses Pharaoh and Sennacherib as the paradigm. CD VIII, 10 interprets the תנינים "dragons" of Deut 32:33 as "the kings of the peoples." Cf. 2 Bar. 29.3–5 which prophesies that the Messiah will destroy "Behemoth" and "Leviathan" at the end; T. Ash. 7.3 has God "breaking the head of the dragon in the water." Neither of these texts make an explicit connection with foreign powers.

[108] Pss. Sol. 2.25–29 employ δράκων to speak of the Gentile ruler (probably the Roman general Pompey) whom God has judged for his sins against Jerusalem and describe him as "pierced on the mountains of Egypt." Sib. Or. 8.88 similarly identifies the "sea dragon" with Rome.

[109] See esp. Sib. Or. 5.28–34.

dragon" of 12:3 *denotes* an evil transcendent being, the image strongly *connotes* evil human empire, including Rome.

Revelation 13 then introduces two beasts, the "beast rising out of the sea" (13:1: ἐκ τῆς θαλάσσης θηρίον ἀναβαῖνον),[110] and the "beast rising out of the earth" (13:11: θηρίον ἀναβαῖνον ἐκ τῆς γῆς). The first beast, the one "from the sea," is set in parallel with the great dragon, since both figures are depicted with "seven heads" and "ten horns" (12:3; 13:1: ἔχον κέρατα δέκα καὶ κεφαλὰς ἑπτὰ). At the same time, the beast is differentiated from the dragon because the dragon gives its "power" and "throne" and "great authority" to the beast, resulting in the beast having "authority ... over every tribe and people and language and nation," being "allowed to make war on the saints and to conquer them," and demanding universal allegiance so that "all who dwell on earth ... worship it" (13:2, 4, 7–8). The dragon, then, is the transcendent evil power which stands behind the beast's evil human empire. Significantly, three observations suggest that this beast's evil power is at least partly manifested in the Roman Empire: (i) the "seven heads" and "ten horns" (13:1: ἔχον κέρατα δέκα καὶ κεφαλὰς ἑπτὰ) allude to the fourth beast in Daniel's vision which, in its original context, is an image of evil human empire opposed to God and his people, and which a range of later Jewish texts identify with Rome (Dan 7:7, 24);[111] (ii) the "ten diadems" (13:1: δέκα διαδήματα) indicate that it is a kingly power which, in first century context, must have suggested Rome; (iii) the beast's arrival "from the sea" (13:1: ἐκ τῆς θαλάσσης) probably evokes the practice of the Roman emperors in annually sending out the Roman proconsul to arrive in Ephesus by boat.[112]

The second beast, the one "from the land," is likewise connected to—but distinguished from—the dragon and the beast from the sea, and is likewise associated with the Roman Empire. It speaks "like a dragon" (13:11: ἐλάλει ὡς δράκων). It "exercises all the authority of the first beast in its presence, and makes the earth and its inhabitants worship the first beast" (13:12). This beast is, however, a different beast, since it looks like a "lamb" with "two horns," and directs its activities towards the worship of the first beast (13:12).[113] Most likely, the "beast from the land" includes reference to either the local Roman governor, or the priesthood of the Roman imperial cults in Asia. This is suggested by three observations: (i) The "beast from the land," rather than coming from afar ("from the sea"), arises in close proximity to the recipients

---

[110] This is almost certainly the same beast described in 11:7 as arising "from the abyss."

[111] Beale, *Revelation*, 684–85 notes the following: Midr. Gen 44:17; 76.6; Midr. Exod 15:6; 25:8; Midr. Lev 13:5; b. Avodah Zarah 2b; b. Shevu'ot 6b; Mekilta Rabbi Ishmael, Bahodesh 9.30–36; Pesiqta Rabbati 14.15; Pesiqta de Rab Kahana 4.9; Pirqe Rabbi Eliezer 28. He further notes that others make the allusion clear enough without citing specific verses from Daniel: Tanh. Gen 12:13; Midr. Ps 11.5; 18.11; 80.5–6; Tg. Zech 4:7 [codex f] with 6:5; Matt 24:15; Luke 21:20; cf. 4 Ezra 12.10; 2 Bar. 39.5–6; As. Mos. 10.8; Josephus *A.J.* 10.203–10 with 10.272–78.

[112] Cf. Rowland, *Open Heaven*, 431–32; I. E. S. Edwards, ed. *The Cambridge Ancient History*, 3rd ed. (Cambridge: Cambridge University Press, 1970/75) 11:581.

[113] The evil of this beast is evident in the way in which it parodies the Lamb of Revelation 5, since it has "two horns like a lamb."

of the book ("from the land") and acts under the authority of, and for the benefit of, the "beast from the sea." (ii) Revelation 13:14–15 announces that this "beast from the land" fosters the false worship of the first beast by commanding the construction of an "image for the beast" (εἰκόνα τῷ θηρίῳ) and by demanding worship (προσκυνήσωσιν) before it on pain of death. This seems to speak directly into the situation in the Roman province of Asia towards the end of the first century when the imperial cult was renewed at Ephesus by the erection of a colossal statue of the emperor Titus in the city, and the requirement that cities across the province make dedications to the new image.[114] (iii) Revelation 13:16–17 speaks figuratively of the beast's requirement that "all, both small and great" alike be "marked on the right hand or the forehead." These references to bearing the "mark of the beast" and "worshiping its image" are then repeated in 14:9–11, 16:2, 19:20 and 20:4 (cf. 15:2). While it is difficult to be certain of what is intended, these texts point to the local expression of the evil human empire (in this case, Rome) requiring both "worship" and some public sign of loyal devotion ("the mark"). The dire consequences of non-participation in this worship are made explicit in Revelation 13:15: the "image of the beast" is given authority so that it might "cause those who would not worship the image of the beast to be slain."

Taken together, it seems clear that these texts in Revelation 12–13 address the threat posed to Christians in the Roman province of Asia towards the end of the first century who refused to participate in the imperial cults.

(c) The Great Prostitute and the Great City (Revelation 17–18)

Revelation 17–18 confirms and extends this understanding of the beasts as evil human empire manifested in Rome and its local representatives or supporters in Asia.[115] Revelation 17:1 announces the "judgment" of "the great prostitute, who is seated on many waters" (17:1: τὸ κρίμα τῆς πόρνης τῆς μεγάλης τῆς καθημένης ἐπὶ ὑδάτων πολλῶν). This evil "woman" is further described as "sitting on a scarlet beast" which has "seven heads and ten horns" (17:3; cf. 17:7). She is finally identified as "the great city that has dominion over the kings of the earth" (17:18: ἡ πόλις ἡ μεγάλη ἡ ἔχουσα βασιλείαν ἐπὶ τῶν βασιλέων τῆς γῆς; cf. 18:10, 16, 18, 19, 21; also 16:19).

Several observations indicate that this "great prostitute" or "great city" includes reference to Rome:[116] (i) mention of the beast with "seven heads and ten horns" connects this vision to that of Revelation 12–13, which already suggests Rome; (ii) the identification of the woman as "the great city that has

---

[114] See esp. Price, *Rituals and Power*, 197–98. Price's assessment is supported by Friesen, "Ephesus: Key to a Vision in Revelation," 24–37 (but cf. n. 61 above).

[115] Cf. Giancarlo Biguzzi, "Is the Babylon of Revelation Rome or Jerusalem?" *Bib* 87 (2006): 371–86 which surveys interpretations of the "great city" and concludes that it is best identified as Rome.

[116] This city is distinguished from the other "great city" mentioned in 11:8 since that earlier city is "symbolically called Sodom and Egypt" and is "where their Lord was crucified," i.e. Jerusalem.

dominion over the kings of the earth" (17:18; cf. 17:15; 18:10, 16, 18, 19, 21), in the context of the first century, cannot but have evoked the largest and most powerful city in the known world; (iii) the further descriptions of the great city's moral degradation and economic prosperity, likewise, must have suggested an identification with Rome (17:2, 4–5; 18:3–4, 7, 9, 11–19, 23); (iv) the woman/city is described as "arrayed in purple and scarlet," the colors of imperial Rome and its wealth (17:4; 18:16);[117] (v) the "name of mystery," "Babylon the great," which is given to the city, is commonly used in early Jewish and Christian texts as a code-word for Rome (17:5; 18:2, 10, 21; also 14:8; 16:19);[118] (vi) the "seven heads" of the beast are interpreted as the "seven mountains on which the woman is seated," which probably alludes to the famous seven hills of Rome (17:9);[119] (vii) the further identification of the "seven horns" and the "ten heads" with "seven kings" and "ten kings" likewise evokes royal dominion of the kind best exemplified in the first century by the Roman emperors (17:10–12); (viii) the description of "the beast that … was, and is not, and is about to rise from the bottomless pit and go to destruction" (17:8; cf. 17:11 with 13:3, 12, 14) has remarkable similarities with the *Nero redivivus* ("Nero living again") or *Nero redux* ("Nero returned") myth, which circulated widely in the late first century, and according to which the dead emperor Nero would return at the head of a Parthian army to reclaim the imperial throne in Rome.[120]

Taken together, these observations indicate that the "great prostitute," which is a "great city," is a symbol of evil human empire opposed to God, manifested in the first century in imperial Rome. Given the repeated references to the "great city's" responsibility for the "blood of the saints" in these chapters (16:6; 17:6; 18:24; 19:2; cf. 20:4), it is again clear that the book

---

[117] See Ludwig A. Moritz, "Purple," in *OCD*, 1280.

[118] Babylon was an appropriate code-word for Rome, since Babylon and Rome had defeated and destroyed Jerusalem in 587 BC and AD 70 respectively. For Rome as "Babylon," see: Midr. Num 7.10; Midr. Ps 137.1, 8; Midr. Lev 6.6; Midr. Cant 1.6 §4; 1QpHab II, 11–12; Tg. Lam 1.19; 2 Bar. 11.1; 33.2; 67.7; 79.1; 4 Ezra 3.2, 31; b. Sanh. 21b; Sib. Or. 5.137–61, 434; 1 Pet 5:13. For discussion, see: Claus-Hunno Hunzinger, "Babylon als Deckname für Rom und die Datierung des I. Petrusbriefes," in *Gottes Wort und Gottes Land. Hans-Wilhelm Hertzberg zum 70. Geburtstag*, ed. Henning Graf Reventlow (Göttingen: Vandenhoeck & Ruprecht, 1965), 67–77.

[119] So also Beckwith, *The Apocalypse of John*, 707–8; George Bradford Caird, *A Commentary on the Revelation of St. John the Divine* (New York: Harper & Row, 1966), 218–19.

[120] Nero was deposed by the Senate and declared a public enemy on 8 June AD 68. He committed suicide the next day, though few witnessed his death. Suetonius, *Nero* 57.1 records that following Nero's suicide some in Rome acted "as if he were still alive and would shortly return and deal destruction to his enemies." The Sibylline Oracles reflect the myth that Nero had escaped to the Parthians and would soon return at the head of an army (Sib. Or. 4.119–22, 137–39; 5.28–34; 137–54, 214–27; 8.68–72; 12.78–94). Dio Chrysostom, *Pulchr.* 10 states "even now everyone wishes that Nero were alive and most people actually believe it." At least three "false Neros" appeared in the following years—(i) AD 69: Dio Cassius, *Hist.* 63.9.3; Tacitus, *Hist.* 2.8–9; (ii) AD 80: Dio Cassius, *Hist.* 66.19.3; (iii) AD 88: Suetonius, *Nero* 57.2. The myth appears to have been stronger in the East than in the West, and gained widespread currency later in the first century. In this connection, it is significant that Juvenal, *Sat.* 4.38 identified Domitian as "Nero."

of Revelation identifies the Roman Empire as a primary manifestation of Satan's transcendent evil power, and indicates that the Roman imperial cults in Asia were a primary cause not only of pressure on Christians to conform to the social norms, but of very real persecution, leading to imprisonment and even death.[121]

3. The Church's Mission in a Hostile World: Worship, Witness, and Wait!

Revelation's apocalyptic prophecy speaks into this world of violence. It is remarkable, then, that rather than calling on its auditors to respond to the violence of the Roman world with further violence, Revelation calls upon its auditors to fight the great spiritual battle by *worshiping* the one true God, by *bearing witness* to him even to the point of death, and by *waiting* for him to deliver his people and judge his enemies.

3.1. Worship!

The book of Revelation calls on its Christian auditors to *worship* the one true and living God as their most fundamental response in a hostile world. Christians faced with persecution, hostility, and violence, rather than "fighting fire with fire," are called first and foremost to worship the Lord who rules over all. This is because the battle in which Christians are engaged is a spiritual battle—a battle of true and false worship. The following brief survey examines, first, Revelation's language of worship, second, the God worshiped in the seven hymns of praise that punctuate the book, and third, the goal of this worship in the book as a whole.

(a) Revelation's Language of Worship

The book of Revelation contains many direct references to "worship." The primary verb προσκυνέω is used twenty-four times.[122] The root idea is that of prostrating oneself before a higher authority to kiss their feet or the ground before them.[123] The word also refers, by extension, to more general reverence shown towards a social superior, and to religious worship of a deity.[124] The

---

[121] This is not to say, however, that the images of the "beast from the sea," the "beast from the land" and the "great prostitute" or "great city" are *exhausted by* reference to Rome. The images are specific enough to make clear that they include reference to the Roman empire and the city of Rome itself, but illusive enough that they are not exhausted by that reference. That is, they retain a trans-temporal and universal horizon. For this perspective, see Beale, *Revelation*, 714, 869.

[122] Προσκυνέω: Rev 3:9; 4:10; 5:14; 7:11; 9:20; 11:1, 16; 13:4 (x2), 8, 12, 15; 14:7, 9, 11; 15:4; 16:2; 19:4, 10, 20; 20:4; 22:8, 9.

[123] See "προσκυνέω," *NIDNTTE* 4:150–54 (150).

[124] Cf. Walter Bauer et al., *A Greek-English Lexicon of the New Testament and Other Early Christian Literature*, 3rd ed. (Chicago: University of Chicago Press, 2000), 882–83.

verb is employed in the classical and Hellenistic Greek literature, as well as in the Greek translations of the Hebrew Scriptures, to describe both reverence towards human persons of superior authority,[125] and reverence toward the gods/God.[126] For our purposes, it is significant that the practice of prostrating oneself before a ruler, which was characteristic in ancient Persia, and taken up in the Hellenistic ruler cults,[127] was also adopted in the Roman imperial cults, particularly in the Greek East.[128]

Revelation often couples the primary verb προσκυνέω with πίπτω, which describes creatures "falling down" before the Lord, so that the two verbs are close to synonymous, describing two elements of a single act of devotion.[129] Right worship of the Lord God and the Lamb in his heavenly temple is also described at two points by use of the verb λατρεύω, which has priestly and cultic connotations (7:15; 22:3). Moreover, Revelation repeatedly speaks of worship in terms of "giving glory" (δίδωμι + δόξα) to God,[130] and at least once depicts the "twenty-four elders ... casting their crowns before the throne" (4:10: βαλοῦσιν τοὺς στεφάνους αὐτῶν ἐνώπιον τοῦ θρόνου), which evokes the practice of conquerors taking or receiving the crowns of vanquished rulers.[131]

The book of Revelation makes clear that people reveal by their worship the identity of their god. The book therefore presents a fundamental division between those who worship God and those who do not. On the one hand, the heavenly beings gathered around God's throne and the faithful among the inhabitants of the world worship the one true God and him alone (4:10; 5:14; 7:11; 11:16; 14:7; 15:4; 19:4, 10; 22:8–9). On the other hand, "the rest of humankind" worship "demons and idols of gold and silver and bronze and

---

[125] E.g., Euripides, *Orest.* 1507; Herodotus, *Hist.* 1.119; 3.86.2; 8.118 // Gen 33:7; 1 Sam 25:5; 2 Sam 9:6; 14:4; 18:21; Dan 2:46 // Matt 2:2, 11.

[126] E.g., Aeschylus, *Pers.* 499; Xenophon, *Anab.* 3, 2, 9; 13; Plato, *Resp.* 3.398a; Polybius, *Hist.* 18, 37, 10; Plutarch, *Pomp.* 626 [14, 4]; Lucian, *Pisc.* 21; *PGM* IV. 649 // Gen 24:26; Exod 12:27; 20:5; Deut 32:43; Ps 5:8. The word also describes image worship in the various polytheistic cults: e.g., Pindar, *Isthm.* 3.2; Athenagoras, *Legatio pro Christianis* 15.1; 2 Clem. 3.1; Diogn. 2.5; Mart. Pol. 12.2; cf. Acts 7:43.

[127] For the early and abortive attempt of Alexander III (the Great) to have the men of his court prostrate themselves before him, see Plutarch, *Alex.* 54.3–6; Arrian, *Anab.* 4.10.5–7; 4.12.3–5; Curtius, *Alex.* 8.5.9–12. See Ian Worthington, *Alexander the Great: A Reader* (London: Routledge, 2003), 236–72 for discussion of competing interpretations.

[128] See, for example, Philo, *Legat.* 116 where Philo denounces the fact that, at the time of Gaius, some people had "even introduced the barbaric custom [τὸ βαρβαρικὸν ἔθος] into Italy of falling down in adoration [τὴν προσκύνησιν] before him" (= the Roman emperor). For προσκύνησις in the Hellenistic ruler cults, see Lily Ross Taylor, "The 'Proskynesis' and the Hellenistic Ruler Cult," *JHS* 47 (1927): 53–62; Taylor, *Divinity*, esp. 256–66.

[129] Προσκυνέω + πίπτω: Rev 4:10; 5:14; 7:11; 11:16; 19:4; cf. 19:10; 22:8. πίπτω alone: 1:17; 5:8. Those who fall are identified as: "the twenty-four elders" (4:10; 5:14; 11:16); "all the angels" (7:11); "the twenty-four elders and the four living creatures" (5:8; 19:4). For the combination in other texts, see: 1 Sam 25:23; 2 Sam 14:4; Dan 3:5, 6, 10, 11, 15; Matt 2:11; 4:9; 18:26; Acts 10:25; 1 Cor 14:25; Apoc. Mos. 27.5; Jos. Asen. 28.9; T. Job 40.6; Josephus, *A.J.* 7.95; 9.11; 10.213.

[130] Δίδωμι + δόξα: 4:9; 11:13; 14:7; 19:7; cf. 16:9.

[131] 2 Sam 1:10; 12:30; 1 Chr 20:2; cf. Ezek 21:26; Plutarch, *Frat. amor.* 488D; cf. Tertullian, *Cor.* 15. For discussion, see esp. Aune, *Revelation 1–5*, 308–09.

stone and wood" (9:20) and especially give themselves to worship "the dragon" (13:4) and "the beast" or its "image" (13:4, 8, 12, 15; 14:9, 11; 16:2; 19:20).[132] The distinction between these two groups is absolute. No syncretism is possible. The faithful are those who not only obey the command to "worship God" (14:7; 19:10; 22:9) but who also do not worship "the beast or its image" (20:4).

(b) The God who is Worshiped: Seven Distinctively Christian Hymns of Praise

The worship of the book of Revelation is concentrated in seven scenes in which true worshipers express their adoration in hymns of praise to God. The presentation of seven hymns is itself probably significant, indicating the complete praise of God.[133] The following table indicates the object of worship in each hymn, the reasons for the worship, and the identity of the worshipers. Taken together, these scenes provide a vision of *distinctively Christian worship*, which is simultaneously distinguished from the worship of Greco-Roman gods and from Jewish worship.[134]

Scene	Object of worship	Reasons for worship	Identity of worshipers
4:8–11	"The Lord God Almighty" "Our Lord and God"	God's holiness and eternal being God's action as Creator	The four living creatures The twenty-four elders
5:9–13	"The Lamb" "The Lamb who was slain" "Him who sits on the throne" and "the Lamb"	The Lamb's sacrifice, ransoming people for God	The four living creatures and the twenty-four elders "Many angels" "Every creature in heaven and on earth and under the earth" with the four living creatures and the twenty-four elders

[132] Two references fall outside this sharp dichotomy: (i) 3:9: the Lord Jesus comforts the church in Philadelphia with the promise that he will make its enemies "come and bow down [προσκυνήσουσιν] before your feet"; (ii) 11:1: John is told to "measure the temple of God and the temple and those who worship there."
[133] This arrangement: (i) counts each of the multi-part songs as a single "composition" (4:8–11; 5:9–13; 7:10–12; 16:5–7 and 19:1–8); (ii) discounts Rev 14:1–5, since the "new song" taught to the 144,000 on Mount Zion, and sung by them, is only reported and not recorded.
[134] For recent studies on the picture of God in Revelation, see Martin Stowasser, *Das Gottesbild in der Offenbarung des Johannes*, WUNT 2 Reihe (T bingen: Mohr Siebeck, 2015).

7:9–12	"Our God who sits on the throne" and "the Lamb"	God's action in salvation	"A great multitude … from every nation" "All the angels"
11:16–18	"The Lord God Almighty"	God's action in judgment	The twenty-four elders
15:3–4	"The Lord God the Almighty" … "King of the nations"	"Great and amazing are your deeds"; "just and true are your ways"; "you alone are holy"; "your righteous acts have been revealed"	"Those who had conquered the beast and its image"
16:5–7	"Holy One"; "the Lord God Almighty"	God's just judgments	"The angel in charge of the waters" and "the altar"
19:1–8	"Our God" "The Lord our God the Almighty"	God's just judgments God's reign consummated in the "marriage of the Lamb"	"A great multitude in heaven" with the four living creatures and the twenty-four elders

Table 1. Worship Scenes in Revelation

The titles and expressions listed in Table 1 communicate God's sole sovereignty, unique holiness, and concern for his people ("… our God"). The God here worshiped is unambiguously the God of Israel's Scriptures: He is the great Creator (4:11; 14:7); the God of Moses and the Exodus (15:3); the God of Israel's King David (3:7; 5:5; 22:16); and the God of Israel's prophets (10:7; cf. 22:6). It is this God and this God alone who is worthy of worship.[135] Revelation, therefore, in keeping with the conviction of Israel's Scriptures—and also of first-century Judaism—distinguishes true worship from the worship of the Greco-Roman deities and of the Roman emperor. The point is made clear by the fact that Revelation not only describes the worship of the

---

[135] For προσκυνέω in the context of exclusive monotheism, see e.g., 1 Kgs 19:18; 2 Kgs 5:18; Esth 3:2, 5. For the concept without the verb προσκυνέω, see esp. Isa 45:20–23. Both Philo and Josephus who, while sometimes employing προσκυνέω in reference to prostration before a human being as a sign of respect (e.g., Josephus, *A.J.* 2.11), also use the verb in the stricter sense of worship of the one true God (e.g., Philo, *Gig.* 54; Josephus, *A.J.* 6.55, 154; 9.267; 20.164). Indeed, Philo, at *Decal.* 64, explicitly affirms a qualitative difference between the respect shown towards human superiors and the worship offered to God when he states that "we must not worship those who are our brothers by nature" (τοὺς ἀδελφοὺς φύσει μὴ προσκυνῶμεν).

one true and living God, but also positively commands it.[136] This command is, indeed, of universal significance. At Revelation 14:6–7 the angel with the "eternal gospel" speaks in a loud voice "to those who dwell on earth, to every nation and tribe and language and people" and commands them that they should "fear God and give him glory [φοβήθητε τὸν θεὸν καὶ δότε αὐτῷ δόξαν] ... and worship [προσκυνήσατε] him who made heaven and earth." In the same way, at Revelation 15:2–4, the worshipers ("those who had conquered the beast and its image") praise the Lord God Almighty as "King of the nations" and declare that "all nations will come and worship you." Similarly, at Revelation 19:5 God himself ("a voice from the throne") commands: "Praise our God [αἰνεῖτε τῷ θεῷ ἡμῶν], all you his servants, you who fear him, small and great." Finally, this Jewish-style exclusive monotheism is further underlined at 19:10 and 22:8–9 when John begins to offer worship to the angel who mediates the revelation to him, and is twice corrected with a firm command: "worship God" (τῷ θεῷ προσκύνησον). Only God is worthy of worship.

Consistent with this perspective, the book categorically condemns worship offered to "demons and idols" (9:20), especially to the symbols of Roman power—"the dragon" (13:4) and "the beast" or "its image" (13:4, 8, 12, 15; 14:9, 11; 16:2; 19:20). Revelation thus rejects the worship of the Greco-Roman deities, and especially any participation in the Roman imperial cult. So comprehensive is this distinction that the faithful may be described as those who have "not worshiped the beast or its image" (20:4). Readers of Revelation are called to worship neither Zeus nor Jupiter, neither Asklepios nor Athena, neither the Roman emperor nor his image, but the Lord God Almighty and him alone. Revelation thus describes and commands the universal and exclusive worship of the one true and living God of Israel's Scriptures.

Revelation also, however, distinguishes the worship it describes and commands from Jewish worship. The "Lord God Almighty" is praised not only for who he is as the eternal, holy, and all powerful Creator (4:8, 11; 15:3–4), but also for what he has done as the righteous King and Judge of the nations and all history (11:16–18; 15:3–4; 16:5–7; 19:1–6), and especially for his gracious work as Savior of his people through the "blood of the Lamb" (5:9–10; 7:10–12; 19:6–8). It is highly significant here that at several points Revelation includes the Lord Jesus in the worship offered to the one true and living God. The stage is set for this remarkable development by the vision the Lord Jesus grants to John in the first chapter. There John describes the one who appeared to him—clearly the risen Lord Jesus—in terms that evoke not only the Danielic "one like a son of man," but also the "Ancient of Days" himself (Rev 1:13–14; cf. Dan 7:9–10, 13–14). [137] John's response is understandable: "I fell at his feet as though dead" (1:17). The explicit worship

---

[136] Προσκυνέω appears in the imperative mood at 14:7; 19:10; 22:9.
[137] Rev 1:14: ἡ δὲ κεφαλὴ αὐτοῦ καὶ αἱ τρίχες λευκαὶ ὡς ἔριον λευκὸν ὡς; Dan 7:9: καὶ τὸ τρίχωμα τῆς κεφαλῆς αὐτοῦ ὡσεὶ ἔριον λευκὸν καθαρόν.

of the risen Lord Jesus first appears in the vision of Revelation 5, which introduces the figure of "the Lion of the tribe of Judah" who is also a slain "Lamb," and a victorious ram (5:5–6). This vision, remarkably, describes how—while all others "fall down" in the presence of God's throne—this Lamb is "standing" (ἑστηκός) "at the center of the throne" (ἐν μέσῳ τοῦ θρόνου), so that the "four living creatures" and the "twenty four elders" fall down in front of him (ἔπεσαν ἐνώπιον τοῦ ἀρνίου) and sing a "new song" of praise directed to the Lamb alone (5:6–10). In singing this song the heavenly creatures are soon joined by a vast multitude of angels (5:11–12). And when the scene reaches its crescendo, they are joined by every creature in the whole of creation, affirmed by the "four living creatures" and the "twenty four elders," who combine praise of God with praise of "the Lamb," declaring "to him who sits on the throne *and to the Lamb*, be blessing and honor and glory and might forever and ever!" (5:13–14).[138] Similarly, at Revelation 7:10 the "great multitude" cry out with a loud voice that "Salvation belongs to our God who sits on the throne, *and to the Lamb*!"—a cry that elicits the affirmation "Amen" from "all the angels" and the "elders" and the "four living creatures" (7:11–12). The book of Revelation, then, affirms, with the Scriptures of Israel and Jewish tradition, that the Lord God alone is to be worshiped, while also— remarkably, and against Jewish tradition—including Jesus in the identity of the one true and living God.[139]

The worship described in the book of Revelation is thus both continuous with the worship commanded and described in the Scriptures of Israel, and remarkably new. For this reason it is no surprise that Revelation 15:3–4 indicates that the first song of praise recorded in the Scriptures, the "song of Moses" in Exodus 15, which celebrates the Lord's victory over that "great dragon" Pharaoh (cf. Ezek 29:3), will also form the basis of the song that the saints will sing for all eternity, now with a new stanza added, celebrating the victory of "the Lamb" over the dragon, Satan. The redeemed will thus sing "the song of Moses, the servant of God, *and the song of the Lamb*" praising the Lord God Almighty because his "righteous acts have been revealed" in a new and startling way (15:3). Indeed, elsewhere, the redeemed sing an entirely "new song," extolling the new redemption that God has won through "the Lamb who was slain" (5:9; 14:3). Moreover, in addition to this new content in the worship offered by the redeemed, there is also a new constituency among the worshipers. While Israel's Scriptures expect and anticipate the universal worship of God (e.g., Psalms 29; 47; 49; 66; 96; 97; 98; 117; 148), Revelation provides a remarkable vision of this expectation fulfilled when it pictures worshipers around God's throne being drawn not

---

[138] Italics added. Indeed, from this point onwards, Revelation repeatedly couples "the throne" or the "one who sits on the throne" with "the Lamb" (5:13; 6:16; 7:9–10), places "the Lamb" at the "center of the throne" (5:6; 7:17), or indicates that the throne belongs jointly to "God" and to "the Lamb" (22:1, 3).

[139] This, of course, is consistent with the book's presentation of Jesus throughout. For a demonstration of the way in which the book as a whole includes Jesus within the identity of the one true God, see especially Bauckham, *Theology*, 54–65.

only from among Israel, the people of God of old, but from "every tribe and nation and people and language" and, indeed, from the entire creation (esp. 5:13; 7:9–12; 15:4).

(c) The Goal of Worship

The purpose of the seven worship scenes, depicting a distinctively Christian worship, is to show auditors the marvel of who God is and what he does, and therefore call them to respond with awe, godly fear, praise, faith, and obedience. God is worshiped primarily in heaven by heavenly creatures (4:8–11; 5:9–12; 11:16–18: the "four living creatures," the "twenty-four elders"; the "angels"; cf. 16:5: an angel; 16:7: "the altar"), but this worship extends first to human beings in heaven (7:9–12; 15:2; 19:1, 6), and then even further to all creatures in every part of the creation (5:13). These expanding circles of worshipers effectively make the point that the worship of the one true and living God is the inevitable destiny of every creature. The scenes, therefore, draw the book's auditors into the worship they hear described, and lead them to join in the praise offered by the heavenly beings, the angels, the saints, and all creation.

In the context of persecution, these scenes also have two more specific functions. First, the worship scenes comfort believers in the knowledge that their worship of the one true and living God—weak and despised as it is—is the reason the whole of creation exists, and the destiny of every creature. In worshiping God, worshipers join with the heavenly creatures, the angels and the whole creation in giving the Creator the honor he is due. Judaism called for worship in the temple in Jerusalem, and the imperial cults included worship choirs composed of elites who entered the imperial temples on regular occasions to sing the praises of the emperor and his family.[140] It is no coincidence, then, that Revelation declares that those who belong to the Lord Jesus have been "made ... a kingdom, priests to his God and Father" (1:6; 5:10; 20:6), or that the book's central vision gives its auditors privileged entry into the heavenly temple to witness and even participate in the worship of the true God (4:1–5:13). Revelation, in this way, comforts the small Christian communities in the cities of Asia: though their choirs are small compared to those of the emperor, and though they are weak, despised, and persecuted, as they join in songs of praise as part of their worship on the Lord's day (cf. 1:10), they participate in the eternal praise of the heavenly creatures around the heavenly throne, and anticipate the worship that every creature in the whole of creation will give the Lord God Almighty, and to him alone, at the end.

Second, the worship scenes challenge believers to declare God's praise in all the earth. Revelation declares that the choirs of the imperial cult are nothing compared to the great choir of creation, announces that the praise of the emperor is to be silenced before that of the living God, and so calls on its

---

[140] See nn. 54 and 55 above.

auditors to join in singing a different song to those around them—the song of all creation praising the Lord God Almighty, the Creator and Redeemer of his people, who rules over all. In praising "the One who sits on the throne" as Lord of heaven and earth, the book proclaims a very different "gospel" from that proclaimed by the imperial cults—an "eternal gospel."[141] It therefore calls on people from every tribe and nation and language to join in the song, worshiping the Lord of all creation (14:6–7). The worshipers affirm that "all nations will come and worship" the one true God (15:4).

Taken together, the worship scenes embody the reality that worship is central to the mission of the church in a hostile world.[142] While the world around refuses to recognize the One seated on the throne and the Lamb at his side, Revelation reveals true reality to the church so that the church can respond with appropriate worship.

3.2. Witness!

The book of Revelation presents Jesus, and those who belong to him, as those who "bear witness" to God in a hostile world. This is the second element of the church's mission envisaged by the book. To bear witness is to faithfully persevere in worshiping the one true God, speaking of him, and living for him, even in the face of persecution and even under the threat of death. This is borne out by a study of the language of "witness" in the book.

(a) Revelation's Language of "Bearing Witness"

First, the book's use of the noun μάρτυς ("witness") makes it clear that a faithful "witness" is one who is loyal to God, even in the face of opposition, and even to the point of death. The noun occurs five times in the book and consistently bears this sense. The first occurrence, which is determinative for the others, presents Jesus himself as "the faithful witness" (1:5: ὁ μάρτυς ὁ πιστός). The reference here is built on Psalm 88:38 LXX (= ET 89:37) and forms part of Revelation's presentation of Jesus as "the faithful witness, the firstborn of the dead, and the ruler of the kings of the earth," which may well summarize the three stages of Jesus' career in terms of his faithful life (and death), his resurrection (and ascension), and his heavenly rule (and return in glory).[143] The presentation of Jesus as "the faithful witness," then, has on view his life of faithfulness even to the point of death (cf. the reference to Jesus'

---

[141] For the language of "gospel" applied by the Council of Asia to the achievements of Augustus, see n. 46 above.

[142] John Piper, *Let the Nations Be Glad*, 3rd ed. (Grand Rapids: Baker, 2010), 17 puts it well: "Missions is not the ultimate goal of the Church. Worship is. Missions exist because worship doesn't. Worship is ultimate, not missions, because God is ultimate, not man. When this age is over, and the countless millions of the redeemed fall on their faces before the throne of God, missions will be no more. It is a temporary necessity. But worship abides forever."

[143] Cf. George R. Beasley-Murray, *The Book of Revelation*, Rev. ed., New Century Biblical Commentary (London: Marshall, Morgan and Scott, 1978), 56.

"blood" in 1:5c), and communicates that in God's economy, those who are faithful in this way will ultimately triumph. Jesus' identity as "the faithful and true witness" is confirmed in his "royal edict" to the church in Laodicea, which contrasts the "lukewarm" faith of the Laodiceans with "the words of the Amen, the faithful and true witness" (3:14: ὁ ἀμήν, ὁ μάρτυς ὁ πιστὸς καὶ ἀληθινός).

The noun μάρτυς is applied not only to Jesus, but to others whose lives are patterned after his. The first such occurrence is at 2:13 where the noun describes "Antipas my faithful witness" (Ἀντιπᾶς ὁ μάρτυς μου ὁ πιστός μου) who "was killed," and whose faithful witness followed that of the Lord himself. The next occurrence of the noun is at 11:3, where it describes "my two witnesses" (δυσὶν μάρτυσίν μου). These two give faithful testimony to God until they have completed their testimony (11:7: ὅταν τελέσωσιν τὴν μαρτυρίαν αὐτῶν), when God allows that "the beast" should "rise from the bottomless pit" and "make war on them and conquer them and kill them" (11:7). Afterwards, however, "a breath of life from God" enters them and they stand up "on their feet" and are called "up to heaven in a cloud" (11:11–12). These faithful witnesses, then, like the Lord himself, are killed for their testimony, and yet are ultimately vindicated by God. The final occurrence of μάρτυς is at 17:6, where it refers in the plural to "the witnesses of Jesus" (τῶν μαρτύρων Ἰησοῦ) whose "blood" had been "drunk" by the "woman" representing "Babylon the great." Again, to bear faithful witness involves suffering even death, but results—ultimately—in vindication by God (cf. 20:4). The noun μάρτυς is, therefore, first applied to Jesus, the one who was faithful to his Father even to death (1:5; 3:14), and subsequently connected in each of its occurrences with faithfulness even to the point of death, enabled by the promise of vindication from God beyond the grave (2:13; 11:3; 17:6).[144]

Second, Revelation's use of the verb μαρτυρέω ("I bear witness") and the cognate noun μαρτυρία ("testimony") emphasizes the role of the "witness" in speaking truth about God. The verb μαρτυρέω occurs four times (1:2; 22:16, 18, 20). Revelation opens with John's assertion that he "bears witness [ἐμαρτύρησεν] to the word of God and the testimony of Jesus Christ" that was revealed to him (1:2). It closes with the Lord Jesus himself, the angel he sent, and John together "bearing witness" to the significance and veracity of what has been revealed in the book (22:16, 18, 20: μαρτυρέω). The verb, then, primarily refers to the activity of Jesus, his angel and John, in faithfully revealing the heavenly truths contained in the book. Related to this is the use of the noun μαρτυρία, which occurs nine times in the book (Rev 1:2, 9; 6:9; 11:7; 12:11, 17; 19:10 (x2); 20:4), six times in the phrase "the testimony of Jesus" (1:2, 9; 12:17; 19:10 [x2]; 20:4: τὴν μαρτυρίαν Ἰησοῦ). The first occurrence of this phrase is most likely a subjective genitive ("testimony Jesus gave") because in its context Jesus is the one who "reveals" and "makes

---

[144] Thus, although the term retains its primary meaning of "witness," the roots of its later sense of "martyr" are to be found in these five uses in Revelation (cf. also Acts 22:20). Cf. Bauer et al., *BDAG*, 620 § 3.

known."[145] If so, then the subjective genitive here might suggest that the other five occurrences should also be read as subjective genitives; that is, primarily as references to the witness *Jesus* bore (to God and his kingdom, or to himself), and which the church *receives*.[146] At the same time, the other five occurrences of the phrase in Revelation may be read as objective genitives, that is, as references to *John/the saints* testifying *to* or *about* Jesus (1:9; 12:17; 19:10 [x2]; 20:4; cf. 6:9; 12:11). Perhaps the ambiguity of the genitive is, in this case, intentionally employed with both connotations: the "testimony of Jesus" is first the testimony Jesus gave, but also the testimony his people give about him. Certainly, the content of this testimony includes that which the Lord Jesus revealed to John and which is now contained in the book of Revelation itself. At the same time, the close association of the phrase "testimony of Jesus" with the "word of God" (1:2, 9; 20:4) and similar phrases at several points (6:9; 12:11, 17), indicates that the "testimony of Jesus" cannot be narrowly associated with the vision John saw, but includes Christians speaking the truth about God, both before and beyond the content of Revelation itself.

(b) Revelation's Call to Faithful Witness in a Hostile World

Taken together, this analysis suggests that, in the context of persecution, Revelation calls its auditors not only to worship the one true and living God, but to bear witness to him by speaking truth about him, and by persevering in this witness even to the point of death. The church's mission in a hostile world is to hold fast to the testimony given by Jesus, that is, to the Word of God, and to hold on to this in the way that Jesus did: in faithful obedience to the Father, even to the point of death. Indeed, Revelation 12:11 explicitly connects these two senses of "bearing witness" when it speaks of those who have "conquered by the blood of the Lamb and by the word of their testimony, for they have not loved their lives even unto death." Osborne summarizes it well: "in Revelation 'witness' refers to fearless public proclamation and authentication, usually in the face of tremendous opposition, of divine realities in word and life."[147] This, together with worship of the One who sits on the throne, is crucial to the mission of the church in a hostile world.

---

[145] Favored by Aune, *Revelation 1–5*, 19 who translates: "who now bears witness to all the visions he saw which is the message from God, that is, the witness *borne by* Jesus" (italics added); cf. Osborne, *Revelation*, 57.

[146] Rev 6:9 might be thought to tell against this interpretation, since it refers to τὰς ψυχὰς τῶν ἐσφαγμένων διὰ τὸν λόγον τοῦ θεοῦ καὶ διὰ τὴν μαρτυρίαν ἣν εἶχον (ESV: "the souls of those who had been slain for the word of God and for the witness *they had borne*"). Even here, however, the primary reference may be to the testimony given *by Jesus* and subsequently "held" (as custodians) by the saints (cf. KJV: "the testimony which *they held*").

[147] Osborne, *Revelation*, 56.

3.3. Wait!

Finally, the book of Revelation also calls on its auditors, as they face persecution, not to take vengeance into their own hands, but to *wait* patiently for God to establish his kingdom.

(a) Revelation's Language of "Patient Endurance"

Revelation's call to wait for God to bring his righteous judgment on the earth takes the form of repeated exhortations to "patiently endure." John identifies himself from the outset as "your brother and partner in the tribulation and the kingdom and the patient endurance that are in Jesus" (1:9). The note of "patient endurance" (ὑπομονή) under suffering is sounded again in the Lord Jesus' encouragement to the churches in Ephesus (2:2), Thyatira (2:19), and Philadelphia (3:10). And it is significant that this same call to "patient endurance" is made twice more in the book, both times in association with the suffering and even death that God's people are to face because of the blasphemous worship of the beast and its image (13:10; 14:12). In the midst of all of this, the book's central vision provides a positive model of what this "patient endurance" might look like when it depicts "the souls of those who had been slain for the word of God and for the witness they had borne" (6:9). These departed faithful have been welcomed into the heavenly throne-room, and yet continue to "cry out with a loud voice [ἔκραξαν φωνῇ μεγάλῃ], 'O Sovereign Lord, holy and true, how long before you will judge and avenge our blood on those who dwell on the earth?'" (6:10). Patient endurance, then, means continuing to worship the One true God, bearing witness to him and word and deed, while crying out to God to establish his kingdom and bring his righteous judgment on the earth.

(b) Revelation's Inaugurated Eschatology: The Lamb Has Conquered

The answer to the prayer of the martyrs in Revelation 6:9–10 is ultimately found in God's action in Christ to conquer his enemies, judge all that is evil, and finally establish his kingdom. The answer, that is, comes in Revelation's inaugurated eschatology, which announces that God has now already triumphed in Christ, and that his victory will "soon" be worked out for the whole creation.

To begin with, Revelation is clear that the Lord Jesus has *already* conquered evil. In the book's opening chapter, Jesus is declared to be "the ruler of the kings of the earth" (1:5). The reference here, built on Psalm 88:28 LXX (= ET 89:27), is to Jesus' present rule over all earthly powers, and is designed to comfort the faithful in their affliction at the hands of those powers. This affirmation that the Lord Jesus already rules is confirmed in the initial vision-commission, when the risen Lord appears to John as the glorious Son of Man (1:12–19), as well as in the seven "royal edicts" to the churches, which repeat key elements of that vision (2:1–3:21). In the initial scene the

Lord Jesus reveals himself in the most exalted manner, and John sees the glory of the Danielic "one like a son of man" merged with that of Ancient of Days himself (Rev 1:13–14; cf. Dan 7:9–10, 13–14). At the same time, the Lord reveals himself in such a way as to demonstrate his supremacy over the powers of the world, including, especially, Rome. He is "the faithful and true witness" (1:5; 3:14); he has "eyes like a flame of fire and feet like burnished bronze" (1:14–15; 2:18); he is "the first and the last" (1:17; 2:8); he has the "keys of Death and Hades" (1:18; cf. 3:7). In all of these ways the Lord Jesus asserts his sovereign power over beginning and end, truth and falsehood, life and death. Most particularly, however, he reveals himself: (i) as the one who holds the "seven stars" in his right hand, using an image that directly challenges Domitian's presentation of himself on his coins as the father of a son surrounded by seven stars (1:16; 2:2; 3:1),[148] and; (ii) as the one with a "sharp two-edged sword" coming from his mouth, using an image that—as we have already had occasion to note—simultaneously evokes the prophetic promise of the Spirit-anointed deliverer of Isaiah 11:2, and declares Jesus' supremacy over the Roman emperor and his governor in Asia (1:16; 2:12, 16; cf. 19:15).

Crucially, the Lord Jesus' present authority is repeatedly grounded in his victory over sin by his faithful obedience to the point of death, and in his victory over death by his resurrection. This starts in the opening chapter, when Jesus asserts that he "holds the keys to Death and Hades" because he is "the living one" who "died" but is "alive forevermore" (1:18). It is repeatedly confirmed throughout the book when Jesus' life, death, and resurrection are shown to be the foundation of his present rule and the means by which he "conquered" the powers of sin and death (2:8; 3:21; 5:5–13; 12:5–10). It is perhaps clearest in the key moment of the book's central vision, when it is revealed that the Creator's plans and purposes for history, symbolized by the "scroll sealed with seven seals," have been unlocked by "the Lion of the tribe of Judah, the Root of David" (5:1–13). In this remarkable scene John hears this mighty Lion described, but then looks to see "a Lamb standing, as though it had been slain" (5:6). This Lamb, to be sure, is also a conquering ram "with seven horns and with seven eyes" (5:6).[149] But the songs of praise that follow celebrate that this Lamb has "conquered" (ἐνίκησεν)—and so can "open the seven seals"—only by the power of his blood shed for others (5:9, 12).[150]

---

[148] See Koester, *Revelation*, 253.

[149] Cf. Osborne, *Revelation*, 255 expresses well the impact of these verses: "It is impossible to overstate the magnificent transformation in 5:5–6: the lion is transformed into a lamb that becomes the slain paschal lamb that is again transformed into the conquering ram (the seven horns)! There is even a certain chiasm: lion—lamb—slain lamb—conquering ram."

[150] Bauckham, *Theology*, 67–69 helpfully points out that here, as elsewhere in Revelation, John draws attention to Jesus' Davidic roots in terms that emphasize the militaristic element of the Messiah's calling, but then declares that his victory over the forces of evil has come not through military might but by his sacrifice of himself (cf. 3:7 "keys of David"; 22:6 "the root and the offspring of David").

This declaration of Christ's victory permeates the book. The result is that while history continues after the victory of the Lamb by his death and resurrection, the ultimate outcome of history has now been revealed.

(c) Revelation's Vision of the Final Victory: The "Rider on the White Horse" Will Conquer

The Lamb "has conquered" by his blood; but his authority in the world is rejected by the "Dragon" and the "beasts" and those who worship them. The final outworking of the Lamb's victory in the world, therefore, remains to be seen. Indeed, Revelation's central vision (4:1–22:5) concerns the outworking of God's rule—the rule of heaven—over the earth, and is divided into three sections. The first and longest section (4:1–16:21) begins with a vision of the heavenly throne room, and a celebration of the victory of the Lamb as the key which unlocks the "scroll" of God's purposes for his creation (4:1–5:13). It then presents a series of four overlapping visions, which repeatedly cover the whole of the church age from a number of different angles (6:1–16:21). The conclusion of each of these four sections presents a complementary vision of final judgment followed by a celebration of eternal salvation (6:12–8:1; 11:15–18; 14:14–15:4; 16:17–21).[151] The second major section (17:1–21:8) then intensifies and extends this pattern of final judgment and salvation so that it becomes the exclusive focus: these chapters present complementary visions of the final return of Christ, and his victory over the powers of evil in the final judgment. The third and final section (21:9–22:5) contemplates the "New Jerusalem" as a picture of the state of eternal bliss to follow the final judgment.

Within this frame, the conflict between the risen Lord Jesus and the earthly powers is a major theme of the book. The evil kings of the earth oppose Christ, but he will utterly defeat them (6:15–17; 10:11; 16:14; 17:2, 14, 18; 18:3, 9–10; 19:18–19). The repeated visions of final judgment and salvation declare that "the kingdom of the world has become the kingdom of our Lord and of his Christ, and he shall reign forever and ever" (11:15; cf. 12:10 and Dan 7:13–14). The enemies of God and his people "will make war on the Lamb," but "the Lamb will conquer them" (17:14). Ultimately, the kings of the earth will "bring their glory" into the heavenly Jerusalem, submitting themselves to Christ's Lordship (21:24). Jesus is the "King of kings and Lord of lords" (19:16; cf. 17:14).[152]

For our purpose, it is particularly significant that in the final vision of eschatological judgment and salvation, in 19:11–16, Revelation speaks of Christ's return as conquering King with daring polemical force. Revelation 19 is sandwiched between the account of the fall of the "evil city," "Babylon the

---

[151] Beale, *Revelation*, 122.

[152] The origins of the title are found in Daniel 4:37 (cf. Deut 10:17; Dan 2:37; 1 En. 9.4; 2 Macc 13:4; 1 En. 63.4; 1 Tim 6:15). The application to Christ here again includes him within the identity of the one true God. For discussion, see Gregory K. Beale, "The Origin of the Title 'King of Kings and Lord of Lords' in Revelation 17:14," *NTS* 31.4 (1985): 618–20.

Great" (17:1–19:5), and the victory of God's city, the glorious "New Jerusalem," which comes down out of heaven from God (21:1–22:5; cf. 3:12). In this context, Revelation 19:11–16 presents the return of Christ as conquering King in a manner that picks up and develops the earlier picture of Christ conquering by the "sword of his mouth" (19:15, 21; cf. 1:16; 2:12, 16). It shows how Christ simultaneously fulfills the expectations of Israel's Scriptures, and challenges the power claims of the Roman emperors. On the one hand, the description of the "rider on the white horse" as the one who "judges ... in righteousness" presents him as the long promised, Spirit-filled, Davidic deliverer (19:11: ἐν δικαιοσύνῃ κρίνει; cf. Isa. 11:4: וְשָׁפַט בְּצֶדֶק).[153] On the other hand, the white horse, the diadems, the title inscribed on the rider, the armies accompanying him, the military imagery, and the description of a decisive victory all evoke common descriptions of Roman military "triumphs."[154] The vision thus speaks out of the Scriptures of Israel and presents a direct challenge to Roman imperial ideology: Jesus is Lord, and Caesar is not. In this context, it is significant that at Revelation 19:11 "the rider on the white horse ... judges *and makes war* in righteousness" (ἐν δικαιοσύνῃ modifies both verbs). Throughout Revelation, the "dragon" (12:9 = Satan) has "made war" (12:7, 17; cf. 16:13–14) and the "beast" (= evil human empire/Rome) has "made war" (11:7; 13:7; 16:14; 17:14; 19:19; cf. 13:4; 16:14) against God and the saints. Now, however, it is Christ who "makes war in righteousness" against his enemies (cf. 2:16; 17:14). As Osborne comments: "If there has ever been a "just" or "holy war," this is the one!"[155] The point is clear: Revelation's auditors, though facing persecution and even death at the hands of Rome or her supporters in the province of Asia, should not give up. Jesus, the world's true Lord, will ultimately triumph.

(d) Imminence and Delay: "How Long O Lord?"

The inaugurated eschatology of Revelation gives rise to a tension between imminence and delay. The "Lamb ... has conquered," but the victory of the "rider on the white horse" is yet to come.

On the one hand, Revelation emphasizes that the final victory will come "soon." The book reveals "what must soon take place" (1:1; 4:1; 22:6: δεῖ

---

[153] In the Scriptures of Israel it is preeminently God alone who has the right to judge (Gen 18:25; Judg 11:27; 1 Sam 2:10; Ps 9:8; 82:8; 94:2; 96:10, 13; 98:9; Isa 33:22). Nevertheless, in Psalm 2:8–12 the Lord's anointed executes God's judgment, and in 1 En. 49.4; 61.9; 62.2–6; 63.11 the "Son of Man" is active in judgment. In the same way, in Revelation it is generally God who judges (6:10; 11:18; 14:7; 16:5, 7; 18:8, 10, 20; 19:2; 20:12–13), even as that role is taken up by the "Son of Man" (14:14–16; cf. Matt 16:27; cf. Matt 13:41–43; 19:28; 25:31–46) and, here, by the "rider on the white horse" (19:11).

[154] Virgil, *Aen.* 3.537; Dio Cassius, *Hist.* 43.14.3; Juvenal, *Sat.* 10.45; Tibullus, *El.* 1.7.5–8. See esp. Aune, *Revelation 17–22*, 1051; cf. already Aune, "The Influence of Roman Imperial Court Ceremonial on the Apocalypse of John," *BR* 28 (1983): 5–26. The Roman "triumph" was a celebratory parade which honored victorious Roman generals upon their return to the capital.

[155] Osborne, *Revelation*, 680.

γενέσθαι ἐν τάχει; cf. 2:16; 3:11; 11:14; 22:7, 12, 20: ἔρχομαι ταχύ).[156] And it speaks of the "time" as "near" (1:3; 22:10: ἐγγύς)[157] and "about to be" (1:19: μέλλει γενέσθαι), using language that echoes Jesus' own announcement of the coming of the kingdom (Mark 1:15: ἤγγικεν; cf. Mark 13:28–29: ἐγγύς; cf. Rom 13:11–12; Phil 4:5; Heb 10:25; Jas 5:8; 1 Pet 4:7).

On the other hand, Revelation also emphasizes that between the victory of the Lamb, through his death and resurrection, and the final outworking of that victory, there will be a period of delay. This is implied already in the three series of seven judgments that fill the central section of the book in Revelation 6–16 (seven seals, seven trumpets, seven bowls): the Lamb has won the decisive victory, but the outworking of that victory remains to be completed in a series of judgments over the earth.[158] The sense of delay created by this literary structure is confirmed at a number of points where a more explicit note is sounded. The "souls of those who had been slain" under the altar at 6:9–10 cry out: "O Sovereign Lord, holy and true, *how long* before you will judge and avenge our blood on those who dwell on the earth?" Similarly, at 11:2 the "temple of God" —a symbol for the church—is to be trampled by the nations for a period of 42 months (3½ years).[159] This assures Christian auditors that their time of trial, though painful, is not indefinite: it is only half of the number of completeness (7), only half of what it could be. Nevertheless, it also communicates that the final victory will not follow immediately. Finally, given the way in which the prayers of the suffering saints function as the impetus for God's judgments in the earth (8:3–5), it seems that the suffering of the righteous, which demands God's intervention, is actually part of God's strategy for establishing his kingdom! His kingdom will come, and "soon," but only when God's purposes for his world are full and complete.

Revelation's emphasis on the "nearness" of the end has led some—despite the indications of delay just noted—to a "Preterist" reading of the book as a whole, according to which its prophecies were all fulfilled in the first century.[160] It is better, however, with Moore, to see that while the New Testament authors, John included, clearly expected the return of Christ to be "soon," and understood the end to be "near," they never delimited this expectation in chronological terms.[161] The references to the "nearness" of the

---

[156] It is also interesting that Jesus uses the phrase δεῖ γενέσθαι in Mark 13:7 parr. in his prophecy of the signs of the "end."

[157] In contrast to the command to Daniel to conceal the words and seal up his book until the end of time (Dan 12:4), John is told the exact opposite: "Do not seal up the words of the prophecy of this book, for the time is near" (Rev 22:10).

[158] In this section of the book the following texts, especially, seem to envisage a significant period of time before the end: 6:1; 7:3; 9:5, 10; 10:11; 11:3; 12:6, 14; 13:5.

[159] Cf. Ps 37:10; Isa 26:20; Heb 10:37

[160] See esp. Ken L. Gentry, *Before Jerusalem Fell: Dating the Book of Revelation* (Tyler: Institute for Christian Economics, 1989); cf. George Bradford Caird, *A Commentary on the Revelation of St. John the Divine* (New York: Harper & Row, 1966), 12.

[161] Arthur L. Moore, *The Parousia in the New Testament*, NovTSup (Leiden: Brill, 1966), esp. 108–59; cf. John P. M. Sweet, *Revelation*, Westminster Pelican Commentaries (Philadelphia:

end are best read as a theological assertion—or, better, a *christological* assertion—that the victory won in Christ's death and resurrection is now, already, a present reality, and that the final manifestation of his victory may therefore take place at any moment.[162]

(e) In the Meantime: Revelation's Call to Conquer by the Lamb

On the basis of the victory won by the Lamb through his death and resurrection, and in anticipation of the final outworking of his victory when he returns, Revelation calls on its auditors to "conquer." Certainly, the Lord Jesus promises eschatological salvation "to the one who conquers" (τῷ νικῶντι) in each of the letters to the seven churches (2:7, 11, 17, 26; 3:5, 12, 21). The content of the promise is different in each case, but always concerns an aspect of the final eschatological reality. It is significant, then, that the promise does not appear again in the same form until the very close of the book (21:7). This has the effect of enclosing the whole book within the call to "conquer" and the promise of eschatological life to those who do.

Crucially, however, the book defines what it means to "conquer" in terms of following in Jesus' footsteps, and in stark contrast to the kind of "victory" celebrated in the Greco-Roman world. The goddess Victory (νίκη) was widely celebrated in the cities of the Roman province of Asia.[163] In Pergamum, to take just one example, victory by military force was worshiped at the temples of Zeus "the Savior" (σωτήρ) and Athena "the victory-bearer" (νικήφορος), who had delivered the city from military peril.[164] Far from conquering through violence or force, however, Revelation praises those who "have conquered ... by the blood of the Lamb and by the word of their testimony, for they loved not their lives even unto death" (12:11). Revelation further describes those who have "conquered" as those who have "harps of God in their hands" (15:2), ready to sing God's praise. In the terms of the categories we have developed in this chapter, "the one who conquers" is the one who *worships* the Lord God Almighty and him alone, and who faithfully bears *witness* to Jesus in word and deed, even to the point of death. In stark contrast to the Roman conquest of the known world by shedding the blood of those conquered, Jesus' victory in the world, and the victory of those who follow him, is won by their self-sacrificial faithfulness to the Lord.

Westminster John Knox, 1979), 58 who notes that Revelation clearly expects the events it depicts to unfold in stages, even if it is difficult to create a precise chronology.
[162] Moore, *Parousia*, 172: "The nearness of the end is bound up with the person of Jesus Christ, in whom the events of the end, including the open, unambiguous manifestation, co-inhere. In him, death, resurrection, ascension and Parousia belong together. They do not belong together as a general principle but as a matter of theological, or more exactly of Christological fact. The Christological unity of the End events is thus the mainspring of the End's nearness"; cf. C. E. B. Cranfield, *The Gospel according to St. Mark: An Introduction and Commentary*, CGTC, 3rd ed. (Cambridge: Cambridge University Press, 1966), 408.
[163] Statues celebrating the goddess have been found in Ephesus, Aphrodisias, and elsewhere.
[164] See n. 94 above.

Revelation, therefore, calls on its auditors to "wait" for the final outworking of God's victory in the world. The final return of Christ to defeat his enemies and vindicate his people is coming "soon," but not before God's purposes in history have been fulfilled. God's people, therefore, must "patiently endure" suffering, worshiping God and bearing witness to Christ in life and deed, confident that those who "conquer" will, in the end, receive the life of the age to come.

4. Conclusion

Revelation addresses the seven churches of Asia in the first century, which lived in a world of violence, and which had faced, were facing, and were about to face persecution for their devotion to the Lord Jesus Christ. The Roman imperial cults in the province were the focal point of this persecution because Christians could not participate in them without denying their most basic confession: "Jesus is Lord." Revelation speaks into this situation and provides the view from the heavenly throne. It unmasks the false claims of the Roman imperial cults, exposes the pretensions of Roman rule, and so empowers is auditors—in the face of pressure and persecution—to *worship* the one true God, to bear *witness* to Christ in word and deed, even at the cost of their lives, and to *wait* for God's final victory in the world.

Recommended Reading

Aune, David E. *Revelation*. WBC. 3 Vols. Dallas: Word, 1997–98.

Bauckham, Richard J. *The Theology of the Book of Revelation*. Cambridge: Cambridge University Press, 1993.

Bauckham, Richard J. *The Climax of Prophecy: Studies on the Book of Revelation*. Edinburgh: T&T Clark, 1993.

Beale, Gregory K. *The Book of Revelation: A Commentary on the Greek Text*. NIGTC. Grand Rapids: Eerdmans, 1999.

DeSilva, David A. *Seeing Things John's Way: The Rhetoric of the Book of Revelation*. Louisville: Westminster John Knox, 2009.

Friesen, Steven J. *Imperial Cults and the Apocalypse of John*. Oxford: Oxford University Press, 2001.

Friesen, Steven J. *Twice Neokoros: Ephesus, Asia and the Cult of the Flavian Imperial Family*. Leiden: Brill, 1993.

Hays, Richard B., and Stefan Alkier. *Revelation and the Politics of Apocalyptic Interpretation*. Waco: Baylor University Press, 2012.

Hemer, Colin J. *The Letters to the Seven Churches of Asia in Their Local Setting*. JSNTSup. Sheffield: JSOT, 1986.

Koester, Craig R. *Revelation: A New Translation with Introduction and Commentary*. The Anchor Yale Bible Commentaries. Vol. 38A. New Haven: Yale University Press, 2014.

Naylor, Michael. "The Roman Imperial Cult and Revelation." *CurBR* 8.2 (2010): 207–39.

Price, Simon R. F. *Rituals and Power: The Roman Imperial Cult in Asia Minor*. Cambridge: Cambridge University Press, 1984.

Winter, Bruce W. *Divine Honours for the Caesars: The First Christians' Responses*. Grand Rapids: Eerdmans, 2015.

13. Roman Political Ideology and the Authority of First Clement

L. L. Welborn

1. Authority

Sometime in the late first or early second century,[1] the church at Rome sought to intervene in the affairs of the church at Corinth.[2] In a struggle over ecclesial office, the Romans sought to intercede, not merely to urge all parties to seek peace and reconciliation, but to take sides in the dispute with a group of deposed presbyters (1 Clem. 44.4–6). The author of the Roman epistle insists upon harsh measures: the exile of the persons who have raised the rebellion (54.1–4; cf. 1.1; 3.3; 47.6),[3] and the restoration of the old presbyters to office, apparently against the will of the majority (44.3, 6; 46.9; 47.6). Such an intervention in the affairs of another congregation is unprecedented in the history of the period.[4] What is the source of the authority that the Roman epistle asserts?[5]

---

[1] Kirsopp Lake, ed., *The Apostolic Fathers,* LCL (Cambridge, MA: Harvard University Press, 1977), 1:5: "It is safest to say that 1 Clement must be dated between 75 and 115 AD." For a critique of the certainty with which 1 Clement is customarily assigned to the year AD 96, see L. L. Welborn, "On the Date of First Clement," *BR* 29 (1985): 35–54; "The Preface to 1 Clement: The Rhetorical Situation and the Traditional Date," in *Encounters with Hellenism: Studies on the First Letter of Clement,* ed. Cilliers Breytenbach and Laurence L. Welborn (Leiden: Brill, 2004), 197–216.

[2] On the subject in general, see R. van Cauwelaert, "L'intervention de l'Église de Rome à Corinthe vers l'an 96," *RHE* 31(1935): 267–306.

[3] Paul Mikat, "Der 'Auswanderungsrat' (I Clem 54,2) als Schlüssel zum Gemeindeverständnis im 1. Clemensbrief," in idem, *Geschichte, Recht, Religion, Politik I* (Paderborn: Schöningh Verlag, 1984), 361–73; L. L. Welborn, "Voluntary Exile as a Solution to Discord in First Clement," *ZAC* 18 (2014): 1–16.

[4] On the exceptional nature of the intervention, see already Adolf von Harnack, *Einführung in die alte Kirchengeschichte. Das Schreiben der römischen Kirche an die korinthische aus der Zeit Domitians (I. Clemensbrief)* (Leipzig: Teubner, 1929), 98: "die Tatsache, dass keine andere reichskirchliche Gemeinde bzw. kein Bischof (auch nicht Ignatius) so im Anfang der Kirchengeschichte gesprochen und gehandelt hat, bleibt bestehen."

[5] Joseph A. Fischer, *Die apostolischen Väter* (Darmstadt: Wissenschaftliche Buchgesellschaft, 1959), 11–12, rightly designates this as the most important question with respect to the epistle. See the discussion in Karlmann Beyschlag, *Clemens Romanus und der Frühkatholizismus* (Tübingen: Mohr Siebeck, 1966), 6–9; Adolf W. Ziegler, "Die Autoritäts und Primatsfrage," in *Neue Studien zum ersten Klemensbrief* (München: Manz, 1958), 102–22; Horacio E. Lona, "Das

We may begin by excluding the possibility that the Roman church already enjoyed the primacy among the churches that it claimed to possess at a later period.[6] Until the outbreak of the Jewish War, the Jerusalem church was the court to which missionaries and apostles turned in the search for ecclesiastical unity (Gal 2:1–10; Acts 15:1–35).[7] Later, the leaders of the urban churches exercised some measure of control over Christians in the surrounding regions.[8] Thus, Ignatius of Antioch refers to himself as "the bishop of Syria" (Ign. *Rom.* 2:2),[9] and addresses the Roman congregation as "the church ... which presides in the place of the district of the Romans" (Ign. *Rom.* Inscr.).[10] To be sure, the power of the Roman bishop grew throughout the second century.[11] In a controversial passage, Irenaeus argues that every church should seek to conform to the tradition of the Roman church, because of its antiquity and authority (*Haer.* 3.3.1–2).[12] According to Eusebius, at the end of the second century, Victor attempted to excommunicate "the dioceses of all Asia, together with the adjacent churches, on the grounds of heterodoxy" (*Hist. eccl.* 5.24.9). He was countered by appeals "to consider the cause of peace and unity and love towards his neighbors" (*Hist. eccl.* 5.24.10). But Victor evidently believed that he possessed the authority for such an action.[13]

That the author of the so-called First Epistle of Clement knew that he did not possess the authority that he asserts is demonstrated by the rhetorical character of the letter: he must persuade by argument (e.g., 14.1–2; 30.3; 47.7; 59.1; 62.2–3) and induce by example (e.g., 5.1; 6.1; 16.17; 46.1; 55.1; 63.1); that is, it is not yet his to command.[14] The author describes his work as an

Eingreifen Roms," in *Der erste Clemensbrief* (Göttingen: Vandenhoeck & Ruprecht, 1998), 82–89.

[6] Contra Otto Bardenhewer, *Geschichte der altkirchlichen Literatur* (Freiburg: Herder, 1913), 1.124–25; more cautiously, Berthold Altaner, "Der 1. Clemensbrief und das römische Primat," in *Kleine patristische Schriften* (Berlin: Akademie Verlag, 1967), 539, who speaks of "einer latenten 'besonderen Apostolizität' der römischen Kirche."

[7] Martin Dibelius, *Studies in the Acts of the Apostles* (London: SCM, 1956), 93–122; Günther Klein, "Galater 2,6–9 und die Geschichte der Jerusalemer Urgemeinde," *ZTK* 57 (1960): 275–95; Gerd Lüdemann, *Paulus, der Heidenapostel II. Antipaulinismus im frühen Christentum* (Göttingen: Vandenhoeck & Ruprecht, 1983), 59–102; Martin Hengel, *Between Jesus and Paul: Studies in the Earliest History of Christianity* (Eugene, OR: Wipf & Stock, 2003), esp. 58–59.

[8] Robert M. Grant, *Augustus to Constantine: The Thrust of the Christian Mission into the Roman World* (New York: Harper & Row, 1970), 154.

[9] See the discussion in William R. Schoedel, *Ignatius of Antioch* (Philadelphia: Fortress, 1985), 171.

[10] Schoedel, *Ignatius of Antioch*, 165–66: "if Ignatius is speaking of the location of the church, he has Rome or Rome and its immediate environs (not the Roman Empire) in mind."

[11] Epiphanius, *Haer.* 33.7.9; Eusebius, *Hist. eccl.* 4.23.9–11.

[12] On this much-debated passage, which is extant only in Latin, see F. Sagnard, *Irénée de Lyon: Contre les hérésie. Mise en lumière et réfutation de la prétendue connaissance. Livre III. Texte latin, fragments grecs. Introduction, Traduction et notes* (Paris: Editions du Cerf, 1952), 414–23.

[13] Grant, *Augustus to Constantine*, 158.

[14] The point is fully appreciated by W. C. van Unnik, *Studies over de zogenaamde Eerste Brief van Clemens. I. Het Litteraire Genre*, Medelingen der koninklijke Nederlandse akademie van wetenschappen, afd. Letterkunde 33 (Amsterdam: N. V. Noord-Hollandsche Uitgevers Maatschappij, 1970), esp. 39–46; English translation by L. L. Welborn in Breytenbach and Welborn, *Encounters with Hellenism*, 115–81. See, more recently, Odd Magne Bakke,

"appeal" (ἔντευξις, 63.2) and urges the Corinthians to heed his "advice" or "counsel," (συμβουλή, 58.2). The hortatory subjunctive is utilized throughout, in preference to the imperative.[15] When obedience is called for, the author appeals to the will of God as revealed in Scripture, to whose authority he is also subject (9.1; 13.3; 14.1; 63.2). If the Corinthians persist in disobedience, they are threatened, not with the ban of the Roman church, but with the judgment of the word of God (58.1; 59.1). Two passages, in particular, illuminate the relationship between the churches. Near the beginning of the argument, the author seeks to clarify his motives: "We are not only writing these things to you, beloved, for your admonition, but also to remind ourselves, for we are in the same arena, and the same struggle is before us" (7.1).[16] And near the end of the letter, the author defines his responsibility: "Then let us also intercede for those who have fallen into any transgression, that meekness and humility be given to them, that they may submit, not to us, but to the will of God" (56.1).[17] The decision to resolve the conflict remains with the Corinthians: those who have given rise to division must themselves decide to submit to the presbyters and to receive the correction of repentance (54.1–2; 57.1).[18] It is not Rome which cuts off from the common unity, but the Corinthians who must take action to quell the sedition (58.1–2; 63.1–2). Thus the emissaries who accompany the Roman epistle are not arbiters of a Roman verdict, but "witnesses between you and us" (63.3),[19] who will "report the sooner the peace and concord which we pray for and desire" (65.1).[20] If the First Epistle of Clement has a place in the history of the Roman primacy, it is as the originative moment in that history.[21] The primacy of Rome cannot be assumed as the basis for the intervention of the Roman church in the affairs of the church at Corinth.[22]

"Concord and Peace": A Rhetorical Analysis of the First Letter of Clement with an Emphasis on the Language of Unity and Sedition (Tübingen: Mohr Siebeck, 2001).

[15] Lona, Der erste Clemensbrief, 37.

[16] Lona, Der erste Clemensbrief, 174: "Die römische Gemeinde wählt eine Ausdrucksform, die jede Art einer unnötigen Demonstration von Autorität vermeidet."

[17] Cf. Andreas Lindemann, Die Apostolischen Väter I. Die Clemensbriefe (Tübingen: Mohr Siebeck, 1992), 157.

[18] On the rhetorical formulation of 54:1–2, see Ziegler, Neue Studien, 91–94.

[19] Robert M. Grant, The Apostolic Fathers: A New Translation and Commentary, vol. 2: First and Second Clement (New York: Thomas Nelson, 1965), 98; Peter Lampe, Die stadtrömischen Christen in den ersten beiden Jahrhunderten (Tübingen: Mohr Siebeck, 1987), 154.

[20] Cf. van Unnik, Studies, 46–53.

[21] Similarly, A. Stuiber, "Clemens Romanus I," Reallexicon für Antike und Christentum (Stuttgart: Teubner, 1950), col. 191; Johannes Quasten, Patrology Vol. 1 (Utrecht: Spectrum, 1950), 46–47; Philipp Vielhauer, Geschichte der urchristlichen Literatur (Berlin: de Gruyter, 1975), 538. On the question in general, see John Fuellenbach, Ecclesiastical Office and the Primacy of Rome: An Evaluation of Recent Theological Discussion of First Clement (Washington: The Catholic University of America Press, 1980).

[22] Similarly, Lona, Der erste Clemensbrief, 84–85.

Nor is there evidence that the Roman church found the warrant for its intervention in the invitation of the Corinthians.[23] Nowhere does the epistle suggest that the deposed presbyters have appealed to the Roman Christians to send a delegation to Corinth as mediators. The one text that might offer support for this supposition proves conclusive in the opposite direction. In an effort to shame the Corinthians, the author claims that the news of their sedition has been widely disseminated: "And this report [ἀκοή] has not only reached us, but also those who dissent from us, so that you bring blasphemy on the name of the Lord through your folly, and are moreover creating danger for yourselves" (47.7). From this formulation one may conclude that the Roman Christians have heard rumor of the conflict, of the "matters which are disputed among you" (1.1), something that is easily conceivable given the frequency of commerce between the Roman province and the capital.[24] But this would seem to exclude an official embassy from the Corinthian community. We are led to conclude that the Roman church has sent the epistle on its own initiative.

It is worth noting that the author of the Roman epistle makes no attempt to place his writing under the authority of the apostles, despite the growth of pseudepigraphy throughout the period.[25] To be sure, the apostles have an exemplary function (5.1–7).[26] Paul is "the model [ὑπογραμμός] of the greatest endurance" (5.7), a term that is usually applied to Christ in the literature of the period (1 Pet 2:21; 1 Clem. 16.17; Polycarp, *Phil.* 8.2).[27] What Paul wrote to

---

[23] Rudolf Knopf, *Die Apostolischen Väter I. Die zwei Clemensbriefe* (Tübingen: Mohr Siebeck, 1920), 44; van Cauwelaert, "L'intervention," 270–71; Beyschlag, *Clemens Romanus*, 6; van Unnik, *Studies*, 10, 46; Lona, *Der erste Clemensbrief*, 82.

[24] Cf. van Cauwelaert, "L'intervention," 305; van Unnik, *Studies*, 46. There is no basis for the interesting conjecture of Thomas M. Wehofer, *Untersuchungen zur altchristlichen Epistolographie* (Wien: Carl Gerald's Sohn, 1901), 140, that a pamphlet had been circulated by the opposition party at Corinth. On the frequency of travel and trade between Rome and Corinth, see, in general, James Wiseman, "Corinth and Rome I: 228 BC–AD 267," *ANRW* II.7/1 (Berlin: de Gruyter, 1979), 497–503; Donald Engels, *Roman Corinth: An Alternative Model for the Classical City* (Chicago: University of Chicago Press, 1990), 19–21, 45, 67–68.

[25] Edgar J. Goodspeed, "Pseudonymity and Pseudepigraphy in Early Christian Literature," in *New Chapters in New Testament Study* (New York: Macmillan, 1937), 169–88; Helmut Koester, *Introduction to the New Testament, Vol. 2: History and Literature of Early Christianity* (Philadelphia: Fortress, 1982), 3–4, 279.

[26] Grant, *First Clement*, 25–26; Lindemann, *Die Clemensbriefe*, 36–39; O. Knoch, "Im Namen des Petrus und Paulus: Der Brief des Clemens Romanus und die Eigenart des römischen Christentums," *ANRW Welt* II.27/1 (Berlin: de Gruyter, 1993): 3–54, esp. 12; Richard I. Pervo, "1 Clement," in *The Making of Paul: Constructions of the Apostle in Early Christianity* (Minneapolis: Fortress, 2010), 127–30. On the Cynic-Stoic origins of the idealization of Peter and Paul in 1 Clement 5, see L. Sanders, *L'Hellénisme de Saint Clement de Rome et le Paulinisme* (Louvain: Peeters, 1943), 8–34; Martin Dibelius, "Rom und die Christen im ersten Jahrhundert," in *Botschaft und Geschichte. Gesammelte Aufsätze II* (Tübingen: Mohr Siebeck, 1956), 199–203.

[27] Clement also uses ὑπογραμμός of the norm provided by the Creator in 33:8. On the accentuation of the image of Paul in 1 Clement 5, see Harnack, *Das Schreiben der römischen Kirche*, 107; Andreas Lindemann, *Paulus im ältesten Christentum. Das Bild des Apostels und die Rezeption der paulinischen Theologie in der frühchristlichen Literatur bis Marcion* (Tübingen: Mohr Siebeck, 1979), 75–80; Pervo, *The Making of Paul*, 130–34.

the Corinthians about partisanship was "by true inspiration" of the spirit (47.3); his advice is held to be applicable, not only to the past, but also to the present situation (47.4–5).[28] It is from the apostles, by succession, that the present ministers derive the legitimacy of their office (42.1–4; 44.1–6).[29] It is more surprising, then, that no attempt is made to connect the writing or the author with one of "the good apostles" (5.3).

The author of the Roman epistle makes no appeal to the authority of his person or his office as the basis for his intervention. In fact, the writing is anonymous, and gives no hint of the name or person of the author.[30] A tradition that goes back to Dionysius of Corinth (Eusebius, *Hist. eccl.* 4.23.9–11) ascribes the authorship of the letter to a certain Clement.[31] Without referring to the epistle, the author of the Shepherd of Hermas mentions a Clement who "will send" his writing "to the churches outside, for that is his function" (Herm. Vis. 2.4.3).[32] This Clement appears to be a secretary of the church at Rome, in charge of foreign correspondence. He may, of course, have held another office, such as that of presbyter.[33] But the tradition that makes him the bishop of Rome, third in succession from the apostle Peter

---

[28] Helmut Opitz, *Ursprünge frühkatholischer Pneumatologie. Ein Beitrag zur Entstehung der Lehre vom Heiligen Geist in der römischen Gemeinde unter Zugrundelegung des I. Clemensbriefes und des "Hirten" des Hermas* (Berlin: Töpelmann,1960), 46: "die Dignität des Briefes ist an die geisterfüllte Apostelpersönlichkeit gebunden"; Grant, *First Clement*, 78.

[29] On the much discussed issue of whether 1 Clement 40–44 reflects the idea of "apostolic succession," see G. G. Blum, *Tradition und Sukzession. Studien zum Normbegriff des Apostolischen von Paulus bis Irenaeus* (Berlin: Lutherische, 1963), 47–49; Karlmann Beyschlag, "1. Clemens 40–44 und das Kirchenrecht," in *Reformatio und Confessio*, ed. F. W. Kantzenbach und G. Müller (Berlin: Lutherische, 1965), 9–22; Hans-Günter Leder, "Das Unrecht der Presbyterabsetzung in Korinth. Zur Interpretation von 1. Clem. 44,1–6," *TL* 10 (1979): 107–27; Lona, *Der erste Clemensbrief*, "Exkurs 7. Amt–apostolische Sukzession–Kirchenrecht," 471–81.

[30] The Greek and Latin mss. attribute the letter to Clement: see the apparatus to the subscription in F. Funk and K. Bihlmeyer, eds., *Die apostolischen Väter* (Tübingen: Mohr Siebeck, 1970), 70. But the Coptic version preserves a form of subscription which is undoubtedly original: ἐπιστολὴ τῶν Ῥωμαίων πρὸς τοὺς Κορινθίους; see the judgment of Lake, *Apostolic Fathers*, 1:121. The best discussion of the authorship of 1 Clement remains that of E. T. Merrill, "On 'Clement of Rome,'" in *Essays in Early Christian History* (London: Macmillan, 1924), 217–41, which includes the *testimonia*. On the person of the author, especially his literary and philosophical training, insofar as it may be inferred from the epistle itself, see Lampe, *Die stadtrömischen Christen*, 172–82; Lona, *Der erste Clemensbrief*, 66–74; Bakke, *"Concord and Peace,"* 1–7.

[31] Eusebius quotes from Dionysius's letter to Soter of Rome whose episcopate extended from ca. AD 166 to 174. It is worth noting that, if Dionysius thought Clement to have been bishop of Rome, like Soter, Eusebius does not represent him as saying so. The testimony of Hegesippus (in Eusebius, *Hist. eccl.* 3.16; 4.22) does not certainly ascribe any individual authorship to the letter.

[32] Merrill, *Essays in Early Christian History*, 221 and Harnack, *Das Sendschreiben der römischen Kirche*, 50 are inclined to identify the author of 1 Clement with the official mentioned by Hermas, finding the testimony of the *Shepherd* simple, clear, and unsuspicious; similarly, Vielhauer, *Geschichte der urchristlichen Literatur*, 539.

[33] Knopf, *Die apostolischen Väter*, 43; Stuiber, "Clemens Romanus I," col. 189; Lindemann, *Die Clemensbriefe*, 13. On the office of presbyter in the church at Rome, see Hans von Campenhausen, *Kirchliches Amt und geistliche Vollmacht in den ersten drei Jahrhunderten* (Tübingen: Mohr Siebeck, 1963), 88–103; Lampe, *Die stadtrömischen Christen*, 336–37.

(Irenaeus, *Haer.* 3.3.3; Origen, *Comm. Jo.* 6.36; Eusebius, *Hist. eccl.* 3.16) is late and without support by corroborative evidence.[34] Whether the author is to be identified with the Clement who was a co-worker of Paul at Philippi (Origen, *Comm. Jo.* 6.36; Eusebius, *Hist. eccl.* 3.15–16) or the Roman consul Titus Flavius Clemens who was put to death on account of "atheism" by Domitian (Suetonius, *Dom.* 15.1; cf. Dio Cassius, *Hist.* 67.14.1) is purely a matter for speculation.[35] Indeed, the attribution of the epistle to a "Clement" may represent nothing more than an early conjecture, based upon Hermas's mention of a person by that name as the foreign correspondent of the Roman Christians.[36]

Instead of appealing to the authority of a person or an office, the First Epistle of Clement presents itself, in the salutation, as a communal writing: "The *ekklēsia* of God which is sojourning in Rome to the *ekklēsia* of God which is sojourning in Corinth" (*praescript.*).[37] The communal character of the authorship is conveyed through the use of first person plural forms throughout the letter.[38] Moreover, early Christian tradition recognized that the sender of the letter was the Roman church as a whole: for example, Irenaeus attests that "the church in Rome dispatched a most powerful epistle to the Corinthians, exhorting them to peace" (*Haer.* 3.3.3); Clement of Alexandria makes reference to "the epistle of the Romans to the Corinthians" (*Strom.* 5.12).[39] That a Christian community should act on its own authority in relation to another group of believers, without invoking the name of an apostle, is a *novum* in early Christian literature, which calls for an explanation.[40]

2. Ideology

In 1935, the Benedictine scholar R. van Cauwelaert put forward the hypothesis that, in its intervention into the affairs of the church at Corinth, the Roman church sought to establish a relationship with its sister congregation like that

[34] Merrill, *Essays in Early Christian History*, 217, 221; Harnack, *Das Sendschreiben der römischen Kirche*, 11; M. Bévenot, "Clement of Rome in Irenaeus' Succession List," *JTS* 17 (1966): 98–107; Lampe, *Die stadtrömischen Christen*, 343.
[35] See the extensive discussion of these possibilities by J. B. Lightfoot, *The Apostolic Fathers I.1: Clement of Rome* (London: Macmillan, 1890; repr. Grand Rapids: Baker, 1981), 21–103. Note the judgment of Lindemann, *Die Clemensbriefe*, 13: "aber alle diese Bemühungen setzen im jeden Fall voraus, dass die Verbindung des Briefes mit dem Namen 'Clemens' zuverlässig ist, was sich nicht erweisen lässt."
[36] See the clear analysis of the matter by Merrill, *Essays in Early Christian History*, 229: "As regards the ascription of the letter to Clement, the gradual development of the tale is to be noted. There was first the indubitable existence of a noteworthy letter, not containing any sign of the personality of the scribe, but addressed by the church in Rome to the church in Corinth; thus the letter is earlier cited without reference to any individual writer; next its actual author is reputed to be Clement; afterward this Clement is thought to have been bishop of Rome; and finally this bishop is identified with a Clement who was a friend of and fellow-worker with Paul."
[37] Cf. Lona, *Der erste Clemensbrief*, 85.
[38] Bakke, *"Concord and Peace,"* 3.
[39] See further Eusebius, *Hist. eccl.* 3.16.1; 3.38.1; 4.23.1. Cf. Grant, *First Clement*, 5–6; Bakke, *"Concord and Peace,"* 3–4.
[40] Pervo, *The Making of Paul*, 127, 326 n. 60, observing that the prescript of 1 Clement is imitated by the *Martyrdom of Polycarp*.

which Rome, as the capital, enjoyed with the provincial cities of the Empire,[41] a relationship like that between mother-city and colony.[42] In advancing this hypothesis, van Cauwelaert was aware that no statement in the text of the Roman epistle permitted its verification. Yet, van Cauwelaert found support in the results of the excavations at Corinth by the American School of Classical Studies which, by the third decade of the twentieth century, were providing impressive evidence of the Roman character of the colony.[43] Subsequent excavations have served to confirm the impression of Roman-era Corinth as a microcosm of the capital, which maintained the closest political and commercial ties with the emperor and the senatorial elite.[44] The names of the *tribus* (e.g., Aurelia, Calpurnia, Vatinia) into which the citizenry was divided reveal the close connections of the original settlers with the family of Caesar, the founder of the colony.[45] Many of the families that monopolized the magistracies were descendants of freedmen of Caesar.[46] Among the earliest Greek notables to be enfranchised were citizens of Corinth, such as the son and grandson of Eurycles, Gaius Julius Laco and Gaius Julius Spartiaticus, who held priestly offices in the Imperial cult, and served as administrators of Imperial estates in Greece.[47] The largest temple in Roman Corinth, Temple E, may have been dedicated to Augustus's sister Octavia, or more generally to the Imperial cult.[48] The Roman-style amphitheater at Corinth was one of the

---

[41] R. van Cauwelaert, "L'intervention de l'Église de Rome à Corinthe vers l'an 96," *RHE* 31 (1935): 267–306, esp. 282–302. See the discussion of van Cauwelaert's hypothesis in Ziegler, *Neue Studien*, 114, 118, 121–22; Lona, *Der erste Clemensbrief*, 85–87.

[42] Jacob Seibert, *Metropolis und Apoikie: Historische Beiträge zur Geschichte ihrer gegenseitige Beziehungen* (Würzburg: PhD dissertation, 1963).

[43] Results of the excavations of the American School of Classical Studies between 1896 and 1931 were published in *Corinth*, Volumes I–VIII (Cambridge, MA: Harvard University Press, 1896–1931), and subsequently in Volumes IX–XX, with further excavation reports in issues of *Hesperia*.

[44] James Wiseman, "Corinth and Rome I: 228 BC–AD 267," *ANRW* II.7.1 (Berlin: de Gruyter, 1979), 438–548; Harry Stansbury, "Corinthian Honor, Corinthian Conflict: A Social History of Early Roman Corinth and the Pauline Community" (PhD diss., University of California Irvine, 1990), 100–375; D. W. G. Gill, "Corinth: A Roman Colony in Achaea," *BZ* 37 (1993): 259–64; Antony J. S. Spawforth, "Roman Corinth: The Formation of a Colonial Elite," in *Roman Onomastics in the Greek East: Social and Political Aspects*, ed. A. D. Rizakis (Athens: Research Center for Greek and Roman Antiquity, 1996), 167–82; A. D. Rizakis, *Greece and the Augustan Cultural Revolution* (Cambridge: Cambridge University Press, 2012), 45, 48, 53, 54.

[45] Wiseman, "Corinth and Rome I," 497–98.

[46] Stansbury, "Corinthian Honor, Corinthian Conflict," 86–88; Spawforth, "Roman Corinth," 178–81; Benjamin W. Millis, "The Social and Ethnic Origins of the Colonists in Early Roman Corinth," in *Corinth in Context: Comparative Studies in Religion and Society*, ed. Steven J. Friesen, Daniel N. Schowalter, and James C. Walters (Leiden: Brill, 2010), 13–36.

[47] Allen B. West, *Corinth VIII.2: Latin Inscriptions 1896–1926* (Cambridge, MA: Harvard University Press, 1931), nos. 49, 51, 52, 53, 67, 68; *IG* 3.805 = *SIG*³ 790. See the discussion in L. R. Taylor and Allen B. West, "The Euryclids in Latin Inscriptions from Corinth," *AJA* 30 (1926): 389–400; Spawforth, "Roman Corinth," 174; Ramsay MacMullen, *Romanization in the Time of Augustus* (New Haven: Yale University Press, 2000), 12, 20.

[48] Mary E. Hoskins Walbank, "Pausanias, Octavia and Temple E at Corinth," *ABSA* 84 (1989): 361–94; Charles K. Williams, "A Re-evaluation of Temple E and the West End of the Forum of Corinth," in *The Greek Renaissance in the Roman Empire*, ed. Susan Walker and Averil Cameron (London: University of London Institute of Classical Studies, 1989), 156–62. On the

earliest built in the Greek world, probably dating to just after the foundation of the colony.[49] Of the 104 inscriptions from Corinth that date prior to the reign of Hadrian, 101 are in Latin and only three are in Greek.[50] When Corinth was damaged by a severe earthquake in AD 77, Vespasian came to the assistance of the survivors and contributed to the restoration of the city's lavish public buildings.[51] Thus, the close political and cultural connections between Rome and Corinth form the context for the intervention of the Roman church, and lend plausibility to van Cauwelaert's hypothesis.[52]

The limits of van Cauwelaert's hypothesis are exposed when one asks: What *mediates* between the structures of power that connected Rome and Corinth, on the political and social level, and the epistolary entreaty of the Roman church for peace and concord (63.2)?[53] The question of mediation between social structures and theological argumentation carries us into the realm of *ideology* in our search for the source of the authority that the Roman epistle asserts, since ideology is the symbolic matrix through which the structures of power impose subjectivity upon individuals and groups in society.[54] As long ago as 1926, in his study *Augustin und der antike Friedensgedanke*, Harald Fuchs argued that the background of the vision of cosmic harmony in 1 Clement 20 was the ideal of universal peace expressed in ancient political philosophy and vigorously defended by orators such as Dio of Prusa.[55] In his Zürich dissertation of 1949, *Die Quellen der politischen Ethik des 1. Klemensbrief*, Christian Eggenberger extended Fuch's insight, tracing the ideological affinities of First Clement with the literary products of the early Empire (not only the discourses of Dio of Prusa, but also the writings

---

Imperial cult at Corinth, see further Mary E. Hoskins Walbank, "Evidence for the Imperial Cult in Julio-Claudian Corinth," in *Subject and Ruler: The Cult of the Ruling Power in Classical Antiquity*, ed. Alastair Small (Ann Arbor, MI: Journal of Roman Archaeology, 1996), 201–14.

[49] Katherine E. Welch, "Negotiating Roman Spectacle Architecture in the Greek World: Athens and Corinth," in *The Art of Ancient Spectacle*, ed. Bettina Bergmann and Christine Kondoleon (New Haven: Yale University Press, 1999), 125–45, esp. 133–40.

[50] John Harvey Kent, *Corinth VIII.3: The Inscriptions 1926–1950* (Princeton: The American School of Classical Studies at Athens, 1966), 18–19.

[51] In gratitude, the Corinthians renamed their city Colonia Julian Flavia Augusta Corinthiensis; see Wiseman, "Corinth and Rome I," 506–7; Barbara Levick, *Vespasian* (London: Routledge, 1999), 141.

[52] Similarly, W. K. Lowther Clarke, *The First Epistle of Clement to the Corinthians* (London: SPCK, 1937), 19; Lona, *Der erste Clemensbrief*, 87.

[53] For critique of van Cauwelaert's hypothesis, see B. Altaner, "Der I. Clemensbrief und das römische Primat," in *Kleine patristische Schriften* (Berlin: de Gruyter, 1967), 534–39, here 539; Ziegler, *Neue Studien*, 121–22; Lona, *Der erste Clemensbrief*, 87.

[54] Louis Althusser, "Ideology and Ideological State Apparatuses," first published in *La Pensée* (1970), reprinted in Louis Althusser, *On Ideology* (London: Verso, 2008), 1–60; see also John B. Thompson, *Ideology and Modern Culture* (Stanford: Stanford University Press, 1990).

[55] Harald Fuchs, *Augustin und der antike Friedensgedanke: Untersuchungen zum neunzehnten Buch der* Civitas Dei (Berlin: Weidmann, 1926), 98–105. The importance of Fuch's insight was recognized by L. Sanders, *L'Hellénisme de Saint Clement de Rome et le Paulinisme* (Louvain: Peeters, 1943), who especially emphasized the Stoic background of Clement's thought, and by Werner Jaeger, *Early Christianity and Greek Paideia* (Cambridge, MA: Belknap, 1961), 12–26.

L. L. Welborn

of Tacitus, Plutarch, Suetonius, and others), in which the order visibly
established in the Imperium Romanum was given theoretical justification.[56]

But it was W. C. van Unnik who contributed most to our understanding of
the ideological framework of First Clement, by raising the neglected question
of literary genre.[57] Van Unnik called attention to the explicit description of the
epistle in 58.2 as a συμβουλή, and argued that the term was used, not in the
ordinary sense of "advice," but with the technical meaning that the term
acquired in the schools of ancient rhetoric, as a designation for one of the
three categories of discourse: the deliberative genre (συμβουλευτικὸν
γένος).[58] As van Unnik observed, a subcategory of the deliberative discourse
is the counsel of concord (συμβουλευτικὸς περὶ ὁμονοίας) by which statesmen
and orators attempted to calm the frequent social conflicts in the cities of the
Roman Empire.[59] Van Unnik explored examples of such speeches by Dio of
Prusa and Aelius Aristides, in which the authors seek to dissuade from discord
(στάσις) and to promote concord (ὁμόνοια), employing various examples
(παραδείγματα), and urging consideration of what is beneficial (σύμφερον).[60]

Van Unnik's analysis of the ideology at work in First Clement focused
upon the combination of terms in 63.2, by which the author expresses the goal
of the letter: "For you will give us joy and gladness, if you are obedient to the
things which we have written through the Holy Spirit, and root out the wicked
passion of your jealousy according to the entreaty for peace and concord
[εἰρήνη καὶ ὁμόνοια] which we have made in this letter." Van Unnik argued
that the phrase εἰρήνη καὶ ὁμόνοια was not an ad hoc creation, but a formulaic
description of the well-being of the Roman state.[61] Out of the abundance of

---

[56] Christian Eggenberger, *Die Quellen der politischen Ethik des 1. Klemensbrief* (Zürich:
Zwingli-Verlag, 1951). Unfortunately, Eggenberger encumbered his work with the theory that
there was no actual dispute over church office at Corinth, but that the strife was a literary fiction.
Nor, according to Eggenberger, was the writing intended for Christian readers in the first place,
but for the Imperial court. The real purpose of the letter was to present Christians as peaceable
and loyal subjects of the Empire. Thus, 1 Clement is an early form of "apology," "eine
Kampfschrift für die rechte Einstellung zum römischen Imperium."

[57] W. C. van Unnik, *Studies over de zogenaamde eerste brief van Clemens, I: Het litteraire
genre* (Amsterdam: Noord Hollandsche Uitg., 1970); English trans. by L. L. Welborn, "Studies
on the so-called First Epistle of Clement: The Literary Genre," in Breytenbach and Welborn,
Encounters with Hellenism, 115–81.

[58] Van Unnik, "Studies on the First Epistle of Clement," 128, 151–63, referencing the
discussions of the rhetorical theorists, e.g., Aristotle, *Rhet.* 1.3–4.8; *Rhet. ad Her.* 1.2.2;
Quintilian, *Inst.* 3.4.15; 3.8.6; [Aristides] *Ars rhet.*, ed. L. Spengel, *Rhet. Gr.* II.503–4. See the
studies by Joseph Klek, *Symbuleutici qui dicitur sermonis historiam criticam per quattuor
saecula continuatam scripsit* (Paderborn, 1919); Ingo Beck, *Untersuchungen zur Theorie des
Genos Symbuleutikon* (Hamburg: Universität Hamburg, 1970).

[59] Van Unnik, "Studies on the First Epistle of Clement," 153–57.

[60] Van Unnik, "Studies on the First Epistle of Clement," 156–57, 164–68.

[61] Van Unnik, "Studies on the First Epistle of Clement," 129. The origin of the formula is not to
be sought in Stoic circles exclusively (contra Sanders, *L'Hellénisme de Saint Clement de Rome*,
129), since it is found on inscriptions recording the arbitration of disputes (e.g., *SIG* 816) and on
coinage propagating the principate and celebrating the end of strife between cities: see M. Amit,
"Concordia: Idéal politique et instrument de propaganda," *Jura* 13 (1962): 133–69; Jean
Béranger, "Remarques sur la Concordia dans la propaganda monétaire impériale et la nature du
principat," in *Beiträge zur alten Geschichte und deren Nachleben*, ed. R. Stiehl and H. E. Stier

sources in which the slogan appears (histories, speeches, inscriptions, coins), van Unnik selected witnesses who were contemporary with First Clement.[62] So, for example, in Dio of Prusa's thirty-ninth oration, "On Concord in Nicaea, upon the Cessation of Civil Strife," one finds: "But it is fitting that those whose city is founded by the gods should maintain peace and concord [εἰρήνη καὶ ὁμόνοια] toward one another."[63] Similarly, in Dio's oration "On Concord with the Apamaeans," delivered in his native Prusa, Dio explains: "For peace and concord [εἰρήνη καὶ ὁμόνοια] have never damaged those who have employed them, but it would be surprising if enmity and contentiousness were not deadly and mighty evils."[64] Examples of the combination εἰρήνη καὶ ὁμόνοια are also found in Plutarch. In his essay "On Garrulousness," Plutarch gives an explanation of a symbolic deed of Heraclitus with the words: "thus demonstrating to them that to be satisfied with whatever they happen upon and not to want expensive things is to keep cities in peace and concord [εἰρήνη καὶ ὁμόνοια]."[65] In "On the Fortune of Alexander," Plutarch argues that the plan of Alexander's campaigns reveals him to be a true philosopher, because he did not seek to obtain luxury for himself, but "to win for all people concord and peace [ὁμόνοια καὶ εἰρήνη] and fellowship toward one another."[66]

The terms "peace and concord" are found together in historians of Rome from the first century BC onward, mutually defining a conception of the well-being of the state, in reaction to bloody civil strife.[67] Dionysius of Halicarnassus narrates the conflict between the patricians and the plebians, in which one of the consuls spoke, "praising concord and peace [ἐπαινῶν μὲν ὁμόνοιαν καὶ εἰρήνην], telling of the great good fortune which each of them brings to states, and inveighing against discord and civil wars, by which, he told them, many cities have been destroyed with all their inhabitants."[68] Diodorus Siculus relates how the inhabitants of Euboea fell into strife and the island was devastated, but "at long last, the parties came into concord and made peace with one another [εἰς ὁμόνοιαν ἦλθον καὶ τὴν εἰρήνην συνέθετο πρὸς ἀλλήλους] having been admonished by their misfortunes."[69] In a speech that Dio Cassius places into the mouth of Cicero, the orator urges: "It is

---

(Berlin: de Gruyter, 1969), 477–91; R. Pera, *Homonoia sulle monete da Augusto agli Antonini* (Genoa: Il Melangolo, 1984); Dietmar Kienast, "Die Homonoiaverträge der römischen Kaiserzeit," *JNG* 14 (1964): 51–64; H. Alan Shapiro and Tonio Hölscher, "Homonoia/Concordia," in *Lexicon Iconographicum Mythologiae Classicae V.1* (Zürich: Artemis, 1996), 476–98.

[62] Van Unnik, "Studies on the First Epistle of Clement," 146–51.

[63] Dio Chrysostom, *Or.* 39.2. See the discussion of Dio Chrysostom's speeches on concord by C. P. Jones, *The Roman World of Dio Chrysostom* (Cambridge, MA: Harvard University Press, 1978), 83–94; Giovanni Salmeri, "Dio, Rome, and the Civic Life of Asia Minor," in *Dio Chrysostom: Politics, Letters and Philosophy*, ed. S. Swain (Oxford: Oxford University Press, 2000), 75–81.

[64] Dio Chrysostom, *Or.* 40.26.

[65] Plutarch, *Garr.* 17.

[66] Plutarch, *Alex. fort.* 1.9.

[67] P. Jal, "'Pax civilis'–'concordia,'" *REL* 39 (1961): 210–31.

[68] Dionysius of Halicarnassus, *Ant. rom.* 7.60.2

[69] Diodorus Siculus, *Hist.* 16.7.2.

necessary for us to do away with enmities and rivalries toward one another, and to return to that ancient peace and friendship and concord [πρὸς δὲ δὴ τὴν παλαιὰν εἰρήνην καὶ φιλίαν καὶ ὁμόνοιαν ἐπανελθεῖν]."[70] A bit later, Dio Cassius calls to mind Roman history: the Romans weakened themselves when they differed from one another; but they were successful in war "when they were able to live in peace and concord [ἐν εἰρήνῃ καὶ ὁμονοίᾳ]."[71]

In Tacitus, one encounters the Latin equivalent of these concepts. During the conflict that brought Vespasian to the throne, the senate selected representatives to go to the armies involved in civil strife "to persuade them in the interests of the state to concord and peace" (*ut praetexto rei publicae concordiam pacemque suaderent*).[72] According to Suetonius, Otho appealed to Vitellius on similar grounds to avoid civil war: "He persuaded the senate to send a deputation to say that an emperor had already been chosen and to counsel peace and concord [*quietem concordiamque suaderet*]."[73] In Plutarch's account of these events, Otho makes it known, in his last speech before he commits suicide, that he wishes to sacrifice himself "for peace and concord" (ὑπὲρ εἰρήνης καὶ ὁμονοίας).[74] How ubiquitous the combination had become is revealed by Tacitus's comment on the negotiations between the Vitelliani and the Othonians: "Finally, when in vain and empty phrases they had bandied back and forth the words 'peace and concord' [*pax et concordia*]..."[75]

In sum, the slogan "peace and concord," or often simply "concord" alone,[76] was the palliative that the orators and moralists of the early Empire applied to the conflicts between social classes and rival factions, in order to reaffirm and solidify the order of society. Most of the conflicts of the first and second centuries, to which the refrain of ὁμόνοια/*concordia* was applied, "arose out of attempts by the non-elite citizenry to retain or regain a measure of control over the running of their communities, and out of anger and suspicion about oligarchic excesses and what the demos perceived as abuses of power by the bouleutic elite."[77] For example, at Aspendus, the rich men (οἱ δυνατοί) artificially induced a food shortage by withholding all the corn for export, instead of selling it on the local market; public anger ran so high that

---

[70] Dio Cassius, *Hist*. 44.23.3.

[71] Dio Cassius, *Hist*. 44.25.3–4.

[72] Tacitus, *Hist*. 3.80.4.

[73] Suetonius, *Otho* 8.1.

[74] Plutarch, *Otho* 15.

[75] Tacitus, *Hist*. 2.20.2.

[76] H. Kramer, *Quid valeat homonoia in litteris graecis* (Göttingen: PhD dissertation, 1915); Eiliv Skard, "Concordia," in *Römische Wertbegriffe*, ed. Hans Oppermann (Darmstadt: Wissenschaftliche Buchgesellschaft, 1974), 173–208; A. Moulakis, *Homonoia. Eintracht und die Entwicklung des politischen Bewusstseins* (Munich: Paul List Verlag, 1973); A. R. R. Sheppard, "*Homonoia* in the Greek Cities of the Roman Empire," *Ancient Society* 15–17 (1984–1986): 229–52; Klaus Thraede, "*Homonoia* (Eintracht)," *RAC* 16 (1994): 176–80; John Alexander Lobur, *Consensus, Concordia, and the Formation of Roman Imperial Ideology* (New York: Routledge, 2008).

[77] Arjan Zuiderhoek, *The Politics of Munificence in the Roman Empire: Citizens, Elites and Benefactors in Asia Minor* (Cambridge: Cambridge University Press, 2009), 68.

the philosopher Apollonius of Tyana was barely able to prevent the burning alive of a magistrate and the looting of large estates.[78] At Prusa, poor citizens stormed the houses of the elite during a food shortage, suspecting the rich of speculative hoarding; Dio delivered an oration on concord in an attempt to restrain the angry demos.[79] At Rhodes, Aelius Aristides found rich and poor locked in a destructive conflict, and urged concord as the most expedient policy for all.[80] As Giovanni Salmeri observes, "It was in the interests of the upper classes for harmony and order to reign in the cities; indeed, it was an indispensable condition for them to be able to enjoy their economic well-being, and to prevent the intervention of the Roman governors."[81] Thus, Plutarch advised the young aristocrat Menemachus of Sardes, who had inquired about the mode of political life appropriate to a subject of the Empire, in which "the affairs of the cities no longer include leadership in wars, or the overthrow of tyrannies, or the conclusion of alliances," as follows: "There remains, then, for the statesman, of those activities which fall within his province, only this—and it is the equal of the other blessings—always to instill concord and friendship in those who dwell together with him and to remove strifes, discords, and all enmity."[82] In urging "peace and concord" in the church at Corinth, the author of First Clement seems to follow the example of upper class orators and philosophers who sought to soothe the tensions that were constantly boiling beneath the surface of civic life. The ideological warrant for such a discursive intervention is the assumption that the well-being of a community is best served by maintaining the existing structure of power.

In recent decades, several scholars have built upon the foundation laid by van Unnik in respect to the literary genre and ideological context of First Clement. In her Harvard dissertation of 1988, Barbara Bowe argued that the use of terms such as ἀλαζονεία and αὐθάδεια to describe the "arrogance" of those who deposed the presbyters from office shows that the author of the Roman epistle "adopts standard Hellenistic rhetoric against seditious people."[83] Bowe also demonstrated that the author of First Clement employs the word group for "danger"—κίνδυνος, κινδυνέω, ῥιψοκινδύνως—in a manner similar to Dio of Prusa and Aelius Aristides in their discourses on concord.[84] In the revision of his Oslo dissertation of 1998,[85] Odd Magne

---

[78] Philostratus, *Vit. Apoll.* 1.15.

[79] Dio Chrysostom, *Or.* 46. See further *Or.* 34 attempting to resolve long standing conflicts between the council and people of Tarsus, and *Or.* 39 urging concord in the aftermath of violent strife in Nicaea.

[80] Aelius Aristides, *Or.* 24.

[81] Salmeri, "Dio, Rome, and the Civic Life of Asia Minor," 74. For the concern of Greek elites about the possibility of Roman intervention, see esp. Dio Chrysostom *Or.* 46.14; Plutarch, *Praec. ger. rei publ.* 814F–815A.

[82] Plutarch, *Praec. ger. rei publ.* 805A, 824C–D.

[83] Barbara E. Bowe, *A Church in Crisis: Ecclesiology and Paraenesis in Clement of Rome* (Minneapolis: Fortress, 1988), 63–67.

[84] Bowe, *A Church in Crisis*, 29.

Bakke added significantly to understanding of the political vocabulary and *topoi* used by the author of First Clement through investigation of the terms στάσις and ἀπόνοια, ἔρις, ζῆλος, and φθόνος, διωγμός and ἀκαταστασία, πόλεμος and αἰχμαλωσία, μιαρός and ἀνόσιος, σχίσμα, etc. Although the primary aim of Bakke's study was to define the rhetorical genre of First Clement as a deliberative discourse on concord,[86] his thorough exploration of the language of unity and sedition in the Roman epistle consistently located relevant parallels in Plutarch, Dio of Prusa, Aelius Aristides, and other political writers, so that much raw material was contributed toward a better understanding of the ideological matrix in which First Clement is situated.

In his commentary on First Clement, Horacio Lona suggested that the Rome-idea, vigorously promoted by the intelligentsia of the Augustan age, supplied the ideological context in which the intervention of the Roman church into the affairs of the church at Corinth becomes understandable.[87] Lona adduced the famous words of the prophecy of Anchises in the *Aeneid* as the best expression of the view of Rome that lies in the background of First Clement:

You, Roman, remember to rule the nations with your power—
these shall be your arts—to crown peace with justice,
to spare the vanquished and to crush the proud.

(*Tu regere imperio populos, Romane, memento—
haec tibi erunt artes—pacique imponere morem,
parcere subiectis et debellare superbos*).[88]

Lona drew an analogy between the task given to the Roman people in the political sphere and the duty of the Roman church toward her sister-congregation in Corinth: in both cases, it was a matter of the imposition of peace and concord by Roman actors with a special aptitude for governing.[89] Lona sought to strengthen the analogy by observing that the idea of *Domina*

---

[85] Odd Magne Bakke, *"Concord and Peace": A Rhetorical Analysis of the First Letter of Clement with an Emphasis on the Language of Unity and Sedition* (Tübingen: Mohr Siebeck, 2001).

[86] Bakke, *"Concord and Peace,"* 15 and passim. Although Bakke acknowledges van Unnik as a predecessor (13–14), he evidently did not regard van Unnik's identification of the rhetorical genre of first Clement as conclusive, and thus stresses the originality of his own contribution. Moreover, there are curious gaps in Bakke's knowledge of the history of scholarship on First Clement: e.g., van Cauwelaert's essay.

[87] Lona, *Der erste Clemensbrief,* 87, citing Harnack, *Das Sendschrieben der römischen Kirche,* 98 as anticipating his suggestion: "Zwar spricht auf den ersten Blick viel dafür, dass die Herrscherin Rom hier redet und handelt—sie mischt sich unaufgefordert in den inneren Streit der Korinthischen Gemeinde." On the Rome-idea, Lona references the essays collected in Bernhard Kytzler, ed., *Rom als Idee* (Darmstadt: Wissenschaftliche Buchgesellschaft, 1993), esp. 13–30, 31–71.

[88] Virgil, *Aen.* 6.851–53.

[89] Lona, *Der erste Clemensbrief,* 87–88.

Roma ultimately stood upon a religious foundation, insofar as Roman politics and Roman religion were inseparably connected.[90]

Lona seems disinclined to attribute self-consciousness to the author of the Roman epistle in his use of the ideology of "peace and concord." He allows that the idea of Rome as the bringer of universal peace may have been an unconscious element in the worldview of Christians living in the capital of the empire.[91] To be sure, ideologies, in their operation, diffuse themselves throughout societies, and are, perhaps, more powerful when they are not entirely conscious.[92] But in the case of the First Epistle of Clement, there are indications that the author is making self-conscious use of the vocabulary of Roman political ideology, and, moreover, that he is aware of the source of the ideas to which he is subscribing, and finally, that he intends to promote subordination to established authority. We shall see that the most impressive instances of the author's awareness and intention emerge at those points where he interpolates politically-loaded words and phrases into the source material from the Septuagint and the New Testament upon which he draws.

We begin with the term στάσις ("sedition" or "rebellion"), which is the principal term by which the author of the Roman epistle designates the conflict in the church at Corinth.[93] At the beginning of the letter, in the *prooimion*, which states the occasion and purpose of the writing, the author speaks of "the abominable and unholy στάσις, alien and foreign to the elect of God, which a few persons, rash and self-willed, have kindled to such a degree of frenzy that your name ... has been seriously maligned" (1.1). The term στάσις, in the sense in which it is used here, derives from the political sphere, where it occurs with the meaning "civil strife" as early as Solon[94] and Democritus.[95] Ancient historians and political philosophers identified στάσις as the central malady of society.[96] Thucydides held that στάσις was endemic to the Greek city-states: he has left a vivid picture of the violent and bloody στάσις at Corcyra in 427 BC,[97] which he regarded as the opening episode in a new age of intensified civil strife.[98] In the *Republic*, Plato defines στάσις as hostility between those who belong together, πόλεμος as hostility toward

---

[90] Lona, *Der erste Clemensbrief*, 88. See further John F. Miller, *Apollo, Augustus, and the Poets* (Cambridge: Cambridge University Press, 2009); Ittai Gradel, *Emperor Worship and Roman Religion* (Oxford: Oxford University Press, 2002).

[91] Lona, *Der erste Clemensbrief*, 87–89.

[92] Miriam Griffin, "*Urbs Roma, Plebs,* and *Princeps,*" in *Images of Empire*, ed. Loveday Alexander (Sheffield: JSOT, 1991), 19–46, here 23.

[93] The noun στάσις is used nine times, the verb στασιάζειν seven times. Cf. Lona, *Der erste Clemensbrief*, 140: "Mit στάσις wird der Vorgang in Korinth zusammengefasst."

[94] Frag. 3.19, Diehl I, 28.

[95] Frag. 29, Diehl II, 195.3–4.

[96] D. Loenen, *Stasis. Enige aspecten van de begrippen partijen klassenstrijd in oud-Griekenland* (Amsterdam: Noord-Hollandsche Uitgevers, 1953); H.-J. Gehrke, *Stasis. Untersuchungen zu den inneren Kriegen in den griechischen Staaten des 5, und 4, Jahrhunderts v. Chr.* (Munich: Beck, 1985). See also Moses I. Finley, *Politics in the Ancient World* (Cambridge: Cambridge University Press, 1983), 95–121.

[97] Thucydides 3.70–81; 4.46–48.

[98] Thucydides 3.82–83, esp. 82.1.

L. L. Welborn

foreign enemies.[99] Aristotle devotes the whole of the fifth book of his *Politics* to an analysis of στάσις: its aim is constitutional change, from oligarchy to democracy, and vice versa;[100] στάσις is connected, on the one hand, with μεταβολή ("revolution"),[101] and on the other hand with quarrels between individuals,[102] which can also lead to political unrest.[103] In an inscription from Dreros, dated 220 BC, the ephebes must swear μηδὲ στάσιος ἀρξεῖν before they are allowed to participate in public life.[104] Philo uses the term in his political pamphlets *Against Flaccus* and *Delegation to Gaius* to describe the civil strife between Jews and Greeks at Alexandria.[105] Josephus uses the word in different connections: to describe the actions of the Zealots on the occasion of the census of Quirinius,[106] the unrest of the Jews in Caesarea,[107] and the principal cause of the outbreak of the Jewish War.[108] In his discourse urging concord between the Nicomedians and the Nicaeans, Dio of Prusa contrasts στάσις, the bringer of war and disease, with ὁμόνοια, which preserves peace and health.[109] In his speech to the Rhodians, Aelius Aristides describes στάσις as the opposite of political concord.[110] The word is also used to describe conflicts within smaller groups in society: for example, a second-century-AD inscription from Ephesus mentions a στάσις among the bakers that led to tumultuous scenes in the agora.[111]

It is in this explicitly *political* sense that the term is used in First Clement, where a στάσις has arisen against the leaders of the Corinthian congregation.[112] According to 47.6, the shameful report has been circulated about the Corinthians that, "on account of one or two persons, the ancient and well-established church of the Corinthians is in revolt [στασιάζειν] against its presbyters." The "leaders of strife and discord" (ἀρχηγοὶ στάσεως καὶ διχοστασίας, 51.1) are described throughout in terms suited to the heads of a political party. The author warns in 14.1–2 against following the rebels in their "pride and disorderliness" (ἀλαζονεία καὶ ἀκαταστασία), for they are "the instigators of abominable jealousy." "We shall incur no common harm," Clement admonishes, "but great danger, if we rashly yield to the purposes of men who rush into ἔρις and στάσις, to estrange us from what is right" (14.2). If the leaders of the opposition are honorable and care about what is happening to the church, they will say: "If στάσις and ἔρις and σχίσμα have

[99] Plato, *Resp.* 5.470B–D.
[100] Aristotle, *Pol.* 2.2, 1302a.
[101] Aristotle, *Pol.* 5.2, 1302a.
[102] Aristotle, *Pol.* 5.4, 1303b28–29, 1304a11–12.
[103] Aristotle, *Pol.* 5.4, 1303b38, 1304a9.
[104] Dittenberger, *Sylloge*³ I, 527.60–61.
[105] Philo, *Flaccus* 135; *Legat.* 113, etc.
[106] Josephus, *A.J.* 18.
[107] Josephus, *A.J.* 174.
[108] Josephus, *B.J.* 1.10, 27.
[109] Dio Chrysostom, *Or.* 38.8, 11, 15.
[110] Aelius Aristides, *Or.* 24.4, 19–21, 41–44, etc.
[111] *I.Magn.* 114.3–4, 11–12.
[112] See already Paul Mikat, *Die Bedeutung der Begriffe Stasis und Aponoia für das Verständnis des 1. Clemensbriefes* (Köln: Westdeutscher Verlag, 1969).

386

arisen on my account, I will depart, I will go away" (54.2). Thus they are admonished in 57.1: "You who laid the foundation of the στάσις, submit to the presbyters and receive the correction of repentance, bending the knees of the heart." But, in all events, the rebels should "cease from this futile στάσις" (63.1).

It is important to note that the term στάσις is not found among the Apostolic Fathers outside of First Clement. Where the term appears in the New Testament, it describes Jewish "insurrection" against the Romans (Mark 15:7; Luke 23:19, 25), "dissension" and "quarrels" among the Jews (Acts 23:7; 24:5), and "uproar" among the people of Ephesus (Acts 19:40), but never depicts strife or discord within a Christian community.[113] In the Septuagint, the word στάσις appears with a "political" meaning only in Proverbs 17:14, where the sage warns against the destructive consequences of "strife."[114] Thus, in the term στάσις, as it is used by the author of First Clement, we have a word that does not derive from the tradition of Hellenistic Judaism or early Christianity, but which is taken from the realm of Greco-Roman politics, where στάσις had an established meaning. By labeling the action against the presbyters at Corinth a στάσις, the author of the Roman epistle characterizes the agents of change in ecclesial office as dangerous rebels, as insurrectionists.

How self-consciously political is Clement's description of the situation in Corinth can be seen by comparison with his account of the conflict in the church at the time of Paul. In keeping with his conception of the early history of the Corinthian church as a "golden age," when all were "sincere and pure in heart, bearing no malice toward one another," the author of the Roman epistle asserts: "All sedition [στάσις] and all schism [σχίσμα] was abominable to you" (2.5–6). The author never refers to the party strife in the time of Paul as a στάσις, but only as an instance of "partisanship" (πρόσκλισις), which entailed less guilt for the Corinthians than the present uprising, for they were then "partisans of distinguished apostles" (47.4). Now, by contrast, the Corinthians have shamefully "revolted" (στασιάζειν) against their presbyters (47.6), and have created danger for themselves (47.7). A similar token of Clement's ideological self-consciousness is his addition to Paul's hymn on love, from which he quotes in 49.5: "love makes no sedition" (ἀγάπη οὐ στασιάζει).

The other explicitly political term employed by the author of the Roman epistle is, as we have seen, ὁμόνοια or "concord." The noun occurs fourteen times in First Clement,[115] but is not found at all in the New Testament. In Paul's epistles, one encounters a less technical vocabulary: τὸ αὐτὸ φρονεῖν ("to think the same thing"), σύμψυχος ("united in spirit"), τὸ ἓν φρονεῖν ("to be

---

[113] In Acts 15:2, the "dissension" (στάσις) is between Paul and Barnabas and "certain people who came down from Judaea."
[114] Gerhard Delling, "στάσις," *TDNT* 7:570.
[115] 1 Clem. 9.4; 11.2; 20.3, 10, 11; 21.1; 30.3; 34.7; 49.5; 50.5; 60.4; 61.1; 63.2; 65.1. The cognate verb is found in 62.2.

L. L. Welborn

of one mind").[116] Again, one might ask whether the author was really conscious of the political character of the term ὁμόνοια. And again, obvious changes in the tradition that the author has inherited make clear how fully and how willingly the author participated in the ideology of concord. For example, in 9.4 the author of the Roman epistle asserts that God saved through Noah the living creatures that entered into the ark ἐν ὁμονοίᾳ ("in concord"). What is peculiar about this formulation is that the emphasis falls not on the salvation of Noah and his family, as in 1 Pet 3:20, but on that of the animals who entered the ark "in concord." There is no tradition, Jewish or Christian, in which the animals are said to have entered the ark "in concord." The notion was doubtlessly suggested to Clement by the "two-by-two" of Gen 6:10. Behind the curious statement lies the desire to tell the Corinthians, as Rudolf Knopf rightly observed, "die Tiere waren einträchtig, die Menschen sind es nicht."[117] But this purpose is foreign to the biblical text. The same motive is apparent in 11.2, where the sin of Lot's wife is said to consist in a difference of opinion with her husband, in her failure to remain ἐν ὁμονοίᾳ with him: thus she was changed into a pillar of salt to make it clear to all that "those who are double-minded fall under condemnation." But nowhere is it said in the biblical text that Lot's wife held different opinions from her husband, that she was not "in concord" with him. Clement has insinuated these political terms into the story, with his eye on the situation in Corinth. So it is everywhere that the Septuagint is cited: the specific regulations are not considered normative, but the ideological principle of concord. Similarly, Clement adds to Paul's hymn on love, from which he quotes in 49.5, precisely what he wishes to say: "love does all things in concord" (ἀγάπη πάντα ποιεῖ ἐν ὁμονοίᾳ).[118]

Turning from vocabulary to *topoi* and arguments, the same ideological awareness is evident. Characteristic of the growth in political consciousness is the way in which Clement treats Paul's appeal for order. In 1 Cor 14:40, Paul advises: "but let all things be done decently and in order" (πάντα δὲ εὐσχημόνως καὶ κατὰ τάξιν γινέσθω). Commentators have noted how secular Paul's sentiment is, and have conjectured that the expression κατὰ τάξιν is drawn from military life.[119] Clement reinforces Paul's emphasis by making the underlying metaphor explicit:

Let us then serve in our army, brothers, with all earnestness, following his faultless commands. Let us consider those who serve our generals, with what good order [εὐτάκτως], habitual readiness, and submissiveness [ὑποτεταγμένως] they perform their commands. Not all are prefects, nor

[116] 1 Cor 1:10; Phil 2:2.
[117] "Animals were peaceable, people are not so." Knopf, *Die apostolischen Väter*, 59.
[118] Jaeger, *Early Christianity and Greek Paideia*, 18 calls 1 Clement 49 "a treatise on civic order in the Christian *politeia*." The political aspects of love are widely discussed in Greek literature: see already Plato, *Leges* 3.678E; Aristotle, *Pol.* 2.1.16, where φιλία is described as "the best safeguard against revolution" (στασιάζειν); Aristotle, *Eth. nic.* 8.1.4, where φιλία is said to promote concord; Dio Chrysostom, *Or.* 38.15, ἡ δὲ φιλία τί ἄλλο ἢ φίλων ὁμόνοια.
[119] E.g., Hans Lietzmann, *An die Korinther I, II*, rev. Werner G. Kümmel (Tübingen: Mohr Siebeck, 1949), 191.

tribunes, nor centurions, nor in charge of fifty men, or the like, but each carries out in his own rank [ἐν τῷ ἰδίῳ τάγματι] the commands of the emperor and of the generals (37.1–3).[120]

When Clement takes up Paul's image of the body and its members (from 1 Cor 12:12–27),[121] he gives it a very different meaning. Paul's use of the body analogy is meant to illustrate the interdependence between the members, despite their differences. Indeed, Paul insists that God has arranged the body so that "the weaker" and "less respectable" members are given "greater honor" (1 Cor 12:22–25).[122] Clement connects the image of the body with that of the army, in which each has his own rank (37.3). More clearly than in Paul, the arrangement of the body is hierarchical: subordination is a necessity and mutual help a duty. Clement stresses the contrast between hand and foot, and the collaboration of great and small (37.5). The point of Clement's body analogy is that "all are united in a common subjection to preserve the whole body" (37.5). Clement's use of the body analogy has more in common with conservative, self-consciously ideological versions of the figure, like that of Menenius Agrippa in Livy, than with the purposes of the apostle Paul.[123]

One may also contrast the solution that Clement offers to the crisis in the church at Corinth with the procedure that Paul recommends in the case of the "wrongdoer" in 2 Corinthians 2 and 7. Paul endorses the punishment decided by the majority as "sufficient," and urges forgiveness and reaffirmation of love (2 Cor 2:5–11).[124] Clement, on the other hand, advises voluntary exile (54.1–4),[125] following the precedent of Roman politics.[126] Exile was the routine punishment for those responsible for civic disturbances in the late Republic and the early Empire.[127] Historical instances of self-banishment have

---

[120] A. Jaubert, "Les sources de la conception militaire de l'eglise en 1 Clement 37," *VC* 18 (1964): 74–84, esp. 79.

[121] The society-as-body *topos* was well established in Greco-Roman political history and in philosophical discussions of concord: the best known version of this figure is the fable of Menenius Agrippa in Livy, *Urb. cond.* 2.32 and Dionysius of Halicarnassus, *Ant. rom.* 6.86; cf. Wilhelm Nestle, "Die Fabel des Menenius Agrippa," *Klio* 21 (1927): 350–60. The body analogy is also employed in a political sense by Cicero, *Off.* 3.5.22–23; 3.6.26–27; Seneca, *Ira* 2.31.7; Dio Chrysostom, *Or.* 40.21; 41.9; 50.3. For additional occurrences, see Margaret M. Mitchell, *Paul and the Rhetoric of Reconciliation: An Exegetical Investigation of the Language and Composition of 1 Corinthians* (Tübingen: Mohr Siebeck, 1991), 218–26.

[122] See the analysis of Dale B. Martin, *The Corinthian Body* (New Haven: Yale University Press, 1995), 94–95.

[123] Cf. Sanders, *L'Hellénisme de Saint Clement de Rome et le Paulinisme*, 85–91.

[124] L. L. Welborn, *An End to Enmity: Paul and the "Wrongdoer" of Second Corinthians* (Berlin: de Gruyter, 2011), 458–60.

[125] Paul Mikat, "Der 'Auswanderungsrat' (I Clem 54,2) als Schlüssel zum Gemeindeverständnis im 1. Clemensbrief," in *Geschichte, Recht, Religion, Politik I* (Paderborn: Schöningh Verlag, 1984), 361–73; L. L. Welborn, "Voluntary Exile as the Solution to Discord in First Clement," *ZAC* 18 (2014): 6–21.

[126] The background in Roman politics has long been recognized: Harnack, *Das Sendschreiben der römischen Kirche*, 82; Sanders, *L'Hellénisme de Saint Clemént de Rome*, 50–52; Ziegler, *Neue Studien*, 99–101; Mikat, *Die Bedeutung der Begriffe Stasis und Aponoia*, 30–36.

[127] See in general G. Kleinfeller, "Exilium," *Paulys Realencyclopädie der classischen Altertumswissenschaft* VI.2 (Stuttgart: Metzler, 1909), 1683–85; Ernst Ludwig Grasmück,

been adduced as relevant to the advice offered in First Clement.[128] The course of action that Clement recommends to the instigators of discord at Corinth brings to mind the exile of Dio of Prusa under Domitian.[129]

3. Politics

The intervention of the Roman church in the affairs of the church at Corinth is modeled on the actions of the Roman senate and the emperor in response to civic disturbances in the provinces. First, the church decided to dispatch a συμβουλή, in much the same manner that philosophers and orators, with the approval or on the instruction of the Roman emperor, were sent to troubled cities to counsel concord.[130] Along with its appeal, the Roman church sent three "witnesses" (63:3–4; 65:1) to observe and report on the restoration of peace. The Roman state proceeded in similar fashion in its efforts to quiet discord in the cities. When a class struggle erupted at Rhodes, Aelius Aristides sent a speech on concord in which he described himself as a "witness."[131] In a symbouleutic discourse ascribed to Julian, but dated by Bruno Keil to the first century AD,[132] the author states that a legation (πρεσβεία) will be sent to Corinth consisting of two philosopher-orators.[133] The senate frequently adjudicated disputes between provincial cities, often employing local agents as arbiters.[134]

In adopting the ideology and strategy of Roman politics, Clement endorsed the Roman imperium. The epistle is characterized throughout by a positive attitude toward the Roman government.[135] The language in which the author praises the Roman military in 37.2–4, "the soldiers in service of our leader,"

Exilium: Untersuchungen zur Verbannung in der Antike (Paderborn: Schöningh, 1978); Giuliano Crifò, *L'esclusione dalla città. Altri studi sull'exilium romano* (Perugia: Università di Perugia, 1985); Gordon P. Kelly, *A History of Exile in the Roman Republic* (Cambridge: Cambridge University Press, 2006).

[128] E.g., Cicero, *Caecin.* 100; see further Cicero, *Mil.* 93. Cf. Ziegler, *Neue Studien,* 91, 94, 100; Lindemann, *Die Clemensbriefe,* 153; Lona, *Der erste Clemensbrief,* 555.

[129] Jones, *The Roman World of Dio Chrysostom,* 46–49, 53–54; Timothy Whitmarsh, *Greek Literature and the Roman Empire: The Politics of Imitation* (Oxford: Oxford University Press, 2001), 156–66.

[130] Salmeri, "Dio, Rome, and the Civic Life of Asia Minor," 53–92.

[131] Aelius Aristides, *Or.* 24, 833D; cf. Carlo Franco, "Aelius Aristides and Rhodes: Consolation and Concord," in *Aelius Aristides between Greece, Rome, and the Gods,* ed. William V. Harris (Leiden: Brill, 2008), 238–48.

[132] Bruno Keil, "Ein ΛΟΓΟΣ ΣΥΣΤΑΤΙΚΟΣ," *Nachrichten der Akademie der Wissenschaften Göttingen,* Philosophische-historische Klasse (1913): 1–41.

[133] Ps.-Julian, *Orationes* 35; cf. Keil, "Ein ΛΟΓΟΣ ΣΥΣΤΑΤΙΚΟΣ," 39.

[134] Texts and commentary in R. K. Sherk, *Roman Documents from the Greek East. Senatus Consulta and Epistulae to the Age of Augustus* (Baltimore: Johns Hopkins University Press, 1969). See the discussion in M. N. Tod, *International Arbitration Amongst the Greeks* (Oxford: Clarendon, 1913); L. Piccirilli, *Gli Arbitrati Interstatali Greci* (Pisa: Fonti e Studi, 1973).

[135] Klaus Wengst, *Pax Romana and the Peace of Jesus Christ* (Philadelphia: Westminster, 1987), 112–15; David G. Horrell, *The Social Ethos of the Corinthian Correspondence: Interests and Ideology from 1 Corinthians to 1 Clement* (Edinburgh: T&T Clark, 1996), 272–80.

as models of obedience, recalls Aelius Aristides's *Eulogy of Rome*.[136] In the solemn liturgical prayer with which the work concludes, the author asks that Christians "may be obedient to our rulers and governors on earth," to whom God has given the sovereignty (60.4–61.1).[137] This prayer for princes is more than a show of loyalty; it expresses the conviction that the Empire and its rulers have been established by God as the earthly counterpart of the heavenly kingdom.[138] Indeed, in the case of First Clement, the endorsement of Roman political ideology is so wholehearted that one must ask whether the effect of the epistle is to inscribe the Roman Empire into the divine economy of salvation, or rather, the latter into the former. Clement's appropriation of the ideology of concord prepared the way for Constantine, whose official correspondence leaves no doubt that the object of his political and religious policy was concord.[139] Following a path made straight by Clement of Rome, Constantine interpreted brotherly love as "the willingness to integrate oneself without reservation into a comprehensive community."[140]

Recommended Reading

Bakke, Odd Magne. *"Concord and Peace": A Rhetorical Analysis of the First Letter of Clement with an Emphasis on the Language of Unity and Sedition*. Tübingen: Mohr Siebeck, 2001.
Bowe, Barbara E. *A Church in Crisis: Ecclesiology and Paraenesis in Clement of Rome*. Minneapolis: Fortress, 1988.
Breytenbach, Cilliers, and Laurence L. Welborn, eds. *Encounters with Hellenism: Studies on the First Letter of Clement*. Leiden: Brill, 2004.
Eggenberger, Christian. *Die Quellen der politischen Ethik des 1. Klemensbriefes*. Zürich: Zwingli-Verlag, 1951.
Horrell, David G. *The Social Ethos of the Corinthian Correspondence: Interests and Ideology from 1 Corinthians to 1 Clement*. Edinburgh: T&T Clark, 1996.
Jeffers, James S. *Conflict at Rome: Social Order and Hierarchy in Early Christianity*. Minneapolis: Fortress, 1991.

[136] Aelius Aristides, *Or.* 26.88 in *Aelii Aristidis Smyrnaei quae supersunt omnia*, Vol. 1, ed. Bruno Keil (Berlin: Weidmans, 1958). Cf. James H. Oliver, "The Ruling Power: A Study of the Roman Empire in the Second Century after Christ through the Roman Oration of Aelius Aristides," *Transactions of the American Philosophical Society* 48.4 (1953): 870–1003, esp. 904–5, 941.
[137] A. Jaubert, *Clément de Rome. Épître aux Corinthiens: Introduction, Texte, Traduction, Notes et Index* (Paris: Éditions du Cerf, 1971), 199.
[138] Wengst, *Pax Romana*, 107.
[139] The primary sources may be consulted in H.-G. Opitz, *Athanasius' Werke 3.1: Urkunden zur Geschichte des arianischen Streites*, GCS (Berlin: Akademie-Verlag, 1934) and Hans von Soden, *Urkunden zur Entstehungsgeschichte des Donatismus* (Berlin: Akademie-Verlag, 1950). Eusebius's *Vita Constantini* is also a valuable source for the emperor's policies: F. Winkelmann, *Eusebius' Werke 1.1*, GCS (Berlin: Akademie-Verlag, 1975). See esp. von Soden, *Urkunden*, 14.75: all must serve God "*concordi observantiae fraternitate*"; 23.44: it is the emperor's office to bring about "*concordem simplicitatem atque meritam omnipotenti deo culturam*."
[140] H. Dörries, *Das Selbstzeugnis Kaiser Konstantins. Abhandlungen der Akademie der Wissenschaften in Göttingen*, Philosophische-hististorische Klasse 34 (Göttingen: Vandenhoeck & Ruprecht, 1954), 318.

Lindemann, Andreas. *Die Apostolischen Väter I. Die Clemensbriefe*. Tübingen: Mohr Siebeck, 1992.

Lona, Horacio E. *Der erste Clemensbrief*. Göttingen: Vandenhoeck & Ruprecht, 1998.

Maier, Harry O. *The Social Setting of the Ministry as Reflected in the Writings of Hermas, Clement and Ignatius*. Waterloo: Wilfrid Laurier, 1991.

Ziegler, Adolf W. *Neue Studien zum ersten Klemensbrief*. München: Manz Verlag, 1958.

INDEX OF ANCIENT PEOPLE

Latin names are generally listed by cognomen